Mutiny on the Bounty

PETER FITZSIMONS

Mutiny on the Bounty

C
CONSTABLE

CONSTABLE

First published in Australia and New Zealand in 2018 by Hachette Australia
(an imprint of Hachette Australia Pty Limited)
Level 17, 207 Kent Street, Sydney NSW 2000
www.hachette.com.au

First published in Great Britain in 2019 by Constable

1 3 5 7 9 10 8 6 4 2

A CIP catalogue record for this book
is available from the British Library.

ISBN: 978-1-47212-897-3

Cover design by Luke Causby/Blue Cork
Cover images: HMS Bounty, Farewell to England © Anthony Saunders
www.militarygallery.com (front cover);
George Tobin 'In Oparrey Harbour – Island of Otahytey',
Mitchell Library, SLNSW (back cover)
Author photo: Peter Morris/Sydney Heads
Diagrams of the Bounty on pp. 5, 10, 15 and 33 © John W. McKay
Maps by Jane Macaulay

Typeset in 11.1/15.1 pt Sabon LT Pro by Bookhouse, Sydney
Printed and bound in Great Britain by CPI Group (UK), Croydon CR0 4YY

Papers used by Constable are from well-managed forests
and other responsible sources.

MIX
Paper from
responsible sources
FSC FSC® C104740

Constable
An imprint of
Little, Brown Book Group
Carmelite House
50 Victoria Embankment
London EC4Y 0DZ

An Hachette UK Company
www.hachette.co.uk

www.littlebrown.co.uk

To Owen Rutter. Over the last 230-odd years this incredible story has had many enthusiasts gathering materials, doing research, trying to work out exactly what happened. None, however, were more dedicated, tenacious or infectiously obsessed than the English historian Owen Rutter and a hundred years later, I salute his work.

CONTENTS

LIST OF MAPS

There never was a mutiny of the Bounty. *Rather there was a revolt of one man against another, Christian against Bligh . . .*[1]

Glynn Christian, author of *Fragile Paradise*,
direct descendant of Fletcher Christian

Awake, Bold Bligh! The foe is at the gate! Awake Bold Bligh! Alas! it is too late![2]

Lord Byron, 'The Island'

INTRODUCTION

It was at a fabulous 60th birthday party in Melbourne, a couple of years ago. Our hostess had placed Lisa and me next to the wonderful acting couple, Sigrid Thornton and Tom Burstall. Over the entrée, Tom raised the story that had long fascinated him, the one he had been gathering material on for 20 years, and had long thought could be the perfect film – Mutiny on the *Bounty*. He was insisting it was the perfect book for me, a *killer* story, which had not yet been done in the fashion I do my historical stuff, making it live and breathe like a novel, but backing it with footnoted fact.

I knew very little about it – not much more than Fletcher Christian rising against Captain William Bligh, before the former reached Pitcairn Island, and the latter returned to England – and was half-interested, at first. But as Tom continued to paint a picture, the contours of the tale, the staggering sexual freedoms of Tahiti, the brilliance of Bligh as a navigator, his bastardry as a Captain, his amazing feat of endurance after the Mutiny occurred; the courage of Fletcher Christian, his extraordinary fate; the division of the *Bounty* crew, first into Mutineers and Loyalists; then the division of the Mutineers into Blacks and Whites, and then most fascinatingly of all, women and men . . . I listened ever more intently.

'What do you think?' he asked when he had finished.

I was both stunned, and sceptical, but didn't know him well enough to express the last part.

Quietly, privately, I couldn't believe the story could be as good as he said. I had always said that the best story in the history of the world was the shipwreck of the *Batavia*, and noted how sad I was when I finished writing it, because I knew I'd never work on a better one. But the history Tom had just recounted had even more – the twists, the turns, the agony, the ecstasy, the endurance, the hatred and love – and lots of situations where the eternal question occurs: *what would I do in that situation?*

But could it possibly all be true, and actually backed up by the kind of original documentation I'd need to believe it was true, to give it the fine detail and dialogue I always cherish most, to make my version of history truly come alive?

A quick cruise trawling the internet later that night gave me the preliminary view – it was true! It was all there. Tom and I corresponded thereafter. He sent me some documents he had collected, I put one of my researchers, my cousin Angus FitzSimons, onto pursuing all the diaries, logs, letters, testimony and transcripts that surrounded the saga. Angus worked hard for three months, getting his head around the whole thing, working out where all the documents were, how they could best be accessed, what had already been done in the field, where we could strike new paths.

When he was finished, we had lunch, which I had scheduled for two hours or so. Four hours later, after I had filled both sides of 15 serviettes and one menu with notes, we got up from the table, and I went home and told Lisa that I had just heard the *new* best story in the history of the world, that this was an important day.

A year later, here we are!

As ever, and as I always recount at the beginning of my historical work, I have tried to bring the *story* part of this *history* alive, by putting it in the present tense, and constructing it in the manner of a novel, albeit with 1500 footnotes, give or take, as the pinpoints on which the story rests. For the sake of the storytelling, I have put the whole account in strong, though not strict, chronological order of events, and I have occasionally created a direct quote from reported speech in a journal, diary or letter, and changed pronouns and tenses to put that reported speech in the present tense. When the story required generic dialogue – as in the things a Captain of that time would say when weighing anchor – I have taken the liberty of using that dialogue to help bring the story to life. Equally, every now and then I have assumed generic emotions where it is obvious, even though that emotion is not necessarily recorded in the diary entries, letters, etc.

Always, my goal has been to surmise what were the words used, based on the primary documentary evidence presented, and what the feel of the situation was. For the same reason of remaining faithful to the language of the day, I have stayed with the imperial system of measurement and used the contemporary spelling, with only the odd exception where it would create too much confusion otherwise. I also note the obvious, that in the eighteenth century displaying a consistency in spelling, particularly with place names and foreign words, was clearly so low on the priority list no-one was remotely fussed. This means that the primary documents have a wide array of different spellings, sometimes from the same person. I have broadly restored consistency, while mostly going with the way Captain Bligh spelt things. In the spirit of depicting the vernacular and thinking of the day, the sailors' terms for Polynesian and Indigenous people – Natives, Indians, or Blacks – have been retained, for the sake of authenticity. And while, at the time, Tahiti was sometimes referred to as Otaheite, I have made it Tahiti throughout, for the sake of consistency.

All books used are listed in the Bibliography, but here I cite most particularly the words recounted by those who lived through the events: James Morrison, William Bligh, 'Jenny' the Tahitian Native, Alec Smith and Peter Heywood. In the modern era, I especially enjoyed the book on Bligh by Rob Mundle – while disagreeing with his fundamental conclusion on Bligh as a leader of men – and also Diana Preston's book, *Paradise in Chains*.

My deepest debt, however – as it is for just about anyone of the modern day who writes about the Mutiny – is to the scholar, writer and editor Owen Rutter who, in the 1930s, produced volume after volume of carefully transcribed and collated documents, trial transcripts, diaries, letters and logs of 'Bountiana' as he put it. Thanks to him we have access to the unfiltered voices of the *Bounty* court martial, the complete stories of James Morrison, John Fryer and especially William Bligh. To indicate the infectious level of his enthusiasm on that maddening man Bligh, I can do no better than to quote his own words, introducing his final volume of Bligh's logs and letters: 'Probing into Bligh's affairs and poring over his papers as I have during a course of years I seem to have come to know him very well: far better, I feel, than I could have known him in life. There have been moments when I could have sworn he was in my room, standing at my elbow as I wrote. Fancy, no doubt; yet at times a fancy that has been curiously real.'* Funny he should say that. For I, too, feel like I know Bligh, and can only hope the reader experiences many such moments before they lay this book down.

I must also thank that Aladdin's cave of Bountyia, the Mitchell Library in Sydney. The Mitchell Library is a national treasure, a place of calm and diligence, a public institution that restores your faith in public institutions. You fill in your request slip for some arcane ancient magazine or incredibly rare, incredibly expensive volume of memoirs, and 45 minutes later, there it is, sitting waiting for you in the collection dock.

To give just one example, William Bligh wrote a Log after the *Bounty* mutiny, a Log full of complaints, arguments, drawn swords and (spoiler alert) further mutinies. This Log was never published by Bligh, there is not any copy of it in the Admiralty records in London, so where is it? The Mitchell Library. Bligh's grandchildren donated it in 1902 and there it sat, waiting for its amazing story to be discovered by researchers like Owen Rutter in the 1930s, who could scarcely believe these scandalous, wonderful records still existed. And they still do, thanks to the Mitchell Library.

For the last decade I have relied heavily on a great team of researchers, and this book owes them as great a debt as ever. Now, if it sounds like nepotism to say I worked on this with my cousin Angus, perhaps it is – and I can only say I am very grateful that, in the name of our very tight extended family – his beloved grandfather was my uncle – *he* agreed to work with *me*. For he was brilliant, working on the story from first to last, around the globe, from north to south and back again, and there are no parts of this whole saga not stronger for his

---

* Rutter, Owen (ed.), *Bligh's Voyage in the Resource*, Golden Cockerel Press, London, 1937, p. 10.

input. Long after my own intellectual resources were spent trying to get to the bottom of something from the frequently conflicting primary accounts, Angus worked on into the night and when I woke up in the morning, there it was! (Bligh *did* have his actual commission handed to him by Christian when he was getting into the Launch, and here is the quote that proves it!)

Dr Libby Effeney has worked with me on the last six books and, again as previously noted, as a researcher and friend she is as good as it gets – she is hard-working, and, curiously, as intellectually strict as she is herself creative in working out how the story can be told better while still remaining within the parameters of *what happened*. Her work on this, going into what we call the FD, Fine Detail, was stronger than ever. From the ground up she took each chapter by the scruff of the neck, worked out what I had, what was not backed up by the historical record, and what else I could add – backed by the historical record. If she were an aeroplane, she'd be a Learjet – fast, and first-class all the way.

My warm thanks also to Dr Peter Williams, the Canberra military historian who first started working with me on my book on Gallipoli, and has stayed with me thereafter. He joined this project late in the piece, but proved to know more about maritime lore, not to mention law, than all of the rest of us put together. As ever, his own commitment to accuracy strengthened the book throughout.

As ever, I also relied on other specialists in their fields, including Dr Michael Cooper for all matters medical, from scurvy through to syphilis.

I am once more indebted to Jane Macaulay for the maps, which you will see throughout. And I offer my thanks once again to Colonel Renfrey Pearson for finding rare documents in archives in the United Kingdom.

My long-time sub-editor, Harriet Veitch, meanwhile, took the fine-tooth comb to the whole thing, untangling hopelessly twisted sentences, eliminating many grammatical errors and giving my work a sheen which does not properly belong to it. She has strengthened my stuff for three decades now, and I warmly thank her.

In all my books, I give a draft of the near-finished product to my eldest brother, David, who has the best red pen in the business. When his interest flags, it is a fair bet so too will the interest of most readers, and I generally slash what doesn't grab him, so long as it is not key to the story. In this book, he was as astute as ever, and I record my gratitude.

My thanks also, as ever, to my highly skilled editor Deonie Fiford, who has honoured my request that she preserve most of the sometimes odd way I write, while only occasionally insisting that something come out because it just doesn't work.

I am grateful, as ever, to my friend and publisher, Matthew Kelly of Hachette, with whom I have worked many times over the last three decades, and who was enthusiastic and supportive throughout, always giving great guidance.

Finally, my thanks to my wife, Lisa. In the midst of this book she had something of a professional upset when, one Monday night, I asked her if, while she was up, she'd mind changing channels . . . and she did! She went from Channel Nine to Channel Ten in about 45 minutes and if that had its challenging moments, it at least meant that there were three glorious months when she was marginally less busy, and we could return to the great days earlier in our marriage when she was able to place her excellent editorial skills at the service of my manuscript, advising on what worked and what didn't. This book also owes those skills an enormous debt.

I hope you enjoy it.

Peter FitzSimons
On the High Seas,
South of Cape Horn,
Late February 2018.
(The waves are *every* bit as high as Bligh said they were.)

DRAMATIS PERSONAE

The crew of the *Bounty* as it leaves Spithead

COMMISSIONED OFFICER

Lieutenant William Bligh, Captain of the HMS *Bounty* but a Lieutenant of the Royal Navy in rank. Age: 33.[1] A brilliant bastard from Plymouth, whose brilliance is narrowly outdone by his bastardry. Having first gone to sea at the age of seven, as a cabin boy, he has salt water in his veins and has risen to become a superb sailor and navigator, who has hauled himself high, despite his common beginnings, to be in command of a mercantile ship from the age of 30, and his first naval command, the *Bounty*, at 32. Of his many undoubted talents, the most singular is an extraordinary capacity to raise the hackles of the men he is meant to lead, against him. In a crisis, few men are better; in tranquillity, none more terrifying.

WARRANT OFFICERS

John Fryer, Master. Age: 34. A stubborn, proud man, born and raised in Norfolk. A good sailor, he is convinced that he is the best sailor on the ship, after Bligh. As Master, he is in charge of running the ship in its day-to-day operations, and also charged with aiding the Captain in matters of navigation.

William Cole, Bosun[2] – the ship's officer in charge of equipment and the crew. Age: unknown, estimated early 30s.

William Peckover, Gunner. Age: 39. Peckover, from London, is the real 'old South Seas hand' on board the *Bounty*. He had been on all three of Cook's voyages and, since Cook had visited Tahiti four times (twice on the second voyage), Peckover's visit on the bread-fruit expedition will be his fifth. He speaks Tahitian fluently and has an excellent understanding of Tahitian customs and ways of thinking.

William Purcell, Carpenter. Age: 26. Proud of his carpentry skills, he works well at them, but – in his first time on a naval, as opposed to merchant, ship – has no interest in other duties.

Dr Thomas Huggan, Surgeon. Age: 43. From Scotland, he is the oldest man on board and the drunkest. 'The drunken sot',[3] as Bligh called him. An obese and incompetent surgeon.

PETTY OFFICERS

Fletcher Christian. Joined the *Bounty* as Master's Mate but was promoted to Acting Lieutenant in March 1788, three months into the voyage. Age: 23. Born in Cumberland. Handsome, charming, popular, proud, moody and prone to secret fits of depression. He had sailed twice before with Bligh, albeit as part of the merchant marine, and not in the Royal Navy as with this trip.

William Elphinstone, Master's Mate. Age: 36. Born in Edinburgh.

Thomas Ledward, Surgeon's Mate. Age: about 30. From Scotland, quiet and conscientious.

John Hallett, Midshipman. Age: 15. Close to Bligh's family.

Thomas Hayward, Midshipman. Age: 20. Born in London. A snippy Loyalist to beat them all.

Peter Heywood, Honorary Midshipman. Age: 15. Born on the Isle of Man. This is his first time at sea.

George Stewart, Honorary Midshipman. Age: 21. From the Orkney Islands. Well educated and experienced. Initially Bligh, who knew his family, considered Stewart a good seaman who 'had always borne a good character'.[4] Shares a mess with Christian, Tinkler and Heywood.

Ned Young, Honorary Midshipman. Age: 21. Born on St Kitts, West Indies. His father was an English gentleman, his mother a native of the West Indies – and he, an illegitimate child of wealth. He is a strong man with dark hair and naturally a dark complexion. There is something slightly unsettling about Mr Young to Bligh, who notes that he has 'a bad look'.[5]

Peter Linkletter, Quartermaster. Age: 30. From the Shetland Islands.

John Norton, Quartermaster. Age: 34. From Liverpool. Functions as the helmsman, responsible for steering the boat. Obese. Previously sailed with Bligh on the *Britannia*.

George Simpson, Quartermaster's Mate. Age: 27. Born in Westmoreland in Cumbria.

James Morrison, Bosun's Mate. Age: 27. A Scot, five foot eight, with a sallow complexion, long black hair, slender. He has been a sailor since he was 18. Although he is qualified as a Master Gunner, that position is already filled on the *Bounty* and so he will serve as the Bosun's Mate, the man who administers the floggings with the dreaded cat o' nine tails. Morrison, who had previously served as a Midshipman, is a cut above your average seaman – a well-educated, witty, hard-working and mischievous man with a rather sardonic and cynical view of life.

John 'Jack' Mills, Gunner's Mate. Age: 38. A cruel bully.

Charles Norman, Carpenter's Mate. Age: 26. Pitted by smallpox.

Thomas McIntosh, Carpenter's Mate. Age: 28. Born in North Shields, England.

Lawrence Lebogue, Sail-maker. Age: 40. Born in Nova Scotia, Canada. Served under Bligh on *Britannia* in 1786.

Charles Churchill, Master-at-Arms. Age: 28. Born in Manchester. In a rogues' gallery, this brutal thug could count on his large portrait hanging in pride of place, in the major salon, before the picture window, so maximum light could fall upon this creature from the dark underworld.

Joseph Coleman, Armourer. Age: 38. Born in Dorking, Surrey. Apprenticed as a blacksmith, he sailed in the *Discovery* (the consort ship to the *Resolution*) on Cook's final voyage.

John Samuel, Captain's Clerk. Age: 26. He was born in Edinburgh and is that rarest of all things, a simpering Scot.

John Smith, Captain's servant. Age: 36. Born in Stirling, Scotland.

Henry Hillbrant, Cooper. Age: 24. Born in Hanover, Germany. 'Sandy hair, strong made, left arm shorter than the other, having been broke . . . speaks bad English.'[6]

Thomas Hall, Cook. Age: 38. Born in Durham. Evidently it was not easy to be a ship's cook under Bligh because of the scanty rations he ordered to be issued to the men.

Robert Lamb, Butcher. Age: 21. Born in London. Served under Bligh on the *Britannia* in 1786.

ABLE SEAMEN

Thomas Burkett. Age: 21. From Bath.

Robert Tinkler, Ship's boy. Tinkler is Mr Fryer's 12-year-old brother-in-law. Born in Norfolk.

William Muspratt, assistant cook and also the *Bounty*'s tailor. Age: 29. From Yarmouth, England.

Michael Byrn, The 'Blind Fiddler'. Age: 28. From Kilkenny, Ireland.

Thomas Ellison, also known as 'Monkey'. Age: 15. Born in Deptford, London. Sailed with Bligh previously on the *Britannia*.

Bill McCoy. Age: 25. Born Aberdeen, Scotland. As hard as nails, but not nearly as sharp.

Isaac Martin. Age: 30. Born in Philadelphia. Served on an American ship during the Revolutionary War, was captured by the Royal Navy and then joined it.

John Millward. Age: 20. From Plymouth.

Matthew Quintal. Age: 21. Cornishman from Padstow.

Richard Skinner. A former hairdresser. Age: 22. Born in Tunbridge Wells, England.

Alec Smith. Age: 20. A working-class lad from Hackney with such a troubled past he has mustered under an assumed name. His real name is John Adams.

John Sumner. Age: 22. Born in Liverpool.

Matthew Thompson. Age: 37. From the Isle of Wight. A violent bastard who is bad to the bone.

James Valentine. Age: 28. Born in Montrose, Scotland.

John Williams. Age: 26. Born in London, grew up on Guernsey.

CIVILIANS

David Nelson, Botanist. Age: Mid-30s. Gardener at Kew Gardens when he accepted the post on the *Bounty* arranged by Sir Joseph Banks. Sailed with Cook on his last voyage. Bligh regards him as a friend. Described by Captain Clerke as, 'one of the quietest fellows in nature'.[7]

William 'Billy' Brown, Assistant Botanist. Age: 26. Born in Leicester, Acting Lieutenant on the *Resolution* with Cook, but changed careers to become a gardener.

PROLOGUE
In Two Scenes

*I, whose ambition leads me not only farther than any other man
has been before me, but as far as I think it possible for man
to go ...*[1]

Captain James Cook, 30 January 1774

Scene I

In the beginning, there was Tane, the Father of Gods, the Maker of
the World, 'the cause of all things; light, darkness, thunder, lightning
and rain'.[2]

And He was Good, and He was Great, and nowhere was His
Goodness or His Greatness better shown to all His children than in
the creation of these islands of *Otaheite*, Tahiti. A sprinkling of land
from His mighty hand sits gracefully atop the impossible blueness of
the ocean, and beneath the sparkling sun, life flourishes. The coconut
palms, plantain plants and bread-fruit trees grow tall and keel over
heavy with their fruits; the grass is verdant, the sand is fine, the birds
roam and chatter, the surrounding sea bubbles with life, and the blessed
people are smiled upon by Tane like no-one else on this earth. The men
of these lands are handsome, strong and supple, able to shinny up the
coconut trees in mere seconds, never putting a foot wrong. The women
are glistening and voluptuous, with round hips, bountiful bosoms and
unrelentingly accommodating natures.

On no-one does Tane more shine, however, than the Tahitian King,
Otoo, whose lineage reaches back to the dawn of time and Tane himself.

Otoo is divine, Otoo can do no wrong. And Otoo will remain King, until such time as a male child is born to his Queen, at which point that child will be King, until such time as he, too, is blessed with a male child.

For so has Tane decreed.

So it has been. So it is. So it will always be.

As Great as Tane is, however, as Divine as King Otoo is, there comes a day in the life of Tahiti, unchanged for centuries, when a Greater Man, a visitor from another land, somewhere far beyond the seas, arrives in a vessel the likes of which the Tahitians have seen only twice before.

His own men call him 'Captain Cook', and he arrives in April 1769, aboard a vessel called the *Endeavour*. Initially, the Tahitians are wary. After all, the first visitors to their shores, two years earlier – Captain Samuel Wallis and the crew of the *Dolphin* – had provided a brutal introduction to how British men might use their power. But this man, Captain Cook, some 40 years of age, is not like that at all. For he comes not to conquer, nor to plunder. No, he comes on a peaceful mission of science. In an effort to pronounce his name, they call him '*Toote*'.[3]

Using sign language, Cook tries to explain to them precisely why he has come, but it is quite beyond the people's understanding. (This is no surprise to Cook. A careless carpenter missing a few digits could easily count on the fingers of both hands how many of Cook's own crew actually understand their reason for being here.)

He has come, you see, to observe the Transit of Venus, an event that occurs with pairs of transits, each pair eight years apart, in a pattern that repeats every 243 years, when for around six hours the planet moves in front of the sun, showing up as a small black disc on its face. When compared with the observations made in London and other points around the globe, it is hoped that the distance from Venus to Earth can be calculated, and that scientists can thereafter use that data to calculate the distance of all the other known planets from Earth,[4] as well as the diameter of the Earth itself.

There are many things in the Tahitian way of life that are quite beyond the understanding of Cook and his men. Things like . . . the *Heiva*, a jigging dance, performed often and complete with costumes, movements and facial expressions the like of which the men have never seen. One Tahitian who explains these strange rituals and rites introduces himself as Hetee-Hetee, a curiously charismatic 40-year-old with a face like a dropped pie, who clearly wants to be of use to these powerful white men, and who makes the effort to learn as many of their words as he can. In the meantime, though Hetee-Hetee, as Cook's surgeon will note, 'was almost constantly drunk with *Kava*',[5] he also gets Kava for the men and anything for the officers.

And then there's something the British *really, TRULY* don't understand . . . the Tahitian women and their overwhelming availability, sexually. Back in England, to get a nice woman to lie with you required a commitment of marriage, while those of easier virtue could be persuaded for a good chunk of your wages, around two shillings. But here in Tahiti, even the comeliest maidens, the most gorgeous creatures, are ready, willing and relentlessly, amazingly able.

Captain James Cook, happily married to Elizabeth Batts, who is waiting for him back in England with their four children, not only declines all offers on the grounds of his marriage vows, but also because he believes it sets a bad example to his men. He is a moderate man.

No matter, one of Cook's trusted associates on the voyage to these shores, the 26-year-old naturalist from the Royal Society, Joseph Banks, is more than happy to take over the skipper's share. Born into a very wealthy family, Banks was educated at Harrow, Eton and Oxford, but his sexual education masters degree takes place on Tahiti. Banks has scarcely set foot on the island paradise, which he records as the 'truest picture of an arcadia of which we were going to be kings',[6] when *two* beautiful women invite him to partake of their considerable charms, *at the same time*, the only problem being they do so in broad daylight!

Banks records the situation as delicately as he can: 'The ladies who shewd us all kind of civilities our situation could admit of, [but] we had not an opportunity of putting their politeness to every test that maybe some of us would not have failed to have done had circumstances been more favourable; indeed we had no reason to doubt any part of their politeness, as by their frequently pointing to the matts on the ground and sometimes by force seating themselves and us upon them they plainly shewd that they were much less jealous of observation than we were.'[7]

Yes, in broad daylight, gorgeous naked maidens are inclined to throw you to the ground to have their way with you. For these extraordinary people, sex is not a matter of shame, nor furtive groping in the dark. It is something to be celebrated, engaged in, *vigorously*. In the same spirit, there is no sense that the job of the woman is merely to succumb to the male's desires. If the women are so inclined, and they frequently are, it is for them to initiate and no eyebrows are raised. No-one pursues the study of this extraordinary cultural phenomenon more than Joseph Banks, who throws himself at the task with enthusiasm, first with the handmaiden of the Tahitian Queen, at which point he is stunned to get an offer from the Queen herself! A few days later, double-canoes arrive bearing more young Tahitian maidens, and just so there can be no mistaking their intentions, one woman disrobes as she walks to him, displaying all her charms, 'and gave me a most convenient opportunity of admiring them by turning herself gradually round'. Well, what is an English gentleman to do? 'I took her by the hand and led her to the tents acompanied by another woman her friend . . .'[8]

Of course Banks recounts his adventures to a bemused Captain Cook, but Cook has no interest in such dalliances himself. He is the Captain, and keeps himself well removed from such activity, for he has serious work to do, in this case starting with the observation of the Transit of Venus which is drawing near.

Banks wishes him well, and when, on 3 June 1769, the Transit of Venus takes place – Cook is certainly occupied with it, as are the astronomer Charles Green and their helpers, but not Joseph Banks. Instead, he closely observes the transit of three Venuses at sunset, with his journal subsequently overflowing with delight:

> 3 hansome girls came off in a canoe to see us . . . they chatted with us very freely and with very little persuasion agreed to send away their carriage and sleep in [the] tent, a proof of confidence which I have not before met with upon so short an acquaintance.[9]

And so, as Captain Cook works through the night making highly detailed observations of heavenly bodies, so too does Banks. Both men are confident they have done fine work, with Banks unable to resist recording the evidence, noting in his journal the following morning:

'We prepared ourselves to depart, in spite of the entreaties of our fair companions who persuaded us much to stay.'[10]

Unfortunately Cook's observations do not go quite so well. His measurements are off. As Cook glumly records, the separate observations taken by himself, the naturalist Dr Daniel Solander and the astronomer Mr Charles Green all differ by 'more much more than could be expected'.[11] A 'dusky shade round the body of the Planet ... very much disturbed the times of the contacts',[12] Cook writes.[13]

It is regrettable, but the opportunity has passed and is not coming around again for over a century. The Royal Society – the most powerful and venerated scientific institution in England, boasting all the leading scientists – will have to make do with the recorded observations; the result will have to be just an approximation, rather than a definitive distance.

With their primary goal achieved, Cook now opens his sealed orders from the British Admiralty – that august institution based at Whitehall, run by the maritime Lords, appointed by the Crown to be responsible for the conduct of the Royal Navy – which were to be read only after the transit observation had been completed. Only now does he find out the second part of his mission.

His secret orders are to seek a Continent or Land of great extent[14] – the long-postulated *Terra Australis Incognita*.

A long journey awaits, and clearly it will take some time to fill the pantries and supply rooms of the *Endeavour* with all the fresh food and water from Tahiti they will need.

Thankfully, there are plenty of exotic fresh fruit and belly-filling roots on this munificent island. And there is one particular plant that has astonished Joseph Banks: the bread-fruit tree, which is so bountiful it has made Tahiti a modern-day Garden of Eden.

It is as big as an apple tree, albeit with enormous multi-pointed leaves and fruit that can grow up to five times the size, and all the Tahitians have to do when hungry is to pick a bread-fruit, bake it in an underground oven, covered in hot coals, or over an open flame and then pick off the black crust of the rind.[15] What remains is, as explorer William Dampier described it in 1688, 'a pure substance like bread'.[16]

Joseph Banks is impressed and intrigued by the possibilities. It has made the Tahitian life so easy:

> Scarcely can it be said that they earn their bread with the sweat of their brow when their cheifest sustenance Bread-fruit is procurd with no more trouble than that of climbing a tree and pulling it down.[17]

Perhaps, he muses, there might be a use for such plants in another part of the British Empire, where they could provide an enormous amount of food, for a minimal amount of effort.

On 13 July 1769, after three months in emerald and azure Tahiti, the Englishmen bid farewell to Obarea, the Queen, and many other acquaintances who have come down to the shore, and now surround the ship with their canoes. The Tahitians farewell Cook as they would a God about to depart for Heaven. From *Toote*'s first days in these islands, despite the extraordinary power of the ship with the big guns that he commanded, he had been kind and benevolent to them, had treated them with respect and honour. He had killed no-one, never betrayed territorial ambitions, had forbidden his sailors to harm the Tahitians or their property in any way, and always made it clear that he was only here for his Transit of Venus observations, and then would go. And now that day has come.

And so farewell. Practically a *God*, we tell you – benevolent, all powerful, the divine *Toote*.

Captain Cook gives the orders. The anchor is weighed, the sailors haul on the ropes, the swathes of heavy canvas unfurl and fill with the light easterly breeze, and the *Endeavour* sails away, many of its crew crowding the stern, gazing back to the green pearl sinking into the blueness, just as the Natives on the shore gaze at the receding white sails until they, too, sink into the hazy horizon.

Among those so gazing is a young girl, Mauatua, the daughter of one of the Chiefs. The impression left by these magnificent officers in their dashing blue coats is so strong that Mauatua will spend many a'night thereafter dreaming of the return of beings just like them.

Scene II

A decade later, in November 1778, James Cook is at the height of his powers, the pinnacle of his fame, but . . . in the depths of his temper.

Yes, the ships he commands, the *Resolution* and *Discovery*, have reached a similar kind of paradise to Tahiti – this one called Hawaii – but he can no longer command a steady mood.

Despite the warm weather, the plentiful food and the agreeable Natives, any sailor can see all is not right with Captain Cook. The warm and rather caring soul of previous voyages seems to be slipping away. He is remote, perpetually irritable, even on a good day, and so prone to losing his temper in such theatrically furious form that his sailors even have a name for it. Captain Cook is doing his *Heiva*, they say of the 'violent motions and stampings on the deck', that little jigging dance of demonic fury and 'the paroxysms of passion',[18] which so resembles the dance the Tahitians used to do, back in ye good olde days.

'The old boy has been tipping a *Heiva* to such and such a one,'[19] the men would remark as they ate their evening meal and recounted the fate of the latest poor officer who had copped a blast from Cook that day, usually unfairly.

It is all *so* reminiscent of those days, the crew-members even call him *Toote*, the name the Tahitians had for him.

At balmy daybreak on 16 January 1779, after more than a month of sailing around and charting this new land, Captain Cook sees a decent bay, fit for anchor. It may just be the place they need 'to refit, and supply ourselves with every refreshment that the place could afford'.[20]

He sends out his Master, a Mr William Bligh, to sound and reconnoitre the harbour. Young Bligh, a Cornishman by birth, is now 24 but has been signed to the Royal Navy since the tender age of seven, and so, having spent most of his life on the water, is a more than worthy Master. Responsible for the ship's navigation, maintaining the Log, setting the sails as required for the conditions, and advising the Captain on the state of the crew and seaworthiness of the ship, he shows a particular aptitude for the technical work of the voyage – sounding and reconnoitring harbours, as well as surveying and charting with remarkable skill. Perhaps seeing a little of himself in the lad, Cook places great value on the young man's abilities. True, Bligh – a man of very humble origins, and, it has to be said, quite common visage, with a head like a potato not plucked at its prime – has an acerbic nature, and often speaks more roughly to the men than Cook would like. But, in the end, his capacity to get the job done is reason enough for Cook to overlook his shortcomings – his rough manner and ever-ready snapping tongue – not to mention the palpable air of tension that too often follows in his wake.

As Cook watches Bligh head off towards the harbour in the ship's Jolly Boat – the smallest boat attending the ship, used as a tender – he notices a canoe making its way towards the ship from shore, followed, yes, by others. *Many* others. Soon there are 50 canoes, all of different length, some being rowed by powerful-looking men, some with a sail, but all full to the gunnels with fierce Natives . . .

These are serious canoes, made by a sophisticated people, their craft carved from single trees, with elaborate carvings on the bow, and the biggest of them holding as many as 50 men, moving at a speed of at least ten knots!

'Before ten o'clock there were not fewer than a thousand about the two ships, most of them crowded with people, and well laden with hogs and other productions of the island. We had the most satisfying proof of their friendly intentions; for we did not see a single person who had with them a weapon of any sort. Trade and curiosity alone had brought them off.'[21]

In the following hours, crowded, loud and joyous – 'the natives singing and shouting, and exhibiting a variety of wild and extravagant gestures' – some of their visitors eventually 'betray a thievish disposition'[22], making off in a canoe with a boat rudder. Cook takes the opportunity to show them, for the first time, the spectacle of firearms. Three muskets and three six-pounders fire over the heads of the men rowing away with the rudder; but it evokes more surprise than fright, and the thieves make no move to turn around.

That evening, of 16 January 1779, Cook notes with satisfaction in his journal:

> In the evening, Mr Bligh returned and reported that he had found
> a bay in which good anchorage and fresh water tolerable easy
> to be come at.[23]

He is not surprised that Bligh has done the job quickly and well, nor that he reported back with almost ceremonial pride, his big green eyes sparkling, the corners of his small mouth turned up in self-congratulation. It is Bligh all over. Responsible yet cocksure.

The following morning, early, Cook gives the orders and the *Resolution* nudges into Karakakooa Bay, just 13 fathoms to the sandy bottom. The busy crew shorten sails so the ship merely bobs forward at one knot, just a mile per hour, before the Master, Bligh, orders the *Resolution* turned into the wind, and gives the order, 'Let go the anchor . . .'

Just 400 yards away, across the bay, the *Discovery* performs the same manoeuvre.

Still the Natives crowd the decks, hang off the sides and the riggings. The clear water around the ships is filled with women and children, 'swimming round the ships like shoals of fish',[24] all day long, never appearing to tire. Many hundreds of Natives also watch from the shoreline.

As the crew get to work, some heading to shore in the ships' Cutters – larger than the Jolly Boat but smaller than the Launch, and used to ferry supplies from shore to ship – to scout for fresh water, others getting to work on fixing the ships, Cook becomes acquainted with the various local Chiefs who are coming on board, even as his concern grows over the sheer numbers and trustworthiness of these new acquaintances.

He is visibly angered when he is gravely informed that the Hawaiians have been swimming under the boats and pulling out nails, something that actually risks sinking them. One of the thieves is caught and flogged on board the *Discovery*. For their part, the Natives are growing curious about when the Europeans plan to leave. They are no doubt wary of the extraordinary amount of supplies Cook and his men are accepting and trading. It has been one thing for them to come and fill their shrunken bellies for a while, but their stay at this bay is now 16 days old, and the sheer quantity of produce they are taking is a worry. If it continues, the Hawaiians will not have enough for themselves, and *they* will go hungry.

Finally, the day of departure arrives – 4 February 1779. Unfortunately, their absence is short-lived, for a few days later a crucial foremast is wrenched from its cradle, which means they must return to damn Hawaii, for repairs.

As they sail into the bay, they find their reception 'very different from what it had been on our first arrival'.[25]

For this time, as they enter the bay, there aren't hundreds of canoes being paddled towards them nor the shouts of thousands of natives welcoming them.

Instead, there are . . . none. *No-one* there at all, 'only here and there a canoe stealing close to the shore'.[26]

The Hawaiians, it seems, are not pleased about something.

'Our return to this bay,' one of the crew-members, John Ledyard, would chronicle, 'was as disagreeable to us as it was to the inhabitants, for we were reciprocally tired of each other . . .'[27]

When King Terreeoboo arrives the following morning and greets Captain Cook, friendly intercourse resumes once more.

Still, sceptical officers like Master William Bligh, and he is not alone, harbour doubts about the depths of this friendship. While Bligh neither knows nor cares what English swabs feel about anything, he has a different approach to Natives, reckoning it is important to both know *and* care, and he prides himself on having nearly a sixth sense as to their collective mood. And today, something is up. He is not sure what it is yet. But it is very likely bad, and he can feel it in his bones.

The common sailor Ledyard feels the same.

'The provisions, both in quantity and quality, plainly informed us that times were altered,' Ledyard records. 'It was also equally evident from the looks of the natives, as well as every other appearance, that our former friendship was at an end, and that we had nothing to do but to hasten our departure to some different island, where our vices were not known, and where our extrinsic virtues might gain us another short space of being wondered at, and doing as we pleased.'[28]

It is the once peaceful Captain Cook who grows unfriendly first and fastest, for on the *Discovery* on this day, tongs and tools are stolen, and on land, some of the Natives throw stones at the men in the watering party.

Captain Cook orders his 2nd Lieutenant, James King, 'in case of their beginning to throw stones or behave insolently, immediately to fire a ball at the offenders'. It is not long before they hear a 'continued fire of muskets from the *Discovery*'. The shots appear to be directed at a canoe, which is escaping towards the shore. Cook, King and some Marines give chase, following the culprits, who are making their escape.

Meanwhile, back on the beach, Thomas Edgar, Master for the *Discovery*, is involved in an unarmed tussle with a young chief, Pareera. Blows are exchanged, an oar is snapped, over a knee or head no-one is sure, but things have now degenerated into danger.

When Captain Cook returns from his fruitless pursuit of the thieves, he is informed of the altercation.

'I am afraid,' he says to 2nd Lieutenant King with anger in his voice, 'that these people will oblige me to use some violent measures; for they must not be left to imagine that they have gained some sort of advantage over us.'[29]

Reluctantly, for violence does not come easily to him, his Master, William Bligh, agrees. Force is the only thing these Natives will respect, the only thing that will bring them to heel. And yet, at least for the moment, other officers intervene, to pacify Cook and delay reckless retribution.

At dawn on 14 February 1779, Cook is woken by a message of troubling news from the *Discovery*: the ship's large Cutter, 'which had been moored to a buoy', 'was missing, and on examining, the Rope which fastened her was found to have been cut . . .'[30] It has been stolen during the night. A whole boat gone!

This is the last straw. Cook moves quickly.

He orders the Marines to arm, immediately, and station themselves across the bay – both on water and land – to 'prevent any of the sailing canoes going out'.[31]

The *Discovery*'s Launch heads to the south point, under the command of 2nd Lieutenant John Rickman, while the large Cutter of the *Resolution*, commanded by Master William Bligh, is sent in chase of a sailing canoe heading out of the bay.

As is Cook's usual practice when things go missing, he intends on pleasantly, politely, bringing the King and his two sons on board the *Resolution*, only to then hold them hostage until such time as the *Discovery*'s Cutter is found and returned. A mean trick? Kidnapping? Yes, but effective.

It is a beautiful, sunny morning, precisely as Hawaii specialises in, when, just after 7.30 am, Cook loads his double-barrelled gun, climbs down into his ship's Jolly Boat, where his 2nd Lieutenant, Molesworth Phillips, the commander of the Marines on the *Resolution*, awaits with nine well-armed Marines, all sitting by their oars, ready to pull their commander to shore, and protect him thereafter. A Launch accompanies the Captain.

Captain Cook heads towards the town of Kavarooa, where King Terreeoboo lives.

•

There they are!

In his large Cutter, perhaps half a mile away, Master William Bligh is catching up to the fleeing canoe in the south end of the bay. At the same time, Lieutenant John Rickman, in the same part of the bay, spots another canoe. Both English officers, and their crews, close fast. But, the thieving 'Indians' are getting away. Desperate to stop them, Bligh orders his men to fire, and with the volley of shots in the far distance, Cook turns.[32]

Unwise?

Perhaps. The boldness of Bligh prompts Rickman to follow suit, he orders his men to fire too, and in short order Nooenemar, a Chief 'of the first rank',[33] – *not* a thief – is killed. Things are spinning out of control. Before Cook has even made land, a Chief is dead. How will the Natives on the beach react when they hear the news?

•

Yes, Cook sees the distant hubbub out on the water, close by the rocks, but he and his men must stay focused.

'The Indians will not stand the fire of a single musket,'[34] he reassures his men, and with that turns his gaze resolutely to the shoreline and beyond, to the cluster of huts where the King is to be found.

Just before 8 am, Captain Cook lands.

He orders the Marines in the Launch to stay put with the Jolly Boat, and marches up the beach with his ten-strong guard, and into the village. The Natives are none the wiser about his intentions as they show him their 'usual marks of respect'[35] as he passes.

Captain Cook waits for the King to emerge, as a matter of courtesy. Out he finally comes, only 'just awoke from a sleep'[36] and greets Cook, who gets straight to explaining the situation with the stolen Cutter.

The King 'squatted down upon his hams as a mark of humiliation'.[37]

The old man tells Cook that he is 'innocent of the Cutter's being stolen'.[38]

Of course. With practised, easy deception, Cook takes Terreeoboo by the hand and asks if he will accompany him to the *Resolution*, to discuss this further?

He will.

Nearby, standing on the beach, Able Seaman William Peckover watches the extraordinary scene closely, as the British Captain and Hawaiian Chief clasp each other's hands tightly, as they purposefully make their way to the shore, even as wild tension flares all around. No, there are no shouts, no stones being hurled. It is much more terrifying than that. Instead, there is a rumble, a murderous murmuring, a strange and sinister noise – not quite of this world – that slowly gets louder as the news spreads among the Natives. *News of death.* A Chief killed, by the Britishers. Shot.

Resolute, Cook continues walking towards the boats waiting by the shore. The youngest of Terreeoboo's sons, Kaoowa, is already waiting in the Jolly Boat. The green pathway under the Captain's and King's feet gives way to the hot black rocks of the beach when, suddenly, the boy's mother – one of the King's favourite wives – comes from the village, and upon reaching Terreeoboo, grabs him by the neck and implores him to stay on land, her tears flowing, her voice strained. Behind her come two Chiefs, who insist the same and eventually force their King to sit down on the ground. They tell him 'he would be put to death if he went on board the ship'.[39] For death has already come today, from one of the British boats!

Bligh. It was that shot that started the volley, the volley that killed a Chief and now Cook can feel the powerful Royal hand in his tighten with rage, the knuckles white.

The King's countenance changes, the Hawaiians seem alarmed, and converse in a manner far too fast for Cook or any of the Marines to follow. People are gathering. Some in the village are seen putting on their war-mats – a native armour made of woven plants then soaked in water – and are 'arming themselves with long spears, clubs, and daggers'.[40]

Captain Cook talks as best he can, trying to persuade the King that no harm is intended, but after no more than 'ten minutes with Terreeoboo he is surrounded by three or four hundred people'.[41]

The situation is not easy. Bligh watches, bobbing in his boat, his glass to his eye, how will the Captain deal with this mob?

Cook can see no way forward. He quickly decides to let the whole ruse go.

'[The King] cannot be forced on board without killing a number of people,'[42] he tells the Marines near him, and they all understand. No-one wants that.

'Lieutenant Phillips,' Cook says quietly, but with urgency. 'Withdraw the men, and get them into the boats.'[43]

A Marine approaches Cook with the news he has been dreading. 'The Indians,' the Marine says, 'will attack in a few minutes. I have just overheard the man I have just stopped say that our boats which were out in the harbour had just killed his brother and he would be revenged.'[44]

The numbers of Natives continues to expand, as does their anger.

Most worryingly, many have started to pick up stones in each hand, and are now knocking them together with an alarming rhythm, the quickening beat of an attack that is surely building.

Clack, clack, clack-clack . . .

The mob starts to close on Cook and his men, swirling around them, beating their rocks, yelling, shaking their fists and weapons. *Steady now, lads, steady.* For Cook knows that to make any sudden move now, show any signs of panic, is to die.

Clack, clack, clack-clack . . .

In the end, however, it is Captain Cook who must act, as he is confronted by 'the insolence of a man armed with a thick mat and a long spike'.[45]

Taking his gun, Cook aims it at the threatening Native and pulls the trigger. As the barrel is loaded only with small shot, it is not intended to kill, merely to hurt – and to warn the others off.

The instant the shot is fired, there is a momentary pause as everyone – Cook, the Native, and the men backing each of them – look to see the result.

He is still standing! The shot did not penetrate the Native's water-soaked war-mat.

Clack, clack, clack-clack . . .

Captain Cook's assailant is now convinced that Cook is *not* invincible, and, worse, aggrieved that Cook has fired at him . . . he charges!

Alarmed, desperate, Cook fires his second barrel, this one 'loaded with a ball'.[46] He misses, but his shot finds another Native, who drops to the ground.

From next to Cook, Lieutenant Phillips shoots at the assailant, killing him.

In an instant, all is chaos. 'A general attack with stones immediately follows'[47] as the numerous Natives close in even more.

Captain Cook hesitates no more.

'Fire!'[48] he calls to the Marines still lined up along the rocks. The muskets are discharged with a thunderous roar. But, as 2nd Lieutenant King later wrote, 'the islanders, contrary to the expectations of every one, stood the fire with great firmness; and before the marines had time to reload, they broke in upon them with dreadful shouts and yells. What followed was a scene of the utmost horror and confusion.'[49]

This haphazard firing, however, will draw fierce criticism from William Bligh, watching contemptuously out in the bay.

'The marines fired & ran,' he will recount, 'which occasioned all that followed, for had they fixed their bayonets & not have run, so frightened as they were, they might have drove all before them.'[50]

All is mayhem and murder, as the musket-balls fly, spears are thrown, and clubs swing. Before long, four of the Marines are cut off amongst the rocks in their retreat, others have taken to the water, while 2nd Lieutenant Phillips, still nearby his Captain, is stabbed between his shoulders with a *pahooa*.

Cook turns his back on the angry Natives and waves his hat to the officers in the boats just offshore.

What does he mean by that?

Exactly.

Lieutenant John Williamson, in the Launch, will ever after claim that Cook was signalling for the men in the boat to retreat, to save themselves. And so Williamson orders his men to retreat, with some enthusiasm – an order that is instantly obeyed – leaving just the Jolly Boat close by.

Lieutenant King, for his part, would insist that Cook waved with his hat for them 'to cease firing, and to pull in'.[51]

Bligh, who swears and curses at the sights in his glass, is *sure* that Cook is calling for their urgent assistance, for them to do the obvious: drive their boats onto the shore, land, and charge at the Indians.

Whatever Cook's intention, there is no doubt as to the result of his turning his back on the crowd. One of the Native Chiefs comes up behind Cook, who is now making his way towards the safety of the Jolly Boat. Wielding a club, the Native strikes Cook in the back of the head.

Cook staggers forward, drops his musket and falls to one knee, hands in the lapping water.

As he rises, another Native Chief brings a dagger right down into the middle of Cook's back. The blade passes 'quite through'[52] James Cook, and his whole body seizes in shock and pain.

In a moment of blurred fury, other Natives rush forward and deal further blows.

Cook falls, face first, into knee-deep clear water.

A dark red stain spreads around him like an ink blot.

But from the Captain himself, the only movement is a slight rising and falling from the wavelets.

Home is the sailor, home from the sea . . .

Captain James Cook is dead.

•

With Cook's death, Captain Clerke, who has been ill for some time, is now in command of the voyage.

After the last retreated sailor is on deck, the urgent task is to retrieve Cook's remains, and give them a Christian burial, before getting out of this duplicitous bay.

And so, at 4 o'clock on the day of Cook's death, Lieutenant King, along with all the boats of the two ships, filled with armed men, proceeds slowly towards the shore 'with view to bring the natives to a parley'.[53]

Gathering and reassembling their Captain's corpse will prove to be a nigh on impossible task, however, as Lieutenant King soon learns that Cook's body has not only been hacked to pieces but then ceremonially presented to different Chiefs, who quickly take the chunks back to their own villages as prizes, to do with as they please.

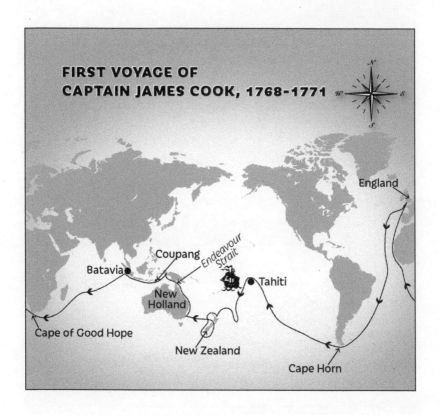

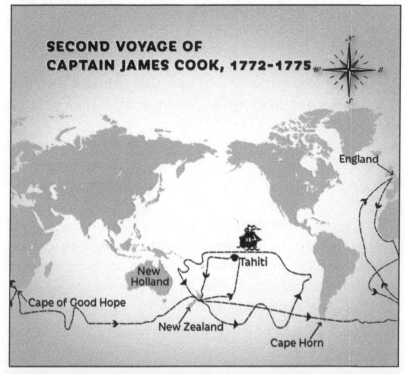

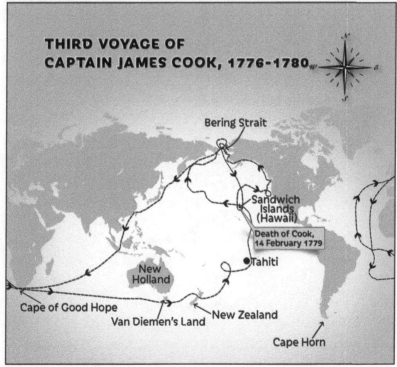

Remnants are painstakingly retrieved and buried at sea, and at 8 o'clock on the evening of 22 February the two European ships leave Karakakooa Bay to find safe harbour elsewhere, before making their second attempt, later in the spring, to find the Northwest Passage.

In the absence of the noble Cook, the chronically ill Captain Clerke removes to the lead ship, the *Resolution*, and is nominally left in charge of the voyage.

And yet Bligh will proudly record the actual situation: 'C. Clerke being very ill in a decline he could not attend the deck & thus he publicly gave me the power solely of conducting the ships & moving as I thought proper.'[54]

As it happens, being in charge is something that William Bligh feels proper from the first. Though saddened by the death of Cook, he feels no responsibility for it. Certainly, it was on his orders that the shot was fired that began the battle, but if only other officers and Marines had shown the same forthrightness, courage and daring, then they would have quickly won the day, and all would have been well. It is an opinion that Bligh is more than happy to share with other officers under his command, just as Bligh is very free with his opinions on all of their failings (something that takes some time). Such forcefully expressed views do not make Bligh popular among his command, but what care he? He is not here to be popular, and he is at least convinced his command will overcome their jealousy long enough for them to observe the consummate skill with which he runs his ships and makes his charts.

On their arrival home, in October 1780, all ship's officers are promoted, with just one exception: William Bligh. The man who ordered the shot that started the fray, which led to the death of Captain James Cook, keeps his current rank.

It does not sit well with Bligh.

But, then again, very few things do.

He is a man who, by his very nature, is dissatisfied, quick to anger and slow to forgive. And everywhere he looks, there are things that make his normal mood move from merely furious to apoplectic with rage.

Ah, but he has seen nothing yet . . .

CHAPTER ONE

IN THE BEGINNING

The natives . . . use it for bread. They gather it, when full grown, while it is green and hard; then they bake it in an oven, which scorcheth the rind and makes it black, but they scrape off the outside black crust, and there remains a tender thin crust; and the inside is soft, tender, and white, like the crumb of a penny-loaf.[1]

William Dampier, 1688, describing bread-fruit

Late November 1787, Portsmouth, England, brothers in arms against a sea of troubles

Those two men, huddled closely together on the table in the corner of this seamen's tavern, The Ship and Castle, at the Royal Navy's anchorage at Portsmouth, have a certain look about them. Clearly, they are peas in a pod, two of a feather, cut from the same cloth, and it is not just the common handsome cut of their uniforms that marks their similarities, nor even the same kind of distinguished, nigh, aristocratic, faces, nor their strong and athletic builds. No, it is that windswept look that all seamen have about them, that slightly squinty gaze that all men possess who have sailed the Seven Seas for many and many a moon, and even more blazing suns, who have faced storms, been through howling gales, and seen sights beyond telling.

It is the intimate way they speak to each other, the instant understanding, the fact that neither man has any hesitation in his words, as they have so many things to say, so little time to say it, and no need for any caution.

If you can't trust your brother, who can you trust?

1

Fletcher Christian has always been like that with his older sibling, Charles, just as they both have been with the eldest brother, Edward, such an accomplished barrister he is to become a Professor of Law at Cambridge. They have loved spending time together even though an occasion like this, when both of their ships are in the one port at the one time, is rare indeed. In a very short time, Fletcher must leave on his ship, the *Bounty*, bound for the South Seas, while Charles is just returned from a mercantile voyage of 20 months to Macao and Madras aboard the East India Company's ship *Middlesex*.

The elder Christian is impressed by just how much Fletch has grown into a man, 'full of professional ambition and hope', in his absence, not to mention actual physical growth, which he delights in showing off!

'This,' says the younger brother, rolling up his sleeves to display his thick forearms, 'has been acquired by hard labour. I delight to set the men an example, I not only can do every part of a common sailor's duty, but am upon a par with a principal part of the officers.'[2]

Charles is not surprised to hear it. In recent times he has come across men who'd sailed with Fletcher, and their reports had been universally glowing – 'he was strict, yet as it were, played while he wrought with the men – he made a toil a pleasure and ruled over them in a superior, pleasant manner to any young officer they had seen'.[3]

Indeed, the sight of Fletcher's familiar, curiously bow-legged walk on deck – it looks like he was born in the saddle, on a fox hunt – brings a smile to the face of any sailor; Fletcher Christian is a friend and a confidant first, an officer second.

Right now, however, he is a brother first and foremost, and, as the drinks flow, the two inevitably trade stories of their adventures upon the Seven Seas, of the things they've seen and done, the women they've loved and lost. (Young Fletcher has always been one for great passions, most particularly since his late teens when he had fallen hard for a beautiful cousin, Isabella Curwen, only to see her marry another man. Her loss has seen him try his considerable luck with dozens of beauties since, but he has found none who can replace her.) But now the conversation turns and Charles Christian makes quite a confession to Fletch, almost by way of warning – a strange tale of mutiny and mayhem on the High Seas. For you see, Fletch, 'when men are cooped up for a long time in the interior of a ship, there oft prevails such a jarring discordancy of tempers and conduct that it is often on many occasions repeated acts of irritation and offence to change the disposition of a lamb into that of an animal fierce and resentful'.[4]

And so it was, Charles confesses, just shy of three months ago, on 5 September 1787, that certain lambs aboard the *Middlesex* had turned to fierce animals. A sailor named Greace had pulled a loaded pistol out of his pocket and aimed it at Captain John Rogers' chest! Greace, maddened by endless minor but multiplying irritations, worsening every day with no relief, shouted that he would kill any man who tried to interfere. Captain Rogers was able to talk him around, and get him to put down the gun, but soon discovered that Greace was not alone! First Captain Rogers found out that his First Officer, Mr Aitken, had been part of the conspiracy to unleash mutiny, which saw Rogers immediately dismiss him from his post and lock him in his cabin. Three hours later, the Second Officer, Mr Fell – appalled at what had happened to both Greace and Aitken – aims a drunken punch at the august form of Captain Rogers, and quickly finds himself also dismissed, and locked in his cabin.

What now?

Captain Rogers had written the answer in his personal journal:

At this time I dismissed the Surgeon, also in the conspiracy.[5]

Fletcher Christian is startled to hear the news. For the surgeon of the *Middlesex* is, of course, his own brother, and the narrator of this tale: Charles Christian.

How on earth, then, is dear Charles here, now, free to tell the tale? Charles has the answer.

Once tempers had cooled, and sobered, you see, Captain Rogers had decided not to report the mutiny to the East India Company![6]

In the extremes of life on the ocean, craziness happens, and men lose their bearings. Rogers had been a brute to his men, and had provoked them to the extremes of mutinying against him. But why have all that come out? Why make an official report on it, which would see all the Mutineers hauled before the courts, and give very damaging testimony against him?

And so, for the moment at least, it had all gone away.

Fletcher listens to the account, transfixed, and his brother is almost amused at how unthinkable his younger sibling finds the whole idea of mutiny.

'I am persuaded,' Charles Christian would recount of the gentle Fletcher, 'that few men had a stronger propensity to beneficence or possessed a greater share of benevolence, or a more anxious disposition to be pleasing and serviceable to all classes of the community, [than he . . .]'[7]

The following morning, Fletcher hurries back to the *Bounty*, with much to do, as he must help the Master, John Fryer, ready the ship for its 18-month journey to the other side of the world.

But, in truth?

The *Bounty* is only just a 'ship'. Much smaller and it would have been rub-a-dub-dub, three men in a tub. For, even allowing for the fact that, at 90 feet long and 215 tons, she is already on the tiny side – some 20 feet shorter than Captain Cook's HMS *Resolution,* and a lot less than half as heavy – no less than a third of that length has been completely refitted so it will no longer hold the crew's crucial berths, but something far more important, a supremely valuable bounty: bread-fruit plants.

Since this extraordinary plant had been discovered and reported back in England, a particular idea had gained enormous traction among merchants and planters in the West Indies. Why not get a thousand or so of the plants from the South Seas and take them to the West Indies, transplant them, and so have a sure and cheap source of food for the slaves working the sugar plantations there? It made sense!

Yes, of course you could continue to feed the slaves with grains bought from America, but that was expensive because they had to be brought from so far, grown by others. Much better to feed the slaves with already proven black man's food that could grow right there in the West Indies!

After all, had not Sir Walter Raleigh's expedition to North America completely revolutionised the cuisine of all of Great Britain simply by bringing the humble potato plant back to England from Virginia in 1586?

HMS *Bounty*

Well then, bread-fruit is the answer here – cheap and self-sustaining.
But how to get King George to agree to the plan?

They know just the man . . .

•

Sir Joseph Banks, the naturalist and botanist who, as a young man, had
accompanied Captain James Cook to Botany Bay, had returned with
so many new flowers, plants, reptiles and mammals – not to mention

memories, as exotic as they are erotic – that his reputation had been made forever. His advancement in the esteem of his country has grown steadily, and he is now one of the most eminent men in England, even becoming a favourite of King George III, and helping His Majesty to establish the wondrously diverse Royal Botanic Gardens at Kew, before going on to advise on several voyages of discovery.

Now installed as the President of the Royal Society, Banks is the *eminence grise*, the acknowledged leader and patron of science in Britain. But yes, very *grise*, he now is. Where once was lustrous tousled blackness, all is now greying curls, at least adding to his air of wisdom. This air is helped by his now jowly countenance – where all was once chiselled precision – bespeaking one who has lived well, and richly, if not always in moderation. Residing in Soho Square, London, he is a wealthy man, a Baronet no less.

Now, though there has been a good gestation period for this grand idea to transport bread-fruit plants to the West Indies, in February 1787 Banks has come up with the grand plan – in fact, it is a plan within a plan – sure to win his country further fame and fortune.

You see, at this time, Britain, after being defeated in the war in which the Americans had won their independence, was losing a means 'for effectually disposing of convicts',[8] whom they had previously shipped off to Virginia's plantations.

What better place could there be as a substitute destination than New South Wales?[9]

On 31 August 1786, Lord Sydney had written to the Lords of the Admiralty, advising: 'The King having pleased to signify his Royal Commands that 750 of the convicts now in this kingdom under sentence of transportation should be sent to Botany Bay . . .'[10]

And so Sir Joseph Banks' first grand plan was set in motion. The government, with the blessing of the Crown, decides to send the well-regarded Captain Arthur Phillip, in charge of a fleet of 11 ships, to establish a penal colony at Botany Bay.

Even as, in the early months of 1787, the fleet at Portsmouth was readied for departure, Banks – pulling the strings in the background, as ever, gliding through the corridors of power – begins to activate his other grand plan: organising a ship to go to Tahiti to secure bread-fruit plants, which can then be taken and transplanted in the West Indies. Perhaps, Governor Phillip could assign one of the ships of the First Fleet to the task, after dropping off its load of convicts at Botany Bay!

On paper, it worked. Two splendid plans combined, very neatly.

Alas, on close inspection, the logistical problems – most particularly how Governor Phillip and his men could turn a floating prison into an airy greenhouse, all in the nether regions of the globe – are overwhelming. And to have them ready to do so, regardless, before their pending departure in just two or three months' time?

In the end, it all proves too much. Reluctantly, Banks realises that getting the bread-fruit will require a separate mission. On 30 March 1787 he writes to the 1st Baron of Hawkesbury, President of the Board of Trade, with the new plan:

> My Lord,
> It is fully my opinion that the plan of sending out a vessel from England
> for the sole purpose of bringing the bread-fruit to the West Indian
> Islands is more likely to be successful than that of dispatching one of
> the transports from Botany Bay, & I am inclined to believe it will be at
> least as economical.[11]

Of course, he also has specific ideas about the route they should follow.

> Her track should be around Cape Horn to the Society Isles [of which
> Tahiti is a part] . . . Thence round the Cape of Good Hope to the West
> Indies, where she may deposit one half of her cargo at his Majesties
> Garden at St. Vincent's . . . & carry the remaining half down to
> Jamaica.[12]

Banks, with supreme confidence in the power of his advocacy, has already taken the liberty of hiring a man who will be key to the voyage's success. Enter the gentle soul of silent David Nelson (if the subject is nothing to do with plants, he has nothing much to say) – the very man Banks had recommended as botanist on Captain Cook's third fateful voyage, who has spent his time since working as silently as a monk in the garden of the King's palace at Kew.

Banks, who has taught Nelson much within the realms of botany, wants him now for his knowledge of the Tahitian language, his capacity with plants and, most particularly, his capacity in 'the art of taking care of plants at sea, and guarding against the many accidents to which they are liable'.[13]

Within weeks, Sir Joseph's whole plan is approved and he gets to work, advising the Admiralty, which then directs the Navy Board. First, he personally approves a collier, *Bethia*, organising for the Royal Navy to buy it for £1950 on 26 May 1787. Within days of its purchase, the ship is at the naval dockyard – Deptford Yard – on the River Thames, with workmen crawling over it like ants, executing myriad tasks, based on Banks' detailed instructions.

The key, as Banks explains to the shipwrights, is to give the plants as much shelter from the salt water and vicious winds as possible, while also giving them a maximum of light, and air, and drainage. Under his guidance, the 'Great Cabin'[14] – normally reserved for the Captain's quarters, where the ship's officers usually eat, meet and make all of the key decisions affecting the course of their venture – is slowly transformed into an aquatic 'greenhouse'.[15] By removing one of the bulkhead walls, the Great Cabin is 'extended as far forward as the after hatchway',[16] making it a third of the length of the ship. Two large skylights are cut into the deck above to let in sunlight, along with stout square windows at the back of the cabin, while three 'scuttles',[17] holes, are cut into either side of the ship to let air flow through. Meanwhile a 'false floor cut full of holes to contain the garden-pots in which the plants were to be brought home'[18] is placed upon the structural floor, which in turn has had a layer of lead sheeting placed upon it, to stop whatever water drips from the pots from seeping to the deck below. Instead, draining holes are cut into the corners, with pipes fitted beneath to gather the excess water to tubs beneath, where it can be recycled to water the plants once more. They also install a heater to be used 'in the case of cold weather in going round the cape', so that the cabin is kept at 'a temperature equal to that of the intertropical countries'.[19]

No expense or effort is spared to make sure the plants will be looked after, and that includes an enormous expense to the comfort of the crew, who are inevitably to be squeezed into a much smaller area than usual.

Things move fairly quickly, most particularly when it comes to finding the right man to command the ship on so unusual a voyage.

Among Sir Joseph's many powerful friends is the very well heeled and well-connected shipowner Duncan Campbell, who swears he has just the man for the voyage – my niece Elizabeth's husband, he explains to Banks, a Navy man by the name of Lieutenant William Bligh.

Ah, yes, Bligh. His time since the notoriously ill-fated voyage with the late, great Captain Cook has not been easy, but still successful. To his endless chagrin, he reflects often on how he was the *only* officer – did he mention? Well, let him tell you again anyway – who'd been on the Cook expedition *not* to be promoted when they arrived home. That notwithstanding, through subsequent voyages, aboard several ships, his undoubted brilliance had so shone through in so many tight spots – including the Battle of Dogger Bank in 1781, when he had been serving aboard HMS *Belle Poule* – he finally got his commission as a lieutenant. What's more, his reputation as a navigator has become ever greater, just as his superb charts are highly prized by the Admiralty. When Bligh gives the longitude and latitude of a particular feature, it can be counted on. (To determine longitude, Bligh uses what amounts to his favourite instrument, his gleaming Kendall chronometer – an extraordinary invention and the first truly accurate timekeeper, just six inches wide with three dials on its face. Cook himself had referred to his own version as 'our trusty watch' and for good reason. The instrument allows them to measure distances travelled along certain courses with such unprecedented precision it has revolutionised navigation in the past decade, allowing seafarers, for the first time, to accurately and quickly measure longitude.) And yet, still the Admiralty has not given Bligh the rank he thought he deserved – Captain.

It does not take Sir Joseph Banks long to be convinced Bligh was born for the position on the *Bounty*. Why, he had not only accompanied Captain Cook to Tahiti on Cook's third voyage, gaining proficiency in the local language – but Cook himself had enthused over his abilities as both navigator and shipmaster.[20]

Bligh will do fine, and Banks will see to it that he receives his commission for the task, with Bligh himself being told – unofficially, by Campbell – when he arrives back in England in early August.

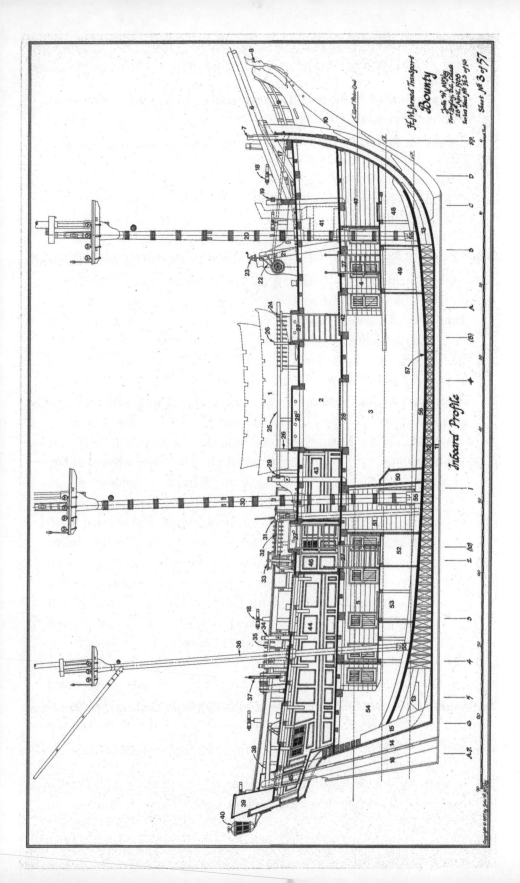

H.M. Armed Transport
Bounty

John M. McKay
for Popham, B.C., Canada
25 April, 1926
Series Sheet No. 3-3 of 6

Inboard Profile

Key

1 Upper deck
2 Lower deck
3 Hold
4 Fore platform
5 Aft platform
6 Bowsprit
7 Knighthead
8 Figurehead
9 Head rails
10 Cutwater
11 Keel
12 Frames
13 Deadwood
14 Stern post
15 Inner stern post
16 Rudder
17 Cathead
18 Half-pounder swivel
19 Fore topsail sheet bitts
20 Foremast
21 Pawl bitt post
22 Windlass
23 Bell
24 Fore pin rail
25 Rail
26 Boat chock
27 Companionway
28 Main hatch
29 Fore brace bitts
30 Mainmast
31 Pump
32 Main pin rail
33 Capstan
34 Mizzen topsail sheet bitts
35 Poop pin rail
36 Mizzen mast
37 Steering wheel
38 Tiller
39 Flag locker
40 Stern lantern
41 Galley stove (starboard)
42 Fore hatch
43 Captain's dining cabin
44 Garden (great cabin)
45 Rudder head housing
46 Lobby
47 Boatswain's store room
48 Boatswain's store room
49 Sail room
50 Shot locker
51 Hold well
52 Spirit room
53 Fish room
54 Bread room
55 Mast step
56 Keelson
57 Ceilings

At last! His own command! And his chance – if he can satisfactorily complete the tasks set him, with his customary brilliance – to prove himself worthy of the rank of Captain.

Immediately, Lieutenant Bligh writes to Sir Joseph:

> *Sir*
>
> *I arrived yesterday from Jamaica . . . I have heard the flattering news of your great goodness to me, intending to honour me with the command of the vessel which you propose to go to the South Seas, for which, after offering you my most grateful thanks, I can only assure you I shall endeavour and I hope succeed in deserving such a trust. I wait your commands and am with the sincerest respect.*
>
> *Sir, Your much obliged and very humble servant,*
> *William Bligh.*[21]

It is the beginning of a long, close relationship. No matter that Sir Joseph is a wealthy aristocrat, while Bligh is of earthy roots, Banks respects the fact that for Bligh – as exemplified by his navigational brilliance – 'close enough' is *not* 'good enough', it has to be correct. No, Bligh is not a man of science, but at least he cares that facts be properly recorded. As for Bligh, to have a man of Sir Joseph's influence pushing his cause is an enormous privilege and he is careful to nurture the relationship.

On 14 August, the *Bounty* is declared ship-shape and ready for service, and two days later the Admiralty officially appoints Lieutenant William Bligh as Commander, and 'orders the Navy Board to have her manned with a crew of forty-five and victualed for twelve months'.[22]

Bligh can barely believe it. Just days ago he was returning from another mercantile voyage for his wife's uncle, and now this – his first sole command of a Navy vessel.

Seeking out Sir Joseph Banks, Bligh questions the great man closely as to the nature of the mission and soon has in his 'possession a copy of the original plan of the voyage and the instructions intended for Governor Phillip'.[23]

Yes, Bligh has certain misgivings about some of the arrangements already made by the powerful botanist but keeps them to himself. For he is, and he knows it, talking to none less than his promoter, patron, *and* defender. With Sir Joseph pushing his cause, there is no limit to the heights he might rise to in the Royal Navy. And for his part, Sir Joseph, just like Cook before him, recognises just what a brilliant seaman and navigator Bligh is and – although recognising he also has a short fuse and high temper – is convinced those positives easily outweigh all negatives.

And now Bligh gets down to the task at hand.

With the usual Captain's quarters being taken over by plants, a small cabin just forward of the Great Cabin, on the starboard side, has been reserved for him to sleep in – at seven foot wide by six foot deep, and no more than five foot high, it is not big enough to swing a dead cat in, but will have to do. His 'dining room' will be not a 'room' at all, just a small section with four canvas walls near his sleeping quarters.

Opposite Bligh's quarters, on the larboard side across the companionway, is a similar cabin for Master John Fryer, essentially the Captain's second-in-command, responsible for the running of the ship, and its security – the latter being the reason he is responsible for the Arms Chest, a sturdy wooden box weighing as much as two men and needing at least that many to lift it. It lies at the foot of the gangway outside the Midshipmen's quarters, and holds no fewer than 40 muskets, a couple of dozen pistols, with assorted bayonets and cutlasses to further make the point if necessary.

Now, although Mr Fryer *should* hold the only key to the chest, because he dislikes being woken in the wee hours for the key, because a shark has been spotted and an officer wishes to shoot at it, or some other such frivolous reason, he gives the key to the ship's Armourer, Mr Coleman.

And where will all the rest of the crew go? Exactly. All are aware that this will be a problem when the ship takes on its cargo.[24]

As ever, they will just have to do the best they can, with the bulk of the 33 seamen hanging their hammocks and placing their sea-chest in whatever spot they can find or wrestle 'before the mast', on the lower deck – in a rough rectangle measuring 22 feet by 36 feet, with some of the 'space also taken up by hatches, companionways and the stove'.[25] As they must eat and live in the same space, if not sleeping they must stow their hammocks so benches and seats may come out. It means they will all be living cheek by jowl by towel with each other once they load the bread-fruit plants on, but they will have to deal with that when the time comes. Behind the seamen are the berths of the Midshipmen.

For his part, Captain Bligh is not worried. He is confident that there is nothing the sea can throw at him that he won't be able to cope with. He always has before. That said, he is concerned that the ship's three masts, although they are regulation Royal Navy size, are too large for the small ship that holds them. Reducing them in height will restrict both the weight on the ship, and the amount of sail that can be put upon them – making the ship a little slower, yes, but much more manageable.

The last is particularly important for the route Sir Joseph Banks has in mind, for this mission – around Cape Horn – might be a bit on the *blowy* side of things.

Bligh also has strong ideas on the inadequacy of the three ship's boats provided by the Navy Board – 'a 20-foot Launch, 18-foot Cutter and a 16-foot Cutter or Jolly Boat'.[26]

No matter that all three boats are already in situ at the Deptford Yards, and ready to be placed on the *Bounty*. With just one glance, Bligh, who has strong views on the virtues of larger boats for the endless ferrying required on long voyages, decides he wants a larger Launch and bigger Cutter, and his requests are granted.

When the larger Launch arrives – a vessel designed to have the capacity for two masts to be fitted – Bligh looks it over. Still no more than 23 feet long, it has a breadth of six feet nine inches, a depth of two feet nine inches and could carry 13 people[27] in relative comfort.

Now, when it comes to filling out that crew roster, the majority of the men, all volunteers, are recommended to him by the Navy Board, but as Captain, Bligh may over-rule those recommendations and also has the capacity to hand-pick many of his men. One of the first so selected is a young fellow, Fletcher Christian.

Hailing from the Isle of Man – that picturesque island, which lies halfway between Great Britain and Ireland, where Bligh's own beloved wife Betsy Betham had been born and raised – Fletcher is a young

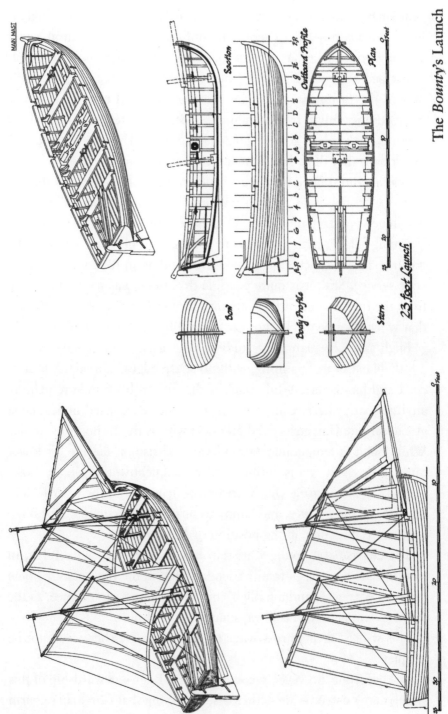

The *Bounty*'s Launch

23 foot Launch

MAIN MAST

Section

Outboard Profile

Plan

Bow

Body Profile

Stern

gentleman who can include no less than King Edward I of England high on his family tree. There is about him the air of a natural leader, a young prince who has not yet found his kingdom, which has deeply impressed Bligh on their previous voyages together, most recently aboard the *Britannia*, when the younger man had been serving as a mere Gunner. Bligh treated him as a Second Mate, an officer in the making, as they had gone to Jamaica and back. The two become such fast friends that Bligh had Fletcher 'to dine and sup every other day in the cabin; and treated him like a brother in giving him every information'.[28] Christian is a Captain's favourite indeed. Of course, as Fletcher is so much younger and junior, Bligh is not remotely threatened by this charming fellow's natural command of the crew, but is aware how useful it can be to have such a highly educated and naturally capable man in your service. Still, it is quite possible that Bligh was *too* fond of him from the first, as one of the Captain's former First Mates would insist that when it came to Fletcher Christian, Bligh is 'blind to his faults'.[29]

Bligh and Christian are a study in contrasts. While Bligh's head is a little like a blurry painting, with no sharp edges, Christian's is chiselled and handsome. While Bligh is the first in his family to achieve anything, anywhere, Christian has a brother ensconced in academia at Cambridge University, and an uncle who is the Bishop of Carlisle. While Bligh is temperamental and vain, Christian, despite his lower rank, leads easily, yet is dutiful. And yet, somehow, the two are close.

And for his part Fletcher Christian is delighted at the offer to join the crew of the *Bounty*, and happy to be under the command of Bligh once more, this time in the position of Master's Mate.

The charismatic young Christian has done so well with Bligh, in fact, that he becomes a family friend, dining in the Bligh family home between voyages, dandling Bligh's infant daughters on his knee, as the toddlers compete for his always laughing attention.

This will be their third voyage together, and Fletcher could not be happier.

Not everyone, however, is convinced that Bligh's stewardship of this young man's career is altogether wise, believing that Christian's charm far outweighs whatever maritime skills he actually possesses.

Among them is the Chief Mate from their latest voyage to Jamaica on the *Britannia*, who cannot believe Bligh has been so seduced once more as to give Fletcher Christian *another* promotion.

For yes, he had seen it all up close, don't you see?

On that last trip, noting Bligh's fondness for the young man, the Chief Mate had gone out of his way to show Christian the ropes, only to find 'he went about every point of duty with a degree of indifference that to me was truly unpleasant'.[30]

And so now Bligh has given him another position?

Of course he has. But the Chief Mate thinks it most unwise.

For his part, Christian is aware that there are those who think he is moving too fast for one so young, but he can still hardly believe his luck at having found a mentor such as Bligh.

As it happens Christian is not the only scion of a well-connected family from the Isle of Man to be hand-picked by Bligh. Peter Heywood, in some ways a younger model of Christian, has never before shinnied up rigging in a storm, never been on a watch, never been out in the open seas, and is still just 15 years old. Bligh's fondness for him – even hosting him in his London home prior to the voyage – and the fact he is from the upper class, has seen him be given the nominal role of 'Honorary Midshipman', which means he can enjoy the privileges of one, even though he doesn't yet know his starboard from his larboard, and barely the bow from the stern. Indeed, Heywood will be well and truly out of his depth on the open ocean and will have to learn fast. No problem, young Peter is much better educated than the usual run of sailors, is a quick learner, and lad of no small talent. As well as a deft artist, he is a poet and very good writer.

•

Inevitably as Bligh spends much of his first weeks as the *Bounty*'s captain overseeing the work, he and the ship's company start to get to know each other. The ship's complement is 46 men in total. Bligh is the only commissioned officer on board, followed by five warrant officers appointed by the Navy Board, experienced men of the sea who are expert in their particular fields: the Master, Bosun, Surgeon, Carpenter, and Gunner. Then there is a swathe of Midshipmen – the young gentlemen, aspiring to one day become officers – and then there are the Able Seamen, enlisted sailors who work the ship at the order of the officers. And of course, the two civilians, the botanists.

The Master for the voyage – the second-in-command, the most senior of the warrant officers and the man upon whom Bligh must rely to take watch and navigate – is a man completely unknown to Bligh, but one who comes with a fine reputation for disciplined navigation. A Mr John Fryer.

From the outset, Bligh notes that Fryer goes about his duties with an air of one who is defensive of his own turf. He is gruff and hard-working, and thanks to a complete lack of charm, he does not make friends easily. But he is more than competent in the technical side of the work, and that is enough for Captain Bligh.

Two other senior men who owe their presence on the ship to Bligh's patronage are the vastly experienced Gunner, Bligh's fellow Cook shipmate, William Peckover, and the Armourer, Joseph Coleman.

The *Bounty*'s oldest crew member, at 43, is the Surgeon – 'sawbones' as the men call him – Thomas Huggan. Though Captain Bligh has been assured from the first that the good doctor is worth his salt, just one look at him raises obvious concerns. Clearly, this is a dissolute, obese man, with the jowls of a bulldog, and a moist pink rim lining his puffy eyes. So they will be starting this long journey with the man in charge of the men's health being the unhealthiest man both before and after the mast. Now, while saying Bligh is not happy is a little like saying Bligh is breathing – it is simply in his nature – in this case he is particularly unhappy. For, of the many things he learnt from James Cook, the need to ensure the health of the crew is among the most important. He will be fastidious about their diet and cleanliness, and hopes to not lose a man to scurvy while on the High Seas. (This is unlike common commanders of the time, who regard men dying from scurvy as being the normal state of affairs.)

So his commitment to good health means he would like to start the journey with a doctor who looks like he is equipped for the task, and this man is far from it. But, we will see.

In contrast to the marked age and experience of Bligh and his top officers, most of the rest of the *Bounty*'s crew are somewhere between merely young, and remarkably wet behind the ears – most of them well under 30, a few on the shy side of 20.

Of particular note is a gaggle of lads on board, the so-called 'Young Gentlemen', including 15-year-old Midshipman John Hallett[31] and 20-year-old Thomas Hayward. Then there are the 'Honorary Midshipmen', lads of little to no seafaring experience who are nevertheless quartered with the actual Midshipmen and given the same privileges as them. Youngest of these aspirants is tiny Tinkler, Robert, the brother-in-law of Master Fryer. (Although the Master has entered Robert on the books as a 17-year-old in order to draw a higher salary, Captain Bligh quickly determines he is no older than 12, and so always addresses him as 'Boy' to needle Mr Fryer, a new favourite pastime of the Captain and one at which he excels.)

A Young Gentleman of note is George Stewart, 21 years old, now living the dream that started a decade before when he was himself a wee lad and his well-to-do father, living at Stromness in Scotland's Orkney Islands, had hosted in their home a young William Bligh and other officers of the late, great Captain James Cook, after their return from the tragic voyage of the *Resolution* and *Discovery*.

On the spot, young George had known what he had wanted to do with his life. He had wanted to be a naval Captain, too, just like these dignified, worldly men. And now, well, here he is, on his way at last, under the command of no less than Captain William Bligh.

Quite the contrary in character to young George is Ned Young, a 21-year-old wild buck of a man with a colourful past, and, as a matter of fact, the only man of colour on the voyage. With a father who is an English gentleman, and a mother who is a native of the West Indies, he is more than usually interested in this mission as it will eventually be taking him back to his homeland. To Bligh, there is something slightly unsettling about Mr Young. This is not simply because he has no fore teeth, nor that all those that remain are rotting, but rather there is a certain malevolent air about him. What is it? His death's-head grin? A devout self-centredness? That, perhaps, is part of it. When, later in the voyage, Bligh comes to note down the tattoos of each man, most of the sailors boast the initials of their sweethearts.

Not Ned Young. His large tattoo under his arm . . .

NY

. . . is in homage to no-one but himself.

An unusual addition to the ship's complement is 27-year-old Irishman Able Seaman Michael Byrn. Cheerful and slender, he is as blond as he is . . . *blind* – a man who can do only one thing well, but that thing makes up for everything else. He is a master of that happiest of instruments, the fiddle, on board to engage the men in the daily dancing that Bligh insists on, yet one more thing Bligh picked up from Captain Cook. As Bligh will note, 'Some time for relaxation and mirth is absolutely necessary [for the crew], and I have considered it so much so that after 4 o'clock, the evening is laid aside for their amusement and dancing. I had great difficulty before I left England to get a man to play the violin and I preferred at last to take one two thirds blind than come without one.'[32] And play Byrn does.

One way or another, between the old and bold, the young and green, and the two-thirds blind, Bligh has no doubt he can successfully complete his mission. The urgent thing now is to complete their preparations, their modifications, and get on their way. With every day, and every step forward, Bligh can feel that rising tingle of excitement that precedes every new voyage.

•

In the early days of September, with Captain Bligh now on board each day and in command of the refit, Sir Joseph Banks receives a letter from Bligh's 'very kind friend'[33] Lord Selkirk, concerning the issue of Bligh's rank.

It appears that Bligh can't quite shake the feeling that he deserves to be made Captain.

Certainly, he is the 'Captain' of the *Bounty* in the sense that no-one will rank higher and he is addressed as 'Captain' by the crew and other officers, but his formal rank remains mere Lieutenant. And it does not sit well with him! On that very subject, he complains to his friend Lord Selkirk of the infamy of his situation, and the good Lord in turn takes up his case with Sir Joseph Banks, writing:

Mr Bligh himself is but very indifferently used, or rather really ill used for he seems to have lost hope of getting any preferement at going out & God knows who may be at the Head of the Admiralty at his return. It would have been simply Justice to him, to have made him Master & Commander before sailing; nay considering that he was, I believe, the only person that was not in some way or other preferred at their return, of all who went out with Captain Cook, it would be no unreasonable thing to make him . . . Captain now . . .[34]

One of the problems is that the *Bounty* is a converted collier-merchant ship, far too small to be considered a warship – its only armaments are four four-pounder carriage guns and five half-pounder swivel guns on each side – meaning its commander can be no more than a Lieutenant, rather than a Captain, and will be the only officer – 'commissioned by His Majesty' – on board.

The small size of the *Bounty* also means, to Bligh's considerable chagrin, that there is no place for the usual contingent of Marines most naval commanders could rely on to defend their person, back up their authority, and defend their ship. This is far from the usual way of things, and it does not sit well with Bligh, even though he has no doubt *his* authority will more than hold its own, regardless, against any internal threats. But what of external? It is irregular, and he does make bitter complaint to the Admiralty. Captain Cook, he knows, would *never* have considered going to areas where sometimes hostile Natives abound, without at least a dozen Marines on deck.

But the Admiralty will not budge. There is no space.

The other factor, of course, both in denying Bligh promotion to Captain, and not giving him Marines, is that they are sending Bligh out on what is little more than a glorified grocery errand, not some massive conquest.

There is to be no promotion, and hence no increase in his salary. For a man with a growing family of one devoted wife and three gorgeous bairns, recently grown used to 'a state of affluence' under his uncle's commercial employ, earning 'five hundred a year',[35] and now on the meagre pay of a Lieutenant, this presents a real problem.

He *needs* extra money for his family's security.

Right now, however, Captain Bligh continues to throw himself into preparations for the voyage to come, now focused on victualling the *Bounty* for 18 months, relying heavily on Deptford's bakery with its 12 large ovens delivering batch after batch of ship's biscuits, or what the men call 'hard tack' – wheat-based and baked hard into thick brown five-inch squares.

Day after day they keep loading the *Bounty* with the supplies destined for her already jam-packed hold, including hundreds of pounds of cheese, tons of preserved meat – heavily salted beef and pork packed into barrels – salted herring, butter, dried peas, dried beans, one month's worth of beer, along with casks of wine and spirits. Enormous barrels of fresh water, each one holding 65 gallons, must also be stored in the hold and secured. And wood, too. Endless bundles of it must be carried on board and stowed – both firewood for the galley, and plank wood for the Carpenter's use when repairing the ship.

Right before leaving, Bligh will also act as a poor man's Noah, of Ark fame, and oversee the bringing on board of many animals, chickens, hogs and sheep that can be slaughtered at sea and fed to the ship's company at the Captain's discretion. Owing to the *Bounty*'s limited space there is simply not enough room to build a pen on the upper deck and all the animals, besides the chickens whose coops can fit onto the after-deck, will have to be housed in the forecastle just forward of the quarters of the Able Seamen, and if that means the sailors' quarters will be right by a pig pen, that is just too bad.

Still, Bligh also orders many barrels of vinegar, for the crew to regularly swab the decks with, to keep things hygienic. There will be no illness on Captain Bligh's watch, and that's an order.

By 3 October, Bligh is able to report to Sir Joseph Banks with some satisfaction:

> *Sir,*
> *I have now 18 months provisions, and which will be the total of what the ship will stow. All other necessaries are on board except a few trifling things . . .* [36]

By 9 October, all the trading goods have been purchased, including everything from chisels, saws and hatchets to looking glasses, beads, and shirts. Captain Bligh must also sign for receiving the sum of 100 ducats in gold coins, to spend in places he will visit after leaving the South Seas.

On 15 October a messenger from Lord Howe gives Bligh formal orders to sail the *Bounty* to Spithead, the safe harbour by the town of Portsmouth. There, they can take on last supplies before receiving final orders, and then sailing out west along the southern coast of the Isle of Wight – where the journey proper will begin. In the first leg, they must complete the long haul south to the treacherous Cape Horn off the tip of South America, where the Atlantic Ocean meets its Pacific and Southern counterparts in a perfect storm of sailors' nightmares. It is a place of monstrous seas, sucking currents, lashing westerly winds that blow strong and constant, whipping up unpredictable williwaws, ushering in sleet, rain, snow, thick fog and clouds that hide protruding rocks, icebergs and shoals; it is the scene of many a ship's doom, and the ocean floor for miles around the Horn is littered with skeleton-filled hulls.

Yes, that is Cape Horn – a place of almost mythological horror, capable of striking a dagger of ice-cold fear into the hearts of even the hardiest seamen, and that certainly includes Captain William Bligh, as his small ship will be taking on this passage of terror from the unfavourable *east*, fighting vicious headwinds all the way. Still, back in 1768 in the *Endeavour*, also going east to west, Captain Cook had managed to round it in three days and Captain Bligh, knowing himself to be a better mariner than his one-time mentor, believes he can do it in the same time, if not better.

However nature itself, in all her many furies, will be conspiring to prevent them getting around the Horn.

Knowing their best hope is to get there early in the season, before the storms are at the height of their fury, Bligh tells Lord Howe's messenger – in his ever short, sharp and even slightly menacing manner – to pass on a message in his own right: 'I beg your Lordship to send me off without delay.'[37]

The messenger, Mr Stephens, slightly shocked at Captain Bligh's presumption, nevertheless gathers himself and assures the mariner he shall have his orders 'in a week'.[38]

Very well then. The main thing for now, is that they are at least off to Spithead. And Bligh is delighted to get moving.

Ahoy, the Captain!

Bligh's small vessel slows down as it draws closer to the *Bounty*, manoeuvres carefully to make its way through the half-a-dozen small craft that are playing tiny cygnets to the glorious mother swan, with dozens upon dozens of men scurrying up and down rope ladders as they go about their duties, more frenzied and important now that the Captain is back in eyeshot, more careful in their language now that he is in earshot.

As Captain Bligh's tender bumps against the side of the *Bounty*, now moored at Longreach, a rope ladder is thrown down to him, and even in their busyness – it would not do to be seen to be slacking off even for a moment – the sailors take pause as Bligh's rather rotund head, balding slightly at the top, pops up like a sprouting potato. He heaves himself upon the deck. Not remotely an athletic man, nor particularly big, still he is intimidating.

It's his eyes. They squint, they glare, they glower, they scan, they calculate, they plot, they judge, they see through bulkheads and are able to spot shirking at 50 yards on a dark and stormy night, right up at the other end of the ship – they miss *nothing*. Bligh, the men know, can spot a loose halyard on a spar in the middle of a gale, during the first watch. He can furthermore know who likely made the error; who should have spotted it long before the Captain did; and how both miserable miscreants should be severely punished under the Articles of War that guide all British warships.

For now, there really are many tasks that he must devote himself to, and he is not a man to be distracted by other trivialities. Arriving back from receiving his orders to sail to Spithead, he drives his men all the harder, eager that their vessel be ship-shape and on its way to Spithead 'ere three days have passed, and then depart for Cape Horn before the end of October at the latest – *hurry, hurry, hurry*, we are already a month delayed!

Yes, there will be many old salts who will tell Bligh that it can't be done, you simply can't get around the Horn if you leave England this late – it is nearly November after all – but Bligh does not care. He is prepared to back his own seamanship, and that of his crew, to accomplish what has not been done before, in order to shave 5000 miles and two or three months off the voyage. Yes, by going around Cape Horn, rather than going with the winds around the Cape of Good Hope and to the south past New Holland, rounding Van Diemen's Land, they might be able to get to Tahiti in seven months, instead of nine or ten, which would mean they may be able to get the plants on board before they germinate, and beyond everything else, he would be back to his beloved Betsy and wee bairns six months earlier than expected. They *must* get around Cape Horn!

In the meantime, the *Bounty* settles ever deeper in the water as more supplies come on board, including sheets of iron, which the Armourer Joseph Coleman will be able to use to do everything from fixing the guns to making nails and axes, not to mention fashioning trinkets for whatever Natives they come across. The sheets of iron can go with the 3000 steel blades, many thousand iron nails, 50 saws, dozens of looking glasses, thousands of beads and 250 ear-rings and shirts that Bligh has already packed away as 'trading goods', with which he will be able to barter with the Natives for the things that they need – hopefully including saplings of bread-fruit! And seeds, in turn, many seeds, with David Nelson carefully storing away everything from corn seeds to seeds for apple and pear trees, tomato vines and so forth.

For their part, the vendors of Portsmouth are eager to supply whatever they can, as quickly as they can. These are not boom times like six months earlier when they had supplied so much for Captain Phillip and the *11* ships of his First Fleet – oh, the money they had made! – but it is precious business at a time when most other ships are settling down for the winter.

Of course, for a captain of the Royal Navy in his home country, there is no problem as Bligh has the Admiralty right behind him, paying whatever bills he presents. Once away from England, however, in far-flung climes, Bligh will have to rely on his commission, that simple but invaluable paper of authority, embossed with the Royal Seal, which should see him granted credit in any foreign port civilised enough to read it.

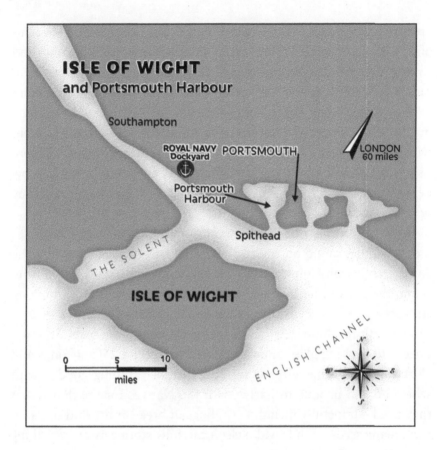

ISLE OF WIGHT
and Portsmouth Harbour

Southampton

ROYAL NAVY PORTSMOUTH
Dockyard

LONDON
60 miles

Portsmouth
Harbour

Spithead

THE SOLENT

ISLE OF WIGHT

0   5   10
miles

ENGLISH CHANNEL

•

The short voyage to Spithead actually proves very difficult as 'a very heavy gale' soon drives the ship 'on the coast of France', and for the first time, the crew are acquainted with the fact that the storm that bursts forth from their Captain will likely be greater than any storm the weather can throw at them. Though testy in readying the ship, once in action like this, he displays a temper and a tempest for the ages.

Nevertheless, as a first test of the ship and her crew, that gale proves handy, and once at Spithead, Bligh is able to report 'with pleasure' to Sir Joseph Banks the *Bounty* 'very capable'.[39]

As to the officers and crew, Bligh is also preliminarily satisfied.

'The Master [Mr Fryer] is a very good Man & gives me every satisfaction,'[40] as do the botanist David Nelson and his assistant William Brown, with both men judged 'very satisfactory'.[41]

As to the crew, Bligh can happily report that, 'we all seem embark'd heartily in one cause which I shall cherish as much as possible'.[42]

There remains, alas, one exception to this glowing first act of the voyage and that is the Surgeon, Dr Thomas Huggan, of whom Bligh writes to Sir Joseph Banks: 'I believe [he] may be a very capable man, but his indolence & corpulency render him rather unfit for the Voyage – I wish I may get him to change.'[43]

To Bligh's mind, it is against nature, against common sense, and against proper naval practice to have the man in charge of maintaining the crew's health guzzling gallons of wine, brandy and rum to get through the day.

Nevertheless, after his attempt to have Huggan replaced fails, Bligh has no choice but to go with the drunken sot he has been given. All he can do is to sign up a Surgeon's Assistant, Thomas Ledward, as backup to Huggan, signing him on, for the moment, as an 'Able Seaman'.

'The Captain,' Ledward writes to a friend soon afterwards, 'is almost certain that I shall get a first Mate's pay, and shall stand a great chance of immediate promotion, and if the Surgeon dies (as he has the character of a drunkard), I shall have a Surgeon's acting order.'[44]

In the meantime, now that the *Bounty* is arrived at Spithead, Bligh is quick to present his credentials and his respects to Vice-Admiral Samuel Hood – the Commander-in-Chief at Portsmouth – and make clear that he wishes to soon be on his way, once he receives those official orders from the Admiralty.

Oddly, as Bligh reports to Sir Joseph, he seems to be the only one with this sense of urgency:

> I have just now waited on Lord Hood who has not yet received
> any orders concerning me. The Commissioner promises one every
> assistance & I have no doubt but the trifles I have to do here [will
> be] soon accomplished. I shall take a pleasure informing you of
> my progress as I go on and I hope by the time my busyness is

over here the Wind will turn favorable – at present I could not move with it.[45]

But to Bligh's stupefaction, and outrage, the orders are slow to arrive. Two weeks later, they are still waiting, and so he writes to Sir Joseph again, pressing his case.

Bounty at Spithead

Nov 18th 1787

Sir

Since my last letter to you wherein I told you of my arrival here, I have been anxiously expecting my Orders. – To see so fine a Wind expending itself and so late in the season as I am, has given me much uneasyness, and it will be particularly hard, if instead of some good reason for detaining the Ship, it has been owing to her being forgot that the orders have not been sent down for me to go to Sea.
I beg Dear Sir to remain with the utmost respect

Your most obliged and very [affectionate].
Humble Servant
Wm Bligh[46]

And yet, day after day, still nothing. The moment of leaving Spithead Harbour should have happened two months ago! And every day's delay, Captain Bligh knows, means a later arrival off the turbulent seas of Cape Horn.

CHAPTER TWO

ON THEIR WAY

The ship was cheered, the harbour cleared,
Merrily did we drop
Below the kirk, below the hill,
Below the lighthouse top.

The Sun came up upon the left,
Out of the sea came he!
And he shone bright, and on the right
Went down into the sea.[1]

Samuel Taylor Coleridge,
'The Rime of the Ancient Mariner'

24 November 1787, Spithead, orders away my boy

The great day has come.

On this morning, the orders arrive from Lord Hood:

> You are . . . hereby required with the first favourable opportunity
> of wind and weather, [to] proceed as expeditiously as possible,
> round Cape Horn, to the Society Islands . . .[2]

Which is one thing. Finally getting away is another, as what has come
with the formal orders is weather so bad – with howling winds, lashing
rain and contrary seas – that Bligh's attempt to get the *Bounty* on its
way is thwarted, they sail just seven leagues over two days before being
forced to return to Spithead.

When they make a second attempt to get away in early December
they are beaten back a second time and Bligh near bursts with fury.

For the last *eight weeks*, his ship has been victualled and ready to go, but here they are, beaten back, stuck. In precisely the kind of towering rage that he specialises in, which sees all underlings cower before him, Bligh writes disgustedly to Duncan Campbell:

> I have been blown back here again with severe winds. I must therefore bear with patience this unavoidable detention. If there is any punishment that ought to be inflicted on a set of men for neglect, I am sure it ought on the Admiralty for my three weeks' detention on this place during a fine fair wind which carried outward bound ships clear of the Channel but me, who wanted it most. This has made my task a very arduous one indeed for to get round Cape Horn at the time I shall be there.[3]

•

With Christmas now just a couple of weeks away, and still no change to the westerly winds, Vice-Admiral Hood is kind enough to turn a blind eye to Bligh briefly leaving the *Bounty* for a last fleeting visit to see his darlings at home, as he also confides to his wife's uncle, 'I could not help revisiting my dear little family for I did not expect a change of Wind, and Lord Hood winked at my absence as he did not imagine it would happen any more than myself.'[4]

In much the same spirit, Captain Bligh even breaks all regulations – punishable by a severe flogging, while bound to the mast if done by an Able Seaman – by helping himself to a couple of fine cheeses in the stores by the galley. And oh, the delight his wife and daughters have to see him so suddenly back among them, bathed in their tears and love, and then to bring out the fine cheeses!

At last, however, two days before Christmas, 1787, there is a change of fortune.

Bligh stirs in his cabin well before dawn. He can sense it even before being quite awake – through the rustle in the rigging, the way the *Bounty* is rolling in the swell. The wind. It has changed!

Quickly dressing, he crawls up the ladder to the quarter-deck, where he is immediately joined by the straight-lipped Master, Mr Fryer, who has sensed the same thing. And there it is. The star-speckled sky confirms it is going to be a clear day, and the strong wind across the waters is from . . . the east!

Captain Bligh barks orders, and things move quickly, starting with the pigtailed Bosun, William Cole, putting his massive lungs to good service by blowing on his pipe to pierce the quiet dawn and rouse the men, even as James Morrison, his mischievous mate, moves from hammock to hammock, calling out: 'All hands! Turn out and save a clue!'[5]

One by one the sleepy sailors emerge and get to work to the urgent tune of the Bosun's whistle.

Moving among them, light on his feet though always perspiring, is Fletcher Christian, shouting orders above the commotion: 'Hove short, sir!'

'Loose the topsails!' Numb hands of the 'top-men', 40 feet above the deck standing on footropes along the spars, fumble to untie frozen stiff knots.

At 6 o'clock, as the twinkling stars give up and disappear and an ethereal glow grows on the eastern horizon, Captain Bligh gives the nod and John Fryer utters the words all the sailors have been waiting for . . . 'Weigh anchor!'

The sailors gather around the capstan and – all together now, *heaaaaave* – throw all their weight on the stubborn bars that jut from it. None strains harder, nor with bigger bulging muscles, than the strongest man on the ship, James Valentine, a 28-year-old Scot, proud of his physical strength, and with every right to be so. Slowly, slowly, the capstan starts to turn and creak, as the rope that pulls the anchor cable pulls ever tighter and, far below, the bower anchor that has been keeping the *Bounty* in position starts to take the strain, as it is hauled from the bottom of the bay six fathoms below.

Heave, lads, *heaaaaave!*

And push to the tune . . .

For now, right by them, Michael Byrn, the 'Blind Fiddler' as he is known, dances his bow across his worthy fiddle, weaving the beloved tune of a 'forebitter', an old sea shanty most sailors know before they get their 'sea-legs' . . .

Loose the forecourse! Christian yells. *Loose the mainsail!*

A great rumbling of canvas and a wild rattling of blocks . . .

The men keep rhythm with the shouted sea shanty, as the Blind Fiddler plays, oh how he plays, while up top, James Valentine – as nimble as he is strong – scrambles along the topgallant yard, one hand manipulating the ropes, the other hanging on – 'one hand for yourself and one for the ship', as the saying goes – as the big beautiful sails unfurl with his efforts, and the ship surges forward.

From the gay wash of the *Bounty*'s blunt-nosed bow hurtles the beautiful, carved figurehead of 'a woman in riding habit',[6] leaping out at all those who would dare to get in her way.

After a squally second day, Christmas Day dawns calm, which, as Bligh would note with satisfaction in his journal, 'allowed us to keep our Christmas with cheerfulness'.[7]

Which is one thing.

Keeping their Christmas dinner down proves to be quite another. For, not long after the sumptuous fare, of beef and plum pudding washed down by copious mugs of rum – which gives their subsequent singing of sea shanties and dancing in happy unison to the Blind Fiddler a certain sway not explained by the roll of the ship herself – it is the turn of the Devil himself to inspire the weather. Yes, in short order, the *Bounty* is beset by sleet, squalls, gales and high seas bad enough to test even the saltiest sailors among them, let alone a wide-eyed, homesick landlubber like young Peter Heywood, who for the first time in his life is away from family, and at Christmas. The next day the weather is worse, and the following day . . . more hellish still, as Bligh records in his Log: 'Very hard Gales and high Sea with Severe Squalls.'[8]

In the extremity of the situation, Bligh is a blur of movement and commands, usurping Master Fryer's usual role, to shout the commands himself.

The murderous maelstrom simply never stops, hour after hour, as the wind howls at them, the thunder booms, the bolts of lightning crack incessantly, the masts bend, and the waves crash over her bow and sides, sending terrifying torrents of water cascading over the decks, sluicing along the entire ship – taking anything not tied down with it, which is why every man topside has a rope around his middle tied to something secure. So pounding are the seas, continually breaking in

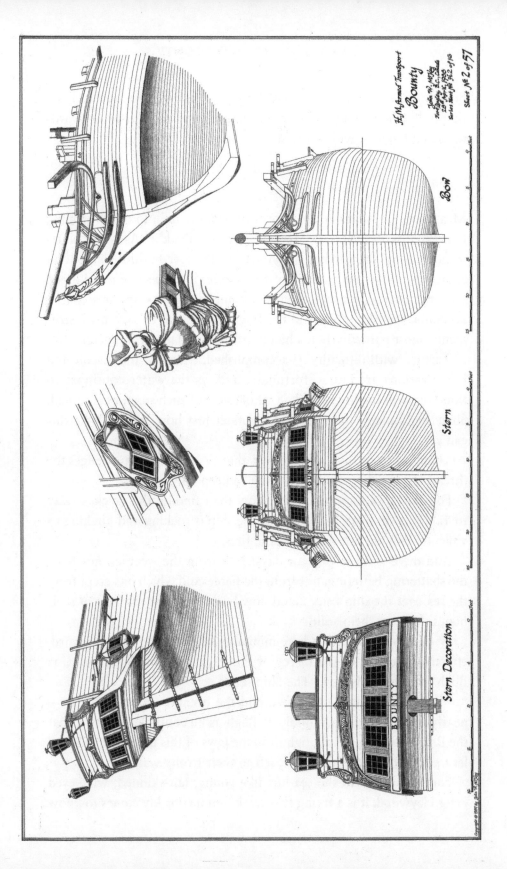

H/M/ Armed Transport *Bounty*

John W. McKay
Montgomery B.C., Canada
23ʳᵈ April, 1988
Series Sheet No 762 of 10

Sheet Nº 2 of 57

Bow

Stern

Stern Decoration

BOUNTY

BOUNTY

huge waves over the sides of the ship, that they knock out the chock that holds the Launch in place on the deck, meaning it slips towards the side, dragging with it the smaller boat, the Cutter.

> It is only with the utmost difficulty and risk that they were saved from being washed overboard.[9]

Meantime, the waves crashing over the sides remain so overwhelming that Bligh writes there is, 'an entire Sea on Deck'.[10] As water starts to pour down the hatches, Bligh yells to his ever faithful clerk, John Samuel – a hovering humbug of a man who lives to serve the skipper, with responsibilities including maintaining all the Captain's charts, accounts, written orders and the Log – to be sure to save his instruments, most particularly his highly prized Kendall chronometer.

This is, 'with difficulty',[11] accomplished. Many of the biscuit and bread rations are not so fortunate, and, as the water continues to flood through the lower deck, a whole slew of such supplies is ruined. Shivering, hungry, wet, the men wonder just how much worse this can get.

Things are so grim, so dangerous, that even Bligh acknowledges the threat, writing they are 'Not daring to keep our Course'.[12]

For, far more important right now than finding the quickest way to Tahiti, is survival. Below decks, the ship is rocking and pitching so violently they do not dare light the fires.

And there is no respite for days! Not from the weather, not from the shattering battering, not from the fierce cold which has crept from the sea over the ship's sides, and now burrows to the marrow of their bones, freezing them solid.

With sails reduced to a bare minimum, the *Bounty* scuds forward, effectively surfing at the mercy of the mighty ocean. Thankfully, as Bligh records in his Log, 'The Ship scuds very well.'[13]

The wind continues to howl, and the ocean continues to roar – nearly, but not quite, as loudly as Bligh as he continues to insist that the *Bounty* keeps pushing right into the jaws of this maritime hell, and let the devil take the hindmost, left in their frothy wake.

For newcomers to the sea-life, like young, fair-skinned, wide-eyed Peter Heywood, it is a trying first week, but he quickly comes to know his way around the ship, how everything fits together, how it all works, and just how *exhausting* it all is. Then, when exhausted, his drenched rudimentary berth hardly offers a place of rest, let alone an appropriate place to draw, sketch and write down his poems, as the ship rocks and moans and the men scurry to bale out as much water as they can.

As for the 33 seamen cramped into the lower deck, all find it hard to sleep, tossing and turning in the foetid darkness, together with myriad rats, cockroaches, fleas and lice, but they simply do the best they can.

At last, on the night of 29 December, the wind drops, the waves calm, the *Bounty* rights herself and, finally, blessedly, the men are able to light a fire in the galley to get a start on drying out all that is wet – everything on the boat bar the cockroaches, which have already dried themselves, and flourish in such conditions.

The next day, the sun comes out in all its glory, and Captain Bligh orders that the whole ship be scrubbed from top to bottom, the beams scoured with vinegar.

> I ordered hot water to be got ready & every man washed his dirty linen &c. and hung up to dry by Noon, having a fresh breeze and fair weather.[14]

In short order, the deck is strewn with sodden bedding, bread, hammocks, hemp, spare sails, socks and sundry.

The bedding can dry and be fine, but not so the bread and biscuits. As a result, Bligh orders every man's daily ration to be cut by a third. It is not quite a starvation diet, but certainly a grumbling one, and while the crew do so relatively freely to each other, so too do the officers, quietly.

Young Peter Heywood finds himself in a mess with the rest of the Young Gentlemen – officers in training, including his fellow Manxman and fast friend, Fletcher Christian, together with George Stewart and Robert Tinkler – where the grumbling is good-natured rather than serious: for it is not right for either an officer like Christian or officers in training like young Peter to speak against the Captain, even in jest.

Beyond both being Manxmen, Heywood and Christian fit together naturally for their common fine education, their common come-down through loss of a family fortune and . . . the fact that these are the only 'common' things about either man.

With that intuitive English feel for one's class, both are aware they are several rungs higher than their Captain, William Bligh, and many rungs higher than most of the ship's company. This, too, brings them together, makes them confidants and messmates who enjoy lingering over their meals.

The old hand Fletcher is quick to show young Peter the ropes, literally and figuratively, and the younger man appreciates it. When Fletcher shows off one of his many crew-pleasing tricks – jumping, with extraordinary athleticism, from one empty barrel on deck into the one right beside it – Peter is front and centre of the applauding throng. How *clever* is Fletcher, and what a fine leader of men, amusing the crew, earning their affection, and not just barking endless orders at them.

The contrast between the approach of the slender, darkly handsome and popular Fletcher to that of Captain Bligh – barking on a bad day, to the point of being barking mad, with a fair skin that simply will not tan and a certain natural rotundity – could not be more marked.

But what cares Captain Bligh? He is not here to be popular, he is here to ensure the ship and crew's survival so they may complete their mission. He doesn't need friends, his own mess is based on rank and prestige – dining nightly with Fryer and Huggan – and they do not discuss personal things.

And so it goes. The sun she rises, the sun she falls. The wind she blows, and the swell rolls on. The *Bounty* proceeds south by south-west at the average rate of four knots, or almost 100 nautical miles a day, her bow sending small, gurgling waves of white scurrying starboard and larboard before her majesty.

At least the weather and seas remain fair for the next few days, allowing the *Bounty* to sail on in relative comfort and arrive in Tenerife's Santa Cruz Harbour on the morning of 6 January 1788.

> As soon as the ship was anchored I sent an officer [Mr. Christian] to wait on the governor and to acquaint him I had put in to obtain refreshments and to repair the damages we had sustained in bad weather.[15]

Rowed back and forth in the Cutter by six good men and true, Fletcher Christian, drying his perpetually sweaty hands with a handkerchief, brings back some good news and some bad news.

Happily, the Governor of the Spanish colony, the Marquis de Branciforte, has sent word that his colony would be pleased to supply Captain Bligh with whatever victuals are needed, and also help with repairs.

But Bligh's message to the Governor, that the *Bounty* would salute His Excellency with several rounds of cannon fire, 'provided an equal number of guns were to be returned . . . I received an extraordinary answer to this part of my message, purporting that His Excellency did not return the same number but to persons equal in rank to himself.'[16]

And that is the end of that.

The *Bounty* enters the harbour with no booming salute to the Governor, and things go little better on shore as they find that Tenerife itself is low on supplies. They simply cannot buy the amount of bread they need to replace that which they have lost, and the quality of the meat and livestock on offer is not only abysmal but offered at prices near double the usual price for such goods.

Three shillings for a single scrawny chicken!

Thankfully, there is corn, onions, potatoes and pumpkins available, and Bligh begrudgingly pays the exorbitant prices to the Spanish thieves. There is one exception to the lack of quality supplies, in the form of casks of delicious wine at reasonable prices.

'My People are all healthy and well,' Bligh informs Banks cheerily, 'and I have taken in some good wines which I think will be better for them in hot Climates than the Spirits.'[17]

The one indulgence Bligh does allow is the purchase of two drip-stones to filter the drinking water that, over time, tends to become slimy in barrels. By pouring the water into the large bowls cut into these remarkably porous pieces of limestone, the water that drips out at the bottom into buckets has had most of its impurities removed, caught in the stone.

The *drip, drip, drip . . . drop*, all day long and into the night from here on is the back . . . *drop* to which the sailors work and sleep around the clock.

Meanwhile, the Carpenter, William Purcell, works hard with his assistants to repair the damage done to the ship by the storms they have gone through. Yes, he works well, but within a narrow parameter. For let this be known to all. He does not, do you hear, do such things as haul supplies or patch sails. He is a highly skilled Carpenter, did he mention, and as a matter of noisy principle, will nary lift a finger to help with any task that is not to do with wood. Still, after just four days, Purcell and his assistants finish their repairs and the ship is back in good order, ready to push on once more.

She weighs anchor on the sparkling morning of 10 January, and the sails of the *Bounty* are soon full with the wind at south-east, and the ship quickly gathers pace across the impossibly azure expanse.

It is good to be underway once more, as they get to grips with the task ahead. On that subject, the following morning the crew is assembled on the aft-deck to be advised of two new orders by Captain Bligh.

Firstly, as the length of this next leg of their voyage is uncertain – there is a real possibility that they will be prevented from rounding Cape Horn so late in the season – the 'allowance of Bread [is] to be reduced to two thirds'.[18]

And secondly: from now, Captain Bligh orders, instead of the two-watch system – the customary 'four on, four off'[19] in which the ship's complement is divided in half and the two groups alternate four-hour shifts; four hours of sailing and work, four hours of rest and sleep, and so on – they will move to a system pioneered by Captain Cook: three watches of eight hours apiece.

Doing it this way, of course, requires a third officer to take charge of a watch, and Captain Bligh is sure he has just the man: Fletcher Christian. Now, to give the affable, hard-working and popular Fletcher Christian proper authority to so oversee the watch, Bligh is effectively appointing him 'to act as Lieutenant',[20] a huge leap up the ranks from mere Master's Mate. Christian will now be in charge of the *Bounty* for a full eight hours each day, unwatched except by himself, with a small group of increasingly loyal men under his command.

This news is well received, as Fletcher Christian is the most highly regarded man on the ship, loved by all, from Captain Bligh down to the most humble Able Seamen.

'We are all in excellent Spirits,' Bligh writes to Sir Joseph Banks, 'and I have still the greatest confidence of success in every part of the Voyage.'[21]

•

As the ship settles down to daily life on the High Seas, a favourite among the crew – particularly Bligh and Fletcher Christian – soon emerges. Young Thomas Ellison, or 'Monkey' as Fletcher calls him, is just over five feet tall, no more than eight stone wringing wet, and has a shock of dark hair that rises in strict contrast to his light-skinned face. He *looks* a little like a monkey, is *mischievous* like a monkey, and with his muscly frame, the 15-year-old can *climb* the rigging like a monkey, scampering hither and thither, with everything the top men require, from flasks of water, to gloves, to wooden mallets. And yet he is also possessed of such a keen intelligence and capacity to learn that even Captain Bligh takes an interest in developing him to the point that, in a relatively rare act of kindness, he instructs the Captain's Clerk, the ever obsequious John Samuel, to teach the boy writing and, as Monkey spells it, Arithmetick.[22] Monkey is always on his best behaviour when within earshot or eye-line of the Captain – and he has a very keen instinct for exactly where the Captain is at all times – and Bligh notes in a letter to Duncan Campbell, who had recommended the lad in the first place, that Monkey 'will make a very good seaman'.[23]

Another on the ship has a slightly aristocratic bearing about him, even though not remotely to the manor, or even manner, born. The 26-year-old Scot and Bosun's Mate, James Morrison, is just like that. Morrison is of slender form but surprising strength. A sailor since he was 18, he has sailed long, toiled hard, and has the kind of wide and deep experience to go with his native intelligence that makes him notable for his resourcefulness. Whatever the problem, Morrison finds a way of solving it, helped along, at least a little, by his deep faith, which allows him to proceed with the confidence that the Lord is watching over him.

This endures despite his mangled hand – which includes missing the upper joint of his right forefinger thanks to an old accident – an injury which affects his handwriting in the journal he keeps. As Bosun's Mate, it is Morrison's task to help the Bosun, William Cole, with maintaining all the sailing operations on the upper deck – from seeing that the deck is swabbed, to maintaining the rigging, looking after the anchors and supervising all the work aloft.

This is on the upside. On the downside is that the Bosun's Mate must also administer whatever floggings Captain Bligh might order – that is, he must personally remove the shirt of the man to be punished, lash his wrists to the mast, and then whip his back to a pulp with the dreaded cat o' nine tails, or in sailor's parlance, make him 'taste the salted eel'.

Another of interest on board – a stranger to each and every one of them before boarding the *Bounty* – is a swarthy, Cockney Able Seaman who was christened John Adams 22 years earlier but these days goes by the name of Alec Smith. Now, precisely why he so changed that which was marked in the Birth Register never actually emerges – any more than how he got a job as an Able Seaman, despite having no such qualifications and this being his first sea voyage of any kind – but it is unlikely to have been by cause of remarkably good behaviour, as opposed to bad. And yet if the blemishes on his record remain unknown, the blemishes on his face are all too apparent, as his face is deeply pitted with smallpox scars. Bligh notes he also 'has a scar on his right foot, where it has been cut with a wood axe',[24] which causes him to limp ever so slightly.

Yes, life has dealt Alec an unending series of very low cards, from being born an orphan, to growing up in a poorhouse in East London as an illiterate, to contracting whatever diseases were going. And yet, he is also a survivor. Standing five feet five inches tall, with a remarkably strong build, he is one who for the most part keeps to himself, who observes rather than participates, who judges which way the wind is blowing rather than causing it to go in one particular direction himself – and acts accordingly.

•

The others?

They comprise a fairly typical rogues' gallery of men who have built their lives sailing the Seven Seas, whoring, fighting, drinking, pissing razor blades with venereal disease, occasionally wielding swords and muskets in shore fights, suffering scurvy, sleeping damp and hot with rats and lice, eating weevils at every meal, swabbing decks, heaving ropes, tying knots until their fingers bleed, shinnying up masts, setting sails, and standing watch as the waves crash, the wind blows, the lightning bolts strike, and the ship surges onward beneath the starry skies and searing suns alike.

There is Charley Churchill from Manchester – nudging 30, and a strapping five foot ten, he has the curious combination of being as strong as a bull and cunning as a sewer rat, all with a head like a friar. Yes, with long light brown hair falling from the ring that marks his entirely bald pate onto his enormous shoulders, Churchill is a formidable character, and one the other crew-members are wary of. And, in the regrettable absence of Marines on the ship, it is an obvious move for Captain Bligh to make him his Master-at-Arms, responsible for basic drill and weapons training for the men above decks, and keeping the crew in line below decks – the logic being that the biggest brute on the ship has the best chance to keep the lesser brutes behaving properly.

Meanwhile, it is hardly surprising that Churchill is as thick as thieves with Matt Thompson, a sailor ten years his senior, as they are both . . . thieves, by nature. Thompson has his own scars from brawls and boozing, it's just they are so numerous and deep it is sometimes uncertain where the scar stops and he begins.

The other bookend of Churchill's bastardry, and a decade younger than him, is the rogues' rogue Matt Quintal, a lusty Cornishman with a fair complexion and light brown hair, who, like his two mentors, would sooner a fight than a feed and is happy to go a good distance out of his way in order to find one. His particular talent is straight out insubordination and he is one of the men that Fryer notes immediately as a troublemaker. Quintal is in turn – and for the same reason – soon in league with Able Seaman Billy McCoy, a 24-year-old whose face and torso bear the marks of many vicious knife-fights.

Yes, rough, tough men – as is to be expected in any crew of the Royal Navy. But they don't worry Captain Bligh. Most of their trouble is committed on land, because, there, the repercussions of punishment are so much less. Here on the water, they are under his total control.

14 January 1788, three days out of Tenerife, a problem with the big cheese

A light breeze is blowing from the south-west, the sun is shining, the *Bounty* is making fair progress covering 100 nautical miles a day, and Bligh takes the opportunity to order the cooper, the man in charge of taking care of the barrels in the hold, to bring some of the casks of cheese up on deck to air, to check they've not spoiled.

But there is a problem.

'Two cheeses have been *stolen*,'[25] Captain Bligh barks like a watch-dog who has just discovered its meat-locker is empty. The officers and sailors respond in kind, stiffening, standing up straight, hoping to avoid being savaged by their own meek immobility. By now, they know that when Bligh barks like this, your only hope is to avoid his scrutiny, for the fit of bad temper that follows, the dark and unpredictable mood that will foul the entire ship, may last mere minutes or days, but you *don't* want to be the object of his focused fury. It is only those aloft, high in the rigging, who can dare to gaze with full interest on the scene below, just as those in the middle of it must stare resolutely at their own shoes.

The cooper, Henry Hillbrant – born Heinrich Heildbrandt in Germany, 27 years earlier, and still with only a minor grasp of English – does not have the option of staying out of it.

Opening and closing the casks is quite a skilled process, requiring the cooper to use his hammer and chisel to remove one hoop, and bend the wood back just far enough to remove the lid – so that gentleman must know something about it? As a matter of fact, he does.

For, when asked, he replies, carefully, hoping this is just some misunderstanding, because the Captain must have forgotten – *Ja?* – 'Zer cask had been opened before while the ship was still in the river by Mr Samuel's order and the cheeses were sent to Mr Bligh's house.'[26]

Well!

Bligh moves quickly.

'I will give you a damn good flogging if you say any more about it!'[27] he tells the startled cooper through clenched teeth.

As to the rest of you scurvy lot, he seethes, 'the allowance of cheese is to be stopped from officers and men until the deficiency is made good!'[28]

The cheese ration is indeed immediately cut, with only butter served, but the seamen refuse it entirely as, 'acceptance of the butter without cheese would be tacitly acknowledging the supposed theft'.[29] The mood darkens further when one of the Able Seamen, John Williams, discloses to the others that he personally had 'taken the cheeses to Mr. Bligh's house with a cask of vinegar and some other things!'[30]

Feelings become even more strained, when, as the ship draws closer to the equator, many of the pumpkins begin to spoil as the weather gets hotter and heavier – and Bligh instructs the cook to prepare for each man one pound of pumpkin per day instead of their daily allowance of two pounds of bread, only for the men to refuse to eat it. They don't want to eat their vegetables, and Captain Bligh can't make them.

Alas, when Bligh's faithful servant – the poor, quivering Mr Samuel – goes to the Commander's cabin to beg his pardon and inform him, Bligh's face flashes hot in 'a violent passion'.[31]

Standing on his dignity and venturing out into that dangerous wilderness that lies on the highwire between high dudgeon and his towering rage – that area where people are known to make the best speeches they will ever regret – Bligh calls all hands on deck to give them a blast that would peel paint and turn oranges into onions, with withering abuse of not just the common sailors but also the officers, even the man thought to be his particular favourite, Fletcher Christian.

'You damned infernal scoundrels!' he roars at them. 'I'll make you eat grass or anything you can catch before I have done with you!'[32]

James Morrison records, 'his speech enforced his orders, and every one took the pumpkin . . . Officers not excepted, who though it was in their eyes an imposition said nothing against it . . .'[33]

In truth, however, Bligh's greatest problem is not any of the common crew-members. No, far more difficult is one of his officers, specifically the medical officer Dr Huggan, he of the flabby form, the ghastly, stale smell, the florid red cheeks, the one who arrives at the table early, leaves late, and drinks four times the amount of wine of any other officer meantime.

> I now find my Doctor to be a Drunken Sot he is constantly in
> liquor, having a private stock by him which I assured him shall

be taken away if he does not desist from making himself such a beast.[34]

February, 1788, Isle of Man, a muse muses

The beautiful young woman in her gracious home on the Isle of Man writes down, scribbles out, writes again, and scribbles once more, as – bit by bit – another of her verses of poetry starts to take form, this one on the dear brother, away on the *Bounty*, who she misses so much:

> *May Heav'n on you its choicest Favors pore*
> *And gentle Breezes waft you safe to Shore*
> *Remember Us – we oft shall think of You,*
> *A thousand Blessings on you all – Adieu.*[35]

Nessy Heywood's poetry is mostly mischievous and witty, but when it comes to her absent brother Peter, there is an aching sadness. Until she is with him once more, smile gaily as she will, Nessy knows she will not be at peace.

Early February 1788, close to the equator, tensions mount

Since Bligh's outbursts of rage over first the cheese and then the pumpkins, the mood on the *Bounty* has blackened, even as tension has grown. Every meal now, to the men's eyes, and more to the point their rumbling tummies, confirms that their portions of meat are beginning 'to appear very light'.[36]

The old salts among them, who recognise this outrage for what it is, appeal to Fryer, 'Examine the business, Mr Fryer. You must procure us redress.'[37]

When Fryer raises the issue with the Captain, his response is swift. It is just not the one they want.

Everyone aft, and gather around the Captain! Now hear him, and hear him well, you ingrates, you curs, you rude ruffians.

'Everything relative to the provisions,' Captain Bligh announces in his jarring way, his potato head glowing red, 'is transacted by *my* orders, and it is therefore needless to make any complaint for *you* will get no redress. *I* am the fittest judge of what is right or wrong.'[38]

Are we clear now?

Looking around – his eyes like glaring slits – he wordlessly dares anyone to speak, to question his command. There is nothing, bar a collective glowering silence.

Very well then. Let me be even clearer.

'I will flog the first man severely who should dare attempt to make any complaint in future,'[39] Bligh threatens, before dismissing them with little more than an imperious wave of his high and mighty hand.

Still, ignoring the growing discontent, the sharp silence that suddenly arises wherever he goes on the ship as the muted murmurings stop the instant he approaches, Bligh blithely drafts a note to Duncan Campbell to be given to a British whaler they come across, noting the crew's 'content and cheerfulness',[40] and another to Sir Joseph Banks where he affirms that 'we are now fit to go round half a score of worlds, both men and officers tractable and well disposed and cheerfulness and content in the countenance of everyone . . . I have no cause to inflict punishments for I have no offenders.'[41]

Or at least, right now, as they are becalmed in the doldrums, where the heat hangs heavy and the wind refuses to blow – they average just a dozen nautical miles a day for as many days – Captain Bligh has no offenders that can be bothered offending with any energy.

On Sunday morning 2 March 1788, the usual religious service takes place, with the entire ship's company gathered around the mizzenmast, as Bligh himself, a pious soul, conducts proceedings. Immediately afterwards, as is the practice every month, the crew are read the Articles of War, so each sailor knows the rule of military law in the Royal Navy and cannot claim ignorance of the penalties for disobeying the Captain.

But, in fact, this morning, as Captain Bligh will record, reading the Articles of War is not the most important part of proceedings.

> I now thought it for the good of the service to give Mr. Fletcher Christian an Acting Order as Lieut. I therefore ordered it to be read to all hands.[42]

Though it involves little more than giving the young man a signed letter confirming his promotion, it is an act of great generosity. For, as Bligh knows, giving Christian such a promotion now – lifting him to the official rank of Acting Lieutenant, in command on the *Bounty*'s third watch – means that upon their return to England, should all go to plan, Fletcher will be virtually guaranteed a full promotion, a commission in the Royal Navy!

And, rare for Bligh, it is a move that is exceedingly well received by the entire ship's company. Congratulations and hearty handshakes abound for the smiling Fletcher, the most popular officer on the *Bounty*.

Fryer is stung. For, incontrovertibly, Christian's promotion sees his own demotion, if not in rank, certainly in pecking order. For Fryer is not a Lieutenant, acting or otherwise. He is the Master of the *Bounty*, a position which is *supposed* to be second only to Bligh.

Now Fryer is feeling a little stormy himself as, a short time later, his composure cracks and he has a vicious quarrel with the troublesome Cornishman, Matt Quintal, prompting the Master to march up to Bligh to report 'insolence and mutinous behavior'.[43] Yes, Captain, one of the rougher sailors, Matt Quintal – that lusty lad when sober, and bruising brawler when drunk – has refused an order.

What?

Refused an order? On *my* ship?

The Articles of War could not be more clear on what must happen next, as Bligh reluctantly notes in the Log: 'I had hopes I could have performed the Voyage without punishment to any one, but found it necessary [to order] 2 dozen lashes for Insolence and Contempt to the Master.'[44]

Within minutes of Fryer's report, the shout goes up around the ship, down the hatches and from deck to deck: 'All hands aft!'

Yes, they must gather to witness punishment, and so form up just forward of the mizzenmast. And now, the glowering Quintal is led forward, his hands bound in front of him by a seizing (a length of cord specifically used to tie the men when needed), wearing only his wide sailor trousers, his shirt already off, exposing his grubby white back and bronzed forearms.

It is now for James Morrison, charged with doing the honours for the dishonoured, to act. Grabbing Quintal's hands, he stretches them out way in front of him, lashing them tightly to a capstan bar, no hint of mischief in his eyes, just detached attention to duty.

In his dress uniform, for this piece of organised, institutionalised brutality is indeed a formal occasion, Captain Bligh stands before his men, and removes his hat, holding it to his heart. The crew do the same, as they all now stand there hatless, out of respect for the King's commandments, as they all must now observe this brutal rite of the Royal Navy.

Bligh, with the slightest hint of pity in his voice – for as much as he knows it is his duty to oversee this punishment, its brutality appals him – orders Morrison to deal out two dozen lashes.

(With the look of one who must now pick up a dead rat – for his own distaste for what he must do goes well beyond displeasure, and even beyond disgust – Morrison plucks the cat o' nine tails from the red baize bag he keeps it in, before dipping the tails in the bucket of seawater handy for the occasion. The crew holds its breath as he now draws the cat high above his shoulders and well back, before flinging it hard, forward and down. There is a furious whistling and now a loud, but fleshy CRACK! as the leather cuts into Quintal's flesh, instantly drawing red stripes across his back.)

All watch until the ritual is complete, a bloody warning if ever there was one.

Bligh returns to his cabin, brooding. Reopening his Log, he adds fresh detail, making it clear that the beating was not his choice. Rather, he was responding to the complaint made by the sailing Master, Fryer. And the charge? Originally, Bligh had marked it down as mere 'Contempt'.[45] But now, on more consideration, he changes it to the heavier charge of 'Mutinous Behaviour'.[46]

They sail the *Bounty* south along the eastern coast of South America, past 40 degrees South latitude and onwards towards the spot where three great oceans – the Pacific, the Atlantic and the frozen Southern Ocean – are in perpetual stormy argument as to which is the greatest of them all.

So tempestuous is their tempest, the men on the *Bounty* are well aware of it, even when on only the distant approaches to Cape Horn.

On 20 March, even as the booming thunder of the trouble up ahead rolls towards them – and our lady of the riding habit is clearly jumping some sharp hedges placed close together – Bligh dictates to his quivering clerk, Mr Samuel, 'the sea became confused and troublesome'.[47]

They are twin conditions that grow by the day, as the winds whip up, the waves rise, and the temperature drops further still. The crew know they are getting close when, out to starboard, in the final week of March, the snow-covered mountains of Tierra del Fuego on the southern tip of South America appear.

Curious whales spout sprays of indignation at their unlikely presence at this time of year, and enormous albatrosses, with wing-spans of up to eight feet, leave their own sprays of a different kind, but similar sentiment. They are joined by 'vast quantities of seals, penguins . . .'[48]

It is the white and black albatrosses though that attract the most attention . . . So huge! So majestic! So *many* of them, gliding high up above the masts, as they follow the ship's progress ever further to the south. And yes, although most of the sailors know the old reckoning that it is bad luck to kill an albatross, neither they nor Captain Bligh care for such superstitions, not when they are this hungry for fresh flesh. So it is that, as Bligh records, 'by floating a line with hooks to it beyond where the bait was placed, and giving a sudden pull when the birds had hold of a piece of meat',[49] they are able to catch them. At other times, when the huge birds sometimes perch on the masts and rigging, the men are able to bring them down with a well-placed musket-ball, being *very* careful not to hit the sails instead.

Just 30 minutes later the albatrosses have been plucked, gutted and are being roasted, with the sailors soon able to fill their gaping maws with great relish and even greater satisfaction – and to hell with the old salts' superstition. We are modern sailors, and do not believe the nonsense about it bringing bad luck.

More than ever, Bligh is aware that they are about to enter what is reputed to be the stormiest patch of sea on earth, the most infamous sailors' graveyard on the planet, from which not even St Elmo, the patron saint of sailors, can save a man. But Bligh is firmly convinced, in his heart, by God, that those reports are exaggerated and . . .

And the BOOM of each wave on the *Bounty* is now followed by a long shudder as the ship tries to shake it off, to compose itself for getting over the next wave. There's no doubt the waves are growing taller, thicker, bigger, more powerful. They crash wildly against the hull, drowning out the subtle *drip, drip, drip* . . . *drop* of the dripstones that once kept the placid rhythm of the voyage. The skies darken; the shrieking westerly winds lift. Thunder rolls over the *Bounty*, rattling the ship's wooden bones to the point that Mr Purcell is concerned. Lightning bolts flash and strike the sea, dead ahead. This time the old salts' warning is vindicated: 'fair weather in this clime is always a fore-runner of foul'.[50] The lady in the riding habit rears up, her beast willing her to turn around. Alas, she cannot. Onwards she rides, further into the maelstrom.

Could it be the curse of the albatross, whose slaughter Captain Bligh has assented to?

Whatever the cause, even Bligh must admit over the next few stormy, tumultuous days, that the previous reports had not been exaggerated at all.

Bligh records in the Log on 29 March that the High Seas 'exceeds any I have seen,'[51] no small claim for one who has been at sea for the better part of three decades.

As March turns to April, and the seas turn fouler still, the *Bounty* finally makes it to 60 degrees of South latitude, which is just far enough south of the latitude of Cape Horn headland that Captain Bligh can at last bark the orders for the ship to tack north-westward – so they may begin the attempt to round the Horn. Right on cue, rising against them, strong winds lash the *Bounty* unceasingly from dead ahead, followed by gales, followed by squalls, teeming with sleet and hail. And soon enough, *snow*. Blanketing snow plummets down upon them, even as the wind roars, causing those on deck – with no protection at all from the flush-deck structure of the ship, nothing to break the wind – to freeze. Still they must keep moving, shovelling snowdrifts from the deck, as their hands falter and their mouths curse and the very marrow of their bones turns to ice.

Theirs is a cold that will not let go, and even when they go below decks and huddle around the smoky fire, there is no respite. For the damp and cold has been seeping into *everything*, their fellow sailors, their meals, the decks themselves, and particularly their bunks and hammocks. Even their *hunger* is cold, a problem as that hunger is getting stronger by the day and their bodies are burning ever more energy in the vain attempt to keep warm. Such is everybody's constant discomfort that tempers are frayed, around the clock, leading to 'frequent broils in the galley',[52] and particularly vicious fighting around mealtimes, when their food is being divvied up and the men circle each other like feuding scavengers intent on getting the best deal.

And still our lady in the riding habit, leading the *Bounty*'s valiant charge, day and night, rocks and rears and then rocks and rears some more, through seas that seem to only grow as they try to head west.

The days are a living nightmare, the nights much worse, and their whole existence only made bearable by what they have to admit is Captain Bligh's solicitude for them, his insistence that the fires are always roaring, that those coming off watch are instantly given hot soup, that their clothes are dried and they have dry clothes ready to get into.

But there remains no sign of relief any time soon.

And Mr Purcell is more worried still, as leaks spring up all over the creaking hull, as ever more water seeps from upper deck to below decks. Bligh records being 'obliged to allot the great cabin, of which I made little use except in fine weather, to those people who had wet berths to hang their hammocks in'.[53]

The most appalling thing for Captain Bligh?

It is that even though it is miraculous enough to have survived such violent weather, even though they could not have worked harder to make headway against all odds, the sad truth is they are getting . . . *nowhere!*

In fact, it is even worse than that.

On 1 April they had made it to 72.5 degrees west latitude.

And now, after three full days of fighting the battering winds, of tacking to starboard then to larboard, and then doing it all again and again – with each tack taking 15 minutes of very hard work, and exhausting everyone – he does fresh calculations and finds they are at 71.9 degrees west.

Yes, all that effort, and they have been blown backwards by 63 nautical miles!

Bligh records his 'mortification to find at the end of every day that we were losing ground; for notwithstanding our utmost exertions and keeping on the most advantageous tacks . . .'[54]

•

Among the ailing sailing men of the *Bounty*, few are suffering more than young Peter Heywood, who beyond staggering sea-sickness, which involves projectile vomiting until there is simply nothing left in his body to give, finds there is something even worse – lighting the fire beneath the ire of Captain Bligh.

Though never quite sure what he has done wrong – it may possibly be being an effortless rung or two higher on the class ladder than his Captain, or even that Bligh begrudges the time Fletcher spends with him – Heywood is all too sure of the punishment. On Bligh's shouted order, Peter is 'mast-headed'.

Mast-*what*?

Mast-headed.

Following the Bosun's barked orders, young Peter learns soon enough, as rung by torturous rung – all as Bligh watches in cruel satisfaction – he must climb the rigging until he reaches the spar on the bottom of the mainsail.

How do you like that then, Master Heywood? Not so fancy, now, lad?

No, indeed.

Not so fancy, Captain Bligh.

With frozen fingers, Peter must fumble to first get a rope around himself, before tying it tight. Praying that his greenhorn knot will hold, he is now hoisted up and up until he reaches the top of the main-mast, hugging tightly to it as the wind howls and he is rocked from side to side in crazy arcs that never cease.

How long must he endure this hell? He has no idea.

An hour passes. The sleet and rain lashing his boyish face are not the only cause of moisture running down his cheeks. Curse Bligh! It is only after one whole watch, eight full hours, that his frozen form is allowed down. He can barely breathe, with a cold in him that goes clear to the core of his being. Quietly, Bligh omits recording the punishment in the Log, as he does not wish a blot on the record of the young gentleman. And here is Bligh all over.

Bligh's 'tornados of temper',[55] as referred to by one of his Lieutenants, are just that. They are violent storms of fury, thunderous curses and endless verbal lashings that nigh blow away the very sanity of the unfortunates who stand quavering and humiliated before them. And then they are gone with the whipping wind, leaving a peaceable Captain Bligh in their wake – often wondering why everyone suddenly seems so silent around him.

In this case, the horrifying scar on Peter's soul is not so easily erased by Bligh's subsequent calm. *Never* will he forget his agonised and freezing fingers clutching the ropes for fear of falling, as the mast swung back and forth on its crazy arc, even as his eyes scanned desperately for a break in the weather that would not come.

Of course it is not just Heywood who is struggling to keep physically and emotionally strong. Nigh on every day, yet one more of the exhausted, terrified crew staggers to his frozen berth or hammock, and, when his next turn comes, is unable to rise again.

During snowstorms, the men on watch are frozen so stiff that they often have to be assisted to come below deck at the end of their eight hours, and are even incapable of speech for some time afterwards. To these men, Bligh remains notably sympathetic.

> I took care to nurse them when off duty with every comfort in
> my power. The invalids I made attend and dry their clothes and
> keep a good fire in every night, so that no man took his watch
> with a wet rag about him.[56]

It is tough going, and on a bad watch it can seem like impossible going, but through it all Bligh orders that, whatever else, they *keep* going and so they do.

Bligh is just made that way, come hell or high water, raging storms or rebellious seas.

Keep going!

CHAPTER THREE

ON THE HORN OF A DILEMMA

Blow wind! come, wrack!
At least we'll die with harness on our back[1]

William Shakespeare, Macbeth, Act 5, Scene 3

'Tho the [Bounty] was an excellent sea boat, it was as much as
she could do to live in this tremendous sea where the elements
seem to wage continual war.[2]

James Morrison, Bosun's Mate,
recalling the attempt of the Bounty to round Cape Horn

Ah! Well a-day! What evil looks
Had I from old and young!
Instead of the cross, the albatross
About my neck was hung.[3]

Samuel Taylor Coleridge, 'The Rime of the Ancient Mariner'

April 1788, off Cape Horn, the *Bounty* battered

In such appalling weather, nothing is simple.

When the wind is so strong and seas so violent that your Captain now has his own person tethered by a rope when on deck, it is a fair reckoning how difficult things must be below, even when one is embarked on something as basic as trying to prepare supper. Coughing and spluttering, the men so assigned can only just manage to cook and serve the food in the dark and cramped confines, due to the thick smoke hanging heavily with no passage to escape, as even though the hatches are battened down, Bligh insists on every fire roaring to try to keep things below as dry as possible.

Still, things get even worse when, in the second week of April, they face mountainous seas the likes of which they have never imagined, let alone seen, as the *Bounty* climbs ever higher up successive monsters, momentarily sheltered from wind as her shortened sails droop wanly, only to climb to the crest, where she is hit by the screaming winds with full force once more, the reefed sails bellowing in protest, the masts creaking to the point of shrieking, begging for release . . . only to plunge down into the valley of water once more . . . before she reaches the terrible bottom. Like the nose of an enormous wooden porpoise, at this point the bow of the *Bounty* is buried in the ocean for a few seconds before, thinking better of the full dive, rises, water cascading from her deck, shuddering with the strain, even as the next wave looms above and she must start her long and agonised climb once more.

As the ocean tries everything to stop her, one wave arrives from a surprise angle and hits amidships with such violence that the ends of the yards take a dip in the ocean and the ship near rolls on her side. She rights herself, but not everyone hurled sideways does, and the cook, Thomas Hall, Bligh is informed, was thrown into the bulkhead so violently he cracks a rib and is knocked stupid. Coming to, it is all he can do to hobble painfully around the galley for a short time, before taking to his berth, no longer able to work. The wretched Dr Huggan also falls and dislocates his shoulder, though Bligh strongly suspects this is more due to him being rolling drunk. There is no way around it. Every day, the weather gets still worse, progress gets even slower – on a bad day, which is just short of every day, they don't advance at all, as although they battle the elements, it is the elements that win, pushing them backwards or off course – and the number of crew injured and invalided continues to rise. Yes, if Dr Huggan were still able to minister to his patients, he would have a lot of them. As it is, Surgeon's Mate Ledward is left in full charge, tending to Able Seaman Skinner's dislocated shoulder after a bad fall, nursing the Quartermaster, Linkletter, who has been hurled by the force of the ocean down into the fore cockpit, wrecking his back, and now must just lie in his bunk and groan as he can do nothing, just as nothing can be done for him.

By mid-April, even Bligh recognises that if the *Bounty* herself doesn't break some time soon, the spirit and bodies of the crew-members will, as he notes on 13 April.

> I now begin to see that this is a most improper time to venture into these seas . . . Upon the whole I may be bold to say that few ships could have gone through it as we have done, but I cannot expect my men and officers to bear it much longer . . .[4]

Just how close that breaking point is, he is too busy and important to know, but Morrison knows. He knows very well. And it is *soon*. If not before. For Morrison is intimate with a story that has been kept from the Captain. That injury of Thomas Hall? That happened during the storm? Well, it actually happened during a storm of angry men, furious at the meagre rations Bligh doles out each day . . . and fighting among themselves over who gets what. At dinner, Hall had been doling out one gallon of cooked wheat into 46 separate lots when some of the men had decided their portion was unfairly small, their tempers exploding in rough rhythm to the fists of the worst of them – big, bruising Quintal – on the ribs of the cook. Of course they hadn't told Bligh. If there is an honour among thieves, so too is there honour among brawlers, even when the brawl-ee gets very badly injured.

All of them know that Bligh's own temper is so white-hot that there is simply no telling what punishment he might mete out, so even Hall agrees to maintain that his broken ribs are due to the storm. Similarly, Churchill, who has his right hand badly scalded in the course of the melee, suffers in glowering silence. Someone is going to pay, but just not yet.

A Captain of more moderate disposition would have learnt thus of the fraying tempers of his own men, but, in this case, Bligh's reputation for incandescent rage means he remains oblivious of what is happening on his ship.

Recognising this, Fryer takes matters into his own hands. When that genuine scoundrel Churchill – the roughest ruffian on the ship, though a couple of others run him close – has his hand scalded in yet another fight about who is to get the first food, Fryer decides something must be done. Saying nothing to Bligh, he decrees that henceforth, at every meal, a mate will be posted at the galley to ensure that the food is shared fairly, and to ensure no fights break out over it.

And so it goes.

A storm without . . . and a storm within. And both of them are getting worse as the days pass, and the *Bounty* continues to plough forward, and backwards, making ever heavier weather of it.

And yet there is one notable exception to those on board the *Bounty* who are demonstrably suffering in the ongoing lashing of the storms – Bligh himself. A man with a chunk of ice for a soul, and a spine of cast iron, he does not shake or shiver or bend in tough times, he just stands out as so much stronger than all those around him who are wilting. Bligh is at his best in a crisis, grows ever stronger as the odds get longer, and is a whirl of action and command! Others go on and off their watch, depleted and defeated, but Bligh is there in the middle of every big storm, no matter how long it lasts.

Meanwhile, though the men on deck continue to struggle through the tons of freezing water that continue to be dumped over the ship's sides, down below those off-watch busy themselves drying their clothes, their hammocks, their bags – everything that is sodden is brought close to the galley fire to be painstakingly dried. Of course, it will all be drenched again soon enough, and to some it seems not worth the effort, but Captain Bligh is insistent.

Bligh can sometimes seem more like a scolding nanny than a fearsome Commander, perhaps because it is Bligh's firm belief that, 'Seamen will seldom attend to themselves in any particular . . . they must be watched like Children.'[5]

And the sailors do indeed display a certain childish joy, when, on occasion, if the wind subsides and the heavens part for long enough, they succeed in what is by now a favourite crew activity, catching and eating albatrosses. Now, instead of killing them immediately to fill out the ship's depleted stocks of food – not a good idea as the flesh tastes too 'gamey' and 'fishy' for the moment – they take the birds below, where they are cooped up and fattened on ground corn for a week or two, and *then* slaughtered. In this manner, Bligh records, the 'albatrosses were as fat, and not inferior in taste to, fine geese'.[6]

Fresh meat, with fat!

'This unexpected supply came very opportunely; for none of our livestock remained except hogs, the sheep and poultry not being hardy enough to stand the severity of the weather.'[7]

And they are not the only ones in trouble. For, can the ship itself withstand the elements?

She's a sturdy ship, a real fighter, but the longer they go, the more the strain on the hull is showing, as the caulking that plugs the seams between the planks continues to work loose, and now the water starts to pour in, to the point that the only way to stay afloat is to have two bilge pumps manned around the clock – something that further exhausts the crew.

The 22nd of April dawns with 'Fresh gales with squalls of snow and cold weather'. And as the day goes on, 'severe squalls of snow' and 'a very high sea'[8] all come at them from the west – the very direction to which they are supposed to be heading. The *Bounty* spends another day going backwards.

Finally, just before 5 pm, with hail battering the hull and snow filling the decks and drenching the men, Bligh comes to the conclusion that most of his men have had for the last four weeks, if not longer. This *cannot* be done. They have made a stunning attempt, they have fought against all odds, they have persevered long past the breaking point of most men and most ships. But . . . now?

He must bow to reality.

The Horn *is* impassable at this time of year.

'I thought I had seen the worst of everything that could be met with at sea,' he will ruefully recount, 'yet I have never seen such violent Winds or such mountainous seas, for they really are beyond every idea I could form of them . . . during this time I suffered the greatest fatigue and anxiety.'[9]

They cannot go on. At least the logbook will stand as proof positive to the Admiralty that he has gone above and beyond the call of duty to fulfil their wishes. (In any case, as Bligh never stops reflecting, it was the infernal, eternal delays of the Admiralty that were responsible for this torturous impasse in the first place.) But as each day now sees them being blown backwards, and with no hope of a change in the weather, sailing sanity must prevail.

Beating to windward for a month has achieved nothing.

On this then, the 33rd day of their attempt to round Cape Horn, Bligh orders Fryer to muster all the men on deck.

One by one, the skinny, ragtag men pop up through the hatchways, eyes wide and wary, like starved, scared bunnies – even as the freezing windblown men aloft leave their frozen ropes and slippery spars to climb down, barely believing they've been given a break.

'I thank you all for your unremitting attention to your duty,' Bligh says once the men are all before him. 'My intention now is to bear away for the Cape of Good Hope as it appears to me an impossibility to get around Cape Horn.'[10]

Suddenly Captain Bligh is surrounded by men who, forgetting protocol, burst out shouting, clapping, cheering, in 'great joy'.[11] Their blowy agony, trying to round a Horn that won't be rounded, is over! Brimming with joy to see the men suddenly so happy, Fletcher Christian hugs young Peter Heywood like a brother. After everything they have been through, all the storms, killer waves, it looks like they will live after all! Once more, they will see their families back on the Isle of Man! The worst of their ordeal is surely over!

'Put the helm a-weather!'[12] Bligh gives the order, quickly whipped away into the shrieking westerly winds. No matter. Master Fryer has caught it, and repeats it in full volume many times, to all the men who need to know, as the *Bounty* is 'instantly put before the wind'[13] at last.

And so it goes, with the frozen figures now back in the rigging eagerly following each order:

'Set the foresail!'

'Set the main topsail!'[14]

The sailors go about their work with the most enthusiasm Bligh has seen in weeks.

In the space of ten minutes, everything changes. The lady in the riding habit charges forward at a gallop. Instead of bashing against a series of aquatic walls breaking all over them, the deafening wind howling straight at them, hurling snow and hail into their ruddy faces, now the wind is in the sweet spot, on the larboard quarter, and they are cascading down the waves. Instead of going nowhere, they are roaring to the east at seven knots, which is close to maximum speed for the *Bounty*. The ride is still rocky, to be sure. And they will still be some time in escaping this boiling cauldron of fury – the lady in her riding habit continues to buck and rear, crashing into the deep troughs between each mountainous wave – but, whatever else, with the wind *behind* them they are actually moving quickly away and not simply battering themselves uselessly against an unmoving weather wall. Below deck, the placid rhythm of the dripstones – *drip, drip, drip . . . drop* – can be heard once more.

Bligh reflects, in his tightly controlled handwriting, very like the man himself – in this case showing a lot of ink blobs, because of the rolling of the sea –

> *It was with much concern I saw it improper and even unjustifiable in me to persist any longer in a passage this way to the Society Islands.*[15]

Under the circumstances, Bligh remains more than ever haunted by the sheer incompetence of the Admiralty and the fact that, 'If we had been one month earlier, or perhaps less, I doubt not but we should have effected our passage',[16] but there is no way back.

Yes, the following morning, the temperature is only just above freezing point, and the storm is still there, but the *Bounty* surges to the north-east, up and down the waves like a whale unleashed from a foetid pond into the wild ocean after long and torturous captivity, and before long the hatches are opened and, as the redoubtable Morrison documents of the following weeks, there is much 'airing and drying the ship between decks, and the sick recovered fast, as we got into a more temperate climate'.[17]

Their new destination is the Cape of Good Hope on the southern tip of the African continent, at a much friendlier latitude of 34 degrees south, after which they will cross the Indian Ocean, going beneath New Holland, stopping briefly at Van Diemen's Land, before heading up its east coast. It is plain sailing all the way. Even the table fare is improved by the men being able to catch some sharks on special shark

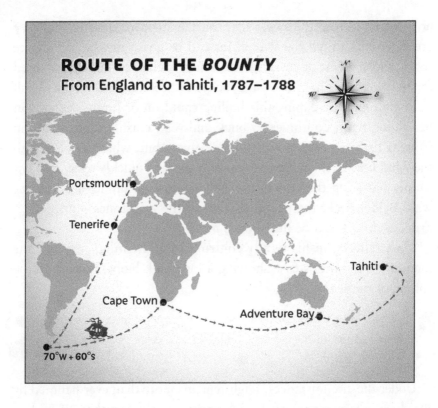

ROUTE OF THE *BOUNTY*
From England to Tahiti, 1787–1788

Portsmouth

Tenerife

Tahiti

Cape Town

Adventure Bay

70°W + 60°S

hooks that are trailed behind the ship, and it takes only a neat, well-fed month after turning back from trying to round Cape Horn until the crew feel blessed to spy the remarkably flat-topped mountain that tells them they have arrived at Cape Town.

On the 24th of May 1788, the *Bounty*'s cannon salute the Dutch Governor van de Graaff and, unlike Tenerife (*sniff*), the salute is returned, gun for gun. At nearby Simon's Bay, the winter season anchorage of the Cape of Good Hope, close to Cape Town, there will be 38 days of much needed rest and repair for both the ship and the men, who have been at sea for five straight months. The most urgent thing is for Purcell, with a little assistance from the local Dutch, to re-caulk the whole ship from bow to stern, to stop the infernal, eternal leaking, even as sail-maker Lawrence Lebogue sees to it that all the damaged sails are again made ship-shape, while Morrison attends to replacing worn rigging.

Still, overall, Bligh is happy with his vessel, noting that, 'upon the whole she is as fine a little ship as ever was at sea. I have suffered much fatigue, but I always thrive best when I have the most to do and I never was better in my life.'[18]

As always when pulling into remote ports, far from the distracting tumult of the ocean, the thoughts of the ship's company turn more than ever to home, wondering how their families are faring, how long it will be before they can be reunited, how much the little ones have grown.

One who feels it more than most, as it happens, is Captain Bligh. For not only is he that rarest of things on this ship, an entirely devoted family man, with an established wife, home and cherished children to return to, but when he had left, his dear Betsy had been four months pregnant – and it is about now, he knows, she will have been confined to have their fourth child.

A small parenthesis, here. Actually, make that *fifth* child, too. Back in Great Britain, at this very time, Betsy gives what she thinks is one last push to deliver a bouncing baby daughter, only to find there are many pushes to go, before a second daughter is also delivered! How thrilled her other three little girls, Harriet, Mary and Elizabeth, are with their new sisters. And yes, it will be difficult, particularly in the early months, without dear William there to help, but, as she tells her girls, he is working hard upon the oceans, so as to return to them next year. Daddy is the skipper of a very big ship, doing very important work for England, and he will be back to them next year. Close parenthesis.

•

Down in the glistening golden cove that is Simon's Bay, right at the foot of a high green mountain just south of Cape Town, the crew of the *Bounty* glisten with sweat themselves as they work all around the ship, and nearly around the clock. They repair and replace the rundown gear, hauling in new supplies for the next leg to Tahiti – 'fresh meat, soft bread, cabbages and celery with onions and leeks and wine'.[19] Oh, and Bligh is also quick to buy 'two very fine red Wings of Flamingoes'[20] which he knows will soon be of great value in Tahiti. And of course other sailors and officers are buying their own things. Very quietly, because it is a little irregular, the ever impecunious Christian – he has never been good with his finances, easy come, easy go – borrows a good deal of money from Bligh to make some purchases and take some pleasures. It can be their small secret. Bligh doesn't hesitate to lend to his friend, despite having very little money himself.

At least Fletcher can now engage a little in the wide commerce of this bustling port, buying ale, curios and the like, a dashingly good-looking man, always smiling, making his way through an always pressing throng in the marketplace. For the snug harbour of this bustling Dutch port is in fact host to *many* Dutch East India men – both outward and homeward bound – and they are joined by several French ships, too.

And what's this now?

Yes, at 9 o'clock in the morning on 13 June, a ship flying the Union Jack from the foremast, the *Dublin*, sails into the harbour. As the men of the *Bounty* gaze towards it, gazing back at them, crowding the deck, are the soldiers and officers of the 77th Regiment under command of Colonel James Balfour, bound for service in India. Among them is an ambitious, highly capable officer by the name of Lieutenant Lachlan Macquarie. A contained, careful officer, Macquarie keeps a contained, careful diary – a white vellum-bound book, each page carefully given margins, numbered and dated before his departure from England – and carefully chronicles today's key event. For, yes, they have met up with 'H.M. Sloop "The Bounty"' commanded by Lieutenant Bligh (who sailed as master with Captain Cook), bound for Ottaheitta in the South Sea, in search of discoveries, but particularly sent to carry and transport the bread-fruit from Ottaheitta to the West India Islands.'[21]

Clearly, Bligh is gilding the lily somewhat, in claiming that he 'is in search of discoveries' rather than the mere grocery errand of getting the bread-fruit, but of course he has nowhere to go in expanding that conversation over dinner, as that adventure is still months away from completion.

In the meantime, while at Cape Town, Bligh is deeply troubled by the sight of manacled black men, in pods of 30 or so, being *whipped* along by brutal French slave traders. These poor brutes, 'imported by the French . . . from Madagascar, Mosambique, Sumatra and Malacca', are forced to traipse naked or barely clothed around this bustling trading town of 'opulence and great abundance'. Each one of them bears a 'weighty burden'[22] on knobbly shoulders covered with open sores due to terrible nutrition, horrible conditions and unceasing labour.

Why, many of these 'poor wretches'[23] are reduced to scooping their sustenance off the street. Bligh has his stomach turned to see many a slave carefully place his cumbersome load on the roadside before roughly falling to his knees, to reaching out a filthy and emaciated arm of skin and bone to 'pick up the most offensive offals and claiming them for food'.[24]

They eat the offending offal quickly, too hungry and exhausted to worry about dignity, lift their loads once more, and stagger off down the road.

On his return to the *Bounty*, Bligh confides in his Log, 'If the Police would oblige the owners of these Poor Wretches consigned to constant drudgery, to clothe and feed them properly it would be much to their honour and humanity . . .' As it is, the slaves are at best in rags, a sight that one 'would imagine could not fail to reproach the owners of a want of decency and compassion in not relieving such a degree of wretchedness of which they were the cause, and had every call on their humanity to remove'.[25]

It is at least something for Bligh to know that when he gets the bread-fruit trees to the West Indies, the British slaves will no longer have to endure such a wretched existence.

At four bells in the afternoon watch of 1 July 1788 the *Bounty* fires its cannon 13 times in a salute to the Governor, receiving 13 cannon roars in reply from His Excellency, and then sets sail.

Four weeks of fast, relatively pleasant sailing ensues, with the notable exception of 22 July when, 'we experienced as heavy a Storm as ever blew hail and sleet, the sea also exceedingly high'.[26]

But for men who are battered veterans of trying for a month to get around Cape Horn, this is no more than a brief inconvenience. They sail on, first passing the island of St Paul – which is roughly the halfway mark between Cape Town and Van Diemen's Land, on 28 July 1788, and then, on 19 August, the Mewstone, 'a high bold rock',[27] which juts 150 yards out of the sea like a massive shark fin, and which, according to Bligh's charts, means that the south-western cape of Van Diemen's land is but five leagues away.

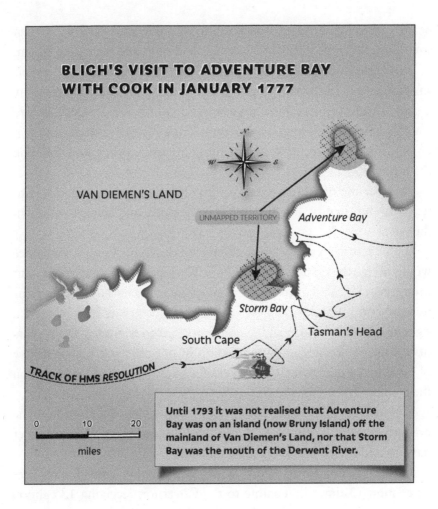

BLIGH'S VISIT TO ADVENTURE BAY
WITH COOK IN JANUARY 1777

VAN DIEMEN'S LAND

UNMAPPED TERRITORY   Adventure Bay

Storm Bay

South Cape   Tasman's Head

TRACK OF HMS RESOLUTION

0   10   20

miles

Until 1793 it was not realised that Adventure
Bay was on an island (now Bruny Island) off the
mainland of Van Diemen's Land, nor that Storm
Bay was the mouth of the Derwent River.

Sure enough, on the morning of 22 August they drop anchor in Adventure Bay, a 'large spacious bay' with 'white sandy bottom',[28] which, Bligh knows from his first visit here with Cook back in 1777, is a place abundant in wood and fresh water.

Most advantageously, as a spot on the east side of Van Diemen's Land, it is protected from the endless westerlies that blow across the Southern Ocean.

And yet, when he had visited here with Cook, the Natives had been apparent on the shore, from the first. This time, Bligh is puzzled to see no sign of anyone at all, bar the odd lazy plume of smoke rising in the distance from the green blanket of forest that covers the surrounding mountains. Not that it matters, particularly. The principal reason they have come is to get fresh water and renew their stores of wood, as they are 'in want of plank'[29] – though they are also hoping for fresh food in the form of crabs, fish, and perhaps a shot kangaroo or two, and even some wild duck – and as soon as the following morning a landing party is sent to the shore on the 23-foot Launch. Under the charge of his best young officer, Christian, the wooding party are soon at work in the spot that Bligh had wooded while on voyage with Cook.

After the trees are felled with an axe, the men dig a sawpit so they can quickly cut the trunks into manageable lengths – with one man standing below pushing and pulling, while the other above pulls and pushes – before they bundle them together and load them into the Launch.

And so it is that the sounds of industry float to the *Palawa*, Natives, as the *raytji*, white people, visiting their homeland, *lutruwita*, cut down the trees with their axes, even as their saws cut them into neat blocks.

And now one of the *raytji*, Midshipman Hayward, breaks away from the work group he is overseeing, and wanders some 20 yards, where his eyes are immediately drawn to something carved on an old dead tree trunk.

A.D. 1773.[30]

Extraordinary. As Captain Bligh will note of the discovery after inspecting it himself, the letters and numbers are carved as freshly as if it had been done just last month, let alone 15 years ago.

> This must have been done by some of Captn. Furneaux crew in March 1773 which is 15 years and 5 months since.[31]

While generally the crew is happy to be here, just as any crew is happy to have time back on shore after almost two months at sea, not all are happy all the time – least of all the ship's Carpenter. Not long after arriving at Adventure Bay, Purcell is also working as part of a wooding party onshore. Of course, to store the maximum amount of wood in the storage space allotted to it on board, the best thing is for the wood to be cut into small, relatively uniform chunks. Coming on shore himself for an inspection, Bligh expresses the view to Purcell that he is cutting up his wooden 'billets' too large and too haphazardly.

Sorry?

You are cutting the pieces too large and haphazardly.

Purcell, not raised in the naval tradition of obeisance to the Captain at all times, pauses. He is a skilled, highly trained, highly accomplished carpenter, and a warrant officer on this ship. He is capable of everything from splinting a damaged mast at the height of a storm, to caulking the hull; from fixing a leak in the Jolly Boat, to replacing a rotten plank in the hull. And now he is engaged in the lowest of all low activities for a skilled carpenter – gathering firewood – and *still* Bligh is presumptuous enough to tell him he is doing it wrong?

Purcell pauses ... just a little ... ... longer. In the end, however, he cannot help himself, muttering that Captain Bligh had only left the *Bounty* and come here, 'on purpose to find fault'.[32]

You challenge me, Sir?

Not outright, no. But having come to the view that William Bligh is no gentleman, in either sense of the word, Purcell does bristle at such high-handedness from one he is happy to look right in the eye as an equal, and brook any challenge that he is not. He aches to say it: *I am as good a man as you, and you will not treat me like a lord condescending to a peasant!*

For now, however, he contents himself with dark muttering only – it has been building for months, and this is merely the release of *some* of his pent-up anger – the result of which is Purcell is sent back to the ship by Bligh, who is quick to pen his official view, for later perusal by the Admiralty.

> My Carpenter on my expressing my disapprobation of his conduct with respect to orders he had received from me concerning the Mode of working with the Wooding Party behaved in a most insolent and reprehensible Manner. I therefore ordered him on board, there to assist in the general duty of the Ship, as I could not bear the loss of an able working and healthy man, otherwise I should have committed him to close confinement until I could have tried him.[33]

Two days later, Bligh is again on shore with the better part of the crew replenishing their supplies of fresh water, gathering wood, and fishing, with their catch including 'many sizeable Rock Cod'[34] for lunch. The watering party, meanwhile, is busy filling empty casks from a stream at the east end of the beach, with none working harder, once they get the barrels back to the ship, than the Master, Mr Fryer, and a Mate and a Quartermaster, who work with ropes and a pulley to manhandle each barrel up on to the deck, before getting it below. It is difficult work, soon requiring help from Mr Purcell . . . Mr Purcell . . . I say, Mr Purcell, are you there?

And that is where the trouble starts. For when, in the late afternoon, Bligh returns to the *Bounty*, it is to be told by Fryer that Purcell had been very clear.

From this day forth, he refuses to do any duties that are not specifically to do with carpentry.

Oh . . . really?

Well, let his Captain see about that. Storming towards Purcell's cabin, Bligh is soon able to remind the Carpenter that he will damn'd well do, sir, whatever you are damn'd well ord'rd to do, sir.

'But my directions and presence had as little effect . . .'[35] Bligh records.

For the cocky Purcell puffs up his strong carpenter's chest and declares, 'I will do anything in my line of duty; but as to this duty, I can not comply.'[36]

Shocked at such obstinance, for the second time in three days, Bligh nevertheless moves quickly. He calls for nearby crew to witness Purcell's refusal to follow his orders, with the obvious purpose of later relying on their testimony in what will now *definitely* be a court martial.

Of course, now, there is ample justification to clap Purcell in irons and leave him in his quarters until they return to England.

However . . .

> It was for the good of the Voyage that I should not make him
> or any Man a prisoner. The few I have even in the good state of
> health I keep them, are but barely sufficient to carry on the duty
> of the Ship, it could then answer no good purpose to lose the use
> of a healthy strong young man in my situation. I therefore laid

aside my power in that particular for the good of the Service I
am on, although it continued in force with equal effect.[37]

But there is an alternative, which just might work. For now, he adds
an order, to all and sundry.

'Until Mr Purcell works once more,' he says firmly, 'he shall have
no provisions. I faithfully promise a severe punishment to any man
that dares to assist him.'[38]

Well then. When Bligh puts it like that, and Purcell can see days
of starvation ahead, it has an amazingly transformative effect on his
commitment to co-operate with orders, if not his mood, which has
fallen still further.

And yet, while the initial problem with Purcell's lack of co-operation
is solved, the overall effect on the ship's atmosphere is far more enduring.

Writing later, Morrison will be clear.

'Here also were sown seeds of eternal discord between . . . Bligh
and his officers. He confined the carpenter and found fault with the
inattention of the rest to their duty, which produced continual disputes,
everyone endeavouring to thwart the others in their duty.'[39]

Given Bligh's prickly presence, his propensity for bursts of temper
that make the very sails billow with rage, each terrified officer has
one clear goal – to stay out of Bligh's way. And when things do go
wrong, the key is to make sure the blame falls on another. It can even
be worth deliberately sabotaging the efforts of another, so as to use
up some of the Captain's rage.

There is at least one upside.

'This made the men exert themselves to divert the storm from falling
on them by a strict attention to their duty, and in this they found their
account and rejoiced, in private, at their good success.'[40]

In the meantime, 11 days after arriving, on the evening of 1 September,
they suddenly see fires in the night 'within the limits of the bay . . . on
the low land near Cape Frederick Henry . . . at daylight . . . we saw
several of them about the beach of the lowland with our glasses'.[41]

Bligh's 'earnest wish to visit them'[42] is without effect, though, as
the southern swell of the ocean on this day is so heavy, so pounding

the surf, there is no way they can land a boat on that part of the cape where they have seen the fires.

The next day, however, the Cutter is able to get within shouting distance of the shore, at which point Bligh, accompanied by the botanist, David Nelson, spot one of their own crewmen, Nelson's assistant, William Brown, who has come this far overland, and he has good news: he has met with some of the Natives, and they are reasonably friendly.

Shortly thereafter, they can hear their voices, 'like the cackling of geese',[43] and a group of 20 or so come out of the wood. While the women – with their impossibly black faces – hang back at the tree-line, the men, much bolder, drop their spears and come down to perch on the rocks by the shore. As one, every man on the boat looks closely at this particularly striking race, all of them, 'perfectly naked'.

> The colour of these people are naturally black. Their skin was scarified about their shoulders and breast. They were of middling stature or rather below it. One of them had his body discoloured with red ochre, but all the others had laid an additional coat of black over their faces and shoulder, and it was laid on so thick that it totally prevented me at this distance, to say anything exact of their features.[44]

Most striking, however, Bligh notes, is the rapidity of their language.

> They made a prodigious clattering of speech, extending their arms over their heads. I made signs for them to come nearer which they did, and placed themselves close to the break of the sea. I could not take up one single word they uttered, their speech being so remarkably quick.[45]

Bligh and Nelson, of course, have met the Natives of Van Diemen's Land before, but as this is all new for Morrison, he sits there in the boat transfixed, observing closely for his later notes on their appearance.

> Their heads were all close shorn, so that we could not tell whether they were woolly or not but thought that the short remains looked more like wool then [sic] hair, their Countenances were by no means agreeable, and their teeth black and uneven: they were quite

naked, and appeared harmless miserable Creatures. Amongst them
was one very much deformed which Mr. Nelson declared to be
the same he had seen here on a former Voyage . . . they talked a
good deal which none of us understood, and would frequently
Jump up & shout seemingly pleased.[46]

Taking the boat in as close as they dare, to within 20 yards of the
rocky shore, they are at least close enough to the Natives that Bligh is
able to hurl to the shore the presents he has brought for them. Lifting
the beads and nails up to show them what he has, he then wraps them
in paper, and throws them on to the beach. The Natives won't touch
them, until such time as the boat starts to move away. Then, and only
then, do they open the parcels, and place the objects on their heads.

On seeing this, Bligh records, 'I then returned again when they laid
everything aside and would not show us they took notice of what we
had given them.'[47]

Bligh throws a few more beads and nails on shore, to no avail – for
they will not pick them up while Bligh is watching – and so he makes
signs for them to come to the ship. They make signs, in turn, for him to
come on shore. Returning to the *Bounty*, Bligh hears Brown's account
of visiting a small Native camp.

He saw some miserable wigwams, in which were nothing but a
few kangaroo skins spread on the ground, and a basket made
of rushes.[48]

Of his overall impressions, Bligh pronounces himself far from impressed:

. . . upon the whole they are perhaps the most wretched and
stupid People existing, yet they are with this no doubt the most
inoffensive.[49]

In Bligh's lexicon, 'the most inoffensive' is as close as he gets to a
compliment.

Yes, their 'wretchedness' may be judged from the fact that they live
in this most isolated part of the world, in inhospitable circumstances,
while their 'stupidity' is evidenced by the fact that they place no value
on the trinkets that make other Natives swoon with desire.

The Tahitians, Bligh knows from his last visit there, become ecstatic over a single red feather – using them on their canoes to please the Gods of war, and on the *marro oora* girdles of their Kings, as a sign of their sanctity. But these Natives just throw far more impressive trinkets away.

Against that, when Bligh does get a closer look at their living circumstances, he is impressed by their sophistication.

> Their wigwams are calculated to repose themselves at full length, the ground being made level and strewed all over with grass, and the roof so disposed with large pieces of bark as to render it perfectly dry on the inside in rainy weather.[50]

Despite himself, Bligh is much struck with the sheer ingenuity.

> Their Wigwams are made with little trouble and afford great convenience.[51]

But, the Natives are welcome to it. Van Diemen's Land itself is little more than a green wilderness, nothing in the way of comfort to a civilised man. It is with a sense of relief that at noon on 5 September 1788, Cap'n Bligh leaves this Godforsaken spot on earth, sailing 'with a light breeze'[52] for the southern tip of the South Island of New Zealand before heading up its east coast.

6 October 1788, just off the coast of New Zealand, Valentine's Day

Captain Bligh's foul mood?

Simple. He has been very badly let down not by one, but by two men.

The first, and most flagrant betrayal, has come from Able Seaman Valentine, who appears ready to irretrievably ruin Bligh's hitherto perfect record by ... dying. Bligh had been earnestly hoping to have the record show that he had completed his mission by taking his ship 25,000 miles and not losing a single member of his crew to ill-health – a sure sign to the Admiralty of his diligence in providing for his men.

And the second one who has let him down, making Bligh even angrier, is his drunken sot of a surgeon, Dr Huggan, who has been until now hiding from Bligh how grave the situation is with Valentine. If Bligh had known earlier he personally could have taken measures to save him. But, through a combination of constant drunkenness, sheer shattering incompetence and shivering fear of the Captain's wrath, Huggan has deliberately kept the true state of Valentine's health to himself. Bligh had only known that Valentine had suffered a 'slight indisposition'[53] at Adventure Bay in Van Diemen's Land, for which he was bled. Back then, Huggan had assured the Captain that the sailor would soon recover. Instead, alas – and unbeknownst to Bligh – because Huggan had taken no precautions, Valentine's arm is now infected and terribly inflamed. In odd moments of sobriety, Huggan has tried to cure the inflammation by bleeding it some more, only to observe through his drunken haze that, 'the inflammation increased considerably' and now young Valentine is in his hammock, barely conscious. He is 'seized with a hollow cough and . . . shortness of breath which continued to increase'.[54]

Bligh had remained oblivious, right up until this very morning, when he is visited in his cabin by Master's Mate William Elphinstone bearing grave news: 'James Valentine is delirious and has every appearance of being in a dying state, Captain.'[55]

How could this be?

'The shock,' Bligh would chronicle, 'was scarce equal to my astonishment.'[56]

One of his crew is at death's door, and he is being told, not by the Surgeon – with whom Bligh dines every day, and whose responsibility it is to prevent precisely this – but a Master's Mate? And yes, what was the most recent thing Huggan had told Bligh on the subject? That's right, only that Valentine was 'getting better'. But in all those seven weeks since the first concern for Valentine had risen at Van Diemen's Land, the Surgeon had 'never expressed the least uneasyness about him'.[57]

Dr Huggan is sent for immediately, and even by Bligh's standards the dressing-down he receives is noteworthy for its sheer fury.

There is no explanation, beyond the obvious – through drunkenness and then fear, Huggan has first botched the care of Valentine, and now hidden the hideous consequences until it is too late to do anything.

'I intended to tell you of it last night,' Huggan offers lamely. 'But as you were not alone I did not think it proper.'

Not *alone*, sir?

I dined with the Officer of the Watch, just as I do every evening – whether that is Mr Christian, Mr Fryer or Mr Peckover. You thought the news you had to bear could not be shared with them? In the meantime, I dine with *you*, Dr Huggan, *every day*! Well, Dr Huggan, what do you have to say to that? Bligh continues, in such a blazing fury, that he will even go on to mildly chastise himself in his Log noting that he was 'perhaps severe for [Huggan's] remissness'.[58]

All Dr Huggan can offer in his own defence is that it was not until the previous night that he had recognised the severity of Valentine's condition. And now, even more bizarrely, he rouses himself to officially inform Bligh of the very thing that the Captain has been berating him for not telling him, *weeks* ago.

'I must inform you,' he says gravely, and almost as if this might make things right between them, 'that Mr Valentine has not many hours to live.'[59]

Bizarre!

'The strangeness of this declaration,' Bligh records, 'as the Man had been daily fed from our Table and he not knowing the tendency of [Valentine's] symptoms gave me very unfavourable Ideas.'[60]

The chief one of said 'Ideas' is that Huggan is so drunkenly incompetent that far from being the salvation of sick sailors, he is overseeing their damnation – precisely as he, Bligh, had warned the Admiralty a year ago. And now a man is knocking on death's door thanks to this fat, negligent, incompetent drunkard, meaning that the record of Bligh as Captain will be blackened. It is *infuriating* to a man who is always only seconds away from a fury in the first place.

•

Now, while the news of Valentine and the sheer incompetence of the wretched Dr Huggan have both tilled the soil for Bligh's rage, it is John Fryer who reaps the full harvest of the skipper's apoplexy three days later.

The message comes from Samuel, a blinking mess of a man perpetually hovering around the Captain, waiting to jump at the next bark.

For yes, if you can believe it, Captain Bligh, the Master, Mr Fryer, is outright *refusing* to sign the 'expense books' – the books which record the ship's economies – and 'the monthly books for August and September',[61] which have already been signed by Bligh himself, just as they have been signed by the Carpenter, Mr Purcell, and the Bosun, Mr Cole. And now Mr Fryer will not add his signature to affirm the Captain's record of events, and that all is in order?

Bligh's blood boils. It is *Fryer's duty to sign the damn'd book! God damn the scoundrel!*

Adding malicious insult to already heavy injury?

Mr Fryer has actually gone well beyond a simple refusal to sign. He has a demand. And a piece of paper for the Captain. As Bligh records contemptuously in his Log: 'The Clerk was then returned with a certificate for me to sign, before the Book could [be signed], the purport of which was that [Fryer] had been doing nothing amiss during his time on board.'[62]

The hideous *hide* of the man!

But what, precisely, is he playing at? Is it an attempt at blackmailing the Captain? If you agree to not mention my misdemeanours, I will sign your dubious books? Bligh will enter into no such bargain.

'As I did not approve of his doing his duty conditionally I sent for him and told him of the consequence.'[63]

Bligh wants Fryer to sign the books. He may make particular comments upon the pages, if he must, but he will sign them. *Now.*

Well, in that case. 'I will not sign the books upon such conditions,'[64] replies Fryer, before turning on his heel very 'abruptly' and leaving the Captain standing. The Master has the air about him, it has to be said, of one who believes that *he* is the one holding the gun. After all, Bligh, if the Master does not sign the books, then the Admiralty will be all over your books like starving ants over a piece of mouldy bread! Fryer is clearly betting that Bligh will prefer discretion to discipline . . .

'Order all hands to be turned up,'[65] Bligh barks, at which point Samuel scurries down the passageways and up the ladder to the deck like a scalded cat, spreading Bligh's orders.

Within minutes, all hands, all men and officers, are on deck, surrounding Bligh, Fryer, and an upturned barrel on which lies the unsigned books, a pen and a small bottle of ink.

Sign the books, Mr Fryer.

Fryer refuses, with a sullen shake of his head. His long, statue-like face remains stoical, his chin high.

Very well then. Bligh has no choice but to read aloud the relevant passages from the Articles of War.

Bligh's point is clear. These Articles spell out, with wording as stark as a cat o' nine tails, precisely what awaits any man who fails to do his duty, or nakedly disobeys Captain's orders. Obviously all traitors, spies, mutineers and sodomites will hang, but they are not the only ones.

For this brings us to you and your situation, Mr Fryer, as Bligh, with a gleam of pure malice, of fierce intent – *just push me on this, Mr Fryer, just give me a chance to see this out* – loudly reads out Article 14, with just his rumbling voice, the flapping of the sails and the swish of the ocean passing by to be heard: 'If when action, or any service shall be *commanded*, any person in the fleet shall presume or to *delay or discourage* the said action or service, upon pretence of arrears of wages, or upon *any pretence whatsoever*, every person so offending, being convicted thereof by the sentence of the court martial, shall suffer death, or such other punishment, as from the nature and degree of the offense a court martial shall deem him to deserve.'[66]

'Now, sir, sign those books,'[67] orders Bligh.

The crew leans forward to see the result, to not miss a word, or a grimace. This is high drama on the High Seas and, whatever else, a wonderful break from the dreadful monotony.

Well, Mr Fryer, what is it to be?

For all of ten seconds there is no movement at all, not even a flicker of the Master's bushy eyebrows as he mulls over the humiliating decision before him.

Finally, Fryer steps forward, takes the proffered quill, stoops over, dips it in the ink and signs, even as he announces to all in an icy voice, 'I sign in obedience to your orders, but this may be cancelled hereafter.'[68]

Insolence! Damn the man.

Nevertheless, Fryer can be dealt with later. The main thing is that the books are now signed. Mr Fryer's bluff has been called, the Captain has won, and the matter, like the book, is closed.

'You are dismissed,' the Captain tells the men. 'Return to your duty.'[69]

Bligh returns to his chamber to write up his Log, all about Fryer, that 'troublesome man'[70] who will *not* dine tonight at the Captain's table, or indeed, ever again. From now on, they will speak when it is their clear duty to do so, 'and even then with much apparent reserve'.[71]

•

Captain, wake up.

Captain . . . ?

Bad news.

It is just after midnight on the following day when Bligh is roused from his slumbers to be told that Valentine is dead. Furious, stupefied and saddened – in that order – the Captain dresses and goes to the lad's hammock to gaze down on the pallid, limp remains of one who was once the strongest man on the ship. After paying his respects, and saying his prayers, Bligh orders that Valentine's body be prepared for a burial at sea on the morrow.

Now, the death of one of his sailors requires a formal record that will be perused by his masters upon the ship's return to England and Bligh frames it carefully in the Log. Not a single word is false, but he is certain to leave out all detail to do with drink, deception and incompetence. For those things to have flourished under his command, to the point of a sailor dying, would reflect badly on him as a commander, and so he must put a much more dignified face on proceedings:

> The loss I met with this day by the Death of James Valentine was
> of equal surprise and regret. This poor man was one of the most
> robust People on board, and therefore the surprise and shock was
> the greater to me . . .[72]

Such is Bligh's disgust with the failure of the drunken Dr Huggan to have properly cared for the tragic Valentine, and so public does he make that disgust, the so-called 'Surgeon' has dined for the last time at the Captain's table.

You, sir, may retire to your cabin, and have your meals there, no doubt washed down by several bottles of wine. Already in an ill-humour, Bligh is now constantly finding furious fault with this wretched bunch of incompetents, low-life scoundrels, frightening fools and bloody blackguards the Admiralty has cursed him with to make up his crew of second-rate sailors.

At least he still has Fletcher Christian to share his table, but Fletcher's regular position on the Captain's table is envied by few. For who wants to be near Bligh when he rolls with rage throughout repast?

•

Bligh remains truly shocked by the death of Valentine, and is intent on watching Dr Huggan very closely from this day forward – observing just how much he drinks, when he does so, and how much it affects his medical care of the crew. They have already lost one man to illness and Bligh is determined there will be no more. In the meantime, Bligh ensures that Valentine's meagre possessions are divided equally between his two sailor friends who actually did care for him, while Huggan was a drunken sot in his cot.

Alas, for Bligh, his determination to watch Dr Huggan more closely does not remotely end the problem. For, feeling himself in exile, the drunken doctor now determines to make his presence felt more than ever. No, not by curing the crew's enduring ailments, but by exercising the one bit of power he has over the Captain: declaring a sailor too ill to perform his duties. Once so declared by the official doctor on a voyage, a Captain risks court martial if he forces any sailor so deemed to work.

Dr Huggan declares man after man in the small, over-stretched crew to be sick, when Bligh can see nothing wrong with them at all!

Nevertheless, as Morrison notes, 'several of the seamen, particularly the oldest, began to complain of pain in their limbs'.[73]

Surely not?

Bligh cannot believe it.

Dr Huggan insists it is so. Scurvy, Dr Huggan informs the Captain on the 14th of October. Three men struck down with it.

On *Bligh's* ship! The captain is appalled as he has prided himself on having learnt from the pioneer in the field, Captain Cook, and it is for this reason that, from the beginning of the voyage, he has gone to such great lengths to insist on obsessive cleanliness – always ordering the cabins aired and surfaces swabbed with vinegar – as well as the consumption of vegetables or sauerkraut and portable soup in lieu of anything fresh, and daily dancing for exercise. And it had worked! Due to his knowledge, and the discipline he had instilled, there have been no cases of scurvy at all. But now, Dr Huggan swears, absolutely *swears*, he can spot the subtle symptoms of scurvy: aching limbs, a pain in the gums, general fatigue . . . all the things that can be claimed, without being proven.

So now, not only does Bligh lose manpower on a ship already strained for lack of it, but the official record risks showing scurvy present on Captain Bligh's ship, to go with the death of a crew-member to illness.

He orders the men be given a treatment for scurvy, a rather unpleasant 'decoction of Essence Malt'.[74]

Four days later, the Captain inspects the three men himself. Just as he thought!

Bligh has a rather different diagnosis: 'on examining the Men who the Doctor supposed had a taint of the Scurvy it appeared to be nothing more than the prickly heat. However their decoction I desired to be continued.'[75]

Yes, whatever their protests, Bligh insists, if you say you have scurvy, then you really must continue to take Dr Huggan's wretched potion. No matter, by the following day, the 'illness' spreads . . . as does the insubordination.

On Sunday 19 October Bligh is told by Cole[76] that two men, John Mills and William Brown, are 'refusing to dance this evening'.[77]

They too, are now sure they have . . . scurvy.

No, you damn well *don't*, Bligh insists. You will dance, gentlemen, and dance well.

'I ordered their grog to be stopped with a promise of further punishment on a second refusal. I have always directed the Evenings from

5 to 8 o'clock to be spent in dancing and that every man should be obliged to dance.'[78]

But it's odd. Despite doing the dancing, and having no grog, and being ordered not to have scurvy, Brown continues to insist – with Dr Huggan's full and public support – that he has scurvy.

Scurvy, you say?

Bligh is sure he means 'Rheumatic Complaints', and writes in the Log as such, only adding afterwards, 'the Doctor insists upon it that it is Scurvy. But I can discover no symptoms to lead me to be apprehensive of it.'[79]

For what would Dr Huggan know?

The same doctor who let Valentine die?

The same one who is yet again drunk, right now?

Bligh demands to see the sick list. Come, come now, Dr Huggan. You have your own official Log to present to the Admiralty and, as Captain, I have the right to see it. Now, sir, where is it?

Dr Huggan hums, he hahs, he drinks some more and delays but, 'with some difficulty I got a Sick list from him'.[80]

And what, in fact, does it demonstrate?

Why, exactly as Bligh had thought all along. That is, that despite all of the Doctor's hand-wringing, his worrying words and the whimperings of Brown, there is one – just one, you may see for yourself, sir – just one man, McIntosh, 'in it under a Rhematic complaint, the others he now seems to think nothing about'.[81]

With proof now of Huggan's deliberate deceptions, Bligh does not hesitate to formalise his accusations in the Log that the Admiralty will read: 'The Doctors Intoxication has given me much trouble these last five days.'[82]

For all that, Bligh still orders that *all* the sailors with rheumatic complaints keep up the treatment for scurvy. And he orders the Surgeon to give him another, full sick list, for his records.

Either way, Bligh is not too anxious. They are but days away from Tahiti, and he is sure that, once there, all the malingerers, once they see a beautiful woman swaying with open arms and more, and beckoning them to come hither, will rise from their sick beds like lepers cured by the healing hand of Jesus Christ, and make full and miraculous recoveries in a matter of minutes.

It takes Huggan two full days, but when at last the sick list is pushed under Bligh's cabin door and the Captain retrieves it, he can't help but notice that the name on top of the list is . . . Dr Huggan. Yes, apparently the Surgeon himself now has rheumatic complaints! So bad, the Captain is informed, the unfortunate fellow has taken to his bed, and can no longer rise. A very red-nosed rheumatism to be sure, and one that makes him sway, and slur his words, but he is certain of it. Dr Bligh, however, offers a second opinion in his Log: 'The Surgeon's complaint has been owing to constant state of intoxication.'[83]

With that, Bligh sends a message to Dr Huggan, and 'in a most friendly manner requested him to leave off drinking, but he seemed not sensible of anything I said to him and it had little effect'.[84]

So little effect, in fact, that, as Bligh finds at nightfall, Dr Huggan has failed to appear at table for dinner, and for a very bad reason. He had already drunk his meal, in his own tiny quarters.

> The Surgeon kept his Bed all this day and always drunk, without eating an ounce of food.[85]

Curse that man!

Making a snap decision, in his ever snappy manner, Bligh stands Dr Huggan down from his post, and replaces him officially with his assistant, Thomas Ledward.

As it happens, just three days without Dr Huggan's medical care really does produce a remarkable result.

'It is with much pleasure,' Bligh records on 24 October, 'that I find the few invalids recovering very fast.'[86]

And this time, Mr Ledward is in full agreement with Bligh that not a single man is showing signs of scurvy! They have no 'eruptions' or 'swellings' and 'Their Gums are as sound as any can be expected after such a length of Salt Diet.' Why, their health is so good that 'their breath is not offensive neither is their teeth loose'.[87]

In truth, however, Mr Ledward is telling an outright lie about one patient – none other than Dr Huggan. Though he has been telling

Bligh that Huggan is getting better and taking the air, he must soon confess he has been, as Bligh recounts, 'deceiving me in respect of the Surgeon's illness. It was now four days since he has seen light and in bed all this time intoxicated.'[88]

Huggan is now officially on the list as suffering 'Paralytic Affection'.

An apoplectic Bligh can bear it no more. Cole! The Bosun, the keeper of discipline, is sent for immediately.

Go to Dr Huggan's cabin. Search it, and see that all liquor is removed. The best way to cure this physician is to remove the liquid illness that so plagues him. It is a moot question whether, in response, Dr Huggan is more surprised, outraged, or . . . drunk. It is probably drunk, though outrage runs it close, and 'the operation was not only troublesome but offensive in the highest degree'.[89]

Later that same day, despite his official diagnosis, Huggan is clearly not nearly so paralysed as he claims, when, shortly afterwards, 'The Doctor . . . was discovered to be able to get out of bed and look for liquor, although represented to have almost lost the use of one side [of his body].'[90]

Fed up, and with nothing left to do to help the insufferable, hopeless old Sawbones, Bligh leaves him to sober up.

The next morning, Saturday 25 October 1788, at half past seven, the *Bounty* passes just to the east and then north of the Island of Maitea, which, Bligh knows, means the island of Tahiti is only one day away with fair winds, two if contrary ones. On Maitea, which Captain Cook had visited on his first voyage nearly 20 years earlier, Bligh can see three dwellings from the deck and a group of 20 Natives waving at them from the shore, but the surf is too high for a landing and so he sails on.

After all, Tahiti is so close now, Bligh can practically smell it, and he cannot wait to get there and get started on the mission proper, and . . .

And now here is another rare sight – Dr Huggan.

> The Surgeon also came upon Deck and was sober, but very weak from the extraordinary manner he has kept himself this week past.

Such an extraordinary recovery, in such a short time!

> His paralytic disorder has been perfectly cured in 48 hours by
> giving him no Spirits to make use of, and only a little Wine and
> water.[91]

Yes, among the most famous of the miracles of Jesus Christ was turning
water into wine. Well, Bligh has performed a miracle of his own, healing
a cripple simply by turning most of his wine into water!

And seeing you are on deck, Dr Huggan, it is time for you to
perform an important medical task, with Tahiti now just 24 hours
away – inspect the men for venereal disease.

Bligh's aim is commendable.

> As I have some reason to suppose the Tahitians have not been
> visited by any ships since Captain Cook, I hope they may have
> found means together with their natural way of living, to have
> eradicated the Venereal disease. To prove this and free us from
> any ill founded suppositions, that we might renew the Complaint,
> I have directed the Surgeon to examine very particularly every
> man . . .[92]

All sailors, and officers, on deck. Now, undo your flies, and let the
doctor see your penises. Let him inspect each one very closely, and press
his thumb and forefinger along the shaft to see if there is any emission.

As the whole process would be described by one of Bligh's officers,
'In the afternoon, with but little distinction, the whole body corporate,
passed through the hands of our worthy associate . . . and never did
the Doctor take a pinch – of snuff, with more solemnity or handle –
a subject, with less risible countenance. It was ever his nature to be
gentle . . .'[93]

Finally it is done.

'He reported every person totally free from the Venereal complaint.'[94]

Not for long though, Bligh suspects.

CHAPTER FOUR

LAND HO!

All the sailors swore that they never saw handsomer made women in their lives, and declared they would all to a man live on two thirds allowance rather than lose so fine an opportunity of getting a girl apiece.[1]

George Robertson, Master of the *Dolphin*,
on Captain Wallis' expedition to Tahiti, 1767

Born under the most beautiful of skies, fed on the fruits of a land that is fertile and requires no cultivation . . . [the Tahitians] know no other Gods but love. Every day is dedicated to it. The entire island is its temple, every woman its altar, every man its priest. And what sort of women? you will ask. The rivals of Georgians in beauty, and the sisters of the utterly naked Graces. There, neither shame nor modesty exercise their tyranny . . .[2]

Philibert Commerson, Botanist on French ship *Etoile*,
under command of Louis-Antoine de Bougainville, 1768

[Tahiti is] certainly the paradise of the world and if happiness could result from situation and convenience, here it is to be found in the highest perfection. I have seen many parts of the world, but Tahiti is capable of being preferable to them all, and certainly is so considering it in its natural state.[3]

Captain William Bligh, 1788

26 October 1788, Matavai Bay, some sunny isle

Cometh the dawn, cometh the vision. For there it is, dead ahead over the translucent blue of the Pacific Ocean. There, do you see? That green smudge, four leagues off and closing . . .

Tahiti! A timeless island in a timeless ocean. Beyond the sparkling translucence, the white waves lap onto the black sands of the beach, even as the palm trees lining the beach wave a green welcome and, beyond them again, the even darker green volcanic peaks soar.

As their worthy ship glides ever closer, skidding down one impossibly blue wave and swiftly climbing the next, the bulbous bow tucking the water 'neath it like the breast of a swan, Bligh gives the orders for Fryer to guide the ship into the gloriously familiar, sparkling, calm waters of Matavai Bay, and to anchor just off Point Venus – the northern tip of Tahiti, where Cook's party had observed the Transit of Venus two decades earlier.

For four men on the *Bounty* – Bligh, his Armourer Joseph Coleman, William Peckover and the botanist David Nelson – it is like a warm

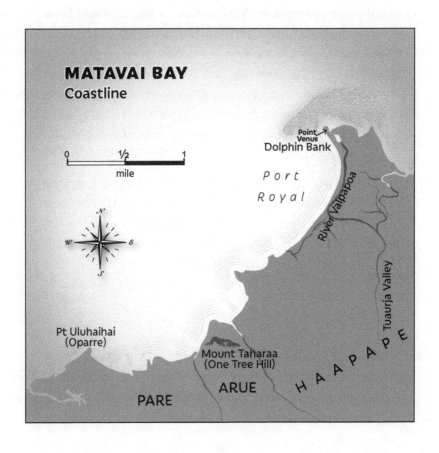

and wonderful homecoming. As they make their way through the break in the reef into the bay proper, all four gaze eagerly to see what they know is coming next.

And . . . sure enough!

'I had no sooner got round . . . Point Venus,' Bligh will note in his log, 'than I was visited by a great number of canoes.'[4]

~~Va'a tele~~! ~~Huge canoes~~! Beautifully constructed ones, carved from Tahitian chestnut, with high ornamental prows moving so fast through the waters that the feathers of red – the colour of the Gods – hanging from those prows are nigh horizontal in the wind as the 20 Natives in each canoe thrust their craft forward, in perfectly synchronised paddling.

And there are *swarms* of these flying vessels! Like an armada of eager seagulls coming at them across the water, the paddles flash high and brightly in the rising sun, before hurtling down and splashing water along the side of their flying canoes.

'Tyos?'[5] those in the first canoes shout up at the incredulous sailors. *Friends?*

Yes! (After all, look at their *bare* breasts! Who would not want to be friends with them? By now the entire bow of the ship is lined with sailors staring down at these semi-naked men and women, but mostly the women, who are brown, lithe, gorgeous, voluptuous and smiling.)

Which prompts the next question.

'Pretanie?'[6] Britain? 'Lima?'[7] Portugal?

'British!' the men call back.

With this answer, the Natives seem to be very pleased indeed – their interactions with the men from that far kingdom of *Pretanie* have been much happier than with those from *Lima* – and in an instant, as Bligh would recount, 'they were no sooner satisfied in this than they crowded on board in vast numbers, notwithstanding our endeavours to prevent it, as we were working the ship in; and in less than ten minutes the deck was so full that I could scarce find my own people'.[8]

Yelling above the tumult of the excited throng, Bligh and Fryer at least manage to bring the ship to a safe anchorage at a depth of 13 fathoms beneath the hull, a mile off Venus Point. The anchor is dropped, ten months and 25,000 miles after leaving Spithead.

To govern local interactions, Bligh has made sure each sailor under-stands the set of rules that he has 'stuck up on the mizzenmast'[9] so all can see. Any failure to follow these rules will result in a lashing.

> Rules to be observed by every Person on Board, or belonging to the Bounty, for the better establishing a Trade for Supplies of Provisions, and good Intercourse with the Natives of the South Sea wherever the Ship may be at.
>
> 1st. At the Society, or Friendly Islands, no person whatever is to intimate that Captain Cook Was killed by Indians; or that he is dead.

(For the Tahitians, Captain Bligh knows, regard *Toote* as a near-God. It will not do for them to know that it is even possible for such a God-like figure to be killed by mere men.)

> 2d. No person is ever to speak, or give the least hint, that We have come on purpose to get the bread-fruit plant, until I have made my plan known to the chiefs.
>
> 3d. Every person is to study to gain the good will and esteem of the natives; to treat them with all kindness; and not to take from them, by violent means, any thing that they may have stolen; and no one is ever to fire, but in defence of his life.
>
> 4th. Every person employed on service, is to take care that no arms, or implements of any kind under their charge, are stolen; the value of such thing, being lost, shall be charged against their wages . . .
>
> Given under my hand, on board the Bounty,
> Tahiti, 25th October, 1788.[10]

Understood?

Understood!

Who would not be happy to abide the rules when there are no restrictions placed on relations with the fairer sex?

Everywhere, all over the deck, joyous and goggle-eyed sailors – many of them missing teeth, heavily pock-marked, and born and raised in cold, dark slums – are surrounded in the bright sunshine by giggling Native women reaching out to touch their strange white skin, the curious shape of their long noses. Encouraged, the sailors reach out to touch the bountiful brown breasts of the females and are awe-struck when their hands are *not* slapped away! Bosom friends!

'Every officer and man in the ship,' James Morrison chronicles, 'were provided with new friends, though none understood the language. Yet, we found it very easy to converse by signs, at which these people are adept.'[11]

Precisely what they are saying with those signs is not detailed exactly by Morrison, but a clue is certainly provided in his next, ironic, notation.

'Some of the women who came on board became very intelligible in a short time and soon brought their former husbands into a method of discourse by which everything was transacted.'[12]

Former husbands?

Well, yes.

For as their sign language makes clear, if the sailor in question would like to be at least the temporary husband of these dusky maidens, or at least have conjugal rights, then neither the maidens, nor their 'former husbands', have any problem with that! But they would like something in return.

What, exactly? Therein lies the beauty of the coming transactions.

For, unlike so many societies around the world, the Tahitians care nothing at all for gold. Yes, gold is shiny. But when you are living in the sunshine, on the most sparkling island in the Pacific, what do you care for a useless metal which merely shines, but has no other particular uses?

No, far more valuable to them – as most particularly explained to the other men by the sun-drenched, leather-skinned old South Seas hand that is William Peckover, who not only understands the language, but also the way of life – is iron, as found in nails. And as the sailors quickly discover, a single nail can easily be exchanged for perfumed paradise!

The Natives like *any* piece of iron they can get their hands on, as well as red feathers and tools such as hatchets and adzes, while Bligh also notes that 'Files, Gimlets, Combs, Knives, [and] Looking Glasses are also in great esteem'.[13]

(One of Bligh's officers will later note of this sexual trade, only half tongue-in-cheek, that while English mothers protect the 'jewel inviolate'[14] of their daughter's virginity and then sell it once for a husband and dowry, in Tahiti, sex is sold all the time to get much smaller things that husbands or mothers want.)

Now, of course, those large swathes of the Tahitian population who simply don't have their voluptuous forms to sell must come up with something else, and it does not take long for a veritable floating market to engulf the *Bounty*.

'We were presently surrounded,' Morrison notes, 'by the natives in their canoes, who brought off hogs, bread-fruit, and coconuts in abundance, and a trade for nails, hatchets, etc., soon commenced.'[15]

The long, arduous voyage from Portsmouth to Tahiti has taken ten gruelling months, but at this moment, for most of the crew, with the wonderful prospect of the *Bounty* soon rocking a little more energetically in the water than the waves alone can explain, it all seems worth it.

Yes, the men of the *Bounty* have arrived in paradise, in the land of plenty, and are taking their fill.

The one man notable among them for having nothing to do with the women is Bligh. He is taking his cue from his marriage vows, his genuine love of his dear wife Betsy, and what he had learnt from Captain Cook a decade earlier: the sailors and officers can sleep with all the women they like, but as the Captain is the 'Chief' of the ship, whoever he chooses to sleep with will have ramifications – and, beyond all that, it simply will not do for the Captain of a ship to show such looseness.

What he is interested in, however, is finding out what has happened to old friends and acquaintances since his last visit here to Tahiti, but a problem soon emerges. For, while Tahiti is still composed of 'seventeen districts called *Venooa* (or Lands)',[16] each one of which has a Chief – and the whole island is still ruled over by a King – not everything about those Chiefs, or King, is so stable.

For just as the Tahitians have what Bligh regards as an unorthodox approach to the exclusive nature of sexual intercourse, so, too, do they take a very different slant on the virtues of keeping the same name. For the nobility of Tahiti, particularly, it turns out, love to change their names every few years!

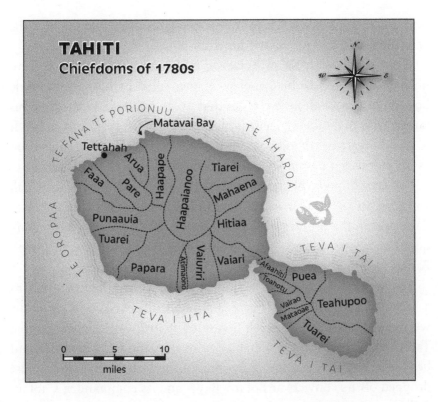

'Almost every individual of any consequence,' Bligh will later note, 'has several names which makes it frequently perplexing when the same person is spoken of to know who is meant. Every chief has perhaps a dozen or more names in the course of thirty years; so that the person who has been spoken of by one visitor will not perhaps be known to another unless other circumstances lead to a discovery.'[17]

It takes, thus, some doing, but Bligh – who is pleased at his enduring grasp of the Tahitian language from his previous visit – eventually works out that Otoo, the 'old' King who ruled when Cook and Bligh were last in Tahiti, in 1777, is currently called 'Tinah', and has a six-year-old son who is the new King called . . . Otoo, while Tinah's father, who had been the King previous to him, who Bligh knew as 'Whappi' is now called . . . Otow.

Otoo, Otoo and Otow. It is all rather confusing, and Bligh decides he will call his old friend – the King of all Tahiti when last they met, over a decade earlier – 'Tinah' to avoid confusion, while the boy, the new King, will be known as King Tu.

What stuns Bligh most, however, is that the King he knew – an unchallenged God to his people – is now ruled by his son, the little boy Tu, just as Bligh now realises that Tinah had taken over from his father, who had taken over from his father before that, and so on. It is an odd system, whereby youth is venerated above all, and as soon as Tu becomes a father to a son, he, too, will lose all of his power.

For now though, Bligh cannot see any King, old or new, as Tinah and King Tu are away from the bay, and so he converses with the older Tahitians on the *Bounty* – 'several inferior chiefs'[18] – who have many questions about old friends, none more than their great *tyo*, Sir Joseph Banks, and their greatest *tyo* of all, *Toote*, Captain Cook.

Yes, well, as soon as the subject of Cook arises, Bligh is quick to assure the Tahitians that *Toote* is wonderfully well, and sends his warmest best wishes . . . which occasions an awkward silence. For the Tahitians now inform them that a British ship, the *Lady Penrhyn*, had been here just four months ago – one of the First Fleet that had just dropped off its convicts at Botany Bay – and its commander, Captain William Sever, had given them the terrible news that *Toote* is dead.

Oh.

Really . . . ?

Dead, you say? Why . . . not at all . . . not at all.

Bligh assures them that Captain Cook is very much alive, and going very well. Alas, Bligh's denial that Cook is dead is confusing to the Tahitians. For aboard the *Lady Penrhyn* was Lieutenant Watts, 'who, having been here in *Resolution* with Captain Cook',[19] was a *witness* from afar to the killing, and had even given them some of the terrible detail.

Salvation comes from *the* most unlikely quarter. For the first man to speak is the botanist, David Nelson, who now points a theatrically dramatic finger at Bligh and says, 'This is the son of Captain Cook!'[20]

All eyes turn to the rather squat figure before them, with the visage a little blurred around the edges, and compare Bligh to the rather tall, distinguished figure of *Toote*, with his chiselled features.

Can it be . . . ?

Yes, that's right! Bligh as the son of Captain Cook – in Tahitian culture, the son of the King is the new King! – is *the* authority on Cook, and if he says that Cook lives then . . . Cook lives!

It makes sense . . . we think. Strange, that neither Cook nor Bligh had mentioned this on their earlier trip to Tahiti. And it is also undeniable that the son in no way resembles the father. A good-looking man, of *Hahy* (great or large) bearing, Cook looks like an impressive *Tata* (man), distinguished, while Bligh looks a little . . . *Etey Etey* (small, little) stunted.

But, still. Who would lie about a thing like that?

And so, he really *is* Cook's son.

All up though, this lie 'seemed to please them very much',[21] Bligh records, and the awkwardness passes.

Meantime, the *Bounty* continues to overflow with Natives. So many, in fact, that as a measure against thieving, Bligh insists that all male Natives must leave the ship that first night, while the women are actively encouraged to stay, and many a hammock bears the weight of two writhing bodies. Several of the hammocks have three (Sir Joseph would be proud).

Welcome to Tahiti.

•

Just one day and the *Bounty* and her men are transformed. The ship is secure, and, after months of deprivation, the ship's company are gorging themselves on the luscious delights of Tahiti delivered to them on ship (and also eating some of the fruit these delights carry with them). The next morning, judging the time right to make their first shore visit, Bligh and his favourite officer, Fletcher Christian, are quickly rowed to land, where they are greeted by Poeeno, the Chief of Matavai Bay, and a swarm of curious chattering Natives.

The son of *Toote* is among them!

The path to Poeeno's residence is a delightful one, beautifully shaded with the bread-fruit trees that Captain Bligh must secure. As they proceed, Bligh with portly paces, Fletcher with his bow-legged bounds, they pass typical Tahitian huts – 'neat thatches made of the palm leaves and supported on posts . . . with coconut leaves woven into a kind of matting [for doors and windows]',[22] filled with happy and welcoming Natives.

Arriving at the house – a quite grand affair, with a thatched roof and elevated floor resting on decorously carved pillars, the whole structure measuring not less than 100 feet from end to end – Bligh and Christian see two women outside, gently bathing a piece of cloth in a tub filled with a red liquid they get from the roots of a native she-oak tree to stain it. These women, Bligh recognises, from his previous trip, as Poeeno's wife and sister.

With hand gestures, the women invite Bligh and Christian to repose themselves on a mat which they have spread out on the floor for them.

Yes, Bligh is welcomed as the King of a visiting tribe, a tribe that the Tahitians respect. And, of course, it does not take long for the word of his presence to spread, as first a couple of Natives, and then some more, and soon dozens at a time, come to see for themselves.

An English Captain, and none less than the son of *Toote*, is here, have you heard?

Soon, even while Bligh and Christian are accepting refreshments, the crowd of Tahitians that has come to see the uniformed Englishmen is so numerous, so pressing, clustering around in such extraordinary numbers, that they 'created a most intense heat'.[23] It is a pressing heat which is all suddenly too much, the portly Bligh can bear it no more. Standing up, he asks the crowd to disperse, accompanying his words with a slightly violent motion with his hands: *Go! Get away! Give me space!*

Reluctantly, they do so, and Bligh and Christian are able to return to their refreshments, offered and served so gracefully by the women of the home. Still, after another hour or so of pleasant talk, Bligh makes his excuses.

'I am to return on board for dinner,'[24] he tells Poeeno. And yet his hosts, with their natural and entirely unaffected manners which so impress Bligh, will not allow him to leave without a present from them. With great elegance, the ladies begin by gathering together some of their finest *tapa* cloth, made from dried pandanus leaves, coconut fibre and bread-fruit bark, with enormous labour, and a sophisticated process passed down through the centuries – with the pulp 'spread in the sun to Dry for one Day, after which it is bleach'd in the Morning Dew till it is perfectly white'[25] – and clothe the Englishman in Tahitian style, with *pareo*, a one-piece wrap-around cloth.

Delighted at his new appearance, they say graciously, 'We will go with you to your boat.'[26]

Thank you, Captain Bligh would be delighted.

It is a pity he has not yet seen Tinah, who is away visiting another village, but Tinah will no doubt come to visit him on the ship, once he returns.

Now clothed in more comfortable – and it must be said, more *regal* – garments of Tahiti, Bligh happily walks back, hand in hand with the two ladies, 'a great crowd'[27] following them along the shore, where his Cutter awaits. Christian, half admiring and half amused – so let us go with bemused – can barely credit how the stiff British officer who had left the *Bounty* just hours before has returned as a quasi Tahitian Chief.

Arriving back on deck, Bligh finds Captain Cook waiting for him.

Well, not quite.

For, of course, it is not the great man in the flesh, but he *is* there, in rather large portrait form. Bligh recognises the portrait immediately as the one of his 'father', done by the sailor-artist John Webber back in 1777, which had been left with the Tahitians to become what is by now no less than a holy relic of Captain Cook's divinity. (Cook, with an eye to helping whoever the next British Captain in these parts would be, had given the painting as a gift for King Tinah – saying that 'When my son comes out, you must show it to him.'[28])

As there has been a little damage done to the frame of the portrait, the Natives had it brought to the *Bounty* in the hope that it might be repaired. The Tahitians know the portrait as '*Toote Earee no Otaheite*, Cook Chief of Tahiti'.

But, can you repair it, Captain Bligh?

Of course he can.

And so, from now on, at every feast, every ceremony, there are the penetrating eyes of Bligh's former Captain gazing at him, assessing him, measuring him against what Cook himself would have done.

And now?

Cook's eyes are coolly appraising his former brilliant young officer to assess how he deals with the drama that has taken place on the *Bounty* while he has been on the shore. For, as Bligh is now apprised, while he has been away, one of the Natives had been caught trying to steal a tin pot, and King Tinah's brother, Prince Oreepyah, is so offended by this offence to their new *tyos* that, he 'flew round the Deck, and with billets of wood he violently beat without mercy and drove over board everyone'.[29]

Yes, the Prince gives a beating to every Native he can reach with his vicious swinging pieces of wood, irrespective of whether or not they had anything to do with the theft. 'This,' the surprised Bligh notes, reeling from such wanton violence, 'was a mode of conduct I never saw in any Tahitian Chief before.'[30]

It was with some difficulty that the thief escaped with his life.

An hour later, Bligh is bemused when now meeting Tinah's youngest brother, Whydooah, who 'appeared stupefied with drinking kava'[31] and seemed 'Stupid and Sulky'. As Bligh soon learns, despite Whydooah's reputation of being a fearsome warrior, he is also regarded as 'being the greatest drunkard in the country'.[32]

(If it were a competition, Dr Huggan would surely be the dark horse, but still.)

In the meantime, although he has still forbidden the crew to leave the *Bounty* to set foot on land, the Captain has come up with a sure-fire method to keep the men happy, and there are no complaints. For, as the Log records: 'Every Night I order all the Natives on shore except the Women, as soon as the Sun is down.'[33]

•

At last, the next morning, the meeting that Bligh has so earnestly been seeking, the one on which the success or failure of his whole mission rests, is clearly approaching. For not long after dawn on this 28th day of October 1788, a glistening Native man in a canoe brings word that Tinah is ready to see Bligh and he would like a boat from the *Bounty*, a boat befitting his royal rank, to be sent to take him to the ship.

Wonderful!

Bligh, in turn, does not merely send the Cutter, he sends it under the command of his best man, Christian.

Only a short time later, thus, Christian is walking through the luxurious greenery of the island, past the turquoise lagoons, by the soaring palm trees – heading towards the dwelling of Tinah – when his eyes happen upon a Tahitian Princess of such striking beauty, such natural poise and elegance, such warmth of expression that he is quite dumbstruck, and stares at her, mesmerised, as if in a trance, before he is able to snap out of it and introduce himself.

'I am Fletcher Christian, Acting Lieutenant of the *Bounty*.'

And I am 'Mauatua', the daughter of one of Tahiti's Chiefs, of the second land of Matavai. And I have been waiting, dreaming of the return of beings in dashing blue coats, just like you.

The softness of her voice! The power of her gaze!

On the spot, Christian decides he has never seen anything so beautiful in his life. She is a statuesque beauty who stands so straight and tall that while Christian himself decides to call her Isabella, named after his only unrequited love, the English rose Isabella Curwen – as he cannot quite master 'Mauatua' – the rest of the *Bounty*'s crew soon christen the gorgeous 18-year-old 'Mainmast'. (She, in turn, calls Christian '*Titriano*', which is how all the Tahitians put their tongue around his name.)

Either way, Christian is completely smitten and, happily, she returns his fervour in kind, the two of them the epitome of falling in love at first sight. Most of the officers and men of the *Bounty* will be with an endless array of different women during their time here, but after meeting Isabella, Christian has no more eyes for another woman than the Blind Fiddler does. There is only one woman for him hereafter, and – he is certain – even in the hereafter.

Isabella! Helping to consolidate their relationship is that Isabella's father, a local Chief, will soon become Fletcher's *tyo*.

In the here and now, however, Christian finally locates King Tinah, and rows the King to the *Bounty* and Bligh, in the company of some of those in the King's court. From the first, it is clear how thrilled Tinah is to see his old friend, engulfing him in his warm embrace, rubbing noses and even desiring that they ... exchange names. Though somewhat confused as to exactly what this name exchange means, Bligh agrees.

'He taking the Name of Bligh, which they could pronounce no way but "*Bry*," and I that of Tinah.'[34]

After all, what else could he do? No longer a King, perhaps, but still very imposing.

> Tinah is a very large man, much above the common stature, being not less than six feet four inches in height and proportionally stout: his age about thirty-five. His wife (Iddeah) I judged to be about twenty-four years of age: she is likewise much above the common size of the women at Tahiti and has a very animated and intelligent countenance.[35]

Iddeah is accompanied by a court of her own.

Among them is 'a woman dressed with a large quantity of cloth in the form of a hoop'.[36] Before Bligh's very eyes, this woman removes her garments and presents them to him as a gift, together with a large hog and some, yes, *bread-fruit*.

Sending his servants, Smith and Samuel, scurrying below, Bligh is quickly able to produce his own presents that he has brought all the way from England. For the delighted Tinah he produces 'hatchets, small adzes, files, gimblets, saws, looking-glasses, red feathers, and two shirts'.[37]

And for you, Iddeah, Captain Bligh has a selection of 'earrings, necklaces, and beads . . .'

Which is all fine. In fact, however, Queen Iddeah makes it clear that what she actually wants is . . . iron. Indeed. Bligh is quick to give her exactly what he has given her husband.

'Much conversation took place among them on the value of the different articles and they appeared extremely satisfied, so that they determined to spend the day with me and requested I would show them all over the ship, and particularly the cabin where I slept.'[38]

Though it goes against the grain, Bligh knows that he really has no choice, and indeed takes them into his cabin, where they evince such a great interest in so many of his personal possessions that, as he would recount, 'they got from me nearly as much more as I had before given them'.[39]

And the cannon, Captain Bligh? Could you fire them, too?

Of course.

Mr Peckover, please fire a cannon for the edification of our guests.

Two minutes later, a massive boom rolls out across the bay, causing a great cry of consternation among the Natives, though their fear turns to wonder soon enough for, 'as the shot fell into the sea at a great distance, all the natives expressed their surprise by loud shouts and acclamations'.[40]

It is a show of power, which is exactly what King Tinah wants.

The fact that Bligh has brought the *Bounty* to anchor in Matavai Bay is a great boon to Tinah's prestige, and a warning to rival tribes.

With everything going so well, Bligh invites Tinah and Iddeah and their entire retinue to stay for a meal, which they readily agree to, at which point Bligh watches, transfixed, as Tinah consumes his meal without touching a single morsel with his hands. For, born a King, since his first mouthful of food as a baby, he has been fed by an attendant, and the practice has never ceased! Even though Tinah is now a grown man, there is still an attendant – himself a big buck of a man – who holds a cup to Tinah's lips, who cuts his food, shapes every perfect morsel and feeds him every mouthful. Again and again and again the spoon goes in, even long after Bligh thinks the King *must* be full.

'I must do him the justice to say he kept his attendant constantly employed,' Bligh notes, 'there was indeed little reason to complain of want of appetite in any of my guests. As the women are not allowed to eat in presence of the men Iddeah dined with some of her companions about an hour afterwards in private, except that her husband Tinah favoured them with his company and seemed to have entirely forgotten that he had already dined.'[41]

Most important for Bligh, however, is not the extraordinary amount of food that Tinah devours, but the even more amazing amount he has brought to the *Bounty*: banana, papaya, guava, bread, kava, goats, 200-pound hogs, all are paddled forth and handed over, in return for just a few nails, or even simple scraps of metal. Even more important are the yams, a kind of Tahitian sweet potato, that is not only delicious but will be able to last for months on the ship, and piles of them under canvas start to grow like pyramids across all decks.

There is in fact such a flood of incoming food that Bligh appoints Peckover as the rough equivalent of a ship customs agent – with quill in hand he carefully notes down exactly what is on board, what is coming on board, who owns what and what might be needed still for the ship to reach the same state of being fully provisioned as it was when it left Portsmouth.

For his part Tinah brings not only food for *Bry*, but an old friend who is that rarest of things in these parts, an old hand used to British ships. His name is Hetee-Hetee, and he is quick to point out to *Bry* that he has been around so long, he sailed with *Toote* before *Bry* did – on Captain Cook's second Pacific voyage, travelling with him to Easter Island, New Zealand and Tonga. *Toote* had liked him so much, he had allowed him to fire the ship's cannon on the King's birthday, and even taught him how to use a musket!

Toote, yes, was a great man, and Hetee-Hetee grieves for him still – an expressed grief, mixed, admittedly, with an endless round of stories, gossip and opinions. There is something so compelling about him. He clearly works all the angles, and had returned from the voyage to Tonga with so many red feathers that Tinah had given him land as a reward. Just what Hetee-Hetee might gain from the latest British ship to arrive on these shores is not yet clear, but for the moment Bligh is happy enough to hear his stories, and laugh at his mischievous memories.

•

Now, while King Tinah and Queen Iddeah are sated at least in terms of what they have eaten, and the gifts they have received, not to mention the one-gun salute in their honour . . .

Still, however, there is one thing they were wondering that Bligh might help them with?

Yes?

A painting of us, perchance, just like the one done of Captain Cook that we and our people have enjoyed so much.

Ah, yes, of course.

Unfortunately, Bligh explains gently, the esteemed artist of the Royal Academy, John Webber, is not with them on this trip and there is no one else with them remotely capable of rendering such a fine likeness.

'Our friends here expressed much disappointment . . .'[42]

It is a bit of a hiccup, true, but it almost seems as if the royal cure for hiccups is eating impossible amounts of food, as the Tahitian King gets busy.

'Tinah continued with me the whole afternoon, in the course of which he ate four times of roast pork besides his dinner.'[43]

The bond between Bligh and Tinah is matched many times over between the *Bounty*'s crew and the rest of the Natives, particularly the females.

'An intimacy between the natives and our people,' Bligh chronicles, 'was already so general that there was scarce a man in the ship who had not his *tyo* or friend.'[44]

Indeed. For this, too, is an important plank in the local culture. While the visiting sailor may form a bond with one or many Tahitian females, as he desires, there is an equal expectation that he will also form a deep relationship with one male, an instant blood brother, a Tahitian male peer who is *tyo*. Officers of rank, like Christian, have great Chiefs pushing to be their *tyo*, but everyone else, right down to the most humble of common sailors, also soon finds themselves embraced by a Tahitian of wealth or rank. Midshipman Thomas Hayward even has a royal *tyo* – the younger brother of King Tinah himself – while the roughest man on the *Bounty*, Charley Churchill, a mere Master-at-Arms, also finds a *tyo* of exalted rank, the Chief of an entire district of Tahiti!

Oh, the glory of it. Only days ago, they were mere British sailors. But now, *now* they are *tyo*, honorary Chiefs, taken right to the bosom (not to mention bosoms) of the Tahitian people.

Tinah has one more request, one more favour to ask, before departing in the late afternoon.

'He requested I would keep for him all the presents I had given to him as he had not at Matavai a place sufficiently safe to secure them from being stolen; I therefore showed him a locker in my cabin for his use and gave him a key to it.'[45]

Still, even after an entire day and evening on board with Tinah, Bligh has not yet found the right moment to bring up the delicate matter of the bread-fruit, and whether they may set about loading their pots with a thousand saplings. All he has been able to do, as a preliminary, is to send Nelson out with his assistant, Brown, to look around the island and determine just how plentiful, and accessible, the bread-fruit plants are, and . . .

And here they are now, already back, being rowed to the side of the ship by several sailors. And they are smiling, which bodes well.

'It was no small pleasure to me,' Bligh will recount, 'to find by their report that according to appearances the object of my mission would probably be accomplished with ease.'[46]

In fact, Nelson reports, the bread-fruit is there in enormous quantities, just for the taking, or perhaps . . . buying. Still, the question remains. How to get a thousand saplings on board, without Tinah realising that they are so priceless to Bligh he will in fact pay the Tahitians almost anything to have them?

On the morning of Wednesday 29 October 1788, Bligh knows he must pay a return visit to King Tinah on land, 'for I found that he expected it'.[47] Bligh makes his way on shore with a bag of gifts especially for the Tahitian children who flock to greet him. For you, little one, some bright beads; and for your friends some toy necklaces that in London had been bought for a penny a dozen, but here are priceless.

It is a sweet sight, a precious parade, as parent after parent lifts their tiny babes up to Bligh so the great man can present his gifts to them. It all goes so well, and Bligh – who, unlike him, even seems to be genuinely enjoying himself – seems to have such a bottomless bag of presents, that the Tahitians soon have a mischievous idea. In short order, amid high hilarity, bigger and bigger children are soon carried to the naval Captain until it ends up with bulky 12-year-olds being carried by their tottering and weak-kneed parents to accept yet more gifts.

Bligh, a family man himself, has a good feel for the antics of these families too, and heartily joins in the laughter and leg-pulling, solemnly presenting each 'little one' with a gift. The whole spectacle 'created much laughter; so that in a short time I got rid of all I had brought on shore'.[48]

Shortly afterwards, Bligh, with Christian, walks to the house of Prince Oreepyah, where he is told Tinah awaits, and, sure enough, there he is, with a large crowd around him who part like the sea before Moses, allowing a passage to be made for Bligh, so he can sit by the great man. And now, a fascinating ceremony takes place. Even as one piece of native *tapa* cloth made from pounded bark – measuring two yards wide by 41 yards long – is spread on the ground, 'another piece of cloth was brought by Oreepyah, which he put over my shoulders and round my waist in the manner the chiefs are clothed. Two large hogs, weighing each above two hundred pounds, and a quantity of baked bread-fruit and coconuts were then laid before me as a present, and I was desired to walk from one end of the cloth spread on the ground to the other.'[49]

As Bligh walks the Tahitians yell as one:

'Tyo! Ehoah! Tyo! Ehoah! Tyo! Ehoah!'[50]

Both words, Bligh knows, mean 'friend', and he is sincerely touched as the 'loud acclamation'[51] echoes about him. Witnessing his old friend so moved by the kindness and acceptance of this ancient people, Fletcher Christian, too, is moved.

Tinah now issues a stream of voluble instructions, which Bligh cannot remotely follow, but, on the instant, dozens of the Natives pick up all the food and start to carry it to where the Cutter has been beached on the shore and begin putting it all in. There is, in fact, so much that the Cutter is 'completely loaded',[52] to the point that there is no room for Bligh himself. No matter, the important thing is that the supplies get safely to the ship, and Bligh is content to wait on the shore, surrounded by the adoring Natives, and talking to King Tinah, until the boat returns to pick him up.

November 1788, Matavai Bay, Aphrodite's Isle

Music, across the water. Gleams of light, slowly bobbing up and down on the swell in the distance.

The sun has fallen, the lanterns on the deck of the *Bounty* are lit. The Blind Fiddler plays, and the well-fed and well-liquored crew dance passionately with bare-breasted Tahitian women, whose hips shake in mesmerising fashion, whose flat bellies are now glistening with the sweat running down from their ample cleavages.

Dance! Dance! Dance!

Young Midshipman George Stewart learns the moves of the *Heiva* with remarkable ease, moving in time with the best of them, while below decks other sailors are becoming expert at different Tahitian rhythms and exertions. Up on the bridge, far enough removed from the bacchanalian scene to remain dignified, Bligh is slowly speaking to one of the slightly older women, who he remembers from the visit 11 years earlier, on a troubling subject – VD, and is it still among the population, as it had been in 1777, after the visit of the men of *Resolution?*

> I was instantly answered in the affirmative, and such a string of descriptive circumstances of the havoc it had made came out, as shocked me to the greatest degree. Many fine Girls she said had died of it . . . [53]

And of course the men, and the officers, have been warned of the dangers they are now running, not that it has made any difference at all. Bligh knows they have all the self-control of alcoholics trapped in a wine cellar. They are more than prepared to take the risk of a grisly death later if it means nights of ecstasy on the *Bounty* right now.

The following morning, Thursday 30 October 1788, there is a new drama aboard the *Bounty*.

There! No sooner has a Native been spotted stealing hooks than the cry goes up, and he darts off, quick to get below decks and mingle with all the other Native men. Which one was he? To Fryer, who was the one who spotted him, they all look much the same – young men with dark brown skin, muscly limbs, fine torsos, grinning countenances and tousled black hair. He simply cannot be sure which one of them is the villain.

Bligh consequently, orders *all* the Tahitian males – except for the attendants of the Chiefs – to immediately remove themselves from the *Bounty*. It is Mr Fryer who has the critical task of distinguishing real 'attendants' from the hoi polloi, but suddenly the nervous thief panics and is revealed, as Captain Bligh would relate in his Log:

... a daring fellow attacked the Centinel ... making several
blows with his stick. As I had not put it in the power of the
Centinel to fire without orders, I was called, when he [the thief]
escaped narrowly with his life among the Crowd where I did
not choose to fire lest an innocent person might suffer, and the
offender after all got clear. Everyone was excessively alarmed at
my determination, and I hope it will be the last provocation I
may meet with among them.[54]

For his part, Fryer is surprised at the Captain's solicitude for the
Tahitian people – *a thief allowed to get away because of the Captain's*
reluctance to permit firing?

But Bligh is still putting into practice the things he has learnt from
Captain Cook, including Cook's biggest lesson of all: it can be dangerous
to provoke the Natives. For Bligh, the most important thing of all is to
maintain good will, so that he can complete his mission for the bread-
fruit. And yet he is also astute enough to quickly realise that there may
be another emotion, beyond good will, that, carefully exploited, may
help his cause: jealousy.

When two other Tahitian 'chiefs of great consequence, Marremarre
and his son Poohaitaiah Otee ... of the districts of Itteeah and
Attahooroo'[55] arrive, Bligh greets them with great ceremony, and offers
them a dinner every bit as sumptuous as the one he had offered Tinah
– who observes closely.

> It was evident that the attention which I showed to these chiefs
> seemed to give uneasiness to Tinah.[56]

Which, in the end, might be useful.

But now to fun!

As the sun goes down, it is decided to hold a race between the
Bounty's Cutter with six oars, and the Natives' fastest double-canoe
with four paddles. The double-canoes are extraordinary vessels, two
canoes side by side, joined together, often with flat platforms between
to carry many people.

A laughing, roaring, Fletcher Christian commands the Cutter, and
with both the crew-members on the *Bounty* and the large crowd of

Natives on the shore cheering themselves hoarse, the two racing vessels match each other stroke for stroke for stroke until right at the end . . . the Cutter pulls ahead and reaches the shore first!

Both sets of rowers warmly congratulate each other in the soft red glow of the falling sun. Before the *Bounty* boys can head back to the ship, however, Prince Oreepyah delays them momentarily, until 'a large piece of cloth that he had sent for was brought . . . which he tied to the boat-hook and desired should be carried off as a trophy of their victory'.[57]

As the *Bounty* lads start to – much more slowly this time – row back, it is to the sound of the 'vast shouts of applause' that are 'given by everyone on shore'.[58]

Whatever the result of the race, the Tahitians' ability to move their canoes through the water is impressive. And yet there is something in this surf that is more impressive still. For the Natives have a favourite sport that soaks up hours of their time when the surf is high. It requires them taking flat pieces of wood, roughly the height and width of a man, out into the waves. The *Bounty* men call these pieces of wood 'paddles', because to get them moving through the waves, the Natives lie flat on them, and use their hands on either side to paddle forth.

> The general plan of this diversion is for a number of them to advance with their paddles to where the Sea begins to break and placing the broad part under the Belly holding the other and with their arms extended at full length, they turn themselves to the surge and balancing themselves on the Paddle are carried to the shore with the greatest rapidity.[59]

Oh, the joy of the Natives, as once they are out to the point where the waves crest, they turn their paddles, catch the breaking wave and *stand* on their paddles, being carried by the surf towards the shore! The best of them can even manoeuvre the paddles back into the wave, sometimes going a little up the face of it, before coming back down.

> The delight they take in this amusement is beyond any thing . . .[60]

Those who are the best at it almost form a group apart within the Natives, as this sport becomes their principal joy and they seem always to be doing one of two things – paddling, or wishing they could be out there paddling.

•

All is now in place for Bligh to begin his plan to gain the bread-fruit. He visits Tinah and tells him of his intent to take the *Bounty* to other parts of Tahiti, to visit other Chiefs.

Tinah's face falls. *He* is the most important Chief. So why not stay here? Tinah pleads with Bligh not to leave Matavai Bay.

'Here,' says Tinah, 'you shall be supplied plentifully with everything you want. All here are your friends and friends of King George: if you go to the other islands you will have everything stolen from you.'

Bligh is not so sure of that, but, seeing as you raise the subject of King George, there is something that occurs to him . . .

'King George sent out those valuable presents to you, and will not you, Tinah, send something to King George in return?'[61]

'Yes,' he says, 'I will send him anything I have . . .'

Tinah then reels off all the different articles he might send, including bark-cloth to make *pareo*, red bird feathers, bread-fruit trees, hogs in abundance, some carvings, any amount of plantains or yams . . .

Bligh pauses, and theatrically thinks for a moment.

The bread-fruit, you say?

Well now, that is interesting.

'The bread-fruit trees are what King George would like,' Bligh says carefully, as if it has just occurred to him for the first time. And if he could get say, a thousand saplings on the ship, right here, he would have no reason to take the *Bounty* to any other part of the islands.

'I promise you,' Tinah replies, 'you can have as many as you can put on board.'[62]

Perfect!

Tinah, as Bligh notes, seems 'much delighted to find it so easily in his power to send anything that would be well received by King George'.[63]

Very well then, that is very kind, Tinah. And Bligh, in turn, reluctantly agrees to keep the *Bounty* anchored exactly where it is, and not go to visit the other Chiefs.

It really is a breakthrough, as it means their bread-fruit mission may now be carried out in the open, *and* with the help of the Tahitians themselves – no small thing when there will be so much work to do to dig out the saplings, being careful not to break the roots, and place them all, with a good fistful of soil, in the pots. After that they will need to constantly water the plants, to nurture them and have them grow larger and sturdier in their pots – with the roots coming through holes in the bottom – before placing them in wheelbarrows and getting them down to the seashore, rowing them to the *Bounty*, getting them on board, and settling them into their allotted and fitted-out spots in the Great Cabin, above the lead-lined floor that will catch whatever water drips through and reticulate it. Yes, the whole thing is an extraordinarily draining operation.

What is not draining for the men after the daily duty is done, however, is spending time in this blessed paradise of Tahiti. Bligh decrees that while all must be back by nightfall, they are otherwise free to be on shore, if they are not on watch. The reverse applies to Tahitian males, as unless given permission by Bligh – usually to a Royal male – they must still leave the ship at nightfall. Tahitian women, Royal or common, however, may stay through the day, and, most particularly, stay through the night. This is not generosity on Bligh's part, but recognition of the facts of life. If he did not allow this, he would risk men deserting every night.

Still, with plants to be grown on shore, there is clearly going to be need for a shore party to base themselves permanently on shore to supervise these precious seeds and saplings, and to protect them – and it is consequently with bated breath that the *Bounty* men wait to see who Bligh will favour to actually live in this paradise, rather than just be granted day leave to visit it.

But now Bligh must pay a key courtesy call. For, as he has been told from the beginning, though Tinah still exercises all the power, he is only the Regent King. The real King, the holy one, is his son Otoo, the *Earee Rahie* King Tu, who – it is explained to the stupefied Bligh – has lived an extraordinary existence since birth.

Like all new Kings, the divine one was taken from his parents at birth, and raised in his own house, on sacred land. As all Tahitians know, everything he touches also becomes sacred, and owned by him. Just the single touch of his hand on the leaf of a tree means the tree will belong to him, forever. It means he is, in essence, such a contagious King Midas he must be kept separate from his subjects and their possessions. Even more extraordinary? To prevent his feet ever touching something so base as the ground, he is carried everywhere by a succession of manservants, human cabs that convey him wherever he wishes. For the alternative, of course, would be problematic. Just one touch of his foot on anyone else's land, and it would become sacred to the King, and forbidden to all others. And so he must live, with his younger siblings, in splendid isolation. Much of it is explained to Bligh by Tinah as they walk to the *fare*, the house where the young King lives. Despite having lived the same existence when he was young, and despite the fact he is speaking about his own son, Tinah speaks of Otoo, the *Earee Rahie*, with a reverential awe. They are about to visit a God on earth.

Now, one thing, *Bry*, just before we get there.

'No person can see my son that is covered above the shoulders,'[64] Tinah says, as he motions for Bligh to stop. Bligh looks sceptical and uncomfortable so Tinah continues to explain and to demonstrate.

'I must do it myself, also my wife. So, you will,'[65] says Tinah as he disrobes and stands expectantly bare-chested before Bligh.

. . .

. . .

Take off his upper garments? In broad daylight?

Besides being undignified, it occurs to Bligh that 'I risked my health in being exposed in such a manner to a burning heat'.[66] Bligh is lily white and determined to remain that way. His gift may proceed, but the Captain of the *Bounty* will not.

'Tinah,' the Captain says to the King, 'if I cannot see your son upon any other conditions, I will leave my present with my best wishes to him.'[67] Tinah is clearly displeased, and Bligh seeks a quick compromise. He will remove an upper garment, the most upper of garments, his hat. As he removes his hat, and says to Tinah, 'I have no objection to go as I would to my own king, who is the greatest in all the world . . .'[68]

Now it is Tinah who pauses. Very well then. Taking a piece of cloth, he drapes it over Bligh's shoulders, as an added sign of his respect, and they proceed. A quarter of a mile onwards, walking through the delightfully dappled light thrown by the bread-fruit trees, they stop by the side of a small serpentine river, on the other side of which they can see, about 50 yards away, a grand house.

Silently, they wait.

And there he is!

From the house now comes the young King, clothed in fine white cloth, serene and silent, carried forth on the shoulders of a servant whose broad feet seem to glide over the ground. Bligh salutes the boy King, addressing him as Tinah has advised: 'Too Earee Rahie,' he calls, 'I bring you gifts.'

On the ground before him, Bligh lays out the finest shiny trinkets he has brought from England. The King looks at them from on high with delight.

A messenger from the other side of the river soon arrives and kneels to collect the gifts in a piece of cloth. Following Tinah's word-for-word instruction, Bligh tells the man in Tahitian: 'It is for the *Earee Rahie*. I am his *tyo*. I hate thieves. I come from Britannia.'[69]

The messenger departs.

In a similar manner, but with different names, Bligh offers presents to the King's two younger siblings.

Still stunned by the exoticness of it all, Bligh strains to see the boy King more clearly and even asks Tinah if he might cross the river to get a better look.

What?

Cross the river?

See the King from close?

Bligh might as well have asked if he could be granted an audience.

The answer is *aima*!

NO.

The land on that side of the river is sacred and he may not step upon it. So, at a distance, Bligh bids farewell to Tu and his two younger siblings, all living in this strange separate palace far from parental care.

Bligh returns to the *Bounty*, quite amazed at the strange beliefs of this people.

For himself, he is quite confident that a woman made out of a rib took an apple courtesy of the evil of a talking snake, and that is where all the trouble started.

1 November 1788, Point Venus, bread of life

On this very morning, Bligh and the botanist, Nelson, are off to inspect Point Venus – a flat, open area where the Transit of Venus was observed by Captain Cook in 1769 – which they have been told will provide the best land on the island to grow hundreds of bread-fruit plants. The landscape is flat, the soil more than usually fertile, even by Tahiti standards, and there is a stream running through it to provide plenty of fresh water.

One look, and Bligh is convinced it is indeed perfect for his purposes.

Captain Bligh's schedule will now be dictated by the growth of the plants.

Nelson's central idea is to transplant the precious bread-fruit root suckers – he selects promising-looking shoots growing from the roots of existing, healthy plants and carefully excises them, along with some of the root, before transplanting them – in a thousand pots filled with rich soil to Point Venus, the whole lot cared for in a large tent made from canvas and sails, a 'greenhouse' to protect them from the elements. Only when the tiny trees have achieved a little hardy maturity – something that should take several months – will they be taken in their pots to the *Bounty*.

Who to put in charge of this important operation? Nelson will provide the horticultural know-how, but has no authority, no rank, to give orders to the *Bounty* men, nor stature to command the Tahitians.

Of course, there can only be one man to do it, Fletcher Christian, who has admittedly been scarce of late. Since meeting Isabella, he has spent every hour he can with her, which has meant only spasmodically, and seemingly reluctantly, returning to the ship. A puzzled Bligh believes that giving Fletcher an important task like this will surely be good for him, refocus this fine young man on the fact that they actually have an important mission to fulfil, and he is to be put at the pointy end of seeing it done. And, of course, Christian could not be more enthusiastic about accepting his new assignment. It means he will live on the island, work on the island, sleep on the island, be *with Isabella* on the island the whole time. He can ask no better than that. And yes, look after the bread-fruit, Captain, very good, Captain. Yes, and of course he also picks his dear friend, Peter Heywood, who has also been enjoying himself more than somewhat in Tahiti and is eager for the task for the same reasons as Fletcher. They will be free Young Gentlemen on this glorious isle, free from the envious eye and caustic tongue of Bligh.

Filling out the shore party is William Peckover – who, with his grasp of the language and customs, is invaluable – the two botanists, David Nelson and Billy Brown, and a rotation of four armed sailors.

And so it begins.

At dawn – a week after arriving at Tahiti – Christian, with his selected group, is dispatched to Point Venus, where they must begin by erecting a tent, both as a nursery for the plants, and as a place for the shore party of sailors to sleep. By the time that Bligh himself arrives, in the company of Tinah, and his fellow Chiefs of Matavai, Moannah and Poeeno, the tent is up. With the consent now of the Tahitian Royals, Bligh marches out the boundary of their new plantation, which soon has ropes and stakes put around it, and the Chiefs comply with Bligh by giving an order that none of the Natives 'are to enter without leave'.[70]

Bligh could not be more pleased with the beginning made and his own cleverness.

'I had now, instead of appearing to receive a favour, brought the chiefs to believe that I was doing them a kindness in carrying the plants as a present from them to the *Earee Rahie no Pretanie* [The King of England].'[71]

That evening, men of the *Bounty* sleep in the tent, few of them unaccompanied, and least of all Christian, who is able to be with Isabella here far more comfortably than he had been on the ship.

After such a good beginning, Bligh invites Tinah to return to the *Bounty* with him that evening to dine. And it goes well, bar one thing.

Without his attendants, there is only one person who can bring the food and wine to Tinah's mouth – that is, Captain William Bligh. It does not sit easily, but Tinah insists – he has never done it himself, and it is not right that he should do so.

So, even as Christian dines with the delectable Isabella in his spacious Point Venus tent, Bligh must feed and water – as to a baby – a grown man on the *Bounty*.

And yet, after dinner, things become more interesting as, at Tinah's insistence, Bligh returns to the shore once more and is taken to visit another sacred, and rarely seen, institution of Tahiti. In a large compound, situated at Tautira, he meets the elite, revered society of the '*Arreoys*', the Tahitian warrior class – instantly identifiable by their notably muscular form, and for the *tata'u*, tattoo of a star, on their left breast – who in wartime must fight all battles, while in peacetime may enjoy all the sensual spoils that their fair islands, and fairer still maidens, can offer. They have no work to do at all, bar prepare for battle. When those battles take place, usually with other tribes, on matters of territorial disputes, they are expected to sacrifice their lives, if necessary, to achieve victory. They are to battles what priests are to religion. Their entire lives are consumed by it.

> The Arreoys are highly respected and . . . the society is chiefly composed of men distinguished by their valour or some other merit . . . Great trust and confidence is reposed in them . . . The Arreoys are allowed great latitude in their amours except in times of danger. Then as they are almost all fighting men (*tata toa*) they are restricted that they may not weaken or enervate themselves.[72]

Tinah explains something of their lives, and one practice in particular horrifies Bligh – just as it had shocked Sir Joseph Banks. Yes, Tinah says, matter-of-factly, all of the newborn babies of the *Arreoys* are strangled at birth. No heirs for them, no child to take their mantle, nothing to distract them from their duty to be ready to fight.

In his private journal – for Bligh vows to himself that this grisly practice shall remain secret, he has little doubt that the British public will have no stomach for such a horror – Bligh adds more grisly specifics:

> The Infant is strangled by the person who receives it the moment
> it is born, and from their representing the Act, it appears to me
> they break its Neck by a twist as is the common way of killing
> a Fowl.[73]

Bligh's revulsion for certain Tahitian ways does not stop there. One that runs institutionalised infanticide close is the brewing of their alcoholic drink, *kava*. 'The operation of making it,' he records, 'is as filthy as the use of it is pernicious. This *kava* is made from a Strong pungent root which few Chiefs ever go without – it is chewed by their servants in large mouthfuls at a time, which when it has collected a sufficiency of saliva is taken and put into a Cocoa nut shell. This is repeated until there is enough chewed – it is then squeezed and given to the principal Men, each of them taking nearly a pint wine measure.'

Captain Bligh, can I offer you a pint of spit?

Don't mind if I don't, Chief, thank you.

This pure beverage of the Gods, however, is only for the King and great Chiefs. Those on the lower tiers of society get a lesser, diluted version, 'mixt with water and again squeezed and strained, it is then delivered to the inferior Chiefs or those of the highest class if they prefer it diluted, and it frequently undergoes a second and third mixture if there is not enough to supply every one'.[74]

God help him, Bligh had not liked the drink to begin with, but, now that he knows how it is made, he cannot *bear* it, and, diplomatic incident or not, outright refuses to drink it.

As it happens, the Tahitians do not feel the same about what the English drink, and have very quickly become partial to both ale, and wine.

So much so that, having noticed that when there is a toast to the King of England, the English always fill their glasses first, it soon becomes quite normal practice to have as many as ten Loyal Toasts to His Majesty in the course of any meal together.

'*King George Earee no Pretanie!*'[75] one or other of the Chiefs will shout, quickly joined in by the others. The English pause, fill their glasses, and join in. 'Gentlemen, the King of England!'

'*King George Earee no Pretanie!*' the cry goes up again. 'Gentlemen, the King of England!'

And so it goes.

Loyal?

Or just royally drunk.

Mostly the latter, but no-one seems to mind.

And this is good piss. Not spit.

3 November 1788, double, double, toil and trouble on the *Bounty*

Trouble on the *Bounty*. Due to the rather thieving nature of the Natives, it has been necessary to place guards on anything and everything they might be able to get their hands on, but on this day, one of those on guard duty – Alec Smith, the Able Seaman with the heavy Cockney accent, notable for his rather stocky pocky-ness and generally lazy disposition – has been found derelict in that very duty. The Cutter had taken Bligh ashore, Smith had been left to guard it, and while he hadn't been looking, a Native had crept forward and taken the 'gudgeon' of the rudder – the key metallic part on which it pivots. It is a problematic loss as it is one of those things that simply cannot be replaced until such time as the *Bounty* gets back to England.

This kind of thing can *not* go on. The point has to be made to the crew that dereliction of duty of any kind is a flogging offence. And Bligh is also of the view that it might be good for the Chiefs to see what a high value the English place on discipline, how seriously they take these troublesome thefts.

'I thought [therefore],' Bligh would recount, 'it would have a good effect to punish the boat-keeper in their presence, many of them happening to be then on board; and accordingly I ordered him a dozen lashes.'[76]

It goes as before.

The surly Smith – a miserable presence at the best of times – is strapped to the grating over the hold, now propped up vertically against the rigging, and again it is James Morrison who is ordered by Bligh, 'under the necessity'[77] of punishing inattention, to do the honours for Smith's dishonour, lashing him a dozen times.

But, instead of being impressed, the Chiefs, led by Tinah, and the Tahitian women who are also present, are terribly upset by the grisly spectacle, begging Bligh to lessen the punishment.

Of course, Bligh does not. Merciless, he insists the punishment is carried out, which clearly does not sit well with the Chiefs, Tinah least of all.

As a matter of fact, Smith himself feels very grim about it, and though he has taken his punishment with barely a whimper – for he is tough all right – there is a look in his eye when it is done, which could peel varnish off the stern. He had done his best to guard the Cutter, had neither been asleep nor drunk, had not been cavorting with a woman. It just so happened that when he was looking one way, a Native had stolen something the other way.

And for *this*, he had been lashed?

You will keep, Captain Bligh, you will keep.

•

Now, while many of the ship's company are making haste slowly to aid their eventual departure – Master Fryer, Mr Cole and above all Mr Nelson – and are looking forward to that day, others take the opposite view and want nothing more than to stay ever longer.

Young 'Monkey', Tom Ellison, is a case in point. He has changed since he has been here – become tanned, put on muscle, perhaps shot up by an inch, known the joys of lying with women. He is a lad from the slums, who can barely fathom that a world like Tahiti existed, and that there is a place in it for such as him – not tugging his forelock, guvnor, as he had to do back in England, and on the *Bounty*, but enjoying it all as a free man.

Another is Peter Heywood, who has also matured remarkably in recent months, most particularly on this magic island – becoming ever stronger and taller, and walking now with the swagger of one who has not merely lost his virginity, but just about everything else of his once childish ways. He is now a *man*, and a proud one. And yet never let it be said that he uses his spare time only for pursuit of Tahitian maidens. For, using his strong education to good effect, he has formed an ambition to create the first dictionary of the Tahitian language. The most obvious words are ones they use every day, like *tyo* for friend, *ae* for yes, *aima* for no, *tane* for man, *vahine* for woman.[78] Other words come, bit by bit. The *hair*, for example, of his favourite maiden, is her *Airooroo*, while her *lips* are her *Aiootoo*, her *tongue* her *Aireroo*, and her *large breasts* her *dahy aai*. When he came to these islands, he was a *peerey peerey*, virgin, but that had not lasted long.

Eno means *bad*, while *myty* means *good*.

Mamu! means *stay silent*!

Mattie means *death*.

Meari'I, Meari'I means *Let me see?*

A *towtow* is a *servant*, man of low degree, while it is noted by even the Natives that Bligh, who they call *Bry*, is frequently very *waureddey* . . . *angry*.

Christian, on the other hand, *Titriano*, is always *matahiti 'āpī*, happy.

Ute'ute, red, is the colour of their God of War, Oro – which is the reason their war canoes are adorned with so many feathers of that colour.

And so it goes. Bit by bit, Heywood's dictionary has filled out, and he is now among the most proficient in the Tahitian language among the ship's company.

Sadly, however . . .

E faarue tatou nei aita i maoro roa . . . We are leaving soon.

Another man making huge strides in learning the language is Christian, courtesy of the fact that, when not supervising the nurturing of the bread-fruit, he spends all his time with Isabella.

Now a few weeks since arriving, he is frankly looking, and sounding, more Tahitian by the day, as his skin becomes deeply tanned, much of his once fine uniform is discarded, his muscles glisten, and he lightly talks to Isabella, who is nearly always with him.

Fletcher's commitment to this new way of life, and the Tahitians' embrace of him, is marked by his request, and their acquiescence, to get a Tahitian tattoo, with a specific design, a star on his left breast, just like the *Arreoy* warriors have. In fact, many of Captain Cook's crew who had visited here 20 years earlier, including Peckover, have such stylish tattoos, and the other crew-members have all long admired them. Now, Fletcher wants one, too, as do his friends George Stewart and James Morrison – the last of whom, as ever a cut above, is freshly tattooed with the famed dictum of the Order of the Garter, *Honi soit qui mal y pense*, 'Shame on him who evil thinks', soon displayed around his left leg. Soon, quite a few of the *Bounty* men are at least displaying the star whereby, the sailors' nascent lore runs, they can identify each other as 'Knights of Tahiti'.

Yes, it is mostly fun, but it will also give them the feeling of being part of a secret club.

Now Fletcher lies down, with his breast bared, and a Tahitian tattooist, who is expert in the field, first marks out the design of the star on his skin using a *niho mano*, a row of shark teeth.

'These marks were made,' the account of Able Seaman John Sumner, who undergoes the same treatment, runs, 'by striking the teeth of an instrument which resembles a comb just through the skin, and rubbing a sort of paste made of soot and oil into the parts thus struck which leaves thereon an indelible stain.'[79]

Soon there is scarce a man on the *Bounty* without a tattoo, just as there is scarce a man who does not have a Tahitian lover.

The exception to both, of course, is that eternal disapproving outsider, glowering in the distance, Captain William Bligh.

CHAPTER FIVE

PARADISE FOUND

Bliss was it in that dawn to be alive,
But to be young was very heaven! Oh! times,
In which the meagre, stale forbidding ways
Of custom, law and statute, took at once
The attraction of a country in romance![1]

William Wordsworth, a schoolmate of Fletcher Christian's, 'The Prelude'

8 November 1788, Point Venus, the *Bounty*'s bounty grows
Captain Bligh is pleased. Two hundred and fifty-two healthy potted plants now sit beneath the awning of the tent made from a spare sail.

God is smiling on his venture at last.

On that note, on this balmy evening, Captain Bligh sits as usual with Tinah, who has brought along his *Taowah* or priest. The leathery elder tells Bligh in a commanding voice that the principal God of the Tahitians is called Oro but that they have 'many others of less consequence'.

'Do you have a God?' he asks Captain Bligh, in Tahitian.

'*Ae*,' replies Bligh, in kind. *Yes.*

'Does he have a son? And who was his wife?'

'Yes, our God had a son but no wife.'

'Who was his father and mother?'

'He never had a father or mother.'[2]

The priest and Tinah try to be polite, really they do. But they simply cannot help themselves as the very *idea* of it sends them into new explosions of mirth.

'You have a God then who never had a father or mother and has a child without a wife!'[3]

117

Yes, that is the sum of it.

The priest and Tinah persist.

'*Aymah timoradee huheine arrami no mydidde?*' Did not a God lie with a woman to get him?

'No.'

'Who was then before your God and where is he? Is he in the Wind or in the Sun?'[4]

There is, of course, no solid answer to be had, and Bligh does not even attempt one.

•

Oh, the pleasures of this life to be had on Tahiti, even beyond the lure of the flesh. The ease with which you can have succulent food! Within days of arriving, the younger lads of the *Bounty*, like 'the boy' Tinkler and 'Monkey' Ellison, had been shinnying up and down coconut trees as if born to it. The men even begin to stockpile the coconuts in neat pyramids below decks on the *Bounty*, against that terrible day they will have to leave this earthly paradise.

Meantime, the bread-fruit plants continue to grow with remarkable vigour, occasioning quite opposite reactions from Captain Bligh, *delight*, and his men, *horror*. For while Bligh, of course, is eager to be on his way, the likes of Fletcher Christian can barely bear to contemplate the day they must part from this sweet land and their new sweethearts.

18 November 1788, *Bounty*, Bligh gets a good Iddeah about the facts of life

After all his time in Tahiti, it takes a good deal to shock Captain Bligh, but this evening it happens. He is joined for dinner by Tinah and his brother, Prince Oreepyah. They are accompanied by the ubiquitous Hetee-Hetee, whose name sounds like laughter, which is appropriate under the circumstances, as he tells riotous story after riotous story. Not all of his stories, however, are funny, and this evening, after Tinah departs a little early, Hetee-Hetee divulges a scandalous truth, blithely confirmed by the Prince.

For you see, Captain Bligh, Iddeah, Tinah's wife, has a regular lover, a servant, *towtow*, and that servant is none other than 'the very person who always fed Tinah at dinner'.[5]

What's more, Hetee-Hetee *insists*, in the face of Bligh's stupefaction it is *Queen Iddeah's* desire for it to be so.

Staggering.

Bligh soon finds out other details. 'Both men cohabited with the Wife in the same hour, and in the presence of one another', enjoying what is essentially a threesome.

'The Virtue and chastity of the chief Women,' writes the scandalised Bligh in his Log, 'is by no means equal to what it has been represented.'[6]

Ah, but Bligh's education in such matters continues to grow. Three days later, he and some of his men are invited to a *Heiva*, a particularly 'lusty dance' in every sense of the phrase, being put on just for Captain Bligh. For, look there now, as 12 glistening and muscly men are divided into four ranks, with two particularly voluptuous women positioned in front of them. A pause now as a priest makes a stirring oration that lasts ten minutes, the audience hanging on every word.

For his part, Bligh sits there a little uncomfortably – of course, the ubiquitous portrait of Captain Cook has been placed by his side – wondering what will happen next. When the priest finishes, two pieces of white cloth are brought forth, one of which is wrapped around the painting, and the other around Bligh. And now an old man steps forward, bearing three mats of plaited coconut leaf. The first is placed at the feet of *Bry*, the second before Tinah, and the final one at the base of the painting. Let the dancing begin!

First, the men jump high, 'throwing their legs and arms into violent and odd motions' as the two women keep time. Bligh can't help but notice that every time the women throw their legs high, 'their [nether regions] were generally exposed to full view, frequently standing on one leg and keeping the other up, giving themselves the most wanton and lascivious motions'.[7]

At least they are a fair distance away, and it is not all right in his face . . .

But now, Iddeah motions for these wildly gyrating, freely perspiring, near-*naked* women to come closer and they 'accordingly advanced with their Cloath up, and went through the same Wanton gestures'.[8]

While Bligh averts his eyes the best he can, everyone else, including Fletcher Christian – and maybe even the eyes of the hitherto exemplary Captain Cook – is mesmerised.

Taking the opportunity – sex is in the air – Hetee-Hetee asks Queen Iddeah to confirm to wide-eyed Captain Bligh that she indeed takes her house servant as a lover.

Laughing, Iddeah indeed confirms exactly that!

Bligh's eyes widen further in disbelief when he learns yet more libidinous social mores.

> I find it is not at all uncommon for brothers to have connection with the wives of each other . . .[9]

For their part, the ship's company of the *Bounty* are less inclined to reel in horror at the Tahitian sexual mores, and more disposed to throw themselves at the Tahitian women with gusto, who continue to throw themselves right back – which comes with attendant problems. That much is evident from the discreet note that Bligh makes in his Log on 4 December, recording 'Three Venereals in the List.'[10]

The *Bounty*'s pay book, though, paints a more complete picture, listing the men who, thus far, have had to draw on a part of their salary as payment for medicine to cure the pains and pus in their penises. (Yes, while if you fall on deck or the like and get injured, the medical care of the Royal Navy is at your service, free of charge, Venereal Disease is on your head, and worse.) The list is long:

> Christian, Peter Heywood, Cole, Purcell, Lebogue, Byrn, Hillbrandt, Hall, Skinner, Alex Smith, John Smith, Burkitt, Millward, Norton, Muspratt, Lamb, Quintal, Brown.[11]

And these are merely the ones who have paid for treatment. The chaste Captain Bligh gets a daily update on exactly what his officers and men have been up to in their hours of leisure and pleasure, and is not pleased. The sooner they can get all the pots on board, and get on their way, back to disciplined shipboard life, the better it will be. But when will the bread-fruit be ready? At the moment, the best he can hope for is April.

4 December 1788, *Bounty*, more trouble at the mill

God damn you, sir, God *damn* you!

To Bligh's infinite outrage, today, for *the third time*, the Carpenter, William Purcell, refuses to comply with a direct order. As ever, he stands on his dignity, reaches for the highest of his high dudgeon and sniffs that the order lies beyond his duties as Carpenter.

And it has all come from nowhere.

This afternoon, Hetee-Hetee brings a particular stone from the shore, begging of Bligh a favour. Can he direct his men to shape the stone, cut the rock with their wondrous tools, to form a proper British carving stone, so it would be smooth enough for them to sharpen their own hatchets on it?

Of course.

Mr Purcell, please use your tools to this effect, and so shape the stone.

Mr Purcell does not hesitate in his response.

'I will not cut the stone for it will spoil my Chisel, and though there is a law to take away my clothes there is none to take away my Tools.'[12]

Stupefied, stunned that once again Purcell refuses a direct order, Bligh instantly metes out a heavy-handed punishment, confining the Carpenter to his cabin.

He would, in truth, like to give the insufferable Purcell a dozen lashes – to go with the dozen lashes that limping rogue Matthew Thompson is also given on this day 'for insolence and disobedience of orders'[13] – but Purcell's rank as Warrant Officer prevents it. In any case it is as well, for as soon as the next afternoon, when the first storm of the monsoon season bursts upon them – coming from their unprotected nor'west – Bligh realises he will need every bit of skill and energy Purcell can muster, to keep the *Bounty* safe.

Again and again waves crash into and over the ship, threatening to break it away from its anchors and hurl it on the shore. All hands on deck! And they all are, at least the best they can, as the ship bucks and rears on the violent, rolling swell.

In desperation, Bligh personally gives the word to Purcell to leave his cabin, immediately, and busy himself securing the ship, battening down the hatches. Bligh adds only one rider, shouting it above the howling wind and thunderous waves that foam all around them, threatening destruction.

'Consider yourself still a prisoner!'[14]

At Point Venus, Fletcher Christian and his party have no time to worry about the *Bounty*, as they too are engulfed in the huge waves that have burst into the usually tranquil bay. Like madmen, up to their knees in surging water, they scramble to get all the bread-fruit plants high enough that they are away from the salt water, which would kill them.

It is a close-run thing.

On the *Bounty*, Bligh is alarmed to see, paddling through the huge surf to get to them, King Tinah, Queen Iddeah, and an old Chief of Matavai by the name of Moannah . . . His alarm, however, is no match for their relief as they climb onto the ship and see that the Captain is still safe, as they take turns to embrace him, each crying and praying, thanking their Gods that he is unhurt. Tinah refuses to leave Bligh, and stays throughout the day, as does the ferocious storm.

It rages on through the long night and Bligh realises he must change their base of operations, so that both the ship and the plants can be assured of safety during the monsoon season, which, he is assured, can deliver far worse storms than the one they have endured this night.

When the weather clears, 30 hours later, a new harbour is found close by at Oparre – just three miles to the south-west of their previous anchorage – which is greeted with great relief by all, as their women remain nearby. Captain Bligh announces that they will move there at the end of the month.

And at least Chief Poeeno is reassuring about what might happen if another storm damages the *Bounty*.

'You shall live with me if the ship is lost,' he tells Captain Bligh, 'and we will cut down trees to build another to carry you to *Pretanie*.'[15]

How very amusing. Cut down trees from this island and craft a vessel sturdy enough to sail to England? Bligh laughs heartily at the notion, for even he would find such a task impossible.

In the meantime, a ten-year-old Tahitian lad is helping the sailors haul the storm-battered Launch onto the beach to be repaired when he slips and falls under it, and is crushed.

Quickly, get the ship's Surgeon! Where is Dr Huggan?

Alas, alas . . .

The Surgeon . . . was found incapable, from being drunk.[16]

Bligh sends for Huggan's assistant, Thomas Ledward, who delivers the good news that the lad will make a complete recovery. The same, however, cannot be said for Huggan, who continues on a long spiral downwards.

In the last few weeks, he has barely stirred from his cabin, refusing Tom Ledward's offer of coconut milk and accepting only liquor.

Captain Bligh orders that he at least be removed from his cabin to get fresh air.

It is done, but it is too late. For within an hour of being carried up on deck, Dr Huggan shuffles off his mortal coil.

Bligh, while publicly mournful, at least the best he can muster, is privately scathing.

This unfortunate man died owing to drunkenness and indolence . . .[17]

When the news becomes known to the Natives the next day, there is a gasp of complete non-surprise from all. The Chiefs, particularly, on their visits to the *Bounty*, had seen enough of this shambling wreck of a man to give an instant summation that he had died due to 'not working and drinking too much *Ava no Pretanie*'[18], too much British grog.

Dr Huggan is at least given a Christian burial in the afternoon, with Captain Bligh ministering, after which Tom Ledward is appointed Surgeon.

The unspoken truth is that the death of the hopeless Huggan – whose only contribution was to drain the cellar – makes them stronger, not weaker.

•

No-one is more relieved than Fletcher Christian that the new safe harbour is only three miles from the first. Though he has only been with her for a short time, the thought of parting from Isabella is anathema. At least now, they should be able to have several more months together. And then?

They will work that out when they get there.

•

As the hot, wet December days pass by, resentment against Captain Bligh from the ship's company grows. The man has no feeling!

Well, Charley Churchill has feeling, it is towards Captain Bligh and it is all bad. How long can he stand this . . . ?

What other Captain, in the history of the Royal Navy, has ever cancelled Christmas?

Ever?!

But that is what Captain Bligh does. Christmas, he decrees, will be celebrated on Sunday 28 December instead!

Of course, it is all to do with his precious bread-fruit – shifting from Matavai Bay to Oparre is far more important than the birth of our Lord and Saviour. Every plant must be loaded onto the *Bounty*, and then, in the company of King Tinah, Queen Iddeah and various important Chiefs eager to experience the thrill of sailing in a British ship, the ship itself will move.

In preparation, on Christmas Eve, Mr Fryer is dispatched to determine the depth of the passage. Several hours later, he returns with a favourable report: '16 and 17 fathoms Water and a good bottom all the way.'[19]

Perfect! That gives 90 feet of safety below the *Bounty*'s keel. Still, Captain Bligh takes extra precautions and places Mr Christian as skipper of the Launch, to proceed just a hundred yards ahead of the *Bounty* and slowly guide it along Fryer's course.

As a final precaution, Mr Fryer is posted at the fore yard, an elevated position up the front mast of the *Bounty*, so that he may keep an eye out for any unforeseen dangers.

A short time after they have weighed anchor on Christmas Day, and Captain Bligh has given the order to proceed slowly under topsails only, Mr Christian in the Launch, 'instead of keeping ahead', makes an unforgivable error and lets the *Bounty* get between him and the wind, which has, literally, 'taken the wind out of his sails', and seen him becalmed.

'Reef the sails!' roars Captain Bligh. 'Drop the anchor!'[20]

Sure enough, the *Bounty* suddenly comes to a stop. But not quite the one intended . . .

For up runs Mr Fryer shouting that the ship has run aground! Bligh's face turns that deep shade of purple the men easily recognise as pure rage.

Somehow, in this simplest of exercises, with no less than the Tahitian Royals on board, he has run his boat aground, all because he has trusted his officers. *Damn Mr Christian* and his stationary Launch, *damn Mr Fryer* and his damn 17 fathoms. Captain Bligh is surrounded by *fools* and *incompetent amateurs* pretending to be sailors.

The only thing that saves Mr Fryer and Mr Christian from vicious censure for the moment is the presence of honoured guests.

And is that not the final humiliation?

To get their *Bounty* off the coral, the once mighty Englishmen are reduced to having the Tahitians help them, hauling on the capstan after another anchor is suitably placed. After no little struggle, and luckily minimal damage, the *Bounty* is at last able to move into its new position, with the bread-fruit once more brought on shore into new premises, safe from the scorching sun and at a safe distance from the ocean's roaring waves. And this time, to ensure there is *no* chance of the *Bounty* drifting onto the rocks – the Captain has had his fill – Bligh insists that the ship is held in place by a strong cable from each end being tethered to two strong trees on shore.

Nothing, however, will save Mr Christian and Mr Fryer from Captain Bligh's scorching tongue, as he excoriates them in front of the crew. The ship is saved, but the same cannot be said for the relationship between Bligh and his two key officers. And yet, while Mr Fryer takes it stoically enough – the lashing is fodder for his naturally lugubrious nature, just another thing that has gone wrong in a lifetime of things going wrong – the same cannot be said for Fletcher Christian. Yes, there had been an error, and yes, it may even have been his fault. But few men are without errors, and here is Captain Bligh publicly humiliating him? Christian can barely contain his rage.

The Natives are not long in noting that where once the sounds coming from the *Bounty* visitors were music and laughter in the day, and much groaning in the night, there are now many raised voices, or rather *one* raised voice many times, that of Captain Bligh, who now finds fault with seemingly everything Titriano does.

Alarmed, some of the Chiefs quietly say to Christian, '*Titriano, Bry worrite beha*', Christian, Bligh is perhaps angry with you.

'No, no,'[21] Christian steadfastly maintains. Just a small misunderstanding.

Later, however, in the otherwise quiet of the evening, with the likes of Peter Heywood and other officers, Fletcher Christian's bitterness flows forth in full stream.

'I would not regard the Captain's cruelty in abusing me,' says he, his brow slick with sweat, 'if he would only do it in private, instead of doing it before the people of this country!'[22]

As 1788 creeps towards 1789, Bligh's public cruelty towards Christian intensifies. The Natives become ever more concerned for their friend, and confused. There is no doubt that *Titriano* is the most loved man on these islands, a favourite with Kings, with Chiefs, most certainly with the women, with men and children.

Indeed, as James Morrison will observe, 'They adored the very ground he trod on.'[23]

Yet, for some reason, *Bry* now seems to hate *Titriano*, and is determined to humiliate him all the time. The worst of it? Bligh insults Christian behind his back, too, as the Acting Lieutenant now finds out.

For one day in late December, Christian is approached by none other than Isabella's father, a man who had been proud to be his *tyo* – bosom friend – because, like the Chief, Christian was an obviously powerful man. So close had they been that they had even exchanged names in the Tahitian custom.

But now, no more!

The Chief is disgusted with Christian for having tricked him into thinking he was a man of power. Tricked him into being *tyo* with a lowly servant! And his own daughter has lain with Christian!

Fletcher Christian is confused. What on earth is the Chief talking about?

The Chief explains.

'I have dined today with Captain Bligh, and was told by him you are only his *towtow*, or servant.'

Though mortified, Christian explains it away, telling the Chief that all of them, including 'Captain Bligh, and all the officers, were *towtows* of the King of *Pretanie*.'[24]

The Chief and Mr Christian are *tyos* again, but Captain Bligh and Mr Christian are more estranged than ever. Deeply angered by this needless humiliation, Christian still bites his tongue. But he will be damned if any man thinks him Bligh's *towtow*.

As it happens, Fletcher is merely one of the *Bounty* men who Bligh now seems to have a set against. In the last days of the year, both Able Seaman William Muspratt and cook Robert Lamb receive a dozen lashes, both for trifles.

Oh, tread lightly, lads, for the Captain is watching us, judging us, *looking* for a reason to let the cat out of the bag – the cat o' nine tails.

5 January 1789, Matavai Bay, fugitives in the night

It is time.

'My watch, Mr Hayward,' says John Fryer.

'Your watch, Mr Fryer,' the outgoing watch-keeper replies, before gratefully heading below deck to sleep.

John Fryer does his usual circuit of the *Bounty* to ensure all is in order . . . when he discovers, it is not.

The Cutter is missing from its usual spot on deck!

After some frantic searching around the ship, as well as wild scanning around the moonlit water, the awful truth dawns. The Cutter has been stolen. With great reluctance, John Fryer rouses Captain Bligh who is up and on deck in a flash, supervising a roll call to quickly establish if any of his crew are missing.

And they are.

There is no sign of Charley Churchill, the ship's Master-at-Arms, and two of the seamen, Muspratt and Millward. It is soon discovered that eight muskets, eight bayonets and eight cartridge boxes are also missing. Beyond that, nothing is known.

Bligh asks the obvious question, first. Who was the Officer of the Watch when these men disappeared, and *why did he not prevent it?*

The answers shock him. For it is Midshipman Thomas Hayward, and he had fallen asleep on duty.

Hayward! Normally so dedicated, and so reliable – and yet it has happened on *his* watch. Bligh has no choice, and sharply orders him to be demoted to a mere Able Seaman and taken below and put in irons, until such times as the deserters are captured and brought back, whereupon they can take his place.

But it is not just Hayward that Bligh is disgusted with. In his current disposition, it is his firm view that all of his 'officers' should be before the mast, as they are useless:

> Such neglectful and worthless Petty Officers I believe never was in a Ship as are in this – No Orders for a few hours together are obeyed by them, and their conduct in general is so bad, that no confidence or trust can be reposed in them – in short they have drove me to everything but Corporal punishment and that must follow if they do not improve.[25]

As ever, to do what needs to be done, Bligh feels he has no choice but to do it himself. He goes to shore to consult with the Chiefs, sure that they will know the whereabouts of these rogues gone rogue.

And of course, they do. The boat has been beached at Matavai, they tell him, near where the *Bounty* was previously anchored, and the fleeing crew-members were last seen in a sailing canoe, heading for the island of Tethuroa, some 30 miles to the north. As it turns out, even before Bligh can send men to the shore to retrieve the Cutter, five of the Natives bring it back to the ship. Now, for the men . . .

From the first, Bligh makes his intentions clear to Tinah and the other assembled Chiefs.

'I expect you will get the deserters brought back,' Bligh remarks calmly but ominously. 'I am determined not to leave Tahiti without them.' *Outou ite?* You understand?

Tinah assures Bligh all will be done: 'Oreepyah and Moannah shall depart in the morning for Tethuroa.'[26]

But Bligh senses something is not being done, that some knowledge is being hidden and he is quick to anger and accusation. He wants his MEN, dammit.

'As you have always been my friends,' he tells Tinah and the assembled Chiefs, 'I expect you to show it in this instance. But unless you do I shall proceed with such violence as to make you repent it.'[27]

Bry Waureddey! Bry Mow Etey! Matow! Bligh is angry! Bligh seizes pistol! Be afraid!

The Chiefs promise to do their best, but still have one pertinent fear. Might Captain Bligh do to them what *Toote* did to Chief Tootaha, keeping him a prisoner on board until such time as the deserters are recovered?

> However they laughed when they asked this question, and I showed them they had no reason to fear . . . [28]

(Another lesson from Cook: trying to imprison Chiefs can end very badly indeed.)

•

Returning to the ship, Bligh orders a search of the absconders' personal effects, which immediately turns up something very interesting indeed. For inside Churchill's chest, a piece of paper is found on which is written Churchill's own name, together with the names of three of the men in the shore party . . . including those of . . . Fletcher Christian and Peter Heywood.

What on earth can the list be?

Perhaps it is of those in the shore party who Churchill had thought might flee with them? But no, that could not be right, because the list includes the name of Fletcher Christian, and that is so out of the question as to be laughable. As a matter of fact, he and his second-in-command do have a laugh about it – a rare occurrence these days – when Captain Bligh visits the shore party that afternoon.

Yes, Bligh upbraids *some* of those stationed on shore: 'Are you in league with Churchill and intending to desert, too?!'[29] he barks at them.

But the Captain never seriously considers Fletcher Christian as being part of it, nor Peter Heywood. That is clearly some mistake. In any case, as James Morrison documents, when it comes to the shore party being confronted by Bligh's charges, 'They persisted in their innocence and denied it so firmly that he was inclined from circumstances to believe them and said no more to them about it.'[30]

For the moment, they must wait to see if the Natives succeed in finding the deserters.

In the meantime, Bligh's education in the ways of the Tahitians continues apace. Arriving on an unannounced visit to Tinah and Queen Iddeah on this morning, 'I found [Iddeah] with a person, who although I was certain was a man, had great marks of effeminacy about him and created in me certain notions which I wished to find out if there were any foundation for.'[31]

Delicately inquiring of Iddeah who, and what, this person is, Iddeah tells him the figure is from 'a class of people common in Tahiti called *Mahoo*'.

Do tell?

Though the Mahoo is, genetically, a man, 'the Men have frequent connections with him and he lives, observes the same ceremonies, and eats as the Women do'.[32]

Bligh is fascinated.

With such effeminacy, surely he is castrated? And is it that, in terms of these 'connections', he is . . . sodomised?

So curious is he that Tinah quickly calls for a dozen Natives, including the Mahoo, to provide answers.

The answers are shocking.

'I was . . . mistaken in all my conjectures [about sodomy],' Bligh records, 'except that things equally disgusting were committed.'[33]

How to put this?

Well, it is not just the Mahoo who does these 'equally disgusting' things.

'It is strange that in so prolific a country as this, Men should be led into such sensual and beastly acts of gratification, but perhaps no place in the world are they so common or so extraordinary as in this island. Even the mouths of women are not exempt from the pollution, and many other as uncommon ways have they of gratifying their beastly inclinations.'[34]

Mahoo, Tinah explains, are selected at a young age and 'kept with the women solely for the caresses of the men'.[35]

Would Bligh like to look at Mahoo's 'connection'.[36]

The offer evinces, aye, a Bligh sigh . . . but . . . yes . . . he would.

> He had the appearance of a woman, his Yard & Testicles being so drawn in under him, having the Art from custom of keeping them in this position; those who are connected with him have their beastly pleasures gratified between his thighs, but are no farther Sodomites as they all positively deny the Crime.[37]

The most amazing thing?

> The Women treat him as one of their sex, and he observed every restriction that they do, and is equally respected and esteemed.[38]

16 January 1789, Matavai Bay, blast the Master

There is news!

Captain Bligh is fussing about the bread-fruit plants on shore when he receives a message from Mr Fryer: The person who carried the deserters off to Tethuroa is on board. Should I detain him?[39]

Let's think.

YES. As if Captain Bligh would ever give any other answer.

But it is too late.

For, as Bligh writes in his contemptuous hand, 'while the Messenger was absent, which was about 10 minutes, he suffered this Offender to jump overboard and escape'. The damn fool Fryer has thus ensured that 'I now lost an opportunity of securing the return of the deserters.'[40]

Bligh, of course, does not miss the opportunity to impart to Mr Fryer exactly what he thinks of him.

But the depths of Captain Bligh's rage at Mr Fryer grow yet deeper the next day, when the skipper orders all the sails to be taken out of the Sail Room and on to the shore, in order to be aired. Now, Mr Fryer has previously assured Captain Bligh many times that the sails – quite important to a sailing vessel, in the scheme of things – have been well looked after, as part of his responsibilities, and are 'in good Order'.[41]

And yet, this proves not to be the case! In fact . . . 'the New Fore Topsail and Fore sail, Main Topmt. Stay sail & Main Staysail were found very much mildewed and rotten in many places.'[42]

Yes, that's it. *Mildewed. Rotten.* Bligh is stunned and enraged in equal measure. Despite Mr Fryer's constant assurances that the sails have been looked after, it is now clear that he was lying and, worse, Captain Bligh realises to his horror that during their whole stay on Tahiti 'these New Sails were never brought out, nor is it certain whether they have been out since we left England'.[43]

Blast the Master! Liar! Dullard! Idiot! Sluggard!

Unable to trust Fryer, Captain Bligh personally oversees the sails being dunked into the sea and hung on shore to dry, ready to be repaired. Sail-maker Lawrence Lebogue will be kept very busy indeed.

If only, Captain Bligh confides to his Log, he could do what he truly wants to do.

> If I had any Officers to supersede the Master and the Bosun,
> or was capable of doing without them, considering them as
> common Seamen, they should no longer occupy their respective
> Stations.[44]

But Bligh has no officers to supersede anybody, he barely has anyone capable of anything. What he has is a scurvy bunch of low-life sailors, obsessed with fornicating with their Tahitian mistresses, and only ever reluctantly attending to their duties. None of them is a sailor born, as he was, none of them is capable of doing every job on the ship as Bligh himself has done ever since he was eight years old.

Somehow, on this oh so important mission, needing competent men who understand that importance and behave accordingly, he finds himself awash with wastrels, rogues, rascals, fools, liars and deserters, most of whom deserve to be lashed.

Captain Bligh is not pleased, and, as ever, expresses his discontent with much the same passion, and even much the same noise, as an exploding volcano.

23 January 1789, the bread-fruit camp at Oparre, it was a dark and stormy night

Hetee-Hetee comes to find his former shipmate Bligh and tells him, in his thick accent, that he has news. The deserters have returned to Tahiti in a native canoe and he knows where they are!

Where?

'The upper part of Tettahah, about six miles to the westward.'[45]

It is late in the afternoon, with just an hour of daylight left. A storm is gathering. The obvious thing for Bligh to do is to garner his resources and set out after the deserters at first light the following morning. But Captain Bligh is not a man for the obvious.

He is a man for *action*, and he wishes to pursue them immediately.

There are none he can trust for such an important task, and so he resolves to do it himself, quickly commanding four men to accompany him, along with Hetee-Hetee. Just to get to the shore at Tettahah requires 'a difficult navigation through the reefs',[46] and although the sea is indeed rough, and the night more than dark, a combination of Bligh's preternatural seamanship and Hetee-Hetee's knowledge of the island shore, means they are able to land on the beach 'at a convenient place for the Boat, but some distance from where the Deserters were'.[47]

In a half-strangled combination of yelling and whispering – making himself heard above the storm, while not wanting to alert those not huddled around him – Bligh tells his sailors to bring the Launch safely around the island to where the deserters are thought to have secreted themselves, while he and Hetee-Hetee land and take a cross-country shortcut through the jungle, beneath a stormy sky. And yet, a new problem quickly emerges. Although they find some brigands . . . they're not British. A group of Tahitians are following them closely, and in whispered hisses, Hetee-Hetee makes it clear to the Captain that he knows what they want: everything Bligh has.

Still the Natives close in, until something has to give.

It proves to be Bligh's temper.

'I will destroy you!'[48] he barks, firing his guns over their head.

The beachside brigands scatter like startled chooks, but they are not the only ones who are now terrified.

> Hetee-Hetee's fears were so great on the occasion, that I could
> scarce get him on, and as I scolded him for leading me into such
> a scrape, it was some time before he got the better of it.[49]

At least better-behaved Natives are nearby, including a Chief, Teppahoo,
and his wife, who greet them warmly and confirm that the deserters
are indeed in a hut nearby.

With the reluctant Hetee-Hetee in tow, assisted by some of Teppahoo's
men, Bligh heads off into the night, confident he is close to securing
the wretched deserters with ease.

Hetee-Hetee clearly – judging by the way he dawdles, the way his
eyes dart around like trapped sparrows in a snare – does not share his
confidence. What has he done, bringing this report to Captain Bligh,
which has seen him now in lock-step with this madman in the middle
of this stormy night. *What has he done?* Onwards they go.

Through the flashes of sheet lightning, they can see in the suddenly
glimmered gloom, just ahead, the hut! A lesser man than Bligh, or at
least a more cautious one, might now position his men around the hut,
or work out a way to minimise the risk to himself. But Bligh cannot
bear it a moment longer.

Taking his pistol in hand and cocking it, he strides forward, calling
on the cursed brigands to give themselves up!

Inside the hut, the voice of the hated Captain appears to paralyse
what last little bit of fight the deserters have left in them. For now, all
of Mr Churchill, Mr Muspratt and Mr Millward run out, their empty
hands in the air.

Bligh glares at them, the flashing sky giving his cocked pistol an
even more sinister edge than usual.

Keeping the muzzle trained on the traitors, Bligh convinces one of
the reluctant Natives, a good swimmer, to go and find the men he
has left in the Launch, now bobbing a hundred yards offshore of the
nearby beach, and tell them to return to their last landing spot. With
copious threats of death and sundry insults, the Captain leads the three
deserters away from the hut and along the beach at gunpoint, until he
finally reunites with the rest of his sodden crew, who bring their own
arms to bear. Judging it unwise to take them in the Launch during the

storm, Bligh arranges for the deserters to be secured in a nearby hut. Of course, it is Bligh himself, not daring to trust anyone else, who sits sentry through the long raging night, his musket trained upon them at all times, allowing his men to sleep.

When morning breaks, so too does the rain, and Bligh is able to make a triumphant return to the *Bounty* with his prisoners in tow – a sure demonstration of his powers to all those who might be thinking of following the deserters' lead. The lesson must be learnt – if you desert the *Bounty*, then Captain Bligh himself, alone, will hunt you down, and bring you to justice.

An even greater reason for would-be deserters to do their duty and stay loyal soon becomes apparent, as the story of the deserters comes out. While it had been one thing to imagine they could live easily on Tahiti and surrounding islands for the rest of their days, their experience, once on their own, had been grim. Not only had their canoe overturned on their way to Tettahah, which had seen them nearly drowned, but in the process they had lost 'One Musquet two Bayonets and some scabbards', with all their powder ruined. Like half-drowned rats, they had washed up on the shores near where they had been found, and got by since, but barely.

The truth is, Bligh's two pocket pistols had been more than enough to overwhelm their remaining arsenal of useless weapons, and it had practically been a relief to be recaptured.

They even claim to a disbelieving Bligh that, 'It was our intention to return to the ship.'[50]

24 January 1789, the *Bounty* moored off Oparre, the cat yowls

For the deserters, it is time to pay the piper.

The crew assemble on the foredeck, the officers wear full naval uniform, and even King Tinah's brother, an unusually sober Prince Whydooah, is here to witness the ceremonies, taking his place just off Bligh's right shoulder as the Captain gravely reads out the Articles of War before getting to the punishments.

And yet, Bligh and all the crew remain oblivious that the person most in danger right now is the Captain himself. For yes, Prince Whydooah, having heard that there are to be lashings this morning, is concerned that his own *tyo,* Thomas Hayward – the officer on the watch when the deserters had got away – will be one of those lashed. And he will *not* have it.

'If Mr. Hayward,' the Prince had secretly vowed to his tribesmen, 'is punished with Churchill, Muspratt, and Millward, I will kill *Bry* . . .'[51]

And he means it!

'Soon as I see Mr. Hayward receive the first blow, I intend to level *Bry* and escape by jumping overboard, and diving till I reach the shore.'[52]

Which is the explanation for the position of Prince Whydooah right now, hovering behind Bligh, seemingly holding his club impassively, but in fact gripping it, ready to swing, the instant his *tyo* Hayward is threatened.

As Bligh begins to announce his verdicts, the punishments each man is to receive, Whydooah's hand further tightens on his club.

Mr Millward is to receive 24 lashes. As is Mr Muspratt. Mr Churchill, strangely, is only to receive a dozen lashes.

Thomas Hayward is to be . . . confined below in chains.

Whydooah relaxes. Bligh lives.

And yet, these lashings Captain Bligh has decided upon are merely the first half of what they are about to receive. After being lashed this time, they will be held below in chains for ten days – right beside Thomas Hayward – until they are strong enough for a second helping, may the Lord have mercy on their souls.

It goes as expected, the attendant sailors wincing as Morrison's lash draws blood, then flesh, then, in the case of Muspratt and Millward, exposes bones. Once Morrison has unleashed his lash for the sixtieth time, and Churchill is cut down, it is time for Captain Bligh to unleash a verbal lashing, aimed at young Mr Hayward in particular.

'This affair,' begins Bligh in grave tones, 'was solely caused by the neglect of the officers who had the watch. However exempt you are at present from the like punishment, yet you are equally subject by the Articles of War . . .'[53]

Bligh's meaning is clear.

True justice would see the officers who let these men escape on their watch whipped every bit as hard as the men themselves.

As to the deserters, it is possible, just possible, they have learnt their lesson. Such at least is their plea, in a letter they soon send Captain Bligh, from one of the previously empty storerooms below, where they are kept in irons.

January 26th, 1789.

SIR,

We should think ourselves wholly inexcusable if we omitted taking this earliest opportunity of returning our thanks for your goodness in delivering us from a trial by Court-Martial, the fatal consequences of which are obvious; and although we cannot possibly lay any claim to so great a favour, yet we humbly beg you will be pleased to remit any further punishment, and we trust our future conduct will fully demonstrate our deep sense of your clemency, and our steadfast resolution to behave better hereafter.

We are Sir,
Your most obedient, most humble servants,

C. CHURCHILL,
WM. MUSPRATT,
JOHN MILLWARD.[54]

Allow them mercy, then, and give them no more lashes?

That is an easy one to decide.

Request denied. As a matter of fact, only a few days before their second flogging takes place, another seaman, Isaac Martin – a native of Philadelphia – is also given 'nineteen lashes for striking an Indian ... though great intercession was made by some of the chiefs'.[55]

Bligh is now intent on his course, every bit as much as he had been in trying to get around Cape Horn, come what may – if the men will not behave of their own accord, he will *beat* the discipline into them.

And all three deserters, plus Martin, can consider themselves lucky that, after their lashes, they are released from their irons. Not so Thomas Hayward, who remains below, with the irons around his ankles and wrists. Unable to flog him, Bligh has decided his only recourse is to *keep* him chained for weeks, perhaps *months*, he is not yet sure.

31 January 1789, *Bounty,* for the sake of the bread-fruit, not the men

Captain Bligh is insistent.

The ship, top to bottom, must be cleared of the cockroaches that infest it.

And for good reason.

'We were constantly obliged to be at great pains to keep the ship clear of vermin,' Bligh notes in his journal, 'on account of the plants.'[56]

But it is not easy. For these vermin have not survived for millennia without being cunning themselves. To escape the clod-hoppers of the sailors, as James Morrison records, 'the cables appeared alive with them, and . . . they flew to the rigging and mastheads and returned as before'.[57]

Ultimately, despite all their efforts and all the vinegar sloshed and swabbed about, the cockroaches appear 'as plentiful as ever in two or three days'.[58]

6 February 1789, Matavai Bay, things drift further

Captain Bligh, come quickly! After a blowy night, as the sun has come up, one of the sailors on shore has noticed something extraordinary, and highly dangerous.

See there, Captain?

> The cable by which the ship rode had been cut near the water's edge in such a manner that only one strand remained whole.[59]

Sabotage!

If the cable had broken in that wind, the *Bounty* would have certainly been swept on the rocks, and likely holed. It would have delayed their departure for months! Mercifully, no damage has been done, and the ship is quickly secured with extra ropes, but it is less certain whether the rapport between the visitors and the hosts will escape equally unscathed.

For, as Bligh notes, the event 'tended greatly to diminish the confidence and good understanding which had hitherto been constantly preserved between us and the natives'.[60]

In fact, when Tinah arrives only shortly after the discovery, Bligh, though convinced that his friend is 'perfectly innocent',[61] still speaks to him sharply, insisting that the perpetrator of this criminal act be found and brought forth for punishment.

Alas, when it emerges two days later that Tinah has had no luck in finding the guilty party, Bligh does not believe him – *Liars, liars all!* – and gives full fire to his ire, which is no small thing.

'King Tinah, I will destroy you if the ship touches the shore!' Bligh thunders.

'I revile you, your people and Tahiti!'[62] he goes on. At this remark the Captain can see the Tahitians buckle with inner distress, and many even begin to cry.

Yes, Bligh's stormy tongue can reduce a King and his subjects to a flood of tears. Taken aback by his own success, Bligh is quick to feel guilt at the pain he has caused, perhaps without cause.

Their tears soften Bligh, and his words soften too. He reveals that his anger was but a test, a trick if you will, to see if any secret was kept hidden around this crime. 'I can no longer keep you people under an idea that I mistrust you,' says the solemn Captain before invoking one King to another. 'I only make a particular request, as you value the King of England's friendship, so use your utmost endeavours to find out the offenders and send them to me!'

By humbug and hook, Bligh wants his crook. King Tinah replies, 'I most sacredly promise',[63] and the pair reconcile over a noontime meal on the *Bounty*.

Very quietly?

While it never occurs to Captain Bligh that the cable had been slashed by a non-Native, some among the ship's company are not so sure.

'It was the private opinion of men as well as officers,' James Morrison chronicles, 'that no native had been so bold as to attempt it . . .'[64]

Which leaves, of course, someone in the ship's company. Those with the best opportunity would be the men in the shore party, like Fletcher Christian or Peter Heywood, but that, too, is unthinkable.

Isn't it?

11 February 1789, Matavai Bay, the puppetry *Heiva*

Another evening, another *Heiva* for Captain Bligh.

This one, however, has a difference – and not only because it involves just four men and two maidens, going wild to a particularly driving drum-beat. Nor because the sole part of the maidens is to come very close to Bligh, before pulling a string, at which point they sway voluptuously before him 'as a present'[65] before walking away . . .

No, this one stands out because of what the men now do. For yes, Bligh has seen many things in his 34 years on this earth, but never has he beheld anything as 'uncommon and detestable'[66] as this.

For now the men, too, drop their clothing, with one man taking the lead as he possesses 'the power and capability of distorting the Penis and Testicles, making at the same time wanton and lascivious motions'.[67]

Using a tightly bound piece of twine at the base of the penis – so tight that it appears to almost cut through – the Native makes his penis erect. The second man wraps his testicles around the head of his penis, and then stretches the whole thing towards his belly. Stretching and stretching until it is nearly one foot long! (No, really.)

Bligh reels.

Could this possibly get any more horrifying, more sickening, more appalling for an English gentleman to have to witness?

Decidedly, yes.

For now, a third man actually yanks his scrotum downwards with such force that, like a startled turtle, the head of his penis retreats to the point that it disappears, even as his testicles swell outwards, trying to burst free of the tightened scrotum.

And so it goes as they dance around the ring for several minutes, making different shapes with their penises and testicles, until Bligh really can bear it no more and shouts for them to 'Desist!'[68]

He stands up and leaves to the sounds of the crowd roaring with laughter at his squeamishness.

These are a strange people, a fact further confirmed a few days later, when, at Iddeah's invitation, Bligh attends a wrestling match for women – which proves to be the same as the male version, except it's . . . more vicious. For a couple of hours, Bligh sits there, progressively more horrified as the usually peaceable and gentle women go at each other with no mercy, 'as savage as Wild Beasts'.[69]

The worst of it is seeing them actually pushing their thumbs into their opponent's eye socket and turning the eyeball out.

Disgusted, Bligh *orders* them to stop!

> When I spoke to Iddeah and other principal people about it, that it was a disgrace to them, they laughed at me and said it was '*Myty Taheite*' – it was customary in Tahiti.[70]

A strange people indeed, with women every bit as violent as they are voluptuous. More than ever, Bligh looks forward to departure, so they can begin the next leg of their journey to Jamaica, and then home to Betsy. Not that there aren't still many problems, and obstacles to overcome.

On 2 March, the Gunner, William Peckover, reports that from his post on the shore, he has had a water cask, part of an azimuth compass, and his bedding stolen!

As ever, Captain Bligh takes an extremely dim view of such thievery – fiercely rebuking the whole shore party for their disgraceful laxness in allowing it to happen – before bitterly complaining to Tinah, telling him that their friendship is now at an end, 'unless the thief is produced, and that must be done in the course of the day'.[71]

Tinah reacts instantaneously.

Steal, from *Bry*? It is a disgrace on them all!

(Quietly, Captain Bligh is a little less aggrieved than he appears, recording in his log on 18 March 1789, 'I now find we are subject to more petty thefts than hitherto . . . it amounts however to no other articles than such as are carelessly left about. I cannot therefore blame the natives for it, as I am perfectly certain that had the ship been lying in the River Thames, a hundred times more would have been stolen in the same time.'[72])

At least Captain Bligh is able to keep himself well-informed of what Tinah is up to, courtesy of Hetee-Hetee, who has become his personal spy, and he is gratified to learn that Tinah is personally leading the charge to find the thief.

Sure enough, only three hours after the theft is reported, Tinah arrives with his entourage, holding a downcast Native by the arm, while one of his men has the water cask and compass.

'There is the thief,' says Tinah, handing him over. 'Kill him. There is no bedding yet, but we will search.'[73]

'You have acted very properly,' Bligh says grandly, 'and have secured my friendship and goodwill . . .'[74]

And no doubt Captain Bligh would have gone on, and at some length. But before he can, Tinah, relieved at such kind words, steps forward to embrace him, even as the whole crowd of Natives cries out, '*Tyo myty!*'

'*Tyo myty!*' Good friend!

'*Tyo myty!*'[75] Good friend!

Indeed.

While Tinah departs to look after the bedding, the thief is sent on board for his punishment, which is every bit the 'severe flogging' that Bligh records in his log, with no fewer than '100 lashes severely given',[76] something that, in a European sailor, would risk death, but leaves this thief only a bloody mess, before he is placed in irons and put below, beside Thomas Hayward who, all these weeks on, is *still* there.

Despite that, however, at 4 o'clock the next morning, the prisoner is able to break the locks of his chains, make his way up the ladder through the hatch, cross the deck and jump into the sea.

> The Officer of the Fore Castle Watch heard the plunge into the water and went off in a boat in search of him but to no effect.[77]

Captain Bligh is, needless to say, appalled once more that such laxness could have occurred.

The young officers have truly let the sunny lassitude of Tahiti seep into their bones, to the point that they are near unrecognisable from the officers of the King who arrived here just five months ago.

> Verbal orders in the course of a month were so forgot that they
> would impudently assert no such thing or directions were given,
> and I have been at last under the necessity to trouble myself with

writing what by decent young officers would be complied with
as the common Rules of the Service.[78]

Of course, Bligh is not remotely surprised to find out who was the
young idiot responsible for the latest escape from the ship.

Mr. Stewart was the Mate of the Watch.[79]

On shore, Stewart is happy as he has never been in his life before,
keeping company with a stunning young maiden by the name of 'Peggy',
who is already proudly pregnant with their child.

Back on the *Bounty*, however, when he can bring himself to answer
the Captain's summons, he must face a Bligh burst of invective that
will seemingly never cease, accusing him of everything up to treason.

He cannot get back to Peggy quickly enough, and, at a lower level,
his experience is common among the ship's company: on the shore,
they are masters of their own domain, living like Kings themselves,
while back on the *Bounty* they are little more than cowering servants
in the Kingdom of Bligh.

Being cooped up with him for another five months, all the way
to Jamaica, then back to cold, dark England? Many of the crew can
barely bear to contemplate it, and George Stewart is a case in point.

For the men staying on the *Bounty*, the most important thing is
preparing for the voyage ahead – loading the ship to the gunnels with
the likes of yams, salted pork and chooks, all for the use of the cooks,
while of course also building up their own supply of coconuts, now
standing in proud pyramids below deck, with Captain Bligh's pyramid
standing tallest of all, so tall only above deck can accommodate it,
courtesy of the efforts of Mssrs Samuel and Smith.

When it comes to procuring provisions, few shine as brightly as
John Fryer, who, beyond being the Master of the *Bounty*, also proves
to be a true master of bargaining with the Tahitians. No man can get
as many goods for as little exchanged and he is particularly partial to
hogs, which he concentrates on securing – as insurance against whatever
outrageous privations Captain Bligh might seek to place upon them on
their way to Jamaica. Mr Fryer's view is that just as the Captain may
not touch Mr Purcell's chisel, as it is the Carpenter's private property,

so too will the Captain be prevented from hogging his hogs. Which is fine, in theory.

Alas, with no explanation and no hint of apology, Captain Bligh suddenly orders that all of Mr Fryer's hogs be slaughtered 'for the ship's use'.[80] Now, given that Mr Fryer has, by James Morrison's count, 'more than forty [hogs] on board of his own',[81] this is no small thing, prompting Mr Fryer to rush to speak to the Captain, so this misunderstanding can be cleared up.

For you must understand, Captain Bligh, that those hogs are my property. I have traded for them, and nurtured them since. They are *mine*.

Yours, Mr Fryer? *Yours?*

Let Captain Bligh give you a little instruction as to what livestock belongs to whom. For he has done some quick calculations, and worked it out.

Let's see.

Dot three, carry four, subtract eight . . .

Yes, he has the answer.

'*Everything* is mine as soon as it is on board,' Bligh tells the stunned Master. 'I will take nine tenths of any man's property, and let me see who dares say anything to the contrary.'[82]

Swallowing his reply, Mr Fryer, like all the other men, does not dare to question his Captain's ruling.

Alas, the three dozen hogs of Mr Fryer prove to be just the beginning of the Captain's plunder: 'Those of the seaman were seized without ceremony, and it became a favour to get a pound extra of his own hog.'[83]

As James Morrison chronicles, Captain Bligh's rapaciousness was not restricted merely to hogs.

'Mr. Bligh seized on all that came to the ship, big and small, dead or alive, taking them as his property and serving them as the ship's allowance at one pound per man per day.'[84]

The Tahitians, of course, soon become aware that the market for their hogs has fallen and 'became very shy of bringing a hog in sight of Lieutenant Bligh either on board or on shore'.[85]

And so they are snuck on board, while he is on shore.

Quickly understanding the ruse, Bligh instructs the Mate of every watch, when he is absent, to note 'the number of hogs ... with the weight of each, that come into the ship'.

Hmmm.

Ever ingenious, the Tahitians change tack to starboard, as Morrison chronicles:

> To remedy this the natives took another method, which was cutting the pigs up, wrapping them in leaves, and covering the meat with bread-fruit in baskets, and sometimes with peeled coconuts. By this means, as the bread was never seized, they were a match for all his industry, and he never suspected their artifice.[86]

The end result is that the alliance between the *Bounty* crew and the common Tahitians is deepened, and placed at the service of thwarting the desires of Captain *Bry*.

March 1789, Tahiti, making Hayward while the sun shines

After no less than seven weeks in chains, Thomas Hayward is released. Like a cowering albino dog – all white and weak, blinking in the sun, scarcely daring to believe his long agony is over – Hayward is quickly put to work on board with all the rest, loading, loading, loading. The time is nearly nigh!

•

The breeze off the bay blows fresh in the blaze of the morning sun.

Beneath Captain Bligh's steely gaze, and according to specific directions from the botanist David Nelson, the process of moving the bread-fruit plants to the ship begins. It is 29 March 1789.

Shuffling single file down to the water, the shirtless shore party – looking like white Natives, which is very close to what they have become, bar their tattered shorts – make their way to the beach, with a pot perched on each of their bronzed shoulders, careful not to let a single splash of salt water get near them. Gently now, they pass the precious pots to the men waiting in the Launch, the Cutter and even the Jolly Boat. Once the living cargo is secure in the bottom of the boats, the crews pull slow and steady on the oars – there can be no splashing – as they glide serenely over the sun-streaked water out to the *Bounty*, where more men lower nets over the gunnels and haul the plants up to the deck, as Bligh watches ever closer.

Easy now, God damn you!

With equal care, the pots are taken to the Grand Cabin cum floating greenhouse, where a bustling David Nelson and his assistant William Brown fuss about, directing the men to place the pots – careful now, please! – in the appropriate spots, according to their size.

It is with satisfaction that Bligh records:

> They were in excellent order: the roots had appeared through the bottom of the pots and would have shot into the ground if care had not been taken to prevent it.[87]

It takes three days, but finally it is done, and by the evening of 31 March, Bligh can write in his Log with some satisfaction, 'Total plants on board 774 pots, 39 tubs, and 24 boxes.'[88]

First week of April 1789, Tahiti, a high-tail by sail

At last, the great day approaches.

The *Bounty* is near fully victualled. The plants are all loaded and secured, the wood is stored, the water barrels all filled to the brim – no less than 47 tons of water, most of which will be dedicated to Bligh's beloved bread-fruit. There are 25 hogs in the pen, and 17 goats. Most importantly, the sea is calm, and all they need is an easterly wind.

Bligh rejoices that they are finally ready to leave. And yet, he is one of a tiny minority of the ship's company who feels that way. For most of the officers and sailors, the last five months has been time spent in paradise, the most glorious time of their lives, and many of them are in love with particular women – some of whom are pregnant with their babies – who they must now leave behind. Some silently beg for the favourable winds to, pray, stay away.

Alas, late on the fourth day of April, an east by north breeze springs up and Bligh resolves to leave first thing the following morning.

On the *Bounty*, all is furious activity.

'The ship,' Bligh chronicles, 'was crowded the whole day with the natives, and we were loaded with coconuts, plantains, bread-fruit, hogs, and goats. In the evening there was no dancing or mirth on the beach such as we had been accustomed to, but all was silent.'[89]

Or, nearly silent.

For in many huts by the shore, many tearful farewells are taking place, and likely none more tearful than the one between Fletcher Christian and Isabella.

Finally, however, the two must untangle their limbs, and Christian, with the others, climbs in the Cutter just as it pulls away from the beach. His eyes glistening, he gazes back on his sweet, beautiful Isabella, her arms outstretched towards him, almost as if she could reach out and bring him back to the shore. Around her, other swaying women weep and wail – a distinctively Tahitian lament – as if in mourning.

On the ship, King Tinah and Queen Iddeah are begging Captain Bligh to stay just one day longer, but he will not hear of it.

They will dine together one more time, and then they must go.

After dinner, Captain Bligh, with great ceremony, gives the Royal couple – who are of course the last of the Tahitians to leave – the thing they have most yearned for: weapons. He hands them 'two muskets, a pair of pistols, and a good stock of ammunition'.[90]

Bry already has in his care two precious *parais*, mourning-dresses – made from the finest *tapa* cloth, gifts to King George from Tinah and Iddeah, with the express desire that 'the King of England might forever remain his friend and not forget him'. And *Bry* has a list, in turn, of the things that King Tinah is hoping King George might send him, including 'a ship full of British ladies'.[91]

Grateful for *Bry*'s kindness in both taking his gift of bread-fruit plants to King George and also his list of required gifts, Tinah offers many fine words, casts many blessings of the Gods upon the great Captain, utters many protestations that their visitors will never be forgotten ... until finally the time comes. As Morrison records, 'Their parting with the lieutenant [Bligh] and officers was truly a tender scene ...'[92]

And now they are gone, being paddled away in their Royal canoe, before ... coming back once more!

For no sooner have Tinah and Iddeah landed back on shore, than they decide to give Captain Bligh one last gift: more coconuts.

Yes, the coconuts are welcome – you can never have too many of them, and this last gift is added atop Bligh's personal coconut pile on the top deck between the guns – but, finally, ultimately, the Royal couple are not.

Gently, delicately, Bligh tells them that they *must* leave, and, this time, stay away.

They understand.

Truly, they do.

Leaving Bligh for the last time, climbing down the rope ladder into their canoe, both Tinah and Iddeah weep as they say to Captain *Bry*, their dearest friend, '*Yourah no t' Eatua tee eveerah*.' May the Eatua protect you, for ever and ever.[93]

At first light the next morning, the order rings out. *Anchors aweigh!*

Out of the shelter of the bay, the sails fill, and the *Bounty* gathers way. The crew wave goodbye to the hundreds of flower-bedecked and canoe-borne well-wishers who bob up and down on their considerable wake.

Yes, of course Tinah has requested that the *Bounty* blast its cannon in farewell, but Bligh has declined 'for fear of disturbing the plants'.[94] Instead, they give Tinah and Iddeah three cheers.

And so they say farewell to Tahiti. 'For twenty-three weeks,' Bligh records, 'we had been treated with the utmost affection and regard, and which seemed to increase in proportion to our stay.'[95]

In a rare moment of generosity of spirit, Captain Bligh gives orders that all of the ship's company be given a double serving of rum. James Morrison notes the oddly happy scene with amused interest:

> Everybody seemed in high spirits and began already to talk of home, affixing the length of the passage and counting up their wages. One would readily have imagined that we had just left Jamaica instead of Tahiti, so far onward did their flattering fancies waft them.[96]

Yes, many of the older men, particularly those with families – like Captain Bligh, Mr Fryer, David Nelson and William Elphinstone – are at least uplifted by the thought that they are now one step closer to getting back to their loved ones in Britain. But for many of the younger men, and none more than Fletcher Christian, their loved ones are those now in the bobbing canoes, wanly watching them disappear – and few can be more bereft than Isabella, who gazes sadly after her disappearing man, the love of her life, her *Titriano*.

Fletcher looks back in turn, to the island paradise where he has spent the most deliriously contented days of his life, thanks to the woman he will in all likelihood . . . never see again! From now, he is *Titriano* only in her heart. Here, on the *Bounty*, he is Acting Lieutenant Christian, the watch awaits and Captain Bligh is watching him closely, his fury festering, ready to find fault and ever eager for Fletcher's failure.

The *Bounty* sails out of Isabella's sight, across the seas, through the day and onward into the night. A trailing whale might note a sole dull gleam coming from high on the stern of the ship. It is Captain Bligh, doing what he loves most – consulting his charts, noting his ship's position against its destination, the obstacles and ports between the two, and reviewing the course he has charted. From Tahiti, they must proceed, broadly west, towards the northern end of New Holland, being very careful to find a way through the formidable barrier of reefs that defends that coastline. Once through, they will push north along the coast to the tip of New Holland, and then – with the prevailing trade winds right behind them – turn west once more, at least after navigating the very narrow, very shallow, Endeavour Strait – first breached by Captain Cook in 1770, going east to west – which will be supremely difficult, but quite doable for a man such as William Bligh. Thereafter they will head towards the Dutch East Indies, before sailing down to the Cape of Good Hope, then into the Atlantic, and up to Jamaica. And then home. Home to England, to his wife and four gorgeous bairns! The whale winks, the lantern fades.

CHAPTER SIX

THE MOOD TURNS MUTINOUS

He that only rules by terror
  Doeth grievous wrong.
Deep as hell I count his error.
  Let him hear my song.

Brave the Captain was; the seamen
  Made a gallant crew,
Gallant sons of English freemen,
  Sailors bold and true,

But they hated his oppression;
  Stern he was and rash,
So for every light transgression
  Doom'd them to the lash.

Day by day more harsh and cruel
  Seem'd the Captain's mood.
Secret wrath like smother'd fuel
  Burnt in each man's blood[1]

Lord Tennyson, 'The Captain', 1865

It was in those violent Tornadoes of temper when he lost himself,
yet, when all, in his opinion, went right, could a man be more
placid and interesting . . . ? Once or twice indeed I felt the
unbridled licence of his power of speech, yet never without soon
receiving something like an emollient plaster to heal the wound.[2]

George Tobin, Royal Navy officer and artist, who also sailed with Bligh

9 April 1789, 120 miles north-west of Tahiti, a whirl of fury

'Ship's companyyyy . . . attennn-shunn!' bawls Master-at-Arms, Charley Churchill to the assembled crew. 'On command you will fix bayonets . . . fix bayonets! On command you will charge bayonets . . . charge bayonets! Orderrrr arms!'[3]

On the foredeck of the *Bounty*, the men are in 'Exercise' – the daily exercise of naval musket drill – when they are interrupted by a small package of fury, whirling towards them, a furious force of nature, terrifying all. Just for once, it is *not* Captain Bligh.

No, this is a water-spout, a kind of mini-tornado that the men of the *Bounty* spot to the east – roughly in the direction they have come from – looming ever more threateningly against a backdrop of angry black clouds.

'As nearly as I could judge,' Bligh would recount, 'it was about two feet diameter at the upper part, and about eight inches at the lower . . . The column, which was higher than our mastheads, and the water below was not otherwise visible than by the sea being disturbed in a circular space of about six yards in diameter, the centre of which, from the whirling of the water round it, formed a hollow; and from the outer part of the circle the water was thrown up with much force in a spiral direction, and could be traced to the height of fifteen or twenty feet.'[4]

And this whirling dervish of weather is coming right for them, a clear and present threat to the ship's masts and maybe more!

'Haul off,' Bligh barks. The helmsman yanks down hard on the wooden wheel and the ship hauls off their westward course to the south, pulling away from the danger.

'Take in all sail bar the foresail,'[5] Bligh roars again and some of the crew start shinnying up the rigging like crazed monkeys – and no-one more than the lovable Monkey himself, springing up in one bound, leaping from spar to spar – even as others haul on the ropes below. In less than ten minutes it is done. And still the water-spout keeps coming, almost as if it is hunting them.

The men watch anxiously as the menacing spout passes just ten yards clear of the *Bounty*'s stern, leaving the ship unscathed.

They are safe from the whirl of fury and the cry goes up, 'Make more sail!'

Alas, the other whirl of fury – Bligh – simply won't let up. Now that they are back at sea, Bligh has not turned a new leaf, calm and content to be on the voyage once more. No. He remains the terrifying tyrant of old – only worse. Thus, even as the ship's company is trying to adjust from the free and easy life at Tahiti, back to the rigid discipline and endless tedium of crossing the ocean, they also must deal with a hissing, shouting, forever furious Captain who finds fault with everybody and everything.

And, there is no doubt about it. One member of the ship seems to attract his ire, almost more than all the others combined.

'Whatever fault was found,' one crew-member would recount, 'Mr. Christian was sure to bear the brunt of the Captain's anger.'[6]

For something indeed has changed in the formerly close relationship of Bligh and the man who was nothing less than his protégé and favourite, Acting Lieutenant Fletcher Christian.

Perhaps Bligh had been disappointed at just how seduced Christian had been by Tahiti in general and Isabella in particular, or perhaps he feels that Christian needs a big injection of discipline, so he can both display it himself and be able to demand it of others – as befitting the rank of Acting Lieutenant, to which exalted level Bligh has *personally promoted him*. Whatever it is, the men are quite stunned at how often, and how publicly, Bligh upbraids the popular officer, frequently including the fact that Christian still owes him *money*. (And, truly, Christian is shocked himself, and humiliated – gritting his teeth, and hoping that it will pass, and soon. For he knows that, one way or another, he cannot bear it for long.)

The ship sails on, but there is a growing uneasiness among her crew, a sense that all is not right, that trouble is festering.

Ah, if only they could know, and . . .

And what now?

Coming across an uncharted island on 12 April, the *Bounty* men are on their guard as several canoes, loaded with Natives, approach. Fortunately, the Natives are friendly, and Bligh even allows some of them to board. Identifying one of them as their Chief, Bligh rubs noses with him, and is rewarded by the Chief removing the 'large mother of pearl shell, which hung with plaited hair round his neck'[7] and fastening it round the Captain's neck.

The name of this island, Captain Bligh is told, is 'Wytootacke . . .'[8] As a gesture of reciprocal good will, Captain Bligh orders 'a young boar and sow to be put into their canoe with some yams and tarro, as we could afford to part with some of these articles'.[9]

Yes, the *Bounty* is a ship of plenty and Bligh can indulge this rare burst of generosity in parting with such gifts.

Such generosity of spirit, however, continues to be elusive for him when it comes to dealing with Fletcher Christian, as their relationship disintegrates by the day.

Meanwhile, Christian is not the only one in trouble, with Bligh recording in his Log on 12 April, 'Punished John Sumner with 12 lashes for neglect of duty,'[10] but his tirades against Christian are just so *constant*, so unending!

One who notes this disintegration is Fryer, who on 21 April 1789, overhears Christian's shaking voice answer back: 'Sir, your abuse is so bad I cannot do my duty with any pleasure. I have been in hell for weeks with you.'[11]

Bligh snaps back, and Fryer hears 'several other disagreeable words',[12] exchanged.

23 April 1789, Latitude 20°23' South, Longitude 174°80' West, taking arms to a sea of troubles

Land ho!

The island of Annamooka, of the 'Friendly' or Tonga islands, appears off the larboard quarter. Bligh knows this island and its Chiefs well, having visited with Captain Cook in 1777. It is the perfect place to replenish their supplies of wood and fresh water.

Ideally, they will be able to drop anchor in Annamooka Harbour, and barter their way over a few days to full supply with these people who have received many visits from European ships over the years. And here is a Chief now, a new one since Bligh was last here, Chief Latoomy-lange, being paddled out to the ship on his fine canoe, soon joined by two older Chiefs well known to Bligh, Chief Noocabo and Chief Kunocappo. Just as at Tahiti, the *Bounty* is quickly *the* place to be, with the Natives flocking to the ship in enormous numbers and bartering anything and everything, from hogs to fowl, from deliciously sweet yams to lovely bunches of coconuts.

A particularity of this island is their sailing canoes, 'formed of two joined together by strong cross-pieces . . . really a wonderful piece of art and contrivance, sailed with great swiftness and managed with much cleverness'. The platform between the two canoes can carry enormous amounts of goods and people, with Bligh noting, 'I have counted 90 passengers on board some of those that have already come to see us.'[13]

And what people they are!

'The men are tattooed from the knee to the waist,' James Morrison chronicles, while, far more importantly, 'the women are handsome but know how to set a price on their favours'.[14]

And yet, while the principal interest of the men in visiting such islands remains unchanged, so too is Bligh's focus exactly the same – breadfruit. Since leaving Tahiti, one of his precious cargo has died and two or three plants are looking sickly. His hope is that Annamooka might have some replacement seedlings that Mr Nelson – another rare being on the ship, for having a focus other than women – might quickly claim.

And oh, what a pleasure it is for Bligh and Nelson to venture ashore once more, just as they had in 1777, to visit the places and houses they had visited with Cook, to remark how little had changed in this timeless land, to meet up with familiar faces, all of which are smiling at them, even as Bligh distributes some 'beads and trinkets to the women and children', and arranges with his oldest ally on the island, a man by the name of Tepa, to send a wood and watering party on shore the next day. At the break of day, Bligh gives his final orders to the two parties – an 11-man watering party under the command of Christian, and a four-man wooding party under Elphinstone.

Christian's watering party may take arms with them, but the arms are 'to be kept in the Boat'.[15] Bligh is firm: 'You will be much safer on shore without them'.[16] As to the wooding party, no arms at all.

'You are to keep yourselves,' he orders, 'unconnected with the Natives.'[17]

Get your wood, and come straight back to the ship.

Yes, Captain Bligh.

Taking the Launch, which can seat his 11-man party, but only just, Christian heads off, closely followed by Elphinstone and his three companions in the Jolly Boat. It shouldn't take long . . .

Hours later, the sailors on the *Bounty* note the steady stomp of Bligh's black boots pacing across the deck, back and forth.

Where *can* Christian be?

He calls to Mr Fryer to ready the Cutter and go ashore: 'Hurry Mr Christian off with the Launch.'[18]

Fryer is soon on his way with half-a-dozen men pulling on oars, guiding the Cutter to where Christian has left the Launch on the shoreline guarded by two of his party, who tell Fryer that Christian and the men can be found over yonder hill, the one covered with plantain trees, about a quarter mile away.

Meanwhile, the arrival of the Cutter has drawn quite a crowd of 'very friendly' Natives, among whom are 'a good looking young man and woman',[19] who appear to be Chiefs.

Taking Mr Fryer by each arm, they kindly offer to show him the way.

Certainly.

He will accompany them, right after snapping off an order for the crew to drag the Cutter just a little up the beach, and to keep the crowding Natives at a safe distance.

'Lay off your oars until I come back,'[20] he instructs.

Only a short time after starting out from the beach in the company of his two helpful, handsome guides, Fryer runs into Matt Quintal who is 'rolling a cask of water down to the boat with a number of natives about him'.[21]

Fryer moves on but not for long as he hears Quintal scream: 'MR FRYER! THERE'S A MAN GOING TO KNOCK YOU DOWN WITH HIS CLUB!'[22]

Fryer whirls around to see the handsome man 'brandishing his club,'[23] about to strike the Master's head, but suddenly stopping, frozen.

The moment, and the movement, hang suspended in time . . . until the man drops his threatening arm, turns on his heel and runs off. To get more men? A surer weapon? What?

Fryer is badly shaken.

'I was not armed,' he would later note, 'even with a stick.'[24]

His best chance of safety, of course, lies with Christian and his men, and he and Quintal race to find them.

Reaching Christian and his party, they see that these men too are having problems, as 'there was a number of Natives about . . . some heaving stones frequently and one chief with a very long spear frequently pointed at Mr Christian'.[25]

At least Christian is personally armed 'with a musket and bayonet',[26] but, despite the danger, he is strictly adhering to the Captain's orders and is not using, or even threatening to use, the weapons on the aggressors.

Under the circumstances, the men are going as fast as they can – eager to fill their water barrels and get away from this hostile environment – and it is hardly necessary to tell them to make haste, but the shaken Fryer cannot help himself.

'Mr Christian, get the casks down to the boat empty or full,'[27] he orders. Fryer quickly gives some of the Natives who are not throwing stones or brandishing spears, 'several small nails'[28] as a bribe. It works. In short order, the watering party is being aided by some of the Natives to roll the barrels down to where the Cutter and Launch await.

Alas, to Fryer's great distress, and against his previous orders, he finds the sailors he has left behind frolicking with the friendly Natives, most particularly the young women. The sailors have landed the Cutter and the small, hooked anchor, known as the grapnel, is planted firmly in the sand of the beach. Or at least it was – for they have no sooner arrived than in the general hubbub one of the Natives manages to cut the rope and whisk the grapnel away. Furious, Mr Fryer questions the Chiefs among the crowd, to be told only that the anchor was 'taken by the people of another island'.[29]

This, at least, is their claim.

It leaves Christian and Fryer brooding darkly as they are rowed back to the *Bounty*, each stroke bringing them closer to what will surely be a brutal burst of Bligh bellicosity that will likely singe their eyebrows. And sure enough . . .

'I will have [the Grapnel] again,' Bligh hisses on receipt of Fryer's quavering news, 'or I will detain some of the chiefs on board until it is brought back.'[30]

Fryer reels. This is precisely the manoeuvre that caused the death of Captain Cook.

'I think,' the Master says carefully, 'it is not worth our while [to] trouble these poor fellows about it that are on board, as they could not know anything about it! We have several more [Grapnels] onboard and plenty of Iron to make one if we should want, therefore our loss is not very great.'[31]

Captain Bligh pounces.

'Not very great, sir? *By God!* Sir, if it is not great to *you*, it is great to *me*!'[32]

'I am very sorry that we have lost the Grapnel, but being sorry I think is of no use,'[33] replies Fryer tartly, his usually stoical face flashing anger.

Bligh's glare could peel paint, but Fryer is his own man, has said his piece, just as he intended to do – and so shuffles off, leaving Christian to give his report.

Well, Mr Christian? Hesitantly, the Acting Lieutenant tells his Captain of the difficulties in gathering water when Natives are throwing stones and brandishing spears at you, and you –

'You damned cowardly rascal!' Bligh roars. 'Are you afraid of a set of naked savages while you have arms?'[34]

Christian is stunned. He is being called a *'coward'*? A *'rascal'*?

Scarcely bringing himself to believe it, he tries to remain calm and explain.

'The arms,' he explains carefully, 'are no use while your orders prevent them being used.'[35]

Insolence! Get out of my sight!

As an old hand, Christian has seen Bligh this angry many times before. But never has Christian seen him so angry at Christian himself. In fact, Bligh is so incandescent with rage that, for the first time, Christian even wonders if he is in physical danger from Bligh?

For now, Christian is dismissed, and stumbles off with a faraway look in his eyes – still trying to comprehend his Captain's diatribe – leaving Bligh to fume, as only he can, on what course of action to take now. Why is he cursed to be so surrounded by such incompetent fools, liars, idlers and fops?

As ever, he decides, it will be up to him to do all the work himself, just as he had done with catching those wretched deserters. And already he has an idea. First of all, he goes in search of the Master, who is in the process of hoisting up the boats when the Captain finds him.

'Mr Fryer,' he says casually, 'anybody that wants to buy curiosities has leave.'[36]

Fryer is more than a little surprised. After his previous foul mood, Bligh now seems almost . . . cheery? Bligh now turns to the *Bounty*'s old Gunner, William Peckover, and affirms: 'Purchase anything. Don't mind what you give for it.'[37]

Even more curious! Peckover agrees to trade generously with the Natives on board, but is none the wiser as to why the Captain is being so generous.

'Mr Fryer, we'll heave the anchor up and go away,'[38] orders Bligh. Perhaps that is the explanation? Perhaps it is simply that, as they are about to get underway, Bligh is keen for the men to replenish their personal stocks to the maximum, whatever might amuse them or feed them, for the long journey to Jamaica.

Fryer is helping to stow the anchor when he hears a very strange and troubling order from Bligh in the distance.

'Hand the Arms up!'[39]

What on earth can be the use of muskets right now?

Worried, Fryer runs aft to investigate.

And here is Bligh in familiar form: furious.

'Why don't you come to assist me, sir?' asks the Captain.

'I did not know you wanted any assistance, Captain,' replies Fryer. 'I only heard you call for the arms, [which] led me to think that something was the matter.'[40]

But now Fryer learns, to his great chagrin, just what the matter is.

'Get the Arms up, Sir,' barks Bligh. '*I'll keep those fellows and see if I can't get the Grapnel!*'[41]

Finally, Fryer understands. Bligh wanted the Natives to stay on board, trading freely, just so he could trap them there, and exchange their liberation for the grapnel. Which poses the obvious question.

Is he stark, staring *mad*?

Yes, it had been a ploy favoured by Captain Cook, but not for trifles such as a grapnel. The great mariner had only used such force when he needed to find deserters, or recover a stolen boat.

This is the worst kind of madness – the unstoppable kind, with a mad momentum all its own. Bligh is blinkered by his own rage as the weapons are distributed among the crew. Fryer is far from the only man dismayed.

'The ship's company was armed and drawn up,' the staggered Morrison records, 'and the chiefs made prisoners. The canoes [of the Natives] were ordered to cast off and keep astern. At this, the chiefs seemed much displeased.'[42]

Now that his intentions are clear and he has the Chiefs secure, Bligh allows one of them to return to the shore, to tell all the Natives: they must find and return the grapnel, or they will never see their Chiefs again. The imprisoned Chiefs await their fate, their number including one young noble by the name of Nagatee, whose eyes glitter at the outrage so suddenly visited upon them. Those eyes meet Bligh's, who does not blink in return.

Just an hour later, the Chief whom Bligh freed reappears, though he refuses to come back on the ship, instead choosing to communicate through words and signs from a safe distance. It is exactly as Fryer had reported; it is Natives from another island who had stolen the grapnel, and it is now long gone.

Very well, then.

The Chief can maintain that, and Fryer can believe him.

But Bligh does not, telling Mr Fryer to, 'Make sail.'[43]

The Master shouts his order. The crew swing into action. The *Bounty* begins to drift.

Yes, Bligh wants the Natives in surrounding canoes to understand the fate of those who steal grapnel anchors from him – they have their Chiefs taken away, never to be seen again. And yet the wails and cries of those Natives are still not enough for Bligh. The humiliation of the detained people and their Chiefs is not complete. He has a more direct and personal punishment for them.

'They were,' Morrison recounts, 'ordered down to the mess room, where Mr. Bligh followed them and set them to peel coconuts for his dinner.'[44]

Once they are set to work, Nagatee's eyes still glittering, Bligh returns to the deck, to deal with his own crew, who clearly think he is going too far.

'You are a parcel of lubberly Rascals!'[45] he bellows. They are the fools, the incompetents, the ingrates, who have allowed this to happen through their own laxness.

'I would be one of five,' he roars, 'who would, with good sticks, disarm all of you.'[46]

Christian and Fryer exchange looks. The Captain is dangerously close to being out of control, as witness his reaction when he notes that Billy McCoy is not looking at him as he speaks.

Instantly drawing his pistol, Bligh aims it at Billy's head and roars, 'McCoy, I will shoot you for not paying attention!'[47]

Now McCoy is paying attention, and close attention at that. Christian watches the whole thing, shaken to his core.

Bligh storms down to his cabin as the *Bounty*'s slow mock 'departure' continues, surrounded by canoes, 'full of People making sad lamentations for their Chiefs',[48] convinced they are about to lose them forever.

Wailing bitterly and with an unearthly intensity, the women slash their own faces and shoulders with knives, the blood soon dribbling into the azure waters around them. The men bash their paddles against their own heads, until they, too, add to the spurting blood.

And that is just the Natives who are free! When Morrison goes below deck he is shocked to see, 'the oldest of the chiefs . . . struck himself several violent blows on the face and cut himself on the cheek bone with his fists'.[49] None of this is apparent to Bligh, who remains in his cabin, fuming, but still confident that his actions will soon see the grapnel returned, for it is the only thing that counts.

As the fiery sun sets, so too does Bligh's temper – he's no longer in an incandescent rage but able to judge things a little more coolly. Given that, despite the Natives' extreme distress, the grapnel has not been returned, it really might be as they have maintained, that it has been taken by other Natives, and is now beyond their powers to retrieve.

Mr Fryer!

Yes, Captain Bligh?

You may let the Chiefs go, and to make the peace, I shall give them some baubles to remember me by.

In his journal, Bligh cheerfully records his mercy and the success of his lesson:

> As this distress was more than the grapnel was worth, and I had no reason to imagine that they were privy to or in any manner concerned in the theft, I could not think of detaining them longer and called their canoes alongside. I then told them they were at liberty to go, and made each of them a present of a hatchet, a saw, with some knives, gimblets, and nails. This unexpected present and the sudden change in their situation affected them not less with joy than they had before been with apprehension. They were unbounded in their acknowledgments and I have little doubt but that we parted better friends than if the affair had never happened.[50]

Well, Bligh may have little doubt, but others on the *Bounty* see it differently, with Morrison caustically noting that the Chiefs 'only smothered their resentment . . . seeing they could not revenge the insult'.[51]

At least, not for the moment.

For now, Bligh orders the *Bounty* northward, away from Annamooka, and retires for the night, recording in his journal before falling to sleep:

> As to the officers I have no resource, or do I ever feel myself safe in the few instances I trust to them.[52]

Into the fine night the *Bounty* sails on, the sea gurgles, the masts creak, the sails flap, the dripstones drip – *drip, drip, drip . . . drop* – and the officer in charge of the watch, Fletcher Christian, stares grimly and with faraway eyes, into the darkness, pondering Bligh's wanton cruelty and insulting words.

27 April 1789, 80 miles south-east of Tofoa, a lovely bunch of coconuts

On this sparkling morning, Christian is completing his brooding night watch when Bligh arrives on deck and immediately notices something amiss.

His pile of coconuts, which had been in a large heap between the guns, seems different.

'Mr Fryer,' barks Bligh. 'Don't you think those coconuts are shrunk since last night?'[53]

'Sir, they are not as high as they were last night,'[54] answers Fryer. 'But the people might have put them down in walking over them in the night.'[55]

'No, Mr Fryer, they have been taken away,' declares the Captain. 'And I will find out who has taken them!'[56]

Churchill, the one-time deserter and Master-at-Arms – the nearest thing on the ship to a Marine, in charge of the ship's security and responsible for enforcing the law as laid down by the Captain – is summoned with a Bligh bellow that makes the ship quaver and its fellows shudder. And so it starts again.

Yes, Captain?

'Master at Arms, I order you to see every nut that is below, on deck.'[57]

Churchill is confused, and says so. Surely Mr Bligh does not mean *all the coconuts*? And from *everybody*?

'Every body, every body, EVERY BODY!'[58] Bligh roars his answer again and again, like one demented, so there can be no doubt. And so Churchill relays the order to all the men . . . and all the officers. *All* men are to come up on deck right now, bringing with them *all* their coconuts. Every single one. Right now.

In double-quick time, thus, every man on the *Bounty* is standing on the swaying deck, before his own pile of coconuts.

Like a General inspecting a parade by a coconut army, Bligh wanders up and down each pile, searching for his missing nuts. Stopping before a notably large pile, he looks around, accusingly.

'Whose are these?' he asks.

'Mine, Captain,' answers Midshipman Ned Young with toothless casualness.

'How many nuts did you buy?'

Young mumbles a large number.

'So many, sir! And how many did you eat?'[59] spits Bligh to Young, a scoundrel, he is sure, whom he has always detested.

'I do not know, sir,' Young replies, before pointing to the coconuts at his feet. 'But there is the remainder, which I have not counted.'[60]

Both Christian and Fryer gaze on, scarcely believing the sheer unhinged absurdity of what they are seeing.

One by one, Bligh moves down the line of seamen, asking each the same question.

How many coconuts have you brought from the island of Tahiti?

How many have you eaten?

Alec Smith? Matt Quintal? Billy Brown?

Each slippery reply is noted down by Bligh's clerk, John Samuel, and finally it is done, as the last slippery sailor gives his last slippery answer.

Or is it not over, after all?

For now, without pause, and still in the presence of the common sailors, Bligh starts to question the *officers*, starting with – yes, of course, it has to be – his second-in-command, Fletcher Christian.

For you, Mr Christian, were the Officer of the Watch last night and if you had attended your duties faithfully you surely should have spotted and apprehended any thief.

Unless of course . . . that very officer *is* the thief.

. . .

. . .

Well, Mr Christian, did you take the coconuts?

. . .

. . .

. . .

Time hangs suspended once more. Can Bligh really have asked him, an officer and a gentleman, and a supposed friend, such a question?

Christian expostulates: 'I hope you do not think me so mean as to be guilty of stealing yours?'[61]

'Yes, you damned hound,' yells Bligh, 'I do. You must have stolen half of them, or you could give a better account of them!'[62]

His words reverberate, rankle and rattle against 1000 years of breeding which has placed the likes of the Christian family so much higher in the social strata than the Bligh family.

Still Captain Bligh goes on, pronouncing from on high the crew's punishment:

'I allow you a pound and a half of Yams,' Bligh hisses. 'But if I do not find out who took the nuts, I will put you on three-quarters of a pound of Yams.'[63]

And, even now, Bligh is not done with his threats.

'I take care of you now for my own good,'[64] he yells at his sullen crew. 'But when I get you through the [Endeavour] Straits you may all go to Hell!'[65]

Now, just in case there is any confusion about how the Captain feels about them, he furthers elucidates his position.

'And if you do not look out sharp I will kill one half of you.'[66]

Oh, Heavenly Father above!

Turning to, and on, his younger officers – the likes of John Hallett, Thomas Hayward and Peter Heywood – Bligh makes sure they know what awaits them, in the unlikely event they survive long enough to get to where they are going now, to drop off their cargo.

'I will leave *you* in Jamaica! You shall not go home with me!'[67]

Christian can bear it no more. Such madness must stop before even more damage is done. So if Bligh really must have a thief, then Fletcher will give him one. As Officer of the Watch, ultimate responsibility must rest with him anyway, so why not go one step further, to spare the men? Taking two bow-legged steps forward, he utters the one lie that might spare all, bar him.

The responsibility is mine, Captain Bligh. I took the coconut.

What? Only one, sir?

Bligh does not believe it.

'Damn your blood,' Bligh roars, perilously close to being completely out of control, 'you have stolen my *coconuts*!'[68]

With a calm that he does not feel – for inside, everything is being pulled apart, including his last shreds of respect for Bligh – Christian replies evenly.

'I was dry, I thought it of no consequence, I took one only, and I am sure no one touched another.'[69]

. . .

All eyes turn to Bligh.

. . .

Will Christian's self-sacrifice be enough to appease the roaring and fiery demon?

'You lie, you scoundrel!' Bligh bellows. 'You have stolen one half!'[70]

The accusation is every bit as absurd as Christian's 'confession', and seemingly everyone on the ship, bar Bligh, can see it – with enormous honour, and courage, Christian is simply trying to protect his men. But in his fury, Bligh sees no honour, only evil. And this last accusation has begun to break down Christian's own control, as he struggles to speak.

'Why do you treat me thus, Captain Bligh?'[71] Fletcher says, in a voice shaking with surging emotion.

In response, Bligh clenches his right fist, and with contempt pure, shakes it in Fletcher's face.

'NO REPLY!'[72] he roars. For he is the Captain of the *Bounty*, and he will not engage in conversation with a lowly 'thief'.[73]

'I desire the people to look after the officers and the officers look after the people,' Bligh spits at his entire crew, 'for never were such a set of damned thieving rascals under any man's command in the world before!'[74]

And that's not all.

'God damn you,' Bligh roars at his officers in particular, 'you scoundrels, you are all thieves alike and combine with the men to rob me. I suppose you will steal my yams next, but I'll sweat you for it, you rascals.'[75]

Bligh's words continue to tumble forth, a volcano of fury now erupting with bile pure, of vile intent – all aimed directly at these lowly curs who dare call themselves officers of the King.

'I'll make half of *you* jump overboard before you get through the Endeavour Strait!'[76]

Really, Captain Bligh? The way Christian feels right now, there will be no need to wait all the way to Endeavour Strait. For he cannot bear this, right now!

'Mr Samuel!'[77] Bligh yells to his personal clerk, his anger in no way spent.

Samuel meekly steps forth, almost like a dog who knows he is about to be beaten. But no.

'Stop these villains' grog,' Bligh snarls, waving a dismissive hand at the seething group of six gentlemen officers – Fletcher Christian, Ned Young, William Peckover, Thomas Hayward, John Hallett and Peter Heywood – 'and give *them* but half a pound of yams tomorrow and if they steal then, I'll reduce them to *a quarter!*'[78]

Yes, and if perchance such rations don't suit you fine 'gentlemen', never fear, for there may be even worse to come.

'I will make you eat grass like cows!'[79] barks Bligh.

With which, he at last seems spent. The snarls are finished and all that remains is his normal scowling countenance, which looks disposed to bite off the heads of passing boobies.

Ah, but Christian's own rage is only just beginning, and he is not the only one, as, by the account of Morrison, 'the officers then got together and were heard to murmur much at such treatment'.[80]

They are officers, they are gentlemen, they are *innocent*, and they are being treated like criminals – in front of their own men!

Beyond rage at Bligh, much of the talk is of the yams, as the crew have brought aboard nearly as many of them as they had coconuts, and it is the obvious next thing for Bligh to seize. Quietly thus, they go to their yam stores and start secreting them where they can.

In a trance throughout the whole afternoon, Fletcher Christian goes about his duties, turning over and over the words of Bligh.

'You damned hound . . . You must have stolen half . . . God damn you . . . You scoundrels, you are all thieves . . . liar, thief, coward.'

The gall of the man!

No, he can take no more.

Instantly, Christian knows two things.

He will *not* go through that again. (While it is one thing to be so abused in private, the humiliation and sheer *dishonour* of being abused in front of the men is excruciating.)

He must *get away*. His honour simply demands it.

Ah, but Christian, Bligh is not yet done with you today. Oh no.

That much is clear to all those sailors within earshot – which is to say just about anywhere on the *Bounty* – as, throughout the entire afternoon, Bligh's grating, screeching, penetrating, pernicious voice is heard screaming time and again at Mr Christian, who can, in turn, be heard protesting. On and on the yelling goes. So intense is the ongoing confrontation, it is clear that something will have to give, and it proves to be the emotions of the Acting Lieutenant.

At 4 o'clock, Purcell is in his cabin, resting for his next shift, when the distressed form of Christian rushes in from the starboard quarter, tears pouring from his eyes in huge drops.

This is staggering. Another man, yes? But never Fletcher Christian, for he is 'no milksop'.[81]

But, clearly, he can bear no more.

'Mr Christian,' Purcell asks, for all the world as if he has not been listening to it all afternoon, 'what is the matter?'[82]

Bligh! *That* is what is the matter!

'Can you ask me and hear the treatment I receive?'[83] Fletcher says.

'Do I not receive as bad as you do?'[84] replies Purcell.

For, of course, Purcell knows more than most just how infuriating Bligh's constant harangues and bullying belittlement can be.

'You have something to protect you,'[85] replies Christian, clearly referring to the fact that Purcell is a warrant officer and Bligh may not subject him to a lashing at the hands of James Morrison, nor strip him of that warrant at sea.

'If I should speak to him as you do, he would probably break me, turn me before the mast and perhaps flog me,'[86] continues Christian. Yes, Purcell is well aware of this, and couldn't agree more with the upset young man's assessment, for he has no doubt that Bligh would do exactly that. But still he is profoundly shocked by Fletcher's next words.

'And if he did,' continues the now suddenly angry Christian, 'it would be the death of us both, for I am sure I should take him in my arms and jump overboard with him.'[87]

What?

Look, it is one thing for Bligh to be a madman when it comes to rage. Purcell knows that. But, Fletcher Christian to match him? To talk openly *of killing a Captain*?

'Never mind, it is but for a short time longer,'[88] says Purcell, as lightly as he can muster.

Fletcher Christian's murmured reply stuns the Carpenter.

Mr Purcell, I need wood, lots of wood, with which I intend to build a raft. I am going to desert the *Bounty* this very night.

You're *what*, Mr Christian? *You're what?*

I am going to build a raft, and cast off in the middle of the ocean.

Why, sir, this is madness, and suicidal madness at that!

No, he does not think he can get all the way back to Tahiti, or even close. As a matter of fact . . .

'He did not expect to reach the shore upon the raft,' one of Christian's men would later explain, 'but was in hopes of being seen and taken up by some of the natives in their canoes.'[89]

Or, maybe, he will be lucky, and the tides will drift him towards Tofoa.

For Christian, what happens afterwards is just a bonus. The first part of the plan, to be separated from Bligh, at any price, will be accomplished the moment he casts off!

This is not the plan of a man thinking right.

In desperation, Purcell goes in search of two men Christian might listen to – two who can be trusted to be silent about this mad plan – Cole, the Bosun, and Stewart, the young Midshipman. They must make Christian see reason!

Both men try, having hurried, hushed conversations with him. But Christian will not see sweet reason.

'I would rather die ten thousand deaths, than bear this treatment,'[90] Christian growls, like a wounded lion. 'I always do my duty as an officer and a man ought to, yet I receive this scandalous usage.'[91]

'Keep your heart up!' encourages Cole. 'Do not mind what has passed.'[92]

'To be counted a thief is more than I can bear,'[93] replies Christian.

But Fletcher . . .

'Flesh and blood,' Christian bursts forth, 'cannot bear this treatment.'[94]
Yes, he insists, he would sooner death before dishonour.

Very well, Purcell and Cole agree to do their bit to help him assemble what he needs.

•

Below, in his small, dark cabin, Bligh is quite calm – as all that unpleasantness is quickly forgotten, as it nearly always is – and has checked his calculations, marked his charts, and now records in the ship's Log the major event of the day.

Served fresh pork and yams as yesterday.[95]

Still, when he thinks about it, perhaps he had been a bit strong on the issue of the coconuts? Should he perhaps do something about it?
Yes, why not . . . ?

•

On deck, the officers, with Christian at their centre, continue to murmur in the wan moonlight breaking through the light rain clouds that hover in the sky as the *Bounty* sails slowly through the gentle swell on a subtle breeze. She leaves a sparkling phosphorescence in her wake, an unlikely trail of elegance for what is now afoot on deck. There is a wonderful purity to sailing like this, the ship gently rocking to a mesmerising natural rhythm, as the three masts slice slow, graceful arcs through the night sky. But are they murmuring too loudly?
Someone is coming!

It proves to be the Bosun's Mate, Morrison. And Morrison, a curious man by nature, has indeed noticed something, and even heard a snatch of strange conversation between Purcell and Cole.

'It won't do tonight,'[96] Purcell says.

What won't do? Morrison is not sure.

Whatever they are doing, it can't be too bad when Fletcher Christian, the ship's nominal second officer, is right there among them.

In the meantime, one more member of the ship's crew is brought to Christian's side, a young fellow who he trusts implicitly – fellow Manxman, young Peter Heywood.

On receipt of the extraordinary news, and witnessing with his own eyes that Christian is quite serious – as he takes a plank stolen from supplies, and lashes it to the two masts of the Launch – young Peter does his best to persuade his friend, his mentor, against pursuing his plan.

Fletcher, *please*!

You must know that:

Captain Bligh will stop at nothing, just as he stopped at nothing to bring back Churchill and the other deserters. And even if he doesn't turn the ship around to scour the oceans, how will you get back to Tahiti and Isabella? How will you survive, Fletcher?

To these questions, Christian has no answers, only his continued commitment. So what can Peter, as a good friend, do?

He helps. In fact, all of them – Christian, Heywood, Stewart, Cole and Purcell – continue to work quietly, lashing the craft together and hastily assembling some provisions for whatever lies ahead.

Now, what else might he need?

Ah, yes.

Of course, on the very off-chance that Christian survives long enough to drift or paddle on to a populated island, he will need something to trade, so Fletcher decides the best thing will be to take the most valuable item: iron nails.

'Take as many as you please out of the locker,' says Purcell.

A shadow falls over them. Christian looks up to see Bligh's cowering clerk, Samuel, gazing upon him.

'Mr Christian, you are asked to dine with Captain Bligh,'[97] says Samuel blithely.

Christian's jaw falls open, stupefied.

'I am unwell,'[98] he offers.

Very well then, Samuel bears the news to Bligh, only to return a short time later.

The Captain wonders whether any officers care to 'join him for dinner?'[99]

There is an uncomfortable pause.

For the truth is, the officers here would sooner put a red-hot nail in their ears than join Bligh for dinner and so they have come to an agreement on this point, privately, as their own gentlemanly form of protest. None shall share the Captain's table, none of the officers so recently insulted would . . . but wait!

One of the officers breaks ranks.

Midshipman Thomas Hayward decides he would like to dine with the Captain and quickly departs, 'hissed by all the rest'.[100] The pathetic Hayward. Such a treacherous toady!

Christian focuses now on the only thing that counts: preparing to depart. While he continues building the raft, one of his friends heads below to his cabin, and returns with his letters and papers, which Christian starts to tear up and throw overboard.

To the few men on deck, who look at him quizzically, the Acting Lieutenant is quick to explain.

'I would not wish everybody to see my letters,'[101] says he, speaking already as a man who knows he will be dead on the morrow, or soon thereafter. In that same spirit Christian gives away 'all his Tahitian curiosities',[102] with his nearest and dearest, Heywood and Stewart, taking their share – though both continue to hope that Christian will soon come to his senses.

Now, while most of the ship's crew are below, eating their supper, Christian and his friends hide the small raft in the *Bounty*'s Launch – *sssshhhh, easy now* – so it can be easily retrieved in the night, once it is Christian's watch.

As it happens, after supper it is Mr Fryer who must take command of the first watch of the night, and the Master is just gazing out to the stern, noting the previously hazy cloud cover giving way to a clear night, when Bligh happens by, and the two actually engage in a brief, civil conversation. Perhaps Bligh *has* realised he has gone too far on this day – Christian has never before refused an invitation to his table – and feels he must do something to dissipate the ill-will. Whatever it is, Fryer indulges his Captain.

'Sir, there is a breeze springing up fare and a young moon, which will be lucky for us to come on the coast of New Holland,'[103] he says.

'Yes, Mr Fryer,' Captain Bligh replies, 'it will be very lucky for us to get on the coast with a good moon.'[104]

For, of course, the new moon frequently brings with it a change to fair weather and Bligh knows that Captain Cook had noted the presence off the coast of New Holland of some rather long and tricky reefs. They will have to navigate their way through them very carefully, before finding their way to Endeavour Strait, off the northern tip of New Holland, and continuing west from there.

The two chat a little more before Bligh gives the night's orders and retires to his cabin.

And now, it seems, even the Gods themselves have concluded it is madness for such a good man as Fletcher Christian to so foolishly throw his life away, and so they intervene. That slight breeze that Fryer had noted? It vanishes with Captain Bligh. Our lady in the riding habit eases and slows from a lazy trot to an ambling walk.

Even Alec Smith, the rough tough from Hackney, East London, who is little given to poetic reflection or the soft contemplation of *anything*, will be moved to note . . .

'It was one of those beautiful nights which characterize the tropical regions, when the mildness of the air and the stillness of nature dispose the mind to reflection.'[105]

All of which means that while it is wonderful weather for reverie, it is horrifyingly hopeless for desertion.

For his part, Christian's mind is as far from quietly reflective as it gets, racing over the insults of the day, the decision he has taken, the risk he will be running . . . and the fact that the fading cloud cover and wind are now conspiring to keep him on the ship!

Could anything more possibly go wrong?

A flare in the distance.

A rumbling across the waters.

Of course. At this very moment, the volcano on the island of Tofoa erupts, casting an unearthly glow on the deck of the *Bounty* and inevitably bringing more crew up from below to gaze upon it. Christian's faint hopes for an unseen departure from an all but deserted deck disappear.

Of all the times!

Of all the nights! So Christian must wait quietly on the after-deck, as the *Bounty* bobs along on the moonlit swell, the old barque creaks, and the glow from the volcano helps to dimly illuminate the sails now starting to give small flaps of interest at the rising breeze, even as

Mr Fryer hands over command of the watch to the Gunner, William Peckover, at midnight.

With that light breeze comes a smell like burnt gunpowder – the sulphurous wafts from the still erupting volcano. But the breeze soon dies away once more, leaving a silent calm – deadly calm, infernal calm – and Christian is left alone to stew once more on the outrages of the previous morning.

'*You damned hound . . . You must have stolen half . . . God damn you . . . You scoundrels, you are all thieves . . . I'll make half of you jump overboard before you get through the Endeavour Strait!*'

The hide of the man! The damn *impertinence*!

Over and over, extreme emotions tumble through his tortured soul. The volcano glows in the distance, its once acute and acrid smell now just the odd passing sulphuric whiff. The ocean laps gently at the hull, the canvas sails flap uselessly, the dripstones . . .

Drip, drip, drip . . . drop.

A mess of jangled nerves, Christian remains intent on launching his raft and making good his escape, but the deck remains too crowded, and at half past three in the morning, just half an hour before he is due to take command of his watch, Fletcher Christian decides to snatch some rest below, so he can indeed be found in his cabin when it is his turn to take watch.

Four bells, and all is not well.

Stewart, who is on the next watch, has something he must say to Christian, just six words that he hastens to get out, for if Fletcher embraces them, the course of history, not to mention the course of the *Bounty*, will change. You see, whispers on the waves in the dead of night, mutinous murmurings, George has been very quietly talking to many of the men.

'The people,' he breathes conspiratorially to Fletcher, leaning in close, 'are ripe for anything . . .'[106]

It is time for the Knights of Tahiti to rise! Let us reveal ourselves, and rule!

Mutiny. The men are ripe for *mutiny*, Fletcher, for seizing the ship, and being done with that bastard Bligh for good.

Stewart makes his case quickly and convincingly.

'Rather than risk your life on so hazardous an expedition, endeavour to take possession of the ship!'[107]

A sparkle flickers in Fletcher's eyes.

'It will not be very difficult,' Stewart continues, 'as many of the ship's company are not well disposed towards the Commander. All will be very glad to return to Tahiti, and reside among our friends in that island!'[108]

Fletcher looks down at the sorry pile of wood and ropes he had been about to trust his chances on, turning himself into a piece of human jetsam, then looks to the mighty masts of the *Bounty* and the sails high above. In an instant, the whole conversation has turned from desertion to mutiny, and their whispers become ever more urgent accordingly.

Yes . . .

Yes . . .

Christian notes that there are only two possibilities: the rising sun will find him commander of the *Bounty* or it will find him dead.

'If I fail,' Fletcher says firmly, 'I will throw myself into the sea.'[109]

To that effect, Stewart watches, dismayed, as Christian takes a deep sea lead attached to a length of rope, and ties it around his own neck, before concealing it all beneath his clothes. His intent is clear. Any mishap on this mutiny, any chance he will be captured, then he will jump to his death first.

Better that than humiliation at the hands of Bligh, a likely shipboard trial, and either being lashed to death, or a hanging.

The pair share an intense glance. Young George Stewart realises how quickly this is all moving. Fletcher Christian thinks of Isabella.

Alea iacta est, the die is cast . . .

CHAPTER SEVEN

MUTINY ON THE *BOUNTY*

Awake, bold Bligh! the foe is at the gate!
Awake! awake!—— Alas! it is too late!
Fiercely beside thy cot the mutineer
Stands, and proclaims the reign of rage and fear.
Thy limbs are bound, the bayonet at thy breast;
The hands, which trembled at thy voice, arrest;
Dragged o'er the deck, no more at thy command
The obedient helm shall veer, the sail expand;[1]

Lord Byron, 'The Island'

Men did not desert because they hated their commanders, or salt
pork, or weevily biscuits; they deserted for love.[2]

John Beaglehole, the historian who was the first
to comprehensively compile and edit Cook's journals

4 am, 28 April 1789, off the Friendly Islands, cometh the hour, cometh the men

Drip, drip, drip . . . drop.

More whispers on the waves in the wee, wee hours . . .

Knowing that everything is moving into place, Stewart returns to his berth as normal. No indication can be given that anything is amiss.

When Fletcher Christian comes back on deck to start his watch, his lead weight secreted under his worn shirt, he looks around at the sailors, the men he must delicately, oh so delicately, test out. Every word he utters, he is keenly aware, puts his life in danger. For merely to suggest a mutiny is to offer a fellow sailor a noose, and invite him to put it over his own neck, or Christian's. If the sailor joins the mutiny the sailor's own life is in peril. If the sailor alerts Bligh, Christian himself will surely swing.

Christian looks around the deck and for once – twice if you count the flagging wind preventing his slow suicide by raft – the Gods are smiling on him. Every man-jack on watch with him this evening has been flogged on Bligh's orders. True, on the *Bounty* the list of those who have been beaten is long, but it really is remarkable to have such a rogues' gallery with Christian at this time, led by the always glowering, resentful Matt Quintal who, just like Christian, has a beautiful young woman he longs to return to.

Surely, he is the most likely to turn? Once the men from the last watch are safely below, Christian slyly approaches the likely lad, and leans in.

He starts by talking in hushed tones of old times on Tahiti, the women they've left behind, the difficulties the ship has known under Bligh since they left, and . . . gaining confidence from Quintal's impassioned and angry responses, finally 'discloses his intentions'.[3]

Quintal's angry eyes flash in the gloom as he silently considers the proposal, and the chance of revenge on that bastard, Bligh. Fletcher Christian is more confident than ever of the response.

'I think,' Quintal finally says, slowly, 'it a dangerous attempt and decline taking a part.'[4]

Christian's heart pounds, and he near gasps. Not even the rough and subversive Quintal will join him? Desperate to show this thug just what level his own commitment is, Christian rips open his shirt to reveal the heavy lead weight.

You see there, Quintal?

The angry eyes open wider just to see it, and Christian seizes the moment.

'Coward!' he accuses Quintal. 'It is fear alone that restrains you.'[5]

'No!' protests Quintal, which is all the opening Christian needs to resume his persuasion.

'Success will restore us all to the happy island [of Tahiti], and the connections we have left behind,'[6] Christian insists.

Quintal, as Machiavellian as he is malevolent, offers a way forward.

Bligh's portrait, c. 1776, by John Webber.
Bligh, in Master's uniform, is about to be
posted to James Cook's ship the *Resolution*.
National Portrait Gallery, Canberra

Fletcher Christian – detail from Robert
Dodd's engraving of the Mutiny on the
Bounty.

Sketch of bread-fruit by George Tobin. Tobin was a Royal Navy officer and artist who accompanied Bligh on HMS *Providence*. Mitchell Library, SLNSW, PXA 563

'Matavai Bay, Island of Otahytey, sunset' by George Tobin. Mitchell Library, SLNSW, PXA 563

'Poedua, the Daughter of Orio', oil painting by John Webber. One of the earliest images of a Polynesian woman produced by a European painter for a western audience.
Royal Museums Greenwich

Hawaiian King's sailing canoes bringing presents to Captain Cook. Engraving by John Webber. commons.wikimedia.org

The death of Captain Cook, as portrayed by George Carter, 1781. National Library of Australia

'In Oparrey Harbour [Oparre Bay] – Island of Otahytey' by George Tobin.
Mitchell Library, SLNSW, PXA 563

'The Observatory, Point Venus, Otahytey' by George Tobin. Mitchell Library, SLNSW, PXA 563

'A young woman of Otaheite, bringing a present'; engraving after a drawing by John Webber, the artist on Cook's third voyage. The girl wears a 'dress' consisting of a prodigious amount of tapa cloth, intended as presents for the visiting Europeans.
Royal Museums Greenwich

OTOO. KING of OTAHEITE.   TYNAI MAI, a principal LADY of OTAHEITE.

Otoo (Tinah) and Queen Iddeah, also known as Tynai-Mai. Engraving from *Complete History of Captain Cook's First, Second and Third Voyages* (1784). Science & Society Picture Library

John Webber's oil painting of Otoo (Tinah), 1777.

commons.wikimedia.org

William Bligh, engraving by Jean Condé after John Russell, 1792. The portrait was drawn for Bligh's book detailing the *Bounty*'s voyage.

National Portrait Gallery, London

'The mutineers turning Lieutenant Bligh and part of the officers and crew adrift from His Majesty's ship the *Bounty*' by Robert Dodd, 1790. The painting is inaccurate in one detail: because the Launch was so weighed down, its lip was only 7 inches above the waterline.

'Someone else should be tried,' he says, indicating others on the watch, just yonder.

Christian leans forward. And who would that be . . . ?

'Isaac Martin.'[7]

Quintal avers that if Martin joins, well, then, he might very well follow.

Quintal watches closely as the Acting Lieutenant walks over for a *very* quiet word. And yet, still, by straining his ears and watching their lips, Quintal understands the response.

'I am for it!' declares Martin. 'It is the very thing!'[8]

With Martin now committed, Quintal agrees to join them. Like a fire on dry grass in a stiff wind, the word rapidly spreads to the trusted and the treacherous, as Christian works his way around the deck, sweating profusely as his mutiny gains momentum. But let us be clear.

Rest assured, lads, there is no foul murder afoot. We are proud British men, not murderers. We are simply going to seize this ship, and put Bligh with his few Loyalists in a boat of his own, the Jolly Boat. They can make their way to nearby Tofoa, where, if they're lucky, they can survive.

The way Christian conceives it, Bligh will be accompanied by his faithful Clerk, Samuel, and two officers, Thomas Hayward and John Hallett, neither of whom Christian wants to remain on the *Bounty*, for they are too true to the Captain.

Quickly, the responses from the other men on the watch come back. Alec Smith, still stinging – both physically and emotionally – from his lashing, is for mutiny.

And what of you, Charley Churchill, your own back not yet quite healed from your meeting with the tails of the cat? If furious nods accompanied by gleaming glares can be counted as, 'Yes, I am with you', then Churchill can be counted on.

Stealthily, carefully, the growing and murmuring mutiny steals its way across the upper deck, down the companionway, from hammock to hammock, turning slumbering sailors into Mutineers with a few chosen words, a look, and a suddenly wide-awake nod. In less than an hour, before the darkness begins to give way to the day, all of Charley Churchill, Matt Thompson, Alec Smith, John Sumner, John

Williams, William McCoy, William Muspratt, Charles Norman and John Mills – a conspiracy of the *Bounty*'s roughest and toughest – are in agreement: *we are with you, Mr Christian.*

Quickly, quietly, he tells them all to keep to their regular duties, but prepare to move, to follow his lead, the instant he gives the word.

Of course, the key source of serious resistance will be Bligh, who is known to have a couple of pistols in his cabin. Since the desertion of the three crewmen, the Master, Fryer, also keeps a brace of pistols by his bunk. All such pistols will have to be secured before the two senior officers are subdued.

What they need to secure first, however, is the Arms Chest, it sits outside the Midshipmen's cabin and is where the muskets, cutlasses and bayonets are stored, and there are two barriers to opening it.

The first is an officer of the watch, Hallett, one of the few on board who remains close to Bligh, and who – by being asleep on duty – is 'securing the Arms Chest' as ordered, by actually slumbering right on top of it.

The second obstacle is that the key to the chest is on a chain hanging around the neck of Coleman, the Armourer, who is responsible for maintaining the weaponry inside.

As Christian ponders what to do, even as he goes below and ponders the sleeping form of Hallett, a sudden alarming cry is heard from on high. Has their plot been discovered?

'There's a Shark on the larboard quarter!'[9] comes the cry.

Which, come to think of it, is perfect. *A shark.*

Putting his hand on Hallett's shoulder, Christian shakes him.

Hallett comes to with a start. Being asleep on duty is an offence punishable by a good flogging. But no, strangely, Christian is smiling, and saying something about a shark.

Come and see for yourself, Mr Hallett, it's just been spotted on the larboard side. See if you can perhaps catch it, with a line.

Hallett, fascinated, and *hungry* as a sailor on three-quarter rations, is on his feet in an instant, and heads up on deck trailing close behind Christian, to see if he can find a way to catch the shark. He immediately comes across Midshipman Hayward who is holding a shark hook and looking over the gunnel, intent on the same thing.

'Do you see the shark, Burkett?'[10] Hayward asks Able Seaman Thomas Burkett, who is busily scrubbing the deck.

'No, sir, I have not seen it forward,'[11] replies Burkett carefully, even as, over Hayward's shoulder he can see the Mutiny getting underway. For here now is Mr Christian, followed closely by Mr Churchill and a slew of others, heading down the fore hatchway, and Burkett hears Mr Christian say to the Armourer, 'Coleman, give me a Musket to shoot a Shark with.'[12]

Of course, Mr Christian.

Coleman takes the key from around his neck, opens the Arms Chest and hands the Acting Lieutenant the first musket that comes to hand.

His reward, he is stunned to find, is to have Christian – after putting powder, ball and wadding down the barrel, and tamping it all down with a ramrod, before sprinkling powder in the firing pan – suddenly cock the primed weapon, and turn it on him, pointing the barrel right at his chest, something only just manageable in the tiny chamber between the Captain and the Master's cabins.

Mamu, Mr Coleman. Stay silent!

It is, for the Mutineers, a key breakthrough – the Arms Chest, with its tens of muskets, bayonets, and dozens of cutlasses, is now firmly in their possession. Taking one of the muskets, Charley Churchill now goes up on deck, to be confronted by a very puzzled Thomas Hayward.

'What are you about?' asks Hayward, 'Are you going to Exercise already?'[13]

'Yes,' Churchill replies, seizing upon the excuse offered. 'I don't know the Captain's reason for it, he has ordered us to Exercise at daylight.'[14]

Churchill moves on, carefully, slowly, keeping an eye on Hayward, who, sure enough, starts to head below, accompanied by Hallett. Surely, he is going to check this unusual order with the Captain, who, if he has given such an order, must be already awake.

Churchill moves quickly.

'Hayward is gone to tell the Captain,'[15] he tells whoever is close enough to hear.

He doesn't have to say more than that. In an instant, he and four other Mutineers, newly armed, run after the pair and bring their weapons to bear. *One move, and we will blow you away. One move.*

The colour drains from the officers' faces, and they submit to being led back up the aft hatchway, and stood captive on the starboard side.

And they are not the only ones to be shocked with this sudden turn of events.

At the other end of the *Bounty*, Burkett is also stunned to see Christian coming towards him, holding a musket with a fixed bayonet *and* a cartridge box in his left hand *and* a pistol *and* cutlass in his right. There is fury in his eyes.

'Here, Burkett, lay hold of this,' says Christian, holding out the musket.[16]

Burkett looks at it as if it were a cobra he was being asked to hold – and it very nearly is. Not only is it deadly to those it is aimed at, but in this situation potentially deadly for whoever holds it as it makes him complicit in whatever treachery is now happening all around him. It is all happening so fast, and all he knows is that it *is* treacherous.

'What must I do with it?'[17] asks the hesitant Burkett.

'Damn your blood, lay hold of it and go aft,'[18] replies the suddenly menacing Christian.

The ever menacing Billy McCoy, meanwhile – a scarred scowl of a man – approaches them, 'loading his piece'.[19]

'Why don't you lay hold of it,' he says, with a vicious gleam in his eyes, 'and go *aft* as Mr. Christian *desires* you?'[20]

Clearly, Burkett has a choice, in the face of what is now, obviously, a mutiny – he can join it, or be subdued and perhaps thrown overboard. He grabs hold of it, and goes aft, joining the Mutineers – and now watches closely in these first streaks of dawn as Christian strides across the deck and waves the cutlass at the officer he likes least on this ship, after Bligh, an officer now seen to be whispering conspiratorially: 'Damn your blood, Hayward . . . *Mamu!*'[21]

Things are moving fast. The Mutineers have the deck, they have the officers of the watch, they have the ship's weapons. Their prime target, however, the key to the whole affair, far more important than the one that had been around Coleman's neck, remains . . .

Bligh.

Are we going to do this?

We are going to do this!

With a quick headcount, Christian sees that they have enough Mutineers with them now to leave some holding the deck, and now, silently, leads his core band of six Mutineers along the lower level of the ship – *drip, drip, drip* . . . *drop* go the dripstones – all the way to the door of Bligh's cabin.

In quick hisses, and hand signals, Fletcher has Alec Smith, holding a musket, stand guard outside the door, to protect their rear.

Meanwhile, Quintal and Sumner, you must deal with Fryer in this cabin, directly opposite Bligh's. Whatever happens, lads, you must get Fryer's pistols, and tie him up. Churchill, Burkett, you come with me, into the Captain's chamber.

And now Christian pauses in front of his mob, with his hand on the doorknob. There is still time to turn back.

Still though, the memory of Bligh's words lashes him forward, stinging with every blow.

You damned hound . . . You must have stolen half . . . Scoundrel! . . . Thief . . . [22]

No, he cannot turn back now.

Instead, he turns the knob with his left hand, a cutlass in his right. It is a quarter past five in the morning, with the rising dawn throwing just enough light through the porthole into Bligh's chamber that it is composed of dark shapes, not pitch blackness. Christian pushes in, ahead of Churchill and Burkett, armed with muskets – making it extremely crowded – ready for the capture of the man who in seconds will no longer be their commander. There is a stirring from the bunk before him, as Bligh wakes from the sudden clamour, the stutter from the clutter of men.

'What is the matter?' the Captain rumbles, and then again. 'What is the matter?'[23]

'Bligh, you are my prisoner,'[24] Christian says quietly.

Bligh's face shows no anger, only confusion. In his half-awake state, it has registered that he has been called 'Bligh' alone, with no rank in front, nor even a 'Mr'. And, he is a 'prisoner'.

What is the meaning of this?

'One noise,' Christian hisses, the point of his sword at the Captain's throat, 'and it is death.'[25]

Now, Bligh is fully awake and all too aware of exactly the infamy at hand.

'MURDER! MURDER!'[26] Bligh cries, calling his bluff.

So much for taking the ship quietly. But Bligh's shouting voice is every bit as common on the *Bounty* as the sound of waves on the hull, creaks in the masts, sails flapping and snapping. How many of the ship's company will this shout have woken? Christian promised death for a single noise, and yet, though he is now a Mutineer, he is not yet a murderer. To drive his sword into the throat of an unarmed man, even a cur such as Bligh, is beyond him.

For his part, however, it is not beyond Churchill to punish 'Bligh' for disobeying the order of 'Captain Christian' – the *insolence* of this bloated bastard of a skipper – and he takes great pleasure in stepping forward and striking a massive blow to Bligh, 'with the flat side of his cutlass'.[27]

It gives Churchill such satisfaction he is about to do it again, but – snapping out of the enormity of what just happened, and shocked that one of his own men would so act, without any orders from his new Captain – Christian will not have it. He jostles Churchill aside, raises his arm to stop the blow, and orders his men to tie the hands of the completely stunned and outraged Bligh behind his back. *Quickly now, quietly now.*

But with no rope or cord to hand – they had not thought of that – Christian orders the glowering Churchill to fetch some – *now, Mr Churchill!* – while he holds the tip of his cutlass to the throat of the glowering Bligh.

•

There is the blackness of a dark night, the blackness of the Black Hole of Calcutta, the blackness of the pitch they use to caulk their ships, and then there is . . . the blackness of two musket muzzles pointed at your face when you wake from a deep sleep.

Such is what Fryer opens his eyes to on this morning as he finds two men he knows well, Sumner and Quintal, pointing muskets at him.

Good morning!

He is instantly fully awake, and it does not take him long to realise that the unspeakable has happened. They are in the middle of a *mutiny*. Looking across to Bligh's cabin, with both doors open, his eyes even meet Bligh's. Wordlessly, Bligh is looking for him to do something, knowing that Fryer has two loaded pistols in his cabin.

But Fryer makes no move. Alec Smith is right there, holding a musket! So is Mr Christian!

Those *muskets*. The sheer blackness of their muzzles, like the blackness of a tomb.

'Sir,' says Quintal, snapping him from his reeling thoughts. 'You are a Prisoner.'[28]

Of course, Fryer attempts to assert his authority as Master of this ship, but Quintal's and Sumner's muskets prevail.

'Hold your Tongue or you are a dead Man,' Sumner snarls at him, before softening a little. 'But if you remain quiet there is no person on board that will hurt a hair of your head.'[29]

Fryer remains very quiet indeed, even as the still glowering Bligh catches his eye once more. This time, Fryer looks away.

Still unhappy that his quarry, the brute, Bligh, is not bound – not to mention that his new skipper has already spoken to him so sharply – Churchill emerges from the cabin to call quietly up the stairs to the Mutineers on high, 'Hand down a seizing to tie the Captain's hands.'[30]

Up on deck, of the Mutineers who are present – Burkett, Mills and Norman – none makes a move.

Nor do the now, perforce, Loyalists, Hayward and Hallett, respond to Churchill's order. At this point it is not clear who Churchill is ordering, just as it is not absolutely clear who is a Loyalist and who is a Mutineer. (Only seconds before, Mills had assured Hayward that he is 'totally ignorant'[31] of any plot to take the ship.)

And so Churchill's voice comes again, much sharper this time, all menacing malevolence: 'You Infernal buggers, hand down a seizing or I'll come up and play hell with you all!'[32]

In response, Mills steps forward and, for the first time, Hayward realised that, 'John Mills was one of the Mutineer's Party.'[33]

'Stop!'[34] Hayward commands him . . . for no result.

For Mills simply takes out his knife and, with a casual if violent swish, cuts the end off a piece of rope hanging from the mizzenmast and hands it down the hatchway.

With the rope in hand, Churchill returns to Bligh's cabin, and after gripping him by the collar of his nightshirt, and hauling him up from the bed, turns him around to tightly bind his hands behind his back.

Here is your prisoner, Mr Christian.

The new leader takes the point of his cutlass and pokes it firmly into Bligh's back. Holding his fallen Captain by the cord, he marches him up towards the deck, as if walking a reluctant dog.

Oh, how the mighty have fallen.

Churchill now enters the Master's cabin and sees the brace of pistols that Sumner and Quintal have already secured.

'I will take care of these, Mr. Fryer,' says Mr Churchill mockingly as he leaves.

'What are you going to do with the Captain?'[35] Fryer asks.

'Damn his eyes!' replies Sumner. 'Put him into the Boat and let the bugger see if he can live on three-fourths of a pound of yams a day!'[36]

'Into the *boat*?'[37] asks Fryer, stunned. So this is not just a mutiny, with the Mutineers holding Captain Bligh and his Loyalists captive on the *Bounty*, they are actually going to set Bligh adrift!

'Mr Christian is Captain of the ship,' barks Sumner. 'Recollect that Mr Bligh has brought all this upon himself!'[38]

'Consider my lads, what you are about!' pleads Fryer, his usually dull grey eyes flashing blue with desperation.

'Oh, sir,' replies Sumner with unseemly glee, a scar on his left cheek giving him the most crooked of smiles. 'We know very well what we are about.'[39]

'I am afraid not,' replies Fryer with all the calm authority he can muster under the circumstances, 'or you would not persist in your intentions. Let me persuade you to lay down your Arms and I will ensure that nothing shall hurt you, for what you have done.'[40]

'Oh, no, sir,' replies Quintal. 'Hold your tongue, it is too late now.'[41]

Alas, despite the circumstances, Fryer cannot hold his tongue.

'What Boat are they going to put Captain Bligh into?'[42] Fryer asks.

'The Jolly Boat,' replies Sumner.

'Good God! The small Cutter's bottom is almost out,' Fryer responds sharply, and with good reason. '[That vessel is practically] eaten with the Worms . . .' [43]

'Damn his Eyes,' Quintal responds, merciless. 'The boat is too good for him.'[44]

'The Jolly Boat will not swim!'[45] Fryer implores, but is quick to realise nobody much cares.

'I hope they are not going to send Captain Bligh adrift by himself?' asks Fryer, his head reeling.

'No, his Clerk, Mr. Samuel, Mr. Hayward and [Mr.] Hallett, are going with him,'[46] replies Sumner.

That's it? The plan is to leave Bligh, and rub-a-dub-dub, three men, for dead in a rickety craft, far from land in the middle of the South Pacific? Whatever his differences with Bligh, Fryer cannot *believe* it has come to this, and is determined to remonstrate with Christian to come to his senses. For this is not mutiny, it is murder, pure and simple.

•

In his berth, Peter Heywood wakes with a start. There are raised voices coming from somewhere near, and they are angry. And it is all before dawn. Right by him, Hallett's and Hayward's bunks are empty.

Rolling out of his hammock, the young Midshipman pulls aside the curtain that cordons off his makeshift cabin, and is confronted by the burly Matthew Thompson holding a musket with a fixed bayonet and sitting 'as a Centinel over the Arms Chest'[47] and gazing at him intently.

'The Captain is a prisoner,' says Thompson simply. 'Christian has taken command of the Ship.'[48]

Good God! I must go up on deck, and see my friend, Mr Christian.

No, Mr Heywood, my bayonet against your superior rank says you will be doing no such thing.

Peter is stunned.

'The spectacle was as sudden to my eyes as it was unknown to my heart,' he will later recall, 'and both were convulsed at the scene.'[49]

What has Fletcher *done*? What is he going to do? How has it come to this?

Many of Heywood's brethren are going through similar emotions. All over the ship there is confusion and alarm, as different reports of the Mutiny, the Mutineers, and the extraordinary fate of Captain Bligh spread from cabin to cabin, deck to deck, man to man.

The old salt Gunner, Peckover, has awoken from a nightmare about bayonets being fixed to sockets on musket barrels. What a strange thing to imagine hearing? He is just putting his trousers on when the worthy botanist, Nelson, pale-faced, flings open his door and blurts out the news.

'The Ship is taken from us!'[50] he says.

What? How on earth could the revenging Natives of Annamooka have pulled off such a feat, this far out to sea! By God, their canoes are extraordinary!

'We are a long way from Land!'[51] he replies, quite astonished.

'By our *own* People!' Nelson responds with uncharacteristic verbosity. 'And Mr. Christian at their head! But we know who is to blame!'[52]

Nelson does not need to say more.

Infernal, tyrannical *Bligh* has driven the usually mild-mannered Christian to this. All of them know it. And no, they can't condone Christian's actions, but they understand them, all right.

'Let us go forward and see what is to be done,'[53] says Peckover, but he and Nelson can go no further than the hatch before they are stopped by Quintal and Sumner guarding the hatchway, and Mr Fryer's cabin door, wielding their muskets and bayonets.

'Mr. Peckover,' says Quintal, his voice cold, '. . . we have Mutinied and taken the Ship, and Mr. Christian has got the Command.'[54]

Peckover and Nelson are ordered to the cockpit.

Meanwhile, Quintal stomps down the passageway – there is no need to creep anymore – and yanks open the door to Purcell's tiny cabin, prodding the sleeping Carpenter awake with his bayonet, to rather make the point. There are new commanders on this ship, and you are now a prisoner, who will do as he is told. In the berth next door, Cole awakes to the hubbub. With malicious glee, Quintal tells Purcell not just the news – about Captain Christian and his men, which include Quintal – but offers an invitation to join them.

'Mr Purcell, you and Mr Cole go on deck and do as you think proper.'[55]

Purcell blinks, confused.

'The Captain is confined,'[56] Quintal continues. 'All resistance will be in vain, if you attempt it you are a Dead Man!'[57]

Having heard everything, Cole now bursts into Purcell's cabin and expostulates, 'For God's sake, I hope you know nothing of this?'[58]

'No!'[59] replies a stunned Purcell.

Both men are thinking the same thing. Just hours ago, they had been helping Christian plan a desertion. And yet, somehow, while they slept, it has turned into a full-blown mutiny.

My God, what has Fletcher done?

What will the Royal Navy think that we *have done?*

Will Captain Bligh believe we have had no hand in it?

Hastily conferring, they know what they must do. They must get to Fletcher quickly, and get him to come to his senses.

•

With little ceremony, ex-Captain Bligh, still in his nightshirt – now fully aware that he is the planned victim of, 'one of the most atrocious and consummate acts of piracy ever committed'[60] – is placed before the mizzenmast by his former Lieutenant. While Christian holds the end of the rope that binds Bligh in one sweaty hand, he holds his cutlass in the other, the point at Bligh's chest.

Such is the scene that many of the crew see as they pop their heads up out of the hatchways like curious bunnies emerging from their burrow, wondering what all the commotion is about. It is a shocking sight. Here is Captain Bligh, held at the point of a sword by Fletcher Christian, while they themselves now have muskets pointed at them by their former crewmates Smith, Churchill and Martin, who are yelling at them as they tumble and stumble onto the deck.

The 16-year-old Monkey, for one, cannot take his eyes off the officer he is so very fond of. The once calm and collected Christian looks 'like a Madman, his long hair loose, his shirt collar open',[61] his eyes 'flaming with revenge'.[62]

And . . . *goodness!*

Shifting his frightened youthful gaze to Captain Bligh, Monkey notices he is half naked! 'Without breeches and with his shirt tail tied up with the seizing that secure his hands',[63] his pale buttocks are exposed. He is being hung out to dry in more ways than one, it seems.

Despite the sheer *indignity* of it all, however, Bligh's expression is one of scorn, and he can still summon the voice of domineering authority, complete with menace.

'What is the meaning of all this?'[64] Bligh demands, for all the world as if *he* is still in charge. Christian can barely believe it.

'Can you ask, Captain Bligh,' Christian growls, 'when you know you have treated us officers, and all these poor fellows, like Turks?'[65]

And yet Bligh appears to be *genuinely* mystified.

'What is the reason for such a violent act . . . ?'[66] he begins to ask again.

'*Mamu*, sir!' roars Christian. 'Not a word, or death's your portion!'[67] *Mamu*.

In that one word, Bligh perceives the root cause of the Mutiny – Tahiti. The lure of lurid paradise is so strong that it has turned dutiful English officers into conniving, conspiring, treacherous and traitorous savages, backed by the common sailors. But not all of them! Bligh is at least pleased to see that among the jeering Mutineers, the wretched traitorous officers, there are bleak faces of men, men of honour, men of integrity, Loyalists, *Englishmen* faithful to King George III and his esteemed officers; men who will risk all to stand by their Captain even as he stands prisoner, bottom exposed. Are there enough Loyalists, perhaps, to retake the ship and throw the brigands in chains? Perhaps! There are enough of them with shocked expressions that it at least has to be a possibility.

And who could lead that re-revolt? Where is Fryer?

•

Mr Fryer sits on his bunk, still staring into the dark abyss of two muzzles, trying to persuade his captors – the menacing Quintal and Sumner – to allow him to leave his cabin, and join Captain Bligh on deck, so he can speak with the skipper before he is cast adrift.

'You cannot,'[68] comes the repeated reply.

'At least, call upon the deck to ask Christian if I may be given permission to come up?'[69]

His captors hesitate, they look at each other. With a rough nod from Quintal, Sumner backs out of the cabin.

On deck, Bligh is still struggling to comprehend the staggering pace of events, and how this has all happened. He twists his hands in agony. The ropes on his wrists are so tight that his hands are turning blue, and his fingertips, which at first roared with pain, are now dully dumb and numb.

And now Christian swaps his cutlass for a bayonet – even more lethal at close quarters – proffered by one of his men, his eyes ever on Bligh, who is trying to speak once again, this time to his former crew:

'Do not persist . . .'[70]

'Hold your tongue, Sir, or you are dead this instant,'[71] repeats Captain Christian, with such a tone and such a look in his eye that even Bligh obeys.

Pock-marked young Burkett, meanwhile, cannot help himself. A most reluctant Mutineer from the first – with his decision taken while at the wrong end of Billy McCoy's pistol – he still has enough respect for Captain Bligh that he insists the deposed leader's bare buttocks should not remain exposed. They have taken the Captain's ship, yes, but let him at least have his dignity.

He lays his musket by the dripstone.

'What are you going to do?'[72] snaps Christian, mystified.

'Let down the Captain's shirt,'[73] replies Burkett calmly, using the rank that, as far as Christian is concerned, Bligh no longer has. With a soft yank, Burkett pulls the shirt free of the seizing, which sees Bligh's bare buttocks covered and his dignity returned to him.

And yet, even after the buttocks are covered to Burkett's satisfaction, he, strangely, leaves his musket lying exactly where he had placed it.

'Take up your arms,'[74] snaps Captain Christian.

But Burkett ignores him, instead walking over to the hatch and calling down to Sumner, who happens to be on his way up. 'Hand me up the Captain's clothes.'[75]

Sumner declines to do any such thing. He is a Mutineer, not a valet. Very well, then. Given that Bligh's actual valet, John Smith, now comes aft, Mr Burkett addresses him.

'Jack, go fetch the Captain's clothes, it is a shame to see him stand naked.'

'Why don't you take up your arms, Burkett,'[76] says Christian sharply, in a tone that will brook no opposition. *I* am the new Captain here, and do not forget it. And here's a pistol pointed at your head, to help you concentrate.

'I would have you take care,'[77] replies the shocked Burkett, though he picks up his musket and points it at Bligh, exactly as ordered.

The point is made, and his fate – for good or bad – is sealed. As the sun breaks free of the horizon, Christian is not just the Captain of the Mutiny, he is also now Captain of the *Bounty*, and all her crew.

Captain Christian?

Yes . . . ?

John Sumner has a request from Master Fryer. He wishes to be allowed to come up on deck.

Captain Christian accedes with a nod.

•

Below deck, Nelson and Peckover are huddled in the cockpit completely stunned by this turn of events, when Mr Samuel, Captain Bligh's ever nervous Clerk, now more nervous than ever, pops his head through the door.

'I am going away in the small Cutter with Captain Bligh, Mr. Hayward [and] Mr. Hallett,'[78] Samuel whispers to the two Loyalists. Always thinking ahead, as to what will make his Master and Commander most comfortable, he seeks advice about what he should provide for Bligh.

After all, just what does one put in one's sea bag, when one is about to be cast adrift?

'If I was in your place,' whispers Peckover, contemplating such an exceedingly small boat, which will need to stay high out of the water on a long journey in stormy seas, 'I should take but very few things.'[79]

Samuel nods in agreement and scurries off.

•

Asleep in his hammock through much of the drama, Morrison is now shaken awake by Cole with the staggering news, and with distinct purpose. Yes, he knows Morrison to be bright and witty, but there is also a mischievous side to him, a scallywag bordering on rogue, and so he must ask him.

'I hope, Morrison, you have no intention to join Christian's party?'[80] asks Cole plaintively.

'No, sir,' Morrison replies convincingly, 'you may depend upon it, that I will not; it is far from my intentions.'[81]

As it happens, waking up right next to Morrison at this time, in the next hammock, is John Millward, who had deserted with Churchill on Tahiti, and will likely be facing even more severe punishment than the punishment already received, once they get back to England. If ever there is a man likely to join the Mutineers, it is Millward, but, right now, he is most anxious to tell Cole he is *not* part of this mutiny.

'As I had a hand in the former foolish piece of business,' Millward says miserably to Cole, 'I suppose that they will make me have a hand in this also.'[82]

Millward is right, for at this very moment, the voice of Churchill bellows down the hatch: 'Millward, I have a musket for you!'[83]

Millward freezes and makes no reply.

'Damn you!' the angry voice comes again, 'come up, there is a musket ready.'[84]

Still nothing.

'Come up on deck, immediately!'[85]

Reluctantly, Millward goes on deck to tell Churchill face to face.

'No, Charles,' he says evenly, 'you brought me into one predicament already.'[86]

Another pause. And now Churchill replies.

'As you like it,'[87] says he with a shrug. Already they have plenty of Mutineers. If Millward is too much of a coward to join them, then so be it.

Morrison, meanwhile, drags on his clothes and goes on deck.

Good God, what a scene it is!

The *Bounty* taken by her own men! Most staggeringly of all, this is not a mutiny only of those before the mast, led by Christian, for he clearly has many petty officers with him, too.

Morrison carefully notes where each armed Mutineer is, and what weapons each sentinel holds. Williams is 'on the Fore Castel with a Musket and fixed Bayonet, William M'Coy and Robert Lamb at the fore-hatchway, Isaac Martin and William Brown on the after part of the Booms, and Henry Hillbrant on the Quarter deck, all armed in the same manner'.[88] (With both the forecastle and quarter-deck being on opposite ends of the ship and slightly raised, Christian has placed an armed man on each, surveying the scene and ready to shoot down the first sign of resistance.)

And the most amazing sight of all, in this early morning light, is noted with sheer stupefaction.

For there is Bligh on the larboard side of the quarter-deck, glaring, and for good reason. His hands are *tied* behind him and while Captain Christian has one hand on his shoulder, the other hand is holding a bayonet pointed at Bligh's chest.

Five feet above them all, up on the boom of the mizzenmast, is the wretch, Churchill, barking orders and swishing his cutlass about, as if to the manner born, the manor itself being far beyond him.

Stunned at this turn of events, the enormity of what the Mutineers are about, and how quickly it has happened, Morrison is making his way to the fore hatchway when he runs into Cole again.

'Mr Cole,' he asks in a low voice, 'what is to be done?'[89]

'By God, James,' Cole replies, equally stunned, 'I do not know.'[90]

•

Put in charge of preparing the Jolly Boat, Churchill – now descended from the booms, with a cutlass in one hand and a pointed pistol in the other – gives an order to the frightened Carpenter's Mate, Charles Norman.

'Norman, clear the Yams out of the Small Cutter.'[91]

'For what?'[92] asks a genuinely puzzled Norman. Yes, of course he knows that Christian has taken Captain Bligh prisoner, but he has not yet heard of him being set adrift on the High Seas. The 'normal' way of such things, if one can so describe something so extraordinary, is for the Captain – if he is not thrown overboard – to be kept prisoner in the bowels of the vessel he used to command. But Churchill is in no mood to either explain or justify Christian's plans.

'Do as I order you,'[93] Churchill growls, menacingly enough that Norman sets to with all speed.

•

Unbowed, Bligh continues to glare balefully at these 'lubberly rascals'.[94] His primary concern right now is to work out a way whereby Christian would find *himself* jerking at the end of a hangman's rope. The way things are turning, however, that event appears likely to be a good way off. For now, giving full vent to his furies, which is really saying something, Bligh expresses himself in such a manner that one of the Mutineers makes a suggestion to the others that they, 'Blow his brains out!!'[95]

In response, a Mutineer close to Bligh cocks his musket, followed by another, and then another, just as if they are readying to unleash a deadly fusillade of fire at him, hoping to see him frightened, perhaps even weep and beg for his life? But Bligh is made of sterner stuff.

'Fire, you ungrateful wretches, I dare you!'[96] Bligh taunts them. They dare not.

Several long seconds pass and some of the Mutineers waver, coming to their senses. Bligh, for all his sins, is a formidable man, with the entire weight of the Royal Navy behind him. Is it really a good idea to throw in your lot with those who would try to take him on?

One such waverer is the tall, bony American Mutineer, Isaac Martin, the first man to wholeheartedly join Christian in the revolt. Sure, he aches to get back to Tahiti, to the wonderful woman he has left behind. But *actually* going through with MUTINY – a crime punishable by death? It all feels too real. Besides that, he is a man who has long survived by compromising his principles when expedient. Why, that is how he came to be serving in the Royal Navy in the first place! When, in the Revolutionary War, his American warship had been captured by the British in 1781, he had turned traitor to join the Royal Navy. It had, therefore, been neither a huge wrench to turn away from it once more as he had when committing to Christian's Mutiny, nor to turn once more, as he is now tempted to do. Suddenly unsure, but very quiet about it, he steps forward to serve Bligh with the breakfast that Mr Christian has allowed him, a large and juicy slice of Tahitian grapefruit.

Yes, just as King Tinah had been fed by a servant, spooning the food directly into his mouth like an infant, so too is Bligh, with his hands still tightly tied behind him, Martin's face just a foot distant.

As he swallows his first mouthful, Bligh is gratified, if stunned, to see that Mutineer Martin is signalling him with his eyes.

I am with you, Captain! I may appear a Mutineer, but I actually want you back in charge!

Sucking on the fruit, savouring the relief it brings to his parched lips, Bligh gives Martin an equally significant look in return. Ten yards away, Joseph Coleman is coming up the fore hatchway, when he runs into Cole, who addresses him.

'Armourer, what do you intend to do?'[97]

'To go with the Captain, go where he will!'[98] replies Coleman.

'So will I,'[99] replies a pleased Cole, before leaning in to add a quiet, stealthy instruction, hopefully before they can be seen or heard.

'Jump down below and put your clothes into a bag. If you have any Trade left, put them into the bag, it might be of service to us.'[100]

•

Fryer is, at last, led up the ladder by his menacing sentinels, Sumner and Quintal. And he can barely believe his squinting eyes: Bligh in his nightshirt, tied by the mizzenmast; the Mutineers with their guns and swords surrounding him; Christian apparently directing proceedings, and another group neither armed, nor seemingly involved. Are they all Loyalists?

It is not possible to tell at the moment, perhaps not even for the 'Captains' Bligh and Christian. What is certain is that it is an explosive situation that could go either way, and Fryer, one of the King's men, does his best to gather the dropped egg and put it back together again.

'Mr. Christian, consider what you are about,'[101] he begs this otherwise fine man, with whom he has always been on collegiate terms, even when Christian had vaulted above him in the chain of command.

'Hold your tongue, sir, it is too late,' Christian replies with unaccustomed roughness, the voice of a man who is desperate and committed to his course.

'I have been in Hell for weeks past,' he continues. 'Captain Bligh has brought all this on himself.'[102]

'You and Captain Bligh not agreeing is no reason for you taking the ship.'[103]

'Hold your tongue, sir!'[104]

'Mr. Christian, you and I have been on friendly terms during the voyage, therefore give me leave to speak. Let Mr. Bligh go down to his Cabin and I make no doubt but that we shall all be friends again in a very short time.'[105]

Christian shoots the Master a quizzical look.

Fryer tries a different tack, straight into the prevailing wind. 'Please, in the name of God, lay down your arms.'[106]

Not a single musket is lowered. Fryer has one card left to play, a difficult one given that the furious Bligh is watching him, but perhaps it is better than nothing?

'If the Captain has done anything,' says Fryer, without being specific about it, 'confine him.'[107]

As in, don't force him from the *Bounty* – which would be akin to murder, under the circumstances, as even such a sailor as he can surely not survive – but keep the Captain a prisoner until they return to England.

'No!' Churchill has a reply. 'Damn you, *you* ought to have done that months ago.'[108]

This proves to be merely his opening remark, as Churchill now bursts forth with every ounce of venomous vitriol vis-a-vis Bligh he has had bottled up for months. The sailors gasp as they listen to the words Churchill dares utter to Bligh.

'Mr. Christian,' Fryer pleads, ignoring Churchill as best he can, 'if you will not grant what I first asked you, do pray give Captain Bligh a better boat than the small Cutter, whose bottom is almost out, and let him have a chance to get on shore.'[109]

'No, that Boat is good enough,'[110] Christian replies flatly.

Amid all the tumult, and Christian being momentarily distracted, Fryer draws in close to Bligh.

'Keep your spirits up, Captain,' he whispers. 'If I stay on board I might soon be able to [seize back the ship].'[111]

'By all means *stay*, Mr. Fryer,'[112] Bligh replies, his words bearing the resonance of *malice*.

Fryer will later note his amazement that Bligh, 'spoke so loud that Christian could not avoid hearing him, but took no notice'.[113]

In fact, Bligh continues to make mischief *sotto voce*, in a stage whisper, intended to be heard.

'Isaac Martin is a friend,'[114] he tells Fryer, *wanting* to be overheard. Oh, yes, Mr Fryer.

'He is aft by the chicken coops,'[115] Bligh goes on, shooting Fryer a look that says to go speak with him.

Oh, and Bligh also has one last instruction for Fryer: 'Knock Christian down!'[116]

Captain, quiet, please!

'*Knock Christian down!*'

'**Knock Christian down!**'[117]

Despite the gravity of the situation, Fryer is bemused by the perversity of Bligh's whole approach. Instead of genuine whispers, and trying to organise a genuine retaking of the *Bounty*, for Bligh what is even more urgent, right now, is to taunt Christian.

But if Bligh thinks Fryer is going to knock Christian down he must be mad. Just one move by the slender Fryer and the armed Mutineers would run him through. No, much better to try to follow Bligh's other, far more reasonable order and speak to Martin.

Alas, just as Fryer takes the first step past Christian, the new commander of the *Bounty* puts the pointy end of the bayonet to the old Master's breast and says firmly, 'Sir, if you advance an inch further, I will run you through.'[118]

Turning to the two men who are clearly now his own key Lieutenants, Sumner and Quintal, Christian says sharply, 'Take him down to his Cabin!'[119]

Fryer walks back to the hatchway where he sees Millward and Morrison preparing to launch the Jolly Boat.

'Morrison,' Fryer challenges him. 'I hope you have no hand in this business?'

'No, sir,' Morrison replies, seemingly mortified at the very suggestion. 'I do not know a word about it.'[120]

Fryer leans in close, and says to him in a low, conspiratorial voice, 'If that's the case, be on your guard. There may be an opportunity of recovering ourselves.'[121]

But Morrison will have none of it. Yes, he really is a Loyalist, but in this instance what counts for much more than that is that he is a REALIST.

Leaning in close himself, he offers sage advice: 'Go down to your cabin, sir, it is too late.'[122]

At Fryer's suddenly crestfallen countenance, Morrison at least makes one promise: 'I will endeavour to do my best.'[123]

Hearing them, John Millward leans in, and whispers, 'I will stand by you if opportunity offers.'[124]

All three quickly shake hands. They are in this together.

Alas, no sooner has Fryer opened his mouth to whisper one more thing, than Quintal's arm is suddenly around his neck, even as a pistol is jammed in his side.

'Come, Fryer, you must go down into your *Cabin*,'[125] says Quintal in a level, calculated voice, as he hauls Fryer away.

Meanwhile, Churchill strides towards Morrison, brandishing his cutlass like a hungry farmer with an axe who wants chicken for dinner.

'What did Mr Fryer say?'[126] demands Churchill.

'He only asked me if they were going to have the Long-boat,'[127] replies and lies Morrison.

Alas, it is now that Alec Smith, who has been standing on the other side of the deck, but still within earshot, speaks up.

'It's a damned lie, Charley,' he says, pointing to Morrison, 'for I saw *him* and Millward shake hands when the Master spoke to them.'[128]

Millward, too?

Of *all* the people, Churchill is most outraged to hear that his former partner in crime and desertion should now be joining in a plot against them. But, let him deal with that cur in due course. First let him deal with a more expected traitor to the cause.

Glaring at Morrison, he pauses for a moment to mass the menace, and then says straight:

'I would have *you* mind how you *come on*, for I have my eye *upon you.*'[129]

As it happens, Smith, with a better eye than most for the popular mood, is certain that more than Charley's eye is needed here, and now roars to all the Mutineers, 'Stand to your arms, for they intend to make a *Rush!*'[130]

Instantly the Mutineers bring their weapons to bear. Just let one of the Loyalists, just *one* of them, make a move right now, and it will be the last thing he ever does. The seconds pass like bugs crawling across the deck, each bug expecting oblivion to fall in an instant, but there is nothing. No-one makes a move. Yes, the Loyalists might indeed rush the Mutineers, but not right now.

With the situation once again in hand, Smith and Churchill corral Morrison and lead him at the points of their cutlasses towards where Christian is standing over Bligh, where they can keep both eyes on him. As they approach, Bligh addresses Smith.

'I did not expect you would be against me, Smith,'[131] the Captain says.

'I act only as the others do,' scowls Smith in reply, as if that is explanation enough. 'I must be like the rest.'[132]

Alec Smith is a survivor, not a hero.

•

In a morning of scarcely credible shocks, Fryer is more than usually shocked. For Christian, after having been informed of Fryer's whispers and handshakes, has placed three guards in his cabin to keep a close eye on him – Quintal, Sumner and . . . Millward!

The very man he and Morrison had shaken hands with, just minutes earlier, sealing a pact to retake the *Bounty*?

Yes. Somehow, the combination of an angry Churchill and a proffered bayonet to his belly had made Millward think again, and he had decided to throw in his lot with Christian after all. They stand, squashed, in Fryer's cabin, looming over him, their pistols pointing at the Master, daring him to try anything.

Still, Fryer has not given up hope. If Millward's loyalty can turn so easily, he might well be able to turn it again. When Sumner's attention wanders momentarily the Master winks at Millward, and with a meaningful nod makes 'a motion for him to knock the man down that was next to him'.[133]

But Mr Fryer is not in luck.

For, despite their previous pact, Millward's sole response is to cock his pistol, and point it straight at Fryer's head.

'Mr Fryer,' he says loudly, to the man who has said not a word, 'be quiet, no one will hurt you.'

Fryer, thus, remains even more silent than before, but notes that his silence is not rewarded, as Millward keeps his pistol trained.

'Millward,' the Master says quietly, 'your Piece is cocked, you had better uncock it, as you may shoot some person.'[134]

Millward smiles, averting the pistol's aim from the Master.

'There is no one who wishes to shoot you,' he tells Fryer quietly.

'No, that was our agreement,' agrees Sumner. 'Not to commit murder.'[135]

Very commendable, gentlemen.

•

Bligh might be tied but his hopes run free. Although the Mutineers have all the weapons, their numbers remain small – just ten in all by his reckoning. If the Loyalists rush them, it will be over. The problem remains, however: though the Mutineers might be overwhelmed, they will certainly be able to kill whichever of the unarmed Loyalists attack them *first*.

Bligh decides his best chance is to appeal to one of the young officers among the Mutineers – like Ned Young, who is coming towards him, a stripling junior officer, who has been seduced by the charm of Christian – to return from treason to reason, by force of his *own* force of personality.

As Ned Young walks by, Bligh ventures gravely, 'This is a serious affair, Mr Young.'

'Yes, it is a serious affair to be starved,' spits Young through the gap in his teeth. 'I hope this day to get a belly full!'[136]

And that is the end of that conversation.

Other officers Bligh does not bother with, as he is already discerning that their feelings run too deep. Stewart, for example, dances up to the bound Bligh and hoots gleefully, 'This is the happiest day of my life!'[137] then starts performing a joyful *Heiva*, until . . .

Until, spotting it, Christian decides that 'dancing and clapping his hands in the Tahitian manner',[138] right in Bligh's face, is not the solemn example to set to already excitable, increasingly reckless Mutineers, and sharply orders Stewart below deck.

But there proves to be no putting this particular genie back in the bottle, now that all fear of Bligh has gone and disrespect no longer risks the lash. Even some of the young men that Bligh had gone out of his way to nurture, hoping to turn them into warrant officers, are now turning on him. Most hurtful is his long-time favourite, young Tom Ellison. For when another volunteer is needed to guard the Captain, the familiar voice of Monkey rings out.

'Damn him,' says he, caught up in the excitement of it all, 'I will be sentry over him.'[139] Bligh's blood boils. He has cared for Monkey, he has invested time in him, teaching him to *read*, to do arithmetic. And this – *this pure betrayal* – is how he repays him?

•

It is time to launch the Jolly Boat. Norman climbs aboard and descends with it.

Christian now gives a sharp order, which the recipients take as tantamount to a death sentence.

'Mr. Hayward and Mr. Hallett, I order you to go into the Boat.'[140]

What! This is news to the young Midshipmen, terrible news, the worst possible news. It is one thing to be loyal to Bligh, but quite another to get into a tiny vessel like that with him, in the middle of the ocean, with so few supplies.

'I hope not, what harm did I ever do you, Mr. Christian, that you should send me in the Boat?'[141] Mr Hayward asks.

For his part, Hallett starts to weep, the tears rolling down his darkly tanned, rough and wrinkly, weathered cheeks.

'I hope you will not insist upon it, Mr. Christian,'[142] Hallett begs.

Hayward also begins to cry, the two grown men suddenly shuddering wrecks.

'GO! Into the Boat!'[143] is Christian's reply.

And now, here is another, Bligh's Clerk, Samuel.

'Mr Samuel, I order you to go into the boat.'

Samuel is not at all surprised, as he had already been told of his fate and had spent the time since gathering his things and, more importantly, those of Bligh's, even as Smith does his best to get his Captain back to basic respectability. Getting his trousers on is not too hard, with Bligh lifting one leg at a time, but, of course, with Bligh's hands tied, the only thing he can do for the top half is to 'lay his jacket over his shoulders'.[144]

And now the new Captain, Fletcher Christian, has a new, and more important, task for him.

'Bring up a bottle of rum, Mr Smith,'[145] orders Christian. For mutiny is proving to be thirsty work.

'Give every man a dram out of Captain Bligh's Case, that is under Arms.'[146]

Bligh is pleased. It will be a quick way to identify who is a Mutineer – whoever takes this criminal communion – and who is a Loyalist: those who decline.

But now, dramatic news comes from below.

'Mr Christian,' calls Norman from the Jolly Boat. 'She is sinking, she has a large hole in her!'[147]

Damn. Fryer was right, the boat has been eaten by worms.

There is nothing to do but to allow Norman to abandon ship – the water is now halfway up his calves – and haul the holey Jolly Boat back on board to be repaired.

'Mr Cole,' Christian says to his co-conspirator of just hours earlier, 'hoist the Boat out.'[148]

Yes, that's it, the Cutter, the second-largest boat available, is the answer.

But Cole makes no move, almost as if his feet are stuck in tar on the deck. It had been one thing to help Fletcher with the raft last night, when it was dark, and there was no-one around. But to follow his orders now, in searing sunlight, with many witnesses, including Bligh, is quite another. You need to be a committed Mutineer to take an order from Christian in front of Bligh – for it is a death sentence if Bligh survives long enough to inform the Admiralty – and Cole is not committed at all.

'Damn you, Mr Cole,'[149] says Christian, shaking his bayonet towards him. 'If you do not do it instantly, I will take care of you.'[150]

Under threat, Cole heads towards the Cutter as Christian turns to Purcell.

'Mr Purcell, get the large Cutter ready.'[151]

Purcell's feet, too, prove to be stuck in tar. Christian's bayonet glints in the bright sunshine.

'Do you get the Boat ready directly?'[152] asks Christian, brandishing the bayonet.

Well, when you put it like that, the answer is also yes, and Purcell is soon helping Cole.

Keenly observing the whole scene, Bligh is slightly puzzled. He has no clue that both men being ordered around by Christian were voluntarily helping the Lieutenant the night before to build his raft and plot his escape, but he nevertheless notes a strange hesitation in Christian's commands to these two men. Of course Christian is not easily disposed to order around two recent, kind allies, but Bligh misreads the reasons and concludes that Christian is hesitant about going through with the whole mutiny. *Now* is the time for another appeal.

'Consider what you are about, Mr. Christian,' says Bligh. 'For God's sake drop it and there shall be no more come of it.'[153]

''Tis too late, Captain Bligh,'[154] says Captain Christian.

'No, Mr. Christian, it is not too late yet,' Bligh responds. 'I'll forfeit my Honour if ever I speak of it; I'll give you my bond that there shall never be any more come of it.'[155]

It is a desperate offer from a man Christian despises nearly as much as he distrusts him. By some measure it is a handsome offer, too, but would he bet his life on William Bligh keeping his word? He would not.

'No, Captain Bligh,' replies Christian. 'If you had any honour things would not have come to this.'[156]

Bligh's face turns ashen. It is one thing to be mutinied against, to have one's buttocks exposed, and wrists tied before the mizzenmast. But it is quite another to have his honour called into question.

'You know, Captain Bligh,' Christian says, 'you have treated me like a dog all the voyage. I have been in Hell this fortnight past and I am determined to suffer it no longer.'[157]

And yet, no sooner do Cole and Purcell overhear the Captain's offer than they too beg Mr Christian to drop the whole thing.

But Christian will not listen.

What was that thing his brother Charles had told him in the dark seamen's tavern back at Spithead, just before he had come on this voyage? He remembers now. Charles had brought his head forward in a conspiratorial *tête-à-tête*, leaned in and told him a tale of mutiny and mayhem on the High Seas.

'When men are cooped up for a long time in the interior of a ship,' his brother had advised, 'there oft prevails such a jarring discordancy of tempers and conduct that it is often on many occasions repeated acts of irritation and offence to change the disposition of a lamb into that of an animal fierce and resentful.'[158]

And that is exactly it, dear brother.

'You know, Cole, how I have been used,' Christian hisses, fierce and resentful.

'I know it very well, Mr. Christian,' replies Cole. 'We all knew it, but drop it, for God's sake.'[159]

Unstated, there is a plea here: Christian, Purcell and I took a huge risk last night, helping you to build a raft. But now, you have escalated this into a full-blown mutiny, perhaps even a murderous mutiny, and you have placed our lives at risk! And make no mistake, Fletcher, to abandon four men in a boat as small as the Cutter *will* be murder. You must think again, Fletcher.

For his part, Hayward is anything but tacit, and actually falls to his knees and begs Christian to change his mind on the whole exercise.

'Consider, Mr. Christian,' he burbles, 'what a dangerous step you have taken.'[160]

Sensing the rising of Christian's humanity, his realisation that it really would be akin to murder, Bligh presses his case, his voice not taunting this time, but almost reasonable . . .

'Can there be no other method taken?'[161] asks the deposed Captain.

The question has been addressed, in an almost genteel manner, to Fletcher Christian – effectively, 'Captain' to 'Captain' – but Churchill, for one, refuses to recognise the protocol and has a sharp answer himself for Bligh's query.

'NO!' he yells. 'This is the best and only method!'[162]

Snapping out of his momentary détente with Bligh, Christian agrees with Churchill. Putting Bligh and his Loyalists into the Cutter is the only way. Hoist the Cutter into the water, men. It can hold up to six men, so there will be plenty of room for Bligh and three Loyalists, together with whatever supplies they take. Certainly, they will not be able to go much beyond the nearest island in such a vessel, and will be marooned there, but that is surely the best thing. They will at least likely survive, and it may well be years before they are rescued, allowing the Mutineers plenty of time to make good their escape, resettle elsewhere, or do whatever it is they are going to do – that part of the plan has not yet been quite worked out.

In the spirit of working much of it out as they go along, Cole, noting that the boat now in the water is bumping alongside the hull of the *Bounty*, orders Michael Byrn, the Blind Fiddler, to climb down into it and to make sure it does not thump against the ship too hard while other preparations are made. Byrn, highly confused as to what is going on, simply does as he is told. Meanwhile, Cole, with Purcell by his side, appeals to Fletcher directly.

'Mr Christian, give us the Long Boat,'[163] pleads Cole referring to the 23-foot Launch. Christian makes no reply.

Us? Christian is shocked. These are good men. They know, and have acknowledged to him, what a brute Bligh is. And yet, instead of coming with him on the *Bounty*, they would choose to bob in the South Pacific with the bastard Bligh? It beggars belief. But it is true, Mr Cole and Mr Purcell will exit now with Bligh.

'Mr Christian, give us the Long Boat,' Cole says again. 'Give us the long boat.'

The words are repeated exactly, with intent, to emphasise the unspoken meaning behind these words.

You are in our debt, Fletcher. We helped you last night. You must help us now.

Still there is no reply. And yet Bligh can sense that Christian is wavering under Cole's pleas, and implores him to go further. 'For God's sake, Mr Cole,' Bligh booms. 'Do all that lays in your power!'[164]

'Mr Christian, give us the Long Boat,'[165] Cole repeats yet one more time, and is quickly followed by Purcell.

'Mr Christian, if you meant to turn us adrift in the boat,' the Carpenter pleads, 'let us have the Launch and not make a sacrifice of us.'[166]

We will not be Mutineers. We wish to return to England, to our lives, our wives. Help us, Fletcher.

All falls silent, as everyone waits on the decision by the man with the sweaty brow, Fletcher Christian.

Drip, drip, drip . . .

The sun beats down. The tension rises. The silence hangs heavier still.

The fact that Christian has said nothing, the men know, means he is wavering. Purcell senses it, and now makes a cryptic comment that Bligh again notes, without understanding.

'I have done nothing,' Purcell says, 'that I am ashamed or afraid of, I want to see my Native Country.'[167]

Christian knows what he means: we helped you last night, to desert, *not* to mutiny. Now *you* must help *us*. We wish to see England once more.

Finally, Christian makes his decision. He has begun this mutiny to defend his honour. And so, in the name of keeping that honour intact, he says in an almost defeated tone, 'Hoist out the Launch, Mr Cole.'[168]

He has decided to be generous, as he will later explain it, 'not for Bligh's sake, but for the safety of those that were going with him'.[169]

Either way, it is done. The Loyalists, whoever they may be, have the Launch! It is possible, just possible, they will survive this, and return to England. Granted, the Launch is designed to hold just 13 men, and will provide them no shelter, but it has two masts for sails, and a rudder, *and* it is in much better condition than the Jolly Boat.

Purcell takes it as a personal victory. If he makes it back home, it will be with a clean bill of health, at least from the point of view of treason.

CHAPTER EIGHT

ADRIFT ON THE HIGH SEAS

If we fairly consider the different situations of a common sailor on board ... and of a Tahitian on his island, we cannot blame the former if he attempted to rid himself of the numberless discomforts of a voyage around the world, and preferred an easy life, free from cares, in the happiest climate of the world, to the frequent vicissitudes which are entailed upon the mariner. The most favourable prospects of future success in England, which he might form an idea, could never be so flattering to his senses as the lowly hope of living like the meanest Tahitian ... he must earn his subsistence in England, at the expense of labour, and by the sweat of his brow, when this oldest curse on mankind is scarcely felt at Tahiti.[1]

German naturalist Johann Forster, who accompanied his father on James Cook's second voyage, 1772–1775

I can only conjecture that [the Mutineers] have ideally assured themselves of a more happy life among the Tahitians than they could possibly have in England, which joined to some female connection, has most likely been the leading cause of the whole business.[2]

William Bligh, journal entry, 28 April 1789

The gallant Chief within his cabin slept,
Secure in those by whom the watch was kept:
His dreams were of old England's welcome shore,
Of toils rewarded, and of danger o'er;
...
The worst was over, and the rest seemed sure,

And why should not his slumber be secure?
Alas! his deck was trod by unwilling feet,
And wilder hands would hold the vessel's sheet;
Young hearts, which languished for some sunny isle,
Where summer years and summer women smile;
Men without country, who, too long estranged,
Had found no native home, or found it changed,
And, half uncivilised, preferred the cave
Of some soft savage to the uncertain wave – [3]

Lord Byron, 'The Island'

Early morning, 28 April 1789, *Bounty*, A choice of deaths . . .

After Bligh has been static under armed guard for well over an hour, all is now flurry, hurry and worry on what was once His Majesty's *Bounty*, as the preparations continue for the Loyalists to depart on the Launch. Just who the Loyalists are, exactly, is still not quite clear – least of all to many of the men themselves, who must make the choice of their lives.

And here is one such mystery man, Peter Heywood, who has only just been allowed up on deck. He turns numb with shock to see his Captain tightly bound and held at the end of Fletcher Christian's glinting bayonet.

It is like coming on deck and seeing a whale walking around, smoking a pipe and chatting with your grandmother – something so completely unbelievable, he can't quite grasp it. But one thing is soon clear – he must choose between the *Launch of Loyalists* and HMS *Mutiny*.

It is, he is certain, little more than 'a choice of deaths'.[4] Suddenly trembling, his mind turns homewards, to his cherished family; his sweet saintly mother, his dear sisters and brothers, all waiting for him. He is too young to die!

All around him, others of the ship's company who have not been involved with either side to this point must also make a snap decision. And there is no doubt which death is proving the more popular.

The vast majority seek to go with . . . Bligh.

To Christian's equal amazement and crushing disappointment, all of Norton, Linkletter, Lebogue, Hall, Ledward, Simpson, Elphinstone, his fellow Master's Mate, and more, are carrying their hastily packed, bulging kits up from their berths and pushing forward to the gangway – for there is a cluttered *crowd* there – to climb down the rope ladder one last time, and clamber into the Launch. Originally, Christian had planned on just four men leaving the *Bounty* – Bligh, Hayward, Hallett and Samuel. But now it seems nearly half the ship, and maybe over half, is prepared to leave the relative comfort and immediate safety of the *Bounty* to go with the infernal Bligh in the Launch.

It is a slap in the face to Christian, and a strong one.

And yet, the truth is, it is not personal.

However high their regard for Christian as a man, however deep their disdain for Captain Bligh, there is no way around the fact that staying on the *Bounty* means never seeing England again, never getting back to home and hearth, never again seeing their wives, their children, their wider family and friends. And there is equally no doubt that to choose, and to be seen to choose, to stay with Christian means betraying the Admiralty, the Country, and King George III. It means they risk ending their lives early, and in disgrace, dangling from the end of a rope. Yes, by choosing to go in the Launch, they may perish – either at sea, or on an island – but at least they will go to their graves as men loyal to England and their families.

Bligh smiles in satisfaction to see the shock, the disappointment, on Christian's face as, one by one, the Loyalists step forward and ask permission to climb down into the Launch – each departure a further rebuke to the leading Mutineer, and his hasty mutiny.

Fletcher Christian is deeply affected.

'Something more than fear,' he would recount, 'had possessed them to suffer themselves to be sent away in such a manner.'[5]

•

It is not as if all the Mutineers are altogether unreasonable.

When Fryer makes the point to the two guarding him that, as he is being guarded in any case, he may as well be guarded in the cockpit, where Peckover and Nelson are now being held prisoner, they agree!

In the cockpit, Fryer finds Nelson fretting.

'Mr. Fryer,' says the botanist, 'what have we brought on ourselves?'[6]

For his part, Peckover, the saltiest man on board, is more disposed to action than reflection.

'What is best to be done, Mr. Fryer?'[7]

'What do you mean to do for the best?'[8] replies Fryer.

'I wish to get home if I possibly can,'[9] replies Peckover. It is his way of saying, he does not wish to stay on the *Bounty*, as it is clear to him, just as it is to the Loyalists climbing down into the Launch, that under Christian it can be bound for England no more.

Take heart, gentlemen. Quietly, ever stoical, Fryer confides to them the conversation he has had with Captain Bligh, and his own plans to stay on the ship, seize back control when the opportunity arises and find the marooned Bligh.

'I flatter myself,' Fryer says confidently, 'that we shall recover the Ship in a short time.'[10]

Peckover furrows his greying brow with concern:

'[Surely] by staying behind we should be reckoned as Pirates, if we should ever be taken.'[11]

'No,' Fryer reassures him, 'I will answer for you and everyone that will join with me.'[12]

Nearby, in the bread-room, Mutineer Henry Hillbrant is fetching some bread to put in the boat – mutineers, not murderers – when he happens to . . . hear every word Fryer and Peckover utter. A rebellion in the midst of the rebellion! Forgetting the bread, he rushes up on deck and, breathless, repeats the conversation to Christian in his heavy German accent. Within seconds, Fryer is being escorted back to his cabin by his armed guard, and they have news for him.

'Christian,' they tell him, 'has consented to give Captain Bligh the Launch, not for his sake but the safety of those who are going with him.'[13]

'Do you know who is going into the Boat with Captain Bligh?'[14] Fryer asks the guard.

'No, but I believe a great many,'[15] is the reply.

A 'great many'? Only an hour ago, there had only been three men due to go with Bligh. But now the numbers have swelled enormously. That is a good sign. He hopes.

Or is it?

How many can the Launch hold exactly?

•

As Bligh's servant John Smith appears on deck bearing a bottle of rum from *his* Captain's cabin as ordered, Captain Fletcher Christian is the first to take a deep swig. Christian orders John Smith to offer a dram to all Mutineers. *Well, this will be interesting.* Bligh observes closely all those who take this criminal communion, deciding to devote all his energies from this point forth to surviving long enough to see each man who drinks with the Devil hanged.

You, Billy McCoy, drink hearty while you may, for you will hang, as will you, John Williams, Thomas Burkett and John Millward and yes, even young Monkey Ellison – perhaps the cruellest cut of all. Oh how busy is John Smith, now the rum steward to traitors, as he continues to serve drams hither and yon, finally ending up near the small Cutter where Morrison is collecting up yams to be handed down to the Launch.

(The irony is more excruciating than exquisite. The very yams designated by Bligh as punishment for his officers are now being gathered up to be put in the Launch as Bligh's new staple diet. Let him eat yams!)

Sweating profusely, exhausted by the events of the morning, Morrison looks longingly at the rum, and licks his parched lips.

'You may as well have a drop, Morrison,' says Smith. 'Though I am ordered to serve none but the sentinels.'[16]

Taking the cup, Morrison throws a slug of restorative rum down his throat, unaware that Bligh, from this point forth, has marked him down on his list of those deserving Eternal Damnation.

Now walking out of Bligh's sight, towards the windlass, Smith comes across young Peter Heywood, his back turned, hands in pockets, staring out at the distant horizon.

'Rum, Mr Heywood?'

'I refuse,'[17] Heywood replies firmly, his decision now taken, albeit unseen and unheard by Captain Bligh who simply presumes that, as Heywood is the best friend of his fellow Manxman, Fletcher Christian, he must have been in on the plot all along.

For, now that Bligh thinks of it (and his mind will think of little else for some time to come), just whose names were on that list of Churchill's when he deserted? He can see it now:

Fletcher Christian, Peter Heywood . . .

How foolish he had been not to see the truth then and there. Christian, Churchill and Heywood were in cahoots from the beginning! No doubt it was they who slashed the cable, in an attempt to cast the ship adrift, back in Tahiti, with their purpose of remaining there, 'effectually answered, without danger, if the ship had been driven on shore'.[18] All those signs, and he has missed them all. Damnation, he has been humbugged!

•

Like a mini water-spout, Purcell, that most unlikely of Loyalists, moves all over the *Bounty*, picking up whatever he can, whatever may prove to be of any use to a group of sailors floating in a little tub in the middle of the ocean, as well as giving out orders.

'McIntosh, Norman,' he says, 'fill a bucket of nails of different sizes, and hand a crosscut and whip saw out of the storeroom.'[19]

Yes, Mr Purcell.

Heading to his own cabin next, he gathers a looking glass and some trinkets which he puts in his wooden clothes chest. He lugs the chest awkwardly up the ladder and onto the deck, then hands it down to the men already in the Launch.

Still there is more. Mr Purcell also lowers down 'Boats' Sails, a lower Studding Sail, Twine, Remnants of Canvas',[20] before getting to the most precious thing of all. That, of course, is his precious tool chest. He begins to lower it . . . eeeasy, lads, slooowly . . . only to be stopped by the rough and chomping Quintal.

'Damn me, if we let them have those things they will build a Vessel in a month!'[21] he says to his fellow Mutineers.

Churchill both roughly agrees, and agrees roughly – viciously barking that Purcell's tool chest must be returned on deck, or there will be trouble. In an instant it is returned and Churchill quickly opens it, rifling through and removing the best of the tools. Purcell, as fiercely territorial as ever defending the privileges and property of the Carpenter, himself – *Mutiny or no mutiny, these tools are mine and anybody who tries to lay even a finger on them, will answer to me, even if he is carrying a loaded musket* – grows red with rage.

•

Meanwhile, Bligh's clerk, Samuel, is securing as many of the Captain's instruments, charts and papers as he can. Dropping the first bundle on the deck, he heads back to Bligh's cabin to collect more when Christian barks at him: 'You are forbidden, on pain of death, to touch either map, ephemeris, book of astronomical observations, sextant, time-keeper, or any surveys or drawings.'[22]

Overhearing, Bligh reels, ashen-faced. In a day of infamy, this is one of the cruellest cuts of all. To not have his precious charts, the very ones he had drawn so carefully on Captain Cook's last voyage of the South Pacific, as well as his latest from this voyage – they are no less than the better part of his life's work – is an unimaginable horror, an irrecoverable loss. As to the loss of instruments, they will render him little more than a blind man on the oceans.

Of course Bligh remonstrates, providing a distraction that allows Samuel to rush below. Rifling through Bligh's various papers, he finds gold. On the reckoning that Fletcher Christian made no mention of the current Log, he tucks it into the bundle and goes on deck once more. Bligh sighs with relief just to see the Log poking out the side of the roughly wrapped parcel – without it, he has no precious documentary proof of what he has done.

'My honour and character might have been suspected,' he would later write, 'without my possessing a proper document to have defended them.'[23]

There are a few other things in the parcel, though, that the dutiful Samuel does not manage to slip past the guard-dogs on deck.

When gruff Churchill finds in Samuel's parcel Bligh's box of 'surveys, drawings, and remarks for fifteen years past, which were numerous', he roars at the clerk: 'Damn your eyes, you are well off to get what you have.'[24]

•

Cole continues to scour the *Bounty*, begging for supplies, scrounging what he can, filling his pockets as he goes, and has just snatched up a compass from the small stand by the helm, when an angry roar from behind makes him jump.

'I'll be damned if you shall have that!'[25] Quintal snarls, mad and despotic, just like Bligh has shown him – the student becomes the master. 'What do you want with a compass when land is in sight?'[26]

The Loyalists are being given a chance to live on the small island of Tofoa, some 30 miles off. They have no use for any instruments!

'There are plenty more in the Storeroom!' Cole begs. 'It is very hard [of you] when there are nine conditioned Compasses below!'[27]

Still Quintal refuses, and so Cole turns his eyes to reluctant Mutineer Thomas Burkett for help.

'It is *very* hard I cannot have *one* out of so many,'[28] Cole pleads.

'Take it,'[29] says Burkett.

'Damn my Eyes, we may as well give [Bligh] the ship!'[30] says Quintal, who realises more than most that in this situation Bligh with a compass is like an angry archer with a bow, a smouldering swordsman with a sword, a seething soldier with a musket – it not only completes him, but makes him dangerous indeed.

Still, reflecting on it, Quintal realises it is of no matter. How are they to survive in that tiny boat, for even a few days, let alone make a grand voyage to a European outpost? Impossible.

So all right then, you may have your single compass, Cole, if it will just shut you up.

The angry archer will have his bow, the smouldering swordsman his sword, the seething soldier his musket and, it seems, the bitter Bligh will have his compass.

•

After being confined to his cabin for what feels like hours, Fryer is at last permitted to receive a single visitor. It is 'the Boy', his brother-in-law, young Tinkler. And the Boy is weeping.

'Mr Churchill has told me that I am to stay aboard,'[31] the Boy sobs. 'To be his servant.'[32]

Fryer will be damned before he lets that happen. He reassures Tinkler that he will intervene, so the young fellow dries his tears on his sleeve, and heads back up on deck.

Fryer remains 'building castles in the air',[33] as he later puts it, working on his schemes to retake the *Bounty*. The fact that Christian has reportedly served out rum is promising.

Could it be possible, Mr Fryer wonders, or maybe even probable, that if the Mutineers get drunk enough, then 'two or three would retake the ship'?[34]

It will depend on how drunk the Mutineers get, who the two or three are, and what weapons they might hold. *Think, man, think.*

There must be a way.

•

On deck, tense voices are heard by the mizzenmast. Purcell and Churchill are going hammer and tongs over, well, over Purcell's hammer and tongs – and other assorted tools. Just as Purcell has insisted to Bligh, on many occasions, that his tools are *not* the property of the Royal Navy, but his own property, he now insists they are even *less* the property of the Mutineers, do you hear? For his property is going into the Launch; that is where it is going, not staying on the *Bounty*. Churchill is less concerned with legal niceties, or Purcell's quirks, and far more concerned with the fact that he has a musket pointed at Purcell's chest, which in his view trumps any argument the Carpenter might care to make.

'Mr. Christian,' Purcell appeals to the only one who can, in turn, trump the view of Churchill. 'I ask for my Tool Chest, Whip, and Cross cut saw!'[35]

Before the new Captain can make reply, Bligh makes a quiet suggestion into his ear, with Loyalist Thomas McIntosh close enough that he can hear every word.

'You let us have that Tool Chest,' Bligh says to his usurper, almost respectfully. 'You have got a very good one in the ship, and you may keep the Carpenter's two mates.'[36]

McIntosh starts. *He* is one of the two mates in question! Yes, even as he listens in, his fate – whether he lives or dies, whether he is with the Loyalists or the Mutineers – is being bargained by Bligh for a set of tools!

Now, although Christian does not reply to Bligh directly, he does indeed order Churchill to let Purcell have his Tool Chest. With all his tools in it.

In reply, Churchill ... pauses ... and glares ... before speaking.

Gesturing towards Bligh, he says, 'I'll be damned if he does not get home if he gets anything with him.'[37]

Still, Churchill finally obeys his new commander, and, though surly to the point of menace, hands the Tool Chest to a puffed up and smirking Purcell, before turning again to give Christian a withering look, which says, *on your head be it.*

Such dumb insolence to Bligh would have been rewarded by the cat o' nine tails on his back, but in this case Christian must let it pass. After all, as an officer who has just declared war on his Captain, he can hardly now invoke the Articles of War he has so flagrantly breached, for his own protection.

Bligh had the entire weight of the English legal system, and centuries of Royal Navy tradition, behind him – Christian has only the weight of the confidence of the majority of Mutineers to rely on – and lashing one of them would threaten that very authority.

So, yes, he has made this decision, and it has got through on his authority alone. But there is no telling how long that authority will last. Clearly, if the decision was put to a vote of the Mutineers, Bligh and his men would be, at best, left on the nearest island with no boat, and a bare minimum of supplies and tools. At worst, it would be *much* worse, with one of the increasingly liquored Mutineers suggesting to Churchill the way to put the whole issue concerning Bligh beyond further debate: 'Blow his brains out!'[38]

No, not on Christian's watch, you won't.

•

Back to the task of rushing around, gathering more materials for their survival, Purcell notices Heywood, frozen again, staring out at the ocean, with his hand resting upon a cutlass that is resting upon the mizzenmast's boom.

'In the name of God, Peter, what do you do with that?'[39] asks Purcell, genuinely gobsmacked.

Young Heywood looks absently down at his hand and drops the cutlass instantly, as if it is red-hot. It falls with a clatter to the clutter on the deck, where materials for the Launch are being heaped.

Shaking, awed by the rapidity of events so far beyond his control that he is no more than flotsam in their wake, the 16-year-old ruefully shakes his head.

The question is still racing through his clouded mind: Which choice of deaths will he choose? Bligh or Fletcher?

What he truly wants, of course, is to choose neither. A firm friend of Fletcher's, he admires everything about him, and can see why he so detests Bligh. But join him as a Mutineer? And so never again see his family – his beloved mother, his cherished sister Nessy? He can barely stand the thought of it. For the moment, he decides to keep his powder dry, not touching any more cutlasses on the way through, and see what happens.

As it happens, he is not the only one who has been doing some hard thinking about which side to take.

Down in the Launch, Purcell is fussing around the supplies, working out how best to stack them, when he is stunned with the arrival of one person in particular. It is the first sailor to agree to the Mutiny, Isaac Martin! With his bag, packed.

'Mr Martin, what are *you* doing here?' asks Purcell, stunned, and angered, to see him.

'I am going in the boat,' replies Martin as a simple statement of fact, for all the world as if he had not thrown in his lot with Christian, just hours ago.

'Mr Martin, if ever we get to England,' Purcell shouts, 'I'll endeavour to HANG YOU MYSELF!'[40]

Attracted by all the shouting, Quintal and Churchill peer over the side of the *Bounty* and are also stunned to see Isaac Martin standing in the Launch.

They train their muskets on the turncoat's turncoat.

'Mr Martin,' says Churchill, so softly and politely, it is truly terrifying, 'we desire you to come out of the Boat.'[41]

You are one of us. Now get up here, or be shot down there.

And so ends Martin's brief career as a Loyalist. Up he clambers on deck, a Mutineer once more.

•

Heywood, his gaze still lost seaward, finally chooses his death. Rather than swing from a noose, he decides it better to die with Bligh. In the Launch. Yes, as much as he likes and admires Christian – and sympathises with what he has done – he does not personally wish to be a Mutineer. He is resolved to either see his mother, sisters and brothers once more or die in the attempt.

Heading below deck thus, to gather his belongings, he passes Cole, who is heading the other way.

'I will fetch a few necessaries in a bag,' Peter says to him quietly, 'and follow you into the boat.'[42]

•

There is no way around it – the combined mass of the Loyalists and the stores they wish to take with them in the Launch is taking the little boat deeper and deeper into the mercifully calm ocean. Morrison observes it all closely.

In addition to all the sails and tools already stowed, Morrison himself now helps to load the boat with . . . two casks of water, four empty breeves, three bags of bread with Mr Bligh's case, some bottles of wine, and several other things, insomuch that she almost sank alongside the *Bounty*.[43]

After all, though a much bigger vessel than the Cutter, the Launch is still only 23 feet long, seven feet wide and three feet deep. And as every Loyalist climbing on board carries a bag full of goods, spare space soon disappears – and it becomes obvious to all. With so *many* Loyalists, Christian has no choice but to keep some of them on the *Bounty* with him.

This is not what he had anticipated, and definitely not what he wished for. Only four men were supposed to go at the outset of the plan – but now that they have divided up, it is clear that there are 22 Loyalists (plus Bligh), and only 21 Mutineers.

And doesn't Bligh know it.

This has been a singularly dark morning for Bligh, but Christian's humiliation is a joyous silver lining. He watches his former Lieutenant squirm with unease as he realises that even so big a boat as the Launch can't accommodate all those who wish to stay true to Bligh, no less than a majority of the crew.

'You can't *all* go in the Boat, my lads,' Bligh yells in a cheerful tone, clearly intended to mock the Captain of the Mutineers and his small mob of traitors. '*Don't* overload her, some of you *must* stay in the Ship.'[44]

As it happens, that is precisely what Morrison is thinking, as he contemplates the tiny and now heavily overladen craft sinking ever lower, so that it now has just a little over half a foot leeway above the sea. One solid wave in a storm, and they would be swamped.

And, after all, Bligh practically had made it an *order*, hadn't he? True, Morrison has made a solid commitment to Fryer that he would try to retake the ship, but now he can't help but notice that most of the Officers are getting into the Launch 'without the least appearance of an effort to *rescue* the Ship'.[45]

Is he really expected to do more than an officer? *Why?*

'I began to reflect on my own situation,' the Bosun's Mate would later recount, 'and seeing the situation of the boat, and considering that she was at least 1000 leagues from *any* friendly Settlement and judging by what I had seen of the Friendly Islanders but a few days before, that nothing could be expected from them but to be *plunder'd*, or *killed*, and seeing no choice but of one evil, I chose, as I thought, the least, to *stay in the ship*, especially as I considered it as obeying Captain Bligh's orders.'[46]

Yes, of course Morrison wants to see England again, but to do that, first he must live, and for him – even as confident as he is that the Lord is always by his side – that means staying with the *Bounty*. Quietly, thus, Morrison takes Cole aside, to tell him that he has kept his promise – he will not be joining Christian and his Mutineers. Now he will stay on the *Bounty* with the Loyalists.

'*God bless you, my boy*,'[47] Cole says warmly, grasping Morrison by the hand, before gingerly climbing down into the ever more cramped Launch. Morrison also bids adieu to Hayward, only to be told something surprising by the hitherto timid Midshipman.

'I intend,' he whispers, 'to knock Charley Churchill down.'[48]

'I will second you,' Morrison replies. In fact, with a wave of his hand towards bulbous wooden clubs they had gathered at the Friendly Islands, he cracks hardy, 'There are tools enough!'[49]

But . . . to Morrison's stupefaction, the suddenly big-talking Hayward has just as suddenly reverted to the blancmange he always was, and makes no move. Instead, he climbs down the swaying ladder into the Launch.

•

Young Peter Heywood is no sooner in his cabin, stuffing his own knife, bowl, spoon, extra shirt, his Bible, drawing pencils and papers, and brooch with a portrait of his mother into a bag than a harsh and hateful voice rings out: 'Keep them below!'[50]

It is Churchill yelling to sentinel Martin – the Launch is too full and the Mutineers risk being too sparse to run the *Bounty*. From now, everyone who remains must stay aboard the *Bounty*.

George Stewart and Peter Heywood, the only two young officers left below, look at each other. The decision, Peter realises, has been taken out of their hands. The fixed bayonet of Isaac Martin, pointed at their soft bellies, says they are not going anywhere, and will be staying on the *Bounty*, unless Christian orders otherwise.

•

There is one person that Fletcher Christian *insists* must go with Bligh and he will not enter into any discussion on the subject.

This way, Fryer, on Captain Christian's orders. Led from his cabin on the end of a musket, the Master is now brought up on deck once more, where, as seagulls caterwaul about and cry at his unhappy fate, he tells Bligh that he wishes to remain on board the *Bounty*. Bligh heartily agrees. (No, he has no expectation that Fryer might actually be able to retake the ship. But at least if Fryer stays on the ship he will be rid of the old woman.)

Most importantly of all, as he already has 16 men on the Launch, there is simply no more room.

'Mr. Christian, let Mr. Fryer and some of the people stay in the Ship,' Bligh says in a tone that is half order and half request, 'as the boat will be overloaded.'[51]

'The people may stay, but Mr. Fryer must go in the boat,'[52] replies Christian in a tone that brooks no negotiation.

'Mr Churchill, see the Officers into the boat and take care that Norman, McIntosh and Coleman are kept in the ship.'[53]

Aye, Aye, Captain Christian.

The three Loyalists Christian has chosen to stay on the *Bounty* have not been chosen by chance. The first two, of course, the Carpenter's Mates, McIntosh and Norman, have been effectively bargaining chips in return for Mr Purcell being allowed to take many of his tools in the Launch. Their skills will be of use. And then there's the Armourer, Coleman, who will be invaluable in making and maintaining tools, weapons and ammunition – something that may well be crucial if, some months or years in the future, the Mutineers find themselves pursued and attacked by the Royal Navy. These three are now prisoners upon their own ship. Still, looking down from the secure deck of the *Bounty*, onto the packed and tiny bobbing boat below, none of them complains too bitterly.

Or, perhaps, their complaints are simply drowned out by Fryer.

'You had better let me stay, Mr. Christian,' he pleads, 'for you'll not know what to do with the Ship.'[54]

Christian is unconvinced and retorts with a sardonic scoff: 'We can do very well without you, Mr. Fryer.'[55]

(Truly, Christian would rather be rid of the tiresome wretch, no matter where his sympathies lie.)

As it happens, it is the sole point of tacit agreement between the leaders of the Loyalists and the Mutineers on this day – they'd be better off without the Master – though Bligh feels it so strongly he even gives the stone-faced Fryer a direct order.

'Mr Fryer, stay in the ship,'[56] commands Bligh.

'No, by God, sir,' commands Captain Christian, displaying his trump card in this ongoing game of one-upmanship – the foot-long spike of a sharpened bayonet pointed cruelly, right at Fryer's breast – 'Go into the Boat or I will run you through.'[57]

'Do let Mr Tinkler go with me, Mr Christian!'[58] Fryer pleads.

The Boy, Tinkler, just 13, is family to him. Fryer will not have him be Churchill's vassal, and so he keeps begging.

'No!'[59] cries Churchill, unwilling to lose his future slave.

'He shall go with you,'[60] says Christian, with a sharp look to Churchill. There are 18 in the boat, and 26 on the *Bounty*. There remains just one man left on the *Bounty* who must disembark – William Bligh.

The leader of the Mutineers turns to him.

'Come, Captain Bligh,' says Christian, 'your officers and men are now in the boat, and you must go with them. If you attempt to make the least resistance, you will instantly be put to death.'[61]

Once mentor and student, Bligh and Christian now stand alongside one another as nothing less than the past and present Captains of the *Bounty*; the betrayed and his betrayer, or the tyrant and the avenger – depending on how you look at it.

Bligh tries one last desperate ploy. For even as the mass of Mutineers joyously jeer and sneer at the crammed, jammed sinking mess of a Launch, Bligh can't help but notice that Fletcher Christian appears to be in almost physical pain at the destruction he has wrought.

Of course, Bligh seeks to deepen whatever guilt his one-time friend is feeling and very softly, in a kind, nurturing voice, twists the knife:

'Is this treatment a proper return for the many instances you have received of my friendship?'[62]

Christian reels, as if slapped.

'That, Captain Bligh – that is the thing – I am in hell – I am in hell!'[63]

Bligh is clearly pleased to hear it. For that is exactly where Christian deserves to be. Perhaps the time is right to give the knife another slow twist? Yes, indeed.

'Consider, Mr Christian,' he says softly, 'I have a wife and four children in England, and you have danced my children upon your knee.'[64]

It is the cruellest blow of all. For, whatever his fury at Bligh, Christian adores kind Betsy Bligh and those innocent little girls. The full realisation of what he is doing to the patriarch of the family hits him like a crack to the head.

'My heart melted,' he would later recount to Heywood, 'and I would have jumped overboard, if I could have saved you, but as it was too late to do that, I was obliged to proceed.'[65]

Rallying, Christian comes up with a fair reply, albeit in a faltering voice.

'You should have thought of them sooner yourself, Captain Bligh! It is too late to consider now, I have been in hell for weeks past with you!'[66]

Christian cuts the rope around Bligh's wrists, and Bligh steadies himself to climb down to the Launch, his aching hands on the gunnels, and his feet on the ladder. He looks at the captive Loyalists and the jeering Mutineers alike and declares: 'Never fear, my lads, I'll do you justice if ever I reach England!'[67]

All of them understand. This is a promise ... and a clear threat. Exoneration for the declared Loyalists on board who are there against their will, and the NOOSE for the rest of you triumphal traitorous dogs, starting with Christian.

They are extraordinary, bold words for one now climbing down into an overcrowded tiny boat with few supplies, bobbing thousands of miles from any European outpost, but ...

But Bligh is an extraordinary man.

•

It has all happened with such raging rapidity.

Two and a half hours ago, William Bligh was the sleeping Captain of the *Bounty*. Now, he is the Captain of a 23-foot, overladen Launch floating just off the stern of the *Bounty*, tethered only by a single rope. And already he is finding fault with the order of things, not least the lack of food and water.

'I request some provisions,'[68] Bligh calls up to the ship.

The cry instantly goes up to give him some lead, for starters.

'Shoot the Bugger!'[69]

Roars of rum-fuelled laughter. But one sharp word from Christian and Morrison runs aft and gets 'all the pork which was in the harness Casks, twenty five or six pieces',[70] which are tossed down, a few lost into the water.

Taking advantage of Christian's momentary humanity, Bligh orders the Launch be rowed closer to the *Bounty*, so more things can be handed down. There are two things in particular he wishes for.

'Mr Christian, my commission and sextant, I beg you!'[71]

Bligh, begging?

So lowering himself?

Yes, and for good reason. It is the one hope he has of getting the sextant, the most crucial navigational instrument of all. The greatest navigator in the world – and Bligh has more than a sneaking suspicion that he is that very man – would be as helpless as hopeless as hapless without at least a sextant to work out where they are.

As for the 'commission', that, too, will be crucial, should they make it to any European outpost or be met by a European ship – as it is the formal paper and badge that conveys the confirmation of the Crown itself. And yet, while Christian hands down the commission to the Launch, he refuses to hand down Bligh's sextant, an instrument, he knows, was a personal gift from Sir Joseph Banks on the eve of the *Bounty*'s departure, and is very likely the finest sextant available in the world. That is fine for the Captain of a ship, but far too good for the Captain of a tiny Launch. No, Bligh can make do, instead, with Christian's sextant, along with a book of nautical tables, and Hamilton Moore's *Seaman's Complete Daily Assistant*, which contains the latitude and longitude of all known lands. They will have to do, in the place of maps.

'There, Captain Bligh,' calls Christian, giving Bligh his rank back, if not his ship. 'This is sufficient for every purpose, and you know the sextant to be a good one.'[72]

Though not satisfied, Bligh is at least quietly pleased. From having nothing, he now has a compass, a sextant, a crew and a half-decent boat. And, of course, he has the unshakeable confidence that, as the Royal Navy's finest Captain, and best navigator, he will find a way, notwithstanding the fact he still has not a single chart, and will have to rely on his nautical tables, but this means he at least has a direction to steer for, and to steer away *from*.

In the meantime, though Bligh is relieved to see Morrison hand a couple of water gourds into the Launch, which are gratefully received by many reaching hands, he decides there is a more precious item they absolutely must have. Guns.

'Mr Morrison,' Bligh calls, 'I desire a musket or two.'[73]

Morrison hurries off, and, encouraged, Bligh tries his luck with another man who has just wandered into view, the very man who had displayed kindness to him, earlier, in covering his bare buttocks.

'Mr Burkett,' he calls up, 'get me a musket or two?'[74]

So it is that, just as Morrison is asking Christian for permission to give Mr Bligh his guns – '*No,*' *comes the firm reply* – Burkett appears.

'Mr Christian, let me give a couple of muskets into the boat?'[75] he asks.

'I'll be damned if you do,'[76] replies Churchill, again with menace, in a manner no seaman or officer would ever have dared speak when Bligh was in charge of this ship.

As it happens, Christian agrees, and says no, for the second time.

Morrison persists: 'Mr Christian, I beg you, let me give *one* into the Boat.'[77]

They are Englishmen. They are our former shipmates, up until just three hours ago. We can't possibly, surely, send them among the savages of the Pacific without a weapon to defend themselves?

'Four cutlasses,' Christian concedes.

Well, it is something. With great care, the wrapped cutlasses are 'thrown into the boat'[78] by Morrison and Churchill. Churchill also throws in a jeer of explanation.

'*There*, Captain Bligh! You *don't* stand in need of firearms as you are going among your *friends*!'[79]

The Mutineers whoop and hoot with laughter.

It is not clear if Churchill is making an unlikely pun on the 'Friendly Islands' – he is not known for his sophisticated humour – or making an observation as to the 'loyalty' of the Loyalists, but either way, Bligh takes an exceedingly dim view of it.

The three captive Loyalists – Coleman, McIntosh and Norman – feel the same, gazing enviously down upon the Launch, weeping and sobbing, as the Mutineers are dancing in delight, a rolling jig of jeerers all around them.

As the Launch moves away, they cry and call out to Bligh to remember that they are on the ship against their will.

'I beg you, Captain,' yells Coleman through his tears. 'Take notice that I had no hand at all in it.'[80]

Bligh gives a further pledge of his long memory.

'My lads, I will do you all justice for I know who is who!'[81]

Mr Coleman yells out once more with a very particular request. 'If ever anybody lives to get to England, I beg you, remember me to a Mr Green in Greenwich.'[82]

Mr *Green* in *Green*wich? Though nobody in the Launch knows who on earth the eponymous Mr Green is or why Mr Coleman is so concerned about this man's opinion, the Loyalists call out that they will.

Now James Morrison, never able to resist a joke, also calls out to the departing Loyalists, 'If *my* friends enquire after *me*, tell them I am . . . somewhere in the South Seas!'[83]

Ah, how the Mutineers laugh. And even in the Launch of Loyalists, there is some snickering, at least until such time as a withering glare from Bligh cuts it dead.

And now another shout, this one of anguish . . . but where is he? Not on the deck, and not in the Launch, though everyone looks around on both levels. It takes a few moments before he is discovered.

Oh. Oh, dear.

It is coming from down there, on the other side, in the Cutter nudged up against the *Bounty*. Why, it is Michael Byrn, the Blind Fiddler, who in all the confusion is still following Mr Cole's order, and sitting, alone, in the large Cutter.

He is, by default, now a *prisoner* of the Mutineers, making him the fourth known Loyalist stuck aboard HMS Mutiny. 'I am detained, Captain!'[84] Byrn yells. The half-soused Mutineers are both amused and pleased at the mix-up.

'We must *not* part with our fiddler!'[85] one yells.

More laughter.

The Blind Fiddler doesn't care. He wishes it noted. He is loyal to Bligh, and he insists it be marked down.

Now, given that the Launch is probably a good ten hours stout rowing to the nearest island of Tofoa, Christian calls out to Bligh, 'I will tow you in towards the land.'[86]

And perhaps Bligh might be tempted.

But the fact that the deck of the *Bounty* has myriad Mutineers with guns upon it, leaning over the gunnels to roar with derision at the Loyalists' predicament, points him the other way. It is becoming ever more obvious they must be on their way, and quickly, as a slurred shout goes up once more from one of the drunken pirates: 'Shoot the Bugger!'[87]

More cackling comes in response, even as his comrades slug back more rum, and Captain Christian shouts to his unruly mob: 'Clear the Great Cabin, throw the bread-fruit overboard!'[88]

Yes, sir, Captain, sir!

William Bligh's humiliation is complete. He watches with disdain as the Mutineers, with hoots of derisive laughter, break into a frenzy of activity the likes of which Bligh never witnessed when they were working for *him*. They throw the precious pots overboard. Out! Out! Out! Everything must go!

Of all the indignities, all the outrages, this is the one that hits Bligh hardest. He must turn away. All that work, all his organisation, now irretrievably gone forever as the pots continue to hurl down, crashing into the water, splashing the Loyalists.

'We had better cast off,' Cole wisely advises the Captain, 'and take our chance, for they will certainly do us a mischief if we stay much longer.'[89]

'*Shoot the Bugger!*'[90] one of the Mutineers cries again.

With that, William Bligh takes a cutlass and with one mighty blow cuts the rope that binds them to the ship.

'Go and see if you can live on a quarter of a pound of yams a day!'[91] Millward shouts maliciously from on high, now every bit as enthusiastic a Mutineer as he is a drunken one.

'Keep right astern,' Bligh orders Fryer, 'to prevent her guns from bearing on us.'[92]

Of course. Bligh would not put it past one of these evil wretches to fire a cannon on them, and be done with the Loyalists and their Launch entirely.

But only moments after they start to haul on the six oars, the Captain of the Launch barks a sharp order: 'Stop!'

Bligh is not quite done.

'I DESIRE TO SPEAK WITH MR CHRISTIAN,'[93] he yells.

Yes, he wishes to make one last appeal.

On the deck of the *Bounty*, Christian is done.

'No person shall answer,'[94] orders Christian quietly.

Almost like naughty schoolboys, hiding from the headmaster behind the woodshed, all duck down and say nothing.

'I WISH TO SPEAK WITH MR CHRISTIAN,'[95] Bligh yells once more.

Still nothing. Yesterday, Bligh screamed 'NO REPLY' into Christian's face as he shook his fist.

Today, Christian's silence pierces the air.

The simple truth dawns on Christian, giving him a rare moment of lightness on this turbulent morning: never again will he hear the raised voice of Captain Bligh, which is slowly fading . . . in . . . the distance.

For this, let the Lord make us truly thankful, for ever and ever, Amen.

Christian orders his men to set sail.

In the Launch, as the men heave hard on the oars, they can hear the chorus of triumphant cheers floating to them over the water in their wake:

'HUZZAH FOR TAHITI! HUZZAH FOR TAHITI!'[96]

Such is not their mood. They are 19 sombre men crammed into a tiny vessel, who, on the orders of their own rumbling volcano, sitting imperiously high at the bow, are bound for the smouldering volcano of Tofoa, some 30 nautical miles away, where they will hopefully find the water they need and, if they're lucky, perhaps even heaps of bread-fruit . . .

And . . . stroke.

And . . . stroke.

And . . . stroke.

And . . . suddenly an enraged shark emerges from the deep and bites off a paddle! (Shakespeare's Claudius is right: '*When sorrows come, they come not in single spies but in battalions.*') There is momentary consternation, followed by some Bligh bellows and order is restored. A spare oar is slid into the rowlock.

And . . . stroke.

And . . . stroke.

And . . . stroke.

Nothing is to be allowed to interfere with the plan to get to Tofoa by nightfall.

No-one speaks. The heavens themselves have been stunned to silence.

The only sound is the constant creak of the oars slotted into the gunnels, and the splash of their paddles. In mid-afternoon, there is the ruffle of a breeze, just enough for the sails to fill not flap, and they are propelled thereafter by the breath of God.

Taking from Hayward the small leather-bound book the young officer has smuggled aboard, Bligh ignores the first two pages which the Midshipman has filled, and begins making careful notes. He needs a plan.

•

As Christian gazes at Bligh's Launch gradually sinking below the northern horizon, his thoughts tumble madly. Everything has happened so quickly.

He is the leader of a bunch of Mutineers aboard the *Bounty*, and Bligh is adrift.

But should he even be the Captain of this ship? With the authority of the law no longer behind him, it is clear that he can only remain Captain if his fellow Mutineers so desire it.

Christian gathers around him the Mutineers – the four Loyalists on board are left out – and puts it to them.

'I have no right to command,' he says firmly. 'I will act in any station you will assign me.'[97]

More than a ripple of surprise moves through the men, who quickly express their view that of course he should be their Captain. As to who should be his second-in-command, here there is genuine debate. Fletcher is firm that he wants George Stewart to fill the role, but most of the other Mutineers are too resentful of his 'former severity' under Bligh – he had been a notably tough superior – to readily agree.

No, their choice is Peter Heywood. Which is one thing. However . . .

'I think Mr Heywood, who is only sixteen, too young and inexperienced for such a charge,'[98] Christian says.

Though surprised, and a little reluctant, the crew bow to the Captain's desires. Henceforth, Fletcher Christian is Captain, and George Stewart is second-in-command, while the crew is to be divided into two watches.

Now, as to their destination . . . that is something that will have to be decided in due course. Obviously they will have to search for a safe haven somewhere in the Pacific, a place beyond the ken of the Royal Navy, its Marines and their guns. But for now, Christian charts a course to an unexplored island with a difficult harbour, called Tubuai. Situated 300 miles south of Tahiti, it is 'out of the track of European ships',[99] and had been mapped but not visited by Cook. If all goes well, they can establish their base there, build huts, ensure it has a fresh water supply and arable land, before heading to Tahiti to pick up the women.

Oh yes, the women. Since they had left Tahiti, the women have been foremost in their minds and in their hearts, perpetually missed.

Sail on, you Mutineers!

CHAPTER NINE

'ALL AROUND THE RUGGED ROCKS, THE RAGGED RASCAL RAN ...'

Red sky at night, sailor's delight.
Red sky in the morning, sailor's warning.[1]

Old British saying

28 April 1789, aboard the Launch, 30 miles south of Tofoa, an island of calm in a sea of madness

Bligh feels an almost unworldly calm. Despite the gravity of their situation, he feels no panic, little danger, and not even a great deal of anger.

'I had scarce got a furlong on my way when I began to reflect on the vicissitude of human affairs ... ,' he will chronicle, 'but in the midst of all I felt an inward happiness which prevented any depression of my spirits; conscious of my own integrity and anxious solicitude for the good of the service I was on, I found my mind most wonderfully supported and began to conceive hopes, not withstanding so heavy a calamity, to be able to recount to my King and country my misfortune.'[2]

In such mind, he does not waste a single second blaming himself, for it is obvious what the cause of the Mutiny was: Tahitian women. Nearly to a man – with the admitted exception of Christian and Heywood – the mutineers 'are void of connections at home',[3] making them so susceptible to being led astray, to crave more debauchery.

He must not dally on such thoughts, for his responsibilities are grave – he must bring the Mutineers to justice, but, more immediately, he must keep safe the good men who have come with him.

This latter duty is supported by the anxious eyes of all the men in the Launch, staring at him, *willing* him to keep them safe.

Row, men, let us make Tofoa by nightfall.

And so he plots – their course, their future, the ultimate revenge on Fletcher Christian and the fall of the Mutineers.

The rattled men pull on their oars with a will, the perfectly cone-shaped, smoking island gradually looming towards them, even as the sun starts to drop, illuminating the luscious green plants that grow thick upon the volcano's mineral black soils in an ethereal red glow.

Hoping against hope, they peer in the dusk-time gloom for some signs of a safe harbour, ideally one with a sandy beach where they can easily come ashore. Alas, all they can see are towering cliffs, against which the waves are crashing – a sure death-trap if they get too close – and so Bligh guides them instead to what is little more than a small indent in the shore, a rough cove, with towering cliffs above, which, although it has no landing spot, at least provides a small amount of shelter from the wind and waves. As the tropical twilight descends on this most extraordinary of days, Bligh orders two of the oars to be secured to the rocks in a manner to give the boat maximum stability in the swell.

They shall sleep on the Launch this night, no easy task when there are 19 of them, crushed one upon t'other, huddled hard amongst their provisions, spare clothes and possessions. There is so little space, you have to stand up just to change your mind – and in the meantime they can neither all sit up or all lie down at the one time, and most must sleep sitting up, slumped against each other. A restless night is thus passed, the sound of the waves crashing on an unseen reef.

At dawn, as Bligh chronicles, they carefully row 'along shore in search of a landing-place, and about 10 o'clock we discovered a cove with a stony beach at the north-west part of the island, where I dropped the grapnel within 20 yards of the rocks'.[4]

Mercifully it is shallow enough that, after Bligh instructs Fryer and two men to stay with the Launch, the rest of them are able to clamber through the surf to the shore, to set foot on land, for some of them for the first time in a month. Using a tinderbox, one of the sailors is soon able to start a fire to warm the sodden Loyalists.

Now, Mr Samuel, if you please. Take a small party with you to scout the surrounds, looking out for Natives, and, most importantly, food and water. Oh, and try not to get killed by an eruption of the volcano.

Two hours later, the foraging party returns with just a few quarts of water, and the news that no bread-fruit plants, or indeed food of any variety, are apparent.

Very well, then, we must move on.

In short order all of them are back in the Launch, at least with the few quarts of fresh water, and continuing their exploration of the island, heading south and sticking close to the shore. By mid-afternoon, though no harbour is apparent, they can see some coconut trees high on some cliffs, which is particularly good news as they know that Bligh is very partial to coconuts.

Sure enough, the Boy and Simpson are quickly dispatched and, after braving the surf, are soon seen first clambering up the towering precipice and then the trees themselves; shinnying up in the manner they had perfected on Tahiti. Shortly thereafter they are able to hurl down – *Watch under!* – no fewer than 20 coconuts to their waiting comrades, who bring the Launch in as close as they dare to scoop them from the turbulent water. It is a small breakthrough in terms of food, but the fact remains that, despite the day's exploration, there is still no discovery of ample food and a good water source, nor have they found a protected harbour or any Natives who may be of help. And so what choice does Bligh have? There is no better option but to return to the cove of last evening, and spend another hideously uncomfortable night bobbing in the sea, safe from whatever dangers the Natives might offer on land. At least, this time, each man receives one coconut for his dinner, and they hand the precious cutlasses around to open them up.

So stormy is the next day that Bligh's plan to set sail for the more bountiful island of Tongataboo must be abandoned, and they instead return to the stony cove where they had landed yesterday, where, after breakfasting on 'a morsel of bread and a spoonful of rum',[5] Bligh, together with Nelson and Samuel, heads off on a more serious search of the island. To begin, they laboriously scale, hand over hand, the twined vines that the Natives have dropped from the cliffs above. As they traipse forward, they find some deserted huts, but with the volcano above still rumbling and smoking continuously it is obvious why the village has been abandoned. Pushing on, they soon find themselves in a deep, dark, ferny gully, their presence causing birds to cry in alarm, and buzzing insects to swarm all around, until the growth thins, the dappled light strengthens, and they emerge on the other side, at the foot of the volcanic peak towering above.

By the time they re-emerge at the top of the cliffs, all their efforts have delivered just nine measly gallons of water collected from nearby dried-up rock pools – likely less than the sweat expended – and three small bunches of plantains. Dispirited, hungry and thirsty, Bligh looks down from the lofty heights at the gruelling climb down and very nearly faints. Only with the help of Nelson is he able to make it safely down. At least in this rare moment of weakness from Bligh – as the shaken skipper sits dazed on the shore, recovering – the other sailors can talk of him, just beyond his earshot.

One of those speaking is David Nelson.

'Our Captain's economy has upset our voyage,'[6] says Nelson grimly to Mr Fryer, referring to the endless privations visited on the ship's company by the skipper.

'Never mind, Mr Nelson, have a good heart!' replies Fryer. 'We shall see old England and tell them our grievances by and by.'[7]

'Aye, Mr Fryer,' he replies. 'Sir Joseph Banks will ask me a number of questions – and be assured that I will speak the truth if ever I live to see him.'[8]

Nelson's words give Fryer great heart and, effectively, strengthen his arm in the struggle with Bligh. Fryer is not alone now, and won't be alone in the future.

For all that, it is not as if Bligh isn't occasionally, *very* occasionally, capable of something that, on a good day, might even pass for warmth. At this moment, as a matter of fact, he is chatting to Cole.

'I have been told, Mr Cole,' he begins, 'that it was through your application to Christian that we got the Launch, instead of the small Cutter with her bottom almost out. Is there any truth in that?'[9]

A little stunned at such acknowledgement, Cole is emboldened to reply with what might even pass for a little cheek . . .

'Truth in it? Yes, you would *never* have got the Launch yourself!'[10]

'Don't you take any notice of that!'[11] Bligh remarks jokingly to the men around them, before adding graciously and gratefully to Cole, 'I will always be a friend to you.'[12]

From a man known for mostly making enemies, and bitter ones at that, this is no small statement. Bligh now decides that while half the men will stay on the Launch to keep it secure, the other half may sleep in a cove cave that they have discovered, about 150 yards from the water's edge, which will afford a perfect place for rest.

But there is to be no relaxation or dropping of standards, even with this momentary relief. Quite the reverse!

For now, Bligh divides his men into three groups, so that, just as it was on the *Bounty*, there can be three watches of eight hours each – with the primary responsibility, here, of keeping the Launch safe. Yes, Bligh is no longer the commander of an actual ship, but he insists that exactly the same order and discipline be maintained, as if he were.

•

What has he done?

What has he *done*?

How *has* it come to this?

Aboard the *Bounty*, in what used to be Bligh's cabin, Fletcher Christian tosses and turns in the night. Time and again he wakes with a start and, courtesy of the moonlight reflecting off the waters through the square windows, he stares at the cracks in the low cabin ceiling as he goes over and over the events of the last week. Could he have handled it differently? Should he not have borne the wretch's insults in the sure knowledge that at least that way he would return to England, and never have to sail with Bligh again?

Will his family understand that? How could they ever find out what happened? If Bligh survives – and Christian has the uncanny feeling that he will – it will be only his side of the story that will be told, and the Christian name will be dragged through the mud, through no fault of his parents, brothers and sisters.

On the other hand, perhaps he *deserves* all the ignominy coming his way? Again and again the words of Bligh come back to him.

'Consider, Mr Christian, I have a wife and four children in England, and you have danced my children upon your knee.'[13]

For it's true. He had done exactly that, with those dear little girls, as wonderful Betsy had laughed gaily at the fun her daughters were having with him. And he, that same man, had cast their father and Betsy's husband adrift on the ocean! Could they ever come to understand? Of course not.

WHY had he done this?

There is no answer, just haunting regrets that leave Fletcher alone with his demons, allowing him snatches of exhausted sleep here and there.

1 May 1789, Tofoa, Latitude 19'71 South, Longitude 175'09 West,[14] Bligh's dead reckoning

Just a couple of hours after another foraging party has set out at dawn, Norton's jowly face appears over the towering cliffs above as he bellows down to those on the shore and in the Launch; 'Good news! Good news! Natives! Here is a man and a woman!'[15]

And sure enough, a couple of Natives indeed appear, making their way to where Bligh and the second watch await them by the shore. Beaming, hopeful, Bligh welcomes them warmly, if awkwardly. For while it is one thing to explain through sign language and the few common words of the Tofoan and Tahitian languages he might know that he is the Captain of a ship from a powerful country, it is quite another to explain just where that ship is now, and why he is no longer in command of it. The best course, he decides, is to indicate that their ship has been sunk, and they are the only survivors.

'They seemed readily satisfied with our account,' Bligh will recount, 'but there did not appear the least symptom of joy or sorrow in their faces, although I fancied I discovered some marks of surprise.'[16]

Whatever the Natives think, the main thing is that the two visitors soon head off to make contact with the rest of their people, who arrive a couple of hours later in their canoes, bearing bread-fruit, plantains, coconuts and a small amount of fresh water – all of which they are happy to trade for buttons and items of clothing. Still watching from the Launch, all the frustrated Fryer can do is cut a button from his jacket and send it to shore, so as to get some extra supplies for himself.

The Natives promise to return on the morrow, and for now the Loyalists – bar those on watch – can sleep easy with bellies full of coconut and bread-fruit.

At dawn, against the probability that the Natives will fail to reappear, Bligh dispatches a foraging party to gather whatever final supplies they can find, only to have many Natives suddenly arrive, just when his own numbers are halved. And now still more arrive, to the point that Bligh and his men are outnumbered many times over. The Loyalists exchange wary glances.

Two Chiefs present themselves to Bligh.

'Maccaackavow,' says the elderly distinguished-looking Chief, introducing himself.

'Eefow,' offers the younger and rather more dangerous-looking buck – there is a troubling look in his eyes, as if he is sizing them up.

Bligh presents each Chief with an old shirt and a small knife. The gifts are accepted, a conversation ensues, and to Bligh's amazement, he finds that the Chiefs already know exactly who he is, and that he and his men had had some trouble at Annamooka recently?

Indeed.

And what of Cook, who, the Chiefs also know, Bligh sailed with?

How *do* they know such things?

Well, that too becomes clear, when yet another young Native Chief suddenly appears, with yet more men, who tells Bligh, he remembers him very well indeed from his recent visit to Annamooka.

My name is Nagatee and I was one of the Chiefs that you held prisoner on the Bounty *when you were so anxious to get your small anchor back.*

. . .

. . .

Well, this could be a little awkward.

And yet, there is no outward aggression, no sense of a desire for unpleasantness due to that unfortunate affair. Indeed, Nagatee seems happy to see Bligh again.

The three Chiefs do have another matter that greatly interests them.

'In what manner have you lost your ship?'[17]

Never have they come across a British Captain without the massive power of a ship, its cannon and muskets at his service.

Ah, yes. Well, then. We actually lost it in a very bad storm, Bligh lies. We salvaged what we could, and got it into the only vessel we could.

Bligh remains cautiously optimistic of the Chiefs' good intentions until Chief Eefow proves 'very inquisitive'[18] indeed – far too inquisitive – as he wades out to the Launch to see what sort of firepower the visitors have, almost as if he is determining the likelihood that an attack on the white men would succeed. That chest, for example. Can it be opened, so he can see inside?

'No, the contents are fire-arms,' replies Fryer firmly in Tahitian, before, for added effect, making a pantomime of the giant explosion that would take place if he even dared to open this mighty chest of arms. Eefow does not look convinced.

'They would kill us,'[19] finishes Fryer.

Eefow is not intimidated and, in fact, does not believe him. Now looking far more acquisitive than merely inquisitive, Eefow wonders if he might at least have the saw that he spies in the Launch?

No.

Eefow grimaces and lets out a guttural growl to the other Natives.

Becoming ever more anxious, Mr Fryer gazes meaningfully at Captain Bligh on the beach, hoping to catch Bligh's eye. He succeeds and Bligh wordlessly indicates he agrees: All hands on deck and everyone be on full alert. The situation is deteriorating; the Natives start to surround Bligh and his men, and they must be ready to react.

No matter that there is, as yet, no overt aggression, no posturing, no shouting. For there is *something* afoot, and just the sheer weight of numbers makes it . . . menacing. It is an atmosphere that Bligh has felt before – once before, in Hawaii, with Captain Cook.

Still more canoes arrive, with still more Natives pulling up on the shore, even as more come clambering down the vine ropes that hang from the cliffs – and, most worrying of all, none of the new arrivals are carrying the hoped-for supplies. They are bearing spears and stones.

Again and again, Bligh and Fryer catch each other's eye from across the water that divides them, wordlessly communicating their rising alarm, and always looking from each other to the path where the foraging party is likely to come from. In part, they need their manpower, should fighting break out. But, more importantly, the sooner they arrive, the sooner they can all get in the Launch and be on their way.

And now Fryer notices that the Launch is coming dangerously close to the shore. How can that be?

There! In the middle of the throng, some Natives are *pulling* on the Launch's stern rope.

'You are discovered!'[20] he roars, motioning the mischievous men to stop.

Startled, the Natives do . . . only to start again within 30 seconds. The time for manoeuvring is coming to an end. Bligh suddenly pulls his cutlass from his scabbard, and tells Eefow that his men must stop pulling on the rope.

Which they do . . . for a time . . . laughing as if this is all a big joke.

Bligh forces a smile to his own face, while still holding the cutlass. This is all so familiar. This is precisely as things had turned for Captain Cook. But Cook had had the protection of two large ships with guns ranged on the shore, smaller boats filled with armed men, while backed up on shore by armed Marines. Bligh has nothing. No guns. No armed Marines. He has just one Launch, one cutlass in his hand, one in the hand of a sailor beside him, and two cutlasses with the sailors on the Launch.

For their part, the 200 Natives have, likely, about 200 spears – as seemingly each and every one of them is armed, forming a solid wall of warriors along the beach. And now many of them pick up large stones, worn smooth by centuries of waves washing over them, and begin knocking them together, in curious rhythm.

Clack, clack, clack-clack . . .

Hold your nerve. Think. Do not turn this into a fight before you have to. Play for time. The sailors in the foraging party must be close now, surely.

Meantime, the sailors who remain with Bligh, though alarmed, take his lead and try to keep things as normal as possible, trading whatever they have for the coconuts and bread-fruit the Natives have brought with them. Bligh, while continuing to talk warily to the Chiefs, whispers to the Boy to start moving the assembled supplies to the Launch in leather buckets with rope handles, by wading them across.

As quickly as you can, Mr Tinkler, make a game of it, all jokes and smiles. A frolic, not a retreat.

Mr Tinkler frolics with the best of them, his extreme youth – he is still only 13 years old – helping him to look the part of a will o' the wisp of no account, remarkable only for the fact he seems to be dancing about, smiling a lot, as he wanders back and forth with another bucket of supplies.

And here, at last, is the foraging party!

Bligh wanders casually with all the crew that are on shore to a nearby cave, and there his manner changes. The hidden hundred feet of cramped space in the cave allow Bligh brief privacy and honesty.

Bligh tells them of their peril.

The Natives are restless. If they attack now, 'our destruction must be inevitable. We shall have nothing left for it but to sell our lives as dearly as we can.'[21] Agreed.

Everyone stay calm. But get ready to fight. Now here is the plan . . .

'I will wait till sunset,' says Bligh, 'by which time something might happen in our favour. For if we attempt to go at present we must fight our way through, which we can do more advantageously at night; and that in the meantime we will endeavour to get off to the boat what we have bought.'[22]

Good luck.

As they exit the cave, all sailors smiling and carefree, with just a glance at the Natives, Bligh can see that the situation has markedly worsened. And it is not just that there are now swarms of Natives lining the beach, it is that they have all now picked up two large stones and are knocking them together, loudly, and in perfect rhythm.

Clack, clack, clack-clack . . .

'I knew very well,' he would later note, 'this was the sign of an attack.'[23]

Steady. Hold your nerve.

The eerie and intimidating sound of the bashed rocks goes on.

Clack, clack, clack-clack . . .

The mesmerising sound of the stones beating together, as well as inducing a rather glazed-eyed look in the Natives, is acting as a siren call for others. More and more arrive on the beach and pick up stones.

The sound of the beat is getting louder, faster; a menacing crescendo all around the *Bounty*'s cast-offs . . .

Bligh remains calm, acting as if none of this is happening.

Rather than looking like a man scheming to save his life, he looks like one who has no greater concern than giving coconuts and pieces of bread-fruit to his hungry men.

Perhaps the Chiefs would like some, too? No, not actually, but they would like Bligh to come and sit with them, and motion for him to do so. Why, Captain Bligh couldn't possibly, as firstly he is too busy feeding his men, and secondly he is sure that if he sits among the Chiefs, they will fall upon him. And so it goes. Smiling all the while, Bligh and his Loyalists eat their dinner standing up, watching the Natives watching them.

Clack, clack, clack-clack . . .

Watching. Watching. Watching.

Now, Boy. Get word to Mr Fryer, if you will, that the moment I and the others start to move to the shore, he is to bring the Launch in close to pick us up.

Trying to affect an air of calm, Bligh takes up his journal and pens an account of events on this day, including the resolution to sell their lives as dear as possible – before asking for the journal to be taken to Fryer. If, as he suspects, he is about to die, let the record show to the Admiralty how courageously he and his men did so.

The Boy takes the precious journal and heads to the Launch, only for a joking Native to grab it from him. Very funny. Peckover, clearly, can barely contain his own mirth, as he now grabs the journal and delivers it back to Bligh, the false smile still frozen on his face.

This is still all fun. No-one must give in to panic.

More Natives keep arriving. With them, more stones, more spears. The black men watch the white men as they beat their rocks together. The white men watch the black men, goggle-eyed. No-one is yet ready to make a move.

The sun begins to set and Bligh – with the small journal now securely back in his inside coat-pocket next to his bosom, safe from the elements – turns his mind to his survival.

'Move now,'[24] Bligh boldly, if quietly, commands.

The calamitous clanging of the rocks becomes more insistent as the sailors move, a precipitous pounding that echoes and shudders along the beach, in rough rhythm to their now pounding hearts. Over and over the Natives smash and bash, just as they might soon smash and bash into the Loyalists' skulls. *Easy, lads, easy. No-one panic. Everyone stay calm.*

CLACK, CLACK, CLACK-CLACK ...

Gently now, steady, slow ...

On Bligh's cue, every sailor on shore suddenly takes up everything he can, walks down the beach to the shoreline and starts to wade through the surf to where the Launch is bobbing. Fryer, watching closely, orders his men to bring the Launch even closer to the shore once more. One of the sailors hauls on the stern rope to back the Launch in towards the deep shallows by the beach, while the others reach over the sides to give a helping hand to haul their fellow Loyalists back on board.

'Will you not stay with us this night?'[25] the Chiefs on the beach ask Bligh, surprised at the suddenness of the move.

'No, I never sleep out of my boat,' Bligh replies, coolly. 'But in the morning we will again trade with you, and I shall remain till the weather is moderate that we may go, as we have agreed, to see Poulaho at Tongataboo.'[26]

Very well then.

It is Maccaackavow who puts things most simply, even though he does not know that Bligh's grasp of the language is strong enough to understand his words.

'You will not sleep on shore? Then ... *Mattie.*'[27]

Mattie, Bligh knows, means Death.

Chief Maccaackavow has given the order, and now leaves, soon followed by the other Chief, Eefow.

Turning to Purcell, Bligh is clear, his words coming over the rocks – *CLACK, CLACK, CLACK-CLACK ...*

'Do not quit me, till the other people are on the boat, Mr Purcell.'[28]

CLACK, CLACK, CLACK-CLACK . . .
Aye, Aye, Captain.

On the Launch, the sailors watch closely, confounded that somehow Bligh is still on the shore, with just Purcell beside him for support.

There would be only a handful of men in Christendom who would stay so long, whatever the orders Bligh has given him, and yet still Purcell stays.

At last, from the side of his mouth, Bligh tells Purcell he may go, and the Carpenter is soon wading towards the Launch.

As the men on the Launch watch, all are moved by Bligh's bravery, his extraordinary *sang-froid*. Yes, sacred Royal Naval lore has it that the duty of the Captain is to be the last one off a sinking ship, to make sure all are safe, but there is no such naval lore about being the last one off the beach in the face of angry Natives to get *back* to the ship.

Now, taking Nagatee by the hand, he walks slowly down to the water, as they all watch, 'everyone in a silent kind of horror'.[29]

Few are more affected than William Peckover, as an eerie horror grips his soul. *He has seen this exact same thing before.* It was on a terrible day long ago in Hawaii, when, right in the midst of a throbbing mass of angry Natives, Captain James Cook had taken a smiling Chief Terreeoboo by the hand and led him down to the shoreline towards a waiting British Cutter, only moments before . . . before . . . before Cook had been brutally struck down and hacked to pieces.

Bligh had been there too. Which makes it all the more extraordinary that his every step seems to put him on the path of Cook – *CLACK, CLACK, CLACK-CLACK . . . CLACK, CLACK, CLACK-CLACK . . .*

Getting close now to the water, Nagatee speaks in the broken English he has learnt from the British ships that have visited since the first days of Captain Cook.

'I want you to stay,' pleads Nagatee. 'To speak to Chief Eefow.'

'No.'[30]

The two keep walking towards the shore.

And now the smiling Nagatee loosens his hand from Bligh's and, speaking in his own tongue, begins to encourage the surrounding Natives to . . . attack.

He has no clue that Bligh is fluent enough in the tongues of the South Pacific to entirely understand the order just given.

Steeling himself for the attack to come, Bligh makes a mental note to kill Nagatee first: 'It was my determination if they had then begun to have killed him for his treacherous behaviour.'[31]

The two keep walking, both still smiling, the words of Nagatee to his fellow Natives to begin their attack evincing in both men an enormous sense of expectation . . .

And yet, while Nagatee's every word on Annamooka is a command that must be obeyed, here on Tofoa, they are more akin to a strong recommendation, and, in this case, not followed. There is no attack and when the two get to the shoreline, with no ceremony, Bligh starts to wade through the breaking waves, out to the Launch.

The stones beat louder and ever faster. The crew keep watching, all the while expecting the attack to come. And yet, still Bligh is able to keep coming closer, until he is just 20 yards from the Launch.

'Oars at the ready, lads,'[32] says Fryer, eager to be underway the instant that the Captain is in the Launch, scarcely believing that, after everything that has happened, they have somehow managed to get all of the men, and most of the supplies, into the Launch intact.

The Natives' stones and angry cries build to a raging climax, but the Loyalists can go nowhere as the Launch's stern rope is still fastened to a rock on the beach.

Stout John Norton knows immediately that there can be only one solution. Someone must go ashore, free the stern rope and that someone is . . . him. So now, just as Bligh is about to jump in the Launch, Norton throws off his jacket, jumps out, and starts running through the water.

In the entire day, it is the first sign of panic to disturb the otherwise tense calm.

'Come back to the ship!'[33] yells Fryer, even as Purcell, still standing waist-deep himself, lifts Bligh into the boat. 'Come into the ship!'[34]

Norton, ignoring the pleas of the Master, charges on regardless, and runs up the rocky beach, right through the throbbing throng of stone-wielding Natives! Fryer yells again, but so loud are the beating stones now, over the sound of the surf, there is no way of knowing if

Norton can hear him. Norton keeps charging . . . even as hundreds of Natives close in on him, their stones in hand.

One unleashes a stone aimed right at Norton, followed by another, and then another. He is knocked down onto all fours in the shallows, blood bursting from a wound in his head, five Natives around him, two of whom kneel beside him and start to beat his head to a bloody pulp with the stones they hold in their hands. Within 20 seconds, he is clearly dead, his lifeless body bobbing up and down, face-down in the water.

And now the Natives are starting to haul on the stern rope, bringing the Launch closer, and within range of the stones they are throwing that are pummelling the white men 'like a shower of shot'.[35]

Cries of alarm. Splotches of blood.

'Cut the rope!' yells Fryer as the men scramble for their oars. 'Cut the rope!'[36]

Bligh whips a knife from his pocket and starts frenetically slashing at the stern rope, even as, with Purcell wading forward and pushing at the boat's stern, the men row for their lives – the Launch caught in a tug of war between the rope that binds it to the shore, and the men pulling on the anchor rope, trying to take them out to sea. After an entire day of high tension, something was always going to break.

Mercifully, it proves to be the stern rope!

For as Bligh at last severs the last strands, the Launch lunges away from the menacing Natives, and it is all Purcell can do to hold onto the stern, his legs still trailing in the water, before he is hauled on board, safe!

Row, lads, row for your lives!

For the struggle is not over.

On the shore, some of the Natives take up as many stones as they can in their arms and join the crowd already leaping into their fast canoes. They start furiously paddling after the Launch, which is drawing away. Of course, it is no contest. For while the heavily laden Launch must be pushed through the water, the light canoes skim effortlessly across the top and soon the Launch is surrounded by men in four canoes. Bligh, standing in the Launch, clutches his cutlass, and is eager to have a swipe, but the Natives are too wise to come that close, and have another plan.

They reach for the stones that line the bottom of their canoes and unleash a sustained hail of potentially deadly rocks. Peckover's head snaps back as a big black stone hits him flush in the face, drawing blood.

The best they can, and with great bravery, Bligh and Fryer – both of whom remain standing – position their bodies so they can shield the rowers from the rain of rocks. Both are struck hard, several times, with Bligh noting, 'I had not an idea that the power of a man's arm could throw stones, from two to eight pounds weight, with such force and exactness as these people did.'[37]

Well, he may not be able to match their strength and accuracy, but he easily has them covered when it comes to fury, and, picking up the very stones that have struck him, now hurls them right back at the Natives, and even scores some direct hits!

Row, you bastards, ROW!

When the stones in the Launch run out, and he is looking for something else to hurl, Captain Bligh is struck by an idea.

Clothes!

On land, just a button will buy a bread-fruit. What might an entire shirt be worth on water – enough to make them give up the pursuit?

Quickly, Mr Nelson, help me!

Now, while Fryer uses an oar trailing in the water as a makeshift rudder – there has not been time to affix the proper rudder – weaving a slightly zig-zagging course that will hopefully thwart the Natives' aim, Bligh and Nelson start to hurl clothes over the side in a furious summer sail: everything must go! Out! Out! Bargain prices! Free, if you will just stop your pursuit!

Aye, these are the very clothes the men had begged from the Mutineers as they were leaving the *Bounty*, the ones that might prove the difference between being wet and freezing to death, or warm and alive, but they can face the consequences later. Far more important is to find a way to stay alive, *now*.

So eager is Bligh to try this method that, to the dismay of Fryer, he even starts to throw at the Natives the provisions they have been bartering for over the last two days. The food, of course, is not a lure, for the Natives already have more food than they know what to do with, but it does lessen the weight of the boat.

Either way . . . *look now!*

The gambit is working! In a choice between killing Englishmen and gathering in their strange garments, the Natives have decided the latter is more precious and have stopped paddling to get the goods before they sink.

What is more, with darkness finally falling, it does not take long before the canoes completely disappear in the enveloping gloom, meaning the white men are unseen by the Natives in turn. With a stream of sharp orders, Bligh orders the foresail set, after which Fryer turns the tiller hard, and they bear away to the south.

Good God, what a day!

Just 12 hours earlier they had been filled with food and high spirits alike, looking forward to friendly Chiefs coming with yet more supplies. It has ended with treachery, murder, the narrowest of escapes, and the sober realisation that previous 'friendships' are worth little when denuded of ships full of muskets and cannon. It is amazing how fire-power can encourage civility, and its lack can cause such unpleasantness.

For now, as the blessed veil of night offers the battered men some precious respite from pursuit as they sail down the coast of the volcanic island, Bligh takes out his small leather-bound notebook. Taking up the one pen the boat possesses and dipping it in the one precious ink bottle they have with them, he writes with a trembling hand:

> I ordered all people and what we had in the boat. When in, I
> followed & the natives began their attack. Killed poor Norton.
> Followed us in canoes. Maimed us very much. Rowed out to sea.[38]

He closes the small leather book and tucks it inside his shirt. Though saddened by Norton's death, there is an undeniable benefit from it, because, as Bligh will note, 'he was the stoutest man in the ship, which circumstance [would] very materially have interfered with the Boat's progress and the allowance of provisions'.[39]

Yes, without him, there will be marginally more food to go round, and just a little more freeboard – the distance between the ocean and the top of the gunnels – for their vessel.

For now, however, the stricken-faced men look to Bligh once more. Where to now, my Captain? It is indeed the question most engaging the brooding, shaken Bligh.

Bligh speaks in hushed tones to his Master, sitting glum as a rum plum next to him in the stern, silently steering the boat while newly attired in the late Norton's jacket, gazing into the darkness ahead.

'Mr Fryer, I desire to go to Tongataboo. There we shall get anything.'[40]

Overhearing, Cole dares to point out that the 'anything' they get may be singularly unpleasant.

'Captain,' he warns, 'we shall be treated the same at Tongataboo as we were at Tofoa.'

'Oh no,' replies Bligh reassuringly. 'They are a different kind of people.'[41]

Fryer shakes his head in disagreement.

'Well then, Mr Fryer, what is best to be done?' asks Bligh.

'Sir, providence may heave us on some friendly shore, by making a fair wind of it sooner than working to windward,'[42] replies Fryer. It is his way of saying we must forget Tongataboo, 100 nautical miles to the south, and rather push to the west, with the easterly winds that prevail in these equatorial climes pushing them along. Sensing Bligh's hesitation – he has not roared at Fryer that he may keep his views to himself – Cole dares to back up his friend.

'I would sooner trust to providence and live on an ounce of bread than go to Tongataboo,' Cole declares. 'If we could get there, I am sure that the Natives would take everything from us if not cut us to pieces.'[43]

Most of the others, with a certain rumbling mumbling, manage to indicate their support of Fryer and Cole, without actually saying anything.

Very well then. In a rare democratic moment, Bligh agrees to forgo Tongataboo. That leaves two options which he now puts before the men – New Holland or the Dutch East Indies.

They could head to New Holland, where, by now, Captain Arthur Phillip and his First Fleet *should* be well established at Botany Bay. But what if they are not? What if there has been a misadventure? What if they have been waylaid, diverted by storms, moved the settlement elsewhere? What if, in short, the Launch would arrive there after a long journey to find no succour? Worse, heading south moves them into colder climes, with uncertain winds and currents that may well conspire to limit their chance of success.

It is at this point in the deliberations that the old salt, William Peckover, makes a quiet suggestion, like a hunter placing a scent before a hungry hound: 'Timor.'[44]

Bligh looks to him.

Ah yes, Timor. Bligh indeed knows of it.

Go on, Mr Peckover?

Well, way back in 1770, the Gunner saw the island of Timor with his own eyes, when he sailed through the straits of New Holland with Captain Cook.

'There is a Dutch settlement,' Bligh remembers, 'but in what part of the island I know not.'[45]

Bligh picks up the *Seaman's Complete Daily Assistant* and the *Tables Requisite* and is at least able to confirm one thing: Timor does indeed lie on a latitude just to the north of Endeavour Strait.

And yes, to get to Timor, some 4000 miles away at Bligh's rough estimate, will be hideously difficult. But, for men in their situation, every option must salute that description. At least this one, with the grace of God, is possible! It offers their best hope and the men are in agreement.

'No hopes for relief for us remain until we come to Timor,'[46] Bligh proclaims.

That is the end of the discussion. Bligh's mind is made up.

At a rough estimate it could take up to eight weeks to reach Timor.

Bligh's thoughts now turn to their provisions, and how he is to ration their meagre supplies.

They are 18 Loyalists with no guns, four cutlasses and enough food for – according to his calculations – less than five days, if they eat and drink normally through the '150 pounds of bread [as in biscuits and hard tack], 28 gallons of water, 20 pounds of pork, 3 bottles of wine and 5 quarts of rum'[47] they are carrying, along with some coconuts and yams that are rolling around the floor of the Launch. (As to the bread-fruit, that which was not thrown overboard has been trampled underfoot in all of the tumult, and from a quick inspection looks barely edible.)

It means, let's see, each man can have, every day, just one ounce of bread, a very small morsel of pork, all of it to be distributed by the Captain himself, to ensure absolute fairness.

True, lads, we may be desiccated skeletons held together by parched skin, blackened by the sun, but we will be alive. As for the water, there is only enough to last for three weeks, at a quarter pint each per day, but that should be less of a problem as in this season, in these parts, there should be a rainy day about once a week.

Bligh now properly understands the situation and asks the men to make a promise. 'Do you all agree,' he asks, addressing every man in the Launch, 'to live on one ounce of bread, and a quarter of a pint of water, per day?'[48]

Aye. Aye. Bligh repeats this solemn vow and commands that they are 'not to depart from their promise'.[49]

We shall not, the men do so solemnly swear.

Very well then, we are agreed.

Bligh looks to Fryer once more, who, for once, looks pleased.

'Let's make a fair wind of it and trust to providence,' says the Master. Bligh nods.

'Shall I put the helm up, sir?'

'Yes, in God's name,'[50] replies the Captain.

•

Unaccustomed as they are to their surroundings, the men settle down for the night in slightly more comfortable circumstances – the absence of poor Norton allows them all another six inches square of space per man – and are well content to have both survived the day and have a plan. And yet, while the men are filled with hope, the Captain himself, the man who has got them this far against all odds, and has been waxing lyrical about their prospects, is filled with quiet doubt, as the fresh breeze makes the sails creak above, even as the small waves regularly thud against the Launch's bow. At least the prevailing winds are pushing them exactly where they want to go – to the west.

But the starkness of their situation remains unaltered, and Bligh knows it. The odds against them surviving long enough to succeed are too great to grasp.

Still, he knows there is no doubt his words have worked, as the quiet, happy chatter in the Launch attests.

> I was happy, however, to see that everyone seemed better satisfied with our situation than myself.[51]

•

At last allowed up on the deck of the *Bounty*, Peter Heywood can barely believe the sheer rapidity of what has happened. Just a short time ago the *Bounty* had its full complement of sailors, had made a good start on its journey to Jamaica, and his dear friend Fletcher Christian had been the most respected and liked person on the ship. And now?

Bligh and 18 Loyalists gone in the Launch, the *Bounty* in the grip of Mutineers, his friend Fletcher the leader of the whole revolt, and his own fortunes now tied to the fate of men who – though many, like Fletcher, are his friends – are intent on a course that he does not want to pursue. But can he express his revulsion, his outrage, his shock at what they have done?

Of course, he cannot. To publicly proclaim himself a Loyalist is clearly to place himself in danger, his friendship with Christian notwithstanding. The likes of Charley Churchill and Alec Smith would more than likely heave him overboard for making a fuss. Besides, while fate has placed him on a ship with Mutineers, rather than where he belongs, with the Loyalists, it is not all bad. At least here, he is in comfort, aboard a solid ship, with plenty of supplies – he cannot imagine what it must be like in the Launch right now . . .

3 May 1789, 86 miles west of Tofoa by Bligh's calculations, a tub in a tempest

As it happens, most of the high morale of the previous evening aboard the Launch does not survive many hours into the next day. At first light Bligh starts making careful records and calculations to plot their course, but it is not at all easy.

For, no sooner has the sun risen 'fiery and red'[52] – a sure indication for sea veterans the calibre of Bligh that a gale is on the way – than they are indeed hit by such a violent storm, with such a heavy and high sea, that 'between the seas the sail was becalmed, and when on the top of the sea it was too much to have set: but we could not venture to take in the sail for we were in very imminent danger and distress, the sea curling over the stern of the boat, which obliged us to bale with all our might'.[53]

Bale, lads, bale!

And bale they do, as if their lives depend upon it . . . because they do.

> A situation more distressing has perhaps seldom been experienced.[54]

It is not simply that the Launch threatens to take on so much water that it will sink – it is that the water will get into the bags holding the bread, and spoil it, in which case they would be as good as dead anyway. The only possible way of surviving is to lighten the boat further, and so, on Bligh's orders, more clothes are thrown overboard, together 'with some rope and spare sails'.[55]

Not only does the Launch immediately sit marginally higher in the water, but with more space, the men have more room to scoop out the water.

Regarding the crucial bread, mercifully, Purcell has a secure and waterproof chest in which he is able to stow it.

Still the waves pound, rocking the boat – as Bligh, on the tiller, uses a lifetime of seamanship to work the boat this way and that, to slide over the waves and not be blindsided by them. If, and it is a real possibility, any part of the tiller or its gudgeon hinges break, the Launch would not survive 30 seconds.

Miraculously, however, despite the extreme stress on both the boat and its crew, everything holds together – just.

Once the worst of the crisis is over, Bligh uses the most sure-fire method to lift the morale of his freezing and sodden crew, serving a single teaspoonful of rum to each man with a quarter of a bread-fruit, which the men try and swallow without gagging, as the slimy mess is both squashed and near-rotten.

And now, where was he, before being so rudely interrupted?

Ah, yes, doing his calculations, as he must do every day at noon. From here, Bligh's reckoning is that they must set a course of west-north-west, so as to pass within 'sight of the islands called Feejee if they laid in the direction the natives had pointed out to me'.[56]

Sure enough, two days later – after a wretched time, marked by yet more storms, bone-chilling nights, and unwavering hunger, with little relief – some previously uncharted islands appear off their starboard quarter. What to do?

Well, given that Christian has stolen from him the last 15 years of his map-making master-works together with his precious copies of Cook's charts, now would appear to be as good a time as any for Bligh to begin again, and taking his pencil in one hand, and small journal in the other, he begins to mark down the coastal contours of what he strongly suspects are the Feejee Islands. And he continues to do so over coming days, a navigator resuming his profession even while survival is his task – also satisfied that as Feejee has shown up almost exactly where expected, it means his calculations have been correct.

Yes, whatever their circumstances, they must maintain discipline and remain vigilant – taking down information at least every hour, allowing Bligh to make a good estimation of their longitude, and thus their position on the globe. Without it, they risk running into reefs, islands and even *continents* in the middle of the night.

Early May 1789, approaching Tahiti, another Mutiny on the *Bounty*?

Whispers on the waves at midnight.

Since they had parted company with the Launch, Joseph Coleman, the Armourer, has been extremely careful to keep his distance from fellow Loyalist James Morrison, for it simply will not do for them to be seen together, for the others to have any sense of them as being united, as well as separate from the Mutineers. It is for the same reason they stay away from Charles Norman and Thomas McIntosh, the two other

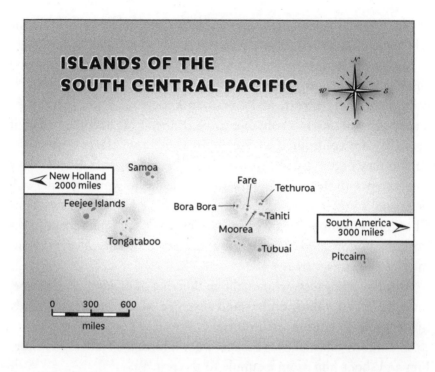

Loyalists. Instead, they must even 'affect a shyness to each other'.[57] But yes, they have managed enough fleeting meetings in the night to hatch something that might very well pass for a plot to retake the ship.

What is clear from the first is that there can be no retaking of it while at sea, because there are just not enough of them to make the ship function. No, they must wait until the night the *Bounty* reaches Tahiti. What will help, apart from the Mutineers being back with their women, is the certainty that Christian will allow them 'an extra allowance of grog',[58] and the double-certainty that most of the Mutineers will so over-indulge they will be incapable of resistance. Ideally, what the Loyalists need more than anything is to turn some of the Mutineers back to their side on the promise that, if successful, they will be spared the noose and likely even be handsomely rewarded.

Alas, alas, despite their certainty that their plans have been kept secret, somehow, somewhere, someone has overheard them and, as Morrison will recount, 'to my unspeakable surprise ... Mr Christian was acquainted with our intentions'.[59]

No, mercifully, Christian does not know precisely who is in on the whole plot, but he knows that Coleman is behind it, and that is enough.

'Coleman,' he says, when the Armourer is dragged before him, 'you shall be left on shore at Tubuai until the ship returns from Tahiti.'[60]

It is an empty threat, and Christian knows it. As the Armourer, Coleman is simply too valuable to be dropped off at Tubuai. For if ever they are confronted by hostile Natives in whatever part of the Pacific they end up, or, worse, a ship of His Majesty's Royal Navy catches up with them, having the *Bounty*'s guns in working order will be crucial to their survival. Coleman does have his keys to the Arms Chest taken from him, and given to Churchill, who puts them in his pocket and, for good measure, now sits down on the chest, with his musket and cutlass by his side.

As for you Loyalists who might be thinking of making your escape, once we get to Tahiti, understand this. We Mutineers have already made a solemn oath to each other:

'Should any one make his Escape, we will force the Natives to restore him and shoot him as an example to the rest.'[61]

Clear, gentlemen?

Yes, very clear, as the Loyalists understand more than ever that they are being watched, and will be watched.

Still, the discovery of the plot means that Christian is henceforth more cautious than ever on his own ship, and not only does he always have a weapon on him, but, on his orders, so too do the other Mutineers.

'Each of Mr Christian's party was armed with a brace of pistols,' Morrison would recount. 'Mr Christian never went without a pistol in his pocket, the same one that Lieutenant Bligh formerly used.'[62]

Yes, though Christian now has Bligh's ship beneath his feet, and his pistol in his pocket, he is determined not to share Bligh's current fate. On Christian's orders, the Loyalists are marked men.

6 May 1789, Feejee Islands, Latitude 17°09' South, Longitude 178°57' East, forbidden fruit, and coconuts and pork and water and . . .

It is a strange thing to be so constantly passing the solution to their woes, without being able to avail themselves of it. For, however hungry and wet the Loyalists might be, however tempting the fertile and inhabited islands they pass might be, the dangers they had only narrowly escaped at Tofoa mean that Bligh refuses to land.

Sail on, Bligh, sail on!

And so they do, as no fewer than a dozen more islands show up on his chart – for the first time in history, their position is formally recorded – and the Launch sails on.

The sodden men, waves forever crashing over them, keep gnawing on their slender rations, while gazing upon columns of smoke, at the base of which the Natives are surely cooking succulent meat. The Loyalists nearly get some flesh of their own to eat when, to enormous excitement, a trailing hook actually catches a fish, 'but we were miserably disappointed by its being lost in getting into the boat'.[63]

Sail on, Bligh, sail on!

And so they do. At one point on 7 May they look up to see two large sailing canoes coming straight for them from one of the islands and, given their previous experience, are alarmed.

> Being apprehensive of their intentions, we rowed with some anxiety, being sensible of our weak and defenceless state.[64]

Do the canoes back off?

They do not.

One of those rowing for his life is Fryer, while Bligh mans the tiller. After a few minutes, Fryer receives the whispered views of both Cole and Elphinstone that the Captain is not steering a course best calculated to get them safely away from their pursuers. Fryer quite agrees but declines to say anything for fear that it would only distract Bligh from the task at hand, and not actually help them.

But now, one of the canoes really does start to close on them 'very fast'[65] and it is Bligh himself who yells.

'Heave away, Lads! If they come up with us they will cut us all to pieces.'[66]

For Lawrence Lebogue, the old salt sail-maker who is rowing right behind Fryer, such words from Captain Bligh are too much, and if he is about to die, it will be with his views at least expressed.

'God damn my eyes, Sir!' he calls loudly, straight at Bligh. 'You frighten us all out of our wits! Let the thiefs come and be damned if they will, we will fight as long as we can!'[67]

Mr Lebogue continues his impertinent mutterings within earshot of Mr Fryer.

'Very pretty indeed, by God,' he mumbles. 'The Captain is the first man frightened.'[68]

Though the Master agrees, he has no choice but to shut such insolence down.

'You old scoundrel!' snaps Fryer. 'If you speak another word I will come and heave you overboard. Pull away!'[69]

For three hours the pursuit goes on, even when they are far out to sea again, and the islands have disappeared, though at last the men of Feejee give way, to Bligh's great relief.

> Whether these canoes had any hostile intention against us is a matter of doubt; perhaps we might have benefited by an intercourse with them, but in our defenceless situation it would have been risking too much to make the experiment.[70]

7 May 1789, *Bounty*, deep dreams of a lost life

Drip, drip, drip . . . drop.

Drip, drip, drip . . . drop.

Drip, drip, drip . . . drop.

All through the silent watch of the darkest hours, the nightmares are getting worse. They are always the same. They are about a young man who threw away a life of promise in an instant, who in a fit of stone-cold rage had launched, yes, a *mutiny*! Is it possible? He, Fletcher Christian, descended from an English King, had actually held a cutlass to the throat of one of His Majesty's commissioned officers, and taken his ship from him. And now, he can never return to England again, never see his family, never see his friends, never . . . sleep in peace again. Time and again he awakes in a cold sweat in a darkness nearly as profound as the dark panic that grips his soul. All he can do, as ever, is restlessly await the dawn, where he heads out on deck, with a crew to order about, a façade of confidence to maintain. But for how long can he maintain it?

9 May 1789, on the Launch, discipline in the balance

As ever, Bligh's core principle applies. Even on this tiny vessel, they must comport themselves with exactly the same discipline as if on the *Bounty*. And this afternoon, in this burst of fine weather, that means cleaning out the entire boat, and hanging everything up to dry. Each man is responsible for his own section of the boat, ensuring it is ship-shape, clean and organised – just as he is responsible for all of his clothes, including the ones he is wearing.

Most men are soon near-naked and happily sweating as they get to work, even as Bligh makes preparations of his own. To this point he has doled out the rations purely according to guess, but now, with the help of Samuel, he fashions a set of scales with half a coconut shell at either end and will henceforth serve exactly equal portions to each man.

It is a good afternoon. The Launch is clean once more, everything is dried, and in the evening Bligh uses a pint cup to give each man a quarter of a pint of water, and a little more than half an ounce of bread, the last measured by putting one pistol ball in one half-coconut – for they have discovered some pistol balls unaccountably in the Launch, and Bligh knows that 25 of them weigh a pound or 16 ounces – and the commensurate amount of bread in the other end.

All the while, Bligh, in an unexpectedly conversational mood, talks to the men about New Guinea and New Holland, giving them as much information in his power so that they may find their own way there, should anything happen to him.

Nothing is to be left to fate.

CHAPTER TEN

HARD TIMES, CHANGING CLIMES

Day after day, day after day,
We stuck, nor breath nor motion;
As idle as a painted ship
Upon a painted ocean.

Water, water, every where,
And all the boards did shrink;
Water, water, every where,
Nor any drop to drink.[1]

Samuel Taylor Coleridge, 'The Rime of the Ancient Mariner'

9 May 1789, two days past Feejee Islands, water, water everywhere AND a drop to drink

It isn't only in the cloistered and comfortable realms of science, music, literature and philosophy that the gentle muse of inspiration may alight on the shoulders of the genius and whisper a master-stroke in their ears. Sometimes, such things may appear in even the direst circumstances, as in when, say, 18 men are on the High Seas in a tiny boat with only eight inches clearance from the sea to the gunnel, at risk of being swamped by just one large wave coming over the sides.

And today, 9 May 1789, is a case in point.

For, after contemplating near-catastrophe for the last fortnight, this morning Bligh – master mariner that he is – comes up with a solution.

Following Bligh's instructions, the men place 'a canvass weather cloth round the boat, and raise the quarters about nine inches . . . which proves of great benefit to us'.[2]

They are just in time, too. That very evening, they are hit by a storm which, though it brings precious rain – allowing them to collect 20 gallons, using spread sails to funnel water into one of the barrels – also brings towering, threatening waves. Even with their new canvas protection, the turbulent seas rear up and crash down, their peaks breaking over the men all night, obliging them to bale like demented monkeys, only ever 50 scoops ahead of disaster.

It is a miserable time, and all the more so as they are living on starvation rations, with Bligh doling out 'one 25th of a pound of bread, and a quarter of a pint of water, at sun-set, eight in the morning, and at noon'.[3]

To make their bread 'a little savoury',[4] the men dip their portion in sea-water, while Bligh, of course, has a different, and rather distinctive, way of doing things.

'I generally broke mine into small pieces, and ate it in my allowance of water, out of a cocoa-nut shell, with a spoon; economically avoiding to take too large a piece at a time, so that I was as long at dinner as if it had been a much more plentiful meal.'[5]

True, it is not necessarily a good look, to be seen still sipping and supping long after the others have finished, but what cares Captain Bligh what they think? Leavening things at least a little is Bligh occasionally doling out a morsel of pork or a single teaspoonful of rum when things are particularly grim, as they are on the morning of 11 May, after a terrible night of squalls, high-breaking waves, relentless baling and biting cold. In their damp clothes, the cramped men shakily fumble with the tiny chunk of biscuit they are served, desperate not to lose a crumb as they bring it to their blue, chapped lips and *ch-ch-ch*attering teeth. Chewing slowly, trying to savour the flavour, treasure the pleasure of having *food* in their mouths, their spirits lift, at least a little. Drinking their water with equal fervour, some take tiny sips, squeezing drops into their parched, unfeeling mouths, while others tip back their heads, take a gulp and swirl the whole lot around their mouths, before finally knocking it back. Oh, the joy! The momentary *relief*.

'At noon,' Bligh records with no little relief of his own, 'the sun appeared, which gave us as much pleasure as in a winter's day in England.'[6]

Ah, but as is the way of such things, the ecstasy of the midday sun soon starts to ebb away as darkness descends once more, the cold gets a grip on their very souls and works its way out from there, and the brooding ocean – which had only, in fact, been resting – starts to snarl once more, throwing yet more waves up and over the gunnels for two long, painful, miserable, freezing days and nights. At dawn on the third day, a gentle angel of inspiration once more alights on Bligh's shoulders, whispering to him what to do.

'I recommend you all to strip and wring your clothes through salt water,'[7] he tells the men. It is less an order, and more a tip, for even the indefatigable William Bligh is suffering so much he can barely be bothered to bark, and must speak softly. When the men look to him quizzically, he explains: 'By this means you shall receive a warmth that while wet with rain you can not.'[8]

Those sitting nearest the gunnel go first, laboriously stripping their heavy, wet clothes off, their lily-white skin now tingling at the sting of rain. Leaning over the side, they trail their garments for a few seconds in the ocean, before pulling them out to wring them out, and put them back on and . . .

And Captain Bligh is right! They really do get a bizarre, and unexpected feeling of warmth – and even a momentary, thrilling sense of purpose.

Mid-May 1789, approaching the island of Tubuai, hello sailors

On this day, the men of the *Bounty* are not merely setting sail, they are cutting spare sails to pieces. The whole thing is Christian's idea. He has decided that in preparation for visiting Tubuai, the men should look the part of a disciplined group, wearing the one uniform, and these old sails will provide the material they need. Christian insists: 'Nothing has more effect on the mind of the Indians as a uniformity of dress . . . as it always betokens discipline especially on board British Men of War.'[9]

The Mutineers busily cut out the correct shapes and begin to sew them into breeches and shirts.

15 May 1789, north of the New Hebrides

The starvation is bad enough. But much more acute is their gnawing agony, when, as on this day, they must pass close by two islands seeming teeming with life, without yet being able to stop.

The only saving grace of the day, as Bligh chronicles in his journal, is that the rain keeps falling, a 'providential blessing', as hot weather would have caused them by now to surely 'have died raving mad with thirst'.[10]

'Water we want none,' he records a few days later, 'for our thirst seems to be quenched through our skin.'[11]

For men who are now mostly skin and bones in any case, it is a good start. But, oh, how enduring and intense is their hunger, how much it depletes their energy, their morale – and how slowly it makes the minutes crawl by, through the long miserable days and devastatingly cold nights.

Sheer exhaustion begets a blurred existence for the Launch Loyalists, with even their eyesight beginning to deteriorate. Filled with hunger, headaches, cramps and shivering, they keep busy conducting running repairs like caulking leaks: cutting away the rotting seam before quickly using a mallet and caulking iron to tamp down oakum – hemp fibre from old rope, soaked in tar – to compress it.[12] Everyone not involved must keep baling, baling, baling.

For his part, though Bligh neither caulks nor bales, nor does he seem to sleep, as whatever time the others wake in the night, there he is in the moonlight, silhouetted against the waters, watching them.

His men are, in his view, 'half-dead',[13] and need constant surveillance. Meanwhile, he continues to make constant calculations, working out just how long it will take to reach the infamous 'barrier of reefs' that lies off New Holland. If they can just find a safe way through, without putting a hole in their vessel, as Captain Cook had with the *Endeavour* in 1770 – they will be in calmer water, and making their way towards the gateway to the west, which is Endeavour Strait, at the northern tip of New Holland.

And now, look there! On this sombre early afternoon of 24 May, almost a month after the Mutiny, they see them. Birds! Big birds, little birds, *lots* of birds! There are boobies, noddies and tropical gulls, cawing, caterwauling, flying about and urging them onwards – *the fact that we are here means that land must be close!*

A few hours later, the weather clears and even the sea begins to run fair – almost as if King Neptune himself is conceding this round to the Loyalists. Blessed with such rare calm, Bligh takes the opportunity to examine the remaining bread supply. It is soon his reckoning that at the current rate of consumption, they have enough to keep going for just 29 more days.

Now, if all goes well, they can indeed get to Timor in that time. But what if it doesn't go well? What if it takes longer, or instead of Timor, they have to go on to Java, a further 1200 miles away? In that case they will need to stay alive for 42 days, and Bligh knows he needs to make allowance for that. The only way forward, thus, is to cut rations by a further third.

> I was apprehensive that this would be ill received, and that it would require my utmost resolution to enforce it . . . [but] it was readily agreed to. I therefore fixed, that every person should receive one 25th of a pound of bread for breakfast, and one 25th of a pound for dinner; so that by omitting the proportion for supper, I had 43 days allowance.[14]

Still, as it turns out, just as fortune favours the brave, so too can it steer towards the starving, as just the next day at noon, a tired noddy bird makes the mistake of coming in for a landing within snatching distance of a Loyalist – who grabs it and snaps its neck in all of two seconds!

A ragged cheer goes up, before Bligh cuts it into 18 equal parts – entrails, beak, legs and all – and hands it out, according to the Royal Navy custom when supplies are limited. That is, Captain Bligh turns his back on the 18 portions, occasioning Mr Fryer to point to one portion and gravely intone, 'Who shall have this?' at which point Bligh names one of the party. The process is repeated until the last piece left goes to Bligh. Each piece is savoured, accompanied by a morsel of ship's biscuit, all with a side of salt water as dipping sauce. True, it is not much. But for starving men it is manna from heaven.

Best of all, dear Providence continues to beam brightly in their direction, as yet more birds are caught over the following days – boobies as big as large ducks! Their blood is given to three men who are struggling badly.

•

It is done. Just a few alterations here and there to allow for different sizes, and the Mutineers on the *Bounty* can try on their new kit. In the end, the common sailors in their new uniforms look every bit as smart, if not smarter, than their officers. Together, they look the part, dressed to kill, ready to face and populate a new world of their own making.

•

It never rains but it pours, and the sun never shines but it burns. As Bligh and his men continue to push on, it feels as if, from dawn to dusk, the sun beats down on them, slowly, agonisingly, sucking the life out of all of them, as surely as a parasite sucks blood, weakening their resolve with every passing hour. Worse, those rays that don't fry you on the way down still zap you on the way back up, beaming brightly from a dozen angles off the moving feast of mirrors that is the sea.

The good news, however, is that they are now regularly passing pieces of driftwood, as well as ever more birds, meaning – together with clouds in the far west that simply do not move – they must be close to New Holland.

With the sun shining, and land getting ever closer, it is time for Captain Bligh to get a particular important project underway. Just before scrambling off the *Bounty*, Mr Cole had grabbed a rough pile of signal flags on the reckoning they might be useful in some manner. And so it now proves! For Captain Bligh now orders the men – Lebogue the sail-maker proving the handiest at the task – to sew them together in a manner that they form a small Union Jack. It is difficult sewing, to be sure, as they constantly fumble with the needle and thread in their trembling, weathered fingers, but finally it is done and Captain Bligh is satisfied. It will serve for the purpose he has in mind.

The Launch continues to make headway thus, and that night, at midnight, Fryer relieves Peckover on watch, and has an hour where nothing much at all happens, when he cocks his ear to the west . . .

There it is!

'Don't you hear a noise like the roaring of the sea against the rocks?'[15] Fryer calls to the seaman manning the tiller.

'Yes, sir, I think I do.'[16]

Standing up, Fryer leans against the mast, cocks his ear to the sound one more time, and peers into the gloom.

There!

There can be no doubt, for he can clearly see now the breakers just up ahead, little explosions of whitish grey catching the moonlight above the black sea.

The waves crash onto the solid reef that sits hidden just below the water's surface, sending spray skywards as the top part of each wave barrels over it like a ball of dirty thunder.

'Captain Bligh!' yells Fryer. 'The breakers are in sight!'[17]

As Bligh sits up, half asleep, Fryer issues a stream of orders to the man steering and the men stirring, 'Port the helm, lower the mainsail!'[18]

Within moments, six men are in position, pulling on the oars, the roar of breakers growing closer. Bligh's voice, with unaccustomed panic, calls out of the darkness, 'Pull my lads! We shall all be swamped!'[19]

In response, Fryer yells himself, seeking to both encourage his men and rebuke Bligh.

'My lads, pull! There is no danger!'[20]

But it is a close-run thing, as the Launch gets within 75 yards of the waves pounding the reef, and risks being sucked into the maelstrom and subsequently hurled onto the coral before . . . the men haul on their oars like mad things. For safety's sake, they pull back a mile off the reef, where they will wait till daylight.

In the morning, as the wind picks up and they row towards the reef once more, it is Fryer who climbs onto the bow of the Launch, and peers to the west.

'Mr Fryer, do you see anything?'[21] asks Bligh, with uncharacteristic anxiety. For they now realise they are surging forward into what is a U-shaped formation of reefs, and there might be no way out of this, with such a wind behind them. They *need* a gap!

'Yes, sir, I see a place where there are no breakers!'[22]

Bligh comes forward in the Launch and sees for himself.

From a distance of a mile, the break in the reef looks very small. But as they approach, it is quite clear that the handsome gap can be easily passed through, for such a navigator as himself. Barking orders to the helmsman about the direction to steer, and to the others to trim the sails, Bligh stays up front and . . .

And they are through!

Suddenly, the water is calm, the sea no longer surges, the reef behind them is keeping away all those treacherous waves of the open ocean. Sweet Providence, once again, has smiled upon them.

•

Land ho! *Reef* ho!

Christian and his Mutineers, all in their new sail-cloth uniforms, have arrived at the north-west tip of Tubuai, the spot marked by Captain Cook on his chart with the island's only possible harbour where a ship might drop sheltered anchor – if they can first get through the small gap in the reef that stands as a barricade in front of it.

It is the morning of 28 May 1789, and just outside the reef, Christian gives the command – 'Let go the anchor' – and sends the Young Gentleman George Stewart with some men in the small Cutter to, 'examine the reef, and find the opening described by Captain Cook'.[23]

Alas, alas, no sooner do Stewart and his men approach the gap than a canoe filled with furious Natives approaches. Within seconds, the Natives jump from their canoe into the Cutter, and a mad melee ensues! Stewart fires a pistol in the air and, as quickly as the Natives had jumped into the Cutter, they now jump out, terrified by the gun's echoing report.

Hearing about what happened, Christian muses on how best to deal with the situation.

Very well then.

Let us use the Cutter in a different capacity. Instead of heading back to the shore, back to the melee, let it go as a pilot, the *Bounty* following close behind, its cannon trained and ready. The plan works. By late afternoon, the *Bounty* is through the reef and anchored, and the Natives are nowhere to be seen. Strange.

Despite the eerie silence, the crew stay busy, cleaning the ship and placing buoys along their passage in through the shallow reef, so they can come and go in the boats with relative ease.

Hoping to establish polite contact, Christian gives orders the following morning for the *Bounty* to move even closer to the shore, anchoring just 400 yards distant so the ship's guns provide cover for a landing party.

And it works! Curiosity seems to get the better of the previously hidden Natives, and in ones and twos and threes they start to emerge.

Soon, the *Bounty* men can see nothing *but* Natives. With vastly increased numbers, both in terms of men and canoes, they are all around the ship, chattering among themselves, and pointing out various features: the sails, the cannon, the crew's uniforms, the portholes and yet . . .

And yet, still there is something about their chatter which is markedly different from the happy chatter of Tahiti's Natives. There is something aggressive about them, like they are working out the best ways to frame an attack, and are using this opportunity to get a close look. The white men get a similar feeling when an old Chief climbs on board, looking every which way with astonishment. He is particularly frightened of the livestock – the hogs, goats, dogs – and every time one of the animals looks up at him, he jumps back in alarm. But there is something predatory about him. Yes, he accepts Christian's gifts with a beaming smile, and assures them he will return the following day, but still something does not seem right – the gleam in his eye, the calculating gaze, indicates he is sizing them up, perhaps even counting their numbers.

On the strength of this suspicion, Christian orders every man to be armed with their muskets loaded and their ammunition pouches full. They must be ready for action, for he is sure an attack is coming.

See there, those Natives on the beach looking our way are now engaging in something of a war dance.

'Their ferocious aspects,' James Morrison would chronicle, 'gave us plainly to understand in what manner we might expect it.'[24]

The armed men wait until noon, and . . .

. . . And what is this now?

Suddenly, from the shore, comes a canoe filled with beautiful Native women. Which is the good news. They are bare-chested, and their gorgeous brown breasts shake and shimmer in the sun as they smile in a manner that whispers softly . . . *come hither!*

With every yard closer they loom ever more gorgeous, with flowers in their hair, and garlands and pearl shells around their necks. And look how they are now all standing as one to sing an island melody, their hips moving to the rhythm of the song. Every single one is 'young and handsome having fine long hair which reached their Waists in waving ringlets'.[25]

Though still cautious, Christian receives the women on deck with courtesy, knowing that the men will likely be close behind.

And here they come; 50 canoes, each with 20 men or so wielding spears, come charging forth. In the fore of each canoe a Native stands holding his conch, an enormous seashell on which they blow clarion calls of battle.

Onwards!

Christian and his men instantly realise that the women have been sent their way as a delightful distraction, diverting their attention from the attack which is sure to come . . .

But, no – none of the spears is hurled and, seemingly on the instant, the Natives become friendly again.

Many climb on board to look over the ship once more, while the Mutineers watch warily. The only way to stop them coming on board is to shoot them, but Christian gives no such order. When Christian catches one Native trying to steal a part of a compass, however, he has had enough, and quickly lashes the man with a handy bit of rope, to send him yelping back into his canoe, with the rest of the wide-eyed Natives soon following.

And that is enough diplomacy for one day. Christian watches as the hundreds of men in 50 canoes take their spears and begin 'brandishing them with many threatening gestures'.[26] He sees one of them cut a buoy free from its anchorage and so trains his musket at the offender and fires, just missing.

But Mr Christian does not have just a musket, he has cannon at his command.

'Fire!' Christian orders a four-pounder gun to be used to disperse the Natives.

With a roar, the cannon fires, sending grapeshot hurtling at the warriors. When the smoke clears, it reveals a shattered canoe, and five bodies in the water.

And again.

'Fire!'

And again!

'Fire!'

Suddenly, many dead Natives, and parts thereof, lie bobbing in the bay, the water around them a ghastly red, before a guttural cry goes out – clearly a command – and the survivors turn around.

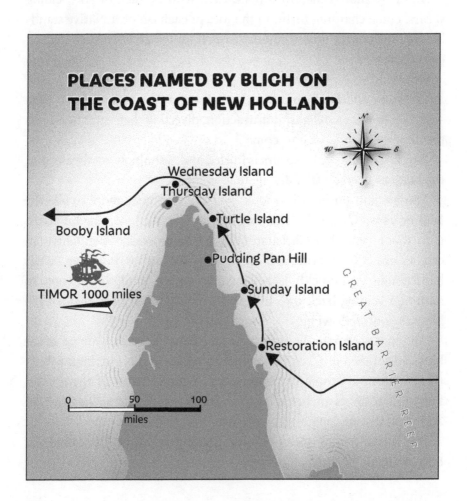

PLACES NAMED BY BLIGH ON THE COAST OF NEW HOLLAND

Welcome to Tubuai. Christian names the new harbour for the *Bounty*: 'Bloody Bay'.[27]

After the cannon-fire retreat, Christian orders the Jolly Boat and the Cutter to follow the canoes to shore, where the sailors force the fleeing Natives into the jungle with hails of musket shot as a chaser. They also examine the contents of the abandoned canoes, finding 'a number of cords in the canoes which', as Morrison chronicles, 'we supposed were intended for to bind us with, had they succeeded in their plan'.[28]

This is not going to be easy. The island Captain Christian has selected for their lifelong home appears to be peopled by Natives who will fight to the death to defend it.

28 May 1789, Restoration Island, the world is not quite Bligh's oyster

At last, land ho!

And this is not just an island that they can see on the horizon, but dare not approach. No, this is a small island just four miles to the west of the enormous reef they have passed through, and just a quarter mile off the coast of what appears to be New Holland.

Most importantly, it appears to be uninhabited, and thus safe for landing – as opposed to the coast of the mainland, where, Bligh already knows, from his close reading of Cook's journals, 'Indians' abound.

But, here? It *looks* safe, though Bligh remains cautious as they approach it in the late afternoon, the setting sun meaning the hump of the island is brilliantly silhouetted against the red sky.

They land the Launch on the sandy shore, and feel solid land beneath their feet for the first time in 26 gruelling days. Alas, no sooner do they set foot on the soft sand than their limp legs wobble. Mr Fryer, watching on, chronicles their tottering footsteps as being 'like so many drunken men'.[29]

For his part, realising he must be careful, Mr Fryer slowly swings his legs over the side and, keeping his emaciated arms hooked over the gunnel for stability, carefully lowers his body down until his feet touch the sand. So far, so good. Letting go, alas, just as he takes his first feeble step, his legs fold like those of a newborn deer and his scrawny body crumples. It is some time before he musters the strength to give it another go. Still, just as a man's 'sea-legs' can return after a short time on a ship, so too can his 'land-legs', and in short order all the men are landed, and, like a small army of human crabs, able to slowly spread out along the shore-line, tottering along in a sideways search for their most urgent need – food.

And they are in luck! For the receding tide at sunset exposes many morsels of magic. Using the tools that Mr Purcell so reluctantly hands over, with dire warnings of their fate if they are damaged, the men are able to pry juicy shellfish from the rocks, and an instant later – barely stopping to rinse off the grit that covers them – send the plump meat sliding down their throats.

'Found oysters & Perrywinkles,'[30] Fryer notes, '[but] it was soon so dark that we could not pick up any great quantity.'[31]

It is enough, still, that their most immediate hunger pangs are satisfied, and, as they bed down for the night – half of the men on the shore, and half on the Launch anchored just *beyond* a stone's throw from shore, in case of an attack – they can enjoy the moment. A month after having been set adrift in the middle of the ocean in a tiny vessel, they are still alive, have covered 2500 miles at an average of 90 miles a day towards their destination, and, tonight, have food in their bellies.

When Bligh returns to the shore at the break of dawn, he is approached by Fryer, whose step is now firm, just as his face has resumed its former flat countenance. Back in control, Fryer advises that all had been calm during the night, and he is confident that there are no Natives on the island, giving the men the opportunity to range wide, and forage freely.

'We had better haul the boat ashore,' Fryer advises, 'and part of us go and see what we can find.'[32]

'Yes, Mr Fryer, let us do it,'[33] says Bligh, though Fryer knows he also means 'you do it', and Fryer sets about the task.

The men are divided into two parties, with one repairing the Launch and scraping the barnacles from its hull, while the other gathers oysters and periwinkles, as well as whatever other food they might find. With just one musket, they could have brought down dozens of birds, as the island abounds with them, but without such weaponry all they can do is gaze longingly – and even angrily – at one particularly plump and fluffy kind of bird that seems to constantly be *laughing* at them.

Oh, the insolence! Alas, they will have to rely on the slightly more meagre terrestrial fare, but with industry even that is enough to fill their starved bellies, which presents problems of its own. For in short order their bodies start to ache, as their intestines – which have lived off crumbs for weeks, only to now gorge – twist and cramp with shuddering pains. Still they keep eating, and presently the pain passes, as do, for many of them, their first evacuations in weeks.

With God's mercy, even the exotic berries that Nelson belatedly warns them not to eat prove harmless; another blessing from Providence.

For yes, despite the disaster of what has happened, the pious Bligh continues to be given reason to believe that the Good Lord is with them – and there is no better example than what they discover on this morning. For, overnight, with the Launch bobbing offshore in gentle, lapping waves, a gudgeon – a small but crucial component of the ship's rudder – had fallen out and drifted away. As Bligh knows only too well, and now glories in, if exactly the same thing had happened while they had been at sea, the rudder would have become next to useless and they surely would have been lost, with no means to steer their Launch they would have just drifted uselessly until they died. As it is, they are safely on land, and Purcell is easily able to repair the rudder, may the Lord be praised.

But not Bligh.

For when, later in the day, Bligh launches himself into a tirade – his first in a while, so perhaps he is coming back to his old self – about how these ungrateful curs don't realise how damn lucky they are to be alive, how if it wasn't for him they wouldn't be here, Nelson mutters what are close to his first unprompted words since his outburst during the Mutiny, and he utters them like they have been festering for a long time:

'Yes,' says he, 'damn his blood, if it wasn't for his economy we *wouldn't* be here!'[34]

30 May 1789, Bloody Bay, Tubuai, a hatchet for your dead husband, madam

Steady now.

Carefully.

It is no small thing to make a landing on an island when you killed more than a few of its male inhabitants just the day before, for who knows what might be about to happen? In the hope that the Natives might be of forgiving nature, the *Bounty* men have brought presents of hatchets with them. But as Christian and his heavily armed companions paddle their boats across the bay, 'carrying a white flag in the bow of one and the Union Jack in the other',[35] and carefully land, there is the strangest thing . . .

Nothing. There is no sign of any Natives, let alone dangerous ones. And even when the men make their way into the lush jungle that abounds to a clearing where they can see the roofs of huts . . . there is no-one there!

The embers of the fires are warm and it is clear people were here as recently as last night, but now, nothing. It is eerie, unsettling. Are they being watched? Very likely.

What to do now?

Christian is not quite sure.

•

At least, among all of Bligh's incompetents, one of their number, just one, has been forward thinking enough to have smuggled on board the Launch a copper pot – and never is it likely to be of more use than right now, as the men return with oysters and periwinkles aplenty, perfect for a stew. In the absence of a flint, Bligh uses his small magnifying glass to concentrate the sun's rays and start a fire (their tinder box long since waterlogged and destroyed). Soon after, aromatic oyster stew is bubbling in their lone pot. To make a real restorative feast of it, Bligh adds some of the ship's biscuit and just a little precious pork. Their mouths watering, the men gaze down upon their coming meal with relish. A hot meal! Their first in a month, and . . .

And what can be the problem, now?

Fryer, backed by Purcell, is taking issue with Bligh. Both men think that Bligh should add more fresh water to the brew, to make it go further, and Fryer, his face flashing rare emotion, is of particularly 'turbulent disposition,'[36] until Bligh orders him to, 'Be silent!'[37]

It is a close-run thing, very close, for Fryer doesn't have a whole lot of silence in him right now, and clearly wants and needs to go on with it. But, by supreme effort of will, he does indeed . . . fall . . . silent. Just.

And so it is.

Bligh and Fryer eat their stew in glowering silence, backed by glaring glances and glancing glares, a perfect fury in the pair of them even as they savour the flavour of the only real meal they have had in a month.

Following the feast there is some relief from the tension, as Fryer heads out with the foraging party to look for more food to take with them, while Bligh and Nelson wander the shore to further investigate the island, which Bligh names Restoration Island for the fact they have arrived on the 'anniversary of the restoration of King Charles the Second, and the name not being inapplicable to our present situation (for we were restored to fresh life and strength)'.[38]

As they continue to walk the white and sandy perimeter of the island, 'about a league in circuit'[39] – occasionally being obliged to leave the beach to clamber around the scrub-covered and rocky headlands that jut into the sea, they are delighted to discover a spring with bubbling fresh water, together with a handful of palm trees that Nelson strips of edible material to take with them on the Launch. They also find some curious tracks of an animal neither has ever seen before . . . but both suspect what it must be.

> Nelson agreed with me that it was the kangooro;[40] but whether these animals swim over from the mainland, or are brought here by the natives to breed, it is impossible to determine. The latter is not improbable as they may be taken with less difficulty in a confined spot like this than on the continent.[41]

More troubling is that they also soon find two wigwams, besides which 'a pointed stick was found, about three feet long, with a slit in the end of it to sling stones with, the same as the natives of Van Diemen's land use'.[42]

If this is a place that the natives frequent – and they clearly do – then it is a place the visitors are best advised to leave, sooner rather than later, as with only four cutlasses, they are perilously close to defence-less. Bligh resolves to leave on the morrow, before noon. Returning to the Launch, another oyster stew is prepared for supper, which causes another row with Fryer, backed by Purcell, who is outraged that this time Captain Bligh adds no biscuit to the meal: 'This occasioned some murmuring with the Master and Carpenter, the former of whom wanted to prove a propriety of such an Expenditure, and was troublesomely ignorant – tending to create disorder among those, if anywise weak enough to listen to him.'[43]

Bligh, of course, does not listen to him.

No biscuit.

As usual, when night falls, the men follow Bligh's orders, with one half sleeping on the Launch and the other half comfortably on shore, by the fire.

The morning brings another foraging party being dispatched for supplies, and . . . yet one more quarrel between Bligh and Fryer. When Bligh discovers that some precious pork has been stolen overnight, he immediately suspects the two men who complained about the lack of food the night before, Fryer and Purcell. Both men hotly deny it. Bligh blazes with fury, hurling accusations and frustrations at this motley crew of ragged ingrates. When Bligh's fury is, if not spent, at least diminished, he retires to the shade of a palm tree to do some writing in his little leather notebook – 'cannot discover the Wretch that did it. Kind providence protects us wonderfully but it is a most unhappy situation to be in a Boat with such discontented People who don't know what to be at or what is best for them'[44] – interspersed with barking orders at his men, as they prepare the Launch for departure and the 1500-mile journey ahead through perilous seas to Timor. And here is Fryer now, returned with his scouting party. Mr Fryer has observed Captain Bligh coolly writing in the shade as they toil in the sun like the navvies they are, but had presumed that the Captain must be performing the complex calculations of navigation to determine the course for the next leg of their journey.

But, no . . .

'Captain Bligh,' Hallett tells Fryer, 'has been correcting the prayer book.'[45]

And there is Bligh in the shell of a stolen coconut! Even the word of God needs some Bligh correction, because it is *just not good enough*!

Oh, the things Fryer could say to him if he was only free to speak. But he is not, of course, and in any case there is much to be done to get ready to leave Restoration Island.

Every available storage vessel – holding some 60 gallons in all – is filled with the spring water, and they not only fill themselves with as many shellfish as they can, but also carry more with them. To try to get them to last longer, they prise the oysters and clams open and dry them in the sun, before packing them tightly into containers in the hope that they can be used in stew. For the bread rations, Bligh calculates they have enough to keep them alive for just 38 more days.

Can it be done?

Perhaps, with the Lord's help. Now they make ready to climb aboard the Launch, and cast off when ... When all at once, they hear some strange shouts in the distance. Have they inadvertently left one of their number behind?

No. There are more men shouting than just one, and in any case it is not even coming from this island. Gazing in the direction of the shouts, they see them!

Over there!

On the mainland, about a quarter of a mile away, they observe with a start 20 or so Natives ... running and yelling, shaking spears and clubs at them from the opposite shore.

Behind them, on the hills, the heads of many more Natives appear, likely their wives and children, told to keep out of sight, but unable to resist peeking at these strange visitors from another world.

Perhaps they are not hostile – they are actually beckoning them to come over – but Bligh is taking no chances. With full bellies, plentiful water, and the best food from the area already harvested, why would he? Instead, he sets a course for two small islands on the far horizon to the north. Helped along by a strong tide, the Launch soon passes between those islands and the shore of New Holland, even as Bligh calls his men for their attention.

In a voice, it must be said, with *no* tinge of Christian humility, he wishes to read to them the prayer he has so recently penned. (He was not actually correcting the Bible, but writing religious prose of his own.)

'Oh Lord . . . We most devoutly thank Thee for our preservations & are truly conscious that only through Thy Divine Mercy we have been saved . . . Thou hast showed us wonders in the Deep, that we might see how powerful & gracious a God Thou art; how able & ready to help those who trust in Thee.'[46]

It goes on and on, with Fryer straining hard not to display his feelings. But they are strong all right. Here is a man thanking the Lord for His provision of their life essentials, when the key contribution of this same man in that provision was to sit pretty under a palm tree, penning pious paeans, and yell orders at the battered, shattered men who were actually doing the work to gather them.

Gratitude, indeed.

The Master broods.

The Captain carries on.

At some length.

31 May 1789, Tubuai, onward Christian's soldiers

By now it is obvious.

Rather than greeting the Mutineers, or even reluctantly helping them, the Natives of Tubuai are determined to hide from the visitors, in the hope that they will go away.

Reluctantly, Christian has decided to oblige them. The *Bounty* will go away. But they will return all right. This place will be their home, despite the hostility of the Natives.

But first they must return to Tahiti, to get supplies, and women.

Making his way back towards the *Bounty* – being hauled along by half-a-dozen good men and true, in the Jolly Boat – Christian's mind turns inevitably to Isabella. Will she be waiting for him? What will she think when she finds out what has happened? Will she be happy to leave Tahiti, her family, everything she has ever known, to come with him to this island? He can only hope so.

And there is only one way to find out.

'Make ready to weigh anchor . . .'

There is a flurry of men moving into position by the capstan.

'Heave cheerily,' comes the first order, followed shortly afterwards by, 'Lay aloft to make sail.'[47]

For his part, Morrison is just glad to leave the Natives of Tubuai, their 'savage aspect & behaviour could not gain favour in the eyes of any Man in his senses, but was fully capable of creating a distaste in anyone'.[48]

Come back here?

Not if he can help it!

Others on the *Bounty* feel the same, and the ship's company leave this tiny island far more divided than when they had arrived, just 24 hours earlier.

31 May 1789, Bligh sails towards the northern tip of New Holland

Across the azure waters off the coast of the far north of New Holland, the Launch proceeds apace, the Loyalists now suffering more than ever from the sun's glare off the water, the wind, and the sheer gut-busting exhaustion of staying alive. Through their red slits of eyes, they gaze to their larboard side to see extraordinarily long stretches of white sandy beaches occasionally punctuated by brown rocky headlands, and beyond them seemingly impenetrable dark green bushland.

True, there has been only a smattering of a scattering of Natives sighted on this stretch of coast – naked, gesticulating wildly, waving tree branches, yelling at them – but even they are enough for Bligh to decline to make a landing. Sail on.

Their best hope is to get to an island, which is far more likely to be entirely uninhabited, and on this Sunday morning just after 8 o'clock, having found just the thing, Bligh gives his emaciated men the order to drop anchor just off its sandy shores.

Now in a choice between naming the island after their condition – 'Starving Island' – or the day of the week, Bligh chooses the latter, but even before they land on 'Sunday Island', Fryer has something to say that has been troubling him.

'Captain,' he says before everyone, 'some of the men were rather idle in picking up oysters at the other place. I think it better for those idlers to have what they get by themselves.'[49]

In other words, finders keepers; idlers weepers.

Now, as an advocate of industry, Bligh considers Fryer's position, even as Elphinstone – who has been quite ill – offers his own view.

'I would rather stay in the boat than go after oysters,'[50] he says mournfully.

Well, when you are genuinely ill, that presents no problem to Fryer.

'Captain Bligh,' he says, gesturing to Elphinstone, 'if any man is sick and can not get any thing for himself, he shall with cheerfulness have part of mine . . . Every one able to go through the fatigue as I am . . . it stands that every man should provide for himself.'[51]

'You are very right, Mr Fryer,' replies Bligh 'I think it best we divide ourselves into three parties and what they [get] shall belong to that party.'[52]

Now, to the Captain's understanding, this means each *party* will have a good incentive to work hard.

The way Fryer sees it, however, it means that, 'what every *man* put into the kettle should take the same quantity out'.[53]

Now, as Bligh, typically, chooses to stay with the Launch, in a moment of rare collegiality Fryer promises him, before heading out in charge of one of the three parties: 'I think I can get a sufficiency for you and myself.'[54]

By Fryer's side is Purcell, who is more than pleased to hear from his friend that, as he understands it, all the oysters he gathers will be his alone.

'I'll be bound that we will provide for ourselves!'[55] he says cheerfully and sets out with his bag.

As it happens, here on Sunday Island, oysters are bountiful and Purcell's bag fills so quickly that he is the first one to head back on his own, where Bligh waits in the beached Launch, pleased to see he has a good haul.

'Hand the oysters aft, Mr Purcell,'[56] the Captain orders blithely.

'The oysters belong to my party,' replies the starving Purcell, a little sharply, as he steps into the Launch. 'That was agreed before we left the boat!'[57]

'Hand the oysters aft, Mr Purcell.'

'No,' replies Purcell.[58]

'You damned scoundrel!' yells Bligh. 'What have I brought you here for? If it had not been for me you all would have perished!'[59]

Purcell recalls the now quietly celebrated quip of Nelson two days earlier, and repeats it, right to Bligh's face.

'Yes, sir,' says Purcell. 'If it had not been for you we should not have been here!'[60]

'What's that you say, sir?' asks a puzzled Bligh, unsure if this is a studied and monstrous insult, or just a rare attempt at a joke from the Carpenter.

Purcell is happy to remove all confusion, and pointedly repeats it, word for word, complete with sneer. 'I say, sir, that if it had *not* been for you we should *not* have been here!'

Bligh now at least understands the tone of insolence, but not the entire purport of the remark.

'You damned scoundrel! What do you mean?'[61] he asks furiously.

'I am not a scoundrel,' replies Purcell. '*I am as good a man as you!*'[62]

There, he has said it. For months, Bligh's assumption of superiority has rankled with Purcell, who knows full well that Bligh is no more a gentleman than he is.

It is a mutinous remark, matching the 'mutinous aspect'[63] Bligh observes in Purcell's eyes, and for a man who has already suffered a mutiny, it proves too much to bear.

'I did not just now see where this was to end,' Bligh would write. 'I therefore determined to strike a final blow at it, and either to preserve my command or die in the attempt.'[64]

Bligh draws his sword, raises it in a threatening manner, and faces Purcell.

'Take hold of a cutlass you rascal, defend yourself!'[65] he roars, even as Fryer, who has returned just in time to bear witness to this extraordinary confrontation, begins to laugh in a slightly deranged manner at the absurdity of it all. Two men in a boat, a beached boat, about to battle! Others too – having heard the shouting, and fearing an attack by Natives – arrive on the gallop, and are also stunned by what they see.

For here is Bligh, 'swaggering with a cutlass over the carpenter's head',[66] while Purcell faces him. The Carpenter is shaking with anger, clearly yearning to do exactly as the perfidious captain has commanded, but unwilling to let go of his prized bag of oysters to do so.

Fryer soon goes from being amused to being profoundly shaken. For Bligh is *serious*. Just 30 days ago Bligh had had a cutlass held to his own throat, on his own ship. And now, here he is, standing in the only boat he has left, with a cutlass to the throat of the first of the Loyalists to truly stand up to him and his vastly diminished reign.

'*Take hold of a cutlass*!' repeats Bligh

'No, sir, you are my officer,'[67] replies Purcell, seeming to calm and come to his senses. For there is no way around it. If he takes up a cutlass, and wins the duel – oh how he'd love to – he would surely be hanged on their return to England for defying his commanding officer. But even his refusal to duel does not make him safe, as Bligh shakes with fury, clearly aching to strike the Carpenter down.

'The Captain is going to kill me!'[68] Purcell yells to all.

With the whole thing teetering on something between mutiny on one side and murder on the other, Fryer decides to take drastic action in his role as Master.

'No fighting here!' he says. 'I put you both under arrest!'[69]

As the men stand, blinking in the sunshine, unsure what to do, Bligh still holds his cutlass as high as his towering rage.

'Mr Cole, place Captain Bligh under arrest,'[70] orders Fryer.

'Mr Fryer,' barks Bligh. 'By God, sir, if you order any to touch me I will cut *you* down.'[71]

'On the contrary, Captain Bligh,' Fryer replies, as he also returns to a certain calm. 'You may rely on me to support your orders and directions in the future.'[72]

Which leaves Purcell, once more, as the only man directly threatened by the cutlass. Changing tack, Fryer tries pleading with the rankled Bligh.

'Sir, this is a very wrong time to talk of fighting,' he says.

'That man,' says Bligh, pointing at Purcell, 'said he was as good a man as I am.'[73]

'When you called me "a scoundrel", I said that I was *not*,'[74] explains Purcell meekly, while still firmly holding on to his bag of oysters.

'As good a man as you in *that* respect,'[75] qualifies Purcell, his remaining resistance collapsing.

Bligh seems to relax, ever so slightly. But what did the man mean by that other remark?

'You said that you had brought us here,' Purcell goes on, carefully, cravenly explaining himself. 'I told you that if it had *not* been for you we should *not* have been here.'[76]

Ah, the Nelson remark. Fryer and Nelson know exactly what he means, as do all those who had heard the Nelson remark whispered. Happily, however, Bligh either remains ignorant of the real meaning, or pretends he is, and accepts this explanation.

'Well then,' says Bligh. 'If you had not any meaning in [what] you said I ask your pardon.'[77]

Purcell gives his pardon, and the oyster mutiny, 'a tumult that lasted a quarter of an hour'[78] as Bligh would describe it, is over. And so to the stew. Bligh orders that it be begun, and Purcell meekly hands over his bag to get it started.

As the stew bubbles away, Bligh approaches Fryer.

'Mr Fryer, I think that you behaved very improperly,' he says.

'I am very sorry for it, sir,' replies Fryer. 'At the same time, beg to know in *what*?'[79]

'In coming . . . and saying you would put us under arrest,' states Bligh.

'Sir, will you give me leave to tell you how far I think *you* were wrong?' asks Fryer.

'Me, wrong?' asks, in turn, an incredulous Bligh.

'Yes, sir, you wrong,' replies Fryer. 'You put yourself on a footing [with] the carpenter when you took up a cutlass and told him to take another. If he had done so and cut you down it is my opinion he would have been justifiable in so doing.'[80]

It is a critique so candid – and quite possibly correct, in hindsight – that even Bligh cannot muster the bluster to counter. And so Fryer dares follow up.

'Captain Bligh, there [are] other methods in making people do as they are ordered without fighting them. You can be assured I will support you in these as far as lies in my power.'[81]

In the pause that follows, as Bligh absorbs his words, a cry comes from the distance. The oyster stew is ready – news that trumps everything else.

Without another word, Bligh and Fryer walk over to eat the meal that nearly sparked a mutiny, nearly caused a murder. At least the fact that it is a big meal, with everyone able to have their fill, helps to lighten the mood, and once it is done, and their water and food supplies are replenished, they quickly cast off.

Sail on.

Bligh sits in his customary spot at the right rear of the Launch – just as he was always to be found at the rear right-hand corner of the *Bounty* – as Sunday Island fades into the distance and the darkness. As they leave, Bligh broods on recent events. Not so long ago, he was a trusting man, never doubting for a moment the loyalty of his men. But Christian's betrayal has changed all that. And so has Peter Heywood's – something that cuts nearly as deep after all that Bligh has done for the lad. If Fletcher and Heywood could betray him, who couldn't?

He broods on it long enough that he will write in the Log a list of the Loyalists who he is sure will remain exactly that, loyal to him, whatever happens, 'well disposed' men, who give 'no uneasiness',[82] men he actually can trust: 'Hallett, Hayward, Nelson, Samuel, Peckover, Ledward, Elphinstone, Cole, Smith and Lebogue.'[83]

Two names are conspicuous for their absence: Fryer and Purcell.

And it is in contemplation of the likes of them that Bligh has come to another decision:

> I now took a cutlass, determined never to have it from under my seat, or out of my reach, as providence had seemed pleased to give me sufficient strength to make use of it.[84]

•

The next morning at dawn, the Loyalists land on another sandy island and go in search of more supplies. At noon, one man has returned from the oyster hunt extremely unwell. It is Nelson, who is so weak he can only hobble back with a man supporting him on each side. He has a terrible fever, bowels that are boiling, he cannot see properly, and cannot walk. Put simply, the heat of the sun, the starvation, has completely sapped the last of the strength he had, and now he has nothing left.

No little alarmed, Bligh oversees the men taking Nelson's clothes off, to help cool him down, as they lay down under some shady bushes before hand-feeding some bread soaked in the precious wine Bligh has saved to help revive him. More alarming still, two others, Cole and Purcell, also soon prove to be crippled by churning stomachs and blinding headaches.

The sick soon outnumber the well, a sure sign that the toll of the journey is starting to tell.

CHAPTER ELEVEN

RETURN TO THE PROMISED LAND

Their sea-green isle, their guilt-won Paradise,
No more could shield their Virtue or their Vice:
Their better feelings, if such were, were thrown
Back on themselves, – their sins remained alone.
Proscribed even in their second country, they
Were lost; [1]

Lord Byron, 'The Island'

6 June 1789, Tahiti, return to Aphrodite's Isle

At last, the promised island lies before them once more. Tahiti!

Though it has only been eight weeks since their departure, for most of the Mutineers it feels like years. Before they come into the familiar waters of Matavai Bay, Christian wishes to give one order in particular. All aft . . .

'Every man,' he says, 'is to remain under arms. It is possible that Captain Bligh has visited some of the neighbouring islands and communicated his misfortunes to Tinah. If so, Tinah will be on his side, and will order his men to recover the vessel.'[2]

. . .

. . .

The men look at each other. Can Christian *possibly* be serious? Just what kind of powers does he think Bligh has? It is the domineering, always bristling Churchill, now emerged as the second-in-command of the Mutineers, who speaks for them all.

'It would have been impossible for Captain Bligh to reach Tahiti,' he says, 'or any of the adjoining islands, without us observing the Launch.'[3]

It is a fair point, from a man known far more for violence than fairness. Nevertheless, Christian insists that everyone remain on their guard, and armed, ready for anything.

But now, Churchill takes him aside. A man practised in lying, speaking to one to whom telling falsehoods does not come easily, Churchill makes the point to Christian that he will need to have something plausible to tell Tinah and the others about why they have returned, for they can hardly tell the Chief that they have cast his beloved *Bry* onto a tiny boat in the ocean.

In response, Fletcher Christian, one of the Mutineers will note, 'seemed quite indifferent about the matter, imagining that any story they thought proper to tell would be credited by the natives'.[4]

Still, he does indeed come up with a story . . .

•

The word spreads quickly around the island.

The big ship! The *Bounty*. It is back, and *Titriano* is with them. Come quickly, Isabella!

And so they all do, with such enthusiasm that even before the anchor of the *Bounty* has touched the harbour floor, Natives are swarming her deck, old friends eager to know what's going on. Minutes later, Christian sets foot once more on the shore, and the two lovers embrace.

You are *back*.

I am back, and will part from you no more. Your shore is my shore, forevermore. For now, however, I must see the Royal family and give to them the extraordinary news of what brings us back to these parts so soon.

King Tinah receives them graciously, if curiously, and Christian excitedly tells them what has happened.

'Where is *Bry*?'[5] asks Tinah.

'He is gone to England,'[6] replies Christian.

'In what ship?'[7] asks Tinah

'In *Toote*'s ship,'[8] replies Christian.

Tinah looks back, stunned. The ship of Captain Cook? Bligh has met up with his father?

'How came you to meet *Toote*,' he asks excitedly, 'and where is he?'[9]

Well, therein lies a quickly invented tale. For as Fletcher now tells it, they had been not long out at sea, when they came across another ship, and it proved to be Captain Cook himself! Yes, wonderful news. Captain Bligh had been quite beside himself to find his father, and now that they are reunited, neither could bear to be parted from the other. And so Captain Cook had insisted that his son come with him to settle the new country of 'Wytootacke'.

'He . . . has sent me for all those who will come and live with him!'[10] Christian continues.

The great *Toote* has also *specifically asked* his great friend Tinah, for 'The Bull and the Cow and as many Hogs as you will send him!'[11]

And yet, King Tinah also has another question that Christian has been expecting.

'What is become of the bread-fruit?'[12]

'He has sent it home to England with Bligh,'[13] Christian quickly explains. King Tinah accepts the explanation without question for the moment.

It is extraordinary. And wonderful.

Toote has asked for *our* help?

The Tahitians feel as if God himself has honoured them by asking for their earthly aid. Of course they can help!

Anything for Captain Cook!

Within mere minutes of the request being made, the Tahitians have hopped to with a haste that is almost unnatural to them, corralling the first of the hogs and goats, leading them like a scene from a poor man's version of Noah's Ark to a makeshift pen on the deck of the *Bounty*. And chickens, you will need lots of chickens, a dog, and the very bull and cow originally brought to these shores by Captain Cook.

In the meantime, of course, the greatest pleasure for most of the Mutineers is to be back among those who love them most and, as Mr Coleman would note, 'It is impossible to describe the pleasure which some of the females felt upon seeing their former gallants.'[14]

Merriment and music is the order of the day, before they get to the pleasures of the night, and the Blind Fiddler, ably accompanied on the flute by a talented Tahitian named Timoa, puts on a virtuoso performance. For many hours, their worries are banished as they immerse themselves in paradise. Certainly, the Mutiny was an extreme measure, but compare all this to being back on the *Bounty* with the bastard, Bligh.

Apart from the general celebrations, there is also a special wrestling match, this one between a man and a woman, 'wherein all difference of sex was lost sight of, for the woman was equally if not more violent than the man, and she almost broke his leg with a fall ... The lady who had thrown him, received universal congratulations, and, indeed, she was not a little proud of her triumph.'[15]

(It is not as if the Mutineers need reminding, but there it is. As voluptuous and available as the Tahitian maidens are, they can be very dangerous indeed.)

June 1789, Tahiti, let no man be put asunder

Dearly beloved, we are gathered here in the sight of God ... to witness the union, of this man, Fletcher Christian, and this woman, Isabella – known to her parents as 'Mauatua', and to the men of the *Bounty* as 'Mainmast'.

Actually, with no Christian priest to preside, most of the ceremony on this splendid day is conducted by a Tahitian priest, though of ceremony itself, there is precious little. That is not the way in Tahiti.

As James Morrison – a man of deep faith, if not *always* faithful to it – notes, in Tahiti the couple 'join, and are called man and wife without ceremony except the greeting of their friends, who present them with hogs, cloths and sundry necessary articles'.[16]

Nevertheless, it is a grand occasion for both the Mutineers and the Tahitians, a union between their best and most beautiful.

Even surly Mr Coleman,[17] one of the four Loyalists on the island, will note his broad approval, starting with the form of Isabella.

'She was young, affectionate, genteel, and ... she might well be accounted handsome. Their mutual affection was remarkable, and the sincerity of their loves indisputable. In short, they were married according to their fashion . . . exchanging mutual promises before all their friends who are on this occasion invited.'[18]

For Christian, his dearest wish has been accomplished. This glorious woman has transformed his life and shown him the extraordinary possibilities of existence. Clearly, Isabella feels the same about him.

Tane, the God of Gods, beams upon their binding, it shall be good, it shall be great, and it will be a love filled with the warmth of the sun above, the lustre of the moon, a love for all time.

Christian's happiness is complete, and he is not the only one. For, shortly thereafter, George Stewart also marries a beautiful maiden, as does Thomas McIntosh marry his beautiful 'Mary', who he can barely bear to be without for even a few minutes. Still, come nightfall, when away from the others, Mary becomes aware of a secret sadness – her husband weeping for William Bligh and the Loyalists they have cast away in the middle of the ocean. Talking to other brides, Mary realises Thomas is not alone, as boys like Monkey Ellison – less able to contain his emotions – even weep at the mention of Bligh's name. As far as they know, Bligh is dead, as are all their crewmates on that Launch. The unknown fate of their former comrades stalks their current happiness, lurking behind each peaceful moment and glorious day.

There is also growing dissension, and even anger, among the Mutineers, on Christian's insistence that they are only to stay in Tahiti for a short time, to re-victual, gather the Tahitians who want to come with them, and then be on their way.

Must they really leave here?

Could they ever have it better?

And while, on the one hand, many of the Mutineers hope the Loyalists are still alive – for then their act would be only mutiny not murder – they must face the truth. There is only an infinitesimal chance that, in that tiny boat, any of them would ever survive long enough to inform the Admiralty of what has happened.

9 June 1789, on the Launch, a dolphin does little to dispel the gloom
In the course of their journey so far, they have caught the odd fish, as well as the odd bird – all to be divided, gizzards and all, with ruthless economy, and eaten raw. For in this realm, beggars are not choosers, they are devourers.

On this sunny afternoon, the sails are full, they have rounded the top of New Holland and they are pushing to the west at a rate of four knots, with a moderate easterly breeze, when suddenly there is a hard jerk on the fishing line they have had trailing behind the boat for most of the journey – without success to this point – and all hell breaks loose with wild thrashing in the waters behind them. They have caught something! Yes, look there, leaping out of the water! A DOLPHIN has swallowed whole the hook.

Haul, me hearties, *haul*, and get it on the boat!

It takes some doing for the much weakened crew to get such a powerful creature on to the Launch – and all the while they are terrified the dolphin will shake loose and free itself – but finally, amid much shouting, it is on board and stabbed until it lies still, with only its gimlet eye staring at them to tell of the brutality of what has just occurred.

No matter. Bligh orders each man to be served with two ounces of dolphin, the awful offal included, and has the rest cut into slices to be dried in the sun. The men gulp down the first serving, unthinking and ravenous.

At daylight, 10 June, of course they beg for more, to stave off the starvation that is once more getting a grip on their very souls, but Bligh insists they must wait till evening.

'A few days and we will be in Timor,' he assures them, masking his own abiding doubt. Looking around he can 'see an alteration for the worse with more than half my people whose looks rather indicated an approaching end to their distresses.'[19]

That end is death, not land, unless he can make such food as they do have, last, just on the top side of starvation rations.

> Served the usual allowance of bread and water and at noon we
> dined on the remainder of the dolphin ... 1 oz, per man.[20]

By the next morning again, 11 June, things are even worse as more and more men appear to succumb to the terrible toll of their trials: ashen faces, swollen limbs, an inability to concentrate and comprehend, a propensity to lie practically comatose at all times.

Noting that Ledward and Lebogue seem the worst, Bligh gives both men a few precious teaspoons of wine, 'out of the little I have preserved for this dreadful Stage',[21] before turning his attention to Cole, who, if he is not quite at death's door, is at least well up the path leading to it, and readying to knock.

And yet, still Cole is not so far gone that he can't summon some compassion of his own.

'Captain, I really think *you* look worse than anyone in the boat,'[22] Cole says.

In response, Bligh cannot help himself, and laughs loudly. Here he is trying to restore life to a man on the edge of death, and that man only has to take one look at Bligh and reckons his Captain will be dead before him!

'I had,' Bligh will record, 'good humour enough to return him a better compliment.'[23]

Thank you, Mr Cole, but, I assure you, I am in better shape than you are!

Death may indeed be their portion, but, in the meantime, the rations will remain as constant as Bligh has deemed.

•

Still, when the sun is at its zenith at midday on this 11th day of June, Bligh, as ever, takes his sextant, and Fryer his old quadrant – and they both take sightings of the sun's altitude, before consulting the nautical tables and doing their calculations. As ever, they both check their calculations twice, before comparing, a practice that, in the past, has sometimes enabled Bligh to determine just how wrong Fryer has got it this time.

Today, however, they are in full agreement and Bligh is happy to share their conclusion: 'allowing the East End of Timor to be 128°00' East [our] distance from it is only 33 leagues'.[24]

A flicker of joy registers on those Loyalists who still have the energy to register anything at all. Just a little over a hundred miles to go . . .

Still, Bligh being Bligh and Fryer being Fryer, their satisfaction is not long in turning into spiteful bickering, as that very evening they catch a booby bird, which, as Bligh recounts, 'I reserved for our Dinner, but I had some difficulty to stop the Master's muttering because I would not serve it for Breakfast, for this ignorant Man conceived he was instantly to be in the midst of plenty'.[25]

We are not at Timor yet, Mr Fryer.

Tension between Mr Fryer and Captain Bligh soon rises further still as a haze descends, and the Master becomes convinced that Captain Bligh is steering them wrong, convinced as Bligh is that the land he can see in the distance is Timor, while Mr Fryer is equally certain – and he says so loudly and with conviction – they are just islands. But Captain Bligh apparently cares so little for what Mr Fryer thinks, that he maintains his course, leaving the Master no choice but to wait to see how long it takes this master of mapping, this bastard Bligh, to realise his mistake.

Still, as the Launch ploughs on, others in the boat begin to feel 'rather uneasy'[26] with their course and with Bligh's decision, for if Bligh is wrong a single day of delay might see more than a couple of men dead. As the hours pass, a muted muttering begins, growing ever louder: *Mr Fryer, speak with the Captain.*

But Fryer will have none of it.

'Captain Bligh,' he tells the mutterers, 'never asked my opinion.'[27]

But, equally, let there be no mistake, as he is happy to share that opinion with them. 'They are islands some distance from Timor,'[28] he says.

'They must be the islands of Roti!' Peckover agrees. 'I remember when I was there with Captain Cook we could see Timor!'[29]

Peckover's words add to the general alarm. For if they continue Bligh's course they risk missing the settlement entirely, and possibly even heading out into the Indian Ocean, to be swept along by the trade winds.

With Bligh now out of earshot, engaged in deep conversation at the back of the Launch with Nelson, Fryer is up the other end, meaning more officers and men can approach him, to now openly voice their fears.

'Mr Fryer, them are islands!'[30] says one man, panicked.

'We are running off from land,' mutters an officer. 'After all our suffering we shall get nowhere!'[31]

Taking matters into his own hands, Peckover carefully threads his way to the stern of the Launch, and dares to interrupt the conversation between Bligh and Nelson, voicing his concerns. Interrupting him, Bligh calls out a question to the front.

'Mr Fryer, what do you think of that land ahead?'[32]

'What I first thought it was,' replies Fryer. 'Islands.'[33]

The dismissive, contemptuous reply, spoken loudly so the whole Launch is left in no doubt what he thinks of Bligh's navigation on this occasion, leaves the Captain infuriated.

'Why did not you give your opinion *before*?'[34] barks Bligh.

'You must have heard me say, sir, that they was islands when we first saw them,' returns Fryer in his deep rhythmic Norfolk accent. 'But as you did not *ask* me my opinion, I did not think it proper to give it.'[35]

'Well, sir,' says Bligh, his voice managing to shake with anger at the same time as it drips with sarcasm, 'What is best to do now?'[36]

Fryer does not hesitate.

'Go in for the land we have been running from,'[37] he says firmly.

In short, Captain Bligh, you damn fool, change your course immediately, and steer us back north-west to Timor proper!

As stormy as Bligh is in response, still he is no match for the weather itself as, with remarkable rapidity, the sea begins to rise and rage.

And yet, despite the sudden danger, the need to reef sails, and to commence baling, still Bligh does not calm but winds up, tighter and tighter, into 'a great passion'.[38]

The skipper *cannot* leave it alone.

'Sir,' says Bligh in that way he has where, though the word is respectful, the tone is a studied insult, 'I suppose that you will take the boat from me?'

'No, sir,' replies Fryer, 'I despise your idea.'

Clearly, too, he despises Bligh personally.

'[It is] far from my intention to take the Boat from you. But, sir, give me leave to tell you that *life to me is sweeter than it has been yet since I left the ship*.'[39]

Again, Fryer's meaning is clear, even if the words are cleverly framed.

For the line between insolence and innocence is simply one of interpretation, don't you see? But *you* get my meaning, now, don't you, Captain Bligh, as do all the men. And that is all that counts: the closer we get to Timor, the sweeter it is for all of us, as we will all soon be able to get away from *you*!

Lightning flashes, thunder roars. And that is just Bligh, livid as never before.

'Oh no, sir,' yells Bligh, his hand going to his sword. 'I am not afraid that you would take the Boat from me, I would soon *cut you to pieces*!'[40]

Fight fire with fire, and a storm with a storm.

For now, the sea rises so fast in this real storm that they are in danger of being completely swamped and sunk, even though they are possibly just hours from safety. For the moment, the verbal clash must take pause, as they bale for their lives, with Fryer noting, 'there was now as much Danger in swamping the Boat as any time since we were turned adrift'.[41]

At least, however, once the storm abates, Fryer has the grim satisfaction of watching as Bligh directs the helmsman of the Launch to change course, away from the islands at their south-west and head north-west, on to what Fryer declares to be Timor.

Yes, it seems that Bligh now agrees that he had been wrong, which, of course, makes him all the more furious at Fryer. For once the course is set, Bligh takes up the verbal cudgels once more to strike rhetorical blows upon Fryer, clearly intent on provoking him to the point that he will respond with unambiguous insolence, just a sentence or two for which he *can* be court-martialled.

'Mr Fryer,' advises Bligh sarcastically. 'You would be dangerously troublesome if not for your ignorance and want of resolution.'[42]

Very well, sir, if you say so, sir.

Fryer refuses to rise to the bait.

The waves lap against the hull.

From a distance comes the cry of seabirds.

Arriving in a sandy bay just as the sun starts to gain momentum on its downward arc, Bligh orders the grapnel to be heaved over the side so he may do some navigational calculations, before committing to following the shoreline.

Gazing to that shore, men can soon see single plumes of smoke rising from several places. Where there are such plumes, there are people. Where there are people, there is food. Food being cooked! A real meal!

Fryer, for one, would like to get to land and explore the possibilities of asking those people to *share* their meal.

Alas, despite all his years at sea, the fact is, the Master can swim no better than a large rock. But, there is another way.

'Captain Bligh,' suggests Fryer. 'If those that can swim take the small line onshore, then I will go overboard and haul myself on shore.'[43]

'Mr Fryer, I will go with you,'[44] says Purcell, to a small rumbling of excitement on the Launch.

All eyes turn to Bligh. What will he decide?

Should he allow the two most infernal men on the Launch to go ashore as a diplomatic party to Natives unknown? Even when they are so close to Coupang and still have bare rations on board?

NO, he replies, firm.

'You keep us from getting supplies!'[45] Mr Purcell dares to complain.

'I give *you* leave to quit the Boat,' says Bligh. 'The *others* I direct to remain.'[46]

His meaning is clear. Both men are free to risk their lives dog-paddling the 40 yards to shore through a current unknown, before heading off, unarmed and unaccompanied, to confront Natives unknown. But everyone else on the Launch is ordered to stay here with him, in relative safety.

Fryer and Purcell have no choice.

'Finding no one to be of their party,' Bligh gleefully notes, 'they chose to be excused.'[47]

They will remain on the Launch, fuming.

•

Fletcher Christian is worried.

Things on Tahiti are not as they were before.

'Several thefts were committed by the natives,' Coleman would recount, 'and the chiefs paid little or no attention to the complaints which were made against them.'[48]

Most worrying of all, 'Tinah, was particularly inquisitive and troublesome . . .'[49]

An astute man, Tinah has clearly been thinking his way through the story. And now, with one eyebrow raised, he has some rather probing questions for *Titriano*.

'I wonder that Captain Cook's death, if he is now alive, was not contradicted long ago?'[50] asks Tinah.

Christian hums and haws, but has no response.

'I am surprised,' Tinah continues, 'that he should fix his residence in Wytootacke.'[51]

After all, *Toote* loved Tahiti, and Tinah knows very well, from the reaction of all Europeans to this shore, that what is offered here is not found anywhere else in the world. So why would *Toote* settle in Wytootacke?

Christian strains for a plausible answer, but, not finding one, remains silent.

'What induces Captain Bligh to settle there too?' Tinah wonders. 'Are the people of that island more friendly and agreeable than the people of Tahiti?

'Has King George consented to it?'[52]

'These questions,' Coleman would observe, 'puzzled Christian not a little, and his palpable confusion did not escape the notice of the enquirer.'[53]

'What time do you mean to leave us?' asks Tinah now.

'Immediately,' replies Christian, carefully, 'if we are already grown troublesome.'[54]

No, no, no, Tinah will not go that far. At least not yet. But now, another Chief speaks up, with yet another question for which there is no answer.

'As Captain Bligh has settled in Wytootacke and seemingly abandoned his own people as well as his foreign friends, it would be equally just in Captain Christian to settle in Tahiti, after the example of your commander?'[55]

'True, true,' answers Christian, seeing a way out here. 'Perhaps I may, I'll consider.'[56]

But this answer only worsens things, as Coleman observes once more. 'Christian's seeming approbation of this advice served to increase their suspicions, and in all probability the proposal was made for the sake of trying him.'[57]

Tinah resumes his questioning, and is even more pointed, his usual jovial expression now inquisitorial.

'Do you intend to abide with us during life?'[58]

'Yes,' replies Christian, forcing a smile.

'Then Captain *Bry* has used me very ill!' cries the King, suddenly outraged. 'He received from me some presents to deliver to King George!'[59]

He refers not to the bread-fruit plants, but his many personal gifts – most particularly the two exquisite *parais*, Tahitian robes, specially made for Royalty. The assembly of those sacred robes had been presided over for days by Tinah himself, and they were then given to Bligh with the prayer that, 'The King of England might forever remain my friend and not forget me.'[60]

So ... where are those sacred robes that were handed to *Bry*, in good faith, to give to King George?

And where is *Bry*?

For having been on the *Bounty*, Tinah knows only too well the truth, and now pronounces it: 'I find that the greater part of [my gifts] remain in the vessel.'[61]

. . .

Well, Captain Christian?

. . .

Well, indeed. Christian has been quite thrown, and is not sure of the way out. But, clearly he must back up.

'I am only joking,' Christian finally declares. 'I am waiting for a more convenient season.'[62]

Once it arrives, he will, as he has said all along, return to Wytootacke, but *then*, by which he means, as soon as possible, 'I intend to proceed for England; and, according to Captain Bligh's directions, deliver those presents to the King in the name of the donor.'[63]

'But,' interrupts Tinah, 'has the captain given you a list of those things which I expect in return, and which are to be sent by the large vessel, in which we are to visit England?'[64]

There is no end to this! It is the way of lies. While truth is free-standing, lies need ever more lies to keep them standing, and those new lies need lies of their own.

But, yes, King Tinah, of course I have that list. It is very important.

Christian cannot get away from this gathering quick enough. Things are becoming completely unworkable, and downright dangerous.

They must leave Tahiti, and as soon as possible.

Afternoon, 13 June 1789, in Roti Channel, the waters off the southern tip of Timor

On their way once more, Captain Bligh and his brooding, starving crew haul up the anchor and set sail out of the sandy and sheltered cove and at 3 pm, they come to a spacious bay, with an entrance some two miles wide.

Just inside this promising entrance, a promising shore is spotted on the eastern side, near which they see a hut, a dog and some cattle. Bligh dispatches Cole and Peckover, who return with five Natives and the good news that they are indeed very near the port of Coupang. The friendly Natives point north-east but add a few hand gestures that clearly mean there are reefs to negotiate on the way.

With his own hand gestures, Captain Bligh convinces one man to come with them as a guide, on the promise of a large reward.

They have a pilot. They have a direction. They have every chance of reaching safety, their salvation against all odds, within hours!

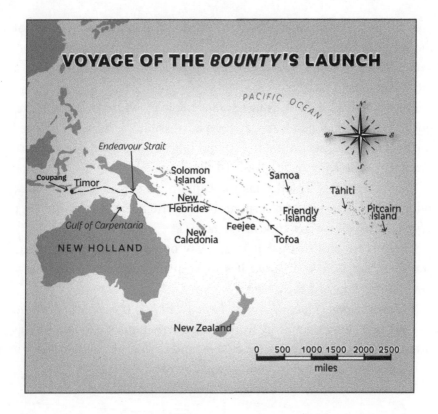

At half past four the Loyalists set sail once more, with wind in their sails, and hope in their hearts. Yes, as night falls so does the wind, but there is to be no stopping now. Bligh simply orders the men to start rowing, and so they do, the very last reserves of their strength being put to the oars and the cause.

Yes, it really is extraordinary how, after seven weeks of privation, now that their journey's end is near, these brittle skeletons of men can somehow summon the strength to not only row, but row hard. Bligh is delighted. Still, by 10 o'clock, his caution re-asserts itself and he orders them to rest, against a current that has suddenly strengthened. Dropping a grapnel anchor, their rest is sweet and all the more so when Bligh, for the first time this whole voyage – and perhaps even since time began – issues a double allowance of bread and a little wine.

It is enough. Their exertions, the food, the wine, all combine with the fact that they really are nearly there, to give the Loyalists 'the most happy and sweet sleep that ever men had'.[65]

Only Bligh stays awake, sitting at the stern, waiting for the tide to turn, and when it does, he rouses the men once more to set the sails, and in the dark early morning they are on their way.

Somewhere in the distance ahead, they suddenly hear the blast of two cannon. The sweet sound of civilisation, of salvation, a clap of man-made thunder that sees a surge of life pouring into every man on board, just to hear it, as throughout the Launch men sit bolt upright, staring straight ahead.

When the wind picks up and begins to blow them off course, their tiny sails no match for its strength, they take to their oars once more and keep rowing until dawn reveals a welcome sight in the near distance. Can it be? Yes, it is!

> A small fort and town, which the pilot told me was Coupang.[66]

For most of the Loyalists, nothing is more important than to arrive, to get off this infernal Launch, to eat, to drink, to be among civilised people again. Ah, but Bligh has different priorities.

He does not wish to arrive in the harbour of Coupang looking like a bunch of bedraggled ruffians, beggars in a boat, on their last legs. No, sir. We are British sailors, proud to be serving in His Majesty's Royal Navy, and we will fly the Union Jack as we make our entrance. The small handmade Jack is duly hauled up the main-mast, and Bligh feels a surge of pride.

There it flaps, ragged and dirty, emblematic of the tattered, starving Loyalists in the Launch – but, like them, it also projects pride.

They have done it!

14 June 1789, Coupang Harbour, a miracle observed

Tropical torpor, be thy name.

Such is the nature of the place where lassitude and apathy gaze at each other wanly every day, idly wondering how it can be so damn hot *again* and if, perhaps, tomorrow might be a bit damn cooler?

Whatever the travails of the colonial outpost, Coupang – based around a heavily manned garrison, situated by a river that flows into a deep harbour – it is at least the centre of some small industry, based around sandalwood and bees-wax, worked by Natives, together with sundry Dutch, Malay and Chinese inhabitants, and it has grown to about 150 houses in total.

Yes, this far-flung trading post is a barely known something in the middle of a vast nothing, and its residents do not receive many visitors . . .

Now, what's *this*?

For, shortly after dawn on this day, 14 June 1789, a strange vessel appears, a ragged boat, peopled by haggard sailors in raggedy clothes – and yet, despite that, from their mast they fly a tattered Union Jack. Look closer still, through your long spy-glass. To a man they are near blackened by the sun, their cheeks sunken, their visages cadaverous, their clothes hanging limply from their bones – men who have lost everything bar the will to live, and some seem to have lost nearly that.

Strange indeed, and many a gun is trained upon them as they slowly, oh so slowly, bob-bob-bob their way up the harbour.

Now, if Bligh feels a certain amount of satisfaction on this day, there can be no doubt he is entitled to. Never, in maritime history, has an open boat been sailed such a distance, through such savage waters – a little more than 4000 miles, a sixth of the Earth's circumference, over 47 days – and all without losing a man, at least not at sea.

Arriving within a hundred yards of the shore, the Loyalists can see plenty of Indians, with the odd European, going to and fro on the cobble-stone streets – which is exciting enough – but still Bligh calls a halt. It would be a breach of naval protocol to just charge to one of the many wharves and get out.

No, he wants to be invited to land. And so there is indeed a pause as both those in the Launch, and those on the shore, get a good look at each other, until finally, the invitation from a white man comes to Bligh.

Most thrillingly, it comes from an Englishman.

Yes, stepping forward from a crowd of Natives, a single English sailor hails them and welcomes them to Coupang. He informs them that the Governor of Coupang, Willem Adriaan Van Este, is at death's door and consequently it is the sailor's own commander, Captain Spikerman – the brother-in-law of the now incapacitated Governor – who is temporarily in charge. If they will come on shore, the sailor says he will be happy to take this fellow dressed in the shattered and tattered remains of what must once have been a magnificent uniform of the Royal Navy – Captain William Bligh, you say? – and his men immediately to see him.

Captain Bligh gives the order and the men pull the oars, gliding the last 20 yards to a wharf.

'Bank oars.'

The bowman secures a line to the wharf and they all clamber out, and onto the ground proper of this European outpost, which is nothing less than the land of their dreams, paradise, salvation and the promise of a better future – at a time when they all would have settled for *a* future – all rolled into one.

Soon enough, seemingly every European in Coupang has heard of their arrival, and has hurried to the shore to witness this extraordinary scene, one that strains even Bligh's own power of description:

> The abilities of a painter, perhaps, could never have been displayed to more advantage than in the delineation of the two groups of figures, which at this time presented themselves. An indifferent spectator would have been at a loss which most to admire; the eyes of famine sparkling at immediate relief, or the horror of their preservers at the sight of so many spectres, whose ghastly countenances, if the cause had been unknown, would rather have excited terror than pity. Our bodies were nothing but skin and bones, our limbs were full of sores, and we were clothed in rags; in this condition, with the tears of joy and gratitude flowing down our cheeks, the people of Timor beheld us with a mixture of horror, surprise, and pity.[67]

Bligh himself can scarcely believe that he has done it.

> Thus happily ended through the blessing of divine providence, without accident a voyage of the most extraordinary nature that ever happened in the world, let it be taken either in its extent, duration, or so much want of the necessaries of life.[68]

Before leaving for Captain Spikerman's residence, however, Bligh insists that one man in particular stay behind in the Launch, to guard it. None other than . . . Master John Fryer. Yes, Mr Fryer, you. We will go off to receive the hospitality Captain Spikerman offers, while you must bear the responsibility of keeping our precious vessel secure. You may choose one man to stay with you.

Shocked and infuriated – does Bligh's vengeance know no bounds, even in triumph? – Fryer chooses the only man whose selection might anger Bligh in turn, the Captain's own servant, John Smith.

Smith's bony shoulders sink with silent disappointment.

And so the furious Fryer and the glumly obedient Smith stay behind, while Bligh and his rag-tag crew of Loyalists walk to comfort, led and, in some cases, helped, through the cobble-stone streets of this fortress town.

They traipse past Malay and Chinese houses at first, which give way to impressive European stone mansions complete with piazzas and fine trees and gardens. Once familiar sights now stun the men. They keep walking towards the wooden walls of the fort itself, its protruding cannon dominating all beneath, its grand residence within. Arriving inside, they are greeted like a platoon of prodigal sons by a very surprised Captain Spikerman. This way, gentlemen, this way!

Within minutes, the Governor's Surgeon himself arrives and starts moving from man to man. Never in the Surgeon's long career has he had to care for such a large group of desperately weak men – just another day or two and some among them must surely have perished.

Back at the Launch, meantime, Fryer waits in the sun, burning up, externally, internally, *eternally*.

The *hide* of the man!

He sits, he rages, he curses. Finally, an hour after the cursed Bligh had left them here, along comes a soldier to offer them tea and cake.

But the soldier is not British, meaning these 'rations' are not official, meaning both Fryer and poor Smith decline to wolf the cakes down as might be expected. For Fryer will take no chances with one so devilishly devious and cruel as Bligh. If he returns and sees them eating on duty, it would provide further fuel to the fire that Fryer expects to soon be facing. And so, though starving, they actually tuck the cakes under their filthy jackets.

Bligh finally sends a messenger to the Launch with a message for Mr Fryer . . . just not the one the Master is expecting.

All Bligh's things are to be brought on shore and the boat is to be brought further into the harbour once the tide turns, he is informed.

In other words, Fryer is to continue to wait, under the sun, with no food and drink, until the tide rises! For the sake of a slightly further berth for the Launch. It is an *unbelievably* petty instruction under the circumstances, *at least to most*. But, of course, Mr Fryer *believes* it. Clearly, Bligh wants him to snap, to do something for which he can be court-martialled, so as to have his final revenge.

No-one knows better than Mr Fryer the heights of bastardry, the depths of venality, of which Captain Bligh is capable, but there it is. As long as Fryer is on this vessel, Bligh is his commander, and he is to remain on this vessel, by Bligh's command. As Bligh's goods are unloaded from the Launch and carried away, Fryer and Smith remain – the former glowering, the latter meekly.

Yes, as the hours slip by, baking in the sun, as Bligh sups and smirks nearby, no doubt in complete comfort, it becomes harder. But still Fryer remains resolute. Wherever Bligh is, the bastard is *not* going to get the better of him, *not* going to make him disobey orders or publicly snarl at him – no matter how much he deserves it!

•

Up in Captain Spikerman's residence the relief of the rest of the Loyalists goes on as, moving on from tea and bread, the men eat their share of pork, and drink more than their share of water and wine. Though their tender stomachs are not sure, they can hardly help themselves.

But now what?

A Dutch merchant arrives to have a quiet word with Captain Spikerman, telling him 'There is an officer [still] in the Boat and one man.'[69]

Really? Extraordinary. It has been well over four hours since the Launch arrived!

'I am very much surprised,' the Captain replies. 'I thought everybody was at my house.'[70] Immediately Spikerman orders that hot tea and loaves of bread be sent to them by way of welcome, with an invitation to come up to his house.

And welcome they are. But while Mr Smith is happy to depart, Mr Fryer refuses. He knows Bligh's tricks, and will *not* be accused of abandoning his duty by Bligh, until he is sure that Bligh cannot pin that charge on him.

Mercifully that order finally comes, when a uniformed man comes down with another message: 'You *must* go to Captain Spikerman's house.'[71]

'Is the English Captain there?'[72] asks Fryer. In other words, did Bligh hear this order?

'Yes,' replies the puzzled man. 'And all the people.'[73]

Fine, then. If there are witnesses, Fryer is prepared to leave the Launch, and does indeed accompany the messenger to Spikerman's grand residence. Staggering inside, for he is completely spent and can barely remain upright, he is instantly more staggered still to find all the men, who just hours ago were ragged ghosts, now living, breathing, eating, drinking, laughing . . . *enjoying* themselves! From the nearby kitchen comes the delicious waft of freshly cooked meat. Servants bearing china plates, covered by silver domes, bustle by towards a dining table groaning under the weight of food.

And there, too, stands Bligh.

'Mr Fryer!' says Bligh cheerfully *'How do you do?'*[74]

And that is Bligh all right, who never saw a wound he didn't wish to pour more salt into.

But Fryer has come too far, is too close to deliverance, and this time will not be goaded.

'I thank you for your compliments, Captain,'[75] replies Mr Fryer tightly, and hobbles, wobbles, past.

And who is this smiling countenance now approaching? Of course, *mijn* host, Captain Spikerman.

'I am sorry,' says this fine Dutch captain, this model of what a commanding officer could be, 'I did not know *who* was left in the Boat.'[76]

Offering Fryer a glass of his finest wine, Spikerman waves an airy hand and says, 'You must stay here, sir'[77] – for nothing is too good for the Master of the *Bounty* – before leading him to the dinner table where a fine, warm meal awaits, with full flagons of wine.

Mr Fryer sits down, pauses, gazes at it all . . . and for the first time this voyage, the famously stoical Master begins to cry.

Mid-June 1789, Tahiti, Nānā Parahi Araua'e . . . goodbye

The time is fast approaching, and they all know it.

Before long, the Mutineers must leave Tahiti for an as yet undetermined destination, although Peter Heywood has no doubt where they must head, and tells Christian time and again.

'Return to England,' he pleads persistently. 'And throw yourselves on the mercy of God!'[78]

Which is all very well. But there is no God that Christian has ever heard of who might make the Admiralty forgive an Acting Lieutenant for seizing a ship and putting her Captain and 18 loyal men in a small boat in the middle of the High Seas. So the answer is no.

Quietly, privately, Christian confides in Stewart – just as he had the night before the Mutiny – and gives free rein to his troubled thoughts, his grief at what has happened, his realisation at the enormity of what they have done. On one thing he is vehement: 'Rather than return [to England],' says he, his low voice a'trembling, 'I would die! . . . Sooner would I suffer massacre, and all the tortures these barbarous natives could inflict, than once set my foot upon English ground to be called to an account, and bear the reproaches that I should surely meet!'[79]

And yet, Heywood persists in his insistence that they must return to England. Coleman also joins in.

'I have considered it well,' says Christian at one point, 'and by God I'll die before I agree.'[80]

'Considered!' replies Heywood, echoing his words sarcastically. 'Would to heaven you had "considered" before you had *acted at all*.'[81]

And so it has come to this.

Does Heywood not understand? Christian never wanted the Mutiny. He was happy to cast off on his raft. But no, he was prevailed upon by the others to join, to lead, what was always *their* mutiny. And now Heywood is publicly blaming *him*? It is as if he had been slapped in the face by a brother.

'This keen reproach stung Christian's soul,' Coleman would recount, 'and he was never afterwards on friendly terms with Heywood.'[82]

Truthfully?

In these difficult times, Christian is seldom on friendly terms even with himself as the full implications of his choices weigh upon him so heavily. And yet, despite his self-condemnation, he remains defiant.

'No, never, never shall I be brought to justice for what I have done: though thousands and ten thousands attacked me, I'd die 'ere I would surrender,' he declares before his men. 'I'd rather meet a host of devils than once see the injured Captain Bligh's [wife and children].'[83]

It is only in the arms and loving embrace of Isabella, losing himself in her soothing touch and soft voice, that he is able to dispel his shame and gloom to find true solace, if only for a short time.

Of course, the state of Christian's mind worries the other Mutineers. He is frequently so depressed they even worry about leaving him on his own, and it is found that only the soothing ministrations of Isabella can lift him up from his remorseful reverie.

More than ever, Christian becomes eager to leave the island forever, to return to Tubuai, perhaps, to establish a new life there. If all goes well, they may even be able to entreat some of the Tahitians to accompany them, so they could liaise with their hosts – for their languages are similar, if not identical – which should help keep the peace. The Tahitians could also do much of the work that will be necessary to establish the new settlement.

But there is fierce resistance from some of the Mutineers – with none more vocal than the increasingly angry Isaac Martin and Charley Churchill.

Are we really to suffer 'perpetual banishment', Martin asks in his American twang, condemned to wander forever like 'vagabonds upon earth'?[84]

For his part, Churchill is insistent – and he seems to have more and more to say lately, and be ever louder about it, almost challenging Christian's leadership – that they could do no better than where they are right now.

'We will have a worse chance with islanders we are unacquainted with,' he insists, 'than with these people we have known for so long.'[85]

But Christian insists. They must leave. Now, as to convincing some Tahitians to come with them, there are varying degrees of difficulty.

For some, like Isabella, despite her strong ties to her family, there is never any question but that she will come with *Titriano* now, whatever he does, wherever he goes, for the rest of his life. Others, too, are coming forward to accompany them, either women who have Mutineer partners, or Native men in search of adventure.

One fact that Christian is determined to hide is his intention to never return to Tahiti, as it is the first place that the Royal Navy will come looking for them, and the Navy will, of course, be merciless. Instead, he makes vague promises of return. Other Mutineers make similar promises to their own women, without knowing if a return is possible or not.

As for the Tahitian men the Mutineers need – primarily for the labour necessary to both run the ship, and, more importantly, to settle Tubuai and till the fields – they are promised adventure, the chance to explore the world beyond their horizons!

•

The *Bounty* is once again fully laden – '460 Hogs, mostly breeders, 50 Goats and a quantity of fowls, a few dogs & Cats',[86] as well as a bull and cow, once gifts to Tahiti from Captain Cook, which stand confused on the upper deck of the gently rocking ship. In the late morning the anchor is weighed, and the *Bounty* is on its way once more, under reefed sails in a strong breeze.

As one, Christian and his fellow Mutineers gaze back at these islands of paradise slowly sinking beneath the northern horizon. And they are not the only ones.

For, also on the ship, are no fewer than 28 Tahitians – nine men, ten women, eight boys and a small female child. Among them, of course, is Isabella, who is feeling as vulnerable as she ever has in her life.

If she could, she would stay tight to Fletcher throughout, but at this time of all times he is busy on the quarter-deck shouting commands – 'Bear Away, Mr Young! Man the helm, Quintal. Mr Churchill, tell the men their watches'[87] – as the winds of change now fill the sails and their ship is soon gathering way.

Others of the 'wives' gazing back at Tahiti getting ever smaller over their stern include Sarah, who is with Matt Quintal, and Teio, who is with Bill McCoy.

Unknown to any of them, meanwhile, down in the furthest reaches of the hold, behind some barrels of water, the *Bounty* has a stowaway, none other than Hetee-Hetee, who, 15 years before, had sailed with Captain Cook, and is now keen to go adventuring once more. As soon as the *Bounty* is out to sea, Hetee-Hetee is out in the open, to the bemusement and amusement of Captain Christian.

Sail on!

•

Captain Bligh, who had been so buoyant at sea, so indomitable, now finds that he is sinking fast on land and can do nothing to stop it.

'Every person is now beginning to recover except myself,' he writes, five days after their arrival at Coupang. 'Great weakness and fever still hangs about me which keeps me confined· A little sago is the only thing my stomach can bear.'[88]

Mr Fryer, in contrast, is in good spirits as he is contemplating the joys of exacting revenge over a villain: Bligh. He has decided the best way will be to gather proof that the wretch has been systematically defrauding the Admiralty.

It is not just the matter of the stolen cheese, all those months ago. For there were also those accounts Fryer was forced to sign in front of the crew and, far more importantly for the moment, the fraud that appears to be going on right now.

Like these new quarters that Spikerman has so kindly provided the Loyalists – a residence that belongs to the good man himself, for which, he is not charging the Englishmen rent. Why, Fryer has heard that from Spikerman himself: 'I never mean to charge you for anything for the house.'[89]

Yet on this day Fryer overhears Bligh mention in passing, 'A house is hired for me.'[90]

Hired? No, it was *given*, Fryer knows. How very interesting.

And it is all the more interesting when Fryer asks Bligh about it.

'I paid for it,'[91] he snaps, in a tone that clearly indicates Fryer would do well to mind his own business.

Really, Captain Bligh?

In Fryer's view, Bligh is up to his old tricks, intent on defrauding the Royal Navy by charging them for expenses that simply do not exist.

Yes, for the moment, Fryer has no proof, but it does not take long, as he starts to discreetly poke around, ask quiet questions, and most importantly record how much things actually cost, and what Bligh actually paid for them. It will be a simple matter, come the time, to compare these facts with whatever Bligh has claimed.

(Is he being disloyal to a man who has successfully guided them across an unprecedented distance in an open boat, to give them their salvation? Not the way he sees it, later maintaining, 'There was others in the boat – that would have found their way to Timor as well as Captain Bligh and made everyone with them more pleasant.')[92]

26 June 1789, Tubuai, back in Bloody Bay

Land ahoy!

On the morning of 26 June 1789, Christian and the Mutineers sail back into Tubuai's Bloody Bay. They stand on deck, wary, looking all around for signs of a revenge attack from the Natives.

And here they come now!

Hands go to muskets and cutlasses. Christian gives a sharp order to man the cannon and train them on the approaching Natives.

But no.

These particular Natives are not remotely hostile. They have no weapons with them, no conch shells, and are all smiles. They even come on board in a peaceable manner.

Over the next few days, by endlessly shuttling the smaller boats back and forth, most of the supplies from the *Bounty* are unloaded on the shore and a start is made on establishing their new settlement. Fortunately, the Tahitian Natives on the *Bounty* waste no time in mastering the local Tubuaian dialect, which helps them make friends, and get information. One of the first things they learn is that Bloody Bay is in the territory of a Chief Tinnarow, who still feels very grim indeed about their last visit, the killing of his people, and he has not forgiven them . . .

Ah, so it is Tinnarow they must be wary of, and all the more so when, via an emissary, the Chief makes it clear he refuses to meet with Christian or any of his murderous Mutineers.

Very well then. Best to prepare for some kind of an attack.

In the meantime, it can be no bad thing to impress upon the Natives around them right now just how powerful the European magical weapons are, and with that in mind, Christian authorises the firing of some of the muskets at designated targets, shattering coconuts at a distance of 50 yards. The Natives are impressed, some even proudly showing the Englishmen the musket balls that now hang from strings around their necks; they collected the balls from the foot of trees after the battle at Bloody Bay.

Despite the fact that Chief Tinnarow is a declared enemy, Christian is welcomed as a friend by another Chief, Tummotoa. They are off to a better start than they might have hoped for.

Of course, two men with a talent for finishing off bright starts are Charley Churchill and Matthew Thompson. Christian is not sure precisely what happened, neither is Heywood, who notes in his journal: 'on 5 July [on Tubuai] some of the people began to be mutinous – on the 6th, two of the men were put in irons by a majority of votes – drunken fighting and threatening each other's life was so common that those abaft were obliged to arm themselves with pistols'.[93]

Churchill at least accepts the majority verdict, as the liquor wears off and the irons begin to wear on his skin. Matthew Thompson, typically, does not. But, no matter. He can stay in irons a little longer, to think about it.

6 July 1789, Coupang, a sour mutiny starts . . .

It has taken three weeks of recuperation, medication and organisation, but now Bligh is seriously turning his thoughts to the next part of the journey, to get to the principal Dutch settlement in these parts, Batavia, on the island of Java, where it should be possible to board a ship bound for Europe – ideally one going to England. The key will be to complete the 1200-mile journey to Batavia before the bulk of the Dutch fleet leave – and with no Dutch ships leaving Coupang any time soon, it leaves only one alternative . . .

In short order, Bligh, courtesy of a Royal Navy promissory note, purchases a small schooner, naming it His Majesty's Schooner *Resource*. The 34-foot long vessel is satisfactory, except for her fittings, and so Bligh orders Purcell to busy himself with making obvious repairs to the boat and getting her ready to sail. Purcell agrees to follow orders, it is just that his definition of 'busy' and Bligh's are not quite the same. For, as soon as the following morning, Fryer finds Bligh fulminating over how slow the Carpenter is, even though some skilled Chinese workers have been organised to help him.

Walking around the room where the Loyalists lounge, still recuperating, Bligh wants to know if any man has seen Purcell do anything at all. Finally, he comes to the Master to enquire what exactly was the last 'work' Purcell has done.

'Mr Fryer. Where did the Carpenter leave off?'[94] asks Bligh.

'Sir, I informed you last night,'[95] replies Fryer, knowing it is no answer at all.

'Have you been down this morning?'[96] asks Bligh.

'No. I am unwell, sir,'[97] replies Mr Fryer.

'What is your complaint?'[98] asks Bligh, not bothering to hide his scepticism.

'The prickly heat is much out on me,' answers Fryer. 'The Doctor told me to take care and not catch cold.'[99]

'Is that all your complaint?' Bligh scornfully asks. 'Take physic!'[100]

Juice of the lime, rubbed into the skin, sir. That is the best method.

Now, perhaps, among the Loyalists, there might be a man – Hayward, most likely – who would be more than happy to hear a medical lecture from Bligh, but Fryer is not of their number.

'The Doctor,' Fryer says carefully, 'is the only man to prescribe on that matter.'[101]

The Doctor, be damned! Bligh can take no more.

'Sir, it is *my* order that you see the Carpenter at work *every* morning *by Daybreak* and keep him at work!'[102]

'Sir, I am not a judge of Carpenter's work,' replies Fryer coolly. 'Neither do I think it my Duty to attend the Carpenter's.'[103]

'It IS your Duty, Sir, and you SHALL do it!' Bligh bellows. 'Sir, you are very impertinent to tell me you are not a judge of the Carpenter's work. Were you in any place where I could try you I would confine you immediately!'[104]

Fryer is not cowed.

'I do not understand that I have any right to attend to Mr Purcell's work,' says he. 'At any rate I shall have an order first.'[105]

'Sir, take care. We are onshore now – mind what you say.'[106]

'If you mean to put yourself on a footing with me, you will find me ready, when I am called on,'[107] Fryer says quietly.

Captain Bligh pauses.

And pauses some more. While it is one thing to call an underling out, it is quite another when the underling comes outside and rolls up his sleeves.

'You take things in a wrong light, sir,' answers Bligh.

'In the course of the Voyage,' Fryer continues angrily, 'you have done and said all you could to provoke me to say something that you might have that opportunity to take hold of.'

'Sir,' Bligh replies, 'if you *was* home now it would rest with me if you stayed *five minutes* in the Service.'[108]

The problem remains, of course, they are not home right now and Bligh – to his clear and infinite regret – cannot act as Fryer's judge and jury. Which means that, for the moment at least, they are stuck with each other. Bligh can barely bear it, but with the insolent Fryer in tow, the two of them head to the harbour foreshore to check on Purcell. He is not there. Apoplectic with rage, Bligh strides with intent back through the town – scattering 'coolies' as he goes – all the way to the Carpenter's quarters, where, sure enough, Purcell is found, resting on his bed.

Bligh's explosion of fury could singe whiskers and peel paint as he hurls accusations at his Carpenter, who, jumping to his feet, returns a key accusation in kind.

'I have seen *you*!' Purcell tells the furious Bligh. 'Frequently when serving the bread [on the Launch] *drop* a piece down and *pick it up* after the bread was served!'[109]

Bligh looks like a thunderstorm of rage, about to burst anew, but Purcell is launched.

'At other times you put a piece of bread in your mouth!'[110] the Carpenter continues.

Bligh, as angry as he has ever been on the entire journey from England, which is no little thing, now grabs Purcell by his jacket and shoves him out of the room.

Things get no better the next morning when Bligh requires some precious chalk – in short supply in these parts – to give to the ailing Governor Van Este, and tells Purcell he would like some, from his tool chest.

The inevitable happens.

'The chalk that is in *my* Chest is *mine*!'[111] roars Purcell. 'You have no right to it, Mr Bligh!'[112]

Very well then, Purcell, have it your way, but now you must face the consequences.

A short time later, Spikerman is interested to see a sole sailor aboard the newly purchased vessel as it bobs in the harbour this evening. It is, of course, none other than Purcell, who Bligh has made his prisoner.

Just as it had been during their visit to Van Diemen's Land, the Carpenter is confined at night to what is effectively his nautical cell, only to be released during the day to work.

Good God, it never bloody ends.

CHAPTER TWELVE

BATAVIA BOUND

During the time men live without a common Power to keep them
all in awe, they are in that condition which is called war; and such
a war, as is of every man, against every man ... where every man
is Enemy to every man, wherein men live without other security
than what their own strength shall furnish them ... and which
is worst of all, continual fear, and danger of violent death; And
the life of man, solitary, poor, nasty, brutish, and short.[1]

Thomas Hobbes, *Leviathan*

7 July 1789, Tubuai, a truce of sorts

The good news is that after weeks of terrible tension, Fletcher Christian
has a formal peace treaty before him, and is about to sign it.

Sadly, however, it is not with the hostile Chiefs of Tubuai – who,
with their warriors, continue to circle and threaten the newcomers – but
with his fellow *Bounty* men. Yes, so divided have the Mutineers become
among themselves in recent weeks, with so many bearing grudges for
acts real and imagined, and with so many differing views as to how
they should proceed, that it is faithfully recorded that, 'Articles were
drawn up by Christian and Churchill specifying a mutual forgiveness
of all past grievances which every man was obliged to swear and to
sign.' All of the white men sign bar one: 'Matthew Thompson excepted
who refused to comply.'[2]

Yes, the ever-glowering Thompson remains a problem. But, at least
for the moment, the others are agreed. They are going to let bygones
be bygones, and they are going to stay here, and really try to make a
go of it on Tubuai.

Christian is pleased to have it signed, and peace for the moment, while acutely aware that pens and paper can only go so far. William Bligh, after all, had been backed by the Articles of War, backed by the King, and centuries of tradition, and even that had not kept him safe in his bed.

18 July 1789, Tubuai, a fortress, by George!

It is now becoming obvious. Tubuai is shaping up to be an extremely difficult place to live in peace. Rather than having arrived in a tropical paradise, they have dropped anchor in the midst of a tribal war.

Tubuai has three main tribes, one headed by Chief Tinnarow (whose men Christian had slaughtered on their first encounter, something the Chief still clearly feels grim about); one by Chief Taroatchoa, and one by Chief Tummotoa. Now, despite all living on the one small island, only 17 square miles, as far as Christian can see, all the tribes, whenever in close proximity to each other – which is often – fight like cats in a sack for control of the island. This could be a useful circumstance, with the tribes taken up with fighting with each other, rather than the Mutineers, bar one thing. Whenever Christian is seen to make a friendly gesture to one tribe, both of the other tribes are mortified by it, and seem to unite against Christian and his prospective allies. For such is the deathly dynamic on the island that he has only to parley peace with one tribe, then the others start circling.

It all comes to a head when he begins scouting the island, looking for a good place to build his fort.

Chief Tummotoa, fancying his own tribe and territory as the most important, is anxious that the white men choose to build on his turf. When Christian finds, however, that none of the available sites suit their needs, the Chief takes it badly.

He becomes angrier still when Christian then goes to the district of Chief Taroatchoa, a minor Chief with a small amount of land, who might be willing to make an alliance to increase his own power. Sure enough, after finding the ideal site, Christian accepts Taroatchoa's offer to build on his land.

Chief Tummotoa does all he can to dissuade Christian from this unwise course of action but, finding his efforts useless, he grows angry.

Very angry . . .

'I will still be your friend,'[3] Christian promises. But a friend of Chief Taroatchoa is no friend of Chief Tummotoa, and Chief Tinnarow feels the same . . . Tummotoa and Tinnarow quickly form an alliance, prohibiting their people from trading or having contact with the white men in any way.

Well, that is just too bad. Tiring of the endless intrigues, Christian decides to embark on building the fort regardless, and quickly at that, but . . .

But hang on!

Where are John Sumner and Matthew Quintal? Gone on shore without leave, he soon learns. It is, if not mutinous behaviour – that term has a different meaning these days – still hugely problematic, and Christian knows he must respond as firmly as Bligh would have.

At least it does not take long to confront them. For when they return to the ship the next morning, after a night spent with Native women, Christian is waiting for them.

'How did you come to go on shore without my leave?' asks Christian.

'The ship is moored,' Quintal replies evenly, 'and we are now our own masters.'[4]

Christian does not hesitate.

Quickly drawing his British light dragoon pistol, and cocking it with ominous purpose, he holds it to Quintal's forehead and says, 'I'll let you know who is master.'[5]

Well, when he puts it like that, there is no doubt that Mr Christian makes a very compelling case.

'Put them in leg irons!' Christian barks. The startled crew fly into motion, escorting the pair down the companionway and locking them up in the brig.

Christian hopes, privately, that his resolute show of force will work.

Mercifully, when allowed back up on deck the next day, both men are indeed hang-dog sorry.

'We beg your pardon,' they plead, before adding, 'and promise to behave better in the future.'[6]

Noblesse oblige, Christian orders their chains to be removed. And so, to work.

On the morning of 18 July 1789, Christian takes a staff with a Union Jack attached and firmly plants it in the selected patch of ground, claiming this territory for Great Britain.

To mark the occasion, he grants an extra issue of rum for the men, and, with all hands joining him in a toast, he solemnly names the place 'Fort George', in honour, of course, of His Majesty George III, by the Grace of God, King of Great Britain, France and Ireland, Defender of the Faith, the very sovereign he has committed mutiny against.

Now, to build the fort.

Marking out the ground by pacing along it and digging in sticks, Christian soon has the basic contours done, the central feature being a 'quadrangular form, measuring one hundred yards on each square outside of the ditch'.[7]

As to that ditch – in front of each wall, Christian wants a ditch that is no less than 18 feet wide, by six feet deep, and the walls made of palm tree trunks must be 12 feet high. The major entrance will be a drawbridge on the north side of the fort, facing the beach. It is, frankly, a ludicrous amount of work for just over 30 men to contemplate, and will obviously take at least six months to build – and will be all the more difficult, as, come to think of it, none of them has ever tried to build a fort before.

For firepower, the four-pounder guns of the *Bounty* are to be laboriously heaaaaaved from the main deck to be placed high on each fort corner, ready to blow apart any attacking tribe, or any ship from England that might try to enter the narrow harbour. Two of the swivel guns are to be permanently placed at the top of each wall, with two kept as reserve, deployed as the occasion might require. By this means, two four-pounders and four swivels can be brought to bear in any direction.

Just let anyone try to dislodge them, and the men of the *Bounty* will show them who rules in these parts.

And so, *back* to work. James Morrison works away with the rest, noting that all are dedicated to their new task: 'Some cut stakes, others made battens, some cut sods and brought them to hand, some built, and others wrought in the ditch. The carpenters made barrows and cut timber for the gates and drawbridge. The work began to rise apace.'[8]

It is a long, exhausting process, and they are so short of manpower to get the job done that – unaccustomed as he is – Christian is obliged to take off his jacket, roll up his sleeves, wield a hammer and saw, and help. It is precisely the kind of heavy manual work that he never would have got close to on the *Bounty*, but now he makes sure to always take part.

The rhythmic sound of axes hitting wood echoes across the isle, followed shortly afterwards by the vision of palm trees falling, men grunting and groaning, sawing and hammering. Huts are constructed to shelter the working *Bounty* men from the heat, crops are planted, with yams and bread-fruit carefully cultivated. Oh yes, what was to sustain the slaves of the West Indies will now sustain the free men of the *Bounty*.

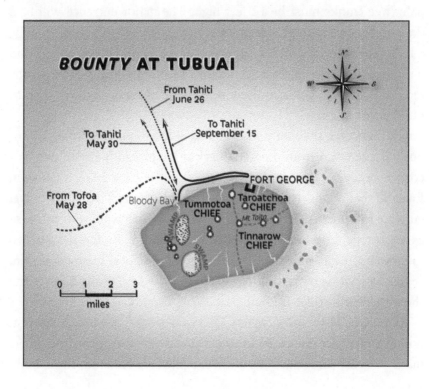

20 July 1789, in the tropical torpor of Timor

Famous last words?

None that are recorded, which is not surprisi

A man who has uttered so few words in this li
up with something memorable just before he sh
coil, and such is the case with the unfortunate
contracted inflammatory fever not long after ar
savagely spiralled earthwards until now, on the
1789, he near silently breathes his last and . . . is

Few deaths could have hit Bligh harder, as, th
greatly admired Nelson's abilities and was sure the
favour and the fervour in kind, and had been com

As soon as the next morning – for funerals in
conducted quickly, before the body decomposes i
is given a grand send-off.

(With the minister of the Dutch Reformed C
followed by Captain Bligh, then ten dignitaries, h
the shoulders of 12 Dutch soldiers dressed in bla
Loyalists and the people of Timor trail behind.
European cemetery behind the chapel, the coffin
grave as the minister leads a sombre burial service

The tragedy is almost more than Bligh can bear
sorrow that he takes up his precious journal and r

> I was sorry to find I could get no Tomb Stone at t
> a . . . man lay there who had surmounted every
> distress for eight and forty days across a dange
> Fortitude and health; but that at last after surm
> difficulty, and in the midst of his humble gratitu
> Almighty God for his preservation; he [died].[9]

Indeed. But could there be any more fitting epita
man than no epitaph at all?

Early August 1789, Tubuai, civility and savagery

The Natives of the South Pacific?

ages?

The experience of the *Bounty* men in Tahiti has made them otherwise. Against that, there is no doubt that some of them *able* of extraordinary savagery – and today at Tubuai is a case it.

rare break from building Fort George, Morrison has been invited ief Taroatchoa to watch an important tribal ceremony.

iving at the scene, he immediately notes young men of the tribe oled in a square at the main *morai*, their place of worship, waiting priests and elders to arrive.

tirring, a rumbling, a wave of excitement, and now here they ke the Red Sea before Moses, the square of young men suddenly on one side, and into the square walk the priests and old men, ch heavy staves in one hand – each staff with a tightly sharpened – and a young plantain sapling in the other. After some holy nces from one of the priests, all of the staves and the saplings rown into a heap in the middle of the square.

ere are more prayers, building to a climax, and now all men – s and elders – retrieve their staves, before one of the priests starts g around the square of men.

pping before one particular young man, the prayer rises to a , there is a flash of the priest's staff. The young man falls to ound. All those with staves crowd forward and start ruthlessly ing his prone form. The young man's blood gushes forth, he is within seconds.

e body,' the stunned Morrison chronicles, 'is instantly dissected bamboo knives.'[10]

is human sacrifice is nothing less than an offering to the Gods. s of the body are now wrapped in leaves, and each elder, accom- d by a priest, carries a piece of the corpse back to his own *morai* a banana tree, while the head, bones and bowels of the victim uried in the main *morai* and a stone is placed to indicate another fice.

ɔw, and only now, is a feast held to celebrate the grand occasion.

16 August 1789, Timor, the pangs of Coupang

Of course Bligh desires to be on his way once more.

And of course, the problem once more is that wretch, Fryer. With the *Resource* now ship-shape, Captain Bligh has made the terrible error of entrusting Fryer to ready the vessel by taking it out to a sheltered spot in the harbour to test its seaworthiness.

Misjudging the tides, Mr Fryer manages to run the vessel aground in the shallows.

Infuriated, Bligh tells Fryer he must stay on board the *Resource* and wait until a sufficiently high tide, so the vessel can be refloated. He is *not* to come ashore, until then, is that clearly understood?

Very well indeed, Captain Bligh. But now Fryer adds a very strange thing:

'When *I* am commanding officer, I shall come ashore when I please.'[11]

Bligh reels.

'The vicious and troublesome disposition of this man can only be equaled by his ignorance and meanness,'[12] Bligh confides to his journal.

And yet, despite the fact that Bligh has the power to confine Fryer to his quarters, it is not as if the Master does not have his own power to hurt the Captain in turn.

That much is apparent when, soon afterwards, the Governor sends quiet word that if Bligh wouldn't mind, they would like a second signature *beside* his own, to sign all bills, so as to verify his credit – so there can be a sense that all of the supplies really are being purchased, and approved, by the Royal Navy, not just one Captain.

What? Him, a Captain of the Royal Navy, and just his signature is not enough? It is an insult! Bligh refuses outright and, in the face of it, Mr Timotheus Wanjon, the son-in-law of the Governor, feels he has no choice but to restore Bligh's credit, and so, personally, becomes his guarantor even without a second signature.

For the moment, Bligh has no proof, but he has little doubt that behind this damn outrage lies Fryer.

> My master, who I am under the necessity to keep strictly to his duty, and is a vicious person, it is hinted to me has been the cause of the Governor's [move] . . . [13]

20 August 1789, Tubuai and Timor, no time to tarry

Though separated by some 4000 miles of open ocean, and the law, it is an auspicious day for the captains Christian and Bligh in their respective small vessels.

On Tubuai, Christian takes a break from building Fort George to go to the other side of the island in his Cutter for his first meeting with Chief Tinnarow, who has resisted his overtures to this point – no doubt still furious over the men killed at Bloody Bay.

Bligh, meantime, on this same morning, is about to set sail in the *Resource* for Sourabaya, the next port on the way to Batavia – with the aim being to get there before October, when the Dutch Fleet will be sailing for Europe.

His last act before leaving is to send off a bundle of letters to go on one of the fast Dutch ships heading for Europe that, though they have no room for Bligh and his crew, can take his missives. The most important of these letters is to the love of his life . . .

Coupang in Timor
Augt. 19th. 1789

My Dear Betsy
I am now in a part of the world that I never expected, it is however
a place that has afforded me relief and saved my life, and I have the
happyness to assure you I am now in perfect health . . . What an
emotion does my heart & soul feel that I have once more an opportunity
of writing to you and my little Angels, and particularly as you have all
been so near losing the best of Friends – when you would have had no
person to have regarded you as I do, and must have spent the remainder
of your days without knowing what was become of me, or what would
have been still worse, to have known I had been starved to Death at
Sea or destroyed by Indians. All these dreadful circumstances I have
combated with success and in the most extraordinary manner that ever
happened, never despairing from the first moment of my disaster but that
I should overcome all my difficulties.

Know then my own Dear Betsy, I have lost the Bounty . . . My
misfortune I trust will be properly considered by all the World – It was
a circumstance I could not foresee – I had not sufficient Officers &

had they granted me Marines most likely the affair would never have happened . . .[14]

As to how on earth the Mutiny occurred, Bligh is mystified: 'The Secrecy of this Mutiny is beyond all conception so that I cannot discover that any who are with me had the least knowledge of it.' Captain Bligh proceeds to recount the horror of what has occurred at the hands of the traitorous Fletcher Christian – yes, the very one who had bounced their dear children on his knee – and 'Beside this Villain see young Heywood one of the ringleaders.'[15]

Yes, Peter Heywood, that young artist boy with the high-bred connections, who slept under their roof, is a traitor too! Bligh lists other protégés who have betrayed him, even the 15-year-old Monkey he was so fond of and was teaching to read, 'even Mr. Tom Ellison',[16] concluding ruefully that, 'I have been run down by my own Dogs'.[17] Bligh's words tell Betsy all of the amazing events of his extraordinary journey to Timor, and how 'through the assistance of divine providence without accident a Voyage of the most extraordinary nature that ever happened in the world,' was achieved, 'let it be taken either in its extent, duration, or so much want of the necessaries of life'.[18]

Bligh assures Betsy that, 'My conduct has been free of blame',[19] and yet, alas, the same cannot be said for some of the 'Loyalists' who remain with him, with young Midshipman Hallett being singled out as a 'worthless impudent scoundrel'.[20] He is now about to leave for Batavia, where he hopes to get on a ship bound for Europe.

> *The next summer will however I trust in God bring me to you and my Dear little Girls and that we shall find our affairs in a flourishing way . . .*[21]
>
> *I know how shocked you will be at this affair but I request of you My Dear Betsy to think nothing of it all is now past & we will again looked forward to future happyness.*[22]

Financially, she need not worry . . .

> *I have saved my pursing Books so that all my profits hitherto will take place and all will be well . . .*[23]

*Give my blessing to my Dear Harriet, my Dear Mary, my Dear
Betsy & to my Dear little stranger & tell them I shall soon be home . . .
     To you my Love I give all that an affectionate Husband can give –
Love, Respect & all that is or ever will be in the power of your ever
affectionate Friend & Husband*

Wm. Bligh[24]

All thus, is in readiness. At Bligh's word, the schooner is pushed away
from the wharf and they set sail out of the harbour – towing the Launch,
as it is, of course, the property of His Majesty – bound for Batavia.

25 August 1789, Tubuai, diplomacy becomes war

Several of Christian's men stagger back to the now half-constructed
fort, dazed and bleeding profusely, reporting that they have just been
set upon by an enraged mob of Chief Tinnarow's tribesmen. One of
the Tahitian Natives they have dragged back with them has been so
badly beaten with a stone they are not sure whether he will survive.

Very well, then. The evidence builds that Christian's meeting with
Chief Tinnarow a few days earlier had not actually changed things.

Christian moves swiftly, ordering an armed party to go to where
the attack took place in search of these tribal ruffians. They rush
back to find several of the Natives still at the scene, still armed with
incriminating spears, and they are quick to fire two muskets in their
general direction, hitting and killing one of them.

No, this is not war.

But it is a skirmish, a way of giving Chief Tinnarow, in the time-
honoured British fashion, 'a taste of Bessie', as in their Brown Bess
muskets, an introduction to the firepower he and his tribe will face
if they continue to resist their settlement on what is now, after all,
declared British territory.

The skirmishes continue over the next few days, with Alec Smith –
who had been unwise enough to visit a maiden in the Tinnarow area
– captured and kept prisoner in the Chief's hut. Other Europeans have
their clothes stolen as they slumber in post-coital bliss.

In an effort to prevent a full-blown war, Christian sends several messengers to the Chief requesting that Smith be released, and the clothes returned.

The answer that comes back is as firm, as it is simple.

E'ita. No.

Very well then, have it your way.

Arming himself and a dozen of his men, Christian leads a party to Chief Tinnarow's hut, firing at any Native who seeks to get in their way, and, finding that the Chief has fled at the news of their approach, manages to free Alec Smith, who is relieved to escape with his life . . . if not his trousers, their whereabouts unknown.

Christian, in the name of justice, orders the hut to be burned.

One end of a burning log from the village fire is thrust out towards the thatched roof when the leader of the Mutineers notices something.

There, hanging on the wall of Chief Tinnarow's hut are, surely, religious icons of some kind, carved images of Gods, 'decorated with pearl shells, human hair, teeth and nails in a very curious manner'[25] surrounded by a heap of prized red feathers.

Take them and secure them, Christian orders. Those red feathers, he knows, are so highly prized by South Pacific Natives, they might well be of great use in negotiating peace. Then, with no more than a nod from Christian – such a gentle gesture, for such a savage result – the Mutineer bearing the torch steps forward and puts it to the roof of the hut, which instantly bursts into flame.

The white men stand back in an arc.

Beneath the light shadows thrown by the billowing smoke now pouring from the hut, Christian agrees to take into his care the desperate young Tubuaian woman who had been sleeping with Smith, and now fears for her life at the hands of her vengeful tribe. She is granted sanctuary on the *Bounty* – Smith is delighted – and the rest of the white men will resume work, cautiously, on the fort, waiting for Chief Tinnarow to make his next move.

Sure enough, three days later, Chief Tinnarow arrives at the fort, flanked by many of his men, all of them weighed down with baskets of food and drink.

They come not to fight.

They come to drink. And to eat. And to make merry. Oh yes, and to ask if the carved Gods of Tinnarow's could please be restored to them.

Christian concedes, 'on condition you restore the things your Men have taken from us. And promise you will not use any of my Men ill when they come into your district.'[26]

Tinnarow promises just that.

Will Fletcher Christian, Chief Tinnarow asks, take this proffered cup of *yava*?

Christian declines.

Never has Chief Tinnarow been more insulted.

He has come here offering the cup of friendship, despite having had his land stolen, 'his island home invaded', his women ravished, his men killed and his house burnt down . . . and the Englishman *refuses* it?

On some quickly uttered, guttural commands, Tinnarow and his men suddenly rush to retrieve the weapons they have hidden nearby, while Christian, a little more calmly it must be said, orders his men to get inside Fort George, and to have their guns at the ready. He also sends one of the Tahitian lads swimming out to the *Bounty*, with specific orders for the Armourer, Mr Coleman, to ready the cannon and give Tinnarow's mob of men more than just a whiff of the grape. Not trusting that Coleman would not hit the fort by mistake, Christian has ordered him to aim for the house, so that no-one will be hurt, but the Natives will understand – this is the kind of firepower we can call on, if we need it.

And so the stage is set.

While a large group of Chief Tinnarow's men – now without the Chief himself, who judges this to be a task for his mighty sacrificial warriors rather than himself – assemble just a little beyond the range of the Mutineers' muskets, the Mutineers ready themselves for the full-blown attack they are sure is coming. As has happened since time immemorial, the men on both sides grimace and glare at each other, mutter darkly, posture menacingly, and prepare themselves for the battle they know must come.

Ten minutes later, a puff of smoke is visible from one of the *Bounty*'s cannon, a boom rolls across the waters, there is a curious whistling, and . . . a four-pound cannon-ball lands on a hut a hundred yards or so away from the threatening Natives. They scatter and disappear back into the jungle.

•

The lusty Mutineers feel ever grimmer about their lonely nights as the Native women are still banned from coming on board, though the men are free to go to them, with all the risks that entails. The men have, thus, come up with the solution of taking Tubuaian women as their concubines, which inevitably make the Tubuaian men feel grimmer in turn.

Perhaps another row of logs on our fort, to make the walls facing the Natives even stronger?

Christian does the best he can, explaining to the Mutineers what should be obvious – that stealing the Tubuaian women can only lead to endless war, and they will never be able to live on this island in peace.

Which is, of course, fine for *him* to say, settling down every night on the *Bounty* with the most gorgeous Tahitian woman of the lot, Isabella. But what of us single, solo sailors?

For safety from attack, Christian still orders all but two men a night to return to the *Bounty* to sleep, so nocturnal visits from Tubuaian women (or more likely *to* such attractive women) are a physical impossibility.

Are we really to live out our lives in this place, with only our machetes and shovels to sleep alongside? Is this all the future holds for us?

In that case, many of us, and we daresay most of us – for we have talked – would much rather go back to Tahiti.

Huzzah for Tahiti!

Huzzah! Huzzah! Huzzah!

Yes, that was exactly their cry when they had first cast Bligh and his Loyalists off, and it had been every bit as much a cry of lust as triumph. For they knew then they were returning to *Tahiti*, where the alluring and voluptuous Tahitian women awaited. But what have they known instead over these last eight weeks? The drudgery of building a fort, amidst hostile Natives, with little to look forward to at night bar a cold bayonet to hold in the silent watch of the night.

The men feel so strongly about it that they down tools and, as Morrison will recount, 'refused to do any more work until every man had a wife'.[27]

Yes, somehow, Christian has to negotiate with the Tubuaian Chiefs to provide wives for them.

Christian, needless to say, refuses their demands.

And so they are at an impasse.

The men will not work. And Christian will not try to get them women.

It is the beginning of three days of deep discussion aboard the *Bounty* – about whether to stay here, or return to Tahiti, all of which makes the men so thirsty, they demand more grog.

Christian refuses, and the result is unequivocal.

The rabble-rousers, led by Quintal and Sumner, simply break the lock of the spirit room and take what they please by force.

You were saying, Mr Christian?

Well, if the men cannot be stopped going in one direction, conciliation is next. Christian orders their grog allowance to be doubled. The debate continues, and more and more men make it clear that they refuse to work anymore on the fort, and wish to return to Tahiti.

This idea, Smith will later recount, is 'much against the inclination of Christian, who . . . expostulated with them on the folly of such a resolution, and the certain detection that must ensue'.[28]

Do they not *realise* the death-trap they will be sailing back to? Even if Bligh has not survived, it is certain that another British ship would arrive within a couple of years, and their fates would be sealed.

Try as he might, however, he cannot bring the majority he needs to his view.

Finally, on 10 September 1789, Christian knows he must bring things to a head, and that they must take a firm decision, by way of a vote.

'All hands aft!'[29]

Now, who wishes to return to Tahiti?

A forest of hands rise. No fewer than 16 of the 25 white men wish to return to Tahiti.

Their number, of course, include the detained Loyalists, Coleman, Norman and McIntosh and blind Byrn. Peter Heywood, George Stewart and James Morrison raise their hands also.

Christian knows, of course, that his once dear friend Heywood wants to return to Tahiti – he has been arguing in favour of it for three days – but still, somehow, his hand going up at this moment comes as a hard slap in the face from someone he holds dear.

But the numbers tell a compelling tale, from which there can be no return. In fact, with such an overwhelming vote, Christian cannot even have confidence that the other eight will choose to stay with him, once they do in fact return to Tahiti.

For there is nothing for it, leave Fort George as a point of no return, and turn their stern to Tubuai, heading back to Tahiti as soon as possible.

And so, deflated, but not yet defeated, Christian rises to give what is no less than the resignation speech of his captaincy:

> Gentleman, I will carry you and land you wherever you please; I desire no one to stay with me, but I have one favour to request, that you will grant me the ship, tie the foresail, and give me a few gallons of water, and leave me to run before the wind, and I shall land upon the first island the ship drives to. I have done such an act that I cannot stay at Tahiti. I will never live where I may be carried home to be a disgrace to my family.[30]

And yet, no sooner has Christian finished speaking than the voice of Midshipman Ned Young rings out: 'We shall never leave you, Mr. Christian, go where you will!'[31]

Hurrah!

And yes, seven other Mutineers do join in – those who have voted against returning to settle in Tahiti – shouting their approval to his words. Could Christian sail the *Bounty* with eight men helping?

Just!

The shouting begins on a separate issue. Just who is to have the spoils of the *Bounty*? While it is one thing for Christian and his core Mutineers to take the ship, they have no right to all of its weapons, munitions and supplies as well. The ever dangerous Charley Churchill, so recently Christian's right-hand Mutineer, now becomes his stout opponent. His point is put with glaring intensity: those who are going to stay on Tahiti may well have to fight the might of the Royal Navy! To do so, they will need weapons, shot and powder more than men sailing in the unknown lands, who will take on, at worst, a smattering of a scattering of Natives armed only with spears.

Finally, it is agreed that such things as tools, clothes, grog, food – both that which walks and that which can be stored in barrels, boxes and piles – must be divided between those who will stay at Tahiti, and those who will look elsewhere.

The first thing then, in preparation for departure from Tubuai, is to take back onto the ship everything that they now have on shore.

And yet, while it is one thing to load back onto the *Bounty* such things as their pots, muskets, saws and sails, it is quite another to round up all their hogs and goats once more, as they are now scattered all over the island.

For now, a party goes out to look for the *Bounty*'s missing cow, only to be fallen upon by a large group of Tinnarow's angry, war-ready men, who pound them with stones and plunder everything they carry.

'Tell your commander, we shall serve him in the same way,'[32] the foremost among the group says, glowering at the beaten white men.

Battered, bruised and bloodied, the men stagger back to Christian to report what has happened, and find that, in the meantime, the Tubuaian woman who had sought refuge with them has disappeared, clearly returning to her own people. It is one more sign that something is up, that the Tubuaians are likely building up to mount a major attack.

13 September 1789, Sourabaya, who goes there?

Arriving at the small Dutch port of Sourabaya, on the north coast of Java, the *Resource* is instructed by flags to proceed no further, to stay put in the outer harbour.

It is not quite the welcome that Bligh and his Loyalists had been hoping for, three weeks after leaving Coupang.

The reason? Pirates.

Really? There is a danger in these waters from armed brutes eager to take over your vessel?

You will have to tell Captain Bligh about it someday.

But wait he must.

•

On the eastern side of Bloody Bay, Tinnarow's men put into motion the Chief's scheme: to rid the island of these troublesome interlopers.

The warriors tie red sashes – the sash of tribal war – around their waists, filling the sashes with flinty, sharp-edged stones. They adorn their torsos with pearl-shell armour, front and back, and they don elaborate helmets made from coconut fibre covered in white cloth and topped by black feathers plucked from the man-o'-war bird.

They sharpen their 20-foot long spears, tapering them to a deadly point designed to pierce flesh. They tend to their clubs, which act as both club and spear as on the head of the shaft is a cut and polished jewel of considerable size, gorgeous craftsmanship with deadly intent.

All about, the men jeer and yell, praying to the Gods, working themselves up to a fight, and the women bring yet more stores of stones, spears and clubs for their brave men to take to battle.

13 September 1789, Tubuai, hunting their animals

And so they are ready.

With the authority that remains to him, until such time as they get back to Tahiti, Christian orders 20 of his men to arm themselves and go in search of the stock . . . and to make hell for those who dare oppose them.

They are quite the posse, as they depart.

Alas, alas, less than a mile inland from their landing spot they find themselves suddenly and formidably surrounded by angry Natives brandishing their clubs, spears and stones. Seven hundred of them!

It is an ambush!

They have been watched all the way, Chief Tinnarow has moved his men into position accordingly, and the *Bounty* men now find themselves outnumbered more than 30 to one.

The men of the *Bounty* at least have their muskets, and now fire them in a frenzy at their approaching tormentors who, in turn, fight 'with more fury than judgement',[33] eventually retreating with great loss. The white men, bruised yet upright, collect some of their stock with no further trouble.

Shocked by how close they have come to being wiped out, Christian decides to have it out with Chief Tinnarow. He issues each man 24 rounds of ammunition, a musket or a pistol. Hetee-Hetee is the only Tahitian to be given a musket – on account of his being an excellent shot – much to the others' offence.

Soon after, news comes to the fort from a young Tubuaian Chief, Taroamiva, who tells Christian that Chief Tinnarow and his warriors are arming a party, too, and are 'determined to dispute his right to the stock'.[34]

Very well then. If it is a battle that Tinnarow wants, he has one.

Christian forms up the same group of men as before. And so they go, marching in silence towards Chief Tinnarow's territory, ready to fight, determined to get the rest of their stock back.

No more than a mile from Fort George, pushing through thick bush, Thomas Burkett hears a slight rustling from a nearby bush, before a spear flies through the startled morning, and pierces him below his left ribs. Groaning, he grips the shaft and is actually able to pull it out, before he sees a club swinging from behind him. It is being swung by one of the Tahitians and is aimed right at the head of the Tubuaian warrior who was about to kill Burkett.

It all happens so quickly that Burkett doesn't have a chance to scream a warning to the others. A moment later, the Tubuaian warriors leap from the jungle like a murderous swarm, their eyes bulging from beneath their fierce helmets, yelling war cries that instil horror in the hearts of the Mutineers.

With commendable discipline – they might be Mutineers, but they have been trained in the finest Royal Navy traditions – the *Bounty* men form a square with their backs to each other, giving themselves a 360-degree arc of fire at the warriors coming at them. *Boom!* go their guns and furious Natives drop before them.

Reload.

Boom!

They keep firing away at Tinnarow's men, but no matter how many are killed, there are hundreds more that pour out of the surrounding jungle, fearless.

For the most part, the warriors are cut down at a good distance and yet, inevitably, with so many of them, some are actually able to get to close quarters. In this case it is Christian who shows the lead, leaping into the fray and suddenly becoming a whirling dervish with his bayonet, thrusting it into warrior after warrior, as the blood spurts and men die – some with a scream, others with no more than a soft gurgle. So fast is Christian's blade of flashing fury, he even cuts his own hand as he wrenches it from the armoured flesh of one massive victim.

And yet, despite the valour of his men, it is soon obvious to Christian that they can only halt such numbers for so long before they will be overwhelmed. Shouting a few sharp orders, the Tahitians act as a rear-guard – arming themselves with the fallen enemies' long spears to hold the Tubuaians off – so Christian and his Mutineers can retreat to some high ground nearby.

And what a job the Tahitians do, as they beat back wave after wave.

Morrison, with the others, successfully makes his way to the high ground, with the brave Tahitians now falling back under their covering fire.

Still, Tinnarow's men keep coming, following up 'with redoubled fury, mocking us (as we were only a handful compared to them) even though many fell by our constant fire as they approached'.[35] With half-a-dozen of the Tahitians badly wounded, as is Burkett, and even Christian bleeding profusely from his hand, it is obvious they must retreat again, but where to?

From their high point, Christian can see about 200 yards off, a '[yam] ground',[36] one of the spots the Europeans have cleared for their agriculture. While lower than their current position, it is clear ground, which is the last hope they have of escaping with their lives – for they must keep the warriors at a distance.

Some more sharp orders from Christian, and, all together, his men begin to fight their way towards it, keeping up a constant fire as they go.

Again Christian barks orders and the men quickly post themselves in the middle of this precious clearing, facing outwards, waiting.

But, suddenly, all is relatively quiet. The attackers, so strong coming at them through the jungle, are suddenly shy when it comes to open ground. The warriors remain hidden, hurling stones in volleys, but not spears. All the fire and fury seems suddenly to have left them as they contemplate the all too apparent reality: death comes from the puff sticks the white men bear, even when they are a great distance away, and so it is best to stay back. At least, most of them feel like that.

Some, however, prove a little braver – or less sensible.

The men of the *Bounty* can see them clearly: several brave warriors trying to rally their men to attack. Whatever they are screaming seems to wash over the others, but none of them makes the move required – which is to charge at the white men, hurling their spears.

There are still more angry yells.

But still no mass move.

Finally, one particularly brave Native, a Chief by the looks of his impressive, shiny pearl-shell helmet, adorned 'with a semicircle of feathers from the wild duck's wings round it',[37] now takes matters into his own hands, and steps forward in violent motions, urging his men onwards while keeping his menacing eyes trained on the white men.

Shoot that man, says Christian coldly.

Beside him there is a sudden *click* as a Brown Bess is cocked, a steadying as one of the Mutineers takes aim at the shiny brown form in the distance, and now a powerful explosion and a puff of stinking acrid smoke as the musket is fired.

And that brave young Chief is no more, felled by a single musketball. Around his felled form there is desperate anguish, many screams and shouts, as his shattered corpse is dragged backwards . . . and of course . . . no attack. Yet.

Is it safe, though, Captain?

That part is not yet sure. A strange stalemate settles as the seconds tick by.

But now, the oddest thing.

Fletcher Christian, in a show of sportsmanship and tribute that would do justice to the schooling he received at the Cockermouth

School (in the company of no less than William Wordsworth), orders 'Three cheers!'[38] and the men of the *Bounty* respond in full cry.

Huzzah! Huzzah! Huzzah!

And something clicks in the Natives . . .

They interpret this as the white man's war cry, meaning they are about to attack. They retreat hurriedly and the battle is finally over.

Huzzah! indeed.

The relief of the Mutineers is palpable.

The important thing now is to get Burkett – who is pasty white and growing faint from the loss of blood from his spear wound – back to the *Bounty*, and Christian orders Skinner to assist him.

Meantime, to the victors, the treasures of triumph are now available, and the Tahitians, particularly, load themselves with spoils, especially with clubs and spears. One of the Tahitian boys suggests removing the jawbones of the corpses, 'to hang round the quarters of the ship as trophies',[39] and frighten future opponents.

But Christian, appalled, is firm.

No.

Still the bloodthirsty boy won't relent, and begs.

Can he cut away just one jawbone for himself?

No.

Just *one*?

NO, says Christian, reaching for his bayonet.

In the end, it was 'only the fear of being put to death that prevented him from setting about it'.[40]

Having recorded the most unlikely victory, against overwhelming odds, the men of the *Bounty* return to Fort George.

With their enemies defeated for the moment, there is no further problem with gathering in the last of the missing stock, whose number even includes their prized cow, now peacefully led back to the fort.

Now, given that the Good Lord has smiled upon them, it seems appropriate: the fatted calf is slaughtered and a feast is given for the Chief Taroamiva, who had sent warning of Tinnarow's attack. As they eat and drink, young Chief Taroamiva is able to give them some detail of just how big their victory over Chief Tinnarow's men has been. No fewer than 60 of them were killed, he gleefully recounts, along with six women who were supplying them weapons.

And what, pray tell, was the decisive point in the battle? Chief Taroamiva is delighted to tell them: It was when Christian, fighting with the strength of two men, felled the brother of Chief Tinnarow!

Toasts all round to our noble leader, and Chief Taroamiva remains delighted to be the bearer of such bad news about Chief Tinnarow.

But now he has a request of Christian.

Yes, Chief Taroamiva?

I would like to go to Tahiti along with two of my men.

Why?

Well, Tinnarow will not lick his wounds forever and, 'I have been Mr Christian's friend so much,' the young Chief states in a worried tone, so 'If I stay on shore I shall be killed.'[41]

All up, it seems a reasonable request from a Chief who has greatly aided them, and Christian has no hesitation in agreeing. The young Chief may come with them when they leave Tubuai for good in a couple of days, and be accompanied by two of his best men: his nephew, Tetaheite, and Ohoo – a Native with muscles that not only bulge, but bristle.

And so to work, one and all, as we load the *Bounty* once more with fresh stores.

CHAPTER THIRTEEN

WHAT SHALL WE DO WITH THE DRUNKEN SAILORS?

Ingratitude, more strong than traitors' arms, Quite vanquish'd him.[1]
William Shakespeare, *Julius Caesar*, Act 3, Scene 3

15 September 1789, Sourabaya, the Captain martials his forces

After waiting four hours at the harbour entrance, Bligh and his Loyalists are allowed to enter Sourabaya, where the Governor, Mr Anthony Barkay, extends them warm hospitality, offering every civility and help, as His Excellency wishes it to be known that, even in the midst of pirate-infested waters, his port is a safe and lively hub.

For Bligh it is a most welcome relief, but after just a few days, he is ready to sail for Batavia, to continue his triumphant path to England.

All is set, and today is the day.

The *Resource* is ready to sail, not alone but – at the insistence of Governor Barkay – in the company of two Dutch vessels, for protection against pirates.

Typically, however, just as the Loyalists are readying to depart, their mood buoyant, Bligh contrives to do something to seriously aggrieve them. Many of the officers – William Peckover, William Purcell, William Elphinstone, William Cole, John Hallett, Peter Linkletter and Thomas Hayward – are having last drinks at an ale house by the harbour when an emissary from the Governor arrives, asking them to take charge of a gift that Bligh has accepted. Ah, yes, and what would that be?

'A small bullock, some poultry and Vegetables . . .'[2]

It is unbelievable! Difficult enough to accommodate cattle on ships, it will be a nightmare in something as small as the *Resource*, and for what purpose? Presumably, it is so Bligh can sell the beasts in Batavia, and pocket the money for himself. Fryer always maintains that Bligh is working some scam, and here is another example.

Well, first things first, as Bligh's men have not yet had their fill of ale, they decide to continue drinking, while the 'presents' remain tethered, cooped and stacked outside, waiting for them.

Finally, the drunken sailors – Elphinstone and Hallett, particularly, being more than three sheets to the wind – stagger out of the ale house, early in the morning, gather in the wretched bullock and the rest, and head to the harbour foreshore, where a ferryman in a strong vessel is indeed eager to take their animals and goods out to the *Resource*. By happenstance, he proves to be an Englishman himself, washed up on these shores years ago. And yes, he will do that for a fee of four 'doits', the equivalent of an English penny.

The drunken sailors are outraged! It is not the penny, it is the principle of the thing. Ever and always, they seem to be reaching into their own pockets to pay for what should be Bligh's cost; sweating and straining to aid Bligh's private ventures.

As ever, though, one man and one man alone, the lackey's lackey, the sycophant's sycophant, the lickspittle's licker of spit, Thomas Hayward, speaks up for Bligh. In fact, more than that, he dresses his fellows down: 'You disobey orders! I shall take the boat off without you all.'[3]

Hayward! Always bloody Hayward!

'Lackey!'[4] they slur his name, in more ways than one.

Flunkey!

Lickspittle!

But he will not resile and, in any case, they have no choice. Hayward pays the ferryman, Bligh's booty is loaded, and they all follow.

Nothing, however, will stop their insults about Bligh and Hayward, and the Sourabaya harbour ferryman listens in horror to their drunken ramblings, which he just knows must be against the law somewhere.

'Captain Bligh,' Purcell says firmly, 'should be hanged.'[5]

Yes, most of the others agree with equally treacherous remarks.

'It will not go well with our Captain when he returns to England,' says Hallett, 'he having ill treated every person under his Command, for which reason he will be tied to the mouth of a Cannon and fired into the Air.'[6]

As it happens, Bligh himself is not far behind them, being rowed on a separate boat, in the company of the Commandant and the Master Attendant, a Mr Bonza, of Sourabaya, who see him safely on the vessel, and then take their gracious leave.

Bligh is not long on board before he hears whisperings, a rumbling grumbling getting louder. Apparently, below, a man is refusing to work. And who would that be?

Two names come to Bligh's ears: William Elphinstone and John Hallett.

Bligh quickly heads to their quarters to confirm it, and, indeed, finds them 'both beastly drunk'.[7] With his furious bark, he orders all men aft, including the two drunkards, even as he himself dashes on deck to confront the Master about this *disgrace*.

'Mr Fryer, what is the cause of you carrying on duty in such a manner? What is the reason you did not see these Officers on deck?'[8] asks Bligh.

'I don't know,'[9] replies Fryer shortly.

'God damn you, sir, why don't you know?'[10] Bligh barks. 'Are they drunk or ill or what is the matter with them?'[11]

'Am I a doctor?' replies Fryer sarcastically, before pointing at the crew surgeon, Thomas Ledward, and saying, 'Ask *him* what is the matter with them!'[12]

But Bligh will not have it.

'What do you mean by this insolence?'[13] booms Bligh.

'It is no insolence,' replies Fryer before finally snapping. 'You not only use me ill but every man in the vessel and every man will say the same!'[14]

Purcell, lips loose from liquor, is quick to join the fray.

'Yes, by God, we are used damned ill!'[15] Purcell growls. 'Nor have we any right to be used so!'[16]

Bligh looks around. Instead of averted eyes, there are eager faces, cries of agreement from the men. Emboldened, Purcell glares at Bligh with 'a daring and Villainous look'.[17]

So it is Purcell, in the place of Fletcher Christian, who is the leader of this fresh mutiny? Egged on by the wide support – including that of the Master himself, whose usually expressionless face has suddenly come alive with contempt – Purcell roars some more: 'You have used me ill! And everybody on board!'[18]

In the midst of the uproar that bursts forth, Bligh does what he was never able to do with Christian – he draws his sword.

You, Mr Fryer, are under arrest. And so are you, Mr Purcell.

In fact, Mr Fryer? I have something even stronger in mind for you, if you dare to glare one more time at your lawful leader.

'If you offer to look up I swear I will run you through,' Bligh sneers. Fryer keeps his eyes down.

Bligh himself – for he simply can trust no-one else – escorts the two scoundrels below, to confine them to their quarters, pausing to order Hayward: 'Call the Commandant back to the *Resource*.'[19]

Shortly thereafter, the Commandant is bemused to see a harried Hayward arrive, insisting that he and the Master Attendant must immediately come back to the *Resource*, and bring some soldiers with them.

Whatever for? I have just left . . . ?

Mutiny.

As fate would have it, the ferryman in charge of the vessel that takes the Commandant is – as he tells them in conspiratorial tones – none other than the man who took the drunken *Bounty* men to the *Resource* just hours before.

Do tell?

So the ferryman does, and in sufficient detail that by the time the Commandant sets foot on the deck of the *Resource*, he is the man with the evidence, not Bligh, and he has the chief independent witness in tow.

'Commandant, I charge the Master with Mutiny,'[20] says Bligh as he steps aboard.

No doubt. But the Master Attendant, Mr Bonza, is able to shock Bligh with his reply.

'We believe you have some villains about you who you do not suspect,'[21] he says.

'Our ferryman has told us your officers and men were saying that you should be hanged or blown from the mouth of a cannon once you get home.'[22]

'I desire everyone be asked if they have said it!'[23] roars Bligh, his voice a shrill shriek, his whole body shaking with rage. The Commandant explains that the ferryman who heard the words is now amongst them.

'Point out those who told you,'[24] he encourages the old Englishman.

There is a pause as the startled ferryman looks around at the men in the line-up before him, as they gaze back at him in turn, aware that their fates may very well hang in the balance.

He lifts his leathery hand and points a thick, gnarled finger at ... Purcell, the Carpenter. There is a collective expulsion of breath, a release of tension.

Ah, but the ferryman is not done.

With the same work-wearied hand, he points to ... *all the men!*

Yes, sir, each and every one of them was cursing Bligh as he ferried them out. And they all agreed that he was the one who was responsible for the Mutiny on the *Bounty*.

Now, even Bligh is taken aback. Such treachery! Such traitors, all around him! *All* of them!

One man, however, aghast, ashen-faced, steps forward to refute the terrible charge.

It is Hayward, who rushes to his Captain, embracing him and tearfully imploring, 'I beseech you, Captain, you will not believe I could be possibly guilty of such infamy and ingratitude.'[25]

Bligh does indeed believe Hayward, knowing he could not be capable of any such thing. For, in the wake of the death of Nelson, if Bligh had to stake his life on one man being loyal to him, it is Thomas Hayward, closely followed by John Samuel, his Clerk.

Tears streaming, Hayward whirls on the others and, caught between shock, misery and fury, roars:

'I dare any one to assert I was guilty of any such baseness or in the least degree privy to it!'[26]

Of course, no-one will make any such assertion. (In the first place, the sycophantic wretch is telling the truth, and in the second place, this is not a time to speak up, it is a time to keep your head down.)

Triumphant at their silence, Hayward whirls back to dear Captain Bligh, noting his disgust for these fellow so-called 'officers', assuring him that he only ever speaks to such an unprincipled lot when he absolutely must.

Of course Bligh not only believes him, but says so, to Hayward's profound relief.

Still, the good Captain has no time to receive Hayward's tearful burblings of gratitude, as he in turn whirls on the wretches who have defied him, and delights in watching them shake and cower in the face of his overwhelming and vindictive anger.

Looking at them, one by one, Bligh decides that so grave are their offences, they cannot possibly wait to face a court martial in England. Oh no. He will have to do it right here, before he sets sail with these traitors again.

'Commandant,' Bligh asks and orders. 'Ask who has any complaints to make against me. Those who have are to go into the Boat to lay such charges before the Governor.'[27]

Bligh is calling the bluff of his officers. If you want to take me on, you heroes in your cups, now is your time. It is classic Bligh – if under pressure from an underling, his instinct is to make a public confrontation of the whole affair, upping the ante. The Commandant is here, the law is here, the crew is here, all are listening, all are watching. You've had some things to say about me in private. *Now*, take me on! In public! And if you don't, let everyone witness your craven cave-in.

Captain Bligh knows, of course, that none of them would dare, and . . . And, what?

To his amazement, it now happens . . .

Thomas Ledward, John Hallett and William Cole step forward.

Wretches! But still Bligh does not buckle. They may be brave now, carried along by the Dutch courage that always sustains such curs, but let's see how they feel after a night in the cells as they contemplate their fates.

'Mr Samuel,' says Bligh, calling for his Clerk. 'Write down what Mr Fryer said. The Gentlemen are to *sign it*. Those that *refuse to sign it* are to go into the Boat and go onshore.'[28]

The five Gentlemen in question – Ledward, Hallett, Cole, Purcell and Fryer – coldly refuse to sign it. Very well then. Their choice. For their trouble, and the trouble they are causing, Bligh draws his sword and hotly escorts them all to the Cutter that will take them to shore. Still, let us give you all one last chance to change your minds before the boat sets off.

Gentlemen, a bargain as we bob? I lay my sword down and offer you my pen.

'Gentlemen, you *will sign* to what Mr Samuel wrote and I will hope you will behave *like men of Honour*.'[29]

Ah, no. Call them dishonourable if you will, but not one of them reaches for the quill, not one is disposed to sign what might amount to their death warrant. Very well then. The boat sets off, Bligh so angry he can barely speak. Clearly considering that the sword might be mightier than the pen after all, Bligh puts down the quill, lifts the sword once more and points the point right at Master Fryer, who . . . offers a smirk so insolent, Bligh nigh explodes.

'Rascal . . . if you speak [one word] I will run you through!'[30] threatens Bligh.

'You are to use your pleasure in doing what you think proper,'[31] replies Fryer tartly, calling his bluff.

'I *will* use my pleasure, *I will break every bone in your skin!*'[32] retorts Bligh.

Just not right now. Bligh will use the law to break them all. The shore reached, the mercurial Captain calms himself just enough to *personally* escort the five insolent crew-members to Sourabaya's barracks, where these ingrates can be held in a dusty room overnight.

And in the morning, Bligh is soon telling the Governor, he wishes all five to face a quickly convened court martial.

•

As they lie uncomfortably in their sweltering, dark cells, the effects of the alcohol wear off, their tempers cool, and each man, each *prisoner*, is left alone with his thoughts.

What have they done? What will Bligh do to them?

After coming all this way, as Loyalists, damn it, are they really about to face the noose? What should they say in the hearing that waits for them on the morrow?

The truth? That Bligh is an unconscionable monster, and it is no coincidence that he has now faced three Mutinies in just the last six months? Or, tell a lie, and say there is no problem with him, it is all just a terrible misunderstanding – effectively throw themselves on the mercy of the court?

•

The morning brings at least one surprise. As Hallett, Ledward and Cole are marched to their court-martial hearing, Fryer and Purcell are told they will face no such thing. Instead, Bligh has decided to keep them in chains all the way back to England so they can face a court martial there.

Of the others, it is Hallett who is the first to be led into the makeshift military courtroom. In the sweltering closeness of it all, mosquitoes hum as the flies buzz around. And now the sound of shuffling footsteps approaching. It is young John Hallett, who now sits on a rickety wooden chair before the three stern judges: the *Commandant des Troupes*, a Captain and the Master Attendant.

'Have you anything to say against your Captain?' the Commandant begins in a thick Dutch accent that lends an air of propriety to every word.

'He beat me once at Tahiti,' Hallett replies, decidedly English, still nasal from the previous afternoon's liquor.

'For what reason?'

'Because I was not got into the Boat.'

'Why did not you go into the Boat?'

'The Water was too deep.'

'Have you no other complaint against your Captain?'

'None.'[33]

Somehow, all the charges of yesterday have disappeared, with the only thing remaining being one long ago trivial complaint. Hallett, clearly, has seen his fate in the cracks in the ceiling the previous night.

The Commandant goes on: 'Why did you then say to an English Sailor now in the service of Holland at this place, that it would not go well with your Captain when he returned to England, he having ill treated every person under his Command for which reason he would be tied to the mouth of a Cannon & fired into the Air?'

'I do not know that I said any such thing and if I did utter such an expression, I was drunk when I did it.'[34]

Hallett now turns to Bligh directly, and pleads openly.

'And I most humbly ask your forgiveness for it, and beg that I may have leave to return to England with you.'

The Dutch Commandant goes on.

'Do you not think the Captain has done his duty in every respect to your knowledge?'

'Yes.'

'Is he brutal or severe so as to give you cause of Complaints?'

'No.'

Hallett steps down, relieved to be freed from this inquisition, and, in the sober light of day, sure that he has done the right thing.

Next is Ledward.

'Have you anything to say against your Captain?'

'I have nothing to say against my Captain only the first time the Boat went on Shore I asked leave to go with him and was refused until he came on board again.'

It is a commendably trivial complaint, from another sage soul who, for the life of him, cannot remember any fault.

Captain Bligh now rises to ask questions himself.

'Have I behaved brutal or severe so as to give cause of complaint?'

'No.'

'Have not I taken every pain to preserve my Ship's Company?'

'Yes, in a very great degree.'

'Was it possible for me to have retaken the Ship or could I have done more than I did?'

'No, certainly not.'[35]

That will be all, Mr Ledward.

Mr Cole now shuffles into the stifling room, his face grim, glistening with sweat, flushed from the heat and the hangover.

'Have you anything to say against your Captain?' Captain Bligh asks him menacingly, barely able to wait for him to take his seat.

'I allege no particular complaint against you, God forbid.'

'Have I behaved brutal or severe so as to give cause of complaint?'

'No.'

'Do you think I have done my duty as an able Officer in every respect?'

'Yes, I do.'

'Was it possible for me to have retaken the Ship or could I have done more than I did?'

'No.'

It is done.

All three accusers have caved in, providing evidence that entirely exonerates Bligh. Their testimony is transcribed and signed by the three judges and they are allowed back on board the *Resource*.

And yet, to Bligh's stupefaction, it is not quite over. For the next afternoon, the Commandant takes Bligh aside to tell him that . . . well . . . how do I put this? . . . well, it seems, the *Bounty*'s Master, Mr Fryer, is of the view that you, Captain Bligh, have been *cheating* the Royal Navy. Yes, Mr Fryer is alleging that you have been fraudulent, that you have in effect been keeping two sets of books, so that you may make private profits at the expense of His Majesty's public purse. More troubling still, Mr Fryer actually has proof of this, as back in Coupang, he got a copy of the true prices demanded for many provisions, signed by the Governor, *Opperhooft* Willem Adriaan Van Este. And when those prices are compared to Bligh's official documents, well, as the furious Bligh himself notes, it seems to show, 'things I bought there for His Majesty's Service for which I had made extravagant charges to Government'.

'This paper will prove it!' an excited Mr Fryer had told the Commandant. 'Bligh will be roughly handled for it on his return to England.'[36]

Oh, and one other thing, Captain Bligh.

You should know that Mr Fryer is also insisting you personally are responsible for the Mutiny on the *Bounty*, because, as Bligh chronicles incredulously, 'I had given my Ship's Company short allowance of Yams and therefore [they] had taken away the Ship.'[37]

So angry he can barely speak, Bligh is, nevertheless, quick to flat-out deny all charges of financial malfeasance. In fact, he is quick to bark orders to the hovering Mr Samuel, who makes off like a scalded cat, doing the Captain's bidding: gathering all of Bligh's financial papers from the ship, including all the receipts and vouchers for all trans-actions in Coupang.

Do you see, *there*, Commandant?

They are all signed by the villainous Master himself! And also signed by Mr Cole and two respectable residents of that port.

Finally, the Commandant tells Bligh, you should know that Mr Purcell is in full agreement with every particular of Mr Fryer's account, as to the cause of the Mutiny.

In the face of such villainy, and he says so to the Commandant, Bligh is more than ever glad that Purcell and Fryer are both prisoners, and that Bligh will not have to share a vessel with them again. They will be travelling on one of the vessels that the Governor has arranged to accompany Bligh on the next leg to Batavia. Or, maybe he should let them rot in Sourabaya, he has not yet decided.

But, Commandant, I will deal with them. Oh yes, I will *definitely* do that.

Observing just how incandescent with rage Bligh is, the Commandant, a reasonable man, of light temperament, visits Fryer in his confinement shortly afterwards to have a quiet word.

'It would be much better for you, and Lieutenant Bligh,' the high Dutch official posits, 'to make it up and be friends.'[38]

. . .

Well, Mr Fryer?

Well, Commandant, you might have a point.

The materials provided, Mr Fryer dips the pen in ink and begins a carefully ambiguous letter, meant to be read between the lines:

Sir

I understand by what the Commandant says that Matters can be settled.
I wish to make everything agreeable as far as lay in my power, that
nothing might happen when we came home.

As I have done everything in my power as far I know to do my duty
& would still wish to do it . . .

Sir
I am Your most
Obedient Humble Servant
Jno. Fryer.[39]

Really, Mr Fryer?

Obedient and humble?

Captain Bligh does not think so.

This is little more than a veiled threat, a villain's bargain, not the grovelling apology he seeks. Bligh throws it down and tells the Commandant that, as Fryer is his prisoner, he desires him to be taken from his cell and put in one of the accompanying vessels, completely on his own. He is not to be placed with Purcell, or any other Englishmen.

Yes, Captain Bligh.

And yet, when the Commandant rather sadly tells Fryer of this decision, the Master is frantic.

'I beg you, Commandant,' he says. 'Tell Lieutenant Bligh that I wish to speak to him before he leaves this place.'[40]

Bligh is delighted to hear of Fryer's panic.

But he is far too busy to talk to common criminals. Instead he will send you a note:

'If you have anything to communicate you must write to me.'[41]

In short, grovel, Mr Fryer, *grovel*, and in writing, so I have legal proof I am right, and then we might have another look at this situation.

Fryer dips his pen in ink once more.

Sir

I have received yours saying that you cannot possibly find time to speak
to me. I most humbly beg of you to grant me that favour if possible it

can be done. I likewise beg of you to take me with you if you confine me in Irons. I will make every concession that you think proper
17th. Sept'r. 1789

Sir I am Your Humble Servant

Jno. Fryer[42]

Now Captain Bligh agrees to see Mr Fryer, and with witnesses present so they may take full account, and confirm the confessions of this scoundrel. When Mr Fryer is brought before them, Bligh is pleased to see that he is pale and trembling 'like a Villain who had done every mischief he could'[43] on the eve of his punishment.

'I humbly ask to be forgiven!' begins Fryer. 'I declare I will make every concession and disavow the infamous report I spread . . . I will give every reparation you please to ask, Captain!'[44]

'I order you away on board the *Prow*,'[45] replies Bligh.

What!

Oh yes, despite this apology, and your grovelling letter, your original punishment must stand – you shall be taken to England in chains on another vessel. And one more thing, Mr Fryer.

'You are to converse no other way with me but by *writing*. All your concessions and disavowals of what you have already asserted must be *by letter*.'[46]

21 September 1789, return to Aphrodite's Isle . . . again

The Tahitians look up to see grand white canvas sails. The *Bounty* has returned!

Their excitement and joy is more than matched by those on the *Bounty* who have chosen to stay in Tahiti. The beautiful people paddling up to them with shouts and laughter are *their* people, and the idea of living here once more is delightful.

For those who have committed to moving on quickly with Christian, however, the scene is upsetting. Even this bare glimpse of paradise is a reminder that they are turning their backs on it. It is the finest place on this earth they have ever seen. What chance there could be another like it, where they could settle just as happily?

What is more, the fact that they are dropping some of their number back in Tahiti indubitably means that – whatever the success or otherwise of Bligh and his own Loyalists in surviving long enough to tell the tale of what happened – their tale will be out regardless, as it can only be a matter of time before another ship arrives, and the likes of Charles Norman, Thomas McIntosh and Michael Byrn tell all. But there is no way around that.

The only exception on the ship is the Armourer, Joseph Coleman, who will not be free to go. Over his howled protests, Christian has decided that his skills as a maker of tools and weapons are too important in the new colony, and he will have to remain on board.

In short order, after dropping anchor, and unloading, Christian addresses them all for the last time.

After advising them that he will not be staying long, he asks for the assistance of all of them the following day to replenish their water supplies, as 'I intended to cruise for some uninhabited island where we can land the stock and set fire to the ship, and where I hope to live the remainder of my days without seeing the face of a European bar those who are already with me.'[47]

Agreed.

The 15 who have chosen to stay in Tahiti are on their way, hauling hard on the oars of the Cutter heading to the shore – the Tahitian men who are returning home to an island they feared they'd never see again, and the likes of Peter Heywood and James Morrison who, for the first time in five months, are away from the custody of Mutineers, and entirely their own men once more.

At last, at long last!

As for Fletcher Christian, he stays resolutely on the *Bounty* and refuses to set foot on Tahiti again – even declining to accompany Isabella as she goes to visit her family.

For yes, it had been one thing to lie to King Tinah last time about *Bry* having met up with *Toote*. But to go and face him now, and be exposed as a liar – for he will surely know all before long – Christian cannot do it.

No matter how much Heywood and Stewart press him to go to see Tinah, to tell him the whole thing, to seek his forgiveness and understanding, Christian will not be moved.

'How can I look him in the face,' he asks plaintively, 'after the lie I told him when I was here last?'[48]

From this position, he will not move and his general mood, his sheer depression, is of great concern to both Heywood and Stewart.

Every time they go out to the *Bounty* to visit him, it is the same thing.

'He was generally below,' Heywood will recount, 'leaning his head upon his hand, and when they came down for orders, he seldom raised his head to answer more than "Yes", or "No".'[49]

It is staggering – and depressing in itself.

The Fletcher Christian they'd known on the island the first time they had been here – the strong, confident, tanned and joyous leader of men, who delighted in every moment of his existence in this paradise – is simply no more.

'[Now,]' Heywood will report, 'he had become such an altered man in his looks and appearance, as to render it probable that he would not long survive.'[50]

Christian appreciates the concern of his friends a great deal, and knows that of the *Bounty* crew, even though they are electing to stay at Tahiti, Heywood and Stewart are, indeed, the only two he can entirely trust.

Which is why on the night of 22 September 1789, just the day after they have returned, he confides in the two a great secret, that he has not even told the Mutineers who will remain with him. He tells them the time of the *Bounty*'s departure.

It means, he tells them, this will be the last time we ever see each other.

'If ever you get to England,' he says with no little emotion, 'inform my friends and country what was the cause of my committing so desperate an act.'[51]

That cause, of course, can be summed up in a single word: *Bligh!*

And you must tell them *everything*. The tempers, the injustices visited upon them all, the insults, the accusations, the hideous charge that, he, Fletcher Christian, the *gentleman* officer from the Isle of Man, would ever have lowered himself to steal coconuts from the perfidious Bligh. How could he not, as a matter of honour, rise up high and proud, against such a low tyrant?

All both men can do is to faithfully promise that, in the unlikely event they do get back to England, and are allowed to speak, they will indeed speak up for the integrity of Fletcher Christian.

And now, Mr Stewart, if you would, Fletcher would like a quiet word with young Peter alone. For there is one other matter which Fletcher would like to entrust to his fellow Manxman.

The pair huddle together, like brothers one last time . . . [52]

•

In the hours after midnight, all falls quiet. Natives of both sexes and crew-members lie, strewn about the quarter-deck. In the wee hours, the rustle of the breeze, the creaking of the masts, and the gentle slapping of the waves against the *Bounty*, receives just a little competition from two things.

The first are the light footsteps of the loyal Armourer, Joseph Coleman, padding to the side of the ship, followed by a small gurgle as he first slides into the water and then starts dog-paddling to the shore, making good his escape.

The second thing, only a short time later, is Fletcher Christian – oblivious to the fact that Coleman has jumped ship – moving among the men on the deck to find the ones he needs, waking them, and telling them very quietly that they must get the ship underway, even before the dawn. He has decided that – given the uncertain reaction of Tinah when he finds out he has been lied to – it is too dangerous to remain here for even another day.

For, what happens when Tinah finds out the truth? And what if the group of Loyalists and Mutineers now on Tahiti – all of them with arms – decide to combine to rise against the *Bounty* men, perhaps indeed with the help of the Natives, led by Tinah, who would be eager to avenge his dear friend, *Bry*?

No, he must leave now, and take with him all those Tahitian men and women who happen to be sleeping on board, even if it is against their wishes. The men they will need for labour and possibly as warriors. The women are needed for love, sex, breeding and labour as the Europeans build their new society on an island unknown.

Taking his cutlass, thus, Christian slashes the rope that binds them to the anchor – he had never been so enamoured of anchors as Bligh, in any case.

Propelled by a favourable current, the *Bounty* begins to drift away from Tahiti, even as the first of his fellow Mutineers start clambering up the rigging, edging out along the spars to unfurl the topsails.

Many of the Natives, of course, are distressed when they wake to find themselves heading out to sea. One maiden is so upset she simply takes a running jump, dives off the stern and is last seen swimming for the smudge of land on the horizon they have come from. Some of the older ladies are wailing, and lashing their faces. As they are not suitable for breeding in any case, and no Mutineer claims them, they are quickly dropped off on the nearest island with a canoe so they can paddle themselves back. They might even be able to pick up a bedraggled swimmer on the way.

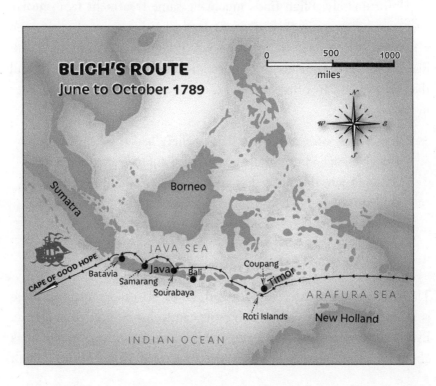

22 September 1789, Samarang, Bligh spreads the word, Fryer concedes all

Oh, the sheer indignity of it!

Waiting to see the Governor – *waiting!* – one of His Excellency's officials insists on making 'many enquiries',[53] and with 'much indelicacy',[54] probes just who Captain Bligh is, and what has happened to him that has brought him to these shores?

It is, of course, a damn impertinence, and Bligh gives the official the very shortest of short shrifts he has in his quiver, making the official quiver in turn. Things hardly go better when he does indeed see the Governor and is stiffly invited for lunch, whereupon another rude official, Mr Grose, also throws questions at him: *How did you lose an entire ship, Captain Bligh?*

Surely there was a sign that your men were unhappy?

Could you not read the mood?

'*Sir,*' Bligh finally barks, 'I find your *ignorance* leading you on so far that I am under the necessity to *put a stop to it*!'[55]

(Unfortunately, Bligh finds much the same treatment from nearly everyone he meets in this town. Instead of being greeted with open arms and storerooms, he must answer impertinent questions about his role in the loss of his ship, questions about his line of credit and the security he can offer for his purchases. Sarcastically, Bligh notes in his Log:

> I have only now to remark that I believe had I not saved my Commission and Uniform, and had been unfortunate enough to have put into this place that the whole of us would have been made prisoners . . . until I could have proved who we were, but at the same time I will do them the Justice to say that had I been a Smuggler loaded with Opium an Article highly Contraband they would have treated me with more politeness and Civility.[56])

The man named Grose, admonished, stops his questions, and Bligh is allowed to relay his story as best he can to his enthralled audience. Ever a man of due process, to ensure there are no misunderstandings about the mutinous tale of His Majesty's Armed Vessel *Bounty*, Bligh has come prepared. He takes from his pocket a particular document he has been working on.

In his neat but ink-smeared script is the whole story, written out in the salt water–stained leather notebook Thomas Hayward had given him. What's more, he has a list of all the Mutineers, together with their distinctive features, with each tattoo, scar and accent carefully noted in order, 'to secure the pirates wherever they might appear'.[57]

> Fletcher Christian, master's mate, aged 24 years, five feet nine inches high, blackish or very dark brown complexion, dark brown hair, strong made; a star tatowed on his left breast, tatowed on his backside; his knees stand a little out, and he may be called rather bow legged. He is subject to violent perspirations, and particularly in his hands, so that he soils any thing he handles . . .
>
> Peter Heywood, midshipman, aged 17 years, five feet seven inches high, fair complexion, light brown hair, well proportioned; very much tatowed; and on the right leg is tatowed the three legs of Man, as it is upon that coin. At this time he has not done growing; and speaks with the Manks, or Isle of Man accent . . . [58]

And so on . . .

Beyond this list being translated into Dutch and disseminated through every port in the Dutch East Indies – ports like Malacca, Batavia, Sunda, Oosthaven – Bligh's desire is that every port they stop at on the way back to England will be given the same list. Whatever happens, if Fletcher Christian and his traitors try to return to European civilisation, they must be captured and arrested as soon as possible.

Everyone must be on the lookout.

(Still, Bligh does take care to name the innocent as well, with Joseph Coleman, Charles Norman and Thomas McIntosh, all noted as 'deserving of mercy, being detained against their inclinations'.[59] Bligh also records that, 'Michael Byrn, the fiddler who is half blind, I am told had no prior knowledge of what was done and wanted to also leave the ship.'[60])

Nodding his approval, the Governor goes on to assure Bligh that there is no need to worry as he will personally take the matter in hand, and see the information circulated.

Satisfied, Bligh returns to his ship, whereupon Mr Samuel hands him a letter that he has just received, marked to the attention of 'Captain William Bligh', in writing that Bligh recognises instantly. For yes, it is the wretched scrawl of the so-called 'Master' of the *Bounty*, Mr Fryer.

Sliding his forefinger along the line of the wax seal, Bligh opens the letter and is soon reading Master Fryer's latest plea, with no little satisfaction.

> *Sir,*
> *. . . you have been informed I uttered things tending to hurt your Character both as an Officer & as a Man. I therefore think it my duty to apologise to you for such conduct. In the first place the paper Signed Wm Adriaan Van Este which I showed was sent to me by Capt. Spikerman for I did not see that Gentleman and I present that paper to you to compare the Signature for I do not wish to hurt the Character of that Man and am sorry for such a transaction.*
> *. . . you have most perfectly in my opinion done your utmost to secure the Health and Happiness of your Officers and Men, that you never have behaved with the least partical of Tyranny or oppression that unless you had been more than a Human Being you could not have foreseen the loss of the Ship . . . I think I am by integrity bound to give you this avowal of my own feelings & to say (conscious that I have done Wrong) I beg your pardon and you may depend I shall ever do my utmost to induce you to forget what is past. I therefore hope you . . . no longer suffer me to be a Prisoner to go to England or have any intention to try me by a Court Martial.*
>
> *Sir*
> *Your much Obliged*
> *& Very humble Serv't.*
> *Jno. Fryer*
>
> *Samarang*
>
> *Sept'r 23rd. 1789*[61]

Very humble?

Indeed. So humble, we might say it is only a small step from there to completely humiliated. Nevertheless, Fryer has half done what needs to be done to save his skin. He has given Bligh a documented statement that he is in no way to blame for the Mutiny, and could not have done better than he did.

Now, as for that other rather unfortunate matter, all those papers, those bills and accounts, the so-called proof that Bligh had been defrauding the Admiralty? Fryer sends the incriminating papers to Bligh the next morning, together with another note: 'I . . . humbly request of you not to mention anything about it at Batavia as it will give me a great deal of uneasiness . . .'[62]

Both men understand exactly what this is about.

In return for leniency, Fryer has positioned himself to be a public advocate for what a good leader Bligh is, and to affirm how well he has done against the curs and cads, the treacherous traitors who had tried to do him down.

Bligh is quick to accept. Fryer's words are recorded word for word in Bligh's journal as a record of his integrity and leadership.[63] Let all who might doubt him, read the words of the Master of the *Bounty*.

There is no need, however, to preserve those 'fraudulent' papers. They are immediately destroyed.

For his trouble – and, in fact, in spite of it – Fryer is liberated, and allowed to resume his position as Master of the *Resource*, as they prepare to depart for Batavia.

Such is not the case, however, for Purcell, who remains prisoner in the other prow.

As far as he is concerned, Bligh can go to the Devil, a sentiment in which Bligh betters him, for, as far as he is concerned, the Carpenter can *go to hell*.

30 September 1789, *Bounty*, South Pacific Ocean, 500 miles south-west of Tahiti

What then, would an eagle eye, high in the sky, in the mother of all crow's nests, now see of the original crew of the *Bounty*?

Directly below, on the ship itself, there are just nine Mutineers, including Christian – in the company of 19 Tahitian and Tubuaian men, women and children – doing their best to manage the many tasks. The one on the quarter-deck rubbing his chin, gazing around the entire horizon, is Christian, trying to work out where to go now. He needs to navigate them to some island in this Pacific Ocean where they can dig in and lead a fruitful life, while also remaining completely hidden from the Royal Navy. And it has to be somewhere in this general part of the world. For, as the expert eagle eye also notes, the movements of the *Bounty* are sluggish, failing to react quickly to shifts in the direction or strength of the wind. With his skeleton crew, only a couple of experienced top-men, it is hard to sail close to the wind and tacking is now a long and arduous process. Christian is forced to sail a much more circuitous route, tacking back and forth sparingly and covering a long zig-zag course instead of a quicker straighter path.

What's more, the crew of a mere *eight* Mutineers – he had been livid to find that the Armourer, Coleman, had slipped away in the dead of night – are soon exhausted and irritable.

Given Christian's feeble authority, orders are not barked, they are posed as requests. His directives are not decrees. They are entreaties, oft earnestly expressed. If they don't mind?

They don't, for the moment. But they're watching you.

•

Six thousand miles to the north-west, meanwhile, Bligh, Fryer and 14 crew – Purcell still in confinement – continue beneath the searing sun to push their way from Samarang to Batavia, cursing their contemptuous Commander under their breath as usual.

•

As the eagle soars over Tahiti, she peers down to focus on the stranded Loyalists, Charles Norman, Thomas McIntosh, the Blind Fiddler and the newly liberated Joseph Coleman – accompanied by Peter Heywood and James Morrison, who claim to be Loyalists – together with the once-were Mutineers, George Stewart, Charley Churchill, William

Muspratt, Henry Hillbrant, Thomas Burkett, Thomas Ellison, John Millward, Richard Skinner, John Sumner and Matthew Thompson.

To their great joy, they are warmly welcomed by King Tinah, who is quick to grant them 'gathering land', where they may collect whatever they like in the way of coconuts, yams, bread-fruit and game. Inevitably, most of the men quickly find their way back to their *vahine*, former lovers, as well as their *tyos*, strong friends who they had previously been staying with.

Now, while it had been one thing to visit Tahiti the first and second time, with the *Bounty*, it is quite another to be living here, full-time, with no link to the outside world, no known chance of leaving.

Such had been the feeling since they had woken up on that terrible morning to find that Christian had cut the rope to the anchor and the *Bounty* had left in the dead of night. The time since for the mix of Loyalists and Mutineers has been uneasy to say the least, with a clear division between them.

For the four indisputable *bona fide* Loyalists, the ones Bligh has promised to mark as innocent, theirs is primarily a feeling of impotent impatience. Hopefully, Bligh will have survived, affirmed their innocence to whoever of the Royal Navy is sent out in pursuit, and they will be safe once that ship arrives.

If he has not survived, however, or hasn't been able to pass on the innocence of some of them, their fate is uncertain and their best hope is that, sooner or later, a ship of the Royal Navy will arrive, looking for what happened to the *Bounty*. That, of course, is not the position of the initial Mutineers, among them the thuggish Churchill and Thompson, both of whom had held their muskets at Bligh, while Stewart had yelled that it was, 'The happiest day of my life!'[64] when he had seen Bligh tied before the mast, and even done a Tahitian celebratory dance to mark the occasion.

For all of them, there is a matter of calculations. If, and it is a very big if, Bligh and the men in the Launch have survived, just how long would it take them to get to a British outpost, where they could raise the alarm? And from there, how long would it take for a ship to be requisitioned, crewed and sent towards what would presumably be their first port of call, Tahiti – at which point Loyalists will be saved.

There is also, of course, the high likelihood that when the *Bounty* fails to appear back at Portsmouth, after a certain amount of time the Royal Navy will send a ship in search of her.

Either way, the best calculations are that the first time a British ship coming to the rescue might reasonably be expected to appear is in the first half of 1791, and the tension rises as the months pass. For the other question that arises, of course, is if a British ship does arrive, just *how much will they know*? If Bligh or any of his Loyalists have survived long enough to tell all to the authorities, they will of course know everything – at least from Bligh's side. (And yes, that reality would point to killing the Loyalists as a solution, but the original decision – *yes to mutiny, no to murder* – holds.)

But the other possibility is that a British, French or American ship will arrive by happenstance, in which case all will turn on whether they are naval or merchant ships, which of the Mutineers or the Loyalists on the island get to them first, and who they will believe – if they are a French or American merchant ship, there is a good chance that they will not care to get involved either way. But they could be a great means of escape!

Not for nothing, thus, is the relationship between the Loyalists and Mutineers on the island a strained one, as they not only look sideways at each other, while keeping another eye on the Natives, but also are perpetually gazing seawards – not only waiting for their ship to come in, but hoping it is the right ship.

In the meantime, as they wait, at least Tahiti is as pleasurable a place as any in the world to be spending time – and not just because of the obvious lusty leisure pursuits available. For there is also feasting, dancing, drinking kava and sleeping it all off under the coconut trees ...

James Morrison, a restless soul, for whom earnest activity provides the only balm, now starts to muse on the possibilities of building ... a boat. And not just any boat. He does not want a mere canoe, nor even his version of a Jolly Boat, Cutter, or Launch. Oh no, he wants nothing less than a yacht, perhaps even big enough to allow them to return to England. To do it, he will need local help and, in the course of his conversations with some of the more influential of the Chiefs, at last the mystery of who had cut the *Bounty*'s cable so many months before is revealed. For while talking to King Tinah's brother, the drunken warrior Prince Whydooah, the royal one blithely reveals it was him, out of loyalty to his *tyo*, Midshipman Thomas Hayward!

For yes, after *tyo* Hayward had been on watch that time the three men deserted, *Bry* had been so angry he might have done anything by way of punishment.

'I cut the cable to let the ship come on shore,' Whydooah recounts to Morrison, 'where I hoped she would . . . receive so much damage as to prevent her going to sea. By that means I wanted to get my *tyo* out of Mr. Bligh's power, as I assumed all hands would be forced to live on shore if the ship received much damage.'[65]

Morrison is stunned.

One way or another, it seems, Bligh and the *Bounty* were destined to be separated at some point. Fletcher Christian did it the hard way, while Prince Whydooah had a much quicker plan.

For their part, the men of the *Bounty* feel the time is now right – or as right as it will ever be – to reveal to Whydooah their own secret, concerning the way Bligh departed their company. It is Heywood who takes it upon himself to delicately break the news to Whydooah.

Slowly, carefully, young Heywood lets it be known that Christian had been lying through his teeth when saying that Bligh is with his father Captain Cook. Firstly, Captain Cook is dead, secondly, Bligh is not his son and, thirdly, well, there has been a mutiny, and in fact Bligh has been placed in a small Launch with his fellow Loyalists and has been set adrift.

For his part, Whydooah's response, while lacking somewhat in delicacy, is clearly nothing if not sincere: 'I curse Fletcher Christian for not killing Captain Bligh. I will kill him myself if he ever comes again to Tahiti!'

For yes, as it turned out, Whydooah had already been apprised of some of the news, courtesy of HMS *Mercury* – a 28-gun ship, three times the size of the *Bounty* and four times the crew – which had visited only three months after Christian had first departed these shores. Its skipper, Captain John Cox, had been astonished to hear that as well as Christian, he had only just missed Captain Cook's son, Captain

Bligh, who had gathered supplies to take to his father in Wytootacke for some . . .

Some mistake in translation?

No, the Tahitians had insisted that *Bry* had gone to see *Toote*, who was very much alive. Gently, Cox explained that Captain Cook had been dead for a decade, and, in any case, had no son by the name of Bligh. When disbelieved, Cox had had the perfect answer. For it so happened that on board the *Mercury*, he had a painting depicting the death of Captain Cook at the hands, and spears, of Hawaiian Natives. The painting had been passed from one to other of the Tahitian royal family, whose grief at the death of Captain Cook had been channelled into rage at the infamy of Bligh's lie.

Bligh has made fools of them.

Most hurt and angered of all is King Tinah, whose trust in Bligh had been so devastatingly betrayed. Well, he will not be so fooled again. Sooner or later, it is obvious, the British will come looking for Bligh and the *Bounty*, and undoubtedly will want some of these white men on Tahiti. Just which of them were loyal to Bligh, and which ones betrayed him is not certain to Tinah, and he does not particularly care. What he wants is to be quit of them all, and in the meantime, keep his distance from them. The best he can do is offer the cautious hospitality of his people, only. Even as he watches them carefully.

•

In the meantime, trouble is brewing on the zig-zagging *Bounty*.

Together with the nine white men, there are six Native men – four from Tahiti and two from Tubuai – making 15 in all, while there are just 12 women from Tahiti on board. In terms of that activity which has been known to soothe the savage breast since the dawn of time – and equally cause rising frustration and ill-will when it is denied – there are three men who will have to go without . . . or share with others. For the moment – as the Polynesian women clearly don't mind sharing themselves, while the men are less proprietorial than whites – sharing will help to settle things.

As it happens, one notably beautiful young woman, Jenny – the prize of the *Bounty*, after Isabella – has *already* transferred her affections.

Despite the fact that she has 'AS 1789' tattooed on her arm in honour of her one-time love of Able Seaman Alec Smith, she had found that behind Smith's surly, violent façade he was . . . even surlier and more violent in private. A strong, smart and highly capable woman, she knows how to get things done, which had included ridding herself of Smith as a partner and taking up with Isaac Martin instead – the American being stunned with her beauty and intelligence – somehow without provoking Smith *too* badly.

With Jenny, perhaps, he does not dare to provoke her too badly in turn. These Tahitian women are beautiful, and none more than Jenny, but so too have the Mutineers come to understand they can also be dangerous. You push *them*, too far, at your peril.

2 October 1789, Batavia, an ill wind blows off the canals

Some mariners who have sailed the Seven Seas think of Batavia as the most dangerous port in the world. No, not because of knife-wielding thugs haunting the back alleys, ready to spring on the unsuspecting passer-by. Rather, it is the 'vapours', the pestilent, stinking air that rises from its stagnant and festering canals, vapours with buzzing insects that bring typhus and malaria, and in a bad year can kill as many as half of all new arrivals, while in a good year it is only one in seven.

Captain Cook had said of Batavia that it was responsible for 'the death of more Europeans than any other place upon the globe'.[66]

As it happens, and exactly as he had feared, Bligh – who arrived in the infamous Dutch port just a day earlier – appears to have caught some of this pestilence.

He takes to his bed.

> My health continues so very bad that the Physician has represented
> it . . . that I should leave Batavia without delay.[67]

Bligh decides to sell, at a maritime auction, both the *Resource* and . . . the mighty Launch.

The funds raised will be enough to buy their passage home, or at least Bligh's.

10 October 1789, Tahiti, of castaways and Mutineers

As it happens, Captain Cox has left behind more than the painting of Captain Cook's death. For yes, he has also left behind . . . a white man!

Here he is now, being paddled ashore in the canoe of Churchill and Millward, who had gone to the other side of the island to visit Tinah, where they had discovered this fellow, John Brown.

He proves indeed to be a former *Mercury* sailor, who had requested to be allowed to stay in Tahiti, and Cox had been only too happy to oblige.

As a matter of fact, Cox had even left Chief Poeno of Matavai Bay a letter to be given to whoever the next ship's Captain is who comes this way, apparently affirming he is no runaway sailor, though the illiterate Brown is not sure.

Could Morrison read it for him?

> John Brown is an ingenious handy man when sober but when drunk a dangerous fellow.[68]

Brown snaffles the letter roughly from the hand of Morrison, who, startled, looks at the hardened castaway with narrowed eyes. This fellow may mean trouble . . .

Brown is, in short, trouble, and as men with plenty enough troubles of their own, both the Mutineers and the Loyalists of the *Bounty* give him a wide berth, both to starboard and to larboard, and never more so than when he is three sheets to the wind, and heading straight for the teeth of a storm, which is mostly.

CHAPTER FOURTEEN

PITCAIRN

Swiftly, swiftly flew the ship,
Yet she sailed softly too:
Sweetly, sweetly blew the breeze –
On me alone it blew.

Oh! dream of joy! is this indeed
The light-house top I see?
Is this the hill? is this the kirk?
Is this mine own countree?[1]

Samuel Taylor Coleridge, 'The Rime of the Ancient Mariner'

WHO IS WITH WHO ON PITCAIRN
(As of the day of landing)
Fletcher Christian (Captain) = 'Isabella' *(Mauatua), nicknamed*
  Mainmast
Ned Young (Midshipman, 2IC) = Teraura
Billy Brown (Gardener Assistant) = Sarah *(Teatuahitea)*
Alec Smith (Able Seaman) = Obuarei
Matt Quintal (Able Seaman) = Tevarua
Jack Williams (Able Seaman) = Faahotu
Isaac Martin (Able Seaman) = Jenny *(Teehuteatuaonoa)*
Bill McCoy (Able Seaman) = Teio *(who also has a baby daughter*
  with her)
John Mills (Gunner's Mate) = Vahineatua
The Tahitians: Talaloo = Toofaiti
  Nehow)
  Timoa) = Mareva *(shared wife of three men)*
  Menalee)

The Tubuaians (referred to by the Mutineers as Tahitians in their
   accounts)

Ohoo)

Tetaheite) = Tinafornea *(shared wife of two men)*.[2]

> The names of the men and their wives, as recorded by Jenny and Alec
> Smith in their written accounts of what happened on Pitcairn Island

10 October 1789, Batavia, a double-Dutch auction

A Dutch auction, Bligh now discovers, is like an English auction in reverse. Whereas with an English auction you start low and keep going higher until there is only one person left standing, with a Dutch auction you start a little higher than your wildest dreams and lower the asked price until the first person puts up their hand, and the new owner is declared.

And so it is that at 9 o'clock on this morning the *Resource* is 'put up at 2000 Rix dollars',[3] about £75, which is, yes, a little beyond Captain Bligh's wildest dreams, for a ship he had purchased for 1000 Rix dollars, just three months earlier.

But when in Rome do as the Romans do, and when in the Dutch East Indies, have the incomprehensible bids in Dutch quickly translated into English for you . . .

1500 Rix dollars then?

No-one.

1000 Rix dollars?

Still no-one.

500 Rix dollars, surely.

To Bligh's stupefaction, hands of potential bidders seem to be pushed more firmly into their pockets than ever.

'Strange as it may appear she only sold for 295 Rix Dollars,' a bewildered Bligh writes in the Log.

Another vessel is sold today. Bligh writes sadly: 'The Launch likewise was sold. The services she had rendered us, made me feel great reluctance at parting with her.'[4] But needs must, and Bligh needs money and so it is that the Launch, the remarkable vessel that carried 19 men on one of the most extraordinary voyages in the history of the world, is sold for a trifling sum.

It is the final page of an extraordinary saga, and, as disappointing as the price is, perhaps, with the ending now, Bligh can at last let himself go a little, to do what he has long wanted to do but not been allowed the luxury – feel sick.

> My health and strength is worse every day so that I am in tortures when I think or write.[5]

And he is not the only one.

For on this day, he records in his Log the fate of another Loyalist, 'At ½ past 11 died at this Hospital Thomas Hall of a Flux. This poor man has never been well since my arrival at Timor.'[6]

Bligh cannot leave this place of pestilence quickly enough and mercifully they are nearly ready to do so.

Before boarding, however, Bligh pauses to write an important letter to Sir Joseph Banks, which will depart on a bigger and faster ship. It is important both that his patron be advised as soon as possible what has occurred, and, even more importantly, can understand how blameless Bligh is, how courageous in the aftermath, and how valiant overall in the service of the Royal Navy, against the curs who had done him down. Most importantly, the letter will stand as testament to what has happened, should his own ship be lost at sea, and the letter even has a word of . . . implied warning.

> *Batavia October 13th. 1789*
>
> *Dear Sir,*
> *I am now so ill that it is with the utmost difficulty I can write to you*
> . . .
>
> *You will find that the Ship was taken from me in a most extraordinary manner . . .*
>
> *Had I been accidentally appointed to the Command, the loss of the Ship would give me no material concern, but when I reflect that it was through you Sir who undertook to assert I was fully capable, and the Eyes of every one regarding the progress of the Voyage, and perhaps*

*more with envy, than with delight; I cannot say but if [it] affects me
considerably.*[7]

Reading his words, Bligh has every right to a certain satisfaction, for
his message, while understated, is clear: When I get back, you would
be well advised to give me your full support, in maintaining that I
am the one wronged. For, the alternative view, that I am a tyrant will
reflect badly on your judgement in putting me there.

As for the cause of Christian's treachery, Sir Joseph . . .

> *I can only conjecture that the Pirates have Ideally assured themselves
> of a more happy life among the Tahitians than they could possibly have
> in England, which joined to some female connections, has most likely
> been the leading cause of the whole busyness.*
>
> *If I Had been equipped with more Officers & Marines the piracy
> could never have happened.*[8]

Ahem. As I *told* you . . .

> *Your most obliged Humble Servant
> Wm Bligh*[9]

Together with this opening letter, Bligh gives a detailed account of
everything that had happened during the Mutiny, and what had
happened thereafter; every adversity, the actions of every Loyalist and
Mutineer, and just how extraordinary each of his nautical triumphs
against the odds was. And yes, he is sorry to close his account with
the tragic news of the death of Sir Joseph's friend, Mr Nelson. Beneath
this news, Bligh adds a note, in the hope that his patron will use his
influence where it counts:

> *I have not given so full an account to the Admiralty you will please
> therefore to attend to it in that particular.*[10]

•

Happy to have the task of writing to Sir Joseph Banks over with, the
ailing Bligh turns his attention to the myriad matters that Samuel is
bringing before him, non-stop.

The paperwork!

The certificates!

The bills! Leaving Batavia, as it turns out, is less a matter of maritime manoeuvres than of navigating through a miserable mountain of paperwork as the Dutch extract their pound of flesh from him with endless bureaucratic procedures, not to mention an unending series of fresh fees to cover the cost of hosting Bligh and his Loyalists, as well as getting them ready for the next leg of their journey. The charges are 'exorbitant', Bligh records in his journal, but 'I had no resource, I must either lose my passage or pay the account'.[11]

It all wouldn't sting so much if any of that which was provided was half-decent, but it is nothing of the kind. Bligh records, 'Batavia is so unhealthy that it is a Miracle if a Stranger remains a Month . . . without a Fever.'[12]

Bligh is particularly irritated with Dutch house 'cleaners' who seem to specialise in spreading dust and dirt with a broom rather than mop with water and vinegar. A different man than Bligh, of course, might be more focused on the fact that he has only just escaped dying of fever thanks to Dutch medical care than the bad housekeeping he must put up with meantime, but this Captain is a special case.

In sum, the sooner they can leave this low citadel of 'contagion and disease', the better.

At last, it is done, with passage booked for himself and Samuel and Smith, and their bags packed, with their bills paid, and their loans guaranteed in a manner such that the Dutch will indeed let them go. The ship that Bligh will be returning to England on, the *Vlydt*, is fully loaded, and will be leaving on the morrow, 16 October 1789.

The rest of the Loyalists can make their way to England on later ships, as berths become available. Which brings Bligh to his final administrative duty.

Mr Fryer, if you please. Here are your formal orders:

Orders to Mr. John Fryer Master

Oct 16, 1789
Whereas from a representation of the Physician General it appears that my life is in great danger to remain here until the Fleet for Europe Sails, and that only myself and two others can be

taken in the Packet which departs on the 16 Instant, I therefore impower you to take command of such remaining Officers and Men & to follow me to the Cape of Good Hope by the first Ships His Excellency the Governor General shall permit you to embark on . . .

You are also upon your embarkation or at a proper time to get a knowledge of what charges are against His Majesty's Subjects under your Command & upon fairly & duly considering them you are to draw Bills for the Amount on the Navy Commissioners for Victualing His Majestys Navy.[13]

The bitter irony of it escapes neither man.

For yes, Mr Fryer, you who so much enjoy gathering documents and bills, and lists of prices, to ensure that every penny is accounted for, can now do this under *my* orders! And yes, you will be doing so, while still under the threat of court martial once you arrive in England, for I have as yet made no formal undertaking to drop all charges. I will decide on my voyage, and you may stew on it meantime.

Now, another thing. You must also ensure safe passage of my bread-fruit plants . . . all . . . three of them.

Yes, they are but three, but who knows . . . the Admiralty might find some way to put these three in a greenhouse and eventually produce a thousand more. It is, to be sure, faintly ridiculous but at least it is something.

Beyond everything else, Bligh is eager to find out if such plants can survive such a long voyage in the first place, as even that will be valuable to know.

Late October 1789, in the South Pacific, fragile command
Drop anchor.

The *Bounty* bobs just off a tiny island, which Christian knows from his chart was discovered by Captain Cook in 1777 and is called Purutea.

They don't have to wait long to find out if it is inhabited. A few minutes after they drop one of their spare anchors, there appears some half-a-dozen Natives in a canoe, bearing a pig and coconuts, paddling steadily towards them. They are unarmed and look friendly, so no-one minds – at least nearly no-one – when one of the bolder of the Natives actually climbs up the anchor chain onto the deck of the ship and walks right up to Captain Christian, half-resplendent in his half heavily patched Master's Mate uniform.

With great wonder apparent in his stupefied countenance, the Native is particularly taken with the shiny pearl buttons on Christian's waistcoat. Rising to the occasion, bemused by his fascination, Christian carefully removes his navy blue jacket, and now takes off his white waistcoat jacket with the white-pearl buttons, before, with great generosity, presenting the waistcoat jacket to the Native as the fine fellow gazes wide-eyed at such a precious gift. So thrilled is he, in fact, that with Christian's help with this unfamiliar garment, the Native immediately puts it on, and jumps up on the gunnel to display it.

From the look of his pride, and their wonder, Purutea very likely has no less than a new *King*, and . .

And suddenly the world stops, a shot rings out. The fine white jacket, with the pearl-shell buttons, sprouts angry red splotches and the resplendent Native – now, *dead* – tumbles from the gunnel and falls, narrowly missing his comrades in the canoe.

Shouts! Screams!

What on *earth* has just happened?

On the *Bounty* stands a Mutineer, grinning, with a still smoking musket, convinced that he has just suitably punished a Native who had stolen the jacket.

Below, the Natives in the canoe, stricken, haul the lifeless body of their dead friend from the waters, and furiously paddle away, wailing wild laments as they go.

Over their shoulders they can hear much shouting, and a quick glance behind reveals it to be the one who had given the coat now yelling at the grinning man with the smoking stick.

The murderer proves to be none other than Alec Smith, who appears to be remarkably unrepentant, even when advised that the Native had not been stealing at all, but merely accepting a gift, graciously given.

Under similar circumstances, just eight months before, Bligh's punishment for Smith would have been swift and merciless lashes.

But now, all is different.

Beyond the tongue-lashing, as one of the Tahitian women, Jenny, who has a gift for observation, would later note, Christian 'could do nothing more, having lost all authority'.[14]

Yes, they call him 'Captain Christian', but the truth is, and they all know it, having cut down Bligh in a mutiny, having taken such extreme action in the cause of correcting injustice, he can hardly demand unquestioned authority from those who have joined him in the same quest. Thus, with tongue-lashing delivered, and the Natives of Purutea now turned entirely against them, there is nowhere else to go . . .

Weigh anchor!

31 October 1789, Indian Ocean, time does not fly on the Fly

Since leaving Batavia, bound for England, on the Dutch packet ship, the *Vlydt*, Bligh's enduring fever had seen him below decks and sleeping for most of the time. But now, feeling stronger, it is time for the unfortunate Dutch captain, Peter Couvert, to be under one of the most critical eyes of this maritime age gazing grimly at every move he makes. For, untroubled by the fact that he is a mere passenger, with no authority, Bligh cannot help himself, and constantly calculates the latitude and longitude every day, to check against Captain Couvert's figures – all so he can tell the remarkably long-suffering Dutchman just how wrong he got it this time. On a bad day, Bligh grimly tells him that he is wrong by 30 miles, while on a good day the Englishman allows Couvert has only miscalculated by six miles. Either way, Bligh's tone suggests that, on his own ship, the best the Dutchman could hope for would be to wash the dishes.

Does Captain Bligh have any kind words for the Dutch sailors, at least? Certainly none that come readily to mind. But, of the *other* kind of words, they simply gush from his pen like an opened duct of bile.

> The Men are stinking and dirty with long beards, and their Bedding a nuisance, as may be conceived when they have not washed Hammocks since they have been from Europe. The Capt. in his person and bedding equally dirty. Some of the people [have]

not a second shift of Cloaths. Cookery so bad I cannot make a meal; such nasty beasts.[15]

Early November 1789, Tahiti, all things ship-shape for the new shipwright

James Morrison is now committed.

He wants to build a vessel, and a good one – good enough to outrun any British vessel that might arrive, and perhaps even good enough to sail all the way back to England. Keeping such a project secret is not possible of course, and when the likes of Churchill and Thompson ask why he is building the boat, Morrison replies carefully that it is a hobby pursuit only, the vessel is 'only for the purpose of pleasuring about the island'.[16]

Anyway, he will need help and now spreads the word among the other *Bounty* men on the island: he wants to build a small vessel. Immediately, there is some interest, particularly from Charles Norman and Thomas McIntosh, Purcell's one-time assistants.

The basic idea is for each man to bring to the boat whatever skills he has, to reproduce on an island in the Pacific, the best of British know-how, to make the best of British vessels, albeit with only the most rudimentary tools and little of the supplies on hand that could be found in even the most rudimentary British docks.

The first and most obvious thing they will need is fine timber, from particular Poorow trees, 'somewhat like Elm',[17] and also bread-fruit trees – for which they need, of course, the blessing of the local Chief.

'We intend to build a little ship,' Morrison tells him, 'as we do not understand the method of handling canoes. When it is built, we could carry you and Tinah with some of your friends to the neighbouring islands.'

The Chief is thrilled.

'*Tapu ra'au*, cut down what timber you please,' he says, 'as there is plenty in Matavai.'[18]

And so it begins.

There remains, however, one particularly notable absentee from Morrison's workforce.

Peter Heywood has no interest in helping Morrison with his boat, as he has nothing to fear and would sooner wait for the first British ship for his salvation. Instead, he devotes himself to compiling his Tahitian dictionary, writing poems and doing his sketches, while also building a hut for himself and the beautiful Tahitian maiden who had been waiting for him. Not content with merely a simple hut in the native fashion, Heywood builds something grander, with more rooms and a higher roof, complete with a garden.

And so back to the dictionary . . .

Tafe poipoi – Breakfast.

Mono'o – Joy.

Ua here vau ia oe – I love you.

Time for *moe*, sleep.

•

And can you hear the rhythmic man-made sound in the distance?

It is the sound of an *axe*, as Morrison and his men keep building their ship.

For within a week or so, Morrison is completely obsessed with his vessel and with the idea that they can build their liberty.

And now, with the final of several dozen strong blows with his axe, yet one more tree – *Timberrrrrr!* – falls to the ground.

And now, together, *lift*.

Covered in dirt and sweat, with chips of wood in their hair and clinging to their clothes, James Morrison and John Millward use the stubs of cut branches to get a grip and, with their axes swinging from their hips, drag their newly felled tree to their rough work yard. There, Norman, Hillbrant and McIntosh are even more covered in grime and woodchips as they keep sawing on the last log brought to the yard, turning it into the long plank that will eventually be the keel, the spine of their grand new vessel.

At 30 feet, it will be seven feet longer than the Launch, with one and a half times its volume and carrying capacity, a formidable vessel, formed up on Morrison's ambitious planning and carefully calculated design:

Length of the keel: 30 feet

Length on deck: 35 feet

Length of the sternpost: 6 feet, 6 inches

Stem: 7 feet, 2 inches

Breadth: 9 feet, 6 inches on the midship frame

Depth of the hold: 5 feet

Breadth of the floors and timbers: 4 inches to 3½, thickness 3¼ to 2½

Keel, stem and sternpost: 8 inches by 4.[19]

First of all, he realises, he must construct a shed with no walls to provide both shade and air to work in. As construction continues, Morrison faces the next challenge – getting maps that may guide their escape. Carefully, he approaches the always menacing Matt Thompson, wondering if he may borrow some of his naval books, the ones he knows contain maps. After all, as Thompson is as illiterate as a brick, the books are no good to him.

And yet, as ill-educated as he might be, Thompson is no man's fool.

'No,' he tells Morrison, 'I have no cartridge paper. The books will answer better for that purpose.'[20]

It is not just the words. It is the way he says it. And the look in his eye. For his message is very clear.

We do not trust you, Mr Morrison, or any man who seeks to leave the island without us. And we are armed, Mr Morrison.

Mid-November 1789, Tongataboo, Fletcher Christian finds a hideout

And these, now, are more of the Friendly Islands – such as this one, Tongataboo.

True to the name, the *Bounty* has no sooner dropped anchor than, again, friendly Natives approach in canoes, with gifts of hogs, yams and poultry. In a halting dialect of the Polynesian language, the Natives proudly tell Christian that none other than the famous '*Toote*', Captain Cook, had visited their island back nearly 200 moons ago – and what is more, they still have some horned cattle that the great man gave them!

Which is wonderful for them, but for Christian, the fact that Cook has been here, the fact that Tongataboo exists on Admiralty maps, is precisely what they don't want. No, it is imperative that they find a dot of an island somewhere within range of the food and water they have, that, preferably, is unknown, but, at the very least, uninhabited. (In the meantime, let them quickly trade with the Natives to stock up on the supplies the *Bounty* needs, before weighing anchor.) True, without the Blind Fiddler and all the others, turning the capstan does not have quite the same feel – it is bloody hard work – but still they sing as they put their shoulders to the wheel . . .

Heave, lads, *heaaaaave!*

And push to the tune . . .

So lean on your bar and walk 'er round
(We're outward bound)
There's a good stiff wind, and we're outward bound!
Thank God boys, we're outward bound!
(Walk 'er round
We're outward bound.)[21]

Early December 1789, somewhere in the South Pacific east of the Friendly Islands, a treasure of an island

Night after night, Isabella had woken to find her *Titriano* sweating profusely, panicky, haunted, full of fear and completely consumed with regret and shame. In recent nights however, it has been less the terrors of his mind that have troubled him, and far more real fears of what might happen now. Obviously, the longer they remain adrift, rootless out on the open ocean, the more they are in peril, and they *must* find a home, a refuge, soon.

But, where? It is this question he now focuses on, frets over, flutters around to the point of total distraction, as Isabella hovers close, trying to soothe him. But she, too, is eager for this to end.

Find us a home, *Titriano.*

Thinking on it, as they push east, staring out at a blurry horizon, Christian realises that being discovered on an island by the British is not the only problem they face. For it would be equally troublesome to be discovered by the Polynesians, as word would spread – and it could only be a matter of time before a visiting British ship would hear of white men in the area and come looking for them. Now, given that the South Pacific Natives can travel more than 300 miles in their canoes, and navigate by the stars, it means that the island they are looking for is not one in this whole *region*, and they must go further afield. But where?

As it happens, Bligh has an extensive library in his *Bounty* cabin, and in one of his books, Hawkesworth's *Voyages*, Christian discovers the possible answer. For there, yes, a Captain Philip Carteret of HMS *Swallow* records a brief visit, in July 1767, to a place he has called Pitcairn Island, after 15-year-old Midshipman Robert Pitcairn, who had first sighted it. It appears uninhabited and, as far as can be determined, no British citizen has ever set foot on the place. Best of all, it is no more than a speck on a dot in the vast ocean, two miles long, and 1500 miles from Tahiti. And, yes, it is on the Admiralty map, but

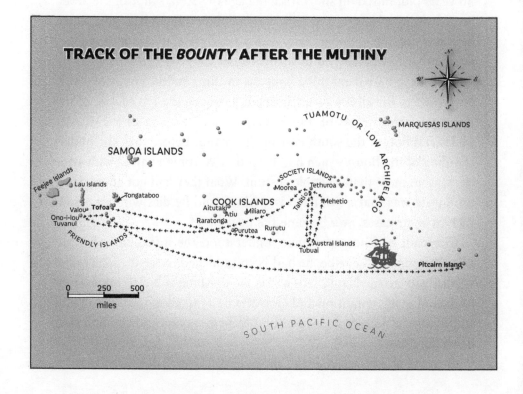

TRACK OF THE *BOUNTY* AFTER THE MUTINY

the fact that Cook could not find it, when looking in 1773, suggests the recorded longitude and latitude is incorrect. Perfect . . . so long as Fletcher can find it now.

Christian realises, of course, that it will strain both the resources left on the *Bounty*, and the temper of its crew and passengers, to get there. But what choice do they have?

Christian sets a course to Captain Carteret's co-ordinates – 25°2'S 133°21'W. It will be an arduous journey, beyond the range of Native canoes, to a place highly unlikely to be visited by British ships, but Christian knows Pitcairn is their only option.

That night, as Isabella is quick to note, instead of tossing and turning, her *Titriano* has his best sleep in weeks.

December 1789, Tahiti, the King is dead, long live . . . King Churchill!

How far you have come, Charley Churchill. Born in Manchester, now 30 years old, raised on ships since the age of seven, sailor of the Seven Seas, bald as a badger, and with a vocabulary as rough as your head, here you are, living in paradise, with a good woman you love, among a tribe that has taken you to their bosom.

And yet, an amazing thing happens in this twelfth month of 1789. For you see, for all his sins, Churchill has been the *tyo* of one of the more powerful Chiefs of Tahiti, Chief Vay-heeadooa of the district of Tyarrabboo in the south-east of the island. Before this, the understanding of the *Bounty* men had been that swapping names with your *tyo* was no more than a simple custom. What they had not appreciated until now was that if your *tyo* is a Chief, and he dies without a son, then in some cases, *you* become the new Chief.

Churchill had not, of course, understood the intricacies of it all. Like everyone in the tribe, he had been saddened to see the Chief take suddenly ill – some Native lads had come to Matavai Bay to inform him of the old man's condition and take him to Tyarrabboo. Churchill had stood hopefully by as the priests had recited prayers and administered decoctions to the Chief.

Even the priests' secret elixir, 'the juice of herbs',[22] does little to help.

The weeping tribe gathers around the ailing old Chief, who, in a lucid moment, shakes his head for them, indicating his inevitable dissolution. Sure enough, the Chief takes one last mighty breath and then ... expires. There is a loud collective wailing from the tribe at this devastating occurrence, the men hit their heads hard enough to draw blood, and the women, screaming, lash their faces with shells and shark's teeth until their own blood flows freely. They cut off all but a single lock of their hair to be buried with the body. The widow and daughters of the dead Chief go further, cutting a square of their scalp completely bare – and bare it will remain for at least the next six moons.

Churchill grieves with all the rest for his *tyo*.

But now, the most staggering thing of all.

'The title and estate of this chief,' Coleman would recount, 'descended to Churchill according to the law of Tyo-ship; and a day being appointed for the ceremony Churchill received all the honours which are paid upon this occasion.'[23]

Eyes right, and all hail Chief Charley Churchill!

•

The wood that Morrison intends to use for his new vessel – his own miniature version of the *Bounty* – is proving problematic. It is entirely unlike good old English wood. Even when seeming as dry as *two* bones, it actually contains moisture, and the results are disastrous.

> We found that several of those [planks] which were already trimmed and fitted, had started, and became straight, so as to alter their form some inches.[24]

There is no choice but to remove the treacherous timbers, a process that keeps Morrison and McIntosh busy for weeks. Again, it will be a process of trial and error, trekking and lugging, splitting and planking, worry and warping, praying and staying, before they have located the best trees that give them the right timber that is then dried enough that it does not warp. No matter how long it takes, this whole thing must be done *perfectly*.

16 December 1789, Cape of Good Hope, Bligh on the Fly

It is something of a cruel reminder for Bligh. Nigh on two years ago, when he had last made his way to the Cape of Good Hope, he had been Commander of his own fine ship, on his way to fulfilling an important mission. This time, aboard this wretched Dutch ship, he is no more than a mere paying passenger, his ship gone, his mission failed. Still, during their brief stop, he manages a meeting with Governor van de Graaff, the same gracious administrator who had been so welcoming to the *Bounty*'s battered crew after they had been beaten back from their attempt to round the Horn. The Governor is suitably appalled by Bligh's shocking tales of mutiny and misfortune on the High Seas, and even more suitably impressed by his guest's triumph in surviving against such overwhelming odds, to be with him here today.

Bligh has not just come here to tell the story, however. What he wants is the wheels of justice to be set in motion and, with that in mind, he hands His Excellency the list of pirates, imploring that should any of them show their scurvy faces in these parts, they be arrested forthwith. And, yes, he would like copies of his account and the description of the pirates to be given to all ships passing through these parts, and be distributed far and wide from there, so that no place on earth will be safe for the brigands of the *Bounty*. No corner of any empire, British or otherwise, is to remain oblivious to the outrage of what has occurred, and Bligh desires that even: 'every port in India will be prepared to receive them, as I informed Lord Cornwallis from Batavia and orders are sent to all the Dutch Settlements'.[25]

There will be no escape.

4 January 1790, Tahiti, a blind test

He is an old man, and a venerable one, a Tahitian elder, now being led forward by some young ones to acquaint himself with the sensation of the day, the vessel being built by the Mutineers.

Carefully, the old man – who feels he has seen it all in his long time on this earth – now feels all over the vessel, asking Morrison careful questions as he goes.

Finally, he is done, and makes his esteemed pronouncement.

'Our canoes,' he says with palpable wonder, 'are foolish things compared to this one.'[26]

And yet there remains a great deal of work to do and many problems to overcome, the chief one of which is finding a substitute for iron nails. Though Coleman has been able to make some from a block of waste iron they'd taken from the *Bounty*, most of that must be used to make various ship parts like eye-bolts and rudder hinges – which is achieved, in turn, by fashioning a bellows from the handle of a frying-pan, clay, canvas and wood. And yes, there is also some iron on Tahiti now, brought by passing European ships, but it is very difficult to secure when the Natives regard it as more valuable than gold. In the end, there is only one possible solution to get the nails they need, and it is Henry Hillbrant, the Cooper, who works it out, making 'nails' out of a Tahitian native hardwood, '*amai*', timber so hard and unyielding it can actually be hammered through the softer planks.

Those planks, though, are still being secured only with enormous effort. With no large saw, just handsaws, and only a few axes and two adzes among the boat builders, fashioning good quality planks from enormous trees way up in the mountains is no small feat. Getting a felled tree down to the work yard takes a full day itself. How many times do they find exactly the tree they need, spend hours sawing and chopping through its thick trunk and start to drag it down, only for one of them to lose his grip and all of them to jump for their lives as they watch the tree tumbling . . . down the precipice.

What do they do in response?

The only thing they can do.

They go back up the next day, and start again, and will keep going – dragging the trunks down to the shed, using 'ships' ropes' made from twined vines – until they have enough planks to build the vessel, sometimes working late, using candles made from goat fat.

Truly, Bligh would be stunned to observe these men he characterised as wastrels, 'lubberly Rascals!',[27] 'scoundrels'[28] and 'villains',[29] the ones he bullied and bellowed at to work till they dropped, now displaying such a single-minded work ethic, such ingenuity, such pride in their craft, with nary a voice raised to harass them.

Matt Quintal's warning that if Carpenter Purcell had been handed his tool chest on leaving the *Bounty* then Bligh would have a new boat constructed in just a month turns out to be a touch on the optimistic side of things.

By James Morrison's reckoning, it will take about six months.

9 January 1790, South Atlantic 500 miles off the African coast, trouble with his Fly

More than ever, Bligh knows he can do better than the idiot skippering the *Vlydt*, writing in his journal . . .

> I am certain that if I had the Command of this Vessel I could run 1½ Knot per Hour more than this Man.[30]

Second week of January 1790, in the Pacific, where in the world can Pitcairn be?

It has taken seven weeks of gruelling sailing east from Tongataboo, with nary the tiniest vision of land in any direction, but at last – after relying entirely on the skills of Christian as a navigator – the *Bounty* is approaching 25 degrees south latitude, 133 degrees west longitude, which is where Captain Philip Carteret had recorded Pitcairn Island. Anxiously, Christian scans the horizon to the east, back and forth, searching for a telltale bump, a smudge of green that will tell them that they have arrived.

And of course his fellow Mutineers are doing the same, while still reserving for him the many sideways glances which pose the unspoken question: *Does Captain Christian know what he is doing?*

But there is no way around it. After checking and checking again, and two more times for good measure, it is clear that, though they are on the exact co-ordinates, there is *nothing* here. There should be . . . but there just isn't . . . and no amount of gazing will change it, just as no amount of sideways glancing, or even hard staring – or even, yes, maybe mutinous muttering – will make Christian believe that *he* has made a mistake. His palms begin to sweat.

No, clearly, the original mistake belongs to Carteret, and there is only one solution. As Christian explains to the ever more restless crew, an error of longitude is most likely. They must, therefore, stay on this latitude, and simply explore along it to the east and west, until they find their target.

And, in the end, it is the way of such things.

Just as it is an enormous thing for a man to become a murderer for the first time, but a much smaller step to do it for the second, so too are some of the Mutineers now contemplating the same heinous act with a lot less troubled emotion than they had the first time.

Does Christian actually know what he is doing?

It has been just over seven days now, exploring along the latitude of 25 degrees south, and still there is *no* sign of any land. The crew are now so restless that, for the second time in nine months, there is the whisper on the waves at midnight and into the day: should they take the ship from the Captain?

Most active in the field are McCoy, Williams and Quintal. Both they and their women, not to mention many others on board, think it is time to return to Tahiti. After all, what likelihood Bligh and the others even survived long enough to sound the alarm? They are likely drowned long ago, or mere bleached bones of starvation on some atoll, all while here the *Bounty* men are, scrambling across the Pacific, trying to get away from a British Naval expedition to punish them that is simply not coming. Christian's hand must be forced, they must go about, and . . .

And what is that?

What?

That! *There!*

It is a small smudge, on the horizon, over the bow. Possibly a low-lying cloud, it is impossible to say. But no, once they get closer, it is clear: it is a beautiful green island – with the clear dome of a volcanic peak, thrusting over a thousand feet from the sea – on exactly the latitude Captain Carteret had recorded, but with three and one quarter degrees further east in longitude, which is to say about 210 miles! In any case, it is perfect for the Mutineers – an obscure, tiny dot on the map, barely known by anyone, and even that dot has been put in the wrong place on the Royal Navy charts.

It is the 15th day of January 1790.

Christian's relief is palpable, and even the perpetually hard-faced McCoy and Quintal soften their countenances and cease their muttering. On this blustery day of howling winds and high seas, it is soon obvious to the men of the *Bounty* that there is no safe harbour at Pitcairn, no sheltered inlets, and no sandy beaches, just towering cliffs and smashing surf staunchly defending the land. It is going to be singularly difficult to land themselves and their supplies, which is something of a problem now – as they are all anxious to get on the island to have a look – but it will be a real advantage for them once they live on shore, should there ever come a time that the Royal Navy arrives. They shall hold the higher ground, and defend it easily.

For now, they are just glad to be here, to see land again, and for this windy, wavy night, Christian is content to drop anchor just off shore, in the hope they can find a way to land on the morrow.

In fact, it is not until the morning of 18 January that they happily wake to calm conditions. Christian orders the Jolly Boat to be lowered, and climbs in, together with Brown, Williams, McCoy and three of the Tahitians. (Among them is the youngest, strongest, and most aggressive of the Tahitians, Nehow. Against the possibility of trouble, he will be a good man to have on their side.)

After grounding the boat in a crunching stop on a thin, rocky, and wonderfully unwelcoming beach, the men gaze up at the steep hills and cliffs that face them. Perfect. With Christian in the lead, they are soon climbing, as stealthy as cats, up and over impossibly narrow passes.

Though they are fairly sure the island is uninhabited, still they are careful, ready as best as they can be for the sudden appearance of hostile Natives. In the first minutes they hold their muskets and cutlasses firmly, ready to leap into action, but . . .

There is nothing. The place really is uninhabited, and instead of the high-pitched battle cries they had feared, there is just the wind whipping their beards, the endless cry of the petrel birds, the rustling of the banyan trees, and the eternal, timeless sound of the waves crashing on the craggy cliffs of this, their timeless hideaway.

With the fact that the island is uninhabited confirmed, Christian and the others look out for the other key features they will need to make this work.

Fresh water is no problem, as the island abounds in springs, creeks, ponds and small waterfalls. In terms of wildlife, there prove to be so many seabirds – gull, tern, frigate-bird, albatross, booby, heron and egret, among others – that as the men approach and the birds take off, they blacken the sky.

There are also plenty of coconuts and even, yes . . . some bread-fruit trees!

When it comes to arable land, they are also blessed, for the soil looks so fertile you could plant a toothpick and grow a pine tree. The island is covered in lush growth, suggesting abundant rainfall, and is dotted with sparkling turquoise lagoons, and though, in terms of establishing fields for corn or the like, a fair amount of clearing will have to be done, it is obvious from the first that they could hardly have hoped for better.

Even the Tahitians are impressed. No, Pitcairn is not exactly like Tahiti. But it is a Pacific island such as they recognise, with steep hills, thick forest, ample tropical fruits and birds, and, as people with millennia of experience in prospering in precisely such an environment, they have no doubt that they can prosper here too.

The men left behind on the *Bounty*, thus, are delighted to note as the Jolly Boat surges back towards them that everyone in it is smiling. Clearly, the exploratory expedition has gone well, and so it proves after all scramble aboard, and burst out with their news.

On the morning of 19 January 1790, Christian directs the ship to 'anchor in a small bay on the northern side of the island'[31] and all is in readiness to begin the arduous process of unloading onto a hazardous, rocky sliver of beach.

Carefully, the *Bounty* is brought as close into the rocky shore as they dare, as they all gaze to the steep and thickly forested hills that come right down to the shore.

And so the most important task of all begins – emptying the *Bounty* of everything that will be of use on Pitcairn, which is pretty much all that is not bolted down, and half of that which *is* bolted down, including the bolts themselves. Far and away the most difficult cargo to get from ship to shore are the hogs and other animals, as the terrified brutes squeal, reel, and have to be held tight to prevent them jumping over the sides.

Though the Jolly Boat is the main work-horse for the task, ferrying back and forth, it is quickly decided that another, bigger, and more stable craft – a raft – is needed.

If only they had someone on board experienced at making rafts from pieces of wood on the *Bounty* . . . ?

Wait!

For it is, of course, Christian who supervises the construction of a sturdy raft, made out of the hatches of the ship, as, once unbolted and strapped together on long beams, they provide exactly the large flat surface needed. Once a rope is tied around a rock on shore, with the other end attached to the ship, all those on the raft have to do is pull over-hand back and forth and the raft moves easily back and forth, as the pile of supplies and the muster of hogs and fowl on the shore grows ever larger.

That evening, around the campfire by the shores of 'Bounty Bay', as it will become known, the Mutineers and their troupe are able to dine well on freshly killed seabirds, washed down by a little wine, and a lot of fresh water, before retiring to shelters provided by the *Bounty*'s sails, strung up on ropes in newly configured ways.

And, of course, the next day, and days thereafter, the process of gutting the *Bounty* continues, with everything from the ship's guns to the *Bounty*'s Bible, an old version first brought on by Bligh, brought ashore.

It takes three days, but finally it is done. Everything bar the *Bounty* itself is on the shores of Pitcairn, which begs the next obvious question.

What should they do with the ship?

Within the camp, there proves to be two camps of thought.

The first one is to destroy it. Burn it. Sink it. It matters not. For it will only take one passing ship to see it, and their hiding place will inevitably be discovered.

Most vociferous in voicing this view, and the debate goes for three intense days, is the ever glowering Quintal, who insists – with an intensity worthy of a roaring fire that simply does not wane, despite no logs being added – that the whole thing must be burnt. For what do they have to gain by keeping it? Nothing. *This* is their home now, and everyone must understand it. Others, led by Christian, and with most of the Tahitians, particularly – as they, after all, have nothing to fear from a British Naval expedition – stand aghast at the whole idea of destroying the only means they have of getting back to Tahiti. And Christian's proposal makes a lot of sense. Instead of destroying it, they could run the *Bounty* aground, allowing them to strip every plank from it and use it for building their huts. They could even preserve the hull, perhaps even drag it out of the water and secrete it. That way, should they ever need to get away from Pitcairn, they could rebuild it from the ground up!

The debate goes for days, getting ever more intense, until it is interrupted by the smell of smoke, and then the vision of flickering flames.

. . .

. . .

Jesus Christ!

The *Bounty* is on fire!

To win the argument beyond all possible doubt, Quintal has slipped onto the fore section of the *Bounty* and set it on fire. He has been joined by two other Mutineers, who have done the same on two other sections of the *Bounty*, and soon the whole ship is ablaze.

As the sun goes down and the night comes falling from the sky, the Mutineers and the Tahitians stand on the shore, their faces lit by the roaring flames – and many of those faces have tears running down their cheeks. For they know they are watching their last link to the world heading to the heavens as smoke.

Some of the men mutter that they should have 'Confined Capt. Bligh and returned to their native country',[32] but hindsight is useless now.

For what will it change?

The whites will never see England again.

The Natives will never see Tahiti or Tubuai again.

They are living on Pitcairn Island and the only thing that will change that fact is their own deaths.

Yes, Christian could try to mete out a terrible punishment upon Quintal, but by what authority?

As Captain of the *Bounty*?

The *Bounty* no longer exists, can't you see?

With the *Bounty*'s destruction, the last vestiges of his authority have gone too. One thing is for certain, they won't be needing his navigational skills anymore. No, all that is necessary, now, is to work out how to get themselves, with their supplies, from this barren shore further inland, where the arable land lies.

'The mountains were so difficult of access,' Alec Smith will record, 'and the passes so narrow, that they might be maintained by a few persons against an army.'[33]

Even better, there are caves, which will make excellent retreat positions should the need arise.

They push on.

2 February 1790, Tahiti, trouble in paradise

First there are squeals, and then come the screams.

Exactly what has happened will be a matter of some dispute. But it will be the fervent claim of John Brown – the caustic cast-off from Captain Cox's *Mercury* – that a Tahitian man has stolen his hog. Which man?

That one, over there, with his hands over the bloody spots where his ears had been, just minutes before.

Yes, in punishment for having stolen his hog, Brown, in high dudgeon, higher temper and low regard for the people who are his hosts on this island, has knocked the man down, fallen upon him, put him in a headlock, and then taken his knife to lop off the man's ears.

What proof does Brown have that this is the man in question?

None.

He just *feels* that this was the man most likely to have done it, and it was important that he be made an example of.

And this is not the only trouble in paradise at the time.

Elsewhere on the island, Matt Thompson – who is bad to the bone – has 'ill used',[34] a phrase meaning 'raped', a Native girl, which has seen the girl's brother knock Thompson down before fleeing from his raging gun.

In return, Thompson has vowed revenge.

The situation is tense, just made for an explosion.

Only four days later, when some Natives from a remote part of the island come visiting, some of them, curious to see a white man in the flesh, gather in front of Thompson's hut, which sees him yell at them: 'Away!'[35]

Ignorant both of his previous threat, and the fact that he fears them to be relatives of the raped girl, they make no move, not even when he raises his musket and points it at them.

What do they know of the Brown Bess musket, or any musket for that matter?

Well, given that he has been limping around with a loaded musket for days now, they are about to find out.

Perhaps drunk, perhaps paranoid, very likely both – and certainly uncaring of human life – Thompson pulls the trigger.

There is a flash, an explosion, a puff of acrid smoke. Thompson's ammunition sprays out of the muzzle in several directions. One Native man, holding his young child, hits the ground with a thud. Both father and infant are covered in blood. Both are dead. To their side a gurgling half-scream comes from a woman who falls to her knees, clutching at her shattered jaw. Another man falls to his stomach, writhing, a piece of musket-ball lodged in his back. The rest of the Natives look to the ground, uncomprehending. They see the blood, the pain, the death. Without a pause, they scatter, running to get away from this devil.

The island seethes.

No, there is no outright explosion now, but it is coming, and they all know it. (Heywood is one who does his best to prevent it, giving a shirt to the widow of the slain man, which is, at least, well received.)

It seems clear to some of the white men that they need to have a recognised leader – to get themselves organised for the attack to come – and it is with that in mind that Charley Churchill offers his services, making a forceful speech to the gathered throng. He is, after all, a Chief in the district of Tyarrabboo.

But, as Morrison will recount, 'as we all looked upon the affair as murder, we declined either making him our chief or taking part in any of the business'.[36]

Very well then. Deciding discretion to be the better part of valour, and absence the better part still, Churchill, Thompson and Brown take their canoes and decamp to Tyarrabboo, where they will be hard to challenge thanks to Churchill's status as a Chief . . .

And yet, that status is not long in being challenged by . . . none other than Thompson himself who refuses – *refuses*, do you hear? – to bow to Churchill the Chief, and is so angry that Churchill should ask it of him, he decamps and moves to a different part of Tyarrabboo.

'I'll shoot him if any difference or distinction is made between us!'[37] he declares to all who care to listen.

•

It happens in an instant, right by a Tahiti lagoon.

On this morning, Heywood is out walking and sketching when, seemingly from out of nowhere, an enormous Tahitian man – as strong as a bull, and twice as angry – grabs him by the hair and throws him to the ground. By the time young Heywood can look up, his assailant – who he recognises as the brother of the man recently murdered by Thompson – is holding a huge rock above his head and is clearly about to bring it down on the Englishman's skull, when . . .

When another Native shouts out: *'Fa auera'a! Stop it!' This is the man who presented the widow with a shirt, this is not the white man who did the killing.*

The rock is held . . . at least momentarily . . . as . . . the avenger . . . considers this new information.

Oh. Well, instead of me killing you, perhaps you'd like to come to my place for dinner tonight? The shaken Heywood declines the polite invitation, carefully, oh so carefully, and returns to his own hut knock-kneed and trembling. No sooner has he walked through the door than he is engulfed by his friends, including Morrison, who embrace him tightly. They had been told with some satisfaction by other Natives that he was already dead.

13 March 1790, off the south coast of England, home is the sailor . . .

Four bells, and all's well. Mostly.

From the previous dusk, and on through the night, they have been sailing blind through the shroud of fog, nudging east by north along the southern coast of England, sounding as they go, to be sure they do not run aground.

42 vademen! 42 fathoms!

35 vademen! 35 fathoms!

38 vademen! 38 fathoms!

And there! For just a minute or so, the rising sun holds hands with the breeze of dawn and rushes the night's mist away for just long enough to give Bligh the briefest glimpse of the land of his dreams, his homeland, some eight leagues distant to their north. It is England. His country. After two years and three months away, Betsy, I am home.

And now it is gone again, as the mist regroups to take back its aquatic empire so briefly lost.

For many hours more, the *Vlydt* keeps sailing through the white haze, hugging the coast, until the Dutch Captain decides it is too dangerous to bring the ship close into land, and so anchors just off the Isle of Wight. Bligh takes destiny in his own hands. After a quick couple of words to the Captain – good riddance – he barks orders to Samuel and Smith to pack his things. Just after noon, with no ceremony and barely a backward glance, Captain Bligh, with his two ever faithful Loyalists by his side, steps on to an English vessel which has come out looking for custom, and orders that he be taken directly to Portsmouth.

So it is that at midnight on 13 March 1790 – nearly 12 months since losing his ship the *Bounty* to the mutinous rabble – Captain William Bligh sets foot on English soil once more, a feat he had always felt he would be able to accomplish without quite realising that he would feel the kind of vindictive joy he does now. Against all odds, he has done it! Though a victim of mutiny most foul, he has overcome each adversity and has been able to return to England once more, with the most amazing story that any sailor has ever had to tell – and a story that, hopefully, will soon see the hounds of the Royal Navy let loose in pursuit of Christian and his Mutineers, wherever they are.

Of course in this, the dead of night, there is not a soul around to utter a single word of welcome, pump his hand in congratulation, bow to his skill and sagacity . . . just a handful of sober sailors going about their duties, mixed with packs of drunken sailors stumbling from the ale houses and whorehouses back to their ships.

Taking the first secure lodgings he can find, Bligh passes an impatient night before, at 10 am on the morrow, as the bells of the Portsmouth churches ring out on this Sabbath to summon the faithful, Bligh – the real miracle of the day, for he is risen from the nearly dead to become an angel of vengeance – is on his way once more. Seated at the back of a post-chaise headed for London at a pace that even our lady of the riding habit could never have approached, he watches this once

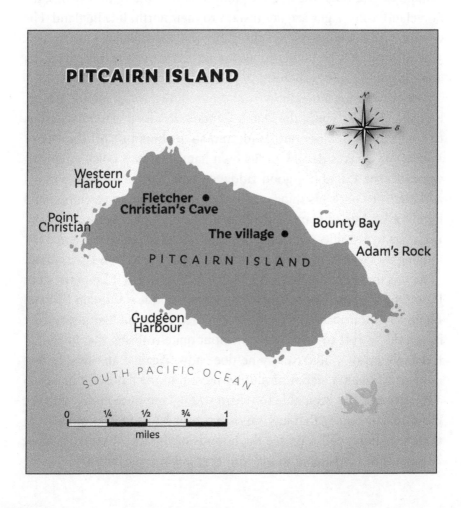

familiar but now strange world slip by him, inevitably comparing it to the extraordinary world he has come from. Here now are so many things he once took for granted, this very post-chaise for example, which he now sees as the very height of sophistication, of modernity.

It is no small thing for a Captain of the Royal Navy to return to England without his ship, and his first step when he arrives in London is to present himself to the Admiralty, and formally hand over every document he possesses concerning the journey.

March 1790, Pitcairn, still they sleep 'neath the *Bounty*'s sails . . .
Some 300 feet above their landing place, Christian and his most loyal Mutineers select a spot for a village entirely invisible from any ships that might happen to pass. From there, each Mutineer marks out for himself and his wife a flat patch of ground to call his own and then erects the tents made from the salvaged sails of the *Bounty*. Laboriously now, and with much squealing, bleating and angry clucking, all of the *Bounty*'s hogs, goats and chickens brought ashore are herded up the precipitous pass to be corralled into makeshift yards. So too are the cats. But no dogs. As Christian explains to the shocked Mutineers, their barking might endanger them all, as it risks forewarning whatever intruders might come to the island just where the Mutineers can be found – so they must be slaughtered.

No!

(They'll put 19 men in a tiny vessel in the middle of the Pacific Ocean, but this, this seems really cruel.)

But Fletcher Christian insists.

Gravely, the Mutineers ordered to carry out the brutal task take up knives and walk towards the dogs, ashen-faced, shoulders slumped. The rest of the crew turn away, but can't help but hear as the dog's playful barks suddenly become alarmed whimpers, harried and harassed yelps, and finally a quick haunted howl before falling silent.

Christ.

Next, they set about clearing land and building themselves farms with the thousand or so acres of cultivable land on higher ground divided nine ways, allocated, and soon planted with the sweet potato and seed yams they had brought with them. While the initial place where they had settled with their tents remains something of a village, where they all may gather, each Mutineer now takes to working his own plot on the farming land, each of the previously unattached men taking a Tahitian woman as his wife. This leaves three Tahitian women for the six Polynesian men to share, with Talaloo taking Toofaiti for his own, the Tubuains, Ohoo and Tetaheite, sharing Prudence (Tinafornia), and Mareva shared between Timoa, Menalee and Nehow. Nehow, the young aggressive warrior, is none too happy about it, and glowers, but is ignored by the white men. The Native men have no option but to share, just as they also must share the rudimentary tenements on the lower slopes, as all the best building materials are reserved for the white men. Under the circumstances, there is soon some tension afoot – disputes over women, and the white men taking the best of everything – but, for the moment at least, it is manageable.

Christian, for one, is far more focused on his own plot and family; Isabella is now pregnant with their first child, yet she works on, tilling the soil, preparing the meals, thatching the roof of their new family hut.

Mid-March 1790, Tyarrabboo, Tahiti, sitting ducks

At Tyarrabboo, Chief Churchill is just taking aim, about to shoot at some ducks sitting on a pond, when they are disturbed by a group of Natives, and fly skyward. And so . . .

So Chief Churchill, in a fit of pique, trains his gun on the Natives instead. Boom! A musket-ball hits one man in the back, and a lad in the heel. Alas, the lad bleeds to death, whereupon, alarmed by the extraordinary power of the man with the stick that shoots fire and kills, together with the fact that Churchill is a Chief, the local Natives make it clear that they are . . . on his side.

Good. Churchill has a clear first instruction to his new subjects: Steal Mr Thompson's gun as he sleeps. (Aware of Thompson's threats, Chief Charley knows he must take action. Thompson is a thief, a murderer, the roughest of rogues, and the natural enemy of authority. Charley himself had been nearly all of those things, but now that he is *himself* the authority, Thompson must be disarmed and dealt with.)

A page from Bligh's notebook listing the mutineers and their physical descriptions. Fletcher Christian's name heads the list. The page is stained with seawater; Bligh was writing while in the Launch on the open sea. National Library of Australia

The coconut shell used by Bligh to eat his ration. It is carved with the words: W Bligh/ April 1789 and inscribed (in ink) 'The cup I eat my miserable allowance out'.
Royal Museums Greenwich, National Maritime Museum

Robert Cleveley's 1790 watercolour depicting Bligh's hasty retreat from Tofoa Island. Norton can be seen kneeling on the beach, about to be killed. National Library of Australia, Rex Nan Kivell Collection, NK2646

'Coupang, in the Island of Timor' by George Tobin. Mitchell Library, SLNSW, PXA 563

Bligh being received in Coupang, Timor. Charles Benazech, 1791. National Library of Australia

Betsy Bligh, portrait by
John Webber. Private collection

John Fryer in later life, a
portrait by Gurtano Calleja.
Mitchell Library, SLNSW

Portrait of Captain Peter Heywood by John Simpson, in 1822 when Heywood was 50.
Royal Museums Greenwich

Peter Heywood in 1793, five years after setting sail on the *Bounty*. commons.wikimedia.org

Engraving of 'Interior of Pitcairn Island', drawn by Frederick Beechey. The picture shows Alec Smith standing in his sailor suit, surrounded by native women and children. The mouth of Fletcher Christian's cave is visible in the hill behind the settlement. National Library of Australia

Typical construction of jollyboats. Royal Museums Greenwich

Engraving based on a sketch by Richard Beechey (brother of Frederick) of Alec Smith/John Adams at age 58. Royal Museums Greenwich

Sketch of Thursday October Christian wearing his signature hat ornamented with black feathers, c. 1810. Alamy

Fletcher Christian's house on Pitcairn Island. Alamy

Fletcher Christian's cave on Pitcairn Island. The cave's inaccessible position, high up on a steep rocky cliff-face, would have given Christian a sense of security – and a 180-degree view of the ocean to watch for any ships that might appear.
Copyright ©Andrew Randall Christian, Pitcairn Island Tourism

Yes, *Arii*, Chief.

His men slip off in a canoe under cover of night, bound for the village where Thompson is staying.

•

How very strange.

Thompson awakes the next morning to find his gun is missing!

Thompson is uneasy – this whole thing must be part of a revenge plot for the father and son he had killed less than a month ago. His life is under threat and he has no gun! With that in mind, Thompson quickly, quietly, sets off in a canoe, paddling along the shores of Tahiti – this once oh so hospitable island, now suddenly turned so dangerous – to where the other Mutineers are living, in the hope of borrowing a musket. On the way, he decides to stop at Chief Churchill's village, to catch up and patch up with Charley, and the two are indeed able to come to an accord of sorts. The real problem, they decide, is that cur John Brown fomenting trouble between them, and now that they have worked that out, maybe they can even resume living together on Thompson's return. Oh and the missing gun, Mr Churchill, do you know anything of it?

Nothing at all, Churchill tells him, it must have been one of the mischievous Natives.

Churchill farewells Thompson cheerily, promising to search high and low for his missing musket.

Early April 1790, Tahiti, eyes right, and all hail the new King!
A few weeks after Thompson's return to Tyarrabboo his gun is restored to him, apparently thanks to Chief Churchill's intervention with the thieving Natives. But what Thomas Burkett would like to know is, if that is really what happened, why is Thompson not more grateful?

When Burkett, who happens to be passing, dines with Chief Churchill and Thompson that evening, he is aware that something is amiss.

Over crispy-skinned roast pig, Thompson mentions, ominously, 'I have found out the thief',[38] without going on to say anything more.

Burkett senses a growing tension between the two men before him, which is uncomfortable, though seemingly not dangerous, until . . .

Until the next morning, Chief Churchill commands – yes, commands – Thompson to fetch him some water.

What?

'Do you know who you are speaking to?'[39] Thompson demands angrily.

'To a *seaman*,' Churchill replies with a glare, 'but perhaps you forget that I am *Master at Arms*.'

'I remember,' Thompson answers, with equal menace. 'I remember what you *were* when Bligh was our commander; but as to what you *are*, I think you are now no better than myself, although the people here have *dubbed* you a chief. To be a servant to a villain is intolerable, for we are all villains alike; perhaps, if the truth were known, you are a greater villain than some among us . . .'[40]

Now Churchill tries to interrupt Thompson with a sneer, but the latter will not be so interrupted, and continues, finishing with his own sneer, a veneer of thin insult, covering what is clearly violent intent.

'Damn you,' Thompson roars, 'though you are a Chief you shall be your own servant for me!'[41]

So noisy is the dispute that some of Chief Churchill's Natives are drawn to it, fearful that their Chief might be in danger. Moving quickly, they encircle the two quarrelling white men, and make very clear to Thompson that they will do what it takes to defend Chief Churchill, and he must leave. Swearing, making threats, Thompson limps off – humiliated and infuriated, but also impatient. Impatient for 'Chief' Churchill's protectors to leave. And as soon as they have, Thompson races back to his own hut, eyes blazing, heart raging, planning his revenge when his eyes fall on the very thing that he needs, and he has just as quickly departed once more.

Moments later, Thompson's loping footsteps come back into earshot – a sound of ill portent in these troubled times. He limps straight up to Churchill, scorning him as 'one of the greatest villains',[42] he has ever had the misfortune to meet. A fraud to boot, what, with all his carry-on with his 'tribe'.

'Oh, what a great chief!' Thompson mocks.

'Hold your tongue, scoundrel, or, by God, I'll kick you.'

'Scoundrel!'[43] echoes Thompson, mockingly, looking Churchill in the eye with a cold-blooded smirk, as he lifts his musket, aims it at Churchill's tattooed breast, and pulls the trigger.

There is a flash, a puff, and a musket-ball bursts forth, hitting Churchill in the chest, and blowing out a part of his back on the other side.

Just a hundred yards away on the beach, Burkett is about to get back into his canoe to head back to Matavai Bay when he hears the shot.

Running back to Churchill's hut, fearing the worst, he finds, sure enough, Thompson standing in the doorway calmly loading his musket, the bloodied body of Churchill lying behind him.

For Thompson has not only found the thief, but the thief has found a musket-ball in his chest.

'Are you angry, Burkett?' Thompson asks, his voice cold.

The unarmed Burkett is very careful in giving the correct answer: 'No.'[44]

There is a pause.

'I hope you don't mean to take advantage of me?'[45] Burkett follows up.

'No, since you are not angry,' replies Thompson. Besides, he adds, with a nod to the bloodied corpse before him, 'I have done him.'[46]

Indeed he has.

Approaching closer, Burkett sees that Churchill is dead, shot through the heart. 'I now thought,' Burkett tells Morrison a short time later, 'it high time to be off.'[47]

Indeed. Can it really be this late, with me still having so much to do before dark?

I must be away.

Still, before leaving, Thompson prevails upon Burkett to help bury Churchill, at which point the murderer is so grateful he raises no objection to Burkett watching him as he goes through Churchill's possessions. They include books, most particularly . . . *the ones that contain the maps.*

Burkett cannot resist.

Carefully, he asks Thompson if he may have those books.

No.

Thompson knows exactly what they contain, and won't hear of it.

Burkett takes leave in his canoe, every stroke that takes him further away singularly powerful, and only when he is out of musket range does he slow at all.

Back in his hut, Thompson looks up to see six of the former loyal royal subjects of Chief Churchill approaching, with a fellow by the name of Patirre.

Trouble?

No.

For no sooner have they approached within easy earshot – Thompson's musket trained upon them the whole while – than the smiling Patirre offers a salute and addresses Thompson as '*Vay-heeadooa*',[48] once the name of the old Chief.

And sure enough . . .

'You are the new chief,'[49] they tell him.

Now *that* is a little more like it.

Gratified, *Vay-heeadooa* Thompson lowers his musket, at which point, Patirre offers his first tribute – a mighty blow to the head that would fell an ox, let alone a seaman, and Thompson has no sooner fallen to the ground than two of the other Natives grab a nearby plank and fall upon him, pinning him, helpless on the ground.

He looks up to see Patirre above him, holding a large stone.

Surely, he's not going to . . . ?

He's not . . .

He is.

The stone comes down like a sledgehammer and splits Thompson's skull with a sickening crunch and a spurt of blood . . .

The old Chief, Churchill, is dead, long live *Vay-heeadooa*, the new Chief, Thompson, for about three minutes.

Still, wanting to be sure of these things, Patirre and his men cut off Thompson's head, before burying the body alongside Churchill.

Only a short time later, James Morrison listens, stunned, as Patirre tells him every grisly detail. As to why Patirre and his men had not brought the murderer back to the other white men at Matavai so he could be punished in their English manner, the Native is clear: '*Te atea I te fare*, the distance was too great,' Patirre explains, 'and our anger would be gone before we could get there; and we should have let him escape when we were cooled and our anger gone, so that he would not have been punished at all, and the blood of the chief would have been on our heads.'[50]

Morrison understands, and agrees with the action.

'You will not be hurt by me for what you have done,'[51] he assures him. For, truly?

'I looked on him,' he will recount, 'as an instrument in the Hand of Providence to punish such crimes.'[52]

And that same Hand of Providence, which has seen them rid of the problematic Thompson, also now delivers to them the precious charts they had wanted, found secure in his hut.

April 1790, London, taking the town by storm

That figure strutting proudly along the streets of London, creating a stir when, time and again, he is recognised by acquaintances who now hail him as a dear friend, pumping his hand and patting him vigorously on the back, is none other than – unaccustomed as he is – William Bligh!

Every newspaper in the land, of course, has delighted in the story of courageous Captain Bligh, commander of the *Bounty* taking on the evil Mutineers, and triumphing against all odds! He is the hero of the hour. 'The distress [Bligh] has undergone entitle him to every reward,' announces *The Scots Magazine*. 'In navigating his little skiff through so dangerous a sea, his seamanship appears as matchless, as the undertaking seems beyond the verge of probability.'[53]

Fletcher Christian, on the other hand, is universally reviled despite being, 'a man of respectable family and connections, and considered a good seaman'.[54]

And there is widespread agreement with Captain Bligh's assessment of the Mutineers' motives: women. 'With regard to the conduct of the conspirators,' goes the story, 'the most probable conjecture is, that, being principally young men, they were so greatly fascinated by the Circean blandishments of the [Tahitian] women, they took this desperate method of returning to scenes of voluptuousness unknown, perhaps, in any other country'.[55]

Nowhere does Bligh create such a stir as in the mahogany hallways of the Admiralty, where the said acquaintances are thick on the ground and all want to congratulate him and hear his story personally. William Bligh is now nothing less than the lion of London, the toast of the Tories and Whigs alike, the hero of the *Bounty*, haven't you *heard*? He is the courageous, brilliant man who, against all odds, made good his journey in a 23-foot open boat from the middle of the South Seas all the way back to the capital of the British Empire. When Sir Joseph Banks squires him and – heavens to Betsy – his wife to Buckingham Palace, it is King George III who hangs on his every word, as this hero of the Royal Navy describes the terrible travails he has been through on His Majesty's Service, only to triumph in the end. Bligh even gives His Majesty a copy of his Log.

Yes, William is the talk of the town, in circles high and low. Novelist Fanny Burney happens to be walking on the streets of London with her beloved brother Lieutenant James Burney, who had sailed on Cook's final voyage, and is stunned to see just how high her brother's reputation has soared, just for the fact that he had sailed with Bligh, known Bligh, talked to Bligh. Coming across a Member of Parliament, William Windham, the parliamentarian suddenly pours praise on the startled James, for this fact alone. Yes, James says uncertainly, he does know Bligh, but . . .

'But what officers you are!' beams Windham effusively. '*You men of Captain Cook*; you rise upon us in every trial! This Captain Bligh – what feats, what wonders he has performed! What difficulties got through! What dangers defied! And with such cool, manly skill!'[56]

For you see, so high is Bligh, even those who know him are heroes! Just to have sailed with the great man is an enormous commendation of your character! In the eyes of the masses, Lieutenant Bligh far outranks in public esteem any Admiral, and every Member of Parliament. Those to the manor born, those to the rough-house raised, *alike,* are united in their acclamation of his heroic feats.

In May, two months after Bligh's return to England, the Royal Theatre in London begins a new play, *The Calamities of Captain Bligh*. Ralph Wewitzer, a veteran of the London stage, plays Bligh and Mrs Alicia Daniel sings 'Loose ev'ry sail', with the whole production including, 'an exact Representation of Bligh's capture' having been 'rehearsed under the immediate instruction of a Person who was on board the Bounty'.[57] (Presumably, John Samuel or John Smith are cashing in.)

Yes, the toast of the town, Bligh is the guest of choice at any number of soirees, constantly on call at the Admiralty as he tells his story on request to intrigued officers of the Royal Navy, and still must make time for his 'Dear Betsy' and his *five* girls – with enormous joy he has found that Betsy has had *twins*, Frances and Jane, now nearly two years old – as well as read, and reply to, the constant correspondence coming his way from any number of sources.

On this day he receives a letter from none other than young Peter Heywood's mother, a fine woman, who is writing to Captain Bligh in the desperate hope that he can give her some news of her beloved boy?

Bligh is glad she asked, and does not hesitate with his reply.

London, 2 April, 1790

Madam,

I received your letter this day, and feel for you very much, being perfectly sensible of the extreme distress you must suffer from the conduct of your son Peter. His baseness is beyond all description, but I hope you will endeavour to prevent the loss of him, heavy as the misfortune is, from afflicting you too severely. I imagine he is, with the rest of the mutineers, returned to Tahiti.

I am, Madam, your obedient servant,
W.M. Bligh[58]

This is not an aberration. It is the attitude that Bligh takes towards all those who have either openly turned against him, or, at the very least, have not been implacably loyal to him.

Bligh also writes a letter to Heywood's uncle, Colonel Holwell, informing him of Peter's 'ingratitude to me of the blackest dye ... I very much regret that so much baseness formed the character of a young man I had a real regard for'.[59]

Even then Bligh is only warming up, ending his blistering note with the words: 'it will give me much pleasure to hear his friends *can bear the loss of him without much concern*'.[60]

And who is this now come to see him?

Ah, yes, here is Captain Taubman, the one who had first steered Fletcher Christian in Bligh's direction, come to ask England's hero why young Fletcher had done what he had done.

Bligh has a curt one-word answer for him: 'Insanity.'[61]

And even then, he is being kind. For when Bligh is shortly afterwards visited by Christian's brother, Edward, he does not ascribe the cur's actions to mental illness, but to moral turpitude.

Your brother, sir, is a cad, a cur, a scoundrel, and a traitor to his country.

Seduced by the carnal temptations of that infernal island, he had betrayed his honour, his Captain and his country.

Edward listens, stunned, refusing to believe it.

The man Bligh describes is not his brother, and there must be another side to the story, he never doubts it for a moment. The question is, how best for him to find out what actually happened, and then get it before the public?

CHAPTER FIFTEEN

OPENING *PANDORA'S* BOX

It is said that by the express command of His Majesty two new sloops of war are to be instantly fitted to go in pursuit of the pirates who have taken possession of the Bounty. *An experienced officer will be appointed to superintend the little command, and the sloops will steer a direct course to Tahiti where, it is conjectured, the mutinous crew have established their rendezvous.*[1]

The London Chronicle, 1 April 1791

Young hearts which languished for some sunny isle
Where summer years and summer women smile;
Men without a country, who, too long estranged,
Had found no native home or found it changed,
And, half uncivilized, preferred the cave
Of some soft savage to the uncertain wave.[2]

Lord Byron, 'The Island'

May 1790, Matavai Bay, waterproofing Noah's Ark

In Tahiti, another ship is gradually taking shape.

For six months now, Morrison, Norman, Hillbrant, McIntosh and Coleman have been working from dawn to dusk on their answer to Noah's Ark, a vessel made all but exclusively from local materials, not the least of which is the sweat off their brow, and every ounce of ingenuity and elbow grease they have in them. This includes getting their hands on 'pitch' to caulk the joints and make the vessel waterproof. After much experimentation, they find the solution and it comes, of all places, wouldn't you know it, from . . . the bread-fruit tree. For, observing the

Natives, Morrison notes how they take a peg of ironwood, 'and with stone drive it through the bark [of the bread-fruit tree] in several places'.[3] A gooey gum runs out, which can be rolled into small balls that, when boiled down, can be turned into a South Pacific pitch, black as the pitch from pine back home. After much trial and error, they determine that when it is mixed with just the right amount of rope fibres, it makes a perfect mixture to caulk their planks. Equally importantly, when they mix the whole lot with pig fat, it forms a kind of waterproof tar which they can thickly slap on to the planks of their vessel, and it doesn't wash away! The only problem is, getting the pitch is so laborious, 'a man can hardly get a pound of it by himself in two days'.[4]

Is there an easier way?

Yes. The ingenious Morrison throws the first of many feasts for the Natives, and rewards all who bring him a ball of gum with delicious chunks of succulent pork – the exchange rate being 50 pounds of pitch gets you 200 pounds of pork – from which they are careful to collect the fat, for their tar.

Everything is starting to come together.

•

On 1 July 1790, the London papers announce that a most fascinating book is newly published and available, which soon sees good folk from all over the British Isles, young and old, rich and poor, rush to buy the account of the Mutiny, written by Captain Bligh himself, which he has comprehensively titled: *A Narrative of the Mutiny, on Board His Majesty's Ship* Bounty; *and the Subsequent Voyage of Part of the Crew, in the Ship's Boat, From Tofoa, one of the Friendly Islands, To Timor, a Dutch Settlement in the East Indies.*

The book is an instant bestseller and foments ever more public outrage towards the mutinous reprobates who have done Bligh down, wherever they are.

•

Six months after the *Bounty*'s arrival at Pitcairn, much of the rhythm of the settlers' lives is well established, with, yet, a clear difference between the ways the white men and black men live.

Each Mutineer has now taken for himself one portion of the habit-able land to build his home, look after his woman, and raise his crops. They are growing bread-fruit, of course, watermelon, bananas, sweet potato and yams. Pens have been built for the hogs, and runs for the chickens. Yes, there is no little labour involved in running it all, but most of the whites have taken the view that if the Natives want to enjoy the fruits of the land – the fruit and vegetables that they are growing – then they must help by working the land . . . under the white man's orders.

'Obliged to lend their assistance to the others in order to procure a subsistence,' Smith records, 'they thus, from being [our] friends, in the course of time became [our] slaves.'⁵

Fletcher Christian, at least, is one exception and is quick to share his food with the Tahitians regardless. He and Isabella have been living very happily in the hut they have built, and she is now heavily pregnant with the first of what they hope will be many children.

Another who does not take the Tahitians as slaves is Ned Young. As a man who is of mixed blood himself – from the West Indies – he refuses to think of himself as better than any man, and makes do with the odd bit of voluntary labour only. Smith also does not.

But Quintal, McCoy, Mills and Brown, particularly, have made it clear that the Native men have been brought with them to work for them, and that is what they must do.

Yes, there are growing tensions between them all, but for the moment their squabbles are manageable, and something of a democratic spirit prevails, at least among the white men.

Another thing that is growing is what effectively amounts to their own language. With no fewer than 28 people, drawn from eight parts of Great Britain, one part of the West Indies, America, Germany, Canada, and two Pacific islands, there are many influences going into the language pot that bubbles furiously and creates, 'Pitkern'. Ultimately it proves to have a simple English for its spine, with Tahitian and Tubuaian words and grammar thrown together with various English dialects, including that of the Scottish Isle of Lewis, the Geordie of Liverpool, and the Manx mouth of Christian all contributing.

For example, the Geordie word for victuals, as in food, is *whittles* and that soon becomes standard Pitkern. *Shep* is ship, *ailen* is island, *morla* is tomorrow and *I kawa* is I don't know. *Ye* is You, and *gwen* is going.

Thus 'How are you?' is 'Whata way ye?' and 'Are you going to cook supper?' is 'You gwen whihi up suppa?'

'Would you like some food?' 'Ye like-a sum whittles?'

'Good!' 'Cooshoo!'

Yes, Pitcairn, which had been a lost island, is now a world unto itself, a kind of Eden in the sea, divided into farming lots, with a common area in the centre of the island, a little 'village' as they come to think of it, with many of the new families building huts nearby one another for safety, if not entirely for neighbourly cheer. Radiating out from the village, up to a mile away for some, the men mark out and plough plots for corn and other staples, just as it is done in the United Kingdom.

6 July, 1790, Tahiti, a *Resolution* kept

Finally their vessel is ready to test for leaks.

Yes, the great day has come. The day to launch their 'ship', which Morrison has christened the *Resolution* after Cook's ship ... with a nod to their own character in getting such a ship built, against all odds.

And now the moment of truth ... sink or swim. No fewer than 300 Natives gather to help push the little ship from the clearing to the beach, nearly a mile away. Now, everyone get a grip on either the ship itself, or the pulling ropes that have been attached.

'A song being given, they all joined in the chorus, and she soon began to move.'[6]

Once they finally get the vessel into the water, James Morrison quickly jumps on board and holds his breath, even as he stares intently at all the seams. No plumes of water! No dribbles. Not even moist!

She is waterproof, and will stay afloat!

As to making sails, it takes a great deal of trial and error, not to mention tribulations, but finally, by 'using the bark of the Poorow for twine, quilting the Matts, & seaming them at every foot distance to strengthen them,'[7] they are able to solve that problem, too.

Now, they just need to make them in sufficient quantity.

A Thursday in October, 1790, Pitcairn Island, if we mutinied on a Tuesday, today must be . . .

It is the Tahitian way.

One of Isabella's friends, as her birth attendant, sits with her knees spread wide, so that Isabella can sit between her friend's legs – and hook her own legs even wider under and outside the attendant's. With everything she has in her, Isabella groans and pushes, and is assisted by the attendant who wraps her arms around under Isabella's and pushes down on the top of her belly with hands spread wide. With one last mighty push, here comes the baby now, and another Tahitian woman is there as the whole baby emerges with a rushing flood, a beautiful baby boy – the first child of British blood to be born on Pitcairn Island.

What shall we call him?

Today is Thursday. Let's call him that.

And so 'Thursday October Christian' – blessed to be born of a Tahitian Princess and a Gentleman of Manx – takes his place in this world, the eldest child of a fugitive family, dug in on an island in the furthest flung reaches of the Pacific Ocean.

Friday 22 October 1790, Spithead, England, court martial of William Bligh et al. for the loss of the *Bounty*

Dressed in his full Navy uniform, all blue and shining, Captain William Bligh strides into the Great Cabin of the guardship HMS *Royal William*, the naval headquarters at Spithead and, with some ceremony, removes his sword. With his right hand holding the hilt, and his left hand the blade, he places the now horizontal sword on the table in front of the officers of the court – three Vice Admirals, six Rear Admirals and three Captains – so that it points towards neither them nor himself.

He is, effectively, relinquishing his command, and it will be for this court martial to decide whether he will take it up once more. Stepping back, he turns, nods to the row of a dozen Loyalists, the round dozen still standing and back in England, from the 19 men who got into the Launch after the Mutiny, 18 months ago.

Bligh sits on the wooden chair placed before the panel, a dozen stern faces above a solid wall of navy blue with gold lace trimmings. He returns their gaze, most particularly that of the presiding officer, Admiral Samuel Barrington, under whom he served during the relief of Gibraltar in 1782.

Let the proceedings being.

The official charge of the court is read out: 'To inquire into the cause and circumstances of the seizure of His Majesty's armed vessel the *Bounty* commanded by Lieutenant William Bligh ... and to try the said Lieutenant Bligh and such of the officers and ship's company as are returned to England for their conduct on that occasion.'[8]

Very well then. Captain Bligh has little fear. He is a national hero. He has done nothing wrong, and surely, the members of the court martial will themselves be disposed to his view. Among other things, with a revolution in France now gaining momentum, this is a time for those in authority to support each other and severely round on those seen to question it.

And so let the formal proceedings for this court martial begin.

'Have you, Lieutenant Bligh,' Admiral Samuel Barrington asks him, 'any objection or complaint to make against any of your Officers and Ship's Company now present?'

This is the moment Fryer has been waiting for, dreading, for many months.

'I have,' Lieutenant Bligh replies, 'no other than charges I have made against the Carpenter.'

Fryer breathes again. Their unspoken agreement has held.

And now the Admiral turns to the surviving Loyalists.

'Have you any objection or complaint to make against Lieutenant Bligh?'

'None.'[9]

Very well then, all Loyalists bar Fryer must leave the court martial. Blinking a little nervously, the Master takes the stand.

'Did you know anything of the Mutiny before it broke out?'

'Not anything.'

'After the Mutiny did break out, did Captain Bligh and the rest of you use your best endeavours to recover her?'

'Everything in our power.'[10]

Now Bligh stands to ask the questions, in a manner Fryer has never heard from him before: authoritative, but gentle; firm but respectful, all of it rather in the manner of a fine Captain of the Royal Navy.

'Did you see me taken out of my cabin?'[11]

Fryer replies in kind, a dutiful Master, who couldn't be happier than to assist the fine Captain in his queries.

'I saw Lt. Bligh going up at the ladder with his hands tied behind him, and Fletcher Christian the Mate following him, holding the cord he was tied with. He had a cutlass in his hand.'[12]

Very clear then – Bligh is the victim, with the perfidious Christian the key culprit.

And so it proceeds with Bligh continuing to guide Fryer as he labours long over just how innocent the Captain was, and just how guilty were Christian and the Mutineers.

Thank you, Mr Fryer, that will be all.

He is followed into the stand by John Hallett as the first of the Loyalists, each one affirming Captain Bligh's blamelessness, as both the court and Bligh put to them the obvious questions.

Finally, the court is cleared so the esteemed officers of the court may deliberate, and now Bligh is called forth.

As he well knows, when he enters the room, if the hilt of his sword, on the table before Admiral Barrington, is pointed towards him it means that it is about to be handed back to him, as an innocent man. If pointed the other way, he is court-martialled and cashiered out of the Royal Navy.

Yes, today has gone well, but still he is nervous as his gaze falls to the sword.

The hilt!

He is acquitted.

As are all – at least for the moment – bar one of the surviving Loyalists.

Which leaves us with you, William Purcell.

After Purcell is put through his own questioning, he is found guilty of six charges of insubordination . . . but given no more than an official reprimand, the lightest possible sentence.

Typically, Bligh claims credit, writing to Banks with news of the court's 'exceeding great leniency . . .' noting that he had withheld, 'a great part of my evidence . . . as it affected [Purcell's] life'.[13]

Unspoken is that Purcell also has the power to affect Bligh's life, by giving evidence against him – but nary a damning word escapes his lips. It is almost as if, as with Fryer, a tacit agreement has been reached, to help each other as the legal process takes its course.

Either way, Bligh is elated at the way things have turned out. His euphoria grows still when, just before Christmas 1790, he at last receives his due, and is promoted to the rank of Captain.

Huzzah!

7 November 1790, Spithead, *Pandora* pursues the pirates

It has taken some doing, but that ship you can see there, making its way downwind at Spithead? An imposing vessel, a fast frigate – pushing towards three times bigger than the *Bounty* at 524 tons, and with 24 cannon, not just four – it is on its way to Tahiti. The distinguished-looking maritime martinet who commands her, Captain Edward Edwards, is not only a hard man – he had stared down his own mutiny in HMS *Narcissus* a decade earlier and seen six men hanged – but he encourages hardness around him, deliberately picking the harshest bastards he can find to fill his ship. On this occasion, however, he has made an exception, carrying a passenger with his 133-strong crew who is not hard at all.

But Captain Edwards is sure he will have his uses . . .

13 February 1791, Tahiti, a sacred day

Today is the day.

After much preparation, on a new ceremonial ground, *Morai*, prepared especially for the occasion, today King Tu, just nine years old, is to be invested with the Royal Sash, the '*Marro Ora*',[14] an important step on his road to manhood, something of a coronation. The exquisite sash is three feet long, made of fine netting and covered in red feathers of the lorikeet. The ends are divided into six tassels, themselves bursting with red, black and yellow feathers, 'for each of which they have a name of some Spirit or Guardian Angel, that watches over the Young Chief'.[15] It is to be worn by the new King for just a single day, the island's equivalent of a crown and throne in one.

Sure enough, on this hot morning all the *Bounty* men are dressed in what remains of their old uniforms, as spruced up the best they can, to carefully observe the ceremony.

Surrounded by his High Priests, dressed in their own colourful finery, King Tu, a slender lad, is placed on the *Morai*. The High Priest makes a long prayer, ties the brilliant sash around King Tu's waist, places a wicker hat on his head and finishes by hailing him 'King of Tahiti'.[16]

'King of Tahiti!'

'King of Tahiti!'

'King of Tahiti!'

And now, three human sacrifices, already dead, are carried forward and placed on the ground, their heads towards the King.

A priest, dressed in coloured robes replete with his own red and yellow feathers, makes a long speech over each of the bodies and lays a young plantain tree next to them. Now, the King above them opens his mouth as the priest, wielding a piece of sharpened bamboo, steps forward. One by one, he places the sharp end of the bamboo on the lower part of the eye socket and, with one shove and an effortless flick, scoops out the eyeball. The severed human eyeballs are all then placed on a plantain leaf, which another priest slowly brings up to King Tu's mouth, so he can receive the souls of the sacrifice. He does not eat the eyeball, but inhales deeply. With that, the bodies are taken away to be buried with great honour.

Still it is not over, however, as also gathered are different Chiefs from different parts of the island, who now offer their own human sacrifices, 'some bringing one Victim & Some two according to the bigness or extent of their districts . . .'.[17]

Within an hour, some 30 eyeballs line the altar in front of King Tu, staring back at the *Bounty* men, whose own eyes are now rather glazed over. By the time the grand feast is ready to take place, most of the men of the *Bounty* are feeling more nauseated than hungry.

•

What on *earth* is that?

On this morning, Christian and Isabella wake to the sound of Alec Smith's hogs rampaging through their garden, causing enormous damage. As calmly as he can, once he has chased the hogs back whence they came, Fletcher seeks out Alec to ask him to at least fix his fence.

Now the fact that Alec is, by nature, a difficult and cantankerous man is relevant to his response.

Go to hell! I will not fix it. If you want it fixed, you fix it.

Christian is free with his opinion: *Very well, if any of your hogs trespass on my land then I will shoot them.*

'Then I will shoot you!'[18] roars Smith.

Such a dispute cannot be easily contained.

A threat to murder from a murderer is not a thing to be taken lightly and the other Mutineers have no hesitation in falling upon Smith and quickly binding him tightly with rope. There is, of course, nothing remotely resembling a prison on Pitcairn. As for justice, Smith's trial amounts to a shouted argument between fearful men. What to do with him? Surely the answer is to do what they did with Bligh. That is, set him adrift on the ocean.

For when the likes of Smith says he will shoot you, they know he means it. He is a man who has killed men for less – including a simple Native who had been accepting Christian's jacket.

Will no-one speak up for Alec, to save his life?

Yes, and it is none other than Christian who does so.

We must free him, and forgive him. We must stay together, must work together, if we are to survive and prosper.

For the moment, things settle down.

Smith promises to mend his fences, and his ways, and is let go.

But they are watching him, hear?

10 March 1791, London, if at first you don't succeed, *Bry, Bry, Bry* again

At last, at last!

Captain Bligh, still the lion of London, receives the orders he has been waiting for. He is to return to Tahiti, in command of a second bread-fruit voyage. He has the support of the King and Sir Joseph Banks, and now he has orders from the Admiralty. It will be for him to find, this time, two ships appropriate to the task, and to set off as soon as possible, this time heading straight around the Cape of Good Hope.

It does not take Captain Bligh long to form up his crew. William Peckover, who loves Tahiti like no man, applies to make what would be his sixth voyage to the island, but – likely because his testimony at the court martial had been so positive for the likes of Peter Heywood – Bligh is merciless. Not only does he refuse Peckover, but takes steps to further punish him.

'Should Peckover my late Gunner ever trouble you to render him further services,' he writes to Sir Joseph Banks on 17 July 1791, 'I shall esteem it a favour if you will tell him I informed you he was a vicious and worthless fellow.'[19]

No, when Captain Bligh has completed his roster, only two men from the original mission are both available, *and* selected, John Smith and Lawrence Lebogue. Oh, and this time, Bligh is going to be sure to take no fewer than 20 marines with him.

23 March 1791, Matavai Bay, mutinous till proven loyal

'Land ho! Fine on the starboard bow!'

After a four and a half month journey from England, around Cape Horn in an easier season than when Bligh had attempted it – they have made the journey in less than half the time it took the *Bounty* – the *Pandora* is reaching its destination. On the bridge, his spy-glass to his eye, Captain Edwards scans the isles ahead for any sign of Natives, or Mutineers.

Meantime, on the shore, Joseph Coleman – one of the three Loyalists identified by Bligh – is so beside himself with joy to see the ship that no sooner has it dropped anchor in Matavai Bay than he is leaving his canoe by the side of the ship and clambering up the rope ladder lowered for him.

Joy, oh joy, oh joy!

In short order he is presented to Edwards, babbling what has happened, and where the Mutineers might be found. Edwards' eyes are on him the whole time, betraying nothing but a certain piercing coldness, though he seems pleased to have so much information confirming so many of the Mutineers are nearby. Still, his gratitude is not completely on show, right now, as he suddenly gives sharp orders that Coleman be placed in irons, and held below!

Coleman is mortified, stunned, scarcely believing it can be happening.

But has not Captain Bligh marked my name as innocent?

Which is as may be, Mr Coleman.

I, Captain Edwards, am not your judge. I am your jailer. I have my orders, and those orders are 'to bring, in confinement, to England . . . Fletcher Christian and his associates . . . in order that they may be brought to condign punishment'.[20]

And so you will be kept in confinement, until such time as we can talk to other white men on this island and work out exactly what has gone on and . . .

And now there are more footsteps upstairs.

New arrivals?

Yes. Two men have just clambered over the side. Both are nearly naked, and so brown and so covered in tattoos that for a few moments they are mistaken for Tahitians.

Lieutenant John Larkin gazes at them, stupefied.

'I am Midshipman Peter Heywood of the *Bounty*,' says the first arrival. 'And I am George Stewart,' says the second.

They speak English! Lieutenant Larkin continues to simply stare back at them, and remains thus for a good 20 seconds.

'I suppose you know my story?' Heywood tries again, breaking the strained silence. Another stare.

'I am of the *Bounty*!' Heywood expostulates.

Stay here. As the other sailors of *Pandora* watch them carefully, Larkin goes below, and informs Edwards that two more men of the *Bounty* have arrived.

'Bring them to my cabin, Mr Larkin,'[21] orders the Captain.

Within minutes, he, too, is gazing suspiciously at these two extraordinary-looking men, each clutching a journal, with Heywood's being the Tahitian–English dictionary he has so laboriously compiled.

'Well, gentlemen, what news?'[22] asks Edwards.

'I suppose you have heard of the affair of the *Bounty*?'[23] Heywood begins, tentatively, unsure what the reaction will be.

As a matter of fact, Edwards has. But what he wants to hear now, and he insists upon it, is their version of just what happened. Heywood cannot oblige quickly enough. While Stewart listens morosely, Heywood bursts forth with his side of the story, how he had *never* wanted to sail with Fletcher Christian at all, don't you understand, Captain Edwards? It was just that, he desired *survival*, to see England once more, to see his beloved family, his mother and sister, dear Nessy and . . .

And Captain Edwards has had enough. It is soon time to bring forth his guest, the man he has brought all the way from England, specifically to test out whatever captured Mutineers might tell him, against the truth.

'Mr Hayward,' Captain Edwards says, 'come out of my Stateroom if you please.'[24]

The door is opened and Lieutenant Thomas Hayward enters to confront the young man he had once been close friends with. It is the first time they have seen each other in nearly two years, but under the circumstances there is not an ounce of hail-fellow-well-met in the air.

Rather, as Edwards notes carefully, Hayward shoots both his former shipmates a look so withering it could curl hair – a clear indication, it would seem, that he gives short shrift to their entire accounts. And why would he not?

Both of these men had put Hayward and all the Loyalists with Bligh on a tiny Launch in the middle of the ocean, knowing that it was very likely they were being left to their deaths. Hayward has come back to Tahiti specifically to see justice done, and that, clearly, includes seeing these two, among others, swing from the end of a long rope.

But Peter Heywood will not have it.

Hayward was there! He knows we are innocent! But now he says nothing. Worse, 'He (like all worldlings when raised a little in life) received us very coolly and pretended ignorance of our affairs.'[25]

'How did you come to stay on the *Bounty*, Stewart?' asks Lieutenant Hayward sarcastically, no doubt picturing Stewart doing his Tahitian dance of joy in front of the bound Captain Bligh.

In response, Mr Stewart, choosing his words carefully, as though he is already waiting for his lawyer, says, 'When called upon hereafter, I shall answer all particulars.'[26] Peter Heywood has no such caution, he is *innocent*! He was *loyal* to Captain Bligh! He was a *prisoner*, Hayward *knows* this, he was there!

Heywood's furious protestations, however, prompt Hayward to tell Peter in turn exactly what he could have done, as the argument escalates . . . until suddenly cut short by Edwards, who has no interest in any such argument. His own mind is made up.

'Sentinel,' he calls to his Bosun's Mate. 'Take these men in to custody. Lt. Hayward you will desist speaking to these men.'[27]

Heywood: 'I shall be able to vindicate my conduct!'

'Place these men in irons,' counters the Captain. 'They are piratical villains.'[28]

Four burly sailors fall upon Heywood and Stewart and lead them below to join Coleman. Back in their hut, Stewart's wife, Peggy, and their baby daughter – still on the teat – wait patiently for him to return.

Meantime, Edwards orders Lieutenants Corner and Hayward to take two of the ship's boats, with the ever friendly and pragmatic Hetee-Hetee as their guide, and go out after the Mutineers. By happenstance, four of the Mutineers who are living at Matavai Bay are away at this time, on a boat built by one James Morrison, visiting seven other Mutineers whose huts are scattered around the shores of Tahiti.

'Get hold of them before they learn of our arrival,'[29] Captain Edwards instructs his officers, who are soon sailing back out of the bay.

•

On the other side of the island, at Papara, where Morrison and his crew are now visiting Burkett, Sumner, Brown and Muspratt, they are just about to sit to have breakfast with one of the Chiefs when Morrison looks up to see a Native hurrying towards him. He has been sent by Hetee-Hetee, with a warning.

'A ship has anchored at Matavai since you left! Those you left there have all gone on board.'[30]

The Mutineers look at each other, ashen-faced, stunned silent.

'The Ship's boats are manned and armed and are on their way after you all. Hetee-Hetee is acting as their pilot but has sent me ahead to give you notice, so you might know how to act.'[31]

Their consternation is immediate, as breakfast is forgotten and most of the men make immediate plans to flee. This is the moment they have dreaded for so long, and it is now upon them.

While John Brown and Michael Byrn, the Blind Fiddler, decide to stay where they are – on the reckoning they have nothing to fear – the other white men are quickly racing to the beach to get into their canoes and paddle furiously to the *Resolution*.

Quickly lads! Haul in the anchor, and get the mainsail up!

Their timing is poor. For even as they get underway, their pursuers are just arriving, and spot them!

Yes, there they are, on the starboard side, three miles off!

At one glance, Lieutenant Hayward is stupefied. The Natives had told him that Morrison had built a *Pahee*, 'a boat'. But what he now sees in the distance, under full sail, is nothing less than a full-blown *schooner* – it must be at least 16 tons! – under full sail, and moving swiftly away from them, perhaps a league out from their current position by the shore. Immediately, they give chase.

Of course, it should be no contest.

Two vessels of the Royal Navy, made by the finest craftsmen of the realm, manned by His Majesty's fine sailors, up against a vessel effectively carved out of the jungle, with mats for sails, and now sailed by scurvy Mutineers?

Hayward sets out with great confidence. His men should haul them in, easily. But he cannot help but notice one thing.

They're not.

The vessel of the Mutineers is slipping away from them, hour by hour by hour, becoming ever smaller on the horizon.

Worse, when the sun begins to fall, they have no choice but to turn back, and do not make it back to the *Pandora* until well after dark, where a miffed Edwards awaits. How *could* they have been outrun by a pirate craft?

And yet, though humiliated, Lieutenant Hayward is not without hope. For in his absence a strange white man has come aboard with blind Byrn, an Englishman by the name of John Brown. He is not a Mutineer, but a free man, and even has the papers to prove it.

Ah yes, Edwards does indeed remember being told by Admiralty to look out for a fellow left at Tahiti by Captain Cox of the *Mercury*. And now Brown can't get his excuses for spending time with these criminals out fast enough.

'I have been under the necessity for my own safety to associate with these pirates,'[32] he declares. 'I took the opportunity to leave them when they were about to embark in the schooner and put to sea. They have very little water and provisions on board, or vessels to hold them in, and, of course, cannot keep at sea long.'[33]

Edwards is as impressed with the possibilities of Brown's help as he is pleased with the information, and immediately has him entered on the ship's books and payroll, as 'guide, soldier and seaman'.[34]

Brown says he knows exactly where they will try to hide on the island . . .

•

Among Morrison and his men, the exultation is overwhelming. They have done it! They have shaken off their pursuers, in the boat they built! And it handles like a dream. All that work, all that ingenuity. And it had all come together in that one superb vessel that had been able to outstrip a vessel constructed in a British dockyard.

But what now?

Upon consideration, they decide to sail back to Papara, where they will split up. While some of the men will go to hide in the mountains, Morrison decides his best option is to go voluntarily to the British ship. After all, sooner or later they would be found in the mountains, and, personally, what has he got to hide? He had never joined the Mutiny, and is confident that will be accepted.

Turning his vessel, however, it is to find strong winds, and it is two full days before they are able to regain the south-west point of the island to again drop anchor at Papara.

Within minutes they are surrounded by concerned Native friends in canoes, led by Chief Tommaree, bearing bad news.

'Mr Hayward, of the *Bounty*, was an officer on one of the boats that you saw,'[35] he declares.

Hayward? On one of the boats we saw? Good God! It is their worst nightmare come to life. If Hayward is alive, and here with the Royal Navy, it means that Bligh and his men did indeed make it back to civilisation and have surely told the Admiralty the whole story. There is no way around it, they are all very likely dead men, unless they can escape. Obviously, their best hope is to get up into the mountains at all speed, where they can either successfully hide or, if the worst comes to the worst, mount a defence.

Burkett, Sumner, Muspratt, Hillbrant, McIntosh and Millward hop into canoes and are taken to shore, whereupon their trek into the high green hills that tower over them immediately begins, while Norman and Monkey Ellison opt to stay with Morrison and the *Resolution*.

Only a few hours later, up north, at Matavai, Edwards is given the word by one of his Native informants: 'The pirates returned with the schooner to Papara. They landed and retired to the mountains to endeavor to conceal and defend themselves.'[36]

Immediately, Edwards orders Lieutenant Robert Corner to go back towards Papara with 26 men in the Launch. The next morning, he sends Hayward, in the company of 20 heavily armed sailors, out to help Corner bring the Mutineers in.

•

Something moving in the dawn! It proves to be three white men coming out of the greenery and making their way down to the beach, where they present themselves to Lieutenant Corner of the *Pandora*, who they find asleep in a canoe. When he comes to with a start, they introduce themselves.

'I am James Morrison of the *Bounty*, sir.'

'I am Charles Norman of the *Bounty*, sir.'

'I am Thomas Ellison of the *Bounty*, sir.'[37]

On the instant, Lieutenant Corner places them in the Launch under guard, while he and 18 of his men set out to find the rest of the missing Mutineers, using Brown as their eager guide.

Many hours later, in the middle of the hot afternoon, Morrison still remains in the Launch, burning up, when he looks up to see new uniformed arrivals. It proves to be none other than Thomas Hayward, arriving in a boat of his own, and surrounded by 20 armed Marines.

With nary a word of greeting, and the only sign that he recognises the prisoners being his look of pure disgust, Hayward simply barks: 'Tie their hands!'[38]

Morrison returns the glare, indignant. Morrison wasn't even involved in the Mutiny, and Hayward knows that! Surely Hayward remembers the last words they spoke to each other, an agreement to attack the Mutineers with clubs?

'There are tools enough!'[39] Morrison had said, only to find Hayward had not the stomach for the act and had slipped away to the Launch instead. But now things have changed. Now Hayward has no further need of courage, for he has the two things that truly count – authority, and an extraordinary capacity to totally forget a past that surely embarrasses him.

'Where are the others?' Hayward snarls to his prisoners.

'We don't know,' they reply.

'Take the men and proceed to the ship,'[40] Lieutenant Hayward snaps to a Midshipman.

With that, Morrison, raging at Hayward's terse treatment of him, is finally getting his wish – to go to the ship.

And yet, of course, no sooner do they arrive on deck than they are placed in heavy manacles and marched below, more Mutineers presumptively locked up on the *Pandora*, while six are still at large on the island.

•

Yes, at large, but living small. High in the Tahitian mountains, the six Mutineers huddle together in the night, knowing what is coming but trying to sleep anyway – unsuccessfully. So far, there is no word of any white men arriving in the mountains to find them, but it can only be a matter of time. Surely.

30 March 1791, Tahiti, the trail goes cold

It is no easy thing to be visitors to a strange land, searching for men who do not want to be found, confronted by locals who have no desire to help. At Papara, the inquiries of Hayward and Corner get them nowhere, and they can find absolutely no trace of the Mutineers. There is nothing for it but to return to the ship, where they find the Carpenter and his assistants sawing, nailing, carrying, constructing – building something that is a cross between a poop and a coop, essentially a small wooden cage on the aft-deck to house the Mutineers on the journey home.

Now all they need to do is to get *all* the Mutineers to fill it.

But it will not be easy. Yes, bits and pieces of intelligence flow to them from various Natives, but they are wildly divergent and no common theme emerges. There remains a cluster of Mutineers at large, likely somewhere in the mountains around Papara. But where, *precisely*, is a mystery.

7 April 1791, Tahiti, closing in on the last Mutineers left standing

'Neath the tropical moon, in the still of the night, suddenly all is . . . not still. Yes, it has been a difficult trip up from the beach at Papara in the darkness for Hayward and his men, but at least they now have a chance to redeem the humiliation of the previous attempts.

Shhhhh!

Just up ahead, beyond the dying embers of the fire, they can see a hut – just where John Brown had said it would be – and, clearly, from the sounds, there are a *lot* of people sleeping inside.

But are these the Mutineers, or are they Natives? Hayward has no way of knowing. Ah, but Brown has. Very carefully, he crawls forward and, with no little delicacy, reaches his hand through a gap and carefully feels around for a naked foot.

They're European feet! These are the Mutineers, right here!

Yes, extraordinary as it might seem, Brown is able to distinguish them from Natives by feeling their toes – 'People unaccustomed to wear shoes are easily discovered from the spread of their toes,'[41] he tells a bemused Hayward in a whisper.

These toes are tight together. They are European.

Very well then, Mr Brown.

Hayward makes his plans, and gives his orders. They are to surround the camp, quietly. They are to wait till dawn. He will fire a shot at first light, and they are to storm forward, surrounding the hut, with bayonets drawn, ready to kill at the first sign of resistance.

•

And . . . *now.*

The sound of the musket shot shatters the dawn, and on the instant, the 20 sailors storm forward, surrounding the Mutineers' hut. It all happens so quickly – from a deep sleep to staring right into the jaws of eternity as you look up into the barrel of a musket pointed right at your face, held by a man – Hayward! – who is clearly just bursting to fire it. He seems so . . . angry.

Well, come to think of it, they had left him in a tub in the middle of the ocean with few supplies and a maniacal commander, laughing and cheering as they sailed away, but still . . .

The captured Mutineers are soon on their way to the *Pandora*, at the point of many guns.

•

May the Good Lord help them all. By 9 April, this construction of the Devil himself, this cage on the quarter-deck, is completed and all of the 14 men who have been kept in irons below are brought up, blinking in the sunlight, scarce believing their eyes at what awaits them.

It is a wooden box reinforced with *lots* of iron; a specially constructed prison, 11 feet by 18 feet and so low that even Monkey, who is just a little over five feet, is peering over it. In the whole wretched thing there are two small windows of nine inches square, with iron grates, to let in a very little air.

From the point of view of Edwards, he is doing no more than following his orders, from the Lords of the Admiralty, to the letter: You are to keep the Mutineers as closely confined as may preclude all possibility of them escaping . . . that they may be brought home to undergo the Punishment due to their Demerits.[42]

Young Peter Heywood, raised in opulence and wide open spaces in that isle of plenty which is the Isle of Man, and a wide-ranging man thereafter, can barely fathom it. It is an outrage that he is in irons in the first place, but now this? *This* box? To hold all of them? All the way back to England?

Yes. One by one, with both their legs and arms trailing their heavy chains, they are shuffled forward, to struggle up a small ladder before being dropped down into the box via a hatch that measures no more than 20 by 20 inches. As the last man drops down, all arms and legs and chains onto this human soup of other arms and legs and chains and groaning, cursing men, the hatch comes down hard above them, and the heavy bolt is thrust into its iron slot. Edwards' description of it as a 'round house . . . airy and healthy'[43] does not quite capture it, but it certainly captures them.

Clutching tightly to his chest the cherished few possessions he has been able to take with him – his book of prayers, his notebooks and his pencils – young Peter Heywood looks around the box with stupefied horror. In these confines, they will have to live, breathe, sleep, eat, drink, urinate and defecate with none for company bar themselves and the tens of thousands of lice that have come with the filthy hammocks that have been thrown in after them. His whole body shudders, his eyes grow misty from welling tears.

To make sure no-one can take pity on them, the Captain has given strict orders that only the Master-at-Arms may speak to the prisoners, and even then it can only be on the subject of provisions – a conversation that surely won't take long, as they are to be given little. Within a day, as the heat rises, a foetid stench comes from the box, as the sweat pours from their persons and flows in streams to the scuppers where, before long, maggots begin to hatch.

Between the heat, the vermin and the lice, the men soon abandon their clothes, to lie naked.

With the last ounce of humour remaining them, they crown their new prison cell '*Pandora*'s box'.

•

And so they come. As the Mutineers have now been living in Tahiti for the better part of the last two and a half years, they have formed many deep bonds with the Natives, and none more so than with the women, some of whom are mothers to their children.

For those women and children, it is a special agony to be on the shore gazing at the wooden prison on the *Pandora* and knowing that their loved ones are inside. And so, as Morrison would recount, their women 'came frequently under the stern (bringing their children, of which there were six born, four girls and two boys; several of the women were big with child). They cut their heads till the blood discoloured the water about them.'[44]

Likely none is more traumatised than Stewart's wife, Peggy.

There is something about Peggy and her baby girl. So extraordinarily upset is she, so imploring of Edwards to allow them to see Stewart for just a few minutes, that even one with so hard a heart as he, wavers . . .

. . .

All right then!

In what would be the sole kind gesture to be marked, Edwards grants a brief meeting.

Stewart is allowed out of the cage briefly, as he, she, and their baby howl in a manner that moves all.

It is all so overwhelming, that after Peggy and her baby have been forcibly extricated from him, and sent back in her canoe, Stewart himself, unable to bear any more heart-rending scenes, begs that she not be admitted on board again.

8 May 1791, Tahiti, paradise lost

A little under two months after arriving in Tahiti, the *Pandora* is ready to leave, its full cargo of naked, swollen, vermin-ridden Mutineers *still* caged in their putrid wooden prison on the aft-deck. On the shore watching them go are many weeping women.

Edwards' task now is to comb the South Pacific looking for Christian and the rest of the Mutineers. Where to begin the search?

After consideration, Edwards charts a course west-south-west for the island of Wytootacke, an island that Fletcher had talked extensively of to the Tahitian Chiefs. Right behind the *Pandora* comes the *Resolution*, officially commissioned by Edwards as his ship's tender – the first Tahiti-built schooner of His Majesty's mighty fleet, an enormous honour for the caged James Morrison – and placed under care of an eight-man crew under 19-year-old Master's Mate William Oliver, in his first command.

And behind both of them?

'Every canoe almost in the island was hovering . . . and they began to mourn.'[45]

Captain Edwards does not care. The *Pandora* carries on. Inside the living hell of the box on the back deck, the prisoners do their best to remain calm. Alas, once out on the open ocean, buffeted by endless waves, they are no sooner squashed up against each other on one wall than they are flung across the box when the next wave hits, with faeces and urine swishing about their naked chained bodies – and of course it is all the worse when they hit storms, as not only is the motion of the ocean so much more violent, but their cage offers no shelter from the weather as they are lashed by wind and rain.

At least in the genuinely calm, dry moments, Peter Heywood takes solace by writing poems and sketching his memories of the outside world – a horse and carriage, a church, a lady with a parasol. Most of his companions, however, just lie there, their eyes firmly shut against the depravity that surrounds them, hoping, usually in vain, to sleep.

In such a situation, there can be few upsides, but at least one is that day after day, they can hear the growing frustration of Captain Edwards and the crew that they can find no sign of Christian and the other Mutineers.

Their relief might be less out of loyalty to them, than fear that Edwards would simply throw more prisoners into *Pandora*'s box, but relief it is.

Edwards first tries Wytootacke, for no result. Pushing west to Palmerston Island things become even worse, as not only is there no sign of Christian and the others, but in shockingly stormy conditions they lose their Cutter and five sailors, never to be seen or heard from again. A remarkably similar thing happens at the Navigators Islands in late June, when they lose contact with the *Resolution* in a storm. No amount of searching reveals the smallest sign of it or its nine crew. They light fires, they fire guns. Still there is nothing. They head to Annamooka in the Friendly Islands, to see if the *Resolution* has turned up at their previously designated rendezvous point, but find that the islands are not so friendly after all. They are not welcome, and one stray sailor, an Irishman, is fallen upon, beaten and stripped naked, to be left with just one shoe ... which he uses to accommodate his dignity, the best he can.

'We soon discovered the great Irishman,' the ship's Surgeon would recount, 'with his shoe full in one hand, and a bayonet in the other, naked and foaming mad with revenge on the natives . . .'[46]

What on earth possesses the Natives to behave so? Lieutenant Hayward knows the answer, as does James Morrison and every man-jack who sailed on the *Bounty*. It is because on Captain Bligh's last visit, he had kidnapped the Chiefs, made them peel pumpkins, and the pumpkin-peelers are not happy about it!

Meanwhile, the *Pandora*'s searches for Fletcher Christian and the Mutineers continue to be fruitless, but not without incident. One memorable day, they have no sooner anchored near the island of Tutuilia than a stunning naked woman comes on board to greet them.

'She was,' the Surgeon would recount, 'six feet high, of exquisite beauty, and exact symmetry, being naked, and unconscious of her being so, added a lustre to her charms; for, in the words of the poet, "She needed not the foreign ornaments of dress; careless of beauty, she was beauty's self." Many mouths were watering for her; but Capt. Edwards, with great humanity and prudence, had given previous orders, that no woman should be permitted to go below.'[47]

And yet, and yet, while orders are orders, and both Captain Cook and Captain Bligh had set the standard when it came to the duty of the Captain to be removed from knowing local women in the biblical sense – through very un-biblical behaviours – Captain Edwards decides that in exceptional circumstances an exception can indeed be made.

The naked Venus is, thus, personally escorted below deck by Captain Edwards and, as the *Pandora*'s surgeon dryly notes in his journal: 'the lady was obliged to be contented with viewing the great cabin, where she was shewn the wonders of the Lord'.[48]

Indeed.

Beyond such excitements, reluctantly, Edwards must resign himself to the fact that Fletcher Christian and his brigands have vanished. Not only that, the nine men and the *Resolution* are very likely lost. He turns the *Pandora* to the west. It is time to head home with such Mutineers as he has, still securely in their cage on the aft-deck.

28 August 1791, Great Barrier of Reefs, beware the breakers

That ship trying to find a way through the extensive barrier of reefs off the coast of New Holland, just after dawn on this 28th day of August, 1791?

It is, of course, the *Pandora* on its journey back to ye olde England.

And they need to get to the calm side of the reef.

But it is not easy. Yes, there are a few gaps, but none large enough to sail the ship through, and when darkness comes, Edwards decides to drop anchor for the night . . . even as a sudden easterly gale whips up.

To the west, Edwards can hear the pounding on the reef, which a strong current is driving *Pandora* towards, aided by the gale. The roar is getting louder! The waves are rising up and crashing onto the solid reef that sits hidden just below the water's surface, barrelling over it like a ball of dirty thunder.

The wind and currents are too strong. The anchor drags on the sandy bottom. They must make sail, and get further away, but . . .

It is too late.

In an instant the wind has captured the sails of the *Pandora* and all who sail upon her, just as the current has gripped the hull, and is hurling her west, towards the jaws of the maw that awaits.

Sure enough . . .

In a split instant there is a mighty explosion of sound, of breaking wood, of screaming men, even as the reef roars out a victory – got another one!

In that moment, everyone on the deck of the *Pandora* is hurtled forward, just as those below are hurled from their bunks and hammocks and the men in the *Pandora*'s box are flung against their prison wall. The wind and waves have smashed the whole ship onto the reef with full force – shattering the wood at the bow on the port side, as the coral continues to tear a hole that is the equivalent of a bayonet slash, long and deep. It all happens so fast that even as the ship groans in its agony on this early evening of 28 August, the *Pandora*'s crew can barely comprehend what is happening.

Everything is conspiring – the wind, the current, the waves, Edward Edwards' incompetence – to keep driving the ship onto the cruel rocks as water pours through the gaping hole and the stricken ship begins to list.

The sea-sprayed air is filled with screams and curses from the sailors and officers, mixed with shouted pleas from those in *Pandora*'s box to be let out, to have a chance to live, all as the wind continues to roar through the now impotently flapping sails, and wave after wave of the Pacific Ocean keep hammering the ship more and more onto the cruel coral barbs. Waves now crash up and over the deck, as the *Pandora* sinks still lower, and, encouraged, the ocean roars still louder at its fallen prey, rushing up, around and over that prey, seeking to devour it whole.

Aghast, Edwards barks orders for the ship's guns to be hurled over the side in the hope that it will sufficiently lighten her and allow her to get off the reef, but it is to no avail. One gun even falls on a sailor in the process, killing him. All is carnage and catastrophe.

'The ship was forced on to the reef with violent and repeated shocks,' Morrison will chronicle, 'and we expected every surge that the mast would go by the board.'[49]

While terror takes hold, nowhere is it greater than in the prison cage, as the whole ship shakes back and forth from stem to stern, a harpooned whale trying to shake itself free with a rhythm and urgency that are soon also its death throes. In the cage, the prisoners are smashed against each other, as the ship sinks ever lower and waves start to cascade over the sides.

'Seeing the ship in this situation,' Morrison would recount of their experience in *Pandora*'s box, 'we judged she would not hold together for long. As we were in danger at every stroke of killing each other with our irons, we broke them so we might be ready to assist ourselves . . . We informed the officers of what we had done.'[50]

Lieutenant Corner is called aft and the prisoners call up to him: 'We shall attempt nothing further . . . we only want a chance for our lives.'

'I promise you shall have a chance,' the Lieutenant calls back through the prison's walls, 'don't fear!' as he goes off to speak with the Captain.[51]

Given that the ship really is rolling, lolling, like a dying whale, with no less than nine feet of water in the hold, and more water gushing in, it is no easy task to remain calm. But at least Corner informs Edwards of the situation, including the fact that the prisoners have broken their chains. And at least Edwards, in turn, desperate, allows three of the prisoners – Coleman, Norman and McIntosh, the very men that Bligh has insisted are innocent, the men Edwards has known all along to be innocent – out of their prison to help with the pumps.

Alas, Edwards shows no such mercy to the rest of the prisoners and orders that they are to be 'handcuffed and leg ironed again, with all the irons that can be mustered'.[52]

Hearing the order, young Peter Heywood stiffens, as the implication hit him hard. Barring a miracle, it is nothing less than a death sentence, and he knows it. Others begin to panic. The caged Mutineers beg for mercy, but Edwards barely blinks. No, his primary concern is that they don't escape, and despite the fact that the water continues to gush in, and there is now no less than 11 feet of water in the hold, still he places an armed guard upon them.

Oh, but it gets worse, still.

For now, the prisoners can see a commotion on deck, together with many calls being made, the tramp of feet, the creak of winches, the sounds of wood hitting wood, surely that of the Launch being lowered over the side!

And now they can hear a sailor say, 'I'll be damned if they shall go without us.'[53]

The awful truth dawns around dawn itself. They are being abandoned. The officers are going over the side to the ship's boats, while in *Pandora*'s box on the aft-deck, they are *still manacled* and locked in their prison! Again there is uproar as the panicked prisoners start to struggle once more with their chains, attracting the attention of none other than the Master-at-Arms, John Grimwood.

'Fire upon the rascals!' he orders the armed guard.

'For God's sake, don't fire!' Morrison roars back. 'There is none here moving!'[54]

All of the prisoners stop their struggling at Morrison's command, now uncertain whether death will come by bullet or by water.

For the moment, it is neither, as the Master-at-Arms moves on, and the armed guard gazes uncertainly after him. For they, too, are keenly aware that while they are stuck, their comrades are making good their escape on the Launch!

All over the *Pandora* now, all is in chaos. The sailors are attempting to salvage whatever they can in the way of supplies, and get them on to the other boats. All of this, even as the ship itself starts breaking up, including a topmast, which suddenly falls and kills yet another sailor.

His shattered body is pushed aside, while the officers gather on deck, preparing to leave.

And still the *Bounty* men are chained!

Is there to be no mercy?

Of a sort.

Finally, Edwards gives the orders for another three prisoners to be unshackled. The Armourer's Mate, Joseph Hodges, removes the bolt, opens the scuttle, jumps down and takes the irons off Muspratt, the Blind Fiddler and Skinner.

And yet, Skinner is *so* desperate to be topside on this hell-hole of a ship that he is hauled up by a sailor with his handcuffs still on.

There are now eight desperate men left in *Pandora*'s box. Hodges, surely an angel come to earth in singularly rough disguise, keeps working frantically, first taking off Stewart's handcuffs, then Morrison's.

With everything he has in him, Morrison now *begs* Grimwood, the Master-at-Arms, who literally holds the keys to their freedom in his hands, to help them out.

'Never fear, my boys,' Grimwood replies with extraordinary callousness from the relative safety of the deck, 'We'll all go to hell together!'[55]

No sooner have the words left his lips than the *Pandora* lists violently. Up goes the cry: '*There she goes!*'[56]

It is sinking *now*.

And yet, in an extraordinary turn of fate, even as the Master-at-Arms is swept overboard to drown, the keys that had been in his hands *fall through the side-hatch of* Pandora's *box!*

With blurring speed, waist-deep in the water, the prisoners start to frantically unshackle themselves.

All is chaos on the *Pandora* now. Without a backward look, Captain Edward Edwards jumps into the water and starts swimming towards a Cutter still floating in the distance. It is clearly every man for himself, but the former Mutineers of the *Bounty* are still trapped in their prison as the entire ship sinks.

Hearing their desperate screams of 'Help! For God's sake!', the Bosun's Mate, William Moulter, shows extraordinary bravery. Swimming to *Pandora*'s box he yells, 'I will set you free or go to the bottom with you!'[57]

Scrambling to the top of the box like a crazed gorilla, grunting with the effort and none too particular if he grazes knees or the like, Moulter quickly pulls back the scuttle so the men can clamber out.

With the whole ship now entirely awash in crashing waves, the prisoners swim their way to the surface. The third last prisoner to leave *Pandora*'s box is none other than Peter Heywood, who has no sooner arrived on the flooded deck than he jams his most treasured *Book of Common Prayer* – the only possession he has salvaged besides his ragged clothes, leaving his sketches and poems behind – between his teeth, grabs a chunk of wood from the shattered topmast and jumps into the raging sea, making his way towards a small sandy set of rocks he can see in the calmer waters on the other side of the reef.

Not far behind him is Morrison, floating on a short flat 'paddle' the way they had seen the Tahitians make their way through the surf, his hands paddling on either side to propel himself.

Others are not so lucky.

George Stewart, he who had first uttered to Fletcher Christian the words 'the people are ripe for anything', and thereafter the First Officer of the Mutineers under Captain Christian, has just dived into the roaring ocean when . . .

When the gangway of the sinking, rolling, *Pandora* comes crashing down into the water . . . smashing into his head. On the instant, George Stewart goes limp, all of the fight gone out of him, as he starts to sink and . . . the water starts flooding into his lungs and the darkness closes in. Slowly, lifelessly, his body drifts down.

In Tahiti, a loving young woman called Peggy is now a widow, and her beautiful baby girl, Charlotte Stewart, forevermore without a father. Yes, they will continue to scan the ocean for years more, hoping for the return of the loving, laughing young man, but he will never come.

•

The survivors hear the haunting sounds from behind, the strangled, fading 'cries of the men drowning in the water'[58] as the last of the *Pandora* breaks up, and sinks to the bottom, taking 31 crew to their deaths, and four men of the *Bounty*; Hillbrant, the sole man left manacled in the box; the handcuffed Skinner; and Sumner, who was also struck by the gangway while in the water; and – hardest of all for young Peter Heywood to accept, his friend and alibi – George Stewart.

•

Captain Bligh is dropping anchor at Tenerife once more, as he makes the first stop on his second bread-fruit voyage.

On board Bligh's flagship, *Providence* – at 406 tons a much more substantial ship than *Bounty*'s mere 215 tons – the men are soon busy hauling aboard wine, water and fresh beef and carrying them to the storerooms below. Among those labouring away so very diligently under the watchful eye of Captain Bligh is one particularly stand-out officer by the name of Matthew Flinders, who – in truth – has his own watchful eye on Bligh in turn.

For, working the angles, and pulling some strings, Commodore Thomas Pasley, Commander of the Channel Fleet, who is Peter Heywood's uncle, has succeeded in having young Flinders – a former Midshipman under his own command – placed on this voyage.

'All that I request in return for the good offices I have done you,' Pasley had written to Flinders, 'is, that you never fail by writing me by all possible opportunities during your voyage and that in your letters you be very particular and circumstantial in regard to everything . . .'[59]

Pasley wants Bligh closely observed, for in the one stormy meeting he has had with him, it is obvious he is a man of fury, of curt rudeness and crass crudeness who, if he can be like that to a Commodore, would be unbearable to a common ship's crew. Commander Pasley has also met with Bligh's Master, Mr John Fryer, who, after some encouragement and assurances that there would be no repercussions, had told him many truths about the people's hero, William Bligh, that had not yet surfaced in the public domain. And so this is where you come in, young Mr Flinders. You are capable of tracing every detail of a coastline to perfection. As your old Captain, I want you now to trace every detail of Captain Bligh's command. Information is power and in the face of young Peter Heywood facing the noose if his court martial goes badly, Commander Pasley will go to great lengths for any possible way out.

For his part, Flinders had long wanted to sail under one with such a reputation for navigational brilliance as Bligh, on the reckoning he could learn from him, and has not been disappointed. That, at least, is when it comes to mapping. When it comes to credit for those maps, there is a lesson that Captain Bligh had learnt at the elbow of Captain Cook, which he now rubs young Flinders' nose in. Brilliant young men are free to make brilliant maps, but the credit for them will remain with their Captain, are we clear?

Either way Midshipman Flinders does indeed learn much of the way that Captain Bligh runs things, and he itches to tell them to Commodore Pasley.

•

For Edwards, Morrison and all the other survivors of the wreck of the *Pandora*, it has been a very difficult few weeks. They had found themselves on a small sandbar, some 60 miles off the coast of the northern tip of New Holland, just four miles inside the reef.

And yes, there is a certain companionship to be found in common misery, but in this case there has also been, in the English fashion, enormous class divisions, too.

For while Edwards and his officers had had tents erected, and even the common sailors had been able to fashion some shelter for themselves, for the Mutineers there had been nothing – stone-cold, motherless nothing.

And even when the Mutineers had delicately approached Edwards, requesting that they be allowed to use some old pieces of sail that had washed up on the shore to build a shelter of their own – the skipper had turned them down cold.

Thus . . .

'The only shelter we had,' Heywood would later recount, 'was to bury ourselves up to the neck in burning sand, which scorched the skin entirely off our bodies, for we were quite naked, and we appeared as if dipped in large tubs of boiling water.'[60]

Compounding their problems is that food is short, and the supply of water shorter still. When one sailor gives in to temptation and drinks seawater, he goes mad. After some time, Edwards reaches the conclusion that the only thing they can do is to get the whole lot of them into the four small boats that remain afloat and head for . . . Timor.

So it is that, from early September onwards, to his stupefaction, Thomas Hayward finds himself, *again*, crammed with too many people into too small a boat, on the open seas, proceeding west, across thousands of miles, towards the pestilential Dutch outpost. This, for the second time in two years, sustained by rainwater and whatever fish they can catch, leavened by the few rations hurriedly grabbed before the *Pandora* sank for good. Again, food is measured by musket-balls alone, and again he near starves.

Could anything make this worse?

Decidedly, yes.

On the last trip, the tension between Bligh and Fryer had been palpable.

In this case, it is perilously close to open warfare between Edwards and Morrison, who are in the Launch together, specifically so that Edwards can keep a close eye on the man he clearly regards as the most dangerous – and certainly most troublesome – of the Mutineers.

Morrison leaves no occasion unspared to needle the skipper. Yes, even when he leads the prayers, the notably pious Morrison manages to pointedly thank the Good Lord Almighty for sparing their lives from such a *terrible disaster*, for, if not for His munificence, they all would have been *killed*, yes, cruelly *thrown into the sea* and *drowned* . . .

On and on he goes, so much that Edwards has to interrupt him and, glowering, incandescent with rage, take over.

Like a starving seagull with the remains of a juicy oyster, day after day, Mr Morrison keeps pecking away at the Captain, until Captain Oyster can take no more.

On 9 September 1791, the Captain explodes and orders that Mr Morrison be tightly bound with rope and left to lie in the centre of the Launch.

'What have I done now to be so cruelly treated?'[61] asks Morrison.

'Silence, you murdering villain!' replies Captain Edwards. 'Are you not a prisoner? You piratical dog, what better treatment do you expect?'[62]

'It is a disgrace for the captain of a British Man of War to treat a prisoner in such an inhumane manner,'[63] complains Morrison.

A disgrace?

A *disgrace?*

Let Captain Edwards show you a disgrace.

Snatching up his pistol, he points it right at Morrison's head and threatens to shoot him dead, if he says *one more word*.

Yes, just one more word, sir.

You may have successfully mutinied against Captain Bligh, you cad, you cur, you traitor, but there will be no mutiny on Captain Edwards' watch, let us be clear about that.

Ah, but when it comes to dealing with angry Captains, Mr Morrison has heard it all before, and, quite unconcerned, starts to speak again, whereupon Edwards roars, 'BY GOD, if you speak another word I'll heave the log with you!'[64]

(That is, he will toss Morrison overboard with a rope attached, and drag him through the water.)

Very well then. At last Mr Morrison decides that discretion really is the better part of valour and falls silent, while maintaining that it was not for fear of Captain Edwards, but because his mouth is 'parched'.[65]

17 September 1791, Coupang, Timor, *Bounty* flotsam flows on

What now? On this day, the Dutch Governor, Mr Timotheus Wanjon, once again happens to be gazing out the window of his quarters to the harbour, when he notices a strange flotilla of small, open vessels arriving.

None of them has the wherewithal to be flying a flag and each is filled with . . . yes, ragged-looking officers and sailors. The whole thing is strangely reminiscent of another sorry lot he welcomed into this port not so long ago and so warrants quick investigation.

Ah-ha. It quickly transpires that these are yet more flotsam drifting their way from the affair of the *Bounty*. Apparently this is what is left of the punitive expedition sent out to find the Mutineers, together with what's been found of the Mutineers themselves.

Quickly, the Timorese colony swings into action.

While the men of the *Pandora* are bathed and fed and put into rooms, the prisoners from the *Bounty* are put into a Dutch prison.

Their fellow prisoners? They are a bedraggled bunch, a curious group of convicts – Mary Bryant, her husband William, their two little kids, Emanuel and Charlotte, and seven male convicts – who have escaped from a place called Sydney Cove in New Holland. Mary explains they had made off with the Governor's Cutter, and travelled for six weeks up the coast of New Holland, through Endeavour Strait, and then to the west, before being arrested for debt in Timor.

Theirs is a stunning story, but still not as stunning as what awaits Captain Edwards and his fellow survivors of the *Pandora* when they sail into the port of Samarang a few weeks later, after their own death-defying journey to, first Coupang and then here. For there as they arrive, bobbing gently in the placid waters, is the *Resolution*! James Morrison, with Peter Heywood by his side, is beside himself to see the very boat he and his mates had built, the one they thought lost with the nine crew-members. But yes, here is the mighty boat, and shortly Edwards and the free men are on the docks embracing nearly all of the *survivors*! After they had become separated from the *Pandora*, 19-year-old Master's Mate William Oliver had taken matters in hand

and, against extraordinary odds, managed to navigate all the way to Timor, losing just one of his men on the way. Edwards will eventually receive a written explanation from the young lad.

> Sir. I have made myself appear foolish. We lost the ship in a gale on 23 June off Navigator's Island [Samoa] and not being able to find her we steered directly for [the rendezvous]. Not seeing anything of the ship . . . we made for Endeavour Strait where we were for 7 days in danger of our lives among the shoals. From thence we proceeded to Timor.[66]

Extraordinary!

For all his joy at seeing his ship once more, Morrison grows happier still when the prisoners of the *Bounty* Mutiny learn they will not have to suffer setting foot on a boat commanded by Edwards again . . .

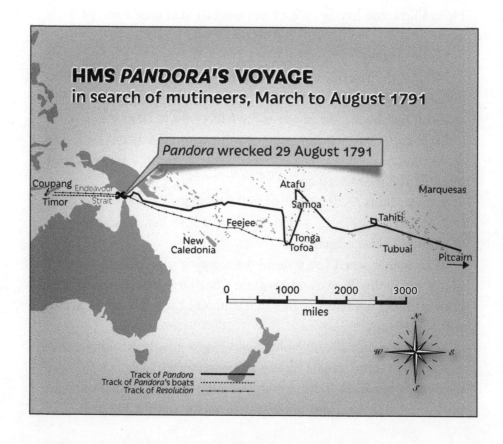

Arrangements for them to go on a ship separate from him have been made.

Hallelujah!

November 1791, Tahiti, poor Peggy

Of course HMS *Chatham* visits Tahiti. In the South Pacific, already on a mission of exploration, why not visit what is now the most fabled paradise in the world? So it is that just seven months after the *Pandora* has departed, the *Chatham* drops anchor in Matavai Bay, to be greeted by the usual flotilla of canoes.

A few days later, however, when things are calmer – the Captain of the *Chatham* has been careful not to allow too much interaction, for obvious reasons – some of the sailors are surprised to see a double-canoe pull up alongside, bearing 'three women, all dress'd in White Linen Shirts, and having each a fine young child in their arms, perfectly white'.[67]

Hello, sailors!

Meet Peggy Stewart, with her beautiful daughter, Charlotte, together with Mary McIntosh, Mary Burkett and their own tiny tots. They seek news of their husbands, last seen departing on the *Pandora*.

Most persistent is Peggy, who returns again and again, with gifts for the sailors, seeking someone who can give her the answer to the question she is obsessed by:

'Do you think George Stewart will be hanged?'

'I do not know,' replies clerk Edward Bell to her, in his cabin, on the last day before departure.

'If he is alive when you return,' the weeping woman begs him, 'tell him you saw his Peggy and his little Charlotte, and that they were both well and tell him to come to Tahiti and live with them, or they will be unhappy.'[68]

In fact, they are already unhappy as Peggy now bursts into tears.

As the *Chatham* weighs anchor and starts moving towards the open sea, still Peggy stays in her canoe, waving, waving, waving until . . . finally, her tiny form sinks beneath the waves and she is gone.

20 November 1791, Batavia, homeward Heywood

Peter Heywood places several sheets of paper on the desk before him, and after dipping his quill in ink, starts the most important missive of his life, his account of the Mutiny, to be sent to his beloved family back on the Isle of Man.

Batavia, November 20th, 1791.

My Ever Honoured and Dearest Mother,
At length the time has arrived when you are once more to hear from your
ill-fated son, whose conduct, at the capture of that ship in which it was
my ill fortune to embark, has, I fear, from what has since happened to
me, been grossly misrepresented to you by Lieutenant Bligh, who, by not
knowing the real cause of my remaining on board, naturally suspected
me, unhappily for me, to be a coadjutor in the mutiny . . .

Oh! my dearest mother, I hope you have not so easily credited such
an account of me; do but let me vindicate my conduct, and declare to
you the true cause of my remaining in the ship, and you will then see
how little I deserve censure, and how I have been injured by so gross an
aspersion. I shall then give you a short and cursory account of what has
happened to me since

How I came to remain on board was thus . . .[69]

And so Peter Heywood, after writing furiously into the night, with a lightened heart pens his final words.

I hope this will be sufficient to undeceive those who have been so
ungenerous as to express, and others who have been so credulous to
believe, all that is laid to my charge. I can say no more, but remember
me to my dearest brothers and sisters &c., and believe me still to be

Your most dutiful and ever obedient son,
Peter Heywood.[70]

Early 1792, Pitcairn, Mutineer wants a wife

The bunk of Jack Williams is achingly cold, every night. His first Native wife, Faahotu, died a year ago now, after a long illness, and sexual desire builds. True, all the women on the island are already taken, but he is not bothered by that detail.

For he is insistent, and at the regular meetings of the Mutineers – they gather at the home of one or other, every couple of weeks to talk things through – makes his position clear.

'If I am not provided with a wife,' he declares, 'I will leave Pitcairn on the *Bounty*'s Jolly Boat.'[71]

Well, then!

In the name of peace, and against the advice of Christian, the Mutineers decide to draw lots, with the wives themselves, of course, not consulted.

And the winner is . . .

Toofaiti, the wife of Talaloo. In fact, she only *used* to be the wife of Talaloo, because the Mutineers all agree she now belongs to Williams.

Fair's fair, after all.

Now while Toofaiti co-operates, and that night takes her few meagre possessions to Williams' hut, and sleeps in his bed, Talaloo takes an exceedingly dim view of proceedings.

Storming away, the distraught and furious Talaloo – trouble on two legs – takes to the hills, plotting revenge.

While this would be a problem in itself, the bigger problem soon emerges.

He is not alone in his outrage.

One by one, all the other Native men on Pitcairn visit Talaloo, sit with him, talk things through, and yes, build on each other's anger at the white men. Finally, it is Ohoo, one of the 'husbands' of Tinafornia who comes up with a possible solution. *Let's kill every white man on the island.* Why should we be slaves to these white devils who pretended to be our friends, only to take us far from everything we knew, work us to the bone, and then take our wives?

Slowly, around the fire with Talaloo, a plan is hatched for the mass slaughter of the Mutineers. Carefully, word is passed to Toofaiti that she will soon be liberated.

Axes are sharpened, spears are fashioned, as a dark cloud of tension descends on Pitcairn. The Mutineers are aware that the Natives are restless, but not overly concerned.

Two people on the island, however, are highly troubled by the way things are heading.

One is Christian, who continues to be a voice of reason, insisting to both blacks and whites that the only way forward is to turn to each other, and not on each other.

The other one who is agitated, naturally enough, is Toofaiti herself. To find herself traded like a sack of potatoes, being handed around between Tahitian and English men alike, with never any question as to her own desires, is more than merely aggravating. She waits for the moment to let all know that she is a woman who can decide her own fate.

So it is that one day, while she is with some of the other women, washing garments in the sea, she starts to sing an improvised song, one with searing words, that makes the other women stop and stare . . .

> *Why does black man sharpen axe?*
> *To kill white man.*
> *Why should the Tahitian men sharpen their axes?*
> *To cut off the Englishmen's heads*[72]

The assistant botanist Billy Brown's wife, Sarah, no sooner hears the song than she instantly grasps its intent, and quickly goes off to find Isabella and tell her the news: murder is coming to Pitcairn. Isabella, in turn, quickly tells *miti Titriano,* dear Fletcher, who has no sooner heard the news than he grabs his musket, loads it, and goes off in search of the Tahitian men to tell them that their plot has been discovered. The afternoon crackles with tension. The island seethes. A storm that has been a long time coming is suddenly about to break all over them.

Only a few minutes walk from the village, Christian comes across the ringleader Ohoo.

'Ohoo!' he calls.

I know all about the plot to kill us. I know that you are behind it.

When Ohoo shouts back at him, clearly entirely unrepentant and intent on going through with the plot, Christian lifts his musket, aims it right at him and pulls the trigger.

There is a flash, a puff of smoke, a massive roar, and the musket's muzzle bursts forth a belch of flame.

Ohoo?

He remains standing.

Christian, wanting only to scare and intimidate, not maim or murder, has loaded his musket with powder alone, not shot.

Alas, rather than be intimidated, Ohoo now appears convinced he has supernatural powers, able to withstand even the white man's weaponry, for he openly mocks Christian.

Against that, he also understands that in such situations discretion really is the better part of valour, and before Christian can reload, Ohoo is on his way to join Talaloo at his hideaway in the hills.

•

Fishing at Pitcairn requires the execution of an ancient art.

The Tahitian women are very good at it. With each one taking a bag and a small net, they form up in a line across the shallows by the shore, up to their middle. Standing tightly side by side, they trap fish in their nets, 'made of the membranous stratums of the coconut tree, sewed together',[73] pluck them up and put them in their bags. Not only have they been raised to it, nurtured on its skills, but they also appear to have a natural patience that does not come easily to the men.

On this day Toofaiti is with the other women, catching fish, when she hears an unmistakable low whistle. It can only have come from one person, and she knows who. Sure enough, gazing into the bushes whence the whistle has come, she sees one branch moving on this otherwise totally still day and makes her way to it.

Talaloo.

He wants her to come back to him, come to live in the hills.

She makes a decision on the spot, and now joins Talaloo and Ohoo at their hiding spot in the hills.

That night, Williams sleeps alone once more, bereft that Toofaiti has left him. He had won her fair and square by drawing lots, and thought he had won her heart, too, but now is alone. When yet one more Tahitian, Timoa, goes off to join the group in the hills, the situation becomes urgent.

The Mutineers are not only losing labour and wives, the island is now forming into two armed camps. Should they send out a punitive expedition to put an end to it?

For the moment, the answer is no. The very features of Pitcairn that encouraged them when they occupied it, the cruel mountain passes and many caves, now aid the black renegades. For they, too, would be able to see the white men coming from a long way off, and, even without muskets, be able to do enormous damage by virtue of spears, hurled rocks, and even landslides prepared above the narrowest of passes.

Instead, the white men send the Tahitian Native most onside, Menalee, as an emissary. His task is, first and foremost, to see if he can find the Tahitians.

It takes several days, but finally Menalee returns with the news.

Yes, he has found two of them, including Ohoo, as cautious as he is cunning, who had hidden himself on the far side of the island. But no, they do not wish to return to the white men, and nothing will convince them to return.

Very well, then. Perhaps a punitive expedition after all? No, not by the white men. That would be too risky. Have Menalee do it. After much discussion with the Native men who are still with them, and who 'finding their plot discovered, purchased pardon by promising to murder their accomplices',[74] the Mutineers decide to send Menalee back to visit Talaloo, Toofaiti and Timoa, bearing three puddings. While two of the puddings would be normal English fare, and given to Toofaiti and Timoa, the one given specifically to Talaloo would be poisoned. Ideally, the poison would be enough to kill him, and show the penalty to the other Natives for disobeying the white men.

One morning late in January 1792, Menalee sets off, with the three puddings, with the normal ones in his left hand and the poisoned one firmly in his right hand, with Christian, by one contemporary account, 'promising to reward him handsomely if he succeeded, but, if he did not, he was to lose his own life'.[75]

Sure enough, Talaloo, Toofaiti and Timoa appear pleased to see him, until such time as he brings out the puddings. This is . . . strange? Men do not bring men puddings. Talaloo is suspicious from the first, and instead of eating the pudding Menalee carefully proffers him, puts it aside, uneaten, while sharing in his wife Toofaiti's pudding.

Mindful of his instructions to kill Talaloo, Menalee comes up with another plan. You all should know that I have left our shared wife Mareva nearby, and she would love to see you. Would you like to come with me through the narrow mountain passes to see her? She is only a short distance off, waiting by a bread-fruit tree!

All three agree, and they are soon on their way, with Menalee carefully positioning himself last on the narrow hill pathway, directly behind Talaloo.

As they approach a particularly narrow pass, where there is no room to manoeuvre left or right, and certainly no way for Talaloo to go forward or back, when he is no more than a sitting duck, Menalee carefully draws his pistol, brings it up to the back of Talaloo's head, meaning he simply can't miss, and, yes . . . pulls the trigger.

What follows is a truly shocking . . . *CLICK.*

The gun has misfired! But Talaloo has heard it all right, and whirls around to see Menalee with the pistol pointed at him, about to have another go. This second, he lives or dies. At this very spot, suddenly, there is a slight opening on the path, enough for him to get past Toofaiti. Like a scalded cat, thus, he takes a bound forward, past his wife, and starts running. Menalee, realising he will never have another chance from this close, also bounds forward, giving chase, and, quickly bringing him down, the two fight on the ground, wrestling, and raining blow after blow on each other.

'*Vahine fa'aipoipo!* Wife!' roars Talaloo. 'Help me kill this man!'

'Toofaiti!' yells Menalee, in turn. 'You must help me kill your husband!'[76]

Toofaiti makes her decision in an instant. Grabbing a rock, she brings it down hard on the head of . . . Talaloo, her first husband, stunning him in two ways and allowing Menalee to get a rock of his own. Together, while the shocked Timoa simply stands witness, the two beat Talaloo to death. When it is done and Talaloo lies still, his crushed-in head a bloody mess, the two stand, covered in blood from head to toe.

Escaping the attention of everyone to this point – most particularly including the entirely oblivious Talaloo – is that Toofaiti has long been in love with Williams! All of the assurances, thus, from her fellow Tahitians, that she would soon be back in the arms of Talaloo had been taunts to her heart. Yes, Williams had won her by drawing lots, but she had felt lucky in turn as he had long before won her heart. And now, as she has so comprehensively demonstrated, she so loves Jack that she will kill to be with him.

•

Here they come!

From the village below, they see three figures emerge from the high mountain passes, a number which is already promising. But who is it?

It does not take long to find out. Once it is clear that Talaloo is not among them, and two of the figures are covered in blood, it is obvious that the mission must have been accomplished in another manner, and the Mutineers rush forward. In short order, the news tumbles out, much as Toofaiti tumbles into the waiting arms of Williams, only minutes before the two return to his house. Toofaiti is now his wife, for now and forevermore, with *no* rivals.

While pleased to hear of the death of Talaloo, still there is a problem. Somewhere out there, Ohoo is still alive and likely plotting to kill one or all of the white men. He, too, will have to be dealt with, but this time they will not bother with poisoned puddings.

•

All is in readiness. After several sorties of a very careful nature, the faithful Menalee knows well Ohoo's hidden camp, in a thick grove on the southern side of the island. On this day in late January, Menalee and Timoa leave together on a visit to Ohoo, with Menalee carefully tucking his primed pistol into his belt, secreted from view by the *marro* around his waist.

And there he is!

Ohoo rises warily as he sees his two Tahitian friends approaching, weeping.

Ohoo, our brother, they call, the tears running down their cheeks. *We have missed you. We are so sorrowful to have been without you for so long.*

Relieved that they come in peace, Ohoo comes forward to embrace them, his arms out wide, at which point Menalee whips out his pistol and shoots him dead.

This time, there is no mistake.

•

The emaciated Mutineers captured by the *Pandora* arrive back at Portsmouth on 18 June 1792, aboard His Majesty's Ship, *Gorgon* – a 44-gun troopship returning from New Holland, which had picked them up at the Cape of Good Hope. No sooner has the ship dropped anchor than the prisoners, in chains, have been dragged into the sunlight, and are soon in a Cutter with a posse of hefty Marines, heading across the harbour to the guardship HMS *Hector*, where they must await their court martial. Among them of course is Peter Heywood, and amazingly, secure among his few possessions, he still has his *Book of Common Prayer* – in which, on the fly leaves he has, in Tahitian, noted events of great importance. *Sept 22nd 1789 Mya Toobooai mye*; *Mar. 25th 1791 We ta Pahee Pandora . . .*[77]

Only three days later, the letter young Peter had, back in Batavia, written to his mother, arrives at the Heywood family home on the Isle of Man. With a start, his frail mother recognises the careful hand-writing – he had always been such a neat, elegant boy – and calls for her daughter Nessy to come quickly!

It is Peter. He has written to us! Taking the letter from her mother's shaking fingers, Nessy composes herself and reads it out loud to her mother, brothers and two younger sisters, stifling a sob of relief at his earnest words: 'I never, to my knowledge, whilst under his command, behaved myself in a manner unbecoming the station I occupied . . .'[78]

She knew it!

She had known all along, and had been telling everyone, her beloved Peter is no Mutineer. And now she quickly pens her own heartfelt response on behalf of the family.

My dearest and most beloved brother,

Thanks to that Almighty Providence which has so miraculously preserved
you, your fond, anxious, and, till now, miserable Nessy, is at last
permitted to address the object of her tenderest affection in England! Oh!
My admirable, my heroic boy, what have we felt on your account . . . !
How blessed did your delightful and yet dreadful letter from Batavia
make us all![79]

For all her expressed love, Mrs Heywood has few illusions – it will
likely need a miracle, some divine intervention, for her son to survive
this. For hanging remains the most likely result for all those accused of
being Mutineers. But at least there is one thing in their favour – Bligh
is still away on his Tahiti venture, completing his mission of getting
the bread-fruit, and, if they move quickly, he will not be back in time,
and so won't be able to give evidence.

In what little time remains, the Heywood family must do everything
they can to save Peter's life. One thing that turns up in their initial
inquiries gives them hope. Apparently, one of his co-accused, a James
Morrison, kept a journal throughout the whole journey, which details
Bligh's bastardry and brutality, and gives context to the Mutiny.

Perhaps, if they could get access to this journal, make copies, and
have it quietly circulated privately amongst the great and the good?

Perhaps that might bring the hero Bligh down from his current
exalted perch and make it clear that, in those circumstances – even
though Peter was *not* involved in the Mutiny – even if he had been, it
would have been justified!

CHAPTER SIXTEEN

TRIALS AND TRIBULATIONS

Mr. Bligh most certainly brands my amiable brother with the vile appellation of 'Mutineer,' but he has not dared to charge you with any crime that could have authoriz'd such an epithet; on the contrary, he has declared, under his own hand, that he had the highest esteem for you till the fatal moment of the Mutiny, and that your conduct during the whole course of the voyage was such as gave him the greatest pleasure and satisfaction.[1]

Nessy Heywood, letter to her brother Peter Heywood, as he awaited trial,
31 July 1792

My dear Nessy, cherish your hope and I will exercise my patience.[2]

Peter Heywood, letter to Nessy as he awaits his sentence, October 1792

H ow sweet is every feature in thy face –
E ach look is fraught with dignity and grace.
S urprising gentleness plays in thine eyes,
T o catch time unwary heart in sweet surprize
E 'en as the voice of Heav'n thine accents flow,
R aising a sweet delight where'er they go . . . [3]

An acrostic poem written for Hester – 'Nessy' – by her beloved uncle,
Captain Thomas Pasley, 1786

But Christian, of a higher order, stood
Like an extinct volcano in his mood;
Silent, and sad, and savage, – with the trace
Of passion reeking from his clouded face;[4]

Lord Byron, 'The Island'

August 1792, Isle of Man, considerable charm and extraordinary energy

They don't come much more beautiful than Nessy Heywood, and few are more accomplished. She is a charming, well-educated 24-year-old with a penchant for poetry, and she and her two young sisters live with their widowed mother on the Isle of Man. Nessy is a happy soul by nature, notwithstanding she has gone through enormous unhappiness in recent times. First she had missed her younger brother Peter terribly, since he had left these shores three years earlier to go on the *Bounty*, and then had come the horrific news of the Mutiny, and that his name was not listed on the line-up of Loyalists!

Worse, just two months ago, he had returned, in chains, and is now being held upon the guardship *Hector*, in Portsmouth, and the common view is that he and the others will soon be tried for mutiny, and hanged.

Surely, there must have been some mistake?

The family is sure of it.

The lad they had so fondly farewelled in 1787 was a polite, well-mannered, confident young man. He was *not* a murderous Mutineer.

> *Oh, my admirable, my heroic boy . . . Oh, my best beloved Peter . . . to fly into your arms . . . I have no joy, no happiness but in your beloved society.*[5]

Nessy asks him to send her a self-portrait so she knows what he looks like these days.

Still imprisoned in the brig of the *Hector*, young Peter is delighted to receive such a warm letter, but not surprised. Such is the nature of dear Nessy. Oh, how he loves her. And now, no matter that the *Pandora* had gone down with all his drawing pencils and colours – not to mention the many dozens of drawings he had completed, and his journals chronicling his wretched voyage – the drawing materials have been replaced by some kind guards, and he happily sets to doing a self-portrait reminding dear Nessy that:

> *I had no Looking Glass and therefore drew it from recollection and 'tis now one year at least since I saw my own face. With these disadvantages you cannot expect a striking resemblance.*[6]

Thrilled in turn with his effort, Nessy writes back, commenting:

> *I am surprised you are not taller – I fully expected you would have been*
> *5 Feet 10 at least, but that is of no consequence.*[7]

Amused, Peter opens a mock-angry reply:

> *And so you are surprised I am not taller? Eh' Nessy? Let me ask you*
> *this: suppose the last two years of your growth had been retarded by*
> *close confinement . . . shut up from the all-cheering light of the sun for*
> *the space of five months and never suffered to breathe fresh air . . . how*
> *tall should you have been my dear? Answer: Four Feet 0. But enough of*
> *nonsense.*
>
> *Adieu, my dearest love – with kind remembrances to all, I remain*
> *yours most affectionately,*
> *Peter Heywood*[8]

Young Peter's letters assure Nessy and the family that he does not deserve to hang, as Captain Bligh has advocated.

Nessy will not have it. Not for a *moment*, do you hear?

And so, with all of her considerable charm, and extraordinary energy, Nessy begins what will be a long campaign to save her brother.

She starts by writing compelling letters, setting out the facts such as are known, which are sent to everyone from the First Lord of the Admiralty, John Pitt, Second Earl of Chatham, to a surprised but polite Midshipman John Hallett (who is set to testify against her brother), and to Nessy and Peter's uncle, the well-connected Naval Commodore Thomas Pasley. To anyone who will listen, Nessy points out the truth: Peter Heywood is a very young man with an impeccable record of good character, caught up in a mutinous monstrosity *not* of his making. Why, if he was guilty of anything mutinous, would he have been among the *first* to board the *Pandora* when she arrived, paddling out to her of his own volition? Was that the act of a guilty man? Surely, in the name of English justice, you men of power and influence can do something to help poor Peter?

Commodore Pasley is in turn among the first to reply to his cherished niece, and in kind terms. But, he must be frank. Having informed himself of the situation, he feels obliged to temper her hopes of a miracle:

> *I cannot conceal it from you, my dearest Nessy, neither is it proper I should – your brother appears by all accounts to be the greatest culprit of all, Christian alone excepted. Every exertion, you may rest assured, I shall use to save his life, but on Trial I have no hope of his not being condemned.*[9]

And nor does it alter his view when Nessy sends the good Commodore Peter's own account of the Mutiny, which shows he nary lifted a hand against Captain Bligh, for he must warn her once more:

> *I will not deceive you, my dear Nessy; however favourable circumstances may appear, our martial law is severe; by the tenor of it, the man who stands neuter is equally guilty with him who lifts his arm against his captain.*[10]

The only saving grace for Peter he can see is that, however scathing Bligh has been in private correspondence about young Peter, his accusations have not been matched in his official reports to the Admiralty – which is important. True, Peter had not been highlighted as one of the men who called out to Bligh from the deck of the *Bounty* to be marked as an innocent Loyalist, but nor has Bligh publicly named him as a Mutineer.

Now, on the specific subject of Bligh, the fact he is now journeying back to Tahiti is significant. For the expert advice that Nessy receives is that it is *imperative* that Peter appear before his court martial before Bligh can return to give testimony. If there is only his written response to go on, Peter might just be able to escape with his life. Here, at least, Commodore Pasley – at Nessy's earnest behest – is able to bring his weight to bear, and ensure that the court martial is hurried up, for Pete's sake, and have it scheduled for just three months after the Mutineers have returned to England, which is before Bligh will be back.

And the good news is that Pasley, meanwhile, is able to find support from surprising areas, even including a man not known for mercy at all, Captain Edward Edwards.

'I have had some conversation on the subject with Pasley,' Edwards writes to a friend, before trial, 'with whose family the young man has some connection ... Whatever might be his conduct in the affair he certainly came to *Pandora* of his own accord almost immediately after we anchored. I believe he has abilities and have been informed he made himself master of the Tahiti language whilst on that island which may be of public utility ...'[11]

Most importantly of all, 'The unfortunate young man ... at present on board a guardship at Portsmouth ... I apprehend ... did not take an active part against Mister Bligh.'[12]

●

In Tahiti, Bligh is busy. Beyond organising the bread-fruit plants, keeping a *very* close eye on the sailors and getting through an inordinate amount of daily cursing, he is spending a great deal of time talking with his old friend Tinah (who, as always, spends much time on board Bligh's ship) and other Natives about their time with the Mutineers, hungry for details of their time on the island, and whatever more they might have divulged about the Mutiny.

Bligh also inspects the huts of his former charges – reluctantly conceding that Peter Heywood, 'the villain who assisted in taking the *Bounty* from me' had 'regulated the garden and the avenue to his House with some taste'[13] – and meets the women and children the Mutineers have left behind.

'A fine child of about 12 months old was brought to me today,' Bligh will recount. 'It is a daughter of George Stewart, Midshipman of the *Bounty*. It was a very pretty creature, but had been so exposed to the sun as to be very little fairer than a Tahitian.'[14]

Few are more helpful than a Native woman called Mary, who had been the wife of Thomas McIntosh. With their baby girl now bouncing on her knee, the heartbroken Mary speaks at length with Bligh in half English, half Tahitian. As Bligh listens, by turns fascinated and appalled, Mary names those men who had mourned the Captain in the belief he was surely dead, even as Bligh chronicles the names of these fine souls in his Log, with the zeal of the Archangel Gabriel in the Good Book:

'McIntosh, Coleman, Hillbrant, Norman, Byrn and Ellison scarcely ever spoke of me without crying.'[15] Nevertheless, Mary says sorrowfully, there were two men who did not shed a single tear in Bligh's general direction. 'Stewart and Heywood were perfectly satisfied with their situation as any two Villains could be.'[16]

And so, Mary, what do you think would be a fitting punishment for Peter Heywood and George Stewart?

'They deserve to be killed,' Bligh records as the considered view of Tahiti's own hanging judge. 'But I hope those who cried for you will not be hurt.'[17]

While pleased to talk to Mary, Bligh is distressed to see how much Tahiti, the one-time paradise, has deteriorated as a direct result of its contact with the outside world.

'Our friends here have benefitted little from their intercourse with Europeans,' he records. 'Our countrymen, have taught them such vile expressions as are in the mouth of every Tahitian and I declare that I would rather forfeit anything than to have been in the list of ships that have touched here since April, 1789.'

And even now, he is just warming up.

'The quantity of old clothes left among these people is considerable, they wear such rags and dirty things as truly disgust us . . . It is rare to see a person dressed with a neat piece of cloth which formerly they had in abundance and wore with much elegance. Their general habiliments are now a dirty shirt and an old coat and waistcoat; they are no longer clean Tahitians, but in appearance a set of ragamuffins with whom it is necessary to have great caution.'[18]

May 1792, Pitcairn, solace to not cave in

While it is one thing for Fletcher Christian to have physically escaped Bligh, it is another to be free of the many things that pursue his spirit. Time and again his haunting regrets meet his worst nightmares head-on and a terrible blackness descends. At such times Isabella packs him some supplies – which includes ammunition for his gun – embraces him, and farewells him to the one place on Pitcairn where he manages to find some kind of solace, a large cave high on a cliff-face, which is dangerously difficult to get to, which is why Fletcher likes it. Once inside, he does not have to speak to anyone, does not have to see or be seen by anyone, and is free to just sit and contemplate, gazing at the extraordinary view of the ocean, and the less pleasing view of his life – what he has done, what might have been, what his lot now is, what he might do in the future. Maybe, one day, a ship might appear on yonder horizons? Maybe it might be Dutch, or Portuguese, or American, and he could actually make his way back to civilisation, and even back to his own family. But what then of Isabella and Thursday? Could he actually leave them? If they came with him, could they ever fit into the life of anonymity he would have to lead while in England? The sad answer to the latter is obviously not. It is a contemplation without answers, but at least he is free to reflect on things without interruption.

And if it proves be a British ship, well, he could perhaps retrieve his family, and – with the cache of supplies he has secreted here – hold out for a very long time.

Usually for three days, from his high citadel, Fletcher stares out to the ocean, thinking of his family and friends in England, missing Isabella and wee Thursday, but simply glad to be alone with his thoughts.

And finally it is time, and a few hours afterwards the moment that Isabella has been waiting for arrives. She looks up, and Fletcher is back, safe. For now.

•

In the lead-up to the court martial, Nessy Heywood seeks learned legal advice, even though, as Commodore Pasley points out, it is just not done in the Royal Navy to have that counsel address the court martial. As ever, Nessy goes after the finest advocate she can find, a renowned naval lawyer who falls within her strong family connections, Mr Aaron Graham. Though too busy, even as jaded a jurist as he can't resist the charms of Nessy Heywood and he agrees to take the case – even adding the professional services of a colleague, Mr Const, to advise on legal strategies, and sit by Peter throughout the trial, even if he cannot argue a case on his behalf.

James Morrison? He has no charming sister to plead his case, no powerful uncle, and barely a bean to pay a lawyer if one could be convinced that his case was not absolutely hopeless.

All he has are his wits and his quill. For, realising that his only chance is to get the true story out – not the fantasy promoted by that brilliant bastard Bligh, whose latest tome, *A Voyage to the South Sea*, is published on 1 July 1792, a mere fortnight after the arrival of the accused Mutineers, and is now being perused with great public interest and sympathy – James Morrison spends his days incarcerated on the *Hector* writing his own version of what happened, first on the *Bounty*, then in Tahiti and then in *Pandora*. It is entitled *Memorandum and Particulars Respecting the Bounty and her Crew*, goes for 42 pages and crackles and explodes on every page as Bligh is seen again and again to succumb to the temptation of losing his temper for trivialities, of imposing outrageous privations on his men, of forcing the Master to sign the books against his will, of, yes, completely alienating the entire ship by blowing up over absurdities.

> In the afternoon of the 27th a number of Cocoa Nuts were missed by Mr Bligh from the Quarter Deck upon which, all the Officers were called and on their declaring, that they had not seen any person take them, he told them they were all thieves alike. He particularly called Christian a Thief and a Villain, and [told the ship's company], 'You Villains, I'll make half of you jump over board before I get through Endeavour Straights.'[19]

There are well-told and endless stories of fury and discord, lacking only one thing – someone of influence to read them, to believe them, to start to get the real story out to others of influence.

Could the very reverent Reverend William Howell, priest at St John's Chapel in Portsmouth, be that man? A kindly pastor, he has made it his business in life to give food to the hungry and hope to the hopeless, and has made a point of coming to visit the prisoners of the *Bounty*, all of whom, he knows, will likely swing. And of course, he talks to Heywood, Muspratt, Morrison and the others about what has occurred, hears all the stories, and is shocked by their consistency, the passion

with which they are told and the fact that they all point to the innocence of the men – or at least an explanation for why they have done
what they've done – and the sheer bloody-minded culpability of Bligh.

So open is Howell in his sympathy for the men that Morrison decides
he can trust him – and is not proven wrong. After the prisoner looks
left, looks right, and slips the preacher the manuscript, the reverend
takes himself to another part of the brig and quietly reads it, before
slipping it back. Shaking the bony hand of the rake-thin Morrison as
he leaves, the truly shocked preacher promises the prisoner that he
will do what he can – and that night, can barely sleep. Of course most
of the story cannot be presented as evidence for the court martial –
as that proceeding is very narrowly framed so that it will be almost
exclusively focused on what happened on the morning of the Mutiny
– but it remains important to get the background story out, and the
Reverend Howell knows he is the man for the job.

•

After the murders and mayhem, comes a kind of calm. The labour of
Talaloo and Ohoo is missed, but in their absence the 'Pitkerners' have
no choice for the moment but to make peace, of a sort, settle down
the best they can, and focus on farming. The sun rises and falls, the
seasons change, a little, and the rhythm of their lives runs to both as
they look after their animals, raise their crops and harvest as hunger
dictates.

By now little Thursday Christian is nearly one year old, he's crawling
and knows both English and Tahitian words – and, by the looks of
things, even speaks a little hog and chicken, to judge by the delight
he takes in playing with both. As it happens, Thursday is one of the
few things absolutely guaranteed to raise Fletcher's troubled spirits,
as even this far removed from the Mutiny he still wakes in the night,
fretting, sweating, letting the horror of what happened wash over him
once more.

Steady, Fletcher, steady.

Holding Isabella more tightly still, he calms at least a little. Whatever
else, he has her, and the sound of Thursday's soft breathing from his
cot beside them is affirmation that he at least has some reasons to live.

12 September 1792, Plymouth, aboard HMS *Duke*, marshal the Mutineers

And so it begins – the court martial to determine whether or not the ten prisoners brought back from the Mutiny on the *Bounty* are deserving of the punishment prescribed in Article XIX of the Articles of War: 'If any Person in or belonging to the Fleet shall make or endeavour to make any mutinous Assembly upon any pretence whatsoever, every person offending herein, and being convicted thereof by the sentence of the Court-martial shall suffer death.'[20]

In the Captain's cabin of the *Duke* – a 90-gun, 2000-ton ship of the line, ten times bigger than the *Bounty* – the eyes of the portrait of King George III that hangs prominently on the wall survey a scene that is a curious combination of ceremony and portent.

Thirteen experienced Royal Navy Captains, esteemed knights of the seas, ranked in importance by their proximity to the President of the court martial, Vice-Admiral Lord Hood, sit behind the long oaken table situated beneath the small stern windows that give glimpses of the horizon swaying up and down with the gentle rock of the boat. They include Sir Andrew Snape Hamond, Sir George Montagu and Sir Roger Curtis, all ready to listen to the testimony, the cross-examinations and sift through the evidence. Captain Albemarle Bertie is also there, a man well ensconced in the Heywood/Pasley network of friends, while at least one other of the group is a friend of Commodore Pasley, and has already been fully briefed by him.

To a man, the presiding members are magnificently groomed and imposingly presented, resplendent in their blue uniforms with gold buttons, the curls of their powdered hair sitting just so beneath their black cocked hats. Such is the importance of the affair, so much hanging in the balance, that every man who had been on the *Bounty* who is alive and in England is present to tell his story – with those accused of mutiny, in chains, sitting side by side in two rows on benches that face their judges. They have been brought here just 30 minutes before, taken from the brig on the *Hector*, and rowed across the waters to the *Duke* under care of the Provost Marshal and an armed guard of Marines. Eyes wide, they take in the sudden opulent airiness of their surroundings, so far removed from the foetid, featureless, fogginess of where they have been kept for months.

Right in the middle of the accused stands Peter Heywood – in the new suit secured for him by dear Nessy, looking regal midst the rags of his fellow defendants – eagerly taking the whole scene in, knowing his day of reckoning has arrived. Nearby is James Morrison, and of course the blind fiddler Michael Byrn, not to mention the glowering Thomas Burkett, and the clearly fearful 'Monkey', Thomas Ellison.

Behind them stands a retinue of armed Marines, glaring at the accused – just on principle.

These are Mutineers. They deserve no respect, only due process, before we hang the guilty high.

The atmosphere crackles as the greatest story of the day builds to its long-awaited climax.

For those fortunate enough to be present – with around 40 people in the room – at least for those who are not accused, there is an enormous sense of privilege just for being here. Overwhelmingly, however, the atmosphere is martial. As this is a closed proceeding, no family or friends are allowed, no public gallery, and not even any journalists. The first the public know of it will be when they hear the verdicts, and the press will carry no account of the evidence presented.

And so let us begin.

After the scripted preliminaries of oaths of the presiding members, the Judge Advocate, Moses Greetham – an appointed civilian judge, present to supervise and superintend the court – calls upon the accused.

All rise.

And so they do, albeit shaking from nerves, and making something of a racket, as the clink and clank of their irons on the hard wood surface clangs around the room until once more silence settles.

'The prisoners are,' the stately Mr Greetham begins in stern tones, 'on a charge of mutiny on the 28th of April 1789, on board His Majesty's Ship *Bounty*, for running away with the Ship and deserting His Majesty's Service . . .'[21]

He goes on to describe the series of events, beginning with the bread-fruit commission and climaxing by reading out Captain Bligh's letter sent from Coupang in Timor on 18 August 1789, detailing the events of the Mutiny:

> *On the 28th April 1789, Fletcher Christian, who was mate of the ship, and officer of the watch, with the ship's corporal, came into my cabin, while I was asleep, and seizing me, tied my hands with a cord, assisted by others who were also in the cabin, all armed with muskets and bayonets. I was now threatened with instant death if I spoke a word . . .*[22]

Every one of the members of the court has himself commanded a ship (and some of them have commanded a fleet), and to a man they seem to glare at these reprobates who would even *think* of doing such a thing. For all of them a 'Mutiny' is the most abhorrent of all crimes and they can be expected to be every bit as penetrating in their questions as they will be fierce in their judgements.

At least four of the ten men assembled before the judges for this trial are innocent. After all, Captain Bligh has placed it on the record that Mr Norman, Mr Coleman and Mr McIntosh had been held against their will on the *Bounty*, while Michael Byrn, the Blind Fiddler, had only missed the boat because he had been stuck in the wrong one. (True, Bligh did not personally hear Byrn's voice, but, in his account, he makes it clear that the other men on the Launch say *they* clearly heard him, and he has no doubt they are telling the truth.)

But no fewer than six of the men are odds on to be hanged, barring extraordinary evidence that might clear them. They are Midshipman Peter Heywood, along with the Bosun's Mate James Morrison, Assistant Cook William Muspratt, and Able Seamen Thomas Ellison, Thomas Burkett and John Millward.

As the trial proper gets underway, the first witness is called: Mr John Fryer.

The one-time Master of the *Bounty* is escorted into the room, holding his black tricorn hat under his right arm, and gazing about him, just as all those in the court gaze at him. His weathered face bespeaks one who sailed the Seven Seas for many years, just as his tightly groomed hair, navy blue coat with long tails, white shirt and trousers, and black shoes with large brass buckles give an air of one who is earnestly trying to make his best impression upon the members of this court. As well, the Mutineers note, he is back to looking a lot more like his old self – no longer hassled, hustled and harried by Bligh to the point of breaking, he now has his emotions much more under control, varying only between a look of slow torture and deep frustration.

Mr Greetham administers the oath, slowly reading the words that Mr Fryer must repeat.

'In the evidence I shall give before the court, respecting the present trial, I will, whether favourable or unfavourable to the prisoner . . . declare the truth, the *whole* truth and nothing but the truth; So help me God.'[23]

So help me, God.

After the preliminaries, Mr Fryer gets to the nub of his testimony – what happened when he realised he was in the middle of a full-blown mutiny.

'When I came upon deck,' he recounts with an air of slow torture, almost as if he can see the scene even now, 'Mr. Bligh was standing by the Mizzen-Mast with his hands tied behind him and Christian holding the cord with one hand and a bayonet in the other. I said, "Mr. Christian, consider what you are about." "Hold your tongue, Sir," he said, "I have been in Hell for weeks past. Captain Bligh has brought all this on himself." I told him that Mr. Bligh and his not agreeing was no reason for his taking the ship. "Hold your tongue, Sir," he said. I said, "Mr. Christian, you and I have been on friendly terms during the voyage, therefore give me leave to speak; let Mr. Bligh go down to his Cabin and I make no doubt but that we shall all be friends again in a very short time . . ."'[24]

Really?

Despite the gravity of the charges, the assembled collection of military eminences might be forgiven for being wryly amused. For as it turns out, Mr Fryer's extreme optimism was a tad . . . well . . . optimistic.

'At the hatchway,' Mr Fryer goes on, 'I saw James Morrison, the Bosun's Mate. He was at that time getting a tackle to hook upon the Launch's stern, apparently, so I said to him, "Morrison, I hope you have no hand in this business?" He replied, "No, sir, I do not know a word about it," or words to that effect. "If that's the case," I said in a low voice, "be on your guard; there may be an opportunity of recovering ourselves." His answer was "Go down to your cabin, sir, it is too late".'[25]

Ah-HA.

As Morrison shifts nervously, his chains rattle and his brow breaks out in a cold sweat. In an instant, he, in the eyes of this tribunal anyway, has clearly moved closer to the core of the Mutineers. If indeed innocent, Morrison must be seen to have resisted the Mutiny, not encouraged others to give in to it.

His only chance now will be to turn up evidence favourable to him in the cross-examination, allowed to all the accused. Before that takes place, however, Heywood makes a request, which the Judge Advocate now reads out.

I would like to listen to the testimony of all those called to the stand, and then, and only then, observe my right to cross-examine those witnesses.

Yes, Midshipman Heywood, your request is granted.

(A brilliant legal manoeuvre, Peter can now make his case as a cohesive whole, not bit by bit as the other accused must do. And it will also mean that my learned friends, Nessy's chosen lawyers, Mr Graham and Mr Const, can assess the whole case against him, work out what the most damaging parts are, and then, and only then, seek to counter them. It is their firm, expert view that this approach will give him the best chance of acquittal.)

Very well, then.

But back to you, James Morrison, as you exert your own right to cross-examine Mr Fryer: 'Are you positive it was me who said, "Go down to your cabin?"'

'Yes, I am positive it was you . . .'[26]

To Morrison's delight, Vice-Admiral Hood himself follows up, carefully, as befitting one bearing the scales of justice on a matter of life and death.

'Might not,' Hood ponders, 'Morrison's speaking to you and telling you to "keep below", be from a laudable motive, as supposing your resistance at that time might have prevented a more advantageous effort?'

'Probably it might,' Mr Fryer agrees, 'had I stayed in the ship he would have been one of the first that I should have opened my mind to, from his good behaviour in the former part of the voyage.'

'Did he speak to you in a threatening tone or address you as advice?'

'Addressed me as advice,'[27] Mr Fryer replies.

So Morrison's hopes survive. Perhaps he is part of the resistance to the Mutiny, perhaps not.

Now, when it comes to Peter Heywood, the Bosun, William Cole, is of the firm opinion, and tells the court so, that Peter *was* trying to get into the Launch.

'I believe Mr. Heywood was, I thought all along he was intending to come away. I did not think anything else – he had no Arms and he assisted to get the boat out and then went below.'

'Have you any other reason,' the prosecutor asks, 'which induces you to think that Mr. Heywood was detained contrary to his will?'

'I heard Churchill call out, "Keep them below." Who he meant I do not know.'

'Do you think he meant Heywood?'

'I have no reason to think any other.'[28]

Heywood could not ask, or hope, for better. This is testimony from one of the men thought to be innocent and it accords exactly with what he said happened: he and George Stewart had helped launch the boats, which they intended to go on, but were both sent below and then finally prevented from leaving their cabin by the armed Mr Churchill and Mr Thompson. The court only has to believe Mr Cole, and it is proof that Peter is innocent.

It concludes the day's proceedings, and with that Vice-Admiral Hood adjourns until 9 o'clock on the morrow. Still manacled, the accused clank their way out and are taken under armed guard back to the brig of the *Hector*, where they must spend a restless night – each man contemplating his chances of escaping the hangman's noose. For his part, Morrison knows that his own chances depend on how well his cross-examination of Mr Cole goes in the first session of the court on the following day.

9 am, 13 September 1792, HMS *Duke*, day two of the Mutineers' court martial

All rise.

And so the accused do – their faces lit by the morning light coming through the stern windows – as Vice-Admiral Hood and his fellow judges once again take their seats.

Now, if it please the court, James Morrison has a question for Mr Cole, hoping his testimony will be equally favourable for himself.

'Do you recollect,' he asks the Bosun, 'that I came to you when you was getting your own things . . . and telling you that the boat was then overloaded, and that Captain Bligh had begged that no more people should go into her, and that in consequence of that I would take my chance in the ship, and that you then shook me by the hand and said, "God bless you, my Boy, I will do you justice if ever I reach England"?'[29]

Take your time, Mr Cole, much hangs on your answer. The Bosun considers, rubs his chin, scratches his brow, and then turns to give his answer direct to the judges.

'I remember shaking hands with him,' Cole tells the judges, 'and he telling me that he would take his chance in the ship. I had no other reason to believe, but that he was intending to quit the ship. I do not remember the whole of our conversation; I *may* have said that "I would do him justice when I got to England" . . .'

Another rub, another scratch, and out comes a reflection that firms things up.

'I make no doubt but I did.'[30]

Morrison breathes again. It is wonderful testimony! As good as he could ask, or hope for.

Well, if Cole appears to be the best life-boat going to get out of here, Thomas Ellison is prepared to attempt to scramble upon it, no matter that it is overloaded, and so asserts his own rights to cross-examine the witness. For, another part of Mr Cole's testimony has it that he personally saw young Ellison bearing arms against Captain Bligh.

'Are you certain whether it was me or not,' he asks, 'as I was then a boy and scarcely able to lift a musket at that time?'

This time it requires no rubbing of the chin or scratching of the brow, for Cole has the answer immediately.

'He,' he says, pointing at Ellison, 'stood by Captain Bligh the best part of the time on the Quarter Deck with a musket and I believe there was a bayonet fixed.'[31]

Oh, God. Again, with just a few utterances, the court's view of what happened has widened, and deepened. For not only did Ellison bear a musket against his Captain, but also a *bayonet*!

And so to the next witness, the Gunner Mr Peckover, the salty old South Seas hand who, during the Mutiny, had instantly sided with Bligh and, thanks to his experience, was the first to suggest they sail for Timor.

Mr Peckover is led quickly to the point where he becomes aware that something is amiss.

'I was awaked out of my sleep by a confused noise,' Mr Peckover recounts. 'Directly after I thought I heard the fixing of bayonets . . . At the door I met Mr. Nelson the Botanist, who told me that the ship was taken from us. My answer was we were a long way from land . . . Mr. Nelson answered, "It is by our own People and Mr. Christian at their head" – or "has got the command," I don't know which . . . "but *we know whose fault it is*".'[32]

Sensation in the court!

Bligh's book had cited the late Mr Nelson as his old and true friend, the most faithful of all the faithful Loyalists, but even *he* thought the blame for the Mutiny lay with the Captain!

Now the court calls Mr Purcell, the ship's Carpenter, the very man who drove Captain Bligh to fury too many times to count. Though among the Loyalists, he is as far from 'a friend of Bligh' as it is possible to get – and it is for that reason that his testimony against the Mutineers is so important.

Most threatened by his words is the nervous Midshipman hanging on his every word, the one who risks to be soon hanging on something much more substantial still.

'Did you see Mr. Heywood standing upon the Booms?' the prosecutor asks him.

'Yes.'

'Had he a cutlass in his hand?'[33]

The court pauses. Leans closer. On his answer, much rests. For the military law could not be clearer: to be proven to bear arms in a mutiny is to be hanged.

So what is it, Mr Purcell? Was he holding a cutlass, or not?

'He was leaning the flat part of his hand on a cutlass on the booms,' Purcell replies, again in the manner of a man without sophistry, simply recalling what he saw, 'when I exclaimed, "In the name of God, Peter, what do you do with that?" when he instantly dropped it. One or two of the people had previous to that laid down their cutlasses, being armed with cutlasses and pistols, to assist in hoisting the Launch out.'[34]

After pursuing other lines of questioning, the prosecutors return to the point of Heywood and his cutlass . . .

'In what light did you look up at Mr. Heywood at the time you say he dropped the Cutlass on your speaking to him?'

'I looked upon him as a person *confused*,' Purcell says, 'and that he did not know that he had the weapon in his hand, or his hand being on it, for it was *not* in his hand.'

'What reason had you for supposing that he was so confused, as not to know that his hand was on it?'

'By his instantly dropping it and assisting in hoisting the boat out, which convinced me, in my own mind, that he had no hand in the conspiracy.'[35]

'When you say Mr. Heywood dropped the cutlass, did it fall down upon his taking his hands from it, or did he lay it down?'

'I think it *did* fall, to the best of my knowledge he did not lay it down.'[36]

Very well then. Watching on, Aaron Graham is clearly pleased.

Much better that he dropped it like a hot potato after realising how things might *appear*, rather than one who had been actively *participating* in the Mutiny, before coming to his senses.

But will this court see things like that? That, of course, remains to be seen as the next witness is called to the stand.

The testimony of Mr Purcell is also strongly in favour of James Morrison, as he attests that before the *Bounty* and the Launch had separated, Mr Morrison had specifically asked him, 'to take notice in the face of the whole of the Mutineers that he was prevented from coming into the Launch'.[37]

And so ends the second day.

The next morning, Midshipman Hayward, or Lieutenant Hayward as the recently promoted officer is now, is called and takes his place with an air of confidence. His has been an extraordinary experience. He is the top-ranking Loyalist present for this affair, an exemplar of duty before devilry, and he knows it. The very man who had waited hidden and listening next to the Captain's cabin in the *Pandora* as Captain Edwards attempted to trap Peter Heywood and George Stewart in a lie is now here, to give his own unvarnished, *untarnished*, account of what occurred – both on the day and, if needs be, on the two subsequent voyages he has taken to both Tahiti, and to Timor, *twice*, did he mention?

For now, while being sworn in, Hayward glowers at his former shipmates and, within the bounds of judicial respect – for they must not veer into anything resembling Contempt of Court – the accused glare back, for they have an expectation that his testimony will not be kind to them.

And they are correct . . .

'I had seen Lieutenant Bligh brought to the gangway held by Christian and surrounded by John Mills, who was at this time Armed,' Hayward begins his most crucial testimony, naming and shaming, condemning those he places right in the middle of the Mutiny. 'Thomas Burkett, the Prisoner, Matthew Quintal, John Sumner, John Millward, the Prisoner, William McCoy, and Thomas Ellison, the Prisoner, who came up rather in a hurry with a bayonet in his hand swearing, "Damn him, I will be sentry over him!"'[38]

Monkey is seen to slump in his seat.

His death sentence, effectively, has just been pronounced. The situation for Mr Burkett and Mr Millward is no better. (And Burkett's truthful claims that he had only ever joined the Mutiny at the wrong end of Billy McCoy's pistol, and then Fletcher Christian's; that he was the one who had covered Captain Bligh's bare buttocks; and if it wasn't for him pushing Quintal, the Loyalists would have had no compass at all . . . make little impression.)

But, for now, the course of the questioning moves on.

For the judges are particularly interested in Lieutenant Hayward's account of the actions of his former friend and messmate, Midshipman Peter Heywood.

Well, Hayward turns to the judges, 'I . . . perceived Peter Heywood . . . in his berth. I told him to go into the boat, but in my hurry do not remember to have received any answer.'[39]

Do you think Peter Heywood was one of the Mutineers?

'I should rather suppose [him] after my having told him to go into the boat and he not joining us, to be on the side of the mutineers.'

And Mr James Morrison? What of him?

At the question, Lieutenant Hayward changes his countenance entirely.

He has no doubt Mr Morrison was a Mutineer he informs the court, because he had closely observed his 'countenance' as he unloaded the Launch and found him 'rejoiced'. This was in strict contrast to Mr McIntosh, who Hayward is sure was not a Mutineer because his face looked, 'depressed'.[40]

And so back to Peter Heywood.

'What was Mr. Heywood employed about in his berth when you went below?'

'Nothing but sitting with his arms folded on his own chest, in the fore part of the berth.'

'Did you from his behaviour consider him as a person attached to his duty or to the party of the mutineers?'

Hayward chooses his words carefully.

'I should rather suppose, after my having told him to go into the boat, and he *not* joining us, to be on the side of the mutineers, but that must be only understood as an opinion as he was not in the least employed during the active part of it.'

'Did you observe any marks of joy or sorrow on his countenance or behaviour?'

'Sorrow.'

'You have said just now that you supposed McIntosh not to be attached to the Mutineers because he had a depressed countenance;

might not the sorrow that you perceived in the countenance of Peter Heywood arise from the same cause?'

'It might be so,'[41] Hayward allows carefully.

After more questioning that leads nowhere in particular, it is time for the accused to cross-examine the witness.

Morrison can barely wait, and wastes no time to get to his key question.

'You say that you observed joy in my countenance and that you are rather inclined to give it as your opinion that I was one of the mutineers,' he says firmly. 'Can you declare before God and this court that such evidence is not the result of a private pique?'

'No,' Hayward replies forcefully, 'it is not the result of any private pique, it is an opinion that I formed after quitting the ship, from the prisoner's not coming with us when he had as good an opportunity as the rest, there being more boats than one.'[42]

Morrison wastes no time in seizing the high ground.

'Can you deny,' he asks plaintively, for he knows that Lieutenant Hayward can do no such thing, 'that you were present when Captain Bligh begged that the Long Boat might not be overloaded and that he did say he would do justice to those who remained?'

'I was present at the time Lieutenant Bligh made such a declaration, but understood it as respecting clothes and other heavy articles with which the Boat was already too full.'[43]

Again, there is a stirring in the court.

In none of the published or circulated accounts, in none of the testimony so far, and nowhere within the parameters of common sense, has such an assertion been made and it is *prima facie*, ludicrous.

It is so ludicrous that Morrison can barely believe Hayward has said it.

And so to his most important question.

'Do you remember,' Morrison asks, 'any time on that day calling upon me to assist you in any point of duty or to give any assistance to retake His Majesty's Ship?'

'I have a faint remembrance,' Lieutenant Hayward allows, 'of a circumstance of that nature.'[44]

'Relate the Circumstance?' asks the prosecutor.

'It is so very faint,' Lieutenant Hayward says, 'that I can hardly remember it or the person who it was – but on seeing Charles Churchill upon the booms I thought that had I had a Friendly Island club, of which there were many on board, I could, had I not been observed, have gone forward, which was behind Churchill, and knocked him down; that was the time after handing the bag up, and the prisoner *might* have been the person whom I called to my assistance.'[45]

In an instant, Morrison follows up with his next question.

'What answer did I give to you?'

'I do not remember.'

'Did I say, "Go it, I'll back you, there is tools enough"?'

'I do not remember.'[46]

Though frustrated, there is nowhere further for Morrison to go, and he must cede the witness to William Muspratt – the only other Mutineer able to afford a lawyer – who has been aching to make his own cross-examination.

'In answer to a question just asked by Morrison,' Muspratt begins, 'you allow Captain Bligh used these words, "Don't let the boat be overloaded, my lads, I'll do you justice," which you say alluded to the clothes and other heavy articles. Do you mean to understand the latter words of "My lads I'll do you justice," to apply to *clothes* or to *men* whom he apprehended might go into the boat?'

Hayward is flustered at the question and becoming cross at being badgered, one after the other, by these (*sniff*) Mutineers.

'If Captain Bligh,' he says irritably, 'made use of the words "My lads," it was to the people already in the boat and not to those in the ship.'[47]

The looks on the faces of the members of the court indicate they are not merely incredulous that Captain Bligh could possibly have meant this, but also underwhelmed and even highly annoyed that Lieutenant Hayward could insist on such an absurdity in sworn testimony.

Midshipman Hallett, or 'that little wretch Hallett',[48] as Nessy Heywood will soon refer to him – and for good reason – is the next to bear witness. For the key to his testimony is indeed focused on his recollection of an episode involving Peter Heywood.

'When he was standing as I have before related,' Hallett says, 'Captain Bligh said something to him, but what I did not hear, upon which he *laughed*, turned round, and walked away.'[49]

Outrageous!

Heywood laughing in the face of a Captain bound to his mast is clearly the action of a scornful Mutineer, and a *scoundrel* at that, not that of a loyal Midshipman trying to find a way to seize back the ship.

Again the fatal pendulum of evidence seems to swing towards the young man being *guilty*.

But Heywood still has a chance to make the pendulum swing back, when his own time to give evidence comes. And at least he has time to prepare, devoting every waking hour of the weekend – which falls at exactly the right time – to writing, rewriting, and then rewriting some more, until he can write no more.

Come Monday, Heywood rises when summoned – the first defendant to be called to the dock on the day – and speaks in a low voice: 'Owing to the long and severe confinement I have suffered I am afraid I am not capable of delivering my defense with the force of expression it requires, and therefore desire one of my friends might read it for me.'

'Granted.'[50]

And so his lawyer, Mr Const, rises to read out Peter Heywood's carefully crafted statement.

Cleverly, Mr Heywood makes it clear from the first: he makes no claim to be a hero. He was a mere 16-year-old in the midst of a situation, the enormity of which was quite overwhelming for a frightened and confused young man.

'Add to my youth and inexperience that I was influenced in my conduct by the example of my messmates, Mr. Hallett and Mr. Hayward, the former of whom was very much agitated and the latter, though he had been many years at sea, yet, when Christian ordered him into the boat he was evidently alarmed at the perilous situation, and so much overcome by the harsh command, that he actually shed tears.'[51]

It is a bold tactic. Heywood is focusing the court's attention on the fact the very officers who have given sworn testimony against him – officers who the court feels kindly to, for their seemingly proven loyalty – in *fact*, had pleaded with the leader of the Mutineers to be allowed to stay with him, and *not* go with Captain Bligh! These men were his superiors, the ones setting the example!

'Such then was exactly my situation on board the *Bounty* – to be starved to death, or drowned, appeared to be inevitable if I went in the boat and surely it is not to be wondered at if at the age of sixteen years, with no one to advise with and so ignorant of the discipline of the service (having never been at sea before), as not to know or even suppose that it was possible that what I should determine upon might afterwards be alleged against me as a crime – : I say under such circumstances, in so trying a situation, can it be wondered at if I suffered the preservation of my life to be the first, and to supersede every other, consideration?'[52]

But to be clear, Heywood is *not* saying he wanted to get into the Launch himself. For, the truth is, no man did.

'Surely I shall not be deemed criminal that I hesitated at getting into a boat whose gunnel when she left the ship was not quite eight inches above the surface of the water. And if, in the moment of unexpected trial, fear and confusion assailed my untaught judgment and that by remaining in the ship I appeared to deny my Commander, it was in appearance only – it was the sin of my head, for I solemnly assure you before God that it was not the vileness of my heart.'[53]

With Mr Const enunciating words in a manner that somehow gives them added legal weight, Heywood's side of the story is put for the first time into the open public domain.

Of course he had wanted to stay loyal to Captain Bligh, but, how? For when he had tried to do exactly that, going with George Stewart back to his berth to collect their belongings, so they could take them onto the Launch, they were confronted with gun-wielding thugs who threatened their lives if they even tried.

Having hopefully established that key point, Heywood now begins his cross-examinations of the witnesses. And yes, his voice is nearly as wispy as his malnourished body. But it is soon apparent that there is absolutely nothing wrong with his sharp mind.

Standing, and only occasionally consulting the copious notes he has been taking throughout in his neat, well-educated artist's hand, Heywood takes on his persecutors, one by one.

Firstly, to Mr Fryer, he puts the critical question: 'If you had been permitted would you have stayed in the ship in preference to going into the boat?'

'Yes.'[54]

After more questions, he finally asks: 'What was my general temper and disposition on board the ship?'

'Beloved by everybody . . .' says Mr Fryer.[55]

William Cole is sworn.

'Did you,' Peter Heywood begins, 'consider me when helping to hoist out the Launch as assisting the Captain or the Mutineers?'

'By no means helping the Mutineers,' Cole replies to their Lordships. 'I thought him to be on the Captain's side.'[56]

Heywood also seeks to have Cole confirm the key pillar on which his innocence rests: he was kept below against his will.

'After I went below accompanied by Stewart, and while we were there, did you hear any orders, given to Thompson the sentinel upon the arms chest, "not to let them come up again" and by whom were such orders given?'

'I heard,' Cole allows, 'Churchill call out "keep them below!"'

'Do you think he meant me as one of them, whoever they were?'

'Yes, I do.'

'Although you cannot positively say it was me he meant to have confined, have you any doubt in your mind but that it was me?'

'None at all.'[57]

'Did you see Mr. Hayward upon deck during the time of the Mutiny?'

'Yes.'

'In what state did he appear to be – was he cool and collected, or did he seem agitated and alarmed?'

'More alarmed.'

'Did you see Mr. Hallett upon deck during the time of the Mutiny?'

'Yes.'

'In what state did he appear to be, was he cool and collected or did he seem agitated and alarmed?'

'Alarmed.'[58]

Heywood's point is eloquently made . . . without him even having to say it. It is all very well for the likes of Lieutenant Hayward and

Mr Hallett to present themselves as cool Loyalists, now capable of recalling precise details and conversations that point to the guilt of others. But at the time they were not like that at all. At the time they were two agitated, alarmed men in tears. So what is their evidence now truly worth?

William Peckover is sworn next and testifies in favour of Heywood's innocence.

Mr Purcell is to be questioned next, which is delicate – for the Carpenter has already told the court he personally saw the hand of Heywood holding a cutlass, at the height of the Mutiny – and that testimony must be either recanted, or at least countered.

'Did you consider me – when assisting to hoist out the Launch – as helping the Captain or the Mutineers?'

'The Captain,' Purcell replies, unequivocally.

With such a good start, Heywood is quick to follow up.

'After what you have said respecting the cutlass on which you say my hand rested, just as the Launch was going to be hoisted out, I would ask you whether, on the most mature consideration of the matter, you did then, or you do now, believe that I could be considered as an Armed Man?'

'No.'[59]

Even better!

The next witness is someone Heywood has longed to question publicly for many months. It is Captain Edwards of the *Pandora*.

'Did I,' Peter Heywood asks pointedly, 'surrender myself to you upon the arrival of the *Pandora* at Tahiti?'

'Not to me,' Edwards replies carefully, again addressing his remarks to the bench of Admiral judges, 'but to the Lieutenant. I apprehend he put himself in my power – I always understood he came voluntarily.'

'Did I give to you such information respecting myself and the *Bounty* as afterwards proved true?'

'He gave me some information respecting the people in the Island, that corroborated with Coleman's. I do not recollect the particular conversation, but in general it agreed with the account given by Coleman.'[60]

Now, as it happens, the court itself has some questions for Captain Edwards about what Midshipman Heywood told him, on one particular matter.

'Did Peter Heywood give you any account of the transactions of the *Bounty* after the boat was turned adrift to her return to Matavai Bay, Tahiti?'

'Yes, I had conversations with Heywood upon that subject, but I do not recollect all the conversation that passed.'[61]

Well, that's all right, because Heywood recalls the conversation down to the tiniest detail, and has had a great deal of time to reflect on its significance.

'When I told you that I went away the first time from Tahiti with the Pirates did I not at the same time inform you that it was *not possible* to separate myself from Christian, who would not permit *any* man of the party to leave him at that time, lest, by giving intelligence, they might have been discovered, whenever a ship should arrive?'[62]

'Yes, but I do not recollect the latter part of it respecting giving intelligence,'[63] Captain Edwards replies.

The only thing that counts, of course, is the 'Yes'.

And finally, at Heywood's prompting, Lieutenant Larkin affirms to the court the young Midshipman had paddled to *Pandora* just after it dropped anchor, and voluntarily gave himself up.

Was this the action of a man who knew himself to be guilty?

The defence of Peter Heywood is complete.

Following Heywood's lead, Morrison now hands over his own written defence, with Judge Advocate Moses Greetham assigned to read it to the court.

'Conscious of my own innocence of every article of the charge exhibited against me, and fully satisfied of my zeal for His Majesty's service, I offer the following narration in vindication of my conduct . . .'[64]

Morrison steadies his gaze on the members of the court.

'My countenance has been compared with that of another employed on the same business. This . . . court knows that all men do not bear their misfortunes with the same fortitude . . . and that the face is too often a bad index to the heart. If there were no sorrow marked in my countenance, it was to deceive those whose act I abhorred that I might be at liberty to seize the first opportunity . . . favourable to the re-taking of the ship.'[65]

All that remains is for the rest of the accused to make final written submissions, in their own hand – and then wait for the verdict to be handed down.

Of all of the written submissions, it is perhaps the one provided by young Thomas Ellison, 'Monkey', which is the most touching . . .

> *I hope your honours will take my Inexpearence'd Youth into Consideration, as I never did or ment any harm to anyone, much more to my Commander . . . Capt. Bligh took great pains with me and spoke too Mr. Samule, his Clark, to teach me Writing and Arithmetick and I believe Would have taught me further had not this hap pend. I must have been very Ingreatfull if I had in any respect assisted in this Unhappy Affair agains my Commander and Benefactor, so I hope, honorable Gentlemen, yo'll be so Kind as to take my Case into Consideration as I was No more than between Sixteen and Seventeen Years of age when this of done. Honourable Gentlemen, I leave my self at the Clemency and Mercy of this Honourable Court.*
>
> *I am with great Respect*
> *Hond. Gentlemen Obt. Humble. Sert.*
> *THOMAS ELLISON.*[66]

Court adjourned.

Mid-September 1792, South Pacific, a feeling of *déjà vu*

For Captain Bligh, it is a strange thing to be passing once more through the islands of the South Pacific, this time on a ship, with plenty of supplies and space – and not fighting for their lives on a tiny Launch. Oh, the memories: scrawling the charts, fighting with Natives and the wretched duo Mssrs Fryer and Purcell, starving, burning up in the sun. It all seems so long ago. What a pleasure it is now – although he has not yet recovered his health – to be sleeping in his own comfortable cabin, dining three times a day, slaking his thirst as he desires, always remaining dry and warm, and able to call on his cannon should ever the soldiers have a problem with the locals!

And, of course, the whole experience is all so much sweeter for knowing that his own conduct has not only been vindicated – he is blameless – but, more than that, he is the toast of London, respected by all men of influence.

18 September 1792, Portsmouth, a decision is made

The president of the court martial, the venerable Vice-Admiral Hood, gazes at the ten Navy men accused of mutiny and asks them in the manner of a deeply disappointed father who cannot quite believe it has come to this: 'Do you have anything more to offer the court in your defense?'[67]

No.

And so the end. The courtroom is cleared, allowing the judges to deliberate and reach their verdict in sacred seclusion. At least deliberations do not last long.

For, look there!

Like a puff of white smoke above the Vatican when a decision has been reached on a new Pope, for this occasion, the yellow flag is taken down on the *Duke*'s foremast to indicate that their honours have reached their verdict.

The prisoners, thus, are retrieved by the Provost Marshal from the brig, still in chains, and obliged to stand in a line before the Admirals and Captains, the audience shuffling in around them, as Vice-Admiral Samuel Hood holds the verdicts in his venerable hands.

He proceeds with little ceremony, voice solemn.

'The charges have been proved against the said Peter Heywood, James Morrison, Thomas Ellison, Thomas Burkitt [sic], John Millward and William Muspratt, and [this court] does adjudge them and each of them to suffer death by being hanged by the neck . . .'[68]

Heywood reels, his breath coming in strangled gasps, his heart beating as if it will burst through his chest. After all that has been done! All the testimony to his good character, to his not bearing arms, to his extreme sorrow on the morning, his willingness to go on the Launch with Bligh, all the work done by dear Nessy and Commander Pasley behind the scenes! After all this, he is to still twist in the wind, lifeless, hanging from a yardarm, not yet 21 years old, while the fleet in the harbour watches?

The other condemned men are having much the same reaction. They slump, as their open grave now yawns before them.

And yet, Vice-Admiral Hood is not finished.

Clearing his throat, he goes on: 'But the court, in consideration of various circumstances, does humbly and most earnestly recommend the said Peter Heywood and James Morrison to His Majesty's Royal Mercy.'[69]

Heywood's and Morrison's breaths regulate a little. Their wild terror lessens just a little. At least there is a reasonable chance they will live, depending on the good graces of King George, who will surely be disposed to take the advice of the wise members of the court martial . . . they hope.

Alas, for some of these men, their brothers of the sea, with whom they have endured so much, their fate is sealed. Theirs has been a short and brutal life, shortly to come to a singularly brutal end, at the end of a rope.

As to the four men singled out by Bligh as innocent, Vice-Admiral Hood duly pronounces: 'The Court further agrees that the charges have not been proved against the said Charles Norman, Joseph Coleman, Thomas McIntosh and Michael Byrne, and did adjudge them and each of them acquitted.'[70]

Joyously liberated, those four are now free men once more and, with their manacles removed by the Marines, are soon filing out of the creaking, wooden room with a newfound spring in their step.

•

That night, as Peter Heywood sits slumped on the *Hector*, grieving for the fate of the condemned around him, living in hope that he will not soon be joining them if the King declines the plea for mercy, his family are at home, none the wiser. For fate has contrived a storm

ENGLAND
Peter Heywood's family waiting to hear news

for the ages that now breaks over the Isle of Man, unleashing such towering seas and contrary winds that, for the better part of a week, no ship can arrive or leave, and the family have no choice but to wait it out in agonising suspense.

On the evening of 24 September, Mrs Heywood and her daughters are in their gracious home, sitting down to their evening meal and discussing what they are always discussing, the possible fate of dear

Peter, and, as ever, are 'fondly flattering themselves with everything being most happily concluded',[71] when there is a clatter in the parlour.

Ah. It is the dear little boy from down the street, who has burst unbidden into their home, so important is the news he is to impart. 'The trial is over!! All the prisoners are to be hanged! Peter is sentenced to be hanged.'[72]

NO! God no! No, the Lord cannot be so cruel!

As her mother wails the wail of mothers through the ages whose young are torn from their breast and about to be thrown to the wolves, it is Nessy who takes the matter in her hands – literally grabbing the boy by both shoulders and questioning him closely.

How do you know this?

I talked to a sailor down by the docks, who had just arrived from the mainland.

Could you find him again?

Probably.

It takes some doing and yet, while Mrs Heywood continues to weep, within the hour *home is the sailor, home from the sea, and the hunter home from the hill,*[73] as Nessy sits him down in the front parlour.

Is it confirmed? Is Peter to hang?

No. No, it is not confirmed.

The little boy has got it wrong.

The way the sailor remembers it, he thinks, but he cannot be sure, that Heywood and one other, may have been 'recommended to mercy'.[74] He had merely scanned briefly a report in a Liverpool newspaper, just before boarding his ship which was bound for here, the Isle of Man, and he had neglected to bring the said paper with him.

It is doubtful if anything could further compound the family's agony of not knowing.

Still the contrary winds blow, cutting off all sea traffic again.

5 October 1792, London, a sister's love is like no other

That elegant young woman with the small bag hurrying with such an evident sense of purpose through the streets of London? It is Nessy Heywood, now making her way to the home of Peter's lawyer, Aaron

Graham. Yes, many have offered their assurances that Peter will be pardoned, but she needs to hear the actual *situation*, not mere speculation, from Mr Graham himself. No more rumours, no more whispers.

Pounding on the door of Graham's stylish terrace house in Great Russell Street, Bloomsbury, she is relieved when it is opened by the man himself, and within seconds has received the confirmation she has dreamed of. At least, after a manner . . .

For, yes!

Peter *has* been recommended for the King's mercy, and there is every chance it will be granted! (Quietly, privately, Graham is not as confident as he makes out to Nessy, for there truly also is a good chance that the King could deny clemency for the overall good of the Royal Navy.)

Nessy Heywood's entire body, her very soul, melts. A good chance that Peter will live, and take his place amongst the family once more!

For his part, Peter Heywood does not allow himself to be so optimistic, soon writing to Nessy:

> *Alas! It is but a broken stick which I have leaned on, and it has pierced my soul in such a manner that I will never more trust to it, but wait with a contented mind and patience for the final accomplishment of the Divine will . . . Mrs. Hope is a faithless and ungrateful acquaintance, with whom I have now broken off all connexions, and in her stead have endeavoured to cultivate a more sure friendship with Resignation, in full trust of finding her more constant.*[75]

One convicted Mutineer, Mr Muspratt, needs no mercy or pardon as he has something just as useful to a guilty man, a very clever lawyer. His counsel, Mr Stephen Barney, has lodged an appeal on the grounds that, despite formal request, Muspratt was not allowed to question either Mr Coleman or blind Byrn, as the court incorrectly treated them as Mutineers, though they were *not* named as such by Captain Bligh. This denial of natural justice is a legal loophole that now leads to Mr Muspratt's head escaping the loop of the noose. A convicted Mutineer, he walks free. Resignation and Hope may be constants, but so is the fact that the Law is an Ass.

10 October 1792, the Mutineer's messenger

James Morrison is relying on the Reverend Howell, who is busy circulating copies of Morrison's narrative among influential naval officers and other men of note.

And so the tales quietly begin to spread.

One copy of his manuscript is even sent to the great Sir Joseph Banks, with the Reverend Howell writing a note to their mutual friend Mr Molesworth Phillips, hoping he will draw Sir Joseph's attention to it.

> It is very natural for Sir Joseph Banks not to think so unfavourably of Bligh as you or I may – there was a time when no one could have a higher opinion of an officer as I had of him – so many circumstances, however, have arisen up against him with such striking marks of veracity that I have been compelled to change that idea of him into one of a very contrary nature.[76]

The efforts of Reverend Howell achieve marked results as the word carries quickly. In the course of his career, Bligh has managed to anger many in the naval service with his thrusting nature, his temper and his abrasive brilliance, and many have had a sneaking sympathy for the Mutineers from the first. Now, as they read and hear of Morrison's account, their suspicions quickly crystallise into convictions – there really is another side to the story.

Some of the newspapers are even sympathetic, starting with the inhuman treatment of the men on the *Pandora*, with the *Times* of London noting:

> The sufferings of the unhappy mutineers of the Bounty were greater than it could be imagined human nature is capable of bearing. They have been upwards of nineteen months in irons, fastened to a bar, five months of which time both legs and hands were secured, when they were entirely without clothing, till the natives of a friendly island procured them such articles as they could part with.[77]

Mid-October 1792, Coupang, Timor, Bligh arrives once more

As the wheels of justice grind slowly but surely forward in England, Captain William Bligh is in Coupang once more – re-victualling his ship – on his way to Jamaica with 1100 bread-fruit plants on board. The trip from Tahiti thus far has been relatively calm, and certainly an easier one than the last time he had travelled in these parts.

And it is good to be back in Coupang, under better circumstances.

Though in the throes of a nasty fever, Bligh has just received happy and unhappy news from the newly appointed Governor, his old friend, *Heer* Timotheus Wanjon, who had helped him so on his first arrival at this lonely port in Timor. Happily, Bligh hears Captain Edwards has found and arrested some of the *Bounty* Mutineers in Tahiti! And even though Edwards had lost his ship off New Holland on the way back, most of them had survived and the captured Mutineers would surely be back in England now facing trial.

Which is to the good.

Alas, Fletcher Christian and much of his band of brigands had not been among those captured, and they are still at large.

Curse, Christian, for the damned, villainous scoundrel that he is! Where on earth can he be?

•

On this morning of 24 October 1792, the blessed news spreads among the Pasley circle in the Royal Navy. In his divine wisdom – and at the recommendation of the fine Navy officers who presided over the court martial – the King has stamped the Great Seal upon a Royal Pardon to Peter Heywood and James Morrison!

Nessy is at Mr Graham's home in London when she hears that her prayers have been answered, and that the official order is now en route to Portsmouth. Immediately, she writes to her mother:

> *Oh, blessed hour! Little did I think, my beloved friends, when I closed my letter this morning, that before night I should be out of my senses with joy! . . . I cannot speak my happiness; let it be sufficient to say, that . . . our angel Peter will be FREE! Mr Graham goes this night to Portsmouth, and tomorrow, or next day at farthest, I shall be – oh,*

heavens! What shall I be? . . . how shall I bear to clasp him to the
bosom of your happy, ah! how very happy and affectionate.[78]

27 October 1792, Portsmouth, the fateful morning is arrived

It is time.

Bright and early, on this exceedingly sparkling day, Portsmouth's Provost Marshal, flanked by a tight knot of grim-faced Marines, drops down the companionway of HMS *Hector* to collect the two potentially pardoned *Bounty* men, Peter Heywood and James Morrison, from the bowels of the ship that has been their prison these last four months.

Blinking in the sudden light, they are brought up on deck before Captain Sir George Montagu, one of the honourable members of the Mutineers' Court Martial – in full regalia, like now, he is the human equivalent of a ship of the realm with billowing sails – who now puffs himself up and stands tall, as he executes his duty, to officially read out His Gracious Majesty's . . . unconditional Pardon. Weak with relief, the two men, who have grown ever closer through their trials and tribulations, warmly embrace each other.

And now, rising to the occasion, Peter Heywood expresses his gratitude, speaking clearly and looking straight at the good Captain:

'I receive with gratitude my Sovereign's mercy, for which, my future life shall be faithfully devoted to His Service.'[79]

Heywood, solemn, says goodbye to the three condemned Mutineers he must leave behind, and is led into the blessedly bright first rays of sunlight on deck, where Mr Graham and Peter's brother James – who has been dispatched to Portsmouth for the occasion – await. The brothers embrace, and are soon whisked away to the shore, Peter Heywood stepping on the shores of England as a free man!

There remains, however, a few more formalities to attend to before they can leave for the shining lights of London, and so the two brothers are accommodated by a friend of Mr Graham's. Still, Mr Graham himself is keenly aware that there is one person who deserves no delay whatsoever, who is even now waiting and agonising, and who it is his duty to inform at least the thrust of the wonderful news. And so he writes a letter to her immediately for delivery by the next fast coach.

My Dearest Nessy,

If you expect me to enter into particulars as to how I got him, when I got him, and where I got him, you will be disappointed . . . suffice it to say, that he is now with me, and well; not on board the Hector, *but at the house of a very worthy man . . .*[80]

He tells her to expect their arrival in two days time. And now Peter wishes to add a note at the end of Mr Graham's letter: 'Be patient my dearest Nessy, a few hours and you will embrace your long-lost and most affectionate brother, Peter Heywood.'[81]

As for skinny, ragged Morrison, though free to go – and yes, he has quietly agreed that, once freed, he will keep the damning narrative that Reverend Howell circulated *out* of the public realm – he has no well-connected relatives waiting with horse and carriage to whisk him away, and stays in Portsmouth, for there is something he still has to do in these parts.

True to his word, on the morning of 29 October, a horse and carriage pulls up outside Aaron Graham's London townhouse, at which point the door bursts open and Nessy Heywood rushes forth. Blind with joy at the sight of her youngest brother James escorting her beloved Peter, she falls into his arms, as they embrace for the first time in over four years, weeping – not like there is no tomorrow, but because there *is* a tomorrow.

Within the hour, again, Nessy writes to her mother:

Great Russell Street, Monday Morning, 29th October, half-past ten o'clock – the brightest moment of my existence!

MY DEAREST MAMMA, – I have seen him, clasped him to my bosom, and my felicity is beyond expression! In person he is almost even now as I could wish; in mind you know him an angel. I can write no more, but to tell you, that the three happiest beings at this moment on earth, are your most dutiful and affectionate children,

And the three children each sign the letter their delighted mother will read:

Nessy Heywood, Peter Heywood, James Heywood

'Love to and from all <u>ten thousand times</u>.'[82]

It is truly the best of times.

•

But even as Nessy and James Heywood are embracing their brother Peter in London, things are being prepared for a grisly ritual that has been a long time coming.

Atop the foremast of HMS *Brunswick*, a yellow flag – 'the signal of death'[83] – flutters in the gentle breeze. The ship Captains in Portsmouth Harbour had drawn lots to see on whose ship the execution would take place. Captain Roger Curtis of the *Brunswick* feels cursed to draw the short straw – it is bad luck to have hangings on your ship.

A signal cannon on the shoreline is suddenly fired, sending a shattering boom rolling out across the waters in all directions. After the *Brunswick* fires its own cannon in reply, vessels of all sizes start to converge from all points of the compass and the ship is soon the central point of a tight circle of boats, with the decks of each one packed with sailors, obliged to witness what happens to those who have violated the Articles of War.

A shroud of deathly silence descends upon the armada, as all wait for what they know must be coming next.

Down below, in the gunroom of the *Brunswick*, the three condemned Mutineers – Thomas Ellison, John Millward and Thomas Burkett – are sitting with a clergyman, when they hear the sound of many boots approaching, marching in deadly unison. And here, now, is the Provost Marshal, with a platoon of red-coated Marines behind him. With a face like granite, he mutters an order to one of the Marines, who quickly steps forward and removes the chains of the condemned, before taking them up towards the deck, the solemn procession led by a clergyman and one other man they have chosen to have present for the occasion . . . Mr Morrison.

Yes, it is none other than James Morrison who the condemned men wish to read the final prayers they will ever hear.[84] Arriving on deck – also blinking despite the rather gloomy day – they see the poop deck, at the rear of the ship, crowded with high officers, including

Vice-Admiral Hood and many of the Captains who sentenced them, come to see their sentence carried out. Around them is a whole sea of grim red-coats, all with their bayonets attached to their muskets. Just let one of them try to make a run for it, leaping over the side, and they will be struck and stuck like a squealing pig, in seconds. There can be no escape.

In the face of it all, two of the three seem to shrink somewhat. But as John Millward alone rises to the occasion, straightening his shoulders and whispering words unknown to the others, they, too, seem to lift themselves.

Still, for 30 minutes, the doomed men kneel with the clergyman, Mr Morrison by their side, as they say their prayers and beg the Holy Father forgiveness of their sins and trespasses, their misdemeanours and . . . mutinies.

At length, however, it is time and after they are led to the quarter-deck where the whole thing is to take place – young Thomas Ellison now recovered enough to even wave to a few of the people he recognises in the surrounding craft – the group divides. While Monkey and Millward are to be hanged from the yardarm off the mizzenmast on the larboard side, Burkett will be hanged from the starboard arm. That way, everyone, all around, will be able to have an unimpeded view of at least one of them hanging. As they take their positions, the attention of each man is inevitably drawn to the noose that waits, swinging lightly, exactly – as per regulation – five feet above the deck. At the other end of each of the three ropes – though looped through the block and tackle that hangs exactly a foot below the mizzen yard, a third of the way up the mast – are 20 sailors in column formation, each gripping their section of rope, grimly contemplating what they are about to do.

After a corporal reads out the charges, the condemned men are asked if they have any last words. Both Burkett and Ellison look to Millward, who in turn nods to James Morrison, who hands him a piece of paper, which, in a booming, confident voice, the condemned man now reads from, hoping all of the assembled crews on the gathered ships may hear.

'Brother Seamen,' Millward begins, 'you see before you three lusty young fellows about to suffer a shameful death for the dreadful crime of mutiny and desertion. Take warning by our example never to desert your officers, and should they behave ill to you, remember: it is *not* their cause, it is *the cause of your country* you are bound to support.'[85]

And now the nooses that have swayed before them are placed by Morrison himself around their necks and tightened, under their chins, so that, when the moment comes, it will not slip off their heads. Morrison also places the blue bags over their heads, whispering as he does so. Both Thomas Ellison and Thomas Burkett bow their heads meekly to allow the bag to be so placed. Their arms are now tied tightly behind them, so there can be no possibility of loosening the noose with their hands.

All is in readiness.

With a nod from Vice-Admiral Hood, at 11.26 am, two of the *Brunswick*'s cannon are fired, belching out simultaneous thunderous roars and a growing plume of smoke. The columns of sailors instantly respond by . . . hauling on the ropes . . . as all three convicted Mutineers are hauled off the ground by their necks . . . For those closest to the men hanging there is a deathly cracking as neck vertebrae break, mixed with an unearthly gurgling as they begin to strangle. The spectators in the boats and on the ships all around squint to see through the haze of smoke, but it is not until some moments later, as the cloud dissipates, that they see three limp bodies dangling from the yardarms above.

Some six yards above the deck, and one yard below the pulleys, the bodies stop rising and swing in the wind, as large stains show up on their trousers now fouled.

It will take another 30 minutes before their legs stop shaking and there are no further signs of life. For the next two hours, the bodies are left swinging there, lightly twisting in the wind, before – in marked contrast to the violence with which they have been raised – their lifeless bodies are lowered with extraordinary gentleness.

CHAPTER SEVENTEEN

BEFORE THE COURT OF THE PEOPLE

I find that two months after I left Tahiti in the 'Bounty', Christian
returned in her to the great astonishment of the natives. Doubting
that things had gone well with me the first questions they asked
were: 'Where is Bry?' 'He is gone,' he replied, 'to England'. 'In
what ship?' asked the natives. 'In Toote's ship.'[1]

Captain Bligh's Log notes on his return to Tahiti, 9 April 1792

Mid-November 1792, Downing College, Cambridge University, a man of letters

A few days after the three Mutineers are hanged, Edward Christian, the dignified-looking Professor of Law, walks into his dark chambers in Cambridge University to find a letter sitting in the middle of his mahogany desk. Opening it, he reads . . .

Sir,

I am sorry to say I have been informed you were inclined to judge too harshly of your truly unfortunate brother; and to think of him in such a manner as I am conscious, from the knowledge I had of his most worthy disposition and character, (both public and private) he merits not in the slightest degree: therefore I think it my duty to undeceive you, and to rekindle the flame of brotherly love (or pity now) towards him, which, I fear, the false reports of slander and vile suspicion may have nearly extinguished.

> *. . . your brother was not that vile wretch, void of all gratitude,*
> *which the world had the unkindness to think him; but on the contrary,*
> *a most worthy character, ruined only by having the misfortune (if it can*
> *be so called) of being a young man of strict honour and adorned with*
> *every virtue and beloved by all (except one, whose ill report is his greatest*
> *praise) who had the pleasure of acquaintance.*
>
> *I am sir, with esteem,*
> *Your most obedient humble servant*
> *P. Heywood*[2]

Peter Heywood's courage in writing such a letter – attempting to right wrongs, even though he is now free, and is risking his own future career – is to be commended, and Professor Christian is determined to meet him. In careful language, he writes back, arranging it.

•

Faraway, on the other side of the world, William Bligh, still bent on revenge, remains unaware that three of the Mutineers have now received what he had always hoped for them – to swing at the end of a rope, disgraced.

But while Bligh sails on contentedly – a hero of his generation, his bread-fruit-laden ship heading at a rate of knots towards the West Indies – Fletcher Christian still tosses and turns in the night, frequently waking in a pool of sweat, panicky, wondering, questioning . . . what *has* he done?

•

Knock, knock.

Professor Edward Christian opens the door and Peter Heywood slips inside, clearly relieved to be away from the public gaze.

They retire to the professor's study to talk, its walls all but leather-lined as its shelves groan under the weight of hundreds of law books, giving an air of august justice to their discussion. Professor Christian listens, rapt, jotting down notes, as this well-spoken young man unburdens himself of all the horrors of the voyage; all of Bligh's capricious viciousness, his explosions over trifles, his needless humiliation of all and sundry. And he also talks of the faithful promise he had made Fletcher, back in Tahiti, that in the unlikely event he got back to England, he would do his best to set the record straight on both Captain Bligh and Fletcher Christian. For his part, Professor Christian is most interested in how his brother Fletcher had reacted to Bligh, how he had tried to temper the temper, calm with balm the searing soul, only to slowly come to the conclusion that there was no other way – for manhood alone demanded it – than to rise against the tyrant.

In response to Heywood's remarkable account, Fletcher's older brother is convinced that more people need to hear the true story.

And so he convenes an informal court of his own, a gathering of eminent citizens of undoubted integrity who he regularly convenes, to hear the evidence of the men of the *Bounty*. Yes, it takes a little persuasion to get the *Bounty* men to speak openly to strangers about what they have only whispered between each other to this point, but all are assured, and come to believe, that their testimony will be treated with the utmost confidence.

Over many evenings, Fryer, Purcell, Lebogue, McIntosh and Heywood make their way to anonymous-looking lodgings, even an inn if necessary, look left, look right, and slip inside, where they are received with enormous warmth. Professor Edward Christian carefully takes down every word.

•

Bligh, meanwhile, is entirely ignorant that this cannon of words against his good name is being loaded, and he continues on his second breadfruit voyage. And yet, there is little doubt that his current officers are becoming aware of what life was like for Fletcher Christian. Even Lieutenant Frank Bond, Bligh's nephew, has found that, once aboard the good ship *Providence*, his formerly kind uncle has become a man transformed, full of scorn, insult and endless criticism – and that is just to a family member.

As Frank writes to his brother, 'Yes Tom, our relative had the credit of being a tyrant in his last expedition . . . The very high opinion he has of himself makes him hold every one of our profession with contempt, perhaps envy; nay the Navy is but a sphere for fops and lubbers to swarm in, without one gem to vie in brilliancy with himself . . .'[3]

Still, for all Bligh's flaws of character, young Frank is impressed by both Uncle William's brilliance as a navigator and, he also can't help but note, how, 'In a time of real danger what a change to cordiality and kindness!' For example, when they are suddenly hit by a howling wind, and thunderous waves, as a storm crashes down upon them, Bligh blames only himself: 'Oh Frank! What a situation! Into what a danger I have brought you! God grant that we may get safe out of it!'[4]

For, precisely as Fletcher Christian had observed, the insufferable Bligh does have a good side, and it is never more apparent than when there is a crisis requiring all of his skills and attributes, whereupon, for some strange reason, the humanity that actually nestles somewhere deep in the wings shuffles forward and takes centre stage. It is only when at leisure that he starts to pick and peck at every scab he can find.

And yet, despite all of the storms, all the squalls, both inside and outside the ship, the expedition is a complete success, with 830 bread-fruit plants delivered alive and well to the islands of the West Indies in the early months of January 1793 and a satisfied Bligh and his infinitely relieved crew arrive back at Deptford on the Thames on 7 August 1793.

•

On Pitcairn Island in this September of 1793, all has been relatively calm, if not quite happy, for the last two years. Well, the Mutineers, at least, have been happy. But the Natives . . . a little less so.

They have been brooding on their lot, and trouble is brewing once more. For the Natives, daily life is an endless round of repetitive chores. Every morning, the most important thing is to catch seabirds to feed their masters, followed by catching more seabirds to feed the hogs of their masters! Their very manhood is insulted. This is not what they were raised to do, and nowhere near what they imagined when they came away on the *Bounty*. A very few of the Mutineers – most notably Fletcher Christian and Ned Young – treat them decently, almost as if they are equals. But the others – with none worse than McCoy and Quintal – are harsh taskmasters.

Such is the level of unhappiness among the Natives that, just as had happened with the death of Jack Williams' wife, it does not take much to set things off. And so it goes when the ever-faithful Menalee, who is so close to the white men he is practically a tenth Mutineer, takes it into his head that he has as much right to Billy McCoy's pig as McCoy has, having done much more than McCoy to look after it for the past four years on Pitcairn.

McCoy takes a different view, as evidenced by those screams you can hear, interspersed with that sickening sound of a whip cutting into flesh. Bound to a post, Menalee is whipped to within an inch of his life by the scarred McCoy, who then rubs salt into every wound for good measure. Menalee's howls of agony manage to haunt the entire island, chill the white men and enrage the Natives. This is nothing less than a slave being tortured by his Master.

Fletcher Christian is appalled, but powerless to stop it. Their paradise is as long gone as his authority. He is now just one farmer hearing another punish a 'thief' who 'stole' his hog.

All that Menalee knows is that it causes him more pain than he has ever known in his life, and he bitterly resents it.

When, shortly afterwards, the faithful Timoa is spotted by one of the women taking yams – just as if he were a white man, and had some right to them – Matt Quintal also administers a beating.

Though a sympathetic Ned Young consoles Menalee and Timoa, these are spiritual wounds that won't heal. The Native men have had *enough*. Are they proud men, or are they beaten slaves? The choice is theirs, and in secret meetings they come to one inalterable conclusion. The white men must be killed. The slaves must become masters of Pitcairn.

•

All up, Bligh finds things since his return very strange.

The last time he had returned to England – after the Mutiny – he had been the hero of the hour, given an audience with King George III. This time? There has been . . . nothing. He waits, day after day, week after week, but still he receives no summons.

Even when he goes to the Admiralty and sits there throughout the day, day after day, nothing happens and, with ever-growing embarrassment, the truth slowly comes to Bligh. This is no unfortunate oversight. This is nothing less than a deliberate snub.

Each night, Bligh returns to the *Providence* – as the mission is not formally complete, and he can only make dashing visits to and from his cherished family – and fumes.

When the Duke of Clarence – who is no less than the son of King George III – calls on the *Providence* and asks Bligh if Lord Chatham has presented him to the King yet, Bligh is embarrassed to inform him that, as a matter of fact, he has not even been presented to Lord Chatham yet.

Bligh is at least pleased with the Duke's obvious shock, as he says in wonder, 'Here is an officer that has acquitted himself in the highest manner, and the First Lord of the Admiralty will not see him!'[5]

Oh, but it is to get worse, still.

In late September 1793, nearly *two months* after arriving in England, Captain Bligh sits fuming in his hated but customary position – waiting unattended in a hallway of the inner sanctum of the Admiralty, desperate to see Lord Chatham – when he looks up to see a familiar figure.

Alas, it is not Lord Chatham.

No, it is Bligh's *junior officer*, Lieutenant Nathaniel Portlock – who commanded HMS *Assistant*, which accompanied the *Providence* – who has been summoned, as his own Captain and Commander waits! It is unheard of, it is outrageous and it is clearly a calculated insult.

All that Bligh is told by way of reason for this infernal delay is that Lord Chatham simply wishes to have sufficient time to receive a full report from Bligh.

Soon enough the word spreads, and everybody in Bligh's naval circles realises what is really going on here.

(Privately, Matthew Flinders, the notably brilliant young Midshipman who'd accompanied Bligh to Tahiti on his second voyage, gets word of his current Captain's standing from his old Captain, Peter Heywood's uncle. Commander Pasley tells him 'Your Captain will meet a very hard reception – he has damned himself.'[6])

Bligh, the Royal Navy Captain who was the hero of England less than a year ago, is now nothing less than *persona non grata*, as word has spread in official circles of what had actually happened, courtesy of the influential Professor Edward Christian's secret gatherings.

For Bligh, it is about to get even worse.

Can you hear it? In the distance, there is that clanking sound, punctuated by regular thumps. That, dear friends, is a printing press pumping out thousands of copies of a document that has one aim – to destroy the reputation of Captain William Bligh.

•

All is in readiness.

For the last few weeks, all of the Natives have been on their best behaviour, working hard and co-operating with every request. At all costs, they must allay the suspicions of the Mutineers, even as they get ready for the big day to come.

But no more; the big day is today. The Mutineers are all separated from each other. The women have gone to the cliffs, to collect eggs and hunt seabirds.

To get things started, the cunning Native, Tetaheite, approaches Jenny's husband, Isaac Martin.

'Can I have your gun,' he asks politely, 'as I would like to go hog shooting today.'

Certainly. Martin hands the gun over, and returns to ploughing his fields.

Taking the gun, Tetaheite meets the waiting Timoa and Nehow at Jack Williams' property.

Are we going to do this?

We are going to do this.

There is Jack Williams now, working in his own fields, the very Jack Williams who had first stolen Talalo's wife, Toofaiti.

He deserves this.

Stealthily, they approach Williams from behind.

Ready?

Now!

As Timoa and Nehow fall upon Williams and cover his mouth, Tetaheite brings the muzzle to Williams' belly and shoots him point-blank, killing him all but instantly.

They return to Isaac Martin, who hails Tetaheite heartily.

'Well done!'[7] he calls out, sure that the Native must have killed his first hog, for he has heard the shot. 'We shall have a glorious feast today!'[8]

With no warning, Tetaheite turns the musket muzzle towards Martin and again pulls the trigger. Isaac Martin too is cut down with one blast.

Several hundred yards away, Menalee is obediently working for Mr Mills and Mr McCoy, just as he has for the last four years, when they all hear the shots.

'May I help the other men bring home the hogs they have just shot?'[9] Menalee asks politely.

Mr Mills gruffly nods his agreement, and Menalee quickly joins his co-conspirators, as planned, at Fletcher Christian's property. If Christian is in a notably happy mood today – even for him – it is because his dear Isabella is so heavy with child that she has already been 'confined', and he is about to be a father for the third time.

As ever, the hard-working Christian – like all of them, dressed in what used to be sails, before they became tents, before they became clothes – is using the time while he waits to till the yam plot and is taking a hoe to it as the four Native men approach from behind with their weapons. Two of them, Timoa and Nehow, are armed with muskets taken from those they have already murdered.

Absorbed by his work, pulling out a stubborn yam, Fletcher hears the rather wildly chattering men – odd, they're usually a lot more circumspect in their conversation – getting closer. For the sake of politeness, at least, he is just about to stand up and turn around to greet them, when . . . . their chattering stops.

Behind him, as the story will be told afterwards, Nehow levels the musket, aims right at Fletcher's back and . . . pulls the trigger.

Fletcher hears the sudden *pffft* sound as the flint on the hammer strikes the very small amount of priming powder in the firing pan and ignites it. Just a split instant later, there is a massive roar, as the main charge of powder inside the barrel is ignited and the musket-ball bursts forth, and catches Fletcher Christian right in the back, hitting him between the shoulderblades and bringing him down, hard. The big puff of dirty white smoke from the muzzle is blown away by the wind, even as Fletcher cries out . . .

He is still alive, but entirely unable to defend himself, and the four Natives are quick to move in to finish the job, shattering his head with an axe. Fletcher Christian's mutilated body, which had been writhing and gushing blood, goes limp. And now it simply lies there in the dirt, ghastly and lifeless, with freshly picked, blood-spattered yams scattered all around him.

•

A few hundred yards to the east, John Mills is working beside Billy McCoy when they hear another musket shot . . . and other strange noises.

It has come from the direction of Fletcher's plot.

Perhaps they should go and see?

'Surely there is some person dying?'[10] McCoy jokes.

No need, replies Mills.

'It is only Mainmast[11][going into labour].'[12]

The two keep working until a few minutes later they see a Native running fast towards them, across the furrowed fields.

It is a breathless Tetaheite, and he has horrifying news . . .

'Mr McCoy, those two rascals Menalee and Timoa, they are stealing things out of your house this very minute! Come quickly!'

Those bastards!

With a roar of anger, McCoy races towards his hut, followed by Mills, and a fair bit further back, the exhausted Tetaheite.

McCoy flings open his front door, whereupon . . .

He has a split second to take it all in – three Natives are waiting for him, with Menalee pointing the gun right at him – before the shot is fired.

Astoundingly, the musket-ball misses McCoy. Dumbstruck, trying to comprehend what is happening, the scarred Scot stands rooted to the spot. With no time to reload, Menalee throws down the musket, grabs McCoy and tries to wrestle him to the ground. But McCoy is the stronger man, and with the added power of one who knows he is fighting for his life, he is able to stagger out with Menalee still clasping and grasping at his body. Out the door they rumble and tumble, with McCoy managing to throw Menalee into a pigsty, before running from the house in terror. No longer is he dumbstruck ...

'Mills!' he shouts as he runs. 'Seek shelter in the woods!' Mills simply stares at him. McCoy clarifies things for the puzzled Mills. 'Run into the bush, the Natives are trying to kill all the white men!'[13]

Extraordinarily, or at least it seems to McCoy, Mills shows no signs of panic, doesn't move a muscle.

'I do not believe,' he calls after McCoy, 'my friend Menalee would kill me.'[14]

Well, good luck to him.

McCoy is not waiting to find out. Instead, he keeps running, knowing how urgent it is to tell Christian that the Natives are rising, that the Mutineers must gather themselves to fight back. As he keeps running, however, he hears another shot fired. Remarkably, though he instinctively steels himself, he is not ripped apart by a musket-ball, and he risks a quick glance over his shoulder.

Jesus Christ!

John Mills had been right.

Menalee would never kill him.

The man standing over Mills' corpse with the still smoking musket is Tetaheite.

Arriving breathless at Christian's patch, the first thing that McCoy sees is Christian's corpse in the field, with a nearly severed head, and without pause he continues running into the house to tell Isabella the news: the Natives are rising! Fletcher is dead, just over there in the field!

Leaving her shattered countenance behind – Fletcher, dead? Really, DEAD? – McCoy pauses only long enough to tell her that she must spread the word to any Mutineers she sees.

Meanwhile, he keeps going, running to find his surest ally, Matt Quintal.

Behind him, he leaves the weeping Isabella, lying prostrate over the shattered form of Fletcher Christian, the woman with a baby in her belly about to burst through, embracing the bloodied form of the love of her life, and the father of that child. Her first lad, Thursday, now just three years old, soon joins her, howling as never before.

•

And here is Quintal now!

We must head for the hills, and head *now*! The Natives are rising. They have already killed Jack Williams, Isaac Martin, John Mills and Fletcher Christian! They tried to kill me, but missed! Within seconds, pausing only to gather their muskets, the two are on their way.

Meanwhile, Alec Smith is working his own patch when he looks up to see Tevarua, Quintal's wife, running across his field.

'Why are you working at such a time?'[15] she calls, wild-eyed, as she passes, with no explanation.

A very odd thing to say?

What is *such a time*? What is happening?

Alec continues working.

•

With four Mutineers murdered, the armed Natives now move to their next target, Billy Brown, and close accordingly on his hut . . . only to come across . . . a spirit!

Well, it is not quite a spirit, but it is the form of a man they thought they had already killed, Isaac Martin.

Though badly wounded, with blood still pouring from his chest, he has crawled over to warn Brown. This time, to make sure of it, Tetaheite shoots Martin in the heart, and to be *doubly* sure, they take a sledgehammer that Brown keeps just inside his house, and stave Martin's head in.

For Billy Brown, it is all happening so quickly. The Natives, murder in their eyes, close in around him.

'Please,' he sobs, 'do not kill me until I have seen my wife!'[16]

Menalee nods his agreement, just a moment before Timoa moves behind Brown and shoots him dead. Timoa did not agree.

Who next?

Well, here he comes now.

Alec Smith has finally laid down his tools and now arrives to investigate all these gunshots, first approaching Brown's hut.

His fierce face flashes dismay.

For there, by Billy's house, he notes four Natives casually standing and, 'leaning on the muzzles of their guns, the butts being against the ground'.[17]

Outrageous! After everything they have done to teach the brutes how to handle a gun safely, and here they are, flagrantly breaching the rules they have put in place and . . .

And, hang on. The Natives have an entirely different aspect about them today. Instead of looking away, or at their feet, they are staring him right back in the eyes, almost as if they are . . . equals? Suddenly a terrible suspicion comes over Smith. But surely, he must be mistaken. They couldn't really be . . .

'What's the matter?'[18] he asks as casually as he can muster.

In an instant, he has his answer.

For instead of an explanation, what Smith gets is one of the Natives lifting his gun, and pointing it right at his chest as he growls, '*Mamu!*' Silence![19]

(Oh, the bitter irony! '*Mamu*', the very word used by Fletcher Christian to bring Captain Bligh to heel – '*Mamu*, sir, not a word, or death's your portion!'[20] – is now being hurled by Natives as they *mutiny* against the *Mutineers*. How amusing the vindictive Bligh would find it, if he could but know.)

Well, Smith wants no part of death being in this portion, or in whatever second helpings might be offered, and in a return to his roots of growing up tough, but not the toughest, on the streets of the downtrodden town of Hackney in Middlesex, his instincts kick in as he turns and runs for his life. Behind him, there is the crack of a musket shot, but, mercifully, there is only a whizzing sound as the ball sails past.

The Natives give only casual pursuit. Having already killed five Mutineers, including their Captain, and having secured their weapons, they need do nothing frantically anymore. From this day forth, they are no-one's servant, nobody's slave.

Smith keeps running, arriving first at Jack Williams' house, hoping to warn him, and also get some thick clothes so they can hide out in the woods, and have some protection from the rain, for as long as this murderous madness goes on. What he finds, of course, is Jack's bloodied corpse.

Good Lord! Taking the clothes, he staggers away, still scarcely believing it can have come to this.

And yet, after three hours hiding in the woods, he realises just how hungry he is and, very carefully, circles back to his own plantation to gather some yams. A ragged rascal, he carefully makes his way round the rugged rocks, hoping to be unseen.

With all quiet now, no sign of anyone, let alone a Native with a gun, he gains a little confidence and ducks back inside his hut to retrieve the cloth bag hanging on the door that he can use to hold the yams. Off in the distance, he can hear his hogs snorting, and – yes, he thinks it is – the sound of women wailing in grief. Or, just maybe, it is Isabella Christian giving birth.

Bag in hand, he returns to the yam patch, staying low to the ground, and starts digging, knocking off the biggest clumps of earth before putting the yams in his bag, when, in the near distance, there is the sudden crack of a gun, and he suddenly feels a stinging sensation in his right shoulder, followed by dribbling wetness as blood starts to flow freely down his front. Yes, a musket-ball has pierced him through the top of his shoulder and come out the side of his neck. The Natives were lying in wait for him to come into the open.

Devils!

Though it is not a mortal wound, the shot has knocked him over. He cannot flee. All he can do is watch as death approaches – in this case in the form of four Natives looming larger. Obviously, they have decided not to waste another musket-ball on the stricken white man, for as he lies there, they soon crowd around, and he can see Tetaheite lift the butt of the musket, ready to dash it down on his skull, and crush it like an egg.

Desperately, instinctively, he flashes his massive right hand out, just in time to deflect the blow, breaking his finger, but leaving his skull intact. Tiring of this, Tetaheite now simply brings the muzzle of his musket down to Alec's chest and ... as Smith holds his breath and steels himself ... pulls the trigger.

(*Click.*)

The hammer has indeed come down on the firing pan, but the attached flint has failed to ignite the gunpowder, and the stunning silence that follows is the sweetest non-noise Alec Smith has ever not heard.

A miracle!

Re-priming it, Tetaheite brings the gun to Smith's side a second time, and pulls the trigger again.

(*Click.*) The gun misfires again.

A second miracle!

Partially recovered from the shock of it, scarcely daring to believe that he is still alive, Smith suddenly leaps to his feet and runs, with the Natives, again, in pursuit.

Ah, but they are not running for their life as he is, and he quickly starts to outstrip them. Tiring, the Natives call out: 'Stop!'[21]

'No,' replies Smith, following up with the rather obvious explanation for his reluctance to halt. 'You want to kill me!'[22]

Extraordinarily, Smith now hears the words that are far more terrifying than the sound of any gunshot would have been.

'No, we do not want to kill you. We forgot what Young told us about leaving you alive to be his companion!'[23]

WHAT?

Ned Young is behind all this?

Even as he continues to run, Smith realises that it makes a certain amount of sense. Young has always been close to the Natives because of his mixed race, and the hallmarks of this attack have his stamp of organisation. It all makes sense. Very well, then. He stops running. The Natives soon catch up, and could easily shoot him down, or at least stave in his skull. But, they don't. They really mean it. In the excitement of all the killing, they really had forgotten Young's instructions to leave Smith alive.

Ned Young is indeed the local Master of Murder, telling the Natives who to kill, how to do it, and in what sequence. After being led, dazed, to Young's house by the Natives, it is to find the former officer of the *Bounty* sitting calmly, chatting with a number of Tahitian women. Ned has always been 'a great favourite with the women'[24] and he is now very popular with the Native men too. He shows no surprise at Smith's arrival, and for his part, Smith makes no mention of the fact that he knows he is only alive because of Young's good graces.

The two talk lightly, of everything bar what has just occurred – though Smith is certainly chattier than usual – even as the four Natives go out into the woods, muskets in hand, to see if they can kill Quintal and McCoy before darkness falls.

This part of their venture remains fruitless, but they have an idea. Might one of the white men be stupid enough to return to his house, just as Smith had done? Carefully, they circle up around the house, high on the hill, belonging to Billy McCoy. Peering in, they find McCoy on one bunk, and Matt Quintal and his wife, Tevarua, on another! All are asleep.

Carefully, a musket is aimed through the window, and the trigger pulled. This time there is no misfire, just a blast to wake the dead . . . but the musket-ball misses all three.

In the mad scramble that follows, McCoy, Quintal and Tevarua manage to flee in only the clothes they are standing up in – or, more accurately, running for their lives in.

The following morning, a gloomy pall has fallen over Pitcairn. In and around the village, the bodies of the dead Mutineers lie as they fell, with Christian still face down in his garden, yam roots still in his hand.

Isabella, of course, would have covered him, or buried him, but only instants after embracing him, the upset of it all had brought on her labour, and she has just given birth.

In fact, Young has carefully noted in his journal the key events on Pitcairn of the last day.

'Massacre of part of the mutineers by the Tahitians'[25] which is true, Young wisely not adding 'orchestrated by me'.

Mary Christian Born.[26]

Of those bloody events of the day before, it will be Smith who sums them up most concisely, from his unique perspective, while perhaps noting that Young is half-black:

'It was a day of emancipation to the blacks, who were now masters of the island, and of humiliation and retribution to the whites.'[27]

And yet, still all is not well in paradise.

For while it is one thing to have killed off five Mutineers and have two of the others on the run, it is quite another to decide who should get their wives. And, as before, while it had been a big step to first start murdering, it is a whole lot less of a step to do it again. As a matter of fact, only a week after the Mutineer massacre, while Young's wife, Teraura, sits outside their hut singing a Tahitian melody, Timoa is sitting by her side, accompanying her on the flute.

It is a pleasant, bucolic scene, spoiled by only one thing.

Menalee, holding a musket, strolls up behind the two of them, points his musket at the back of Timoa – with whom he has been in dispute over the favours of one of the widows – and pulls the trigger.

This time there is no misfire, no mistake, and Timoa goes down hard, bleeding from his side.

'Teraura!' he calls. 'Bring me my gun.'

And perhaps she even might have done so. But it all proves to be beside the point, as even before she can move, Menalee has reloaded and calmly shoots Timoa again. Shoots him dead.

There is, of course, pandemonium, with everyone running every which way, including Teraura, who runs to Tetaheite and, weeping, tells him that Menalee has murdered 'her favourite black'.[28]

As it happens, Menalee is not far behind her, intent on killing Tetaheite. But the Native women will not have it. Seeing what is about to happen, they rush from all parts to surround Tetaheite for protection, even as he calls to Nehow for help.

When Nehow arrives, it is suddenly Menalee who is outnumbered, and he makes a strategic retreat, heading out into the same hills where his former quarries, Billy McCoy and Matt Quintal, are still hiding.

On an island this small, it does not take long for Menalee to find them, and he is quick to propose a new understanding. Instead of trying to kill each other, why not join forces?

Really?

McCoy and Quintal, who have been living off what they can forage, wondering if every day will be their last, are unsure. Here is the very man who had wanted to kill them, who had tried to hunt them down, now being hunted himself. And now he wants to join forces?

After a quick parley, the two make him an offer.

To prove your bona fides, we want you to lay your musket down at your feet, and move away from it.

Carefully, Menalee bends forward, places the gun on the ground and shuffles back a couple of steps, staring all the while at the white men, wondering if he is about to be betrayed, as . . .

As with a rush, the two Mutineers snatch the musket. Armed, at last!

Now, kill Menalee, or not?

They decide not to. For while there may be no honour among thieves, there is a bond between fugitives when pursued for their lives, and the three men begin to talk. Menalee makes a proposal. He would like Quintal and McCoy to join him in killing the other two Tahitian men – at which point there would be peace among all survivors. Menalee promises!

Quintal and McCoy consult with each other, and cautiously agree.

Slowly, thus, not quite trusting Menalee, or the situation, McCoy and Quintal head back to the village with Menalee in the lead, stopping right at the edge of the woods, just near the huts. They can see the glow from the communal fire up ahead, hear the low rumble of white men talking – clearly Smith and Young – as well as the sing-song voices of the Native women.

What now? What should they do?

Before they can decide, Menalee catches sight of Tetaheite and Nehow and immediately rushes forward, intent on attacking them. Convinced, however, that Menalee is intent on betraying their presence, so all three Natives can attack *them* – there have been so many betrayals in the last while it is difficult to keep track – McCoy and Quintal rush back into the woods.

Not long afterwards, Menalee joins them. He has indeed attacked Tetaheite and Nehow, convinced McCoy and Quintal were right behind him. But the second he had found himself alone and outnumbered, he had extricated himself and raced away. He is *very* disappointed by the lack of faith displayed by McCoy and Quintal, and says so.

What now?

Frustrated, tired, hungry, the three decide to at least express some of their emotion by climbing to a ridge above the village, and firing a shot down into it. And if they hit one of their wives or children, that is too bad, for they must deliver the message:

Yes, you have the village, but we have a musket, and don't you forget it!

Fortunately the musket-ball hits no-one, but it is enough to start a panic. Young and Smith immediately decide on an extreme course of action – with Smith, though talkative, always deferring to Young. For he knows more than most just how ruthless the West Indian is, how heartless, with the exception of his desire to keep Smith alive, so he will have someone to talk to. So Smith talks, and talks some more, but whatever Young would like to do is fine with him.

Tetaheite and Nehow, we need to talk to you. Here is the proposal.

If Menalee is killed by Quintal and McCoy, they will be allowed to return to the village and live in peace. Do you agree to that?

They do. But how to get this message to the two Mutineers?

•

The following morning, early, Quintal is in their fugitive camp with Menalee and McCoy, when he looks up to see his Tevarua approaching. She has a letter with her, written by Young. And of course she cannot understand the strange shapes on the paper any more than Menalee can, but, as asked, faithfully hands it over.

Quintal and McCoy read the missive silently:

> If you kill the black man and return to
> the village, we will all be friends again.[29]

The two look at each other, and have a wordless conversation with their eyes, and finally with a mutual nod of their heads. It makes sense.

What does it say?

It is the last question asked on this earth by Menalee, as Quintal[30] simply takes the musket – already primed and ready for action – and pulls the trigger. The black man is indeed killed.

Down in the village, Smith and Young hear the shot, and look at each other.

Has the job been done?

The job has been done! Quintal and McCoy know that. Should they simply turn up, back at the village to advise that Menalee has been killed, and expect there to be peace, and for all the killing to stop?

On reflection, they decide against it.

Tetaheite and Nehow have made no secret of their hatred for the white men, have tried to kill them just days ago, and now they're expected to lay down their weapons, and for them all to live in peace? *AIMAH.* NO.

They decide not to return to the village while the two Native men remain there.

It proves to be a sound instinct, for already, down in the village, armed with muskets provided by Young, Tetaheite and Nehow walk purposefully away from the huts and into the thick forest, to go looking for Quintal and McCoy.

Now, though it takes the better part of a morning, the same rule applies: on an island this small, it is simply not possible to remain hidden for long. For, there they are now. Just up ahead through the trees, Tetaheite and Nehow can see the two white men resting under a tree, Quintal nursing the one musket they have. This is going to need a clean shot, as the Native men want to avoid being caught in cross-fire at all costs. Going down on his belly, Nehow steadies the musket, drawing a bead on Quintal's chest, and pulls the trigger.

The sudden roar in the thick shroud of the forest causes birds as far as 500 yards away to take flight. Shouting in shock, McCoy and Quintal jump to their feet and start running away from where the sound of the shot has come. So little is their care for anything other than frantic flight that McCoy manages to badly cut his foot on a jagged jutting barb from a tree-stump. Clutching at the wound, he limps on, as the warm blood flowing out of the deep cut leaves a red path. Following on, the two Natives see such a trail of blood it is obvious that one of the white men is badly wounded and won't be able to get far.

That, at least, is what they tell Young when – after abandoning the chase when the trail takes them into an area where they are the ones most at risk of being ambushed – they return to the village in the late afternoon. But is McCoy *really* that badly wounded?

If it is a part of the human condition that the most devious of men are the least likely to trust others – because they know better than anyone how easy it is to deceive – then let Young be the exemplar. For he refuses to trust the word of the Native men, and instead asks Jenny, Isaac Martin's widow, to see what she can find out.

But, careful now. It is one thing for Young to ask her to leave the village to go and find the white men, but Jenny refuses to go anywhere unless she has the permission of Tetaheite and Nehow. Then, and only then – for they do indeed give her their blessing – does she venture up into the hills to look for the white men. Despite her show of seeking male permission, the truth is that Jenny is on a mission on behalf of the Native women, who, after long discussion, have come to their own conclusions.

The Native women, and this includes Tetaheite and Nehow's two 'share-wives', want the last two Native men killed. (Yes, the only way to stop all the killing is to kill the killers, or at least the two still alive who have killed most often.)

Finding Quintal and McCoy, Jenny puts the proposal to them, and they agree. They will, they say, co-operate with the women, and come down from the hills, to shoot the last two Native men tomorrow morning.

•

Throughout the morning, even as they do their chores, the Tahitian women, including Isabella, Jenny and Tevarua, keep gazing to the distant hills, and the near woods. Where are they? Quintal and McCoy have promised to come, but there is no sign. Again and again, the women manage to position Tetaheite and Nehow so they are isolated – human bait, placed so that Matt and Billy will come out to kill them. But by now, Quintal and McCoy are wary indeed when it comes to the ways of the Native women, so even when offered a human gift they are *expecting* treachery and these paranoid men will not be so lured.

And so the women quickly come up with another solution. In short order, Young and Smith are in deep conversation with Teraura, Jenny and Tevarua. It will be for Tevarua to invite Tetaheite, the strongest and most dangerous of the two Natives, to come to her bed at noon.

'I caution you,' says Young. 'On no account put your arm under Tetaheite's head as you go to sleep.'

For Young's wife Teraura will be secreted nearby, will have an axe, and knows what to do once Tetaheite has *taoto maitai*, fallen asleep after sex.

Once she has done it, she must yell 'Shoot', and Young, in turn, will know what to do.

And so it goes.

When it comes to that look a woman gives to indicate to a man she is in the mood for love, Tevarua is not only expert, but irrefusable, and – even as Teraura stays by the fire, sharpening an axe with her file – Tetaheite is soon noted trailing the seductress to her hut. Some 15 minutes later, Teraura, too, heads that way. With no doors on the huts, bar light curtains of grass matting or canvas, entrance is easy and silent. And yes, it takes Teraura a moment or two to adjust her eyes to the relative dimness, but she quickly sees everything that she needs.

There is the naked Tevarua, on the right, her eyes wide, knowing what is coming. And there, on the left, is Tetaheite, conveniently on his side, asleep, his neck exposed. As requested, Tevarua has kept her arm well away from him. Teraura moves forward, silently, her large padded feet making no noise at all on the brushed dirt floor.

She steels herself, even while lifting the gleaming steel blade high above her head.

•

In the hut next door, Young is keeping Nehow talking, even while loading his gun. Young doesn't want to talk much himself, he mostly wants to listen, waiting for the cry that must come.

Nehow is bemused at Young's gun, wondering why he is loading it.

Oh, just some hog shooting.

'Make sure you put in a good load,' suggests Nehow.

'Yes, I will,' replies Young.

•

Gathering her strength, Teraura lifts the axe high, and with one sharp move brings the axe down hard and . . . Instead of hitting Tetaheite clean in the neck, the blade has struck the hard part of his skull. Though blood gushes out, he is not dead, and he is even able to partially sit up in bed, confused anger in his eyes . . . just before Teraura swings her axe down for the second time, and this time kills him clean, nearly severing his head.

'SHOOT!' she yells, which is the very call Young has been waiting for.

For he now does exactly that, shooting Nehow at near point-blank range, and very nearly blowing his head right off his shoulders. The last two Native men on the island are dead.

That afternoon, Smith, his hands empty, and raised in peace, is able to approach Quintal and McCoy high in the hills, and advise that the last of the Tahitians have been killed.

'But so many instances of treachery had occurred,' Smith would recount, 'that they would not believe the report.'[31]

How to resolve their lack of trust? How to prove it to them?

Quintal and McCoy give their conditions.

Bring us their heads. And their hands, for good measure. Yes, that's it. Cut off the dead men's heads and hands 'as a sort of certificate that the two Tahitians are really dead'[32] and then Quintal and McCoy will return in peace.

Very well then. Late that afternoon, Young hacks away the two heads – at least what is left of them – and Smith returns with the grisly, dripping proof. Finally, Quintal and McCoy believe, and do indeed return to the village.

While they are glad to be back, and welcomed by the likes of Young and Smith, there is no doubt things have changed . . . and not in a good way.

With just four men left on the island, and 11 women, there is a clear change in approach from the women. They become much more free with their opinions, much less eager to serve the men, and are frequently off together, talking. Are they conspiring?

Is there danger to the men?

It is too early to tell, but, certainly, it is this very possibility which keeps Young tossing and turning at night, worrying – and for very good reason.

For the women of the island their sudden majority is a heady thing. As a matter of fact, the question has to be asked – on this island, do they even need men at all?

Well, yes, there is one thing they need them for, for the moment, and in this field, the four surviving men notice a real change.

When they had first landed on Pitcairn, most of them had just one woman, and that was enough. They lay with them when they liked, which was often, and the frequency of lying together was never determined by when the woman felt like it. The woman's job was to submit, simple as that.

But now, things are . . . different.

With 11 virile women, in the prime of their lives, and only four men, it is the women who have expectations of them, who make sexual demands that they sometimes have trouble filling. And yes, each of the four men retains a wife, but the thing is, these wives don't mind sharing their men with the widows, and a certain promiscuousness takes over. But it is no longer the women submitting. They are done with that. It is the men who must submit to them. And such is the new mood on the island, they dare not say no. The women are powerful. They must be pleased, and therefore appeased.

And so it is now the men who are chosen at will for sex and then discarded when the women are satisfied.

Meantime, though often exhausted by their nocturnal activities – not to mention day-time, when the mood strikes one or other, or several of the women – the four Mutineers occupy themselves with their fields and animals. Among the things they must do is to divide the original ten plots among the four of them, and build new fences, new gates, to accommodate their new domains, while also doing such things as 'constructing pits for the purpose of entrapping hogs'.[33]

It is not a bad life, if only they could quell their nagging doubts about the women, who seem progressively more discontented – after all they have done, and are doing for them – and more obviously disobedient.

•

Come January 1794, Captain William Bligh is still without a commission for his next ship and his potato head glows constantly red with rage. It is not a good time, then, for Professor Christian to begin circulating a most intriguing document he calls the Appendix.

Legally, it is cleverly framed, as one might expect from a Cambridge professor.

That is, while it bears the name of Edward Christian on the cover and title page, the testimony within is unsigned – though it is clear who has contributed to this new version of events: 'It will naturally be asked from whom, and how have these facts been collected?' Professor Christian writes. 'The following circumstances have been collected from many interviews and conversations, in the presence of several respectable gentlemen, with Mr Fryer master of the *Bounty*, Mr Heywood, midshipman, Mr Peckover, Gunner, Mr Purcell, carpenter, John Smith, cook, Lawrence Lebogue, sail maker . . . and Joseph Coleman, armourer, Thomas McIntosh, carpenter's mate, Michael Byrne, seaman . . . the writer of this has received also letters upon the subject from James Morrison.'[34]

It is . . . well, almost every *Bounty* man worth his salt who is in England.

Perhaps most devastating for Bligh's reputation is that the Appendix includes the privately taken minutes of the previously unpublished court martial, obligingly provided by Muspratt's lawyer.

The Appendix is sold on the streets of London for sixpence a pop and is an instant bestseller, a literary bombshell that shows Bligh at his worst, in the words of his own 'loyal' men!

Captain Bligh, of course, cannot help himself, and soon shuffles up to a street seller to – much as it grates – buy his own copy. Folding it in a manner that it can be secreted inside the pocket of his coat – for he does not want to be seen possessing it – Bligh returns home to Betsy and begins reading, feeling a rising rage with every page. And also there is hurt.

Could it really be that his friend, Nelson – his late *friend*! – could have made such remarks as those reported by the others? Could he have really announced that while Christian had mutinied, 'we know whose fault it is'[35] – and Fryer's report of Christian having said, 'I've been in Hell for weeks past; Captain Bligh has brought all this upon himself . . .'[36]

Of course, there is a whole lot more, all of it damaging and the whole lot lovingly curated by that infernal penny professor, Edward Christian!

They declare that Captain Bligh used to call his officers 'scoundrels, damned rascals, hounds, hell-hounds, beasts and infamous wretches';[37] that he frequently threatened them that when the ship arrived at the Endeavour Strait 'he would kill one half of the people, make the officers jump overboard and would make them eat grass like cows'.[38]

Damn the Christian name!

Yes, indeed. For those who read it, and they are many, a very different Bligh emerges to the hero they have previously read all about. This Bligh is not a saint, standing up to evil ruffians. This is *not* one who deserves to be hailed as the Lion of London, the Royal darling, the one-man miracle who outwitted that Judas, Fletcher Christian, to guide his small band of Loyalists on their frail craft, against impossible odds, all the way to Timor, rallying all good men and true to the greatest, most courageous navigational feat in all history. This Bligh is a foul-tempered, foul-mouthed fury who is a disgrace to the Royal Navy, and the King whose Commission he bears.

As for Fletcher Christian.

How different a man he is, as he appears in the Appendix, to the one portrayed by Bligh!

For, in direct contrast to the careful listing of Bligh's blemishes and blunders, his many instances of callous cruelty and incandescent rages over trivialities, Christian receives a paean of praise from shipmates outdoing each other in their eagerness to set the record straight about this very fine man indeed. Their admiring anonymous quotes glow with warmth:

His Majesty might have his equal, but he had not a superior officer in his service.

He was a gentleman; and a brave man and every officer and seaman on board the ship would have gone through fire and water to have served him . . .

He was adorned with every virtue and beloved by all . . .

He was a gentleman, every inch of him, and I would still wade up to the arm pits in blood to serve him . . .

As much as I have lost and suffered by him, if he could be restored to his country I should be the first to go without wages in search of him.

He was as good and generous a man as ever lived.[39]

Oh, and lest there be any remaining doubt about Christian's manners, as compared to the low-brow Bligh?

Mr Christian was always good natured, I never heard him say 'Damn you' to any man aboard ship . . .[40]

Christian, the public is now told, is first and foremost an officer and a gentleman, a man of honour tormented by a tyrant who is, let's face it, his social inferior. And what true gentleman could be so abused, so humiliated, by such a cruel despot and not rise against it?

Edward Christian is so determined to defend his brother's reputation that he does not so much gild the lily, as plant an entirely new one, in Fletcher's case a lily-white one, even maintaining that he had – no, really – no female favourite to return to in Tahiti. For you see, yes, some men (*sniff*) might engage in such un-Christian behaviour, but not Bligh's second-in-command.

And while Bligh had recounted that the Mutineers had shouted 'Huzzah for Tahiti!',[41] not one of the men interviewed for this account can recall it. For you see, the point that must be made is that what caused the Mutiny had nothing to do with the lure of lusty Tahiti, and everything to do with Bligh's barbed tongue and lusty lash.

Ah yes, Captain Bligh. Not a single man in the Appendix can think of a single good thing to say about him, and can't even commend him for his seamanship. But bad memories, and damaging quotes? They abound.

And, of course, Bligh is not alone in having his reputation damaged by the contents.

The Appendix is likely to be so ruinous to Bligh's reputation that none other than Sir Joseph Banks – who has mentored and championed

Bligh from the start, and whose own judgement is now under severe question – insists to Bligh that he must lower himself to the fray and write a public reply.

12 March 1794, Pitcairn, of skulls and cross-bones

On this day, Young is off to visit Smith to borrow a rake when he comes across a group of the women walking together – as they seem to be doing ever more often these days, and in ever more intense conversations – and there, right in the middle of them, is Jenny, carrying in her hands a human skull.

'Whose skull is that, Jenny?' asks Young.

'Jack Williams',' she replies.

'I desire that be buried,' commands Young.

'It should not!' answers another of the women, and although her English is imperfect, her meaning is crystal clear: NO.

'It should and I demand it accordingly!'[42] Young insists, going on to explain that to keep such a skull is 'not decent', and 'not Christian'.

(True, it had not been particularly 'Christian' of Young to have ordered the slaughter of Williams in the first place, together with the other Mutineers, but for the moment, at least, this point passes him.)

Well, they will consider it. But the problem soon emerges that, even if the women do agree to bury the skull, they have retained the heads of the other dead Mutineers as well. And they don't quite understand why they should bury them.

This strange Tahitian practice has already been chronicled by James Morrison who recorded that, 'Some, who have a great veneration for the deceased, wrap up the skull and hang it up in their house, in token of their love.'[43]

So yes, of course they resist the idea of burying Williams.

'Why should you, in particular,' they ask Young, 'insist on such a thing, when the rest of the white men do not?'

'If they give you leave to keep the skulls above ground,' Young replies haughtily, 'I do not!'[44]

Meeting with McCoy, Smith and Quintal shortly afterwards, he tells them what he has seen.

'I think if the girls do not agree to give up the heads of the five white men in a peaceable manner, they ought to be taken by force and buried.'[45]

Very well then. But, take by force? Against 11 women? Two of whom are blooded axe-murderers?

When it comes to dealing with 'the girls',[46] things are no longer straightforward.

And, as it turns out, the girls – including Isabella, with a six-month-old baby at her breast, the daughter born on the day of Fletcher's death – have been having meetings of their own, and soon afterwards make their own demand. They wish to leave Pitcairn, to return to Tahiti, and so, they wish the men to build a boat, starting . . . *now*.

The men look at each other.

While it is all very well for the women to return to their island, they are in a much different position from the men. They are not Mutineers. They are not going to swing from the nearest yardarm if caught. True, they still do not know if Bligh has survived long enough to tell of the Mutiny, but they really do not want to take that risk. The men are now well settled into Pitcairn, and reasonably happy, beyond the damned restlessness of the women. There is nothing that Tahiti can offer the men, bar danger. They do not want to go.

But dare they say that to the women?

All things considered, they dare not.

Let us instead, find reasons why we can't do it.

Most importantly, there is only one boat still left to us, the Jolly Boat of the *Bounty* – a very small affair, of dubious seaworthiness for a long haul. Though we *could* build a bigger and more solid one, in theory, it will take time, and it requires wood and nails that we simply don't have. Where on earth could we get the English wood, nails, pitch and tar that we need?

A cry from Jenny is their reward, as she immediately starts tearing her hut apart, and 'in her zeal'[47] encourages the other women to do the same.

In short order, though the village is reeling somewhat, a pile of wooden boards and a collection of nails have materialised, and, with the women hovering – almost *menacingly*, you know? – the sound of hammering and sawing breaks out once more over Pitcairn.

•

Bligh is in his natural state: pure fury, and for very good reason. The one-time Lion of London is being savagely attacked by Christians. That tuppenny Professor of Law, Edward Christian, and his cursed 'Appendix', that compendium of slurs, lies, insinuations, exaggerations, and, yes, perhaps one or two tragic truths, is devoured each and every day by ever eager eyes as the word spreads of the contents of the explosive document. And of course everyone who reads it repeats it to others. Suddenly people are crossing the street to avoid him, eyes are being averted and he has the growing sense that he is nothing less than an embarrassment to the Royal Navy. Though the world was once his oyster, he is now in danger of becoming the Bligh barnacle.

All because of a damned booklet!

Well, Bligh is now convinced that Sir Joseph is right. He really must stoop to conquer, lower himself to answer these cads. And so, with the same dogged determination that marked his long voyage on the Launch to Timor, against similar overwhelming odds, he sets out to restore his tattered and battered reputation.

Taking up his quill, he sits at his desk, day after day, and writes long and hard to restore his good name. Betsy, ever faithful Betsy, is sure to administer plentiful tea and sympathy.

It will be all right, dear William.

•

One afternoon in mid-1794, the feeble London sun is shining its last rays for the day when Bligh signs the title page of his reply to Professor Christian's Appendix. His stiff, ink-stained hand replaces the mighty quill in its stand. He reads the title page one last time with pride:

> *An Answer to Certain Assertions contained in the Appendix to*
> *a Pamphlet*

Before long, his latest treatise hits the streets, and people are buying it with delight, eager to take in this newest instalment of drama on the High Seas.

It starts quite directly:

> It is with no small degree of regret, that I find myself under the necessity of obtruding my private concerns on the Public . . . the respect I owe to that Public in whose service I have spent my life; as well as regard to my character, compel me to reply to such parts of Mr Christian's Appendix, as might, if unnoticed, obtain credit to my prejudice.[48]

Bligh does not stoop to making his case in his own prose. Why would he when the testimony of others in his support is so much more powerful? So, he is supposed to be a cruel tyrant?

Well, how does this fit with this posted list of instructions forbidding cruelty to any Tahitian?

And let the reader digest the contents of a letter from one of the Mutineers, Mr Charles Churchill, acknowledging that he had done the wrong thing in deserting, but thanking Captain Bligh for his kindness in response!

Oh, so you want the specifics of what occurred in the Mutiny? Look no further than this transcript of the Court of Inquiry in Batavia. You cannot do better, surely, than an account that every sober man swore to and *signed*. Yes, signed. Of course it is different from what they told Mr Edward Christian when he plies them with drink in inns. Who could be surprised? And here, too, is an extract from Mr Peter Heywood's sworn testimony in England, the very testimony your penny Professor Edward Christian chose to *omit*, where Peter tells of Bligh's 'very kind treatment of me, personally, I should have been a monster of depravity to have betrayed him'.[49] Indeed. A letter is also reprinted, from a Mr Edward Lamb, an old shipmate of Captain Bligh and Mr Christian, who writes of his amusement at one claim: 'In the Appendix it is said, that Mr. Fletcher Christian had no attachment amongst the women at Tahiti; if that was the case, he must have been much altered since he was with you in the *Britannia*; he was then one of the most foolish young men I ever knew in regard to the sex.'[50]

And now, for his final trick. With a quasi-judicial zeal, Bligh uses his accusers' own words to dent their credibility.

For Bligh has conducted his own little chats. Mr Coleman, Mr Smith and Mr Lebogue; all Loyalists previously 'interviewed' by Professor

Edward Christian were recently interviewed in turn by Captain Bligh. And wouldn't you know it? For it now turns out that they insist – (admittedly prodded by legal threats, career threats, and even *actual* threats, mixed with reminders that *he* saved *their* miserable lives) – they had been misquoted! To re-set the record straight, an exhaustive list of things they deny is now printed:

> I never saw Captain Bligh shake his hand in Christian's face, or hear him damn him for not firing at the Indians.

> I never said Christian or Stewart was equal to Captain Bligh in abilities, I never thought any such thing.

> I never heard the Captain damn the officers and call them names.[51]

Page after page of it!

True, there remain *other* men of the *Bounty* whose previous accusations are not countered, but at least Bligh can now demonstrate that their experience was not universal, and there really are loyal sailors who will speak for him.

Most helpful to Captain Bligh is Lawrence Lebogue, who says that all the good things he told Edward Christian had been left out of the Appendix! Whereas Professor Christian had portrayed Captain Bligh as a sadist with the lash, nothing could be further from the truth:

> I said Captain Bligh was not a person fond of flogging his men; and some of them deserved hanging, who had only a dozen . . .[52]

And as for the noble celibacy of Fletcher Christian at Tahiti?

> I remember Christian had a girl, who was always with him . . .[53]

(Reading it, Professor Edward Christian is truly shocked by the turnaround of Lebogue, the sheer depth of his calumny of lies, calling it 'the most wicked and perjured affidavit that was ever sworn before a magistrate, or published to the world'.[54])

Nevertheless Bligh's effort to right the record, by releasing his own document, containing the testimony of others, along with a slew of private letters to men of influence, achieves precisely what he intends.

The press react positively, as does the public. Bligh is declared to have fully vindicated his character. The influential *British Critic* now insists that the whole affair is over and adds by way of advice, 'We cannot help thinking that the friends of Christian will act the wisest part, in throwing as much as possible into oblivion, the transaction in which that young man played so conspicuous and so criminal a part . . .'[55]

No, the amazing tale of the *Bounty* will never die, but much of the extraordinary heat of attention and anger that had come with it, that had even threatened to burn Bligh's career to the ground, begins to pass.

13 August 1794, Pitcairn, time to launch

It has taken five months, but at last, the boat requested by the women is finished – at least after a fashion. For although the men have been careful to make it look like a fine boat, they have also been keen to ensure that it is not *too* fine – and in fact have deliberately left many cracks and holes to let the water in.

Sure enough, down at Bounty Bay, when they all heave together to push the boat into the water – the excited women, led by Isabella, Tevarua, Jenny and all of their excited children – they achieve the desired outcome.

For as Young notes in his journal, 'according to expectation, she upset',[56] which is to say that, just as the Mutineers had planned, the boat immediately takes on water, and sinks.

That's that, then.

But not as far as the women are concerned. For 'she', the boat, is far from the only one upset. The Tahitian women, no fools, are soon seen to be in deep consultation once more. They never stop.

On 16 August 1794, three days after the boat had been finished, and the day after they have failed to leave Pitcairn, the Mutineers achieve at least one thing – the women, accepting that they will never leave this place, agree to bury the bones of all the people murdered on Pitcairn.

3 October 1794, Pitcairn, joy in the old town tonight!

It is the party to beat them all, and Matt Quintal throws it. For today, don't you know, is the first anniversary of the day they had killed the last of the Tahitian men. And yet while Quintal is happy, believing that with the death of the Natives, he had eliminated the two most likely sources of his own demise, both Smith and Young are not so sure, and, in fact, are particularly uneasy on this night. For they have come to realise that both Quintal and McCoy have continued to beat their wives – something that endangers all of the remaining Mutineers.

'McCoy and Quintal,' Smith will record, '[were] of very quarrelsome dispositions.'[57] It is Quintal, in particular, who is the most fierce, proposing 'not to laugh, joke, or give any thing to any of the girls'.[58]

For the women, all the women, are angry, and there is no telling what they might do. So yes, Quintal can laugh and joke and carry on, but the knot of Native women on the side, in deep discussion, tells Young that something bad is brewing.

CHAPTER EIGHTEEN

PITCAIRN – A RECKONING OF ACCOUNTS

Those people cannot enjoy comfortably what God has given them because they see and covet what He has not given them. All of our discontents for what we want appear to me to spring from want of thankfulness for what we have.[1]

Daniel Defoe, *Robinson Crusoe*

The book of female logic is blotted all over with tears, and Justice in their courts is forever in a passion.[2]

William Makepeace Thackeray, *The Virginians*

No man is an island,
Entire of itself,
Every man is a piece of the continent,
A part of the main.
If a clod be washed away by the sea,
Europe is the less.
As well as if a promontory were.
As well as if a manor of thy friend's
Or of thine own were:
Any man's death diminishes me,
Because I am involved in mankind,
And therefore never send to know for whom the bell tolls;
It tolls for thee.[3]

John Donne

11 November 1794, Pitcairn, the plot thickens

A stirring in the village. Averted looks. Mutterings in the dark. Bit by bit, Ned Young discovers there is a plot to kill all the Englishmen in their sleep.

Kill all four of them at once?

Why, it is *monstrous*!

After everything the men have done for the women, this, *this* is their reward?

Well, the men must strike first.

On this morning, after all the women are gathered in the village, the four Mutineers train their muskets on them.

Confess!

You planned to kill us all, didn't you?

Yes.

Bit by bit, talking to them separately, the plan comes out. All four men were to be killed with an axe as they lay in their beds. Young winces – it had been exactly the plan he'd used to kill Nehow and Tetaheite. The women know it works.

Try as they might, however, the Mutineers cannot get to the bottom of who is behind the plot, who is the driving force. It almost seems as if it is a collective plan, put together by all of the women, over months.

What to do?

Well, what *can* they do?

Punish one or two of them?

Kill them *all*, then?

It is out of the question. Firstly, it is unlikely such a massacre could be organised. And besides that, for all the trouble that comes with the women, it would risk being a very long few decades ahead without them.

In the end, once the women repent, and promise only good behaviour from now on – the first and most important rule to be observed is that there is to be *no* axe-murdering, and that's a promise – the men have a private meeting and, as Young notes, while there is to be no punishment for now, it is agreed, 'that the first female who misbehaves should be put to death, and this punishment is to be repeated on each offence until we discover the real intentions of the women'.[4]

Can the men trust the women?

They simply have to, but what sleep they gain is restless at best. For the next two days, Young records in his journal, he is 'bothered and idle'.[5]

How can he sleep, close his eyes and get real rest, when, at the tiniest sound, he opens his eyes with a start to see if a woman with an axe is looming above him, about to chop his head off with the sharp side, or dash his brains out with the blunt end?

After four days of this, with a menacing mood still gripping the village, Young takes two loaded muskets, with extra ammunition, and secretes them behind a well-known tree in the forest, returning to tell the other three men where they are. Now, if the women attack, those muskets will be, 'for the use of any person who might be so fortunate as to escape, in the event of an attack being made'.[6]

Before the month is over, the women do attack, but are beaten off by the white men. Again they beg forgiveness, and again they are pardoned.

The cycle continues. Strengthening the women's hand is the fact that they are united, making it clear that he who punishes one of them, punishes all of them, and will have to face all of them. Given their far greater number – 11 of them, to just four Mutineers – this is no small threat. And yes, the Mutineers at least have more weapons and are more skilled with them, but when the women start to equip themselves with firearms, and head off into the hills for days at a time, that advantage, too, begins to dissipate. With women out there, with muskets, the men have to remain vigilant, at all times, a state of perpetual wariness that, indeed, begins to wear them down.

One way or another, it is a situation that cannot endure for long.

•

It is morning on 27 December 1795 when a sail appears on the horizon.[7]

A ship! A ship!

Fear grips the Mutineers to a man.

Scarcely daring to breathe, secreted in their hideaways, mentally rehearsing where they might flee, how they would defend themselves, what they would do, they watch the sails come closer and now . . .

shrink before their eyes, until they disappear! Whoever these sailors were – it had not been possible to see which flag they flew – they have gone away.

The Mutineers breathe again, but this visitation is not a one-off. At a later point, they spy another distant sail that passes without coming closer, while still another one actually comes so close that they can see men on deck, staring curiously in their direction. Mercifully, Pitcairn's rugged nature, with no easy landing spots, no shelter, and many steep cliffs dissuades the passers-by from attempting a landing.

Again, the Mutineers breathe, while the women groan and wail with disappointment.

September 1796, England, gone is the sailor

Now seven years since the Mutiny, Captain William Bligh resumes his life as a sea Captain. His career prospers as he commands HMS *Calcutta* and *Director* in the French Revolutionary War.

If only he could be allowed to forget the whole dreadful episode.

But, clearly, no-one else wants to. Fascination from the rest of Great Britain, about just what happened to Fletcher Christian, does not abate, and is lifted further in September 1796 by fresh revelations.

Published in the newspaper *The True Briton*, and devoured by a ravenous readership, '*The Letters of Fletcher Christian*' – though entirely fraudulent – purport to be the true account of the dashing buccaneer's adventures after the Mutiny, an extraordinary swashbuckling tale full of sword fights, gun battles, piracy and a safe port found in South America.

There is no doubt in the account that Fletcher Christian is the hero to beat them all – even though it is mixed with a fetching bitter regret that it had come to mutiny. Perhaps the person most shocked and infuriated to read it is Bligh.

His strong suspicion is that the perfidious wretch Christian has sent these letters to his duplicitous brother, who has in turn conspired to have this new set of slurs also published, just to embarrass Bligh. Apoplectic with rage, he immediately writes to Sir Joseph Banks:

Is it possible that wretch can be at Cadiz and that he has had
intercourse with his brother, that sixpenny professor, who has more law
about him than honour? My dear Sir, I can only say that I heartily
despise the praise of any of the family of Christian, and I hope and
trust yet that the Mutineer will meet with his deserts.[8]

No less than William Wordsworth, the famed poet and one-time schoolmate of Fletcher Christian, has no illusions that his old friend has re-emerged. In fact, when Fletcher's supposed autobiography is published in 1796, for the first and only time in his life Wordsworth writes a letter to a newspaper:

There having appeared in your Entertainer *. . . an extract from a*
work purporting to be the production of Fletcher Christian, who headed
the mutiny on board the Bounty, *I think it proper to inform you, that*
I have the best authority for saying that this publication is spurious.
Your regard for the truth will induce you to apprize your readers of this
circumstance.

Yours,
William Wordsworth[9]

Now, just how Wordsworth could have 'the best authority' for saying the publication is spurious, when even Bligh is unsure, he does not make clear. The truth remains, however. Despite such fanciful accounts – of unknown source – no-one has the first clue where the remaining Mutineers are, and what has become of Fletcher Christian.

•

For four long years the women continue to treat the Mutineers with a troubling, sometimes sinister, indifference, and the uneasy truce continues. Sleep still does not come easy to Young, and so he comes up with a plan to improve their spirits by . . . making some.

Ten years ago, as a young man, in St Kitts, he had been taught how to make spirits out of sugarcane, distilling it using jars. Which is fortuitous. For McCoy had worked in a Scottish distillery many years before, and between them they are able to pool their knowledge in order to make a pool of liquor for parched throats, idle hands and bored brains of Pitcairn. After all, they still have the biggest copper cooking pot from the galley of the *Bounty*, and, by boiling up tea root and fermenting it for a week, followed by distilling it to concentrate the alcohol, they might be able to get roaring drunk.

For you see, given that tea root grows everywhere on the island it should be easy to do for men so inclined, and Young begins to teach the method to the other men. It takes a little trial and error, and the women hover suspiciously – but finally it proves possible to concoct a potent beverage .... *whish* .... *shtartsh* ... *to have quite* ... *a sherioush* ... *shimpact.*

Before long, heavy drinking among the men becomes as much a normal part of life on the island as seagulls cawing, waves pounding on the shore, and brutal, uncaring sex.

It becomes more a matter of remark when they are not drunk than when they are drunk, for sobriety is soon a rarity, but ...

But hark!

What is that?

In the distance a scream is heard ... which proves to be the last earthly sound emitted by Matt Quintal's wife, Tevarua, who, while trying to collect eggs from bird nests nestled high in the cliffs, has lost her purchase and fallen to her death.

Suddenly lonely, Quintal decides he would like a new wife, and, despite the fact there are many available widows on the island, *in vino veritas*, announces he wants, nay, *demands*, either Young or Smith's wife, it doesn't matter much. One or other man must hand his woman over or he will kill one of the men.

Young and Smith take the threat to heart, and decide to embark on what has become Pitcairn's traditional method of settling strong arguments. Murder. The next time that Quintal falls dead drunk, which is only a day or so after he has made the threat to kill them, Young and Smith loom over his sozzled form, each with an axe in hand.

Two savage blows, and that is the end of that conflict – the bloodied life of Matt Quintal comes to an appropriately bloody end. (Despite that, only a short time later, Teraura, Young's wife, has a son she names ... Quintal! Yet one more sign of a Pitcairn family tree completely covered in interconnecting vines.)

And now there are just three men left on the island: Ned Young, Alec Smith and Billy McCoy. Having murdered together, Young and Smith become even closer, and take to spending many hours every afternoon sitting in the shade, with Young even taking the trouble to teach Smith how to read and write by transcribing the Bible – likely skipping over the 'Thou Shalt Not Kill' bit.

Billy McCoy? He has no interest in either reading or writing, and only cares about drinking to try to take away the pain of being unhappy, lost on an island in the Pacific, leading a pointless existence. He is so miserable that not even Christmas could cheer him up, for it is on the Eve of that sacred day in 1799 – 12 years and a day since he sailed on the *Bounty* from Spithead – McCoy decides to give up the uneven struggle. Tying a large weight around his neck, just as Fletcher Christian had on the day of the Mutiny, he leaps off towards the beckoning finger of Davy Jones. This is a man who had been determined to manage his own death, rather than wait for it to come in the night at the hands of either the men, or the women.

Merry Christmas, Ned Young. Having once planned to kill all the men except his mate, Alec Smith, he now finds that McCoy's suicide has spared him the trouble of another murder.

Alas, alas, Young has very little time to enjoy this gift of the Gods. For with the dawn of Christmas Day, he is hit by such an asthma attack that, despite all but coughing up a kidney, he simply cannot catch his breath and . . . succumbs to that rarest of all things for a Pitcairner – a natural death.

Merry Christmas, Mr Smith! Yes, 12 years since leaving England and nine years on from the burning of the *Bounty*, Alec Smith is the last man standing, his sudden solitude attended by an epiphany. The depressive delirium and suicide of drunken Billy McCoy shocks Smith so much that he swears off liquor for life. (Helping that decision is the fact that he is now one man with ten women, who have already shown a propensity to kill what they don't like – and they don't like drinking.)

A certain quiet descends on Pitcairn, with none quieter than Smith, a sole patriarch surrounded by potentially murdering matriarchs, keenly aware that every night as he goes to sleep, his only chance of waking again is that none, not one, of these women has anything against him. He must treat them well.

•

The fact that there is nobody left to kill – and on the reckoning that the women are not inclined to kill the one being capable of giving them children – life proceeds relatively calmly for the next decade.

Both the women and the 14 children alike come to address him as 'father'. Growing into the role, Smith becomes what he has never been before, a good and peaceful leader. For their part, the women, too, change their approach. With no men fighting over them, and none working the fields, they are both happier and busier than ever before. They work, they raise their children, they take turns spending the night with Alec, they become ever closer to each other.

All proceeds calmly until one midnight, in the early years of the new century, when Smith receives an unexpected visitor. The way he will recount it ever afterwards, his visitor is no less than the Archangel Gabriel come 'down from heaven' to warn him of his danger 'for his past wickedness'.[10]

Now, when it comes to wicked sins, Smith knows only too well that, high in the Kingdom of Heaven, his register doth overflow and the Lord has had to put another man on, just to keep track. Mutiny and murder are only the beginning of it. He has taken the Lord's name in vain more times than he can remember, been violent on the innocent, stolen, lusted in his heart, coveted his neighbour's wife before sleeping with her, after knocking his neighbour on the head, he has fornicated before wedlock more times than he can remember, and committed adultery after marriage – all that, and while this island of Pitcairn has been baptised in blood, not a single one of the children now running around has been baptised at all!

The result is that, when Smith awakes, he has the fear of God in him, and, with the Archangel Gabriel as his guide, becomes if not quite a tub-thumping Christian, at least his perception of what a tub-thumping Christian should be.

Now, where did he put that Holy Bible that Ned had used to teach him how to read and write?

Here.

Now, though Smith does his best to read and understand it, Young's lessons had not quite been finished when he had died, meaning that Smith – acting as parishioner, priest and Pope – does not always grasp the full intent, or extent, of the Bible's lessons, and so mistakenly forms a few new Christian traditions of his own.

Luke 5:35, for example – 'But the days will come, when the bridegroom shall be taken away from them, and then shall they fast in those days'[11] has long been used by Christians as a reason to fast on Good Friday. Smith, though, interprets it differently. Using notes from a Prayer Book that had come to him from Young – 'Good Friday: fast, Ash Wednesday: fast'[12] – Alec comes to the conclusion that they must fast *every* Wednesday and Friday.

Such fasting is no easy thing, and many times the Pitcairn women and children faint from hunger, but as they are all soon converted to a life of strict faith, they know that Jesus died for their sins, that God is watching, and they must stay with it. And so they do, praying every day, fasting twice a week, and attending services conducted by Smith every Sunday. A pious Christian community grows up on the same bloodied ground that has seen the massacre of Mutineers, and the annihilation of the Native men.

Meanwhile, Smith's dreams continue, or, more particularly, nightmares, as he suffers the 'recurrence of another vision' in which he is 'carried away to view the flames and torments of the bottomless pit'.[13] These infernal visions drive his devotion deeper still. Soon, every woman and child on Pitcairn can not only recount the Lord's Prayer, but does so every day. And from having church services only on Sunday, they move to having morning and evening Christian services every day with a third added on Sunday. Not a man to do things by halves, when Smith delivers his Sunday sermon, he doesn't just do it once, he repeats it twice more in the same service – three times in total – so that every word has the best chance of being remembered. Though they don't know it, as they have no contact with the outside world, Pitcairn becomes one of the most devout Christian communities in the world.

But still, so isolated, will the world ever find out?

•

It is the most extraordinary thing.

For on the afternoon of 6 February 1808, an American sealer, the *Topaz*, under the command of Captain Mayhew Folger from Boston, spots an island on the far horizon south-west by west, where none is marked on his chart, and, after steering towards it, he finally drops the anchor in the wee hours of the following morning. Shortly after dawn he puts off two boats to look for seals and is in one of them approaching the beach when he sees a Tahitian-style canoe boat paddling towards them with three Natives aboard. He is stunned when they hail him.

'Who are you?' one of them asks in perfect English, and even with an English accent.

'This is the ship *Topaz* of the United States of America. I am the master, Captain Mayhew Folger, and American.'

Incredulous, they fire off rapid questions: 'You are an American?' 'You come from America?' 'Where is America?' 'Is it in Ireland?'

But enough. For now, Folger has a question for them.

'Who are you?' Folger asks them.

'We are Englishmen . . .' they reply.

'Where were you born?'

'On that island which you see.'

'How then are you Englishmen?'

'We are Englishmen, because our father was an Englishman.'

'Who is your father?'

'Alec.'

'Who is Alec?'

'Don't you know Alec?'

'How should I know Alec?'

'Well then, did you know Captain Bligh of the *Bounty*?'[14]

As a matter of fact, Captain Folger does. Everyone in the English-speaking maritime world knows of the *Bounty*.

Landing on the beach, Folger follows the three young men up to the village, to be greeted by the last surviving Mutineer, Alec Smith, with white hair, surrounded by – Folger counts them – a dozen or so wives, and a gaggle of children. There are about three dozen in all.

To begin with, Smith is ravenous to know details of what has happened in the world, and Folger tells him, among other things, of the French Revolution, the rise of Napoleon and Admiral Horatio Nelson's subsequent victory over the French at Trafalgar in 1805.

Smith is so delighted at the news that, as Captain Folger would recount, he rises, 'from his seat, took off his hat, swung it three times round his head, threw it on the ground sailor-like and cried out "*Old England forever!*"'[15]

Captain Folger likes him. And is clear: 'Whatever may have been the Errors or Crimes of Smith the Mutineer in times Back, he is at present in my opinion a worthy man and may be useful to Navigators who traverse this immense ocean.'[16]

As to what happened during the Mutiny on the *Bounty*, Smith, in turn, gives a comprehensive account, making clear that he barely had anything to do with the Mutiny himself, having awoken to find it already going at full tilt – led by Fletcher Christian, due to 'the overbearing and tyrannical behaviour of the captain'[17] – and when arms were pressed into his hands, he had no choice but to take them up, or risk being killed by the Mutineers himself, don't you see?

At the end of their conversation, Smith gives Captain Folger a present to take with him, nothing less than the *Bounty*'s prized Kendall chronometer and the azimuth compass that had not only survived the Mutiny, but had had pride of place on Smith's mantelpiece for most of the last two decades.

Grateful, stunned to have come across such a story, Folger sails away only ten or so hours after arriving and a few months later tells the whole story to a British Royal Navy officer he meets in the Chilean port city of Valparaiso, and that officer, fascinated, writes up his own report, makes a copy of the *Topaz*'s Log covering the relevant date and forwards the lot to the British Admiralty, who receive the report on 14 May 1809.

Nothing happens. Either disbelieved, or at least placed at the bottom of the list of priorities while Great Britain is at war with France, it is not until a year later that a report appears in the literary and political journal, *The Quarterly Review*.

'If this [claim] rested solely on the faith that is due to Americans,' the *Review* notes, 'with whom we say, with regret, truth is not always considered as a moral obligation, we should hesitate in giving it this publicity.'[18]

But the editors had checked. And the *Bounty* really did have a Kendall chronometer with it when it disappeared, just as there had been an Alec Smith on the ship's muster who had disappeared and was presumed to be a Mutineer.

Still, the reaction is strangely muted. After all, the Mutiny on the *Bounty* was two decades earlier, with many of the principals now dead, and the broad mass of the population not necessarily familiar with the story. As for the Royal Navy, there proves to be little interest in sending out a punitive expedition on the chance of capturing one Mutineer who is now no more than a little old man, and a Christian one at that, leading a model Christian community.

Still, mystified at the lack of response from the British Admiralty – *do you understand, I have FOUND them?* – Folger writes a further missive, recounting his experience on Pitcairn, adding: 'I am sending you the azimuth compass which I received from Alex Smith. I repaired and made use of it on my homeward passage. I now forward it to your lordship.'[19]

No response.

•

At 2.30 am on Saturday 17 September 1814, Captain Philip Pipon on the quarter-deck of his ship the HMS *Tagus*, on a mission to hunt down the American ship USS *Essex*, for its part in the Second War of Independence, is awoken in his cabin to news that originated from an eagle-eyed seaman in the crow's nest who has been gazing into the moonlight: 'Land ahoy, abeam on the lee!'[20]

It is some six leagues to their south.

With no such island marked on his map, Pipon is curious to take a closer look – at least such islands should be marked, with their co-ordinates taken for the British Admiralty so other British ships can know of shoals, reefs, safe harbours etc.

And so, at dawn, after dropping anchor in the closest to a safe harbour he can find – it is a rocky cove – he sees two Natives paddling a canoe towards his vessel. That is not the shock. Many such tiny islands have Natives.

But look what happens now.

For as they get close, one of them calls up in *English*, 'Won't you heave us a rope, now?'

Of course they do, and as the curious crew stand gaping, the two brown young men shinny up the rope as if born for the task, and Pipon gets a closer look at them.

The first fellow to make it up on deck is a handsome dark-haired six foot youth, whose 'well shaped muscular limbs were displayed to much advantage'.[21] The only thing that saves him from being naked is the cloth bound around his loins.

'Who are you?' asks the Captain.

'I am Thursday October Christian,' the lad replies, even as the second lad makes it to the top and stands by his side.

'Thursday October', indeed? And also a Christian, you say? No doubt some missionary has previously come to this land . . . and yet the lad continues.

'I am the son of the late Fletcher Christian.'[22]

It takes a moment for Pipon to comprehend what the lad has just said. *Fletcher* Christian?

Suddenly it all makes sense. That is why the handsome young man with the slightly regal bearing – he carries himself as if of many more years, a natural leader – is more light-skinned than most Natives. That is why he speaks a strange kind of English, with lots of odd, hybrid words. And that is why his last name is Christian. At last, nigh on 25 years after the infamous Mutiny on the *Bounty*, they really have discovered the secret land of the Mutineers; it is Pitcairn Island.

Captain Pipon gazes at Thursday even more closely.

'He was . . . about twenty-five years of age, a tall fine young man about six feet high, with dark black hair, and a countenance extremely open and interesting; he wore no clothes except a piece of cloth round his loins, a straw hat ornamented with *black cock's feathers*, and occasionally a *peacock's*, nearly similar to that worn by the Spaniards in South America, though smaller.'[23]

And the second lad? Who are you?

'George Young,' the lad replies with similarly accented English, 'son of Midshipman Young of the Bounty.'[24]

And now it is the turn of the lads to exult, for when the ship's dog runs up, panting and barking, both Thursday and George yell with delight.

'Oh, what a pretty little thing it is!' cries George Young. 'I know it is a *dog*, for I have heard of such an animal!'[25]

Pipon, stunned at this sudden turn of events, is rowed ashore and is soon struggling up a steep path, which finally flattens to something of a plateau. At this point, he is suddenly greeted by a strange and wizened white man, who introduces himself as ... Alec Smith.

'When he learned we had landed without arms,' Pipon would recount, 'and were not come to seize his person, he met us on the road ... His wife accompanied him a very old woman, blind from age. They were at first extremely alarmed, lest our visit was intended against him, but as we observed to him, we were not even aware of his being then living, and that we had no intention of that nature, he was soon relieved from all his apprehensions.'[26]

So much so, the visitors are invited to Mr and Mrs Smith's house.

Here, Pipon listens to much of the story – the Mutiny, the hunt for an island, the arrival at Pitcairn, the burning of the *Bounty*, the murder of so many men, including Fletcher Christian – whose widow, and Thursday's mother, Isabella, is one of the very quiet women gathered around, part of a throng of the 40 people now living on the island – and the saga thereafter until there had been just one white man left, with ten women and their children, and a single Jolly Boat all that is left of the famous *Bounty*.

Pipon is stunned to discover such a strong Christian community can have been built on the foundations of foul mutiny. Of course, there is no trace of the man who had wrought that mutiny, but even now Pipon can hear his echoes in this community, in a very odd way.

> They know the Lord's Prayer and, I believe, the Creed. They
> frequently call upon our Blessed Saviour, saying, 'I will arise
> and go to my father, and will say, Father, I have sinned against
> heaven and before thee, and am no more worthy to be called thy
> son.' This, I may imagine, was early taught them by Christian,
> with reference to the shameful part he had acted, both against
> God and his country; but it was truly pleasing to see, that there
> poor people are so well-disposed as to listen attentively to moral
> instruction and believe in the divine attributes of God.[27]

It is like a parable brought to life. While the Mutineers have clearly
destroyed themselves with lust, liquor and murder, this community,
built around faith in the Lord, has transformed itself into a model of
how man should live.

And, it has to be said, they live very well!

> Their habitations are extremely neat ... The little village at
> Pitcairn forms a pretty square. [Alec Smith] occupies the house
> at the upper end, and Thursday October Christian one opposite
> to him; the centre is a fine lawn where the poultry wander; but
> it is fenced in so as to prevent the intrusion of hogs, &c. It
> was easily to be perceived that in this establishment the labour
> and ingenuity of European hands had been exerted ... In their
> houses they have also a good deal of decent furniture, consisting
> of beds, and bedsteads, and covering; they have also tables and
> large chests; their clothing and linen are made from the bark of
> a certain tree ...[28]

Now, strictly speaking, Alec Smith should be taken back to England
and tried for the Mutiny of a quarter-century earlier.

And yet, this old man swears on his well-thumbed Bible, 'I was
sleeping in my hammock'[29] when the Mutiny occurred. Indeed, this
poor pious soul stumbled up on deck to find 'everything in great confusion',[30] a confusion which included a bound Captain Bligh being held
by those *evil* Mutineers! (This would be news to Bligh. To this day,
when he wakes in the night, it is not to the vision of the Archangel

Gabriel, but the memory of Smith aiming a musket at his chest, after Christian broke into his cabin, unleashing the Mutiny.)

As to the fate of the leader of the Mutineers, the old man has news: 'Fletcher Christian was never happy after the rash and inconsiderate step he had taken, but became sullen and morose, and having, by many acts of cruelty and inhumanity, brought on himself the hatred and detestation of his companions, he was shot by a black man whilst digging in his field, and almost instantly expired.'[31]

No doubt about it, Smith makes clear. Christian was a deeply troubled man after that very unfortunate mutiny.

But what he stresses again and again is his own innocence. And, really, who, in good conscience, could be so cold of heart, so un-Christian in charity, to separate this Christian *paterfamilias* from his clearly devoted flock, by arresting him? Certainly not such a man as Pipon.

'Although in the eye of the law [we] could only consider him in the light of a criminal of the deepest dye,' the good Captain would note, '[yet Alec Smith's] exemplary conduct and fatherly care of the whole of the little colony cannot but command admiration.'[32]

Take him back to England, to face justice?

Decidedly, no.

'It would have been a heart-breaking circumstance to have torn him from those he most dearly loved, as well as cruel to a degree, to have left a young colony to perish without such a protector and adviser as he was in all their concerns, both with respect to the tilling of the ground, and the private and domestic concerns of all.'[33]

Besides which, by informing the Admiralty of this outpost, passing British ships of the future would have a place to wood and water and re-victual, as the *Tagus* does now.

Captain Pipon is confident he has made the right decision.

And so, just six hours after arriving, the *Tagus* is on its way, leaving the small Christian community exactly as it had found them, bar two things. First, it has corrected their mistake.

'On our arrival here we found that [Alec Smith] was mistaken in the day of the week and month: he considered it to be Sunday, the 18th of September, whereas it was Saturday, the 17th.'[34]

And it has relieved them through trade of 'many valuable refresh-ments . . . such as a few small pigs, yams, cocoa-nuts. bananas, &c'[35] that young Thursday and George manage to guide through the surf on their canoe, to the side of the ship.

As the British ship sails off, Smith remains free on Pitcairn Island, surrounded by his faithful family flock. He and his pious people weep with joy. Truly, the Lord has smiled upon him. Yea, He is good. Yea, He is great. Yea, He has shown the greatest mercy to them.

Now, time for church service, everyone.

The *Tagus* leaves in its happy wake a people who are no longer English, Scottish, Irish, American, Tahitian or Tubuaian. They are, instead, a people all their own, a little flock descended from Mutineers and Natives, the people of Pitcairn, living at last in promised peace, a life of fabled faith on a tiny, beautiful island.

Theirs is a world apart, and they are a people apart, the children of the revolution, the progeny of one of the most compelling stories the world will ever know, the Mutiny on the *Bounty*.

Sail on.

EPILOGUE

For never can true reconcilement grow where wounds of deadly hate have pierced so deep.[1]

John Milton, 'Paradise Lost'

The Byronic hero, incapable of love, or capable only of an impossible love, suffers endlessly. He is solitary, languid, his condition exhausts him.[2]

Albert Camus, *The Rebel*

For the rest of his long career in the Royal Navy, **Captain William Bligh**'s brilliance continued unabated, as did his monumental bastardry, despite the fact that – even beyond the three mutinies he'd suffered in 1789 – still more mutinies were recorded on his watch. For four weeks in 1797 the crews of no fewer than 20 ships of the Royal Navy mutinied in Nore harbour in a dispute over pay and conditions. The crew of HMS *Director*, under the command of Captain Bligh, was the last to surrender. Although his abrasive manner of leadership continued to rankle with his men, still his brilliance and bravery shone through. At the Battle of Copenhagen in April 1801, where the British Fleet fell upon the Danish Fleet, just outside the harbour of Copenhagen, he performed so well that Lord Nelson publicly thanked Bligh for his judgement, skill and bravery on deck after the battle was won.

So overwhelming did his bastardry become, however, that, on 26 February 1805, he faced a further court martial because of it. It was convened aboard HMS *San Josef* and Bligh's accuser was Lieutenant John Frazier, who the year before had sailed under Bligh on the *Warrior* – a 74-gun, 1600-ton ship of the line, with a complement of

600 men – and because of his scarifying experience brought charges of abuse against Bligh for language, threats and behaviour unbecoming to an officer.

Giving testimony with the force of the truly scandalised, Lieutenant Frazier paints a picture that is very familiar to those who know Bligh and have had the misfortune to serve under him.

Gentlemen, in the course of honourably fulfilling my duties, Captain Bligh called me a 'damn'd rascal', and a 'damn'd scoundrel', and in front of the crew bitterly complained that 'never was a man troubled with such a set of blackguards as I am'. He, furthermore, shook his fist in my face, called me a 'liar', yelled that I 'bore false witness', and declared every man in the *Warrior* constituted 'a parcel of villains and scoundrels'.[3]

These proved to be his opening remarks.

For Bligh goes on to call others, 'an infamous scoundrel, an audacious rascal, a vagrant and a dastardly villain', and 'a damn'd long pelt of a bitch'.[4]

And so it goes.

After two days the examinations and cross-examinations are complete, and the court retires to consider its verdict. It does not take long.

All rise.

Their Honours find the charges, 'part proved'. Captain Bligh is officially reprimanded and instructed to 'be in the future more correct in [your] language',[5] the best result he could hope for, under the circumstances of the damning testimony that has been delivered.

The fact that it does little to damage Bligh's career is revealed just two months later, when – due to the efforts of the relentless Sir Joseph Banks pushing his case once more – Bligh is asked to become the next Governor of New South Wales, the notoriously corrupt colony that is a disgrace to the British Empire.

After all, as Sir Joseph writes to his protégé, the incumbent Governor, Philip Gidley King, is exhausted, having 'carried into effect a reform of great extent, which militated much with the interest of the soldiers and settlers there. He is, consequently, disliked and much opposed, and has asked leave to return.'[6]

Who better to command and regain the confidence and respect of a group of soldiers who disliked and were much opposed to the old Governor than Captain Bligh?

(Seriously, Sir Joseph? *Seriously?*)

It did not end well.

For, once in New South Wales – with Betsy and all but one of their daughters remaining in England – it was not long before the mother of all mutinies against Bligh took place, this one the infamous Rum Rebellion, but that is another story (and, I hope, another book).

Not surprisingly, well before Bligh has made landfall in Sydney, his reputation has preceded him, moved in and made itself uncomfortable. There was always going to be a clash, and this time the man leading the rebellion against Bligh's rule was that most fascinating of Australian heroes and villains, John Macarthur. Wealthy, well-connected, influential and ruthless, Macarthur quickly laid the foundations for the only successful military coup in our national history. And Bligh helped, quickly rousing both the people and the soldiers against him.

As Bligh began reforming the Rum Corps, and slicing away at Macarthur's power, graffiti showed up all over Sydney Town:

> Is there no CHRISTIAN in New South Wales to put a stop
> to the tyranny of the Governor?[7]

At the next confrontation with Macarthur, after Bligh had confiscated Macarthur's industrial-scale still for producing rum, Sydney's wealthiest man threatened the Governor that he'd better return it, as 'if you do not, you will perhaps get another voyage in your Launch again'.[8]

Funny he should say that.

For not long afterwards, Macarthur was indeed instrumental in having the Rum Corps rise against Bligh and having him held prisoner in Government House, before he would agree to return to England as Captain of HMS *Porpoise*. Bligh did so agree, but, once on the ship, turned his guns on Sydney Town before heading to Van Diemen's Land instead, where he held out, blockading the state before sulkily returning to a Sydney finally prospering under a popular Governor, the former Lieutenant Lachlan Macquarie who had met Captain Bligh so many years and so many miles ago. (As I say, it is another fascinating story that needs another book.)

As Bligh's successor as Governor of New South Wales, Lachlan Macquarie had to put up with the pompous presence of his predecessor for many an awkward month and was not long in spotting the problem, noting in a letter to his brother: 'Governor Bligh certainly is a most disagreeable person to have any dealings, or public business to transact with; having no regard whatever to his promises or engagements however sacred, and his natural temper is uncommonly harsh and tyrannical in the extreme.'

In the same letter Macquarie wrote it was 'an undoubted fact that he is a very improper person to be employed in any situation of Trust or Command, and he is certainly detested by high, low, rich and poor'.[9] Poor William Bligh, at sea when not at sea, returned home, perhaps dimly aware that history would remember him mostly as a tyrant twice overthrown, a little as the brilliant navigational genius he most certainly was, and not at all as the national hero he felt himself to be.

At least, in his twilight years, he was given a final promotion, to Vice-Admiral of the Blue, before retiring from duty to live in Kent – sadly without Betsy for the last part, as she died in 1812, leaving him as the head of a household with four unmarried daughters.

Whatever else, he was an old man with many extraordinary memories.

Writing well over half a century later, in the 1870s, the Reverend Alfred Gatty would recount how, as a small boy, his parents had taken him to see the famous Captain Bligh. Ushered into the great man's study, wee Alfred is suddenly in another world, one filled with maps, models, compasses, chronometers, and yes, Captain Bligh himself!

Spellbound, the young lad sits on the old man's knee as he tells tales from long ago, of places faraway, of heroes, pirates and *scoundrels*! Noticing an odd object hanging around Bligh's neck, Alfred asks about it.

What, this, lad?

Why this, young fellow, is a musket-ball and I once used it to measure the tiny food rations we had each day for 18 men crammed into a tiny Launch, as we sailed towards a place thousands of miles away called Coupang.

We were making good our escape from a villain by the name of Fletcher Christian and his band of brigands. Let me tell you the story.

As the afternoon passes, and the shadows outside lengthen, the lamps are lit and Captain Bligh goes on, telling a thrilling tale that the lad will never forget: of an island kingdom filled with dusky maidens, a boy King who is carried on the backs of men and rules his own parents – Alfred likes that detail, particularly – of piracy, mutiny, starvation, wild Natives they only just escaped from, lashings, drownings and a great Captain who, betrayed by a man he thought a friend, triumphed anyway, against unbelievable odds, by completing a journey of 4000 miles in an open boat! (A feat that will never be surpassed.)

It is an amazing story, of wild twists and turns, great heroes, terrible villains, extraordinary characters, unbelievable endings ... and it is all true, every word of it.

Though the grand old man of the sea settles easily into country life, by 1817, just seven years after returning from New South Wales, he has fallen ill, and while consulting his doctor in London's famed Bond Street, collapses and dies. Where to spend eternity? Of course, right by dear Betsy, in the graveyard that lies behind St Mary's Church at Lambeth.

How significant was the Mutiny episode in his story? Significant enough that, presumably at his request, a small bread-fruit in stone adorns the top of his tomb. (In the meantime, one tragic irony of the whole bread-fruit saga was that, despite the extraordinary efforts of Bligh to complete that mission, and despite the plants flourishing in those climes, the slaves did not like the taste and it never did become the cheap source of food the slave masters had hoped for.)

Nearby Bligh's tomb, his and Betsy's home is still standing, right opposite what is now the Imperial War Museum but what, back in the day, was Bethlehem Hospital for the Insane, otherwise known as 'Bedlam'.

Farewell, Captain Bligh. Whatever else we'll say about you, you were the most compelling character in this stunning saga, a brilliant bastard like they don't make anymore, a tornado of temper, a superb survivor and undoubtedly the finest navigator of your generation.

And whoever took your coconuts that morning really has a case to answer ...

•

Sir Joseph Banks, the puppetmaster behind so much of what happened on the *Bounty*, as well as the aftermath, remained an enormously influential figure in British society for a good 30 years after the Mutiny on the *Bounty*.

What a life he led, what an influence he wielded. The dashing young scientist who cut such a swathe through the Tahitian maidens on his first visit with Captain Cook in 1769 went on to be perhaps the most influential man of science of his time and President of the Royal Society for an extraordinary 42 years.

Today few realise how much this founding father of Australia was involved in the affair of the *Bounty*. Bligh was his hand-picked hero and it was Banks who rode shotgun on his career and reputation thereafter (in the process defending his own judgement). And he did it all very well. Like Bligh, he was a man of genius, but Banks had two invaluable skills that Bligh never had: diplomacy and discretion. He lived to the ripe old age of 77, finally dying at his home, in London, on 19 June 1820.

•

Perhaps even more remarkably, despite having only narrowly escaped the noose, and then being publicly associated with Edward Christian's attempts to set the record straight about Bligh, **Peter Heywood** also rose in the ranks of the Royal Navy and was even promoted to Captain in 1803 at the age of 31, five years younger than Bligh was when he first gained that honour. (Tragically, the woman who had done so much to see Peter freed, his sister, **Nessy Heywood,** was not there to see his triumph, as she had died within 12 months of his liberation, a fever and inflammation of the lungs leading to an early grave. I *weep*.)

Why was Peter Heywood such a good Captain, and promoted so rapidly? One can't help but speculate . . .

Perhaps, just as Michelangelo is celebrated for having said that it was easy to sculpt the statue of David, as all he had to do was start with a block of marble and chip away anything that didn't look like the lad, so too did Heywood know that the art of man-management was to use Bligh as the example of what not to do. In any case, Heywood went on to a quarter-century of captaincy, with a distinguished career entirely untouched by reprimand or scandal, let alone anything that even looked like a mutiny.

One episode in his career, however, bears particular repeating. It occurs in 1816, just months before his retirement, when he is in command of HMS *Montagu*. Having just dropped anchor at Gibraltar, he hears an intriguing story from one of his fellow Captains in one of the popular taverns. Apparently two Natives from a distant island in the Pacific had been kidnapped as slaves by a Spanish ship, only to escape. They have made their way here, and now are begging for help from the nearest British ship, the *Calypso*.

Do tell?

And what island in the Pacific are they from?

I believe it is called Tahiti.

Excited, Captain Heywood sends for the men, and the two wild-eyed escapees, so far from home, so brutalised by what has occurred, are brought to his cabin.

What now? Are they to be shot, perhaps? Tied to the mast, and lashed some more?

But no, strangely, this grand-looking man, this Captain of this enormous ship, rises as they enter, throws his arms wide and says: *'Ma now, wa, Eho maa! Yowra t'Eatooa te hare a mye!'* (Welcome my friends! God save you in coming here!)[10]

Yes, even after all this time, Heywood can still speak the Tahitian language, just as he still harbours wonderful memories of his time in the island paradise. What a pleasure, thus, to be able to welcome, speak to, and help two men from this place of his dreams. Later, he would recount:

> They could scarce believe their ears when I accosted them in a
> language so dear to them, and which, except by each other, they
> had not heard pronounced since they were torn from their country.
> They seemed at the moment electrified. A rush of past recollec-
> tions at once filled their minds, and then, in a tone and with an

expression peculiar to these people; and strikingly mournful, they sighed out together and in unison:

'*Attaye, huoy ay! Attaye huoy to tawa Venooa, my tye ay! Ita rota ye heo ay!*' (Alas! Alas! Our Good country, we shall never see it more!)

I took each by the hand and told them, that if I lived they should be sent home to their country, and assured them, that in the mean time they should remain with me, and that I would be their countryman, their friend and protector. Poor fellows! They were quite overwhelmed – their tears flowed apace – and they wept the thankfulness they could not express.[11]

For now, the men stay in the Captain's cabin late in the night, talking of Tahiti, of their experiences, of how Captain Heywood will get them home once more. Despite the unhappiness they have been through, the Englishman is struck forcefully by the realisation that these two Natives are so much more innately happy than the civilisation into which they have been dragged. Writing a letter to a friend that chronicles the encounter, he notes the depth of longing these men have to return to Tahiti, 'and God knows . . . so do I, that is not to be wondered at'.[12] His empathy and immediate sense of brotherhood with these two exiles is instant and profound: 'But there is no describing the state of one's mind in witnessing the sensibilities of another fellow being, with a *conviction*, at the same time, that they are *true and unaffected*. And *good God!* With what ease is that discovered. What an amazing difference there is between these children of nature and the pupils of art and refinement!'[13]

Captain Heywood cannot help himself, and suddenly remembering what he had back then, now laments the state of the modern world 'where polish teaches to conceal, except among the poor and untaught "*savages*" of the island which gave these men birth – where plenty and content are the portion of all, unalloyed by care, envy or ambition. Where labour is needless and want unknown. At least, such it was twenty-five years ago. And after all that is said and done among us great and wise people of the earth, pray what do we all toil for . . . but to reach, at last, *the very state to which they are born* – ease of circumstances and the option of being idle or as busy as we please? But if I go on this way you will say I am a *savage*, and so I believe I am, and *ever shall be* in *some* points, but let that pass . . . Upon the whole, there is more general happiness among them, than among any people I have met with on earth; so that I am very sure, the less we teach them of our arts and sciences, the better for themselves . . . But of this matter I have said more than enough, perhaps, and more than I intended.'[14]

Heywood keeps his word, and does indeed ensure these two Tahitian men return to their island, though personally he will never set foot there again. Instead, he retires, returns to England and settles back to an easy life in his London home, surrounded by family, his aristocratic wife, Francis – they were married in 1816 – and fine friends. Peter Heywood died at home in England, in February 1831, aged 58, of a stroke. A decade before that he'd privately published a dictionary of the Tahitian language, though no copy has survived to the present day.

•

James Morrison also returned to naval service and, like Peter Heywood, continued to rise through the ranks. By 1806 he had achieved the rank of Master Gunner when, alas, the ship he was serving on, the *Blenheim*, sank with all hands off Madagascar in 1807.

As to the journal that he had penned, that, too, very nearly sank without trace courtesy of the efforts of Sir Joseph Banks, who – with all the damaging information therein about Bligh – reportedly did everything possible to prevent its publication. He would have succeeded entirely, bar one thing. Peter Heywood had kept a copy of this means of his redemption, and long after he had died, his step-daughter was rummaging in the attic one afternoon when she came across it, started reading, and was instantly transfixed. And so it was that, 63 years after his death, the prose of James Morrison was finally put in the public domain by being published, and that step-daughter, Lady Belcher, became one of the first *Bounty* historians.

Undoubtedly, however, Morrison's greatest legacy was less his writing and much more his Tahitian-built boat, the Cutter *Resolution*. For after it had delivered those stranded sailors of the *Pandora* to safety at Samarang, it was sold to the Captain of HMS *Providence*, who placed it on board his ship. In 1797, when the *Providence* was wrecked off the coast of Formosa and sank, the *Resolution* knew its finest hour, going back and forth taking 112 shivering British sailors to safety, on dry land, instead of drowning. Sir John Barrow, one of the earliest chroniclers of the whole *Bounty* saga, loved the story of the *Resolution* and the wonderful postscript it provided, noting that, according to the men he spoke to, 'she was a remarkably swift sailer, and being afterwards employed in the sea-otter trade, is stated to have made one of the quickest passages ever known from China to the Sandwich Islands'.[15]

A good effort for a 30-foot vessel, knocked together with perspiration, elbow-grease, bread-fruit sap and hog lard.

Bravo, James Morrison.

•

Memories of the other characters, of course, would also live on. **George Stewart** – who left Tahiti in *Pandora*'s box, with his beloved Peggy and infant daughter Charlotte in his wake – had a sister, Margaret. She was still alive in 1869, when at the age of 92, an ancient Victorian lady, she said of the tattooed 21-year-old young buck of a brother she'd last seen some 80 years earlier, 'whether or not the *Bounty* was the first ship George sailed in I do not know, but, poor fellow, it was his last'.[16]

•

Another Royal Navy ship arrived in Pitcairn in November 1825, when Captain Frederick Beechey of HMS *Blossom* dropped anchor and came ashore, finding the Christian community thriving, as reported, and still presided over by **Alec Smith**, who, 'in his sixty-fifth year, was unusually strong and active . . . He still retained his sailor's gait, doffing his hat and smoothing down his bald forehead whenever addressed by the officers . . .'[17]

Captain Beechey talked to him extensively, taking notes, and later provided a full report titled *Narrative of a Voyage to the Pacific and Beering's Strait*, regarded as the most reliable report of events on Pitcairn as Smith, now assured he would never be prosecuted, 'Apprehension for his safety formed no part of his thoughts',[18] was much more forthcoming about what had occurred.

For his part, once he has established that Beechey is no danger, Alec Smith is even more delighted at his arrival as he now asks a favour of the Captain: 'It would add much to my happiness if you would read a marriage ceremony for me and my wife. I cannot bear the thought of living with her without it being done.'[19]

Sure enough, the following day, 17 December 1825, old Alec Smith and his bed-ridden, blind wife are able to stop living in sin, and are finally united in the eyes of God, as Captain Beechey conducts a Christian ceremony with all the trimmings. The Christian conscience of Alec can now be put to rest on this point, at least.

In March 1829, the day after his 66th birthday, Alec was ailing badly. He is still unchallenged as the *paterfamilias* of the whole Pitcairn tribe, and no fewer than 140 Pitkerners are hoping he will pull through.

Alas, alas, late in the day, as the light fades, he takes a turn for the worse. 'He said in a whisper,' a family member would recount, 'as his countenance lighted up with joy "Let go the anchor" and fell back upon his pillow and died.'[20]

And here endeth, friends, the final psalm beneath the palms, of an extraordinary life.

•

Jenny turned out to be one of the great sources, and shrewdest observers, of what happened at Tahiti, on the *Bounty*, and then at Pitcairn. Interviewed first for a daily Sydney newspaper and then for a United States naval magazine, she proved to be a fount of information, including providing the precious names of all the original women on Pitcairn and which of the men they were matched to, voluntarily or otherwise. Even her silence could be remarkably telling. For example, Jenny has a crystal-clear recollection of who killed who on the island, but does not name who so dismayed Fletcher Christian by shooting one button-admiring Native on the way there. I have drawn the conclusion it is Alec Smith, *because* she does not name who it was. There is only one Mutineer left alive when Jenny is interviewed; Alec Smith, her former partner and still a possible threat. Jenny is also atypically vague when it comes to naming who set fire to the *Bounty*. Alec Smith says it was Matt Quintal, but again I would wager that, at the very least, Alec Smith helped with this arson. Nearing the end of her life, in 1820, Jenny actually left Pitcairn on the American ship *Sultan*, sailed to Chile, the Marquesas and then returned to Tahiti 'after an absence of thirty one years'.[21]

•

Isabella – my favourite, with Nessy! – never took another lover after Fletcher's death, and never remarried. She died on Pitcairn on 19 September 1841, likely of influenza. She was about 72 years old. An extraordinary woman, whose life had encompassed the historic visit of Captain Cook to Tahiti in 1777, the visit of Bligh, the revisit by the Mutineers, the flight to Pitcairn and establishment of their colony there, she was one of the last survivors of all those who sailed with Christian, the matriarch of 200 Pitkerners.

•

Isabella's death left **Teraura** as the last person left standing from those who had first landed on Pitcairn from the *Bounty*, before it was burnt. Ned Young's first wife, she had decapitated Tetaheite while he slept, and, aged 30, she married 15-year-old Thursday October Christian, thereby bearing grandchildren to the Mutineers as well as children. She died in 1850.

•

Master **John Fryer** and Captain Bligh never repaired their relationship. Years after returning to England, Fryer asked Bligh for a reference. Bligh declined. Fryer remained in the Royal Navy until 1812. He was never promoted. He died in 1817 aged 63.

•

Having survived the wreck of the *Pandora*, **Thomas Hayward** was lucky once more, four years later, when he also survived being shipwrecked in the *Diomede* off Ceylon. Alas, just two years later, when his first command, the *Swift*, sank in the South China Sea in 1797, Captain Hayward was lost with all his men. He was just 30 years old.

•

Many survivors, even Loyalists – perhaps *particularly* Loyalists – tried to forget the whole dreadful episode. When **Lawrence Lebogue** was encountered by a member of the Bligh family and was asked about his voyage in the Launch, his response was quick: 'Oh damn me, I never think about the boat.'[22] Lebogue drowned in 1795, when HMS *Jason*, which he was serving on, was shipwrecked.

•

Although the court martial of **Captain Edward Edwards** for losing the *Pandora* exonerated him, he was never appointed to a sea-going naval command again. Nevertheless, like a character from a Gilbert and Sullivan musical, his career on land prospered remarkably regardless, as he rose steadily through the ranks, eventually being made an Admiral in 1810. Upon retirement, he ran a lodging in Cornwall which he called, yes, *The Pandora Inn*. I do wonder if any of the men he put in *Pandora*'s box, who survived, ever passed by and stayed there? He died in 1815, aged 73.

•

After the court martial, **Michael Byrn**, the **Blind Fiddler**, served on the *Prompte* with Bligh's nephew Francis Bond. At his uncle's behest, Bond interviewed Byrn to see if his testimony might counter the lies being put out by the wretched Professor Christian.

For example, on the morning of the Mutiny, did you hear Midshipman George Stewart clap his hands together and say that this was the happiest day of his life?

Byrn thinks for a moment then says, 'No.'

Oh well.

'I heard Mr Heywood say so.'[23]

Good Lord! Such testimony at the court martial would have seen Peter Heywood swinging from the end of a rope, and one can only imagine how furious Uncle William would have been to hear it, long after Peter Heywood had been pardoned.

The fate of the Blind Fiddler thereafter is lost.

•

Few were more helpful to Edward Christian after the court martial than **William Purcell,** as he went well above and beyond the call of duty to put on the record that the real cause of the Mutiny was the bastardry of Captain Bligh himself. He then went off to spend the rest of his working life on ships in the West Indies. Sir John Barrow, in *The Eventful History of the Mutiny and Piratical Seizure of HMS Bounty*, claims Purcell was in a 'madhouse' in 1831 – perhaps Bedlam, right opposite Bligh's grave, I can't help but wonder? – and George Mackaness, in *The Life of Vice-Admiral William Bligh*, says Purcell died at Haslar Hospital on 10 March 1834. I do hope they buried him with his tool box, or, even better, *in* it. Mr Purcell was very fond of that tool box, and there surely could have been no better resting place for it than with him for eternity. That way, the bastards could never get their hands on it. Either way, he died as the last officer left standing of the *Bounty*.

•

Matthew Flinders, of course, went on to great fame as the first to circumnavigate Australia, which voyage he completed in 1803. One episode of that feat bears repeating here. For the coast off what we now know as North Queensland, Flinders had two maps – one by Captain Cook and one by Captain Bligh.

Whose map, do you suppose, proved to be more accurate? The one made by the starving Bligh, in a rocking, packed Launch? Or the one done by Cook, in full comfort of a ship, with all instruments?

Bligh's was better.

Flinders, comparing the accurate map he had drawn, with those of Cook and Bligh, was firm. His own map had 'less agreement both in situation and appearance with Captain Cook's Chart, than they have with that made by Captain Bligh in the Bounty's launch'.[24]

Flinders was stunned.

> It has been to me a cause of much surprise, that under such distress of hunger and fatigue, and of anxiety still greater than these, and whilst running before a strong breeze in an open boat, Captain Bligh should have been able to gather materials for a

chart; but that this chart should possess a considerable share of accuracy, is a subject for admiration. [I] pride myself in being, in some sort, [Captain Cook's] disciple; my first acquirements in nautical science having been made under one who mostly gained his from that great master himself: untoward circumstances shall not prevent me repeating the name of Bligh.[25]

•

Glimpses of the fate of **Tahiti** itself come through the ages, with the deterioration spotted by Captain Bligh in 1792 continuing with alarming pace. By the mid-1790s whalers and other ships started arriving once or twice a year and by 1800 the population had halved as a result of European diseases.

Sir Joseph Banks noted in 1806:

Tahiti is said to be at present in the hands of about one hundred white men, chiefly English convicts [from New South Wales] who lend their assistance as warriors to the chief whoever he may be, who offers them the most acceptable wages payable in women, hogs etc; and we are told that these *banditti* have by the introduction of diseases, by devastation, murder and all kinds of European barbarism, reduced the population of that one interesting island to less than one tenth of what it was when the *Endeavour* visited it in 1769.[26]

When the missionaries arrived in the 1820s it must have been a hard sell – particularly to the older Natives – to maintain that the Lord was smiling upon them, but virtually the whole population was indeed converted to Christianity.

On the famous voyage of the *Beagle* to the South Pacific in 1835, Charles Darwin himself defined Tahiti as 'that fallen Paradise', while still being impressed by the surviving Natives, recording 'there is a mildness in the expression of their countenances which at once banishes the idea of a savage; and an intelligence which shows that they are advancing in civilization'.[27]

Geopolitically, in the 1840s, Tahiti came under the French sphere of influence and was annexed as a territory of France in 1843. In 2004 the status was upgraded and Tahiti became *un Pays d'Outremer*, overseas land, making all Tahitians French citizens, just as they have been in New Caledonia since 1853.

Today the economy thrives, and an international airport and a university are at Oparre, not far from where the *Bounty* was moored in Matavai Bay.

•

The fate of the **Tasmanian Aborigines**, who Captain Bligh gave us such a penetrating, poignant glimpse of, would be devastating. The brief, curious and peaceful pen portraits provided by James Cook and William Bligh of that people are rich in pathos for the fact that their entire way of life would soon be overwhelmed by a cataclysm of bloody, brutal and fatal events stemming from British engagement with the most remote people on earth.

•

The future of **Pitcairn** would be problematic, as by the early 1830s its population of 135 had outgrown the capacity of the island to sustain them. Hearing of their plight, with great generosity, Tahiti's Queen Pomare offered a return to her island's wayward children – all of them, after all, having descended from Tahitian women – and in February 1831, they were welcomed back. It was, alas, a disaster. So long isolated, their resistance to disease common to Tahitians was all but non-existent and their numbers were decimated in the six months before they decided to return to Pitcairn. Those who died included none other than **Thursday October Christian.**

In 1838, the island was formally made a colony of Great Britain, which saw such a flood of immigrants that, together with the natural population expansion by the descendants of the Mutineers and the Natives, by the mid-1850s, the population had effectively outgrown the island again.

The solution, for the British government, was to move them all to the just abandoned penal colony of Norfolk Island, a slightly bigger island some 3500 miles to their west. On 3 May 1856, the entire population of 194 people set sail for Norfolk on board the *Morayshire*, arriving on 8 June after what they thought was a merely miserable five-week trip. Ah, but *true* misery would only come on Norfolk Island. They were so homesick that two brothers, Moses and Mayhew Young – descendants of Ned Young – took their wives and 12 children and led what would be an exodus once more to Pitcairn, with another 27 following them by 1864.

As to how things worked on such a small island as Pitcairn, with such a small population, as the generations passed, it was Mark Twain himself who summed it up in 1879, reminding readers that when the population are descended from such a small base, there are inevitably tight connections between just about everyone. 'The relationships are wonderfully, even astoundingly, mixed up and complicated. A stranger, for instance, says to an islander: "You speak of that young woman as your cousin; a while ago you called her your aunt."

'"Well, she is my aunt, and my cousin, too. And also my stepsister, my niece, my fourth cousin, my thirty-third cousin, my forty-second cousin, my great-aunt, my grandmother, my widowed sister-in-law – and next week she will be my wife."'[28]

Pitcairn Island would once again gain infamy as in the late 1990s it became apparent that an abhorrent culture of underage sexual abuse was entrenched in certain circles on the island. Defenders claimed such an approach to underage sex was a legacy of the Tahitian libertine approach in the late 1700s. Prosecutors countered it had no place in the modern era and the judge and jury agreed. Six male residents were successfully prosecuted and served time in a specially constructed prison on the island.

•

Which leaves us with . . . **Fletcher Christian**. As the decades rolled past, other theories of the true story of the Mutiny emerged.

One particularly far-fetched one maintained that when Christian made Heywood and Stewart promise to find his family should they survive, to tell them the real reason he mutinied, that reason was one that 'dare not speak its name'.

In 1965, in her book *Captain Bligh in Wapping*, the writer Madge Darby speculated that it might have been because Bligh, 'made his young friend pay for privilege with his body'.[29]

I strongly reject this as a possibility. All indications are that Bligh was totally devoted to Betsy and Fletcher Christian had a long record of heterosexual relationships.

Far more likely is something to do with Christian being in monetary debt to Bligh, as the original Captain of the *Bounty* had indeed lent money to the Master's Mate, in Cape Town. Either way, there is no doubt that Peter Heywood, as revealed in Chapter 17, did indeed seek out Christian's family, most particularly Edward Christian. Had he made any revelations of Captain Bligh committing the 'detestable sin of buggery' as the Articles of War indelicately put it, then a sin punishable by death in the Royal Navy – it is inconceivable that the Professor would not have at least hinted at that behaviour, if not necessarily applying it to his own brother. If it were true, can we believe that Peter Heywood, on trial for his life, would not have raised it in his defence, or, at the very least, have told his influential relatives in the Navy?

When, at the time, people pressed Heywood on the 'secret' he intimated that, though it was not scandalous, it still could not be told. Again, that fits with debt being the most likely secret – a want of money that 'dared not speak its name'. But the reason it had to be whispered only is because of the embarrassment of a gentleman like Fletcher Christian owing money to a man of the lower classes, like Bligh.

Bligh himself wrote of this to Sir Joseph Banks, complaining of Edward Christian's impudence given the fact that the Professor 'knows from his Brother's Note of Hand (which he received) that he was supplied by him [*Bligh*] with that money he wanted'.[30]

So why did Fletcher Christian rise up? Not because of sexual abuse, just outright abuse: mental and verbal. The bizarre coconut episode was the last straw, for a man worn down to what amounted to an only tentative hold on mental equilibrium. The fact that Fletcher Christian seriously considered getting off a ship and on a raft in the middle of the ocean is as sure a sign as exists that he was not stable at the time of the Mutiny.

On the matter of his stability, allow me to float another theory, courtesy of one of my researchers, Dr Peter Williams. Bligh, you will recall, notes that his one-time favourite, Fletcher, 'is subject to violent perspiration and particularly in his hands so he soils anything he handles'.[31]

Is that the clue? For Dr Williams notes that, 'studies show that a third of those with this condition, "hyperhydrosis", also have mental health issues, including occasional outbursts of irrational behaviour and depression. Perhaps Fletcher Christian had such an outburst at the time of the Mutiny?'

And was Christian's fate, indeed, the generally accepted one, described earlier in this book? For there remains an intriguing theory about his actual fate that has endured through the centuries. As a prelude to revealing it, allow me to note I write this as one who has long pooh-poohed many modern conspiracy theories. I do believe that President John F. Kennedy was shot by a loser named Lee Harvey Oswald, and it was neither the Russians, nor the Mafia, nor the CIA or FBI, wot dunnit. I think Elvis died, just as reported, from eating too many cheeseburgers. And I think the most salient factors in the tragic death of Diana, Princess of Wales, were that she was in the car with a drunken driver, and was not wearing her seatbelt – rather than a hit ordered by the Queen or Prince Philip or MI5.

So I don't easily embrace anything other than the traditional conclusion that Christian died at the hands of the Natives.

But . . . a few things really don't add up.

In 1809, in his official report to the Admiralty, Sir Sydney Smith recorded what the second mate of the *Topaz* was told: 'Christian the ringleader became insane shortly after their arrival on the island and threw himself off the rocks into the sea.'[32]

Yet the diary of one of Captain Mayhew Folger's close friends equally firmly records, 'Folger was very explicit in his statement that Alec Smith told him Christian got sick and died a natural death.'[33]

Another version comes from Captain Pipon, who reported he was told about a 'sullen & morose' Christian, who, after his wife died, 'forcibly seized on one belonging to the Tahitian men', whereupon he was murdered for his trouble, 'whilst digging in his own field'.[34] (At least one part of this is demonstrably false, as we know that the only wife Christian ever had survived until 1841.)

Finally, Alec Smith would report to Captain Beechey that Christian was 'always cheerful a happy and active'[35] leader who was very popular.

My point is that it is extraordinary that the accounts of the key player in the piece, Fletcher Christian, should vary so much from so many eye-witnesses, or at least people intimately familiar with events. Does it not stand to reason that a very public, plebeian death would lend itself to a uniformity of accounts, while mystery lends itself to variance? Is it not also more than passing odd that such a man as Christian would have no known grave, if indeed he died in the manner accepted? Would it make sense that, if so killed, Smith would go to the effort of destroying almost all written records and journals?

And where was the missing boat? On arrival at Pitcairn, the Mutineers had the *Bounty*, the Cutter and the Jolly Boat. But when Captain Folger gets there in 1808 only the Jolly Boat is left. What happened to the Cutter? Could a sailor as experienced as Christian – perhaps on the day of the murders – have escaped, to navigate as far as an island more frequently visited by French, Dutch, Portuguese or Spanish ships, presented himself as the survivor of a shipwreck and gone on to live happily, if quietly, ever after? After all, Christian has all of Bligh's personal maps of 20 years work, plus every single map that Bligh brought on the *Bounty*. With the right vessel, he could sail anywhere in the world. But when the Americans and English arrive at Pitcairn, Bligh's entire library of prose books is preserved, with 'Fletcher Christian' having written his own name neatly under Bligh's to indicate he now owns them, but all the maps are gone. Why? Could it be that Christian has taken them? Smith, of course, has no reason to destroy them.

And so, try the alternative, that he got away to remake his life elsewhere. Would that not fit with a variation of accounts, of no known grave, of destroying records so nothing would point to that escape from the island?

And how was William Wordsworth so sure that the purported 'autobiography' of Fletcher was a fake, when not even Bligh was sure?

Could it be because he has either spoken to Fletcher Christian, or at least knows he is back in England?

Though Wordsworth will never write again of his friend – perhaps consistent with having him be forgotten – it seems another of Wordsworth's close friends, Samuel Taylor Coleridge, very well may have, famously penning 'The Rime of the Ancient Mariner', the key character of which is able to tell the tale of a nightmarish sea tragedy. For you see, over a century later, a scholar going over Coleridge's notebooks found a scribble in one of them, just prior to composition, noting 'Adventures of Christian, the MUTINEER.'[36]

The parallels between the poem and Christian's story are obvious, as witness some of the quotes from the poem in the opening chapters in this book. And those similarities could well include that the key protagonist survived to tell the tale.

Whatever else, let the record show, many roughly contemporary chroniclers came to much that conclusion, led by Sir John Barrow, who delicately observed in 1831, in the first version of the story, 'the manner of Christian's death has been reported differently to each different visitor'.[37]

So much so, in fact, that Sir John suggests so many differing accounts 'might render his death on Pitcairn's Island almost a matter of doubt'.[38]

There are other inconsistencies.

When the *Bounty* landed at Pitcairn it had a small fortune of ducats and Spanish dollars on board, as currency in the South Seas with anyone they could find to trade with. To this day, *none* of the coins has been found.

As to whether, most intriguingly, Christian made his way back to England, there is also evidence that supports this.

In 1808, Peter Heywood, now a respected Captain of the Royal Navy, confided in the secretary of the Royal Navy, Sir John Barrow, a story he would never put in the public domain – but Sir John makes a note of it, and will reveal it just after Heywood dies.

For you see, one afternoon back in 1808, Heywood had just returned from a voyage and was down near Plymouth Dock, up Fore Street way, you know the place, when he suddenly notices the man walking up yonder, well in front of him. Those shoulders! That trim! That strange, distinctive bow-legged way he is walking!

He has no doubt. It is Fletcher Christian!

Of course, Heywood breaks into something of a trot to catch him, but this alerts the man, who turns quickly to see who is after him. Heywood sees his face.

It is him.

It was him, I tell you, Sir John!

And yes, of course Sir John is stunned, and seems disbelieving, but Captain Heywood insists.

'The face was as much like Fletcher as the back!'[39]

Now whether the man in front recognises Heywood is not certain. But he at least sees that he is being pursued by a Captain of the Royal Navy, and that is enough. He starts to run. Heywood does the same.

'Both ran as fast as they were able,' Sir John would later recount of the conversation, 'but the stranger had the advantage and after making several short turns, disappeared.'[40]

It is a moment fleeting, but an impression enduring, and Heywood will believe it for the rest of his life.

That *was* Fletcher Christian! Somehow, despite reports, he had made it back to England. (And this is consistent with another rumour that Sir John Barrow also records: 'About the years 1808 and 1809, a very general opinion was prevalent in the neighbourhood of the lakes of Cumberland and Westmoreland, that Christian was in that part of the country, and made frequent private visits to an aunt who was living there. Being the near relative of Mr. Christian Curwen, long member of Parliament for Carlisle, and himself a native, he was well known in the neighbourhood.')[41]

After all, a curious house, mostly hidden by trees, on an island in those lakes was called *Folly*, the whole lot owned by Fletcher Christian's beautiful and wealthy cousin: Isabella Christian Curwen – the very woman that Fletcher had named his Tahitian wife after. If Fletcher did make his way back to England, there could surely be few better places to live in comfort, but relative isolation – where you could venture out as you chose, always with a safe place to retreat to.

Buttressing evidence? Try this . . .

A century and a half pass, it is 1965, and an editor is in the dusty depths of the Bodleian Library at Oxford, going through the letters of the late Poet Laureate, Robert Southey, when he comes across one from 1808, written to Southey's friend Charles Bedford about a man whose name is so sensitive, he dares only use the initials:

> F. is a native of this country. One of our country gentleman . . . who was his schoolfellow . . . told me, that about five or six years ago, as he was walking near his own house with his daughter, he saw two Gentlemen riding towards him, and recognized one of them in time to say to his daughter – look at this man – it is F.C. – and also to consider it would be better not to speak to him. There was a dog with the horsemen, and presently afterwards some boys came along who had picked up a collar, bearing the name of F.C.'s father. My friend had no doubt before of his identity, and this was a confirmation of the fact. What is become of him since God knows . . .[42]

There is also a little more circumstantial evidence. Take the actions of Edward Christian, for example. While he had led a spectacular defence of his brother in the early 1790s, even while tearing down Captain Bligh's reputation, thereafter he goes completely silent and says not another public word on either subject.

Could such be the actions of a man keen for the whole story to die, because his brother is now back in England and the less interest the better? It is also surely odd that neither Christian's mother, Ann, or either of his brothers – one of whom is not just a professor of law but a judge with a family and many possessions – leaves a will. Perhaps, they had a key reason for privately sorting out their estate? Perhaps familial splitting of assets could not be done in the public domain, when one member of the family was presumed to be long dead?

Could that also be why, after Edward Christian passed away in 1823, relatives of his wife found an exceedingly peculiar thing in his belongings: 'a strange native hat',[43] from Pitcairn Island.

Admittedly, one simply *wants* to believe these pieces of 'evidence', because the alternative – to accept that Christian was simply smashed in the back of the head while gathering yams – seems against nature. Such a plebeian end for such an extraordinary man? Surely not!

That would be like saying that the Princess of Wales died because she didn't have her seatbelt on.

Oh, wait . . .

Yes, I guess, the likelihood is that Fletcher Christian really was murdered on Pitcairn Island. But those other bits of evidence do intrigue me. And I'd love to know if there is a quiet gravesite, somewhere around *Folly*, which is his *true* resting place. Vale, Captain Christian.

ENDNOTES

1 Christian, Glynn, *Fragile Paradise*, Book Club Associates, London, 1983, p. 14.
2 Byron, *The Works of Lord Byron Complete in One Volume*, H.L. Brönner, Frankfurt am Main, 1837

Dramatis Personae

1 Author's note: The ages provided in this list are those at the time of the *Bounty*'s departure from England.
2 Author's note: For the sake of clarity I have used the more familiar term of 'Bosun' throughout this book rather than the now archaic Boatswain.
3 Bligh, Log of the Proceedings of His Majesty's Ship Bounty (1 Dec. 1787 – 22 Oct. 1788), 23 January 1788, State Library of NSW.
4 Bligh, *The Bounty Mutiny*, p. 10.
5 Bligh, *The Bounty Mutiny*, p. 162.
6 Bligh, *The Bounty Mutiny*, p. 164.
7 Maiden, *Sir Joseph Banks*, William Gullick, Sydney, 1909, p. 124.

Prologue

1 Beaglehole, *The Life of Captain James Cook*, Stanford University Press, USA, 1992, p. 365.
2 Morrison, Journal on HMS Bounty and at Tahiti, SLNSW, p. 269.
3 Williams, *Captain Cook: Explorations and Reassessments*, Boydell Press, Suffolk, 2004.
4 Author's note: At this point in modern history, only Mercury, Venus, Mars, Jupiter and Saturn were known to European scientists. Uranus was added in 1781, Neptune in 1846 and Pluto in 1930.
5 Salmond, *Aphrodite's Island: The European Discovery of Tahiti*, University of California Press, Berkeley, 2009, p. 429.
6 Tobin, Beth, *Colonizing Nature*, University of Pennsylvania Press, Philadelphia, 2004, p. 33.
7 Banks, The *Endeavour* Journal of Joseph Banks (25 August 1768 – 12 July 1771), 14 April 1769, SLNSW, [no page numbers].
8 Banks, The *Endeavour* Journal of Joseph Banks, 12 May 1769.
9 Banks, Joseph, The *Endeavour* Journal of Joseph Banks, 3 June 1769.
10 Banks, Joseph, The *Endeavour* Journal of Joseph Banks, 4 June 1769.
11 Cook, James, Journal of H.M.S. Endeavour, 1768–1771, 3 June 1769, NLA, MS 1.
12 Cook, James, Journal of H.M.S. Endeavour, 3 June 1769.
13 Author's note: They later found out that observers from all over noted a haze or 'black drop' that seemed to follow Venus, making it very difficult to record accurate times. Nonetheless, the Royal Society was very disappointed with Cook's report and data.
14 Stephens, 'Secret Instructions for Lieutenant James Cook Appointed to Command His Majesty's Bark the Endeavour', 30 July 1768, NLA, MS 2, p. 1.

15 Author's note: Bread-fruit trees are productive for around 50 years and can be harvested several times a year. The fruit is very nutritious. Each fruit can weigh up to five kilograms and a single tree might yield over a hundred fruit per year.

16 Barrow, *The Mutiny and Piratical Seizure of HMS Bounty*, Folio Society, London, 1831, p. 50.

17 Banks, 'Manners and Customs of the South Sea Islands' in The *Endeavour* Journal of Joseph Banks, 25 August 1768 – 12 July 1771, SLNSW, Papers of Sir Joseph Banks, Section 2, Series 03.354, [no page numbers].

18 Beaglehole, *The Journals of Captain James Cook on his Voyages of Discovery*, Vol II, Part 1, Cambridge University Press, London, 1967, p. cliii.

19 Beaglehole, *The Journals of Captain James Cook on his Voyages of Discovery*, p. cliii.

20 Cook, James, *The Voyages of Captain James Cook*, Vol. 2, W. Smith, London, 1842, p. 369.

21 Cook, James, *The Voyages of Captain James Cook*, p. 369.

22 Cook, James, *The Voyages of Captain James Cook*, p. 370.

23 Cook, James, *The Voyages of Captain James Cook*, p. 369.

24 Cook, James, *The Voyages of Captain James Cook*, p. 369.

25 Cook, James, *The Voyages of Captain James Cook*, p. 383.

26 Cook, James, *The Voyages of Captain James Cook*, p. 383.

27 Ledyard and Sparks, *Travels and Adventures of John Ledyard*, Henry Colburn, London, 1834, p. 140.

28 Ledyard, *Travels and Adventures of John Ledyard*, pp. 140–41.

29 Cook, James, *The Voyages of Captain James Cook*, p. 385.

30 Burney, Journal, SLNSW, Safe 1/64; Safe 1/79, Vol. 3, p. 253.

31 Burney, Journal, p. 253.

32 Author's note: Bligh's role in the events that led to the death of Cook is a fascinating example of how one small action can lead to another. So many things led to Cook's death, but the fact that William Bligh ordered the first shots fired in this day of death was noted by his contemporaries. Lieutenant King, Cook's eventual successor as Commander of his final voyage, was careful to note that the first shots from Bligh's and Rickman's Cutters gave 'a fatal turn to the affair'. The author Richard Hough was also struck by the careful note made by William Bayley, Cook's astronomer, that 'a man arrived in a small canoe from the opposite side of the bay with the account of a chief of some note being killed by our people in the boats at that side. This intelligence seems to have spread the alarm, as they all began to arm themselves with clubs and spears'. That William Bligh, the towering figure of the *Bounty* affair was to start the chain of events that ended in Cook's demise is one of those fascinating coincidences, or perhaps precursors, of history.

33 Cook, James, *The Voyages of Captain James Cook*, p. 386.

34 Burney, Journal, p. 254 [reported speech].

35 Cook, James, *The Voyages of Captain James Cook*, p. 386.

36 Cook, James, *The Voyages of Captain James Cook*, p. 386.

37 Jarves, *History of the Hawaiian or Sandwich Islands*, Boston, Tappan and Dennett, 1843, p. 125.

38 Burney, Journal, p. 255.

39 Samwell, David, *A Narrative on the Death of Captain Cook*, G.G.J. & J. Robinson, London, 1786, p. 12.

40 Samwell, *A Narrative on the Death of Captain Cook*, p. 11.

41 Ledyard, *Travels and Adventures of John Ledyard*, p. 146.

42 Cook, James, *The Voyages of Captain James Cook*, p. 386 [reported speech].

43 Account of John Ledyard, in Jarves *History of the Hawaiian or Sandwich Islands*, p. 126 [reported speech].

44 Account of John Ledyard, in Jarves *History of the Hawaiian or Sandwich Islands*, p. 126 [reported speech].

45 Burney, Journal, p. 256 [tense changed].

46 Cook, James, *The Voyages of Captain James Cook*, p. 387.

47 Cook, James, *The Voyages of Captain James Cook*, p. 387.
48 Burney, Journal, p. 257 [reported speech].
49 Cook, James, *The Voyages of Captain James Cook*, p. 387.
50 Mackaness, *The Life of Vice-Admiral William Bligh*, Angus & Robertson, Sydney, 1951, p. 23.
51 Cook, James, *The Voyages of Captain James Cook*, p. 387.
52 Jarves, *History of the Hawaiian or Sandwich Islands*, p. 126.
53 Cook, James, *The Voyages of Captain James Cook*, p. 393.
54 Mackaness, *The Life of Vice-Admiral William Bligh*, p. 25.

Chapter 1

1 Barrow, *The Mutiny and Piratical Seizure of HMS Bounty*, p. 50. William Dampier was one of the earliest European explorers to discover the value of bread-fruit as a food source.
2 Christian, *Fragile Paradise*, p. 69.
3 Christian, *Fragile Paradise*, p. 69.
4 Christian, *Fragile Paradise*, p. 69.
5 Christian, *Fragile Paradise*, p. 71.
6 Preston, *Paradise in Chains: The Bounty Mutiny and the Founding of Australia*, Bloomsbury, New York, 2017, p. 80.
7 Christian, *Fragile Paradise*, p. 69.
8 Phillip, *Historical Records of New South Wales*, Vol. I, Part 2, 1783–1792, Charles Potter, Government Printer, Sydney, 1892, p. 22.
9 Phillip, *Historical Records of New South Wales*, p. 22.
10 Phillip, *Historical Records of New South Wales*, p. 20.
11 Chambers, *Letters of Sir Joseph Banks*, 1768–1820, World Scientific, 2000, p. 86.
12 Chambers, *Letters of Sir Joseph Banks*, p. 86.
13 Chambers, *Letters of Sir Joseph Banks*, p. 87.
14 Bligh, *A voyage to the South sea, undertaken by command of His Majesty, for the purpose of conveying the bread-fruit tree to the West Indies, in His Majesty's ship the Bounty, commanded by Lieutenant William Bligh*, G. Nicol, London, 1792, p. 2.
15 Banks, 'Instructions for a Vessel from Botany Bay', circa. February 1878, SLNSW, Sir Joseph Banks Papers, Series 45.03, p. 2.
16 Bligh, *A voyage to the South sea*, 1792, p. 2.
17 Bligh, *A voyage to the South sea*, 1792, p. 2.
18 Bligh, *A voyage to the South sea*, 1792, p. 2.
19 Banks, 'Instructions for a Vessel from Botany Bay', p. 2
20 Mackaness, *Life of Vice-Admiral Bligh Sometime Governor of N.S.W.*, Vol. 1, Angus & Robertson, Sydney, 1931, p. 37.
21 Bligh to Joseph Banks, Letter, 6 August 1787, SLNSW, Sir Joseph Banks Papers, Series 46.02, p. 1.
22 McKay, *The Armed Transport BOUNTY*, Conway Maritime Press, London, 2001, p. 7.
23 Banks to George Yonge, Letter, 9 September 1787, SLNSW, Sir Joseph Banks Papers, Series 45.08, p. 3.
24 McKay, *The Armed Transport BOUNTY*, p. 9.
25 McKay, *The Armed Transport BOUNTY*, p. 12.
26 McKay, *The Armed Transport BOUNTY*, p. 11.
27 McKay, *The Armed Transport BOUNTY*, p. 11.
28 Christian, *Fragile Paradise*, p. 53.
29 Bligh and Christian, *The Bounty Mutiny*, Penguin, New York, 2001, p. 181.
30 Mackaness, *Life of Vice-Admiral Bligh Sometime Governor of N.S.W.*, p. 46.
31 Author's note: Sometimes also spelt Hallet. I have gone with Bligh's spelling, Hallett.

32 Bligh, Extract from the logbook HMS Bounty (16 August 1787 – 20 August 1789), 11 January 1788, The National Archives, Kew, ADM 55/151, p. 20.

33 Bligh to Joseph Banks, Letter, 15 September 1787, SLNSW, Sir Joseph Banks Papers, Series 46.03, p. 2.

34 Lord Selkirk to Joseph Banks, Letter, 14 September 1787, SLNSW, Sir Joseph Banks Papers, Series 45.11, p. 1.

35 Bligh to Duncan Campbell, Letter, 10 December 1787, SLNSW, Safe 1/40, p. 2.

36 Bligh to Joseph Banks, Letter, 3 October 1787, SLNSW, Sir Joseph Banks Papers, Series 46.05, p. 1.

37 Bligh to Joseph Banks, Letter, 20 October 1787, SLNSW, Sir Joseph Banks Papers, Series 46.07, p. 1 [reported speech].

38 Bligh to Joseph Banks, Letter, 20 October 1787, p. 1.

39 Bligh to Joseph Banks, Letter, 5 November 1787, SLNSW, Sir Joseph Banks Papers, Series 46.08, p. 1.

40 Bligh to Joseph Banks, Letter, 5 November 1787, p. 1.

41 Bligh to Joseph Banks, Letter, 5 November 1787, p. 2.

42 Bligh to Joseph Banks, Letter, 5 November 1787, p. 2.

43 Bligh to Joseph Banks, Letter, 5 November 1787, p. 2.

44 Mackaness, *The Life of Vice-Admiral William Bligh*, p. 7.

45 Bligh to Joseph Banks, Letter, 5 November 1787, p. 3.

46 Bligh to Joseph Banks, Letter, 18 November 1787, SLNSW, Sir Joseph Banks Papers, Series 46.09, p. 2.

Chapter 2

1 Shedd (ed.), *The Complete Works of Samuel Taylor Coleridge*, Harper and Brothers, New York, 1853, p. 230.

2 Bligh, William, *A Voyage to the South Sea*, Hutchinson, Richmond, 1979, pp. 1–8.

3 Bligh to Duncan Campbell, Letter, 10 December 1787, SLNSW, Safe 1/40, p. 1.

4 Bligh to Duncan Campbell, Letter, 22 December 1787, SLNSW, Safe 1/40, p. 1.

5 James Norman Hall and Charles Nordhoff, *Mutiny on the Bounty*, 1932.

6 Bligh to Joseph Banks, Letter, 13 October 1789, SLNSW, Sir Joseph Banks Papers, Series 46.27, p. 5.

7 Bligh, *A Voyage to the South Sea*, 1979, p. 14.

8 Bligh, Extract from the logbook HMS Bounty, 27 December 1787, p. 8.

9 Bligh, Extract from the logbook HMS Bounty, 27 December 1787, p. 8.

10 Bligh, Extract from the logbook HMS Bounty, 27 December 1787, p. 8.

11 Bligh, Extract from the logbook HMS Bounty, 27 December 1787, p. 8.

12 Bligh, Extract from the logbook HMS Bounty, 27 December 1787, p. 8.

13 Bligh, Extract from the logbook HMS Bounty, 27 December 1787, p. 8.

14 Bligh, Extract from the logbook HMS Bounty, 29 December 1787, p. 10.

15 Bligh, A voyage to the South sea, 1792, p. 15.

16 Bligh, A voyage to the South sea, 1792, p. 15.

17 Bligh to Joseph Banks, Letter, 9 January 1788, SLNSW, Sir Joseph Banks Papers, Series 46.20, p. 1.

18 Morrison, Journal on HMS Bounty and at Tahiti, p. 2.

19 McKinney, *Bligh!: The Whole Story of the Mutiny Aboard H.M.S. Bounty*, Touch Wood Editions, Canada, 1999, p. 28.

20 Morrison, Journal on HMS Bounty and at Tahiti, p. 2.

21 Bligh to Joseph Banks, Letter, 9 January 1788, p. 2.

22 Rutter, Owen (ed.), *The Court-Martial of the 'Bounty' Mutineers*, Canada Law Book Company, Toronto, 1933, p. 177.

23 Bligh to Duncan Campbell, Letter, 9 January 1788, p. 3.

24 Bligh, *Mutiny on Board HMS Bounty*, Bloomsbury Publishing, London 2014, p. 132.

25 Morrison, Journal on HMS Bounty and at Tahiti, p. 2 [reported speech].

26 Morrison, Journal on HMS Bounty and at Tahiti, pp. 2–3.

27 Morrison, Journal on HMS Bounty and at Tahiti, p. 3 [reported speech].

28 Morrison, Journal on HMS Bounty and at Tahiti, p. 3 [reported speech].

29 Morrison, Journal on HMS Bounty and at Tahiti, p. 3 [reported speech].

30 Morrison, Journal on HMS Bounty and at Tahiti, p. 3.

31 Morrison, Journal on HMS Bounty and at Tahiti, p. 3.

32 Morrison, Journal on HMS Bounty and at Tahiti, p. 4.

33 Morrison, Journal on HMS Bounty and at Tahiti, p. 4.

34 Kennedy, *Captain Bligh: The Man and His Mutinies*, Duckworth, London, 1989, p. 27.

35 Heywood, Peter and Heywood, Nessy, *Innocent on the Bounty*, McFarland & Company, London, 2013, p. 156.

36 Morrison, Journal on HMS Bounty and at Tahiti, p. 4.

37 Morrison, Journal on HMS Bounty and at Tahiti, p. 4 [reported speech].

38 Morrison, Journal on HMS Bounty and at Tahiti, p. 4.

39 Morrison, Journal on HMS Bounty and at Tahiti, pp. 4–5.

40 Mackaness, *The Life of Vice-Admiral William Bligh*, p. 54.

41 Dening, *Mr Bligh's Bad Language*, Cambridge University Press, Melbourne, 1992, pp. 66–67.

42 Bligh, Extract from the logbook HMS Bounty, 2 March 1788, p. 47.

43 Kennedy, *Captain Bligh: The Man and His Mutinies*, p. 27.

44 Bligh, Extract from the logbook HMS Bounty, 10 March 1788, p. 52.

45 Mackaness, *The Life of Vice-Admiral William Bligh*, p. 54.

46 Kennedy, *Captain Bligh: The Man and His Mutinies*, p. 27.

47 Bligh, Extract from the logbook HMS Bounty, 20 March 1788, p. 58.

48 Morrison, Journal on HMS Bounty and at Tahiti, p. 7.

49 Bligh, Extract from the logbook HMS Bounty, 5 April 1788, p. 71.

50 Morrison, Journal on HMS Bounty and at Tahiti, p. 7.

51 Bligh, Extract from the logbook HMS Bounty, 29 March 1788, p. 66.

52 Morrison, Journal on HMS Bounty and at Tahiti, p. 8.

53 Bligh, A voyage to the South sea, 1792, p. 31.

54 Bligh, A voyage to the South sea, 1792, p. 31.

55 Mackaness, *Fresh Light on Bligh*, Review Publications, Dubbo, 1976, p. 33.

56 Bligh, Extract from the logbook HMS Bounty, 22 April 1788, p. 86.

Chapter 3

1 Shakespeare, William, *Macbeth*, Lyons and Carnahan, New York, 1913, p. 114.

2 Morrison, James, Journal on HMS Bounty and at Tahiti, p. 7.

3 Shedd (ed.), *The Complete Works of Samuel Taylor Coleridge*, p. 233.

4 Bligh, Extract from the logbook HMS Bounty, 13 April 1788, p. 76.

5 Bligh, Extract from the logbook HMS Bounty, 24 May 1788, p. 106.

6 Bligh, *A Voyage to the South Sea*, 1979, p. 32.

7 Bligh, *A Voyage to the South Sea*, 1979, p. 32.

8 Bligh, Extract from the logbook HMS Bounty, 22 April 1788, p. 85.

9 Bligh to Campbell, Letter, 26 May 1788, p. 3.

10 Morrison, Journal on HMS Bounty and at Tahiti, p. 9 [reported speech]. Author's note: Morrison gives this description for the events of 18 April 1788, when Bligh first ordered the *Bounty* to bear away for the Cape of Good Hope. I have adapted the dialogue to 22 April 1788 as it would likely have been a very similar scenario.

11 Bligh, Extract from the logbook HMS Bounty, 17 April 1788, p. 80.

12 Bligh, Extract from the logbook HMS Bounty, 22 April 1788, p. 86 [reported speech].

13 Morrison, Journal on HMS Bounty and at Tahiti, p. 9.

14 Author's note: These orders have been adapted from James Morrison's journal recalling the *Bounty* bearing away from Cape Horn on 18 April 1788. I presume similar orders would have been used on 22 April, given they were sailing in similar conditions.

15 Bligh, Extract from the logbook HMS Bounty, 22 April 1788, p. 85.

16 Bligh, *A Voyage to the South Sea*, 1979, p. 34.

17 Morrison, Journal on HMS Bounty and at Tahiti, p. 10.

18 Bligh to Banks, Letter, 24 May 1788, p. 5.

19 Bligh, Extract from the logbook HMS Bounty, 26 May 1788, p. 109.

20 Bligh, Extract from the logbook HMS Bounty, 28 October 1788, p. 188.

21 Macquarie, *Journal No. 1: 15 December 1787 – 24 March 1792*, 13 June 1788, SLNSW, pp. 87–88.

22 Bligh, Extract from the logbook HMS Bounty, 1 July 1788, p. 114.

23 Bligh, Extract from the logbook HMS Bounty, 1 July 1788, p. 114.

24 Bligh, Extract from the logbook HMS Bounty, 1 July 1788, p. 114.

25 Bligh, Extract from the logbook HMS Bounty, 1 July 1788, p. 114.

26 Bligh, Extract from the logbook HMS Bounty, 22 July 1788, p. 128.

27 Bligh, Extract from the logbook HMS Bounty, 20 August 1788, p. 144.

28 Morrison, Journal on HMS Bounty and at Tahiti, , p. 13.

29 Bligh, Extract from the logbook HMS Bounty, 27 August 1788, p. 149.

30 Bligh, Extract from the logbook HMS Bounty, 28 August 1788, p. 149.

31 Bligh, Extract from the logbook HMS Bounty, 28 August 1788, p. 149.

32 Alexander, *The Bounty*, HarperCollins, London, 2003, p. 97.

33 Bligh, Extract from the logbook HMS Bounty, 23 August 1788, p. 146.

34 Bligh, Extract from the logbook HMS Bounty, 26 August 1788, p. 148.

35 Bligh, Extract from the logbook HMS Bounty, 26 August 1788, p. 148

36 Bligh, Extract from the logbook HMS Bounty, 26 August 1788, p. 148

37 Bligh, Extract from the logbook HMS Bounty, 26 August 1788, p. 148.

38 Bligh, Extract from the logbook HMS Bounty, 26 August 1788, p. 148 [reported speech].

39 Morrison, Journal on HMS Bounty and at Tahiti, p. 15.

40 Morrison, Journal on HMS Bounty and at Tahiti, p. 15.

41 Bligh, Extract from the logbook HMS Bounty, 1 September 1788, p. 150.

42 Bligh, Extract from the logbook HMS Bounty, 1 September 1788, p. 151.

43 Bligh, Extract from the logbook HMS Bounty, 2 September 1788, p. 151.

44 Bligh, Extract from the logbook HMS Bounty, 2 September 1788, p. 151.

45 Bligh, Extract from the logbook HMS Bounty, 2 September 1788, p. 151.

46 Morrison, Journal on HMS Bounty and at Tahiti, p. 14.

47 Bligh, Extract from the logbook HMS Bounty, 2 September 1788, p. 151.

48 Bligh, *A Voyage to the South Sea*, 1979, pp. 49–52.

49 Bligh, Extract from the logbook HMS Bounty, 2 September 1788, p. 151.

50 Bligh, Extract from the logbook HMS Bounty, 31 August 1788, p. 150.

51 Bligh, Extract from the logbook HMS Bounty, 31 August 1788, p. 150.

52 Bligh, Extract from the logbook HMS Bounty, 4 September 1788, p. 152.

53 Mackaness, *The Life of Vice-Admiral William Bligh*, p. 68. Author's note: This portion of the Log was crossed out by Bligh, but it is still able to be read. He wrote a censored/more formal account of Valentine's death later in the Log.

54 Bligh, Extract from the logbook HMS Bounty, 10 October 1788, p. 174.

55 Mackaness, *The Life of Vice-Admiral William Bligh*, p. 68.

56 Mackaness, *The Life of Vice-Admiral William Bligh*, p. 68.

57 Mackaness, *The Life of Vice-Admiral William Bligh*, p. 68.

58 Mackaness, *The Life of Vice-Admiral William Bligh*, p. 68.

59 Mackaness, *The Life of Vice-Admiral William Bligh*, p. 68 [reported speech].

60 Mackaness, *The Life of Vice-Admiral William Bligh*, p. 68.

61 Bligh, Extract from the logbook HMS Bounty, 9 October 1788, p. 173.

62 Bligh, Extract from the logbook HMS Bounty, 9 October 1788, p. 173.
63 Bligh, Extract from the logbook HMS Bounty, 9 October 1788, p. 173.
64 Bligh, Extract from the logbook HMS Bounty, 9 October 1788, p. 173 [reported speech].
65 Bligh, Extract from the logbook HMS Bounty, 9 October 1788, p. 173 [reported speech].
66 McKinney, *Bligh!: The Whole Story of the Mutiny Aboard H.M.S. Bounty*, p. 172.
67 Morrison, Journal on HMS Bounty and at Tahiti, p. 16.
68 Morrison, Journal on HMS Bounty and at Tahiti, p. 16.
69 Morrison, Journal on HMS Bounty and at Tahiti, p. 16 [reported speech].
70 Bligh, Extract from the logbook HMS Bounty, 9 October 1788, p. 173.
71 Morrison, Journal on HMS Bounty and at Tahiti, p. 16.
72 Bligh, Extract from the logbook HMS Bounty, 10 October 1788, p. 174.
73 Morrison, Journal on HMS Bounty and at Tahiti, p. 15.
74 Bligh, Extract from the logbook HMS Bounty, p. 176.
75 Bligh, Extract from the logbook HMS Bounty, 18 October 1788, p. 178.
76 Author's note: I presume he was told by Cole, whose job it was to ensure order and obedience among the crew.
77 Bligh, Extract from the logbook HMS Bounty, 19 October 1788, p. 179.
78 Bligh, Extract from the logbook HMS Bounty, 19 October 1788, p. 179.
79 Bligh, Extract from the logbook HMS Bounty, 19 October 1788, p. 179.
80 Bligh, Extract from the logbook HMS Bounty, 20 October 1788, p. 179.
81 Bligh, Extract from the logbook HMS Bounty, 20 October 1788, p. 179.
82 Bligh, Extract from the logbook HMS Bounty, 20 October 1788, p. 179.
83 Bligh, Extract from the logbook HMS Bounty, 23 October 1788, p. 182.
84 Kennedy, *Captain Bligh: The Man and His Mutinies*, p. 41.
85 Kennedy, *Captain Bligh: The Man and His Mutinies*, p. 42.
86 Bligh, Extract from the logbook HMS Bounty, 24 October 1788, p. 183.
87 Bligh, Extract from the logbook HMS Bounty, 24 October 1788, p. 183.
88 Bligh, Extract from the logbook HMS Bounty, 24 October 1788, p. 183.
89 Bligh, Extract from the logbook HMS Bounty, 24 October 1788, p. 183.
90 Bligh, Extract from the logbook HMS Bounty, 24 October 1788, p. 183.
91 Bligh, Extract from the logbook HMS Bounty, 25 October 1788, p. 184.
92 Bligh, Extract from the logbook HMS Bounty, 25 October 1788, p. 184.
93 Oliver, *Return to Tahiti*, University of Hawaii Press, Honolulu, 1988, p. 32.
94 Bligh, Extract from the logbook HMS Bounty, 25 October 1788, p. 184.

Chapter 4

1 Robertson, *The Discovery of Tahiti: A Journal of the Second Voyage of H. M. S. Dolphin Round the World, Under the Command of Captain Wallis, R.N., in the Years 1766, 1767 and 1768*, Volume 98, Hakluyt Society, London, 1948, p. 167.
2 Preston, *Paradise in Chains*, p. 8.
3 Bligh, Extract from the logbook HMS Bounty, 1 November 1788, p. 194.
4 Bligh, Extract from the logbook HMS Bounty, 26 October 1788, p. 185.
5 Bligh, *A Voyage to the South Sea*, 1979, p. 59.
6 Bligh, *A Voyage to the South Sea*, 1979, p. 59.
7 Bligh, *A Voyage to the South Sea*, 1979, p. 59.
8 Bligh, *A Voyage to the South Sea*, 1979, p. 59.
9 Morrison, Journal on HMS Bounty and at Tahiti, p. 18.
10 Bligh and Christian, *The Bounty Mutiny*, pp. 157–58.
11 Morrison, Journal on HMS Bounty and at Tahiti, p. 22.
12 Morrison, Journal on HMS Bounty and at Tahiti, p. 22.
13 Bligh, Extract from the logbook HMS Bounty, 27 October 1788, p. 186.
14 Oliver, *Return to Tahiti*, pp. 72–73.

15 Morrison, Journal on HMS Bounty and at Tahiti, p. 18.
16 Morrison, Journal on HMS Bounty and at Tahiti, p. 252.
17 Bligh, *A Voyage to the South Sea*, 1979, p. 82.
18 Bligh, Extract from the logbook HMS Bounty, 26 October 1788, p. 185.
19 Bligh, *A Voyage to the South Sea*, 1979, p. 62.
20 Bligh, Extract from the logbook HMS Bounty, 26 October 1788, p. 185 [reported speech].
21 Bligh, Extract from the logbook HMS Bounty, 26 October 1788, p. 185.
22 Morrison, Journal on HMS Bounty and at Tahiti, p. 308.
23 Bligh, Extract from the logbook HMS Bounty, 27 October 1788, p. 187.
24 Bligh, Extract from the logbook HMS Bounty, 27 October 1788, p. 187 [reported speech].
25 Morrison, Journal on HMS Bounty and at Tahiti, p. 243.
26 Bligh, Extract from the logbook HMS Bounty, 27 October 1788, p. 187.
27 Bligh, Extract from the logbook HMS Bounty, 27 October 1788, p. 187.
28 Bligh, Extract from the logbook HMS Bounty, 27 October 1788, p. 188 [reported speech].
29 Bligh, Extract from the logbook HMS Bounty, 27 October 1788, p. 187.
30 Bligh, Extract from the logbook HMS Bounty, 27 October 1788, p. 187.
31 Bligh, *A Voyage to the South Sea*, 1979, p. 64.
32 Bligh, *A Voyage to the South Sea*, 1979, p. 66.
33 Bligh, Extract from the logbook HMS Bounty, 27 October 1788, p. 188.
34 Bligh, Extract from the logbook HMS Bounty, 28 October 1788, p. 188.
35 Bligh, *A Voyage to the South Sea*, 1979, p. 66.
36 Bligh, *A Voyage to the South Sea*, 1979, p. 65.
37 Bligh, *A Voyage to the South Sea*, 1979, pp. 65–66.
38 Bligh, *A Voyage to the South Sea*, 1979, pp. 65–66.
39 Bligh, *A Voyage to the South Sea*, 1979, pp. 65–66.
40 Bligh, *A Voyage to the South Sea*, 1979, pp. 65–66.
41 Bligh, *A Voyage to the South Sea*, 1979, p. 66.
42 Bligh, *A Voyage to the South Sea*, 1979, p. 67.
43 Bligh, *A Voyage to the South Sea*, 1979, p. 67.
44 Bligh, *A Voyage to the South Sea*, 1979, p. 67.
45 Bligh, *A Voyage to the South Sea*, 1979, p. 67.
46 Bligh, *A Voyage to the South Sea*, 1979, p. 67.
47 Bligh, *A Voyage to the South Sea*, 1979, p. 68.
48 Bligh, *A Voyage to the South Sea*, 1979, p. 68.
49 Bligh, *A Voyage to the South Sea*, 1979, p. 69.
50 Bligh, *A Voyage to the South Sea*, 1979, p. 69.
51 Bligh, *A Voyage to the South Sea*, 1979, p. 69.
52 Bligh, *A Voyage to the South Sea*, 1979, p. 69.
53 Bligh, Extract from the logbook HMS Bounty, 29 October 1788, p. 190.
54 Bligh, Extract from the logbook HMS Bounty, 30 October 1788, p. 191.
55 Bligh, *A voyage to the South sea*, 1792, p. 70.
56 Bligh, *A Voyage to the South Sea*, 1979, p. 70.
57 Bligh, *A Voyage to the South Sea*, 1979, pp. 70–71.
58 Bligh, Extract from the logbook HMS Bounty, 31 October 1788, p. 191.
59 Bligh, Extract from the logbook HMS Bounty, 28 November 1788, p. 221.
60 Bligh, Extract from the logbook HMS Bounty, 28 November 1788, p. 221.
61 Bligh, *A Voyage to the South Sea*, 1979, p. 73 [reported speech].
62 Bligh, *A Voyage to the South Sea*, 1979, p. 73.
63 Bligh, *A Voyage to the South Sea*, 1979, p. 73.
64 Bligh, Extract from the logbook HMS Bounty, 1 November 1788, p. 193 [reported speech].
65 Bligh, Extract from the logbook HMS Bounty, 1 November 1788, p. 193 [reported speech].
66 Bligh, Extract from the logbook HMS Bounty, 1 November 1788, p. 193.
67 Bligh, Extract from the logbook HMS Bounty, 1 November 1788, p. 193 [reported speech].

68 Bligh, Extract from the logbook HMS Bounty, 1 November 1788, p. 193 [reported speech].

69 Bligh, *A Voyage to the South Sea*, 1979, p. 74.

70 Bligh, *A Voyage to the South Sea*, 1979, pp. 76–77.

71 Bligh, *A Voyage to the South Sea*, 1979, p. 77. Author's note: I have standardised the spelling of Pretanie, for Britain, as there are two versions.

72 Bligh, *A Voyage to the South Sea*, 1979, pp. 77–79.

73 Bligh, Extract from the logbook HMS Bounty, 2 November 1788, p. 195.

74 Bligh, Extract from the logbook HMS Bounty, 2 November 1788, p. 195.

75 Bligh, *A Voyage to the South Sea*, 1979, p. 91.

76 Bligh, *A Voyage to the South Sea*, 1979, p. 83.

77 Bligh, Extract from the logbook HMS Bounty, 4 November 1788, p. 197.

78 Tobin, *Captain Bligh's Second Chance*, UNSW Press, Sydney, 2007, pp. 128–30. Author's note: Peter Heywood's dictionary was never published for public consumption. It was apparently used by Christian missionaries on Tahiti at one point, but no copy of it has survived into the 21st century. I have, therefore, gone with Tobin's dictionary, as he was there just two years later with Bligh and so has the best contemporaneous recording of vocabulary.

79 *Walker's Hiberian Magazine*, Part Two, R. Gibson, Dublin, 1794, p. 418.

Chapter 5

1 Wordsworth, *Wordsworth: The Major Works*, Oxford University Press, UK, 2000, p. 550.

2 Bligh, Extract from the logbook HMS Bounty, 9 November 1788, p. 202.

3 Bligh, Extract from the logbook HMS Bounty, 9 November 1788, p. 202.

4 Bligh, Extract from the logbook HMS Bounty, 9 November 1788, p. 202.

5 Bligh, *A Voyage to the South Sea*, 1979, p. 95.

6 Bligh, Extract from the logbook HMS Bounty, 18 November 1788, p. 211.

7 Bligh, Extract from the logbook HMS Bounty, 21 November 1788, p. 216.

8 Bligh, Extract from the logbook HMS Bounty, 21 November 1788, p. 216.

9 Bowker and Bligh, *Mutiny!! Aboard H.M. Armed Transport 'Bounty' in 1789*, Boerker and Bertram, Sussex, 1978, p. 311.

10 Bligh, Extract from the logbook HMS Bounty, 4 December 1788, p. 227.

11 Bowker and Bligh, *Mutiny!! Aboard H.M. Armed Transport 'Bounty' in 1789*, 1978, p. 266.

12 Bligh, Extract from the logbook HMS Bounty, 5 December 1788, p. 227.

13 Bligh, Extract from the logbook HMS Bounty, 5 December 1788, p. 227.

14 Bligh, Extract from the logbook HMS Bounty, 6 December 1788, p. 228 [reported speech].

15 Bligh, Extract from the logbook HMS Bounty, 8 December 1788, p. 230.

16 Bligh, Extract from the logbook HMS Bounty, 10 December 1788, p. 232.

17 Bligh, Extract from the logbook HMS Bounty, 10 December 1788, p. 232.

18 Bowker and Bligh, *Mutiny!!* 1978, p. 270.

19 Bligh, Extract from the logbook HMS Bounty, 24 December 1788, p. 242.

20 Author's note: These are generic commands, consistent with the terminology of the time.

21 Bligh and Christian, *The Bounty Mutiny*, p. 143.

22 Bligh and Christian, *The Bounty Mutiny*, p. 143 [reported speech].

23 Bligh and Christian, *The Bounty Mutiny*, p. 143.

24 Bligh and Christian, *The Bounty Mutiny*, p. 143.

25 Bligh, Extract from the logbook HMS Bounty, 5 January 1789, p. 251.

26 Bligh, *A Voyage to the South Sea*, 1979, p. 113 [reported speech].

27 Bligh, Extract from the logbook HMS Bounty, 5 January 1789, p. 251.

28 Bligh, Extract from the logbook HMS Bounty, 5 January 1789, p. 251.

29 Morrison, Journal on HMS Bounty and at Tahiti, p. 26 [reported speech].

30 Morrison, Journal on HMS Bounty and at Tahiti, p. 26.

31 Bligh, Extract from the logbook HMS Bounty, 15 January 1789, p. 257.

32 Bligh, Extract from the logbook HMS Bounty, 15 January 1789, p. 257 [reported speech].

33 Bligh, Extract from the logbook HMS Bounty, 15 January 1789, p. 257.

34 Bligh, Extract from the logbook HMS Bounty, 15 January 1789, p. 257.

35 Bligh, Extract from the logbook HMS Bounty, 15 January 1789, p. 258.

36 Bligh, Extract from the logbook HMS Bounty, 15 January 1789, p. 258.

37 Bligh, Extract from the logbook HMS Bounty, 15 January 1789, p. 258.

38 Bligh, Extract from the logbook HMS Bounty, 15 January 1789, p. 258.

39 Bligh, Extract from the logbook HMS Bounty, 16 January 1789, p. 258 [reported speech].

40 Bligh, Extract from the logbook HMS Bounty, 16 January 1789, p. 258.

41 Bligh, Extract from the logbook HMS Bounty, 17 January 1789, p. 259.

42 Bligh, Extract from the logbook HMS Bounty, 17 January 1789, p. 259.

43 Bligh, Extract from the logbook HMS Bounty, 17 January 1789, p. 259.

44 Bligh, Extract from the logbook HMS Bounty, 17 January 1789, p. 259.

45 Morrison, Journal on HMS Bounty and at Tahiti, p. 26.

46 Bligh, Extract from the logbook HMS Bounty, 23 January 1789, p. 262.

47 Bligh, Extract from the logbook HMS Bounty, 23 January 1789, p. 262.

48 Bligh, Extract from the logbook HMS Bounty, 23 January 1789, p. 262 [reported speech].

49 Bligh, Extract from the logbook HMS Bounty, 23 January 1789, p. 262.

50 Bligh, *A Voyage to the South Sea*, 1979, p. 119 [reported speech].

51 Morrison, Journal on HMS Bounty and at Tahiti, p. 101 [reported speech].

52 Morrison, Journal on HMS Bounty and at Tahiti, p. 101 [reported speech].

53 Bligh, Extract from the logbook HMS Bounty, 24 January 1789, p. 264 [reported speech].

54 Bligh and Christian, *The Bounty Mutiny*, pp. 158–59.

55 Bligh, *A Voyage to the South Sea*, 1979, p. 120.

56 Bligh, *A Voyage to the South Sea*, 1979, p. 121.

57 Morrison, Journal on HMS Bounty and at Tahiti, p. 25.

58 Morrison, Journal on HMS Bounty and at Tahiti, p. 25.

59 Bligh, *A Voyage to the South Sea*, 1979, p. 124.

60 Bligh, *A Voyage to the South Sea*, 1979, p. 124.

61 Bligh, *A Voyage to the South Sea*, 1979, p. 124.

62 Bligh, Extract from the logbook HMS Bounty, 8 February 1789, p. 275 [reported speech].

63 Bligh, Extract from the logbook HMS Bounty, 8 February 1789, p. 275 [reported speech].

64 Morrison, Journal on HMS Bounty and at Tahiti, p. 27.

65 Bligh, Extract from the logbook HMS Bounty, 11 February 1789, p. 277.

66 Bligh, Extract from the logbook HMS Bounty, 11 February 1789, p. 278.

67 Bligh, Extract from the logbook HMS Bounty, 11 February 1789, p. 278.

68 Bligh, Extract from the logbook HMS Bounty, 11 February 1789, p. 278.

69 Bligh, Extract from the logbook HMS Bounty, 17 February 1789, p. 283.

70 Bligh, Extract from the logbook HMS Bounty, 17 February 1789, p. 283.

71 Bligh, Extract from the logbook HMS Bounty, 2 March 1789, p. 293 [reported speech, tense changed].

72 Bligh, Extract from the logbook HMS Bounty, 18 March 1789, p. 307.

73 Bligh, Extract from the logbook HMS Bounty, 2 March 1789, p. 293. Author's note: The last sentence of this quote is reported speech.

74 Bligh, Extract from the logbook HMS Bounty, 2 March 1789, p. 293.

75 Bligh, Extract from the logbook HMS Bounty, 2 March 1789, p. 293.

76 Bligh, Extract from the logbook HMS Bounty, 2 March 1789, p. 294.

77 Bligh, Extract from the logbook HMS Bounty, 7 March 1789, p. 298.

78 Bligh, Extract from the logbook HMS Bounty, 7 March 1789, p. 298.

79 Bligh, Extract from the logbook HMS Bounty, 7 March 1789, p. 298.

80 Morrison, Journal on HMS Bounty and at Tahiti, p. 19.

81 Morrison, Journal on HMS Bounty and at Tahiti, p. 19.

82 Morrison, Journal on HMS Bounty and at Tahiti, pp. 19–20 [reported speech].

83 Morrison, Journal on HMS Bounty and at Tahiti, p. 20.

84 Morrison, Journal on HMS Bounty and at Tahiti, p. 19.
85 Morrison, Journal on HMS Bounty and at Tahiti, p. 20.
86 Morrison, Journal on HMS Bounty and at Tahiti, p. 20.
87 Bligh, *A Voyage to the South Sea*, 1979, p. 138.
88 Bligh, Extract from the logbook HMS Bounty, 1 April 1789, p. 315.
89 Bligh, *A Voyage to the South Sea*, 1979, p. 140.
90 Bligh, *A Voyage to the South Sea*, 1979, p. 140.
91 Bligh, *A Voyage to the South Sea*, 1979, p. 85.
92 Morrison, Journal on HMS Bounty and at Tahiti, pp. 29–30.
93 Bligh, *A Voyage to the South Sea*, 1979, p. 141.
94 Bligh, *A Voyage to the South Sea*, 1979, pp. 140–41.
95 Bligh, *A Voyage to the South Sea*, 1979, pp. 140–41.
96 Morrison, Journal on HMS Bounty and at Tahiti, p. 30.

Chapter 6

1 Tennyson, *The Complete Works of Alfred, Lord Tennyson*, Frederick A. Stokes, New York, 1891, p. 97.
2 Author's note: Tobin's original spelling is 'plaister' for 'plaster'. This letter was first published by Mackaness in *Fresh Light on Bligh*, p. 33.
3 Author's note: These are generic commands, consistent with the terminology of the time.
4 Bligh, *A Voyage to the South Sea*, 1979, pp. 144–45.
5 Author's note: These are generic commands, consistent with the terminology of the time.
6 Bligh and Christian, *The Bounty Mutiny*, p. 135.
7 Bligh, *A Voyage to the South Sea*, 1979, pp. 146–47.
8 Author's note: Wytootacke is the island now known as Aitutaki in the Cook Islands.
9 Bligh, *A Voyage to the South Sea*, 1979, p. 147.
10 Bligh, Extract from the logbook HMS Bounty, 12 April 1789, p. 337.
11 Rutter (ed.), *The Voyage of the Bounty's Launch*, p. 54.
12 Rutter (ed.), *The Voyage of the Bounty's Launch*, p. 54.
13 Mundle, *Bligh: Master Mariner*, Hachette, Sydney 2010, p. 153.
14 Morrison, Journal on HMS Bounty and at Tahiti, p. 36.
15 Bligh, Extract from the logbook HMS Bounty, 25 April 1789, p. 350.
16 Bligh, Extract from the logbook HMS Bounty, 25 April 1789, p. 350 [reported speech].
17 Bligh, Extract from the logbook HMS Bounty, 25 April 1789, p. 350 [reported speech].
18 Rutter (ed.), *The Voyage of the Bounty's Launch*, p. 53.
19 Rutter (ed.), *The Voyage of the Bounty's Launch*, p. 53.
20 Rutter (ed.), *The Voyage of the Bounty's Launch*, pp. 53–54.
21 Rutter (ed.), *The Voyage of the Bounty's Launch*, p. 54.
22 Rutter (ed.), *The Voyage of the Bounty's Launch*, p. 54.
23 Rutter (ed.), *The Voyage of the Bounty's Launch*, p. 54.
24 Rutter (ed.), *The Voyage of the Bounty's Launch*, p. 54.
25 Rutter (ed.), *The Voyage of the Bounty's Launch*, p. 54.
26 Rutter (ed.), *The Voyage of the Bounty's Launch*, p. 54.
27 Rutter (ed.), *The Voyage of the Bounty's Launch*, p. 54.
28 Rutter (ed.), *The Voyage of the Bounty's Launch*, p. 54.
29 Rutter (ed.), *The Voyage of the Bounty's Launch*, p. 54.
30 Rutter (ed.), *The Voyage of the Bounty's Launch*, p. 54.
31 Rutter (ed.), *The Voyage of the Bounty's Launch*, p. 54.
32 Rutter (ed.), *The Voyage of the Bounty's Launch*, p. 55.
33 Rutter (ed.), *The Voyage of the Bounty's Launch*, p. 54.
34 Morrison, Journal on HMS Bounty and at Tahiti, p. 33 [reported speech].
35 Morrison, Journal on HMS Bounty and at Tahiti, p. 33.

36 Rutter (ed.), *The Voyage of the Bounty's Launch*, p. 55.

37 Rutter (ed.), *The Voyage of the Bounty's Launch*, p. 54.

38 Rutter (ed.), *The Voyage of the Bounty's Launch*, p. 54.

39 Rutter (ed.), *The Voyage of the Bounty's Launch*, p. 55.

40 Rutter (ed.), *The Voyage of the Bounty's Launch*, p. 55.

41 Rutter (ed.), *The Voyage of the Bounty's Launch*, p. 55.

42 Morrison, Journal on HMS Bounty and at Tahiti, pp. 36–37.

43 Author's note: These are generic commands, consistent with the terminology of the time.

44 Morrison, Journal on HMS Bounty and at Tahiti, p. 37.

45 Morrison, Journal on HMS Bounty and at Tahiti, p. 37 [reported speech].

46 Morrison, Journal on HMS Bounty and at Tahiti, p. 37 [reported speech].

47 Morrison, Journal on HMS Bounty and at Tahiti, p. 37 [reported speech].

48 Rutter (ed.), *The Voyage of the Bounty's Launch*, p. 55.

49 Morrison, Journal on HMS Bounty and at Tahiti, p. 37.

50 Bligh, *A Voyage to the South Sea*, 1979, pp. 152–53.

51 Morrison, Journal on HMS Bounty and at Tahiti, p. 37.

52 Bligh, Extract from the logbook HMS Bounty, 25 April 1789, p. 350.

53 Rutter (ed.), *The Voyage of the Bounty's Launch*, p. 54.

54 Rutter (ed.), *The Voyage of the Bounty's Launch*, pp. 55–56.

55 Rutter (ed.), *The Voyage of the Bounty's Launch*, pp. 55–56.

56 Rutter (ed.), *The Voyage of the Bounty's Launch*, p. 56.

57 Rutter (ed.), *The Voyage of the Bounty's Launch*, p. 56.

58 Rutter (ed.), *The Voyage of the Bounty's Launch*, p. 56.

59 Rutter (ed.), *The Voyage of the Bounty's Launch*, p. 56.

60 Rutter (ed.), *The Voyage of the Bounty's Launch*, p. 56.

61 Morrison, Journal on HMS Bounty and at Tahiti, p. 39.

62 Morrison, Journal on HMS Bounty and at Tahiti, p. 39.

63 Rutter (ed.), *The Voyage of the Bounty's Launch*, p. 56.

64 Rutter (ed.), *The Voyage of the Bounty's Launch*, p. 56.

65 Rutter (ed.), *The Voyage of the Bounty's Launch*, p. 56.

66 Rutter (ed.), *The Voyage of the Bounty's Launch*, p. 56

67 Rutter (ed.), *The Voyage of the Bounty's Launch*, p. 56.

68 Bligh and Christian, *The Bounty Mutiny*, p. 136.

69 Bligh and Christian, *The Bounty Mutiny*, p. 136.

70 Bligh and Christian, *The Bounty Mutiny*, p. 136.

71 Bligh and Christian, *The Bounty Mutiny*, p. 136.

72 Bligh and Christian, *The Bounty Mutiny*, p. 136.

73 Bligh and Christian, *The Bounty Mutiny*, p. 136.

74 Bligh and Christian, *The Bounty Mutiny*, p. 136.

75 Morrison, Journal on HMS Bounty and at Tahiti, p. 39.

76 Morrison, Journal on HMS Bounty and at Tahiti, p. 39.

77 Morrison, Journal on HMS Bounty and at Tahiti, p. 39 [reported speech].

78 Morrison, Journal on HMS Bounty and at Tahiti, p. 39.

79 Bligh and Christian, *The Bounty Mutiny*, p. 135.

80 Morrison, Journal on HMS Bounty and at Tahiti, p. 39.

81 Bligh and Christian, *The Bounty Mutiny*, p. 137.

82 Bligh and Christian, *The Bounty Mutiny*, p. 136.

83 Bligh and Christian, *The Bounty Mutiny*, pp. 136–37.

84 Bligh and Christian, *The Bounty Mutiny*, p. 137.

85 Bligh and Christian, *The Bounty Mutiny*, p. 137.

86 Bligh and Christian, *The Bounty Mutiny*, p. 137.

87 Bligh and Christian, *The Bounty Mutiny*, p. 137.

88 Bligh and Christian, *The Bounty Mutiny*, p. 137.

89 Bligh and Christian, *The Bounty Mutiny*, p. 138.
90 Bligh and Christian, *The Bounty Mutiny*, p. 137.
91 Bligh and Christian, *The Bounty Mutiny*, p. 137.
92 Rutter (ed.), *The Voyage of the Bounty's Launch*, p. 61.
93 Rutter (ed.), *The Voyage of the Bounty's Launch*, p. 61.
94 Bligh and Christian, *The Bounty Mutiny*, pp. 136–37.
95 Bligh, Extract from the logbook HMS Bounty, 27 April 1789, p. 352.
96 Morrison, Journal on HMS Bounty and at Tahiti, p. 47.
97 Rutter (ed.), *The Voyage of the Bounty's Launch*, p. 61 [reported speech].
98 Bligh, *A Voyage to the South Sea*, 1979, p. 164 [reported speech].
99 Rutter (ed.), *The Voyage of the Bounty's Launch*, p. 61 [reported speech].
100 Rutter (ed.), *The Voyage of the Bounty's Launch*, p. 61.
101 Rutter (ed.), *The Voyage of the Bounty's Launch*, p. 61.
102 Bligh and Christian, *The Bounty Mutiny*, p. 137.
103 Rutter (ed.), *The Voyage of the Bounty's Launch*, p. 56.
104 Rutter (ed.), *The Voyage of the Bounty's Launch*, p. 56.
105 John Adams's story in Bligh and Christian, *The Bounty Mutiny*, p. 238.
106 Author's note: Morrison records it as 'The people are ripe for anything' (Morrison, Journal on HMS Bounty and at Tahiti, p. 46). Bligh, and hence his officers, used 'People' to describe all sailors who were not officers. Still, multiple secondary sources (such as Anne Salmond and David G. Williams) have it as 'The men are ripe for anything'.
107 Bligh and Christian, *The Bounty Mutiny*, p. 239. Author's note: Alec Smith goes further and says George Stewart proposed that Fletcher Christian, instead of going away on a raft, should capture the ship.
108 Bligh and Christian, *The Bounty Mutiny*, p. 239.
109 Bligh and Christian, *The Bounty Mutiny*, p. 239.

Chapter 7

1 Byron, *The Works of Lord Byron Complete in One Volume*, p. 311.
2 Beaglehole, *Captain Cook and Captain Bligh*, The Dr W. E. Collins Lecture delivered at the University on 3 August 1967, The Victoria University of Wellington, 1967, p. 19.
3 Bligh and Christian, *The Bounty Mutiny*, p. 239.
4 Bligh and Christian, *The Bounty Mutiny*, p. 239.
5 Bligh and Christian, *The Bounty Mutiny*, p. 239 [reported speech].
6 Bligh and Christian, *The Bounty Mutiny*, p. 239 [reported speech].
7 Bligh and Christian, *The Bounty Mutiny*, p. 239 [reported speech].
8 Bligh and Christian, *The Bounty Mutiny*, p. 240.
9 Rutter (ed.), *The Court-Martial of the 'Bounty' Mutineers*, p. 172.
10 Rutter (ed.), *The Court-Martial of the 'Bounty' Mutineers*, p. 184.
11 Rutter (ed.), *The Court-Martial of the 'Bounty' Mutineers*, p. 184.
12 Rutter (ed.), *The Court-Martial of the 'Bounty' Mutineers*, p. 185.
13 Rutter (ed.), *The Court-Martial of the 'Bounty' Mutineers*, p. 185.
14 Rutter (ed.), *The Court-Martial of the 'Bounty' Mutineers*, p. 185.
15 Rutter (ed.), *The Court-Martial of the 'Bounty' Mutineers*, p. 185.
16 Rutter (ed.), *The Court-Martial of the 'Bounty' Mutineers*, p. 185.
17 Rutter (ed.), *The Court-Martial of the 'Bounty' Mutineers*, p. 185.
18 Rutter (ed.), *The Court-Martial of the 'Bounty' Mutineers*, p. 185.
19 Rutter (ed.), *The Court-Martial of the 'Bounty' Mutineers*, p. 185.
20 Rutter (ed.), *The Court-Martial of the 'Bounty' Mutineers*, p. 185.
21 Rutter (ed.), *The Court-Martial of the 'Bounty' Mutineers*, p. 185.
22 Morrison, Journal on HMS Bounty and at Tahiti, p. 39.
23 Rutter (ed.), *The Court-Martial of the 'Bounty' Mutineers*, p. 186.

24 Rutter (ed.), *The Court-Martial of the 'Bounty' Mutineers*, p. 186.

25 Bligh, Extract from the logbook HMS Bounty, 28 April 1789, p. 352.

26 Rutter (ed.), *The Court-Martial of the 'Bounty' Mutineers*, p. 186.

27 Bligh and Christian, *The Bounty Mutiny*, p. 240.

28 Rutter (ed.), *The Voyage of the Bounty's Launch*, p. 57.

29 Rutter (ed.), *The Voyage of the Bounty's Launch*, p. 57.

30 Rutter (ed.), *The Court-Martial of the 'Bounty' Mutineers*, p. 186.

31 Rutter (ed.), *The Court-Martial of the 'Bounty' Mutineers*, p. 113.

32 Rutter (ed.), *The Court-Martial of the 'Bounty' Mutineers*, p. 186.

33 Rutter (ed.), *The Court-Martial of the 'Bounty' Mutineers*, p. 113.

34 Rutter (ed.), *The Court-Martial of the 'Bounty' Mutineers*, p. 113 [reported speech].

35 Rutter (ed.), *The Voyage of the Bounty's Launch*, p. 57.

36 Rutter (ed.), *The Court-Martial of the 'Bounty' Mutineers*, p. 72.

37 Rutter (ed.), *The Court-Martial of the 'Bounty' Mutineers*, p. 72.

38 Rutter (ed.), *The Court-Martial of the 'Bounty' Mutineers*, p. 72.

39 Rutter (ed.), *The Court-Martial of the 'Bounty' Mutineers*, pp. 72–73.

40 Rutter (ed.), *The Court-Martial of the 'Bounty' Mutineers*, p. 73.

41 Rutter (ed.), *The Court-Martial of the 'Bounty' Mutineers*, p. 73.

42 Rutter (ed.), *The Court-Martial of the 'Bounty' Mutineers*, p. 73.

43 Rutter (ed.), *The Court-Martial of the 'Bounty' Mutineers*, p. 73.

44 Rutter (ed.), *The Court-Martial of the 'Bounty' Mutineers*, p. 73.

45 Rutter (ed.), *The Voyage of the Bounty's Launch*, p. 57.

46 Rutter (ed.), *The Court-Martial of the 'Bounty' Mutineers*, p. 73.

47 Rutter (ed.), *The Court-Martial of the 'Bounty' Mutineers*, p. 138.

48 Rutter (ed.), *The Court-Martial of the 'Bounty' Mutineers*, p. 138.

49 Rutter (ed.), *The Court-Martial of the 'Bounty' Mutineers*, p. 138.

50 Rutter (ed.), *The Court-Martial of the 'Bounty' Mutineers*, p. 94.

51 Rutter (ed.), *The Court-Martial of the 'Bounty' Mutineers*, p. 94.

52 Rutter (ed.), *The Court-Martial of the 'Bounty' Mutineers*, p. 94.

53 Rutter (ed.), *The Court-Martial of the 'Bounty' Mutineers*, p. 94.

54 Rutter (ed.), *The Court-Martial of the 'Bounty' Mutineers*, p. 94.

55 Rutter (ed.), *The Court-Martial of the 'Bounty' Mutineers*, p. 100.

56 Rutter (ed.), *The Court-Martial of the 'Bounty' Mutineers*, p. 100.

57 Rutter (ed.), *The Court-Martial of the 'Bounty' Mutineers*, p. 100.

58 Rutter (ed.), *The Court-Martial of the 'Bounty' Mutineers*, p. 82.

59 Rutter (ed.), *The Court-Martial of the 'Bounty' Mutineers*, p. 82.

60 Bligh to Banks, Letter, 13 October 1789, p. 9.

61 Rutter (ed.), *The Court-Martial of the 'Bounty' Mutineers*, p. 175.

62 Morrison, Journal on HMS Bounty and at Tahiti, p. 41 [tense changed].

63 Rutter (ed.), *The Court-Martial of the 'Bounty' Mutineers*, p. 186.

64 Bligh and Christian, *The Bounty Mutiny*, p. 143.

65 Bligh and Christian, *The Bounty Mutiny*, p. 143.

66 Bligh, Extract from the logbook HMS Bounty, 28 April 1789, p. 352 [reported speech].

67 Morrison, Journal on HMS Bounty and at Tahiti, p. 41.

68 Rutter, *The Court Martial of the 'Bounty' Mutineers*, Hodge and Company, Glasgow, 1931, p. 73 [reported speech].

69 Rutter, *The Court Martial of the 'Bounty' Mutineers*, Hodge and Company, Glasgow, 1931, p. 73 [reported speech].

70 Bligh, *A Narrative of the Mutiny on board his Majesty's Ship Bounty*, Smith, London, 1838, p. 39 [reported speech].

71 Bligh, *A Narrative of the Mutiny on board his Majesty's Ship Bounty*, Smith, London, 1838, p. 39.

72 Rutter, *The Court Martial of the 'Bounty' Mutineers*, Hodge and Company, Glasgow, 1931, p. 186 [reported speech].

73 Rutter, *The Court Martial of the 'Bounty' Mutineers*, Hodge and Company, Glasgow, 1931, p. 186.

74 Rutter, *The Court Martial of the 'Bounty' Mutineers*, Hodge and Company, Glasgow, 1931, p. 186.

75 Rutter, *The Court Martial of the 'Bounty' Mutineers*, Hodge and Company, Glasgow, 1931, p. 186.

76 Rutter, *The Court Martial of the 'Bounty' Mutineers*, Hodge and Company, Glasgow, 1931, p. 186.

77 Rutter, *The Court Martial of the 'Bounty' Mutineers*, Hodge and Company, Glasgow, 1931, p. 186.

78 Rutter (ed.), *The Court-Martial of the 'Bounty' Mutineers*, p. 94.

79 Rutter (ed.), *The Court-Martial of the 'Bounty' Mutineers*, p. 94.

80 Rutter (ed.), *The Court-Martial of the 'Bounty' Mutineers*, p. 162.

81 Rutter (ed.), *The Court-Martial of the 'Bounty' Mutineers*, p. 162.

82 Rutter (ed.), *The Court-Martial of the 'Bounty' Mutineers*, p. 83.

83 Rutter (ed.), *The Court-Martial of the 'Bounty' Mutineers*, p. 86.

84 Rutter (ed.), *The Court-Martial of the 'Bounty' Mutineers*, p. 86.

85 Rutter (ed.), *The Court-Martial of the 'Bounty' Mutineers*, p. 83.

86 Rutter (ed.), *The Court-Martial of the 'Bounty' Mutineers*, p. 195.

87 Rutter (ed.), *The Court-Martial of the 'Bounty' Mutineers*, p. 83.

88 Rutter (ed.), *The Court-Martial of the 'Bounty' Mutineers*, p. 162.

89 Rutter (ed.), *The Court-Martial of the 'Bounty' Mutineers*, p. 163.

90 Rutter (ed.), *The Court-Martial of the 'Bounty' Mutineers*, p. 90.

91 Rutter (ed.), *The Court-Martial of the 'Bounty' Mutineers*, p. 173.

92 Rutter (ed.), *The Court-Martial of the 'Bounty' Mutineers*, p. 173.

93 Rutter (ed.), *The Court-Martial of the 'Bounty' Mutineers*, p. 173.

94 Morrison, Journal on HMS Bounty and at Tahiti, p. 37.

95 Brunton, *Awake, Bold Bligh!*, Allen & Unwin, Sydney, 1989, p. 27. Author's note: Bligh did not include this detail in the first letter to Betsy, but in the first letter to her uncle. Clearly, Bligh does not want his wife to know all the details or how many times he came close to death; he is a devoted husband and does not want to upset her more than he has to.

96 Bligh, *A Voyage to the South Sea*, 1979, p. 156.

97 Rutter (ed.), *The Court-Martial of the 'Bounty' Mutineers*, p. 136.

98 Rutter (ed.), *The Court-Martial of the 'Bounty' Mutineers*, p. 136.

99 Rutter (ed.), *The Court-Martial of the 'Bounty' Mutineers*, p. 136.

100 Rutter (ed.), *The Court-Martial of the 'Bounty' Mutineers*, p. 136.

101 Rutter (ed.), *The Court-Martial of the 'Bounty' Mutineers*, p. 73.

102 Rutter (ed.), *The Court-Martial of the 'Bounty' Mutineers*, p. 73.

103 Rutter (ed.), *The Court-Martial of the 'Bounty' Mutineers*, p. 73 [reported speech].

104 Rutter (ed.), *The Court-Martial of the 'Bounty' Mutineers*, p. 73.

105 Rutter (ed.), *The Court-Martial of the 'Bounty' Mutineers*, p. 73.

106 Rutter (ed.), *The Court-Martial of the 'Bounty' Mutineers*, p. 102.

107 Rutter (ed.), *The Court-Martial of the 'Bounty' Mutineers*, p. 102.

108 Rutter (ed.), *The Court-Martial of the 'Bounty' Mutineers*, p. 102.

109 Rutter (ed.), *The Court-Martial of the 'Bounty' Mutineers*, p. 73.

110 Rutter (ed.), *The Court-Martial of the 'Bounty' Mutineers*, p. 73.

111 Rutter (ed.), *The Court-Martial of the 'Bounty' Mutineers*, p. 73.

112 Rutter (ed.), *The Court-Martial of the 'Bounty' Mutineers*, p. 73.

113 Rutter (ed.), *The Court-Martial of the 'Bounty' Mutineers*, pp. 73–74.

114 Rutter (ed.), *The Court-Martial of the 'Bounty' Mutineers*, p. 74.

115 Rutter (ed.), *The Court-Martial of the 'Bounty' Mutineers*, p. 74.

116 Rutter (ed.), *The Court-Martial of the 'Bounty' Mutineers*, p. 74.
117 Rutter (ed.), *The Court-Martial of the 'Bounty' Mutineers*, p. 74.
118 Rutter (ed.), *The Court-Martial of the 'Bounty' Mutineers*, p. 74.
119 Rutter (ed.), *The Court-Martial of the 'Bounty' Mutineers*, p. 74 [reported speech].
120 Rutter (ed.), *The Court-Martial of the 'Bounty' Mutineers*, p. 74.
121 Rutter (ed.), *The Court-Martial of the 'Bounty' Mutineers*, p. 74 [reported speech].
122 Rutter (ed.), *The Court-Martial of the 'Bounty' Mutineers*, p. 74.
123 Rutter (ed.), *The Court-Martial of the 'Bounty' Mutineers*, p. 163 [reported speech].
124 Rutter (ed.), *The Court-Martial of the 'Bounty' Mutineers*, p. 163 [reported speech].
125 Rutter (ed.), *The Court-Martial of the 'Bounty' Mutineers*, p. 163.
126 Rutter (ed.), *The Court-Martial of the 'Bounty' Mutineers*, p. 163.
127 Rutter (ed.), *The Court-Martial of the 'Bounty' Mutineers*, p. 163.
128 Rutter (ed.), *The Court-Martial of the 'Bounty' Mutineers*, p. 163.
129 Rutter (ed.), *The Court-Martial of the 'Bounty' Mutineers*, p. 163.
130 Rutter (ed.), *The Court-Martial of the 'Bounty' Mutineers*, p. 163.
131 Rutter (ed.), *The Court-Martial of the 'Bounty' Mutineers*, p. 163.
132 Bligh and Christian, *The Bounty Mutiny*, p. 241. Author's note: Morrison remembers Bligh's question but says he could not hear the answer. Twenty-five years later, Alec Smith gives the answer to the question on Pitcairn in his own account, completely independent of Morrison's evidence. The events of that morning made an impression that does not fade.
133 Rutter (ed.), *The Court-Martial of the 'Bounty' Mutineers*, p. 74.
134 Rutter (ed.), *The Court-Martial of the 'Bounty' Mutineers*, p. 74.
135 Rutter (ed.), *The Court-Martial of the 'Bounty' Mutineers*, p. 74.
136 Bligh and Christian, *The Bounty Mutiny*, p. 136.
137 Bligh and Christian, *The Bounty Mutiny*, p. 145.
138 Bligh and Christian, *The Bounty Mutiny*, p. 136.
139 Rutter (ed.), *The Court-Martial of the 'Bounty' Mutineers*, p. 114.
140 Rutter (ed.), *The Court-Martial of the 'Bounty' Mutineers*, p. 186.
141 Rutter (ed.), *The Court-Martial of the 'Bounty' Mutineers*, pp. 186–87.
142 Rutter (ed.), *The Court-Martial of the 'Bounty' Mutineers*, p. 187.
143 Rutter (ed.), *The Court-Martial of the 'Bounty' Mutineers*, p. 187.
144 Rutter (ed.), *The Court-Martial of the 'Bounty' Mutineers*, p. 129.
145 Rutter (ed.), *The Court-Martial of the 'Bounty' Mutineers*, p. 129.
146 Rutter (ed.), *The Court-Martial of the 'Bounty' Mutineers*, p. 75.
147 Rutter (ed.), *The Court-Martial of the 'Bounty' Mutineers*, p. 187.
148 Rutter (ed.), *The Court-Martial of the 'Bounty' Mutineers*, p. 83.
149 Rutter (ed.), *The Court-Martial of the 'Bounty' Mutineers*, p. 83.
150 Bligh, Extract from the logbook HMS Bounty, 28 April 1789, p. 353 [reported speech].
151 Rutter (ed.), *The Court-Martial of the 'Bounty' Mutineers*, p. 101.
152 Rutter (ed.), *The Court-Martial of the 'Bounty' Mutineers*, p. 101.
153 Rutter (ed.), *The Court-Martial of the 'Bounty' Mutineers*, p. 187.
154 Rutter (ed.), *The Court-Martial of the 'Bounty' Mutineers*, p. 187.
155 Rutter (ed.), *The Court-Martial of the 'Bounty' Mutineers*, p. 187.
156 Morrison, Journal on HMS Bounty and at Tahiti, p. 42.
157 Rutter (ed.), *The Court-Martial of the 'Bounty' Mutineers*, p. 187.
158 Christian, *Fragile Paradise*, p. 69.
159 Rutter (ed.), *The Court-Martial of the 'Bounty' Mutineers*, p. 187.
160 Rutter (ed.), *The Court-Martial of the 'Bounty' Mutineers*, p. 187.
161 Rutter (ed.), *The Court-Martial of the 'Bounty' Mutineers*, p. 187.
162 Rutter (ed.), *The Court-Martial of the 'Bounty' Mutineers*, p. 187.
163 Rutter (ed.), *The Court-Martial of the 'Bounty' Mutineers*, p. 84.
164 Rutter (ed.), *The Court-Martial of the 'Bounty' Mutineers*, p. 84.
165 Rutter (ed.), *The Court-Martial of the 'Bounty' Mutineers*, p. 84.

166 Rutter (ed.), *The Court-Martial of the 'Bounty' Mutineers*, p. 101.
167 Rutter (ed.), *The Court-Martial of the 'Bounty' Mutineers*, p. 84.
168 Rutter (ed.), *The Court-Martial of the 'Bounty' Mutineers*, p. 101.
169 Rutter, *The Court Martial of the Bounty Mutineers*, Canada Law Book Company, Toronto, 1933, p. 75.

Chapter 8

1 Forster, *A Voyage Round the World: in His Britannic Majesty's Sloop, Resolution, commanded by Capt. Cook, during the years 1772, 3, 4 and 5*, Vol. II, B. White, London, 1777, pp. 108–109.
2 Bligh, Extract from the logbook HMS Bounty, 28 April 1789, p. 356.
3 Byron, *The Works of Lord Byron Complete in One Volume*, p. 311.
4 Rutter (ed.), *The Court-Martial of the 'Bounty' Mutineers*, p. 140.
5 Morrison, Journal on HMS Bounty and at Tahiti, p. 45.
6 Rutter (ed.), *The Court-Martial of the 'Bounty' Mutineers*, pp. 74–75.
7 Rutter (ed.), *The Court-Martial of the 'Bounty' Mutineers*, p. 75.
8 Rutter (ed.), *The Court-Martial of the 'Bounty' Mutineers*, p. 94.
9 Rutter (ed.), *The Court-Martial of the 'Bounty' Mutineers*, p. 94.
10 Rutter (ed.), *The Court-Martial of the 'Bounty' Mutineers*, p. 74.
11 Rutter (ed.), *The Court-Martial of the 'Bounty' Mutineers*, p. 94.
12 Rutter (ed.), *The Court-Martial of the 'Bounty' Mutineers*, p. 74.
13 Rutter (ed.), *The Court-Martial of the 'Bounty' Mutineers*, p. 74.
14 Rutter (ed.), *The Court-Martial of the 'Bounty' Mutineers*, p. 74.
15 Rutter (ed.), *The Court-Martial of the 'Bounty' Mutineers*, p. 74.
16 Rutter (ed.), *The Court-Martial of the 'Bounty' Mutineers*, p. 129 [changed to evoke his Cockney accent].
17 Rutter (ed.), *The Court-Martial of the 'Bounty' Mutineers*, p. 130 [changed to represent Manx accent].
18 Bligh, *The Mutiny on Board HMS Bounty*, Airmont, New York, 1965, p. 98.
19 Rutter (ed.), *The Court-Martial of the 'Bounty' Mutineers*, p. 101.
20 Rutter (ed.), *The Court-Martial of the 'Bounty' Mutineers*, p. 102.
21 Rutter (ed.), *The Court-Martial of the 'Bounty' Mutineers*, p. 85.
22 Bligh, *A Voyage to the South Sea*, 1979, p. 156 [reported speech].
23 Bligh, *A Voyage to the South Sea*, 1979, p. 157.
24 Bligh, *A Voyage to the South Sea*, 1979, p. 157. Author's note: Although Bligh does not specify, I assume this is Charley Churchill speaking.
25 Rutter (ed.), *The Court-Martial of the 'Bounty' Mutineers*, p. 92 [reported speech].
26 Rutter (ed.), *The Court-Martial of the 'Bounty' Mutineers*, p. 188.
27 Rutter (ed.), *The Court-Martial of the 'Bounty' Mutineers*, p. 92.
28 Rutter (ed.), *The Court-Martial of the 'Bounty' Mutineers*, p. 188.
29 Rutter (ed.), *The Court-Martial of the 'Bounty' Mutineers*, p. 188.
30 Rutter (ed.), *The Court-Martial of the 'Bounty' Mutineers*, p. 188.
31 Rutter (ed.), *The Court-Martial of the 'Bounty' Mutineers*, p. 79.
32 Rutter (ed.), *The Court-Martial of the 'Bounty' Mutineers*, p. 79.
33 Rutter (ed.), *The Voyage of the Bounty's Launch*, p. 57.
34 Rutter (ed.), *The Voyage of the Bounty's Launch*, p. 57.
35 Rutter (ed.), *The Court-Martial of the 'Bounty' Mutineers*, p. 102.
36 Rutter (ed.), *The Court-Martial of the 'Bounty' Mutineers*, p. 180.
37 Bligh, Extract from the logbook HMS Bounty, 28 April 1789, p. 355.
38 Bligh, Extract from the logbook HMS Bounty, 28 April 1789, p. 353.
39 Rutter (ed.), *The Court-Martial of the 'Bounty' Mutineers*, p. 104.
40 Rutter (ed.), *The Court-Martial of the 'Bounty' Mutineers*, p. 102.

41 Rutter (ed.), *The Court-Martial of the 'Bounty' Mutineers*, p. 102.
42 Rutter (ed.), *The Court-Martial of the 'Bounty' Mutineers*, p. 145.
43 Morrison, Journal on HMS Bounty and at Tahiti, p. 43.
44 Rutter (ed.), *The Court-Martial of the 'Bounty' Mutineers*, p. 164.
45 Rutter (ed.), *The Court-Martial of the 'Bounty' Mutineers*, p. 164.
46 Rutter (ed.), *The Court-Martial of the 'Bounty' Mutineers*, p. 164.
47 Rutter (ed.), *The Court-Martial of the 'Bounty' Mutineers*, p. 164.
48 Rutter (ed.), *The Court-Martial of the 'Bounty' Mutineers*, p. 165.
49 Rutter (ed.), *The Court-Martial of the 'Bounty' Mutineers*, p. 165.
50 Rutter (ed.), *The Court-Martial of the 'Bounty' Mutineers*, p. 87.
51 Rutter (ed.), *The Court-Martial of the 'Bounty' Mutineers*, p. 188 [reported speech].
52 Rutter (ed.), *The Court-Martial of the 'Bounty' Mutineers*, p. 188.
53 Rutter (ed.), *The Court-Martial of the 'Bounty' Mutineers*, p. 188 [reported speech].
54 Rutter (ed.), *The Court-Martial of the 'Bounty' Mutineers*, pp. 188–89.
55 Rutter (ed.), *The Court-Martial of the 'Bounty' Mutineers*, p. 189.
56 Rutter (ed.), *The Court-Martial of the 'Bounty' Mutineers*, p. 75.
57 Rutter (ed.), *The Court-Martial of the 'Bounty' Mutineers*, p. 75.
58 Rutter (ed.), *The Voyage of the Bounty's Launch*, p. 59.
59 Rutter (ed.), *The Voyage of the Bounty's Launch*, p. 59.
60 Rutter (ed.), *The Voyage of the Bounty's Launch*, p. 59.
61 Bligh, *A Voyage to the South Sea*, 1979, p. 158.
62 Bligh, *A Voyage to the South Sea*, 1979, p. 161.
63 Bligh, *A Voyage to the South Sea*, 1979, p. 161.
64 Bligh and Christian, *The Bounty Mutiny*, p. 142.
65 Bligh and Christian, *The Bounty Mutiny*, p. 142.
66 Bligh and Christian, *The Bounty Mutiny*, p. 142.
67 Rutter (ed.), *The Court-Martial of the 'Bounty' Mutineers*, p. 189.
68 Rutter (ed.), *The Court-Martial of the 'Bounty' Mutineers*, p. 165.
69 Rutter (ed.), *The Court-Martial of the 'Bounty' Mutineers*, p. 76.
70 Rutter (ed.), *The Court-Martial of the 'Bounty' Mutineers*, p. 165.
71 Morrison, Journal on HMS Bounty and at Tahiti, p. 44 [reported speech].
72 Morrison, Journal on HMS Bounty and at Tahiti, p. 44.
73 Rutter (ed.), *The Court-Martial of the 'Bounty' Mutineers*, p. 165 [reported speech].
74 Rutter (ed.), *The Court-Martial of the 'Bounty' Mutineers*, p. 189.
75 Rutter (ed.), *The Court-Martial of the 'Bounty' Mutineers*, p. 189.
76 Rutter (ed.), *The Court-Martial of the 'Bounty' Mutineers*, p. 189.
77 Rutter (ed.), *The Court-Martial of the 'Bounty' Mutineers*, p. 165 [reported speech].
78 Bligh, Extract from the logbook HMS Bounty, 28 April 1789, p. 357.
79 Rutter (ed.), *The Court-Martial of the 'Bounty' Mutineers*, p. 165.
80 Rutter (ed.), *The Court-Martial of the 'Bounty' Mutineers*, p. 86.
81 Rutter (ed.), *The Court-Martial of the 'Bounty' Mutineers*, p. 177.
82 Rutter (ed.), *The Court-Martial of the 'Bounty' Mutineers*, p. 86.
83 Rutter (ed.), *The Court-Martial of the 'Bounty' Mutineers*, p. 127.
84 Rutter (ed.), *The Court-Martial of the 'Bounty' Mutineers*, p. 161.
85 Rutter (ed.), *The Court-Martial of the 'Bounty' Mutineers*, p. 161.
86 Rutter (ed.), *The Court-Martial of the 'Bounty' Mutineers*, p. 125.
87 Rutter (ed.), *The Court-Martial of the 'Bounty' Mutineers*, p. 76.
88 Morrison, *After the Bounty*, Potomac Books, Dulles, 2010, p. 41 [reported speech].
89 Rutter (ed.), *The Court-Martial of the 'Bounty' Mutineers*, p. 76.
90 Rutter (ed.), *The Court-Martial of the 'Bounty' Mutineers*, p. 76.
91 Rutter (ed.), *The Court-Martial of the 'Bounty' Mutineers*, p. 115.
92 Rutter (ed.), *The Court-Martial of the 'Bounty' Mutineers*, p. 76.
93 Rutter (ed.), *The Court-Martial of the 'Bounty' Mutineers*, p. 165.

94 Rutter (ed.), *The Court-Martial of the 'Bounty' Mutineers*, p. 165.
95 Rutter (ed.), *The Court-Martial of the 'Bounty' Mutineers*, p. 165.
96 Bligh, *A voyage to the South sea*, G. Nicol, London, 1792, p. 160.
97 Bligh and Christian, *The Bounty Mutiny*, p. 145.
98 Bligh and Christian, *The Bounty Mutiny*, p. 145.
99 Bligh and Christian, *The Bounty Mutiny*, p. 145.

Chapter 9

1 Dolan, *The Old Farmer's Almanac Book of Weather Lore: The Fact and Fancy Behind Weather Predictions, Superstitions, Old-time Sayings, and Traditions*, Yankee Books, New Hampshire, 1988, p. 11.
2 Bligh and Christian, *The Bounty Mutiny*, p. 10.
3 Bligh and Christian, *The Bounty Mutiny*, p. 11.
4 Bligh, Extract from the logbook HMS Bounty, 29 April 1789, p. 361.
5 Bligh, Extract from the logbook HMS Bounty, 30 April 1789, p. 362.
6 Rutter (ed.), *The Voyage of the Bounty's Launch*, p. 63.
7 Rutter (ed.), *The Voyage of the Bounty's Launch*, p. 63.
8 Rutter (ed.), *The Voyage of the Bounty's Launch*, p. 63.
9 Rutter (ed.), *The Voyage of the Bounty's Launch*, p. 63.
10 Rutter (ed.), *The Voyage of the Bounty's Launch*, p. 63.
11 Rutter (ed.), *The Voyage of the Bounty's Launch*, p. 63.
12 Rutter (ed.), *The Voyage of the Bounty's Launch*, p. 63.
13 Bligh and Christian, *The Bounty Mutiny*, p. 142.
14 Author's note: For the record, and in the old money, Bligh was 15 miles out in this estimation.
15 Rutter (ed.), *The Voyage of the Bounty's Launch*, p. 64.
16 Bligh, *A Voyage to the South Sea*, 1979, pp. 169–70.
17 Bligh, *A Voyage to the South Sea*, 1979, p. 171 [reported speech].
18 Rutter (ed.), *The Voyage of the Bounty's Launch*, p. 64.
19 Rutter (ed.), *The Voyage of the Bounty's Launch*, p. 64 [reported speech].
20 Rutter (ed.), *The Voyage of the Bounty's Launch*, p. 64 [reported speech].
21 Bligh, *A Voyage to the South Sea*, 1979, p. 175 [reported speech].
22 Bligh, *A Voyage to the South Sea*, 1979, p. 172 [reported speech].
23 Bligh, *A Voyage to the South Sea*, 1979, p. 172.
24 Bligh, *A Voyage to the South Sea*, 1979, p. 173 [reported speech].
25 Bligh, *A Voyage to the South Sea*, 1979, p. 173 [reported speech].
26 Bligh, *A Voyage to the South Sea*, 1979, p. 173.
27 Bligh, *A Voyage to the South Sea*, 1979, p. 173.
28 Bligh, *A Voyage to the South Sea*, 1979, p. 174.
29 Bligh, *A Voyage to the South Sea*, 1979, p. 173.
30 Bligh, *A Voyage to the South Sea*, 1979, p. 173 [reported speech].
31 Bligh, *A Voyage to the South Sea*, 1979, pp. 173–74.
32 Rutter (ed.), *The Voyage of the Bounty's Launch*, p. 65 [reported speech].
33 Bligh, *A Voyage to the South Sea*, 1979, p. 174.
34 Rutter (ed.), *The Voyage of the Bounty's Launch*, p. 65. Author's note: Fryer writes he said 'Come into the ship' but Bligh has it as 'called him to return'.
35 Bligh, *A Voyage to the South Sea*, 1979, p. 174.
36 Rutter (ed.), *The Voyage of the Bounty's Launch*, p. 65.
37 Bligh, *A Voyage to the South Sea*, 1979, p. 175.
38 Bach, *The Bligh Notebook*, Allen & Unwin, Sydney, 1987, p. 47.
39 Mackaness, *The Life of Vice-Admiral William Bligh*, p. 141. Author's note: Bligh tells this to his uncle after returning to England. His uncle is so struck by these words that he writes them down in his own private copy of Bligh's 'Narrative'.

40 Rutter (ed.), *The Voyage of the Bounty's Launch*, p. 66 [reported speech].
41 Rutter (ed.), *The Voyage of the Bounty's Launch*, p. 66 [reported speech].
42 Rutter (ed.), *The Voyage of the Bounty's Launch*, p. 66.
43 Rutter (ed.), *The Voyage of the Bounty's Launch*, p. 66.
44 Rutter (ed.), *The Voyage of the Bounty's Launch*, p. 67 [reported speech].
45 Bligh, *A Voyage to the South Sea*, 1979, p. 176.
46 Bligh, *A Voyage to the South Sea*, 1979, p. 176.
47 Bligh, Extract from the logbook HMS Bounty, 3 May 1789, p. 367.
48 Rutter (ed.), *The Voyage of the Bounty's Launch*, p. 66.
49 Bligh, *A Voyage to the South Sea*, 1979, p. 176.
50 Rutter (ed.), *The Voyage of the Bounty's Launch*, p. 66.
51 Bligh, *A Voyage to the South Sea*, 1979, p. 176.
52 Bligh, *A Voyage to the South Sea*, 1979, pp. 177–78.
53 Bligh, *A Voyage to the South Sea*, 1979, pp. 177–78.
54 Bligh, *A Voyage to the South Sea*, 1979, pp. 177–78.
55 Bligh, *A Voyage to the South Sea*, 1979, p. 178.
56 Bligh, *A Voyage to the South Sea*, 1979, pp. 177–78.
57 Morrison, Journal on HMS Bounty and at Tahiti, p. 50.
58 Morrison, Journal on HMS Bounty and at Tahiti, p. 50.
59 Morrison, Journal on HMS Bounty and at Tahiti, p. 50.
60 Morrison, Journal on HMS Bounty and at Tahiti, p. 50 [reported speech].
61 Heywood, *Innocent on the Bounty*, p. 38.
62 Morrison, Journal on HMS Bounty and at Tahiti, p. 50.
63 Bligh, Extract from the logbook HMS Bounty, 6 May 1789, p. 370.
64 Bligh, Extract from the logbook HMS Bounty, 7 May 1789, p. 371.
65 Rutter (ed.), *The Voyage of the Bounty's Launch*, p. 68.
66 Rutter (ed.), *The Voyage of the Bounty's Launch*, p. 68.
67 Rutter (ed.), *The Voyage of the Bounty's Launch*, p. 68.
68 Rutter (ed.), *The Voyage of the Bounty's Launch*, p. 68.
69 Rutter (ed.), *The Voyage of the Bounty's Launch*, p. 68.
70 Bligh and Christian, *The Bounty Mutiny*, p. 25.

Chapter 10

1 Shedd (ed.), *The Complete Works of Samuel Taylor Coleridge*, pp. 232–33.
2 Bligh and Christian, *The Bounty Mutiny*, pp. 26–27 [tense changed].
3 Bligh, *A voyage to the South sea*, 1792, p. 185.
4 Bligh, *A voyage to the South sea*, 1979, p. 195.
5 Bligh, *A voyage to the South sea*, 1979, p. 195.
6 Bligh and Christian, *The Bounty Mutiny*, p. 27.
7 Bligh, *A voyage to the South sea*, 1792, p. 185 [reported speech].
8 Bligh, *A voyage to the South sea*, 1792, p. 185 [reported speech].
9 Morrison, Journal on HMS Bounty and at Tahiti, p. 51 [reported speech].
10 Bligh, *A voyage to the South sea*, 1792, p. 197.
11 Bligh, Extract from the logbook HMS Bounty, 20 May 1789, p. 384.
12 Author's note: This was a standard method for caulking ships in the 18th century. I presume it was used by the *Bounty* men although there is no detailed record of them using this precise method.
13 Bligh and Christian, *The Bounty Mutiny*, p. 31.
14 Bligh and Christian, *The Bounty Mutiny*, p. 33.
15 Rutter (ed.), *The Voyage of the Bounty's Launch*, p. 68.
16 Rutter (ed.), *The Voyage of the Bounty's Launch*, p. 68.
17 Rutter (ed.), *The Voyage of the Bounty's Launch*, p. 68.

18 Rutter (ed.), *The Voyage of the Bounty's Launch*, p. 68.
19 Rutter (ed.), *The Voyage of the Bounty's Launch*, p. 68.
20 Rutter (ed.), *The Voyage of the Bounty's Launch*, p. 68.
21 Rutter (ed.), *The Voyage of the Bounty's Launch*, p. 69.
22 Rutter (ed.), *The Voyage of the Bounty's Launch*, p. 69.
23 Morrison, Journal on HMS Bounty and at Tahiti, p. 51.
24 Morrison, Journal on HMS Bounty and at Tahiti, pp. 52–53.
25 Morrison, Journal on HMS Bounty and at Tahiti, p. 53.
26 Morrison, Journal on HMS Bounty and at Tahiti, p. 54.
27 Morrison, Journal on HMS Bounty and at Tahiti, p. 54.
28 Morrison, Journal on HMS Bounty and at Tahiti, p. 54.
29 Rutter (ed.), *The Voyage of the Bounty's Launch*, p. 69.
30 Bach, *The Bligh Notebook*, p. 115.
31 Rutter (ed.), *The Voyage of the Bounty's Launch*, p .69.
32 Rutter (ed.), *The Voyage of the Bounty's Launch*, p. 69.
33 Rutter (ed.), *The Voyage of the Bounty's Launch*, p. 69.
34 Rutter (ed.), *The Voyage of the Bounty's Launch*, p. 70.
35 Morrison, Journal on HMS Bounty and at Tahiti, p. 55.
36 Bligh, Log, 29 May 1789.
37 Barrow, *The Mutiny and Piratical Seizure of HMS Bounty*, p. 111 [reported speech].
38 Bligh, *A Voyage to the South Sea*, 1979, pp. 205–206.
39 Bligh, *A Voyage to the South Sea*, 1979, p. 203.
40 Author's note: Joseph Banks was the first to obtain the name 'kangaroo' from a native on 23 June 1770.
41 Bligh, *A Voyage to the South Sea*, 1979, p. 203.
42 Bligh, *A Voyage to the South Sea*, 1979, p. 203.
43 Bligh, Log, 30 May 1789.
44 Bligh, Notebook and List of Mutineers, 1789, NLA, MS 5393, 30 May 1789, [no page numbers].
45 Rutter (ed.), *The Voyage of the Bounty's Launch*, p. 70.
46 Bligh, Notebook and List of Mutineers, [no page numbers].
47 Author's note: These are generic commands, consistent with the terminology of the time.
48 Morrison, Journal on HMS Bounty and at Tahiti, p. 56.
49 Rutter (ed.), *The Voyage of the Bounty's Launch*, p. 70 [reported speech].
50 Rutter (ed.), *The Voyage of the Bounty's Launch*, p. 70 [reported speech].
51 Rutter (ed.), *The Voyage of the Bounty's Launch*, p. 70 [reported speech].
52 Rutter (ed.), *The Voyage of the Bounty's Launch*, pp. 70–71 [reported speech].
53 Rutter (ed.), *The Voyage of the Bounty's Launch*, p. 71.
54 Rutter (ed.), *The Voyage of the Bounty's Launch*, p. 71 [reported speech].
55 Rutter (ed.), *The Voyage of the Bounty's Launch*, p. 71.
56 Rutter (ed.), *The Voyage of the Bounty's Launch*, p. 71.
57 Rutter (ed.), *The Voyage of the Bounty's Launch*, p. 71.
58 Rutter (ed.), *The Voyage of the Bounty's Launch*, p. 71 [reported speech].
59 Rutter (ed.), *The Voyage of the Bounty's Launch*, p. 71.
60 Rutter (ed.), *The Voyage of the Bounty's Launch*, p. 71.
61 Rutter (ed.), *The Voyage of the Bounty's Launch*, p. 71.
62 Rutter (ed.), *The Voyage of the Bounty's Launch*, p. 71.
63 Bligh, Extract from the logbook HMS Bounty, 31 May 1789.
64 Bligh, *A Voyage to the South Sea*, 1979, pp. 209–10.
65 Bligh, *A Voyage to the South Sea*, 1979, p. 210.
66 Rutter (ed.), *The Voyage of the Bounty's Launch*, p. 71.
67 Rutter (ed.), *The Voyage of the Bounty's Launch*, p. 71.
68 Barrow, *The Mutiny and Piratical Seizure of HMS Bounty*, p. 111.

69 Rutter (ed.), *The Voyage of the Bounty's Launch*, p. 71.
70 Barrow, *The Mutiny and Piratical Seizure of HMS Bounty*, p. 111.
71 Rutter (ed.), *The Voyage of the Bounty's Launch*, p. 71.
72 Barrow, *The Mutiny and Piratical Seizure of HMS Bounty*, p. 111.
73 Rutter (ed.), *The Voyage of the Bounty's Launch*, p. 71.
74 Rutter (ed.), *The Voyage of the Bounty's Launch*, p. 71.
75 Rutter (ed.), *The Voyage of the Bounty's Launch*, p. 71.
76 Rutter (ed.), *The Voyage of the Bounty's Launch*, p. 71.
77 Rutter (ed.), *The Voyage of the Bounty's Launch*, p. 71.
78 Barrow, *The Mutiny and Piratical Seizure of HMS Bounty*, p. 111.
79 Rutter (ed.), *The Voyage of the Bounty's Launch*, p. 72.
80 Rutter (ed.), *The Voyage of the Bounty's Launch*, p. 72.
81 Rutter (ed.), *The Voyage of the Bounty's Launch*, p. 72.
82 Kennedy, *Captain Bligh: The Man and His Mutinies*, p. 159.
83 Dening, *Mr Bligh's Bad Language*, p. 104.
84 Dening, *Mr Bligh's Bad Language*, p. 104.

Chapter 11

1 Byron, *The Works of Lord Byron Complete in One Volume*, p. 318.
2 *Walker's Hibernian Magazine*, p. 326 [reported speech].
3 *Walker's Hibernian Magazine*, p. 326 [reported speech].
4 *Walker's Hibernian Magazine*, p. 325.
5 Oliver, *Return to Tahiti*, p. 54.
6 Oliver, *Return to Tahiti*, p. 54. Author's note: This remarkable dialogue was recorded by William Bligh himself. Fascinated by all aspects of Fletcher Christian's treachery and deception, Bligh was a ceaseless inquisitor about Christian and the Mutineers on his eventual return to Tahiti. This exchange was carefully noted, word for word in the form of a dialogue, in Bligh's Log on 10 April 1792, his first full day back on this island. No doubt Bligh was already imagining this evidence forming part of the court martial of Fletcher Christian once the rascal was caught.
7 Oliver, *Return to Tahiti*, p. 54.
8 Oliver, *Return to Tahiti*, p. 54.
9 Oliver, *Return to Tahiti*, p. 54.
10 Oliver, *Return to Tahiti*, p. 54.
11 Oliver, *Return to Tahiti*, pp. 54–55.
12 Oliver, *Return to Tahiti*, p. 55.
13 Oliver, *Return to Tahiti*, p. 55.
14 *Walker's Hibernian Magazine*, p. 327.
15 *Walker's Hibernian Magazine*, p. 327.
16 Morrison, Journal on HMS Bounty and at Tahiti, pp. 285–86.
17 Author's note: These Tahitian anecdotes are undated but occurred in Tahiti during the Mutineers' stay there. The source of these anecdotes is a long article from 1794 in *Walker's Hibernian Magazine*. The journalist does not say explicitly which of the sailors has been interviewed, but as the article criticises everybody except wise Mr Coleman, good Mr Coleman, Mr Coleman who forbore liquor and was beloved by all, it is my assumption that the key source is Mr Coleman himself. As one of the three marked, detained Loyalists, Coleman is there throughout, and free to give his observations without fear of self-incrimination.
18 *Walker's Hibernian Magazine*, p. 328.
19 Bligh, Extract from the logbook HMS Bounty, 10 June 1789, p. 413.
20 Bligh, Extract from the logbook HMS Bounty, 9 June 1789, p. 412.
21 Bligh, Extract from the logbook HMS Bounty, 11 June 1789, p. 414.
22 Bligh, Extract from the logbook HMS Bounty, 11 June 1789, p. 414 [reported speech].

23 Bligh, Extract from the logbook HMS Bounty, 11 June 1789, p. 414.
24 Bligh, Extract from the logbook HMS Bounty, 11 June 1789, p. 414.
25 Bligh, Extract from the logbook HMS Bounty, 12 June 1789, p. 415.
26 Rutter (ed.), *The Voyage of the Bounty's Launch*, p. 73.
27 Rutter (ed.), *The Voyage of the Bounty's Launch*, p. 73.
28 Rutter (ed.), *The Voyage of the Bounty's Launch*, p. 73.
29 Rutter (ed.), *The Voyage of the Bounty's Launch*, p. 73.
30 Rutter (ed.), *The Voyage of the Bounty's Launch*, p. 73.
31 Rutter (ed.), *The Voyage of the Bounty's Launch*, p. 73.
32 Rutter (ed.), *The Voyage of the Bounty's Launch*, p. 74.
33 Rutter (ed.), *The Voyage of the Bounty's Launch*, p. 74.
34 Rutter (ed.), *The Voyage of the Bounty's Launch*, p. 74.
35 Rutter (ed.), *The Voyage of the Bounty's Launch*, p. 74
36 Rutter (ed.), *The Voyage of the Bounty's Launch*, p. 74.
37 Rutter (ed.), *The Voyage of the Bounty's Launch*, p. 74.
38 Rutter (ed.), *The Voyage of the Bounty's Launch*, p. 74.
39 Rutter (ed.), *The Voyage of the Bounty's Launch*, p. 74.
40 Rutter (ed.), *The Voyage of the Bounty's Launch*, p. 74.
41 Rutter (ed.), *The Voyage of the Bounty's Launch*, p. 74.
42 Kennedy, *Captain Bligh: The Man and His Mutinies*, p. 166.
43 Rutter (ed.), *The Voyage of the Bounty's Launch*, p. 74.
44 Rutter (ed.), *The Voyage of the Bounty's Launch*, p. 74.
45 Bligh, Extract from the logbook HMS Bounty, 13 June 1789, p. 417 [reported speech].
46 Bligh, Extract from the logbook HMS Bounty, 13 June 1789, p. 417 [reported speech].
47 Bligh, Extract from the logbook HMS Bounty, 13 June 1789, p. 417 [reported speech].
48 *Walker's Hibernian Magazine*, p. 503.
49 *Walker's Hibernian Magazine*, p. 503.
50 *Walker's Hibernian Magazine*, p. 503.
51 *Walker's Hibernian Magazine*, p. 503.
52 *Walker's Hibernian Magazine*, p. 503.
53 *Walker's Hibernian Magazine*, p. 503.
54 *Walker's Hibernian Magazine*, p. 503.
55 *Walker's Hibernian Magazine*, p. 503.
56 *Walker's Hibernian Magazine*, p. 503.
57 *Walker's Hibernian Magazine*, p. 503.
58 *Walker's Hibernian Magazine*, p. 503.
59 *Walker's Hibernian Magazine*, p. 503.
60 Bligh, *A Voyage to the South Sea*, 1979, p. 138.
61 *Walker's Hibernian Magazine*, p. 503.
62 *Walker's Hibernian Magazine*, p. 503.
63 *Walker's Hibernian Magazine*, p. 503.
64 *Walker's Hibernian Magazine*, p. 503.
65 Bligh and Christian, *The Bounty Mutiny*, p. 60.
66 Bligh and Christian, *The Bounty Mutiny*, p. 60.
67 Bligh and Christian, *The Bounty Mutiny*, p. 61.
68 Bligh to Banks, Letter, 13 October 1789, p. 19.
69 Rutter (ed.), *The Voyage of the Bounty's Launch*, p. 76.
70 Rutter (ed.), *The Voyage of the Bounty's Launch*, p. 76.
71 Rutter (ed.), *The Voyage of the Bounty's Launch*, p. 76 [reported speech].
72 Rutter (ed.), *The Voyage of the Bounty's Launch*, p. 76.
73 Rutter (ed.), *The Voyage of the Bounty's Launch*, p. 76.
74 Rutter (ed.), *The Voyage of the Bounty's Launch*, p. 77.
75 Rutter (ed.), *The Voyage of the Bounty's Launch*, p. 77.

76 Rutter (ed.), *The Voyage of the Bounty's Launch*, p. 77.

77 Rutter (ed.), *The Voyage of the Bounty's Launch*, p. 77.

78 *Walker's Hibernian Magazine*, p. 504.

79 *Walker's Hibernian Magazine*, p. 504.

80 *Walker's Hibernian Magazine*, p. 504.

81 *Walker's Hibernian Magazine*, p. 504.

82 *Walker's Hibernian Magazine*, p. 504.

83 *Walker's Hibernian Magazine*, p. 417 [reported speech].

84 *Walker's Hibernian Magazine*, p. 416.

85 *Walker's Hibernian Magazine*, p. 416 [reported speech]. Author's note: I have taken Coleman's rather more literate account of his words, and put them the way I believe the far less educated Churchill would have said them.

86 Morrison, Journal on HMS Bounty and at Tahiti, p. 59.

87 Author's note: These were nautical terms of the time that any Captain might give upon the launching of a vessel. The 'Dogwatch' was the period from 4 pm to 8 pm, split into two-hour periods, the first dog watch and the last dog watch.

88 Bligh, Extract from the logbook HMS Bounty, 19 June 1789, p. 423.

89 Rutter (ed.), *The Voyage of the Bounty's Launch*, p. 77.

90 Rutter (ed.), *The Voyage of the Bounty's Launch*, p. 77.

91 Rutter (ed.), *The Voyage of the Bounty's Launch*, p. 77.

92 Rutter (ed.), *The Voyage of the Bounty's Launch*, pp. 67–68.

93 Kennedy, *Captain Bligh: The Man and His Mutinies*, p. 97.

94 Rutter (ed.), *The Voyage of the Bounty's Launch*, p. 79.

95 Rutter (ed.), *The Voyage of the Bounty's Launch*, p. 79.

96 Rutter (ed.), *The Voyage of the Bounty's Launch*, p. 79.

97 Rutter (ed.), *The Voyage of the Bounty's Launch*, p. 79.

98 Rutter (ed.), *The Voyage of the Bounty's Launch*, p. 79.

99 Rutter (ed.), *The Voyage of the Bounty's Launch*, p. 79.

100 Rutter (ed.), *The Voyage of the Bounty's Launch*, p. 79.

101 Rutter (ed.), *The Voyage of the Bounty's Launch*, p. 79.

102 Rutter (ed.), *The Voyage of the Bounty's Launch*, p. 79.

103 Rutter (ed.), *The Voyage of the Bounty's Launch*, p. 79.

104 Rutter (ed.), *The Voyage of the Bounty's Launch*, p. 79. Author's note: This dialogue is taken directly from the accounts of Fryer and Bligh of their angry conversations, but I have added capitals and italics where I saw fit to give some impression of the sound, fury and sarcasm of these two ever quarrelling men. It is fascinating that both kept such careful accounts of each other's quips and insults, both so infuriated they felt they must be preserved for history, or rather for a future trial that did not eventuate. Bligh had a gift for memorable invective and from the *Bounty* to the Rum Rebellion we are again and again treated to the vivid recall of the many men lashed by his tongue and temper.

105 Mackaness, *The Life of Vice-Admiral William Bligh*, p. 161.

106 Rutter (ed.), *The Voyage of the Bounty's Launch*, p. 79.

107 Rutter (ed.), *The Voyage of the Bounty's Launch*, p. 79.

108 Rutter (ed.), *The Voyage of the Bounty's Launch*, p. 79.

109 Rutter (ed.), *The Voyage of the Bounty's Launch*, p. 78.

110 Rutter (ed.), *The Voyage of the Bounty's Launch*, p. 78.

111 Rutter (ed.), *The Voyage of the Bounty's Launch*, p. 78.

112 Mackaness, *The Life of Vice-Admiral William Bligh*, p. 161.

Chapter 12

1 Hobbes, *Leviathan*, Collier, New York, 1972, p. 100.

2 Alexander, *The Bounty*, p. 14.

3 Morrison, Journal on HMS Bounty and at Tahiti, p. 62 [reported speech].
4 Morrison, Journal on HMS Bounty and at Tahiti, p. 64 [reported speech].
5 Morrison, Journal on HMS Bounty and at Tahiti, p. 64.
6 Morrison, Journal on HMS Bounty and at Tahiti, p. 64 [reported speech].
7 Morrison, Journal on HMS Bounty and at Tahiti, p. 66.
8 Morrison, Journal on HMS Bounty and at Tahiti, p. 67.
9 Bligh, Extract from the logbook HMS Bounty, 22 July 1789, p. 437.
10 Morrison, Journal on HMS Bounty and at Tahiti, p. 90.
11 Kennedy, *Captain Bligh: The Man and His Mutinies*, p. 171.
12 Mackaness, *The Life of Vice-Admiral William Bligh*, p. 163.
13 Mackaness, *The Life of Vice-Admiral William Bligh*, p. 162.
14 Bligh to Elizabeth Bligh, Letter, 19 August 1789, SLNSW, p. 1.
15 Bligh to Elizabeth Bligh, Letter, 19 August 1789, p. 2.
16 Bligh to Elizabeth Bligh, Letter, 19 August 1789, p. 4.
17 Bligh to Elizabeth Bligh, Letter, 19 August 1789, p. 4.
18 Bligh to Elizabeth Bligh, Letter, 19 August 1789, p. 4.
19 Bligh to Elizabeth Bligh, Letter, 19 August 1789, p. 5.
20 Bligh to Elizabeth Bligh, Letter, 19 August 1789, p. 5.
21 Bligh to Elizabeth Bligh, Letter, 19 August 1789, p. 4.
22 Bligh to Elizabeth Bligh, Letter, 19 August 1789, p. 5.
23 Bligh to Elizabeth Bligh, Letter, 19 August 1789, p. 5.
24 Bligh to Elizabeth Bligh, Letter, 19 August 1789, p. 5.
25 Morrison, Journal on HMS Bounty and at Tahiti, p. 68.
26 Morrison, Journal on HMS Bounty and at Tahiti, p. 69 [reported speech].
27 Morrison, Journal on HMS Bounty and at Tahiti, p. 72.
28 John Adams's story in Bligh and Christian, *The Bounty Mutiny*, p. 244.
29 Morrison, Journal on HMS Bounty and at Tahiti, p. 72 [reported speech].
30 Bligh and Christian, *The Bounty Mutiny*, p. 146.
31 Bligh and Christian, *The Bounty Mutiny*, p. 146.
32 Morrison, Journal on HMS Bounty and at Tahiti, p. 73 [reported speech].
33 Morrison, Journal on HMS Bounty and at Tahiti, p. 74.
34 Morrison, Journal on HMS Bounty and at Tahiti, p. 74.
35 Morrison, Journal on HMS Bounty and at Tahiti, p. 75.
36 Morrison, Journal on HMS Bounty and at Tahiti, p. 75.
37 Morrison, Journal on HMS Bounty and at Tahiti, p. 89.
38 Morrison, *After the Bounty*, Potomac Books, Dulles, 2010, p. 57.
39 Morrison, Journal on HMS Bounty and at Tahiti, p. 76.
40 Morrison, Journal on HMS Bounty and at Tahiti, p. 77.
41 Morrison, Journal on HMS Bounty and at Tahiti, p. 78 [reported speech].

Chapter 13

1 Shakespeare *Julius Caesar*, H. Altemus, Philadelphia, 1890, p. 114.
2 Bligh, 'Log of the Proceedings of His Majesty's Ship Bounty Lieut. Wm Bligh Commander from Otaheite towards Jamaica, signed 'Wm Bligh', 5 Apr. 1789 – 13 Mar. 1790', 17 September 1789, SLNSW, Safe 1/47 (Microfilm CY 274), p. 304.
3 Bligh, 'Log of the Proceedings of His Majesty's Ship Bounty' 17 September 1789, p. 304 [reported speech].
4 Bligh, 'Log of the Proceedings of His Majesty's Ship Bounty', 17 September 1789, p. 304 [reported speech].
5 Bligh, 'Log of the Proceedings of His Majesty's Ship Bounty', 17 September 1789, p. 305 [reported speech].

6 Bligh, 'Log of the Proceedings of His Majesty's Ship Bounty', 17 September 1789, p. 308 [reported speech].

7 Rutter (ed.), *Bligh's Voyage in the Resource*, p. 64.

8 Rutter (ed.), *Bligh's Voyage in the Resource*, p. 64.

9 Rutter (ed.), *Bligh's Voyage in the Resource*, p. 64.

10 Rutter (ed.), *The Voyage of the Bounty's Launch*, p. 81.

11 Rutter (ed.), *Bligh's Voyage in the Resource*, p. 64.

12 Rutter (ed.), *Bligh's Voyage in the Resource*, p. 64.

13 Rutter (ed.), *Bligh's Voyage in the Resource*, p. 64.

14 Rutter (ed.), *Bligh's Voyage in the Resource*, p. 64.

15 Rutter (ed.), *Bligh's Voyage in the Resource*, pp. 64–65.

16 Rutter (ed.), *Bligh's Voyage in the Resource*, p. 65.

17 Rutter (ed.), *Bligh's Voyage in the Resource*, p. 65.

18 Rutter (ed.), *Bligh's Voyage in the Resource*, p. 65.

19 Rutter (ed.), *The Voyage of the Bounty's Launch*, p. 81 [reported speech].

20 Rutter (ed.), *The Voyage of the Bounty's Launch*, p. 81.

21 Rutter (ed.), *Bligh's Voyage in the Resource*, p. 65.

22 Rutter (ed.), *Bligh's Voyage in the Resource*, p. 65.

23 Rutter (ed.), *Bligh's Voyage in the Resource*, p. 65.

24 Rutter (ed.), *Bligh's Voyage in the Resource*, p. 65.

25 Rutter (ed.), *Bligh's Voyage in the Resource*, p. 65.

26 Rutter (ed.), *Bligh's Voyage in the Resource*, p. 65.

27 Rutter (ed.), *Bligh's Voyage in the Resource*, p. 65.

28 Rutter (ed.), *The Voyage of the Bounty's Launch*, p. 81.

29 Rutter (ed.), *The Voyage of the Bounty's Launch*, p. 81.

30 Rutter (ed.), *The Voyage of the Bounty's Launch*, p. 81.

31 Rutter (ed.), *The Voyage of the Bounty's Launch*, p. 81.

32 Rutter (ed.), *The Voyage of the Bounty's Launch*, p. 81.

33 Rutter (ed.), *Bligh's Voyage in the Resource*, p. 66.

34 Rutter (ed.), *Bligh's Voyage in the Resource*, pp. 66–67.

35 Rutter (ed.), *Bligh's Voyage in the Resource*, p. 67.

36 Rutter (ed.), *Bligh's Voyage in the Resource*, p. 68 [reported speech].

37 Rutter (ed.), *Bligh's Voyage in the Resource*, p. 68.

38 Rutter (ed.), *The Voyage of the Bounty's Launch*, p. 81.

39 Rutter (ed.), *Bligh's Voyage in the Resource*, pp. 68–69.

40 Rutter (ed.), *The Voyage of the Bounty's Launch*, p. 82.

41 Rutter (ed.), *Bligh's Voyage in the Resource*, p. 69.

42 Rutter (ed.), *Bligh's Voyage in the Resource*, p. 69.

43 Rutter (ed.), *Bligh's Voyage in the Resource*, p. 69.

44 Rutter (ed.), *Bligh's Voyage in the Resource*, p. 69.

45 Rutter (ed.), *Bligh's Voyage in the Resource*, p. 69

46 Rutter (ed.), *Bligh's Voyage in the Resource*, p. 69.

47 Morrison, Journal on HMS Bounty and at Tahiti, p. 99 [reported speech].

48 Bligh and Christian, *The Bounty Mutiny*, p. 147.

49 Bligh and Christian, *The Bounty Mutiny*, p. 148.

50 Bligh and Christian, *The Bounty Mutiny*, p. 148.

51 Bligh and Christian, *The Bounty Mutiny*, p. 147.

52 Author's note: What was actually said in this exchange was not recorded. Heywood later recounted: 'At that last interview with Christian, he also communicated to me, for the satisfaction of his relations, other circumstances connected with that unfortunate disaster, which, after their deaths, may or may not be laid before the public.' (Barrow, *The Mutiny and Piratical Seizure of HMS Bounty*, p. 85.)

53 Rutter (ed.), *Bligh's Voyage in the Resource*, p. 81.

54 Rutter (ed.), *Bligh's Voyage in the Resource*, p. 81.

55 Rutter (ed.), *Bligh's Voyage in the Resource*, p. 81.

56 Rutter (ed.), *Bligh's Voyage in the Resource*, p. 86.

57 Rutter (ed.), *Bligh's Voyage in the Resource*, p. 82.

58 Bligh and Christian, *The Bounty Mutiny*, p. 162.

59 Bligh and Christian, *The Bounty Mutiny*, pp. 162–65.

60 Bowker and Bligh, *Mutiny!! Aboard H.M. Armed Transport 'Bounty' in 1789*, p. 356.

61 Rutter (ed.), *Bligh's Voyage in the Resource*, pp. 82–83.

62 Rutter (ed.), *Bligh's Voyage in the Resource*, p. 83.

63 Author's note: The curious thing is that, according to Owen Rutter, this Log (or, as I have called it, a journal) was *not* given to the Admiralty. There is no copy of it with the Admiralty or in the Public Records. Bligh's Admiralty Log ends with him leaving Timor in the *Resource*, before Fryer and Purcell are arrested for mutiny and the brief trial of Hallett, Cole and Ledward. It is unknown what happened to these intended-to-be official volumes. Perhaps on returning to England, Bligh thought better of making mutinies seem like a habit on his watch. Similarly, all mention of this remarkable uprising was left out of Bligh's published narrative of his travels. The logs vanished and only reappeared via Bligh's grandchildren, who gave them to the Mitchell Library in 1902.

64 Bligh and Christian, *The Bounty Mutiny*, p. 145.

65 Morrison, Journal on HMS Bounty and at Tahiti, p. 101 [reported speech].

66 Cook, *First Voyage Around the World: Captain Cook's Journal*, Salzwasser, Paderborn, 2013, p. 486.

67 Rutter (ed.), *Bligh's Voyage in the Resource*, p. 97.

68 Morrison, Journal on HMS Bounty and at Tahiti, p. 106 [reported speech].

Chapter 14

1 Coleridge, *The complete poetical works of Samuel Taylor Coleridge*, The Clarendon Press, Oxford, 1912, p. 192.

2 The names of the Mutineers, and their initial consorts, as described by 'Jenny' in her 1819 account in the *Sydney Gazette*, 17 July 1819, p. 3.

3 Rutter (ed.), *Bligh's Voyage in the Resource*, p. 97.

4 Bligh, *A Voyage to the South Sea*, 1979, p. 256.

5 Rutter (ed.), *Bligh's Voyage in the Resource*, p. 98.

6 Rutter (ed.), *Bligh's Voyage in the Resource*, p. 98.

7 Bligh to Banks, Letter, 13 October 1789, pp. 1–2.

8 Bligh to Banks, Letter, 13 October 1789, p. 3.

9 Bligh to Banks, Letter, 13 October 1789, p. 3.

10 Bligh to Banks, Letter, 13 October 1789, p. 24.

11 Rutter (ed.), *Bligh's Voyage in the Resource*, p. 68.

12 Rutter (ed.), *Bligh's Voyage in the Resource*, p. 101.

13 Rutter (ed.), *Bligh's Voyage in the Resource*, p. 106.

14 Bligh and Christian, *The Bounty Mutiny*, p. 230.

15 Rutter (ed.), *Bligh's Voyage in the Resource*, p. 113.

16 Morrison, Journal on HMS Bounty and at Tahiti, p. 107.

17 Morrison, Journal on HMS Bounty and at Tahiti, p. 221.

18 Morrison, Journal on HMS Bounty and at Tahiti, p. 108 [reported speech].

19 Morrison, Journal on HMS Bounty and at Tahiti, p. 109.

20 Morrison, *After the Bounty*, p. 74 [reported speech].

21 Kemp, *Chanteys and Ballads, Sea-chanteys, Tramp-ballads and Other Ballads and Poems*, Brentano's Publishers, New York, 1920, pp. 32–33. Author's note: It is not recorded what shanty the men sang on this day, but I have taken the liberty of using a common 'capstan shanty' that is thought to have been sung around this period in the Royal Navy.

22 Morrison, Journal on HMS Bounty and at Tahiti, p. 361.
23 'Narrative of the Adventures of the Mutineers aboard his Majesty's Ship Bounty', *The Edinburgh Magazine*, June 1792, p. 438.
24 Morrison, Journal on HMS Bounty and at Tahiti, p. 111.
25 Rutter (ed.), *Bligh's Voyage in the Resource*, p. 126.
26 Morrison, Journal on HMS Bounty and at Tahiti, p. 113.
27 Morrison, Journal on HMS Bounty and at Tahiti, p. 37.
28 Morrison, Journal on HMS Bounty and at Tahiti, p. 39.
29 Morrison, Journal on HMS Bounty and at Tahiti, p. 39.
30 Rutter (ed.), *Bligh's Voyage in the Resource*, p. 131.
31 Bligh and Christian, *The Bounty Mutiny*, p. 245.
32 Bligh and Christian, *The Bounty Mutiny*, p. 231.
33 John Adams's Story in Bligh and Christian, *The Bounty Mutiny*, p. 245.
34 Morrison, Journal on HMS Bounty and at Tahiti, p. 118.
35 Morrison, *After the Bounty*, p. 81.
36 Morrison, Journal on HMS Bounty and at Tahiti, p. 119.
37 Morrison, Journal on HMS Bounty and at Tahiti, p. 128.
38 Morrison, Journal on HMS Bounty and at Tahiti, p. 130 [reported speech].
39 *Walker's Hibernian Magazine*, p. 419 [reported speech].
40 *Walker's Hibernian Magazine*, p. 419 [reported speech].
41 *Walker's Hibernian Magazine*, p. 419.
42 *Walker's Hibernian Magazine*, pp. 419–20.
43 *Walker's Hibernian Magazine*, p. 420.
44 Morrison, Journal on HMS Bounty and at Tahiti, p. 130 [reported speech].
45 Morrison, Journal on HMS Bounty and at Tahiti, p. 130.
46 Morrison, Journal on HMS Bounty and at Tahiti, p. 130.
47 Morrison, Journal on HMS Bounty and at Tahiti, p. 130.
48 Morrison, Journal on HMS Bounty and at Tahiti, p. 131.
49 Morrison, Journal on HMS Bounty and at Tahiti, p. 131 [reported speech].
50 Morrison, Journal on HMS Bounty and at Tahiti, pp. 132–33.
51 Morrison, Journal on HMS Bounty and at Tahiti, p. 133 [reported speech].
52 Morrison, Journal on HMS Bounty and at Tahiti, p. 133.
53 *The Scots Magazine*, March 1790, pp. 146–47.
54 *The Scots Magazine*, p. 146.
55 *The Derby Mercury*, 18 March 1790, p. 2.
56 Alexander, *The Bounty*, p. 165.
57 Alexander, *The Bounty*, pp. 164–65.
58 Barrow, *The Mutiny and Piratical Seizure of H.M.S. Bounty*, p. 114.
59 Barrow, *The Mutiny and Piratical Seizure of H.M.S. Bounty*, p. 114.
60 Barrow, *The Mutiny and Piratical Seizure of H.M.S. Bounty*, p. 114.
61 Alexander, *The Bounty*, p. 167.

Chapter 15

1 *The London Chronicle*, 1 April 1791
2 Byron, *The Works of Lord Byron Complete in One Volume*, p. 311.
3 Morrison, Journal on HMS Bounty and at Tahiti, p. 135.
4 Morrison, Journal on HMS Bounty and at Tahiti, p. 135.
5 Bligh and Christian, *The Bounty Mutiny*, p. 245.
6 Morrison, *After the Bounty*, p. 91.
7 Morrison, Journal on HMS Bounty and at Tahiti, p. 144.
8 Galloway, *The Bounty Mutiny Courts Martial: William Bligh, The Carpenter, Edward Edwards, The Mutineers*, James Galloway Ebook, 2014, [no page numbers].

9 Galloway, *The Bounty Mutiny Courts Martial*, [no page numbers].

10 Galloway, *The Bounty Mutiny Courts Martial*, [no page numbers].

11 Galloway, *The Bounty Mutiny Courts Martial*, [no page numbers].

12 Galloway, *The Bounty Mutiny Courts Martial*, [no page numbers].

13 Bligh to Banks, Letter, 24 October 1790, SLNSW, Sir Joseph Banks Papers, Series 46.31, p. 1.

14 Morrison, Journal on HMS Bounty and at Tahiti, p. 169.

15 Morrison, Journal on HMS Bounty and at Tahiti, p. 169.

16 Morrison, Journal on HMS Bounty and at Tahiti, p. 170.

17 Morrison, Journal on HMS Bounty and at Tahiti, p. 169.

18 Christian, *Fragile Paradise*, p. 197.

19 Bligh to Banks, Letter, 17 July 1791, SLNSW, Sir Joseph Banks Papers, Series 50.05, p. 2.

20 Admiralty Orders for Captain Edward Edwards of HMS Pandora, 5 October 1790, in *The United Service Magazine and Naval and Military Journal*, Part 1, Henry Colburn, London, 1843, p. 413.

21 Barrow, *The Mutiny and Piratical Seizure of H.M.S. Bounty*, p. 215 [reported speech].

22 Barrow, *The Mutiny and Piratical Seizure of H.M.S. Bounty*, p. 215 [reported speech].

23 Barrow, *The Mutiny and Piratical Seizure of H.M.S. Bounty*, p. 215 [reported speech].

24 Barrow, *The Mutiny and Piratical Seizure of H.M.S. Bounty*, p. 215 [reported speech].

25 Heywood, *Innocent on the Bounty*, p. 39.

26 Rutter (ed.), *Bligh's Voyage in the Resource*, p. 116.

27 Barrow, *The Mutiny and Piratical Seizure of H.M.S. Bounty*, p. 215 [reported speech].

28 Barrow, *The Mutiny and Piratical Seizure of H.M.S. Bounty*, p. 215 [reported speech].

29 Edwards and Hamilton, *Voyage of H.M.S. 'Pandora' Despatched to Arrest the Mutineers of the 'Bounty' in the South Seas, 1790–1791*, Francis Edwards, London, 1915, p. 31 [reported speech].

30 Morrison, Journal on HMS Bounty and at Tahiti, p. 173 [reported speech].

31 Morrison, Journal on HMS Bounty and at Tahiti, p. 173 [reported speech].

32 Edwards and Hamilton, *Voyage of H.M.S. 'Pandora'*, p. 31 [reported speech].

33 Edwards and Hamilton, *Voyage of H.M.S. 'Pandora'*, p. 31 [reported speech].

34 Clune, *Journey to Pitcairn*, 1966, p. 55

35 Morrison, Journal on HMS Bounty and at Tahiti, p. 174 [reported speech].

36 Edwards and Hamilton, *Voyage of H.M.S. 'Pandora'*, p. 32 [reported speech].

37 Author's note: These words are assumed as Morrison wrote: 'we waked him and delivered ourselves up to Him, telling Him who we were', Morrison, Journal on HMS Bounty and at Tahiti, p. 178 [reported speech].

38 Morrison, *After the Bounty*, p. 112.

39 Rutter (ed.), *The Court-Martial of the 'Bounty' Mutineers*, p. 87.

40 Morrison, *After the Bounty*, p. 112.

41 Edwards and Hamilton, *Voyage of H.M.S. 'Pandora'*, p. 106 [reported speech].

42 Instructions from the Lords of the Admiralty to Capt Edwards, Papers of Edward Edwards as Captain of HMS Pandora, 1790–1792, Admiralty Library Manuscript Collection: MSS 180.

43 Edwards and Hamilton, *Voyage of H.M.S. 'Pandora'*, p. 34.

44 Morrison, Journal on HMS Bounty and at Tahiti, p. 181.

45 Edwards and Hamilton, *Voyage of H.M.S. 'Pandora'*, p. 119.

46 Hamilton, *Voyage Round the World in His Majesty's Frigate Pandora*, W. Phorson, London, 1793. p xx.

47 Hamilton, *Voyage Round the World in His Majesty's Frigate Pandora*, p xx.

48 Hamilton, *Voyage Round the World in His Majesty's Frigate Pandora*, p xx.

49 Morrison, Journal on HMS Bounty and at Tahiti, p. 187.

50 Morrison, Journal on HMS Bounty and at Tahiti, p. 187.

51 Morrison, Journal on HMS Bounty and at Tahiti, p. 187 [reported speech].

52 Morrison, Journal on HMS Bounty and at Tahiti, p. 187.

53 Morrison, Journal on HMS Bounty and at Tahiti, p. 188.

54 Morrison, *After the Bounty*, p. 118.
55 Morrison, Journal on HMS Bounty and at Tahiti, p. 189.
56 Morrison, Journal on HMS Bounty and at Tahiti, p. 189.
57 Barrow, John, *The Mutiny and Piratical Seizure of HMS Bounty*, p. 135.
58 Edwards and Hamilton, *Voyage of H.M.S. 'Pandora'*, p. 145.
59 Pasley to Flinders, 3 June 1791, in The Flinders Papers: Letters and documents about the Explorer Matthew Flinders (1774–1814), National Maritime Museum, p. 1.
60 Letter, 16 July 1792, in Tagart, *Memoir of the late Captain Peter Heywood, R. N.*, Effingham Wilson, London, 1832, p. 71.
61 Morrison, Journal on HMS Bounty and at Tahiti, p. 196 [reported speech].
62 Morrison, Journal on HMS Bounty and at Tahiti, p. 196.
63 Morrison, Journal on HMS Bounty and at Tahiti, pp. 196–97 [reported speech].
64 Morrison, Journal on HMS Bounty and at Tahiti, p. 197.
65 Morrison, Journal on HMS Bounty and at Tahiti, p. 197.
66 Papers of Edward Edwards as Captain of HMS *Pandora*, 1790–1792, Admiralty Library Manuscript Collection: MSS 180.
67 Alexander, *The Bounty*, p. 36.
68 Alexander, *The Bounty*, p. 36 [reported speech].
69 Tagart, *Memoir of the late Captain Peter Heywood, R. N.*, pp. 23–24.
70 Tagart, *Memoir of the late Captain Peter Heywood, R. N.*, p. 37.
71 Bligh and Christian, *The Bounty Mutiny*, p. 246 [reported speech].
72 Brodie, *Pitcairn's Island and The Islanders in 1850*, Whittaker and Co., London, 1851, p. 53.
73 Morrison, Journal on HMS Bounty and at Tahiti, p. 235.
74 Bligh and Christian, *The Bounty Mutiny*, p. 246.
75 Bligh and Christian, *The Bounty Mutiny*, p. 232.
76 Brodie, *Pitcairn's Island and The Islanders in 1850*, p. 54.
77 Alexander, *The Bounty*, p. 35.
78 Tagart, *Memoir of the late Captain Peter Heywood, R.N.*, p. 24.
79 Tagart, *Memoir of the late Captain Peter Heywood, R.N.*, p. 58.

Chapter 16

1 Nessy Heywood to Peter Heywood, Letter, 31 July 1792, in Heywood, *Innocent on the Bounty*, p. 78.
2 Tagart, *Memoir of the late Captain Peter Heywood, R.N.*, p. 142.
3 Moore, *Nessy Heywood*, Brown and Sons, Douglas, 1913, p. 14.
4 Byron, *The Works of Lord Byron Complete in One Volume*, p. 319.
5 Nessy Heywood to Peter Heywood, Letter, 29 June 1792, in Tagart, *Memoir of the late Captain Peter Heywood, R.N.*, pp. 58–59.
6 Peter Heywood to Nessy Heywood, Letter, 4 August 1792, in Heywood, *Innocent on the Bounty*, p. 82.
7 Nessy Heywood to Peter Heywood, Letter, 31 August 1792, in Heywood, *Innocent on the Bounty*, p. 82.
8 Peter Heywood to Nessy Heywood, Letter, 6 September 1792, in Heywood, *Innocent on the Bounty*, 82.
9 Pasley to Nessy Heywood, Letter, 8 June 1792, in Mary Heywood – letter-book, SLNSW, MLMSS 5719 (Safe 1/127), Item 10, p. 85.
10 Pasley to Nessy Heywood, Letter, 15 July 1792, in Mary Heywood – letter-book, p. 144.
11 Papers of Edward Edwards as Captain of HMS *Pandora*, 1790–1792, Admiralty Library Manuscript Collection: MSS 180 (no page numbers).
12 Papers of Edward Edwards as Captain of HMS Pandora, 1790–1792, Admiralty Library Manuscript Collection: MSS 180 (no page numbers).
13 Alexander, *The Bounty*, p. 309.

14 Alexander, *The Bounty*, p. 309.

15 Bligh, Log, 2 May 1792, quoted in Oliver, *Return to Tahiti*, p. 139.

16 Bligh, Log, 2 May 1792, quoted in Oliver, *Return to Tahiti*, pp. 139–40.

17 Bligh, Log, 2 May 1792, quoted in Oliver, *Return to Tahiti*, p. 140.

18 Lee, *Captain Bligh's Second Voyage to the South Sea*, Longmans, Green and Co., London, 1920, p. 87.

19 Morrison, *Memorandum and Particulars Respecting the Bounty and Her Crew*, in William Bligh – Papers relating to HMS Bounty, 1787–1794, undated, State Library of NSW, Safe 1/33, p. 33.

20 McKinney, *Bligh!: The Whole Story of the Mutiny Aboard H.M.S. Bounty*, TouchWood Editions, Canada, 1999, p. 173.

21 McKinney, *Bligh!*, p. 142.

22 Barney [compiled by], *Minutes of the Proceedings of the Court-Martial held at Portsmouth, August 12, 1792. on ten persons charged with mutiny on board His Majesty's Ship the Bounty*, J. Deighton, London, 1794, p. 2.

23 Falconer, *Falconer's Marine Dictionary*, T. Cadell, London, 1815, p. 109.

24 Rutter (ed.), *The Court-Martial of the 'Bounty' Mutineers*, p. 73.

25 Rutter (ed.), *The Court-Martial of the 'Bounty' Mutineers*, p. 74.

26 Rutter (ed.), *The Court-Martial of the 'Bounty' Mutineers*, p. 81.

27 Rutter (ed.), *The Court-Martial of the 'Bounty' Mutineers*, p. 81.

28 Rutter (ed.), *The Court-Martial of the 'Bounty' Mutineers*, p. 87.

29 Rutter (ed.), *The Court-Martial of the 'Bounty' Mutineers*, p. 90.

30 Rutter (ed.), *The Court-Martial of the 'Bounty' Mutineers*, p. 90.

31 Rutter (ed.), *The Court-Martial of the 'Bounty' Mutineers*, p. 92.

32 Rutter (ed.), *The Court-Martial of the 'Bounty' Mutineers*, p. 94.

33 Rutter (ed.), *The Court-Martial of the 'Bounty' Mutineers*, pp. 103–4.

34 Rutter (ed.), *The Court-Martial of the 'Bounty' Mutineers*, p. 104.

35 Rutter (ed.), *The Court-Martial of the 'Bounty' Mutineers*, p. 107.

36 Rutter (ed.), *The Court-Martial of the 'Bounty' Mutineers*, p. 109.

37 Rutter (ed.), *The Court-Martial of the 'Bounty' Mutineers*, p. 111.

38 Rutter (ed.), *The Court-Martial of the 'Bounty' Mutineers*, p. 114.

39 Rutter (ed.), *The Court-Martial of the 'Bounty' Mutineers*, p. 114.

40 Rutter (ed.), *The Court-Martial of the 'Bounty' Mutineers*, p. 121.

41 Rutter (ed.), *The Court-Martial of the 'Bounty' Mutineers*, p. 121.

42 Rutter (ed.), *The Court-Martial of the 'Bounty' Mutineers*, pp. 121–22.

43 Rutter (ed.), *The Court-Martial of the 'Bounty' Mutineers*, p. 122.

44 Rutter (ed.), *The Court-Martial of the 'Bounty' Mutineers*, p. 122.

45 Rutter (ed.), *The Court-Martial of the 'Bounty' Mutineers*, p. 122.

46 Rutter (ed.), *The Court-Martial of the 'Bounty' Mutineers*, p. 123.

47 Rutter (ed.), *The Court-Martial of the 'Bounty' Mutineers*, p. 123.

48 Tagart, *Memoir of the late Captain Peter Heywood, R.N.*, p. 140.

49 Rutter (ed.), *The Court-Martial of the 'Bounty' Mutineers*, p. 126.

50 Rutter (ed.), *The Court-Martial of the 'Bounty' Mutineers*, p. 137 [reported speech].

51 Rutter (ed.), *The Court-Martial of the 'Bounty' Mutineers*, p. 139.

52 Rutter (ed.), *The Court-Martial of the 'Bounty' Mutineers*, pp. 140–41.

53 Rutter (ed.), *The Court-Martial of the 'Bounty' Mutineers*, pp. 145–46.

54 Rutter (ed.), *The Court-Martial of the 'Bounty' Mutineers*, p. 148.

55 Rutter (ed.), *The Court-Martial of the 'Bounty' Mutineers*, p. 149.

56 Rutter (ed.), *The Court-Martial of the 'Bounty' Mutineers*, p. 150.

57 Rutter (ed.), *The Court-Martial of the 'Bounty' Mutineers*, p. 150.

58 Rutter (ed.), *The Court-Martial of the 'Bounty' Mutineers*, p. 151.

59 Rutter (ed.), *The Court-Martial of the 'Bounty' Mutineers*, p. 153.

60 Rutter (ed.), *The Court-Martial of the 'Bounty' Mutineers*, p. 156.

61 Rutter (ed.), *The Court-Martial of the 'Bounty' Mutineers*, p. 156.
62 Rutter (ed.), *The Court-Martial of the 'Bounty' Mutineers*, p. 158.
63 Rutter (ed.), *The Court-Martial of the 'Bounty' Mutineers*, p. 158.
64 Rutter (ed.), *The Court-Martial of the 'Bounty' Mutineers*, p. 166.
65 Rutter (ed.), *The Court-Martial of the 'Bounty' Mutineers*, p. 166.
66 Rutter (ed.), *The Court-Martial of the 'Bounty' Mutineers*, pp. 177–78.
67 Rutter (ed.), *The Court-Martial of the 'Bounty' Mutineers*, p. 198 [reported speech].
68 Rutter (ed.), *The Court-Martial of the 'Bounty' Mutineers*, p. 198 [reported speech].
69 Rutter (ed.), *The Court-Martial of the 'Bounty' Mutineers*, p. 198 [reported speech].
70 Rutter (ed.), *The Court-Martial of the 'Bounty' Mutineers*, p. 198 [reported speech].
71 Barrow, *The Mutiny and Piratical Seizure of HMS Bounty*, p. 191.
72 Tagart, *Memoir of the late Captain Peter Heywood, R.N.*, p. 123 [reported speech].
73 Lines from Robert Louis Stevenson's *Requiem*.
74 Barrow, *The Mutiny and Piratical Seizure of HMS Bounty*, p. 191.
75 Barrow, *The Mutiny and Piratical Seizure of H.M.S. Bounty*, p. 257.
76 Howell to Phillips, Letter, 25 November 1792, Papers of Sir Joseph Banks, SLNSW, Series 48.01, p. 1.
77 Preston, *Paradise in Chains: The Bounty Mutiny and the Founding of Australia*, p. xx.
78 Barrow, *The Mutiny and Piratical Seizure of H.M.S. Bounty*, p. 272.
79 Heywood, 'Spoken by Mr Peter Heywood to Captain Montagu after he had read him his Majesty's unconditional Pardon Octr 27th 1792.' in Heywood, Letter-book, p. 308.
80 Graham to Nessy Heywood, Letter, 27 October 1792, in Heywood, Letter-book, p. 283.
81 Graham to Nessy Heywood, Letter, 27 October 1792, in Heywood, Letter-book, p. 284.
82 Heywood, *Innocent on the Bounty*, p. 148.
83 McArthur, John, *A treatise of the principles and practice of naval courts-martial*, Whieldon and Butterworth, London, 1792, p. 161.
84 Alexander, *The Bounty*, p. 300.
85 Bligh and Christian, *The Bounty Mutiny*, p. 128.

Chapter 17

1 Lee, *Captain Bligh's Second Voyage to the South Sea*, p. 43.
2 Heywood, *Innocent on the Bounty*, pp. 203–4.
3 Francis Bond to Thomas Bond, Letter, undated, printed in Mackaness, George, *Fresh Light on Bligh*, p. 69.
4 Christian, *Fragile Paradise*, p. 189.
5 Bligh to Banks, Letter, 30 October 1793, SLNSW, Papers of Sir Joseph Banks, Series 50.32, p. 2.
6 Salmond, *Bligh: William Bligh in the South Seas*, Penguin, New Zealand, 2011, p. 433 [reported speech].
7 Bligh and Christian, *The Bounty Mutiny*, p. 247.
8 Bligh and Christian, *The Bounty Mutiny*, p. 247.
9 Bligh and Christian, *The Bounty Mutiny*, p. 247 [reported speech].
10 Bligh and Christian, *The Bounty Mutiny*, p. 247.
11 Author's note: The words Mills is recorded as saying are that 'It is only Mainmast calling her children to dinner', but I have interpreted this as an archaic joke, Mills jesting that her yells of labour are her 'calling' her child.
12 Bligh and Christian, *The Bounty Mutiny*, p. 247.
13 Brodie, *Pitcairn's Island and The Islanders in 1850*, p. 56.
14 Brodie, *Pitcairn's Island and The Islanders in 1850*, p. 56.
15 Bligh and Christian, *The Bounty Mutiny*, p. 248.
16 Bligh and Christian, *The Bounty Mutiny*, p. 232.
17 Brodie, *Pitcairn's Island and The Islanders in 1850*, p. 58.
18 Brodie, *Pitcairn's Island and The Islanders in 1850*, p. 58.

19 Brodie, *Pitcairn's Island and The Islanders in 1850*, p. 58.
20 Morrison, Journal on HMS Bounty and at Tahiti, p. 41.
21 Brodie, *Pitcairn's Island and The Islanders in 1850*, p. 58.
22 Brodie, *Pitcairn's Island and The Islanders in 1850*, p. 58.
23 Brodie, *Pitcairn's Island and The Islanders in 1850*, p. 58.
24 Bligh and Christian, *The Bounty Mutiny*, p. 248.
25 *Mutiny on the Bounty 1789–1989 [Magazine]*, Manorial Research PLC, London, 1989, p. 130.
26 *Mutiny on the Bounty 1789–1989*, p. 130.
27 Bligh and Christian, *The Bounty Mutiny*, p. 248.
28 Bligh and Christian, *The Bounty Mutiny*, p. 249.
29 Bligh and Christian, *The Bounty Mutiny*, p. 249.
30 Author's note: Although which of the two men was the gunman is not revealed by the existing sources, I have assumed here that his identity is Matt Quintal, given Quintal's relentless love of violence and cold-blooded murder. A man unbothered by conscience, Matt Quintal is one of the most brutal men to board the *Bounty*, which, given his competition, is saying something.
31 Bligh and Christian, *The Bounty Mutiny*, pp. 249–50.
32 Brodie, *Pitcairn's Island and the Islanders in 1850*, p. 61.
33 Bligh and Christian, *The Bounty Mutiny*, p. 250.
34 Bligh and Christian, *The Bounty Mutiny*, p. 135.
35 Bligh and Christian, *The Bounty Mutiny*, p. 93.
36 Bligh and Christian, *The Bounty Mutiny*, p. 77.
37 Bligh and Christian, *The Bounty Mutiny*, p. 135.
38 Bligh and Christian, *The Bounty Mutiny*, p. 135.
39 Bligh and Christian, *The Bounty Mutiny*, p. 149.
40 Bligh and Christian, *The Bounty Mutiny*, p. 149.
41 Bligh and Christian, *The Bounty Mutiny*, p. 10.
42 Bligh and Christian, *The Bounty Mutiny*, p. 250.
43 Morrison, Journal on HMS Bounty and at Tahiti, p. 369.
44 Bligh and Christian, *The Bounty Mutiny*, p. 241.
45 Bligh and Christian, *The Bounty Mutiny*, p. 250.
46 Bligh and Christian, *The Bounty Mutiny*, p. 250.
47 Bligh and Christian, *The Bounty Mutiny*, p. 250.
48 Bligh and Christian, *The Bounty Mutiny*, p. 155.
49 Bligh and Christian, *The Bounty Mutiny*, p. 168.
50 Bligh and Christian, *The Bounty Mutiny*, p. 181.
51 Bligh and Christian, *The Bounty Mutiny*, pp. 173–74.
52 Bligh and Christian, *The Bounty Mutiny*, p. 176.
53 Bligh and Christian, *The Bounty Mutiny*, p. 177.
54 Bligh and Christian, *The Bounty Mutiny*, p. 189.
55 *British Critic*, December 1794, F and C Rivington, London, 1794.
56 Bligh and Christian, *The Bounty Mutiny*, p. 250.
57 Bligh and Christian, *The Bounty Mutiny*, p. 251.
58 Bligh and Christian, *The Bounty Mutiny*, p. 251.

Chapter 18

1 Defoe, *The Life and Adventures of Robinson Crusoe*, Thomas Kelly, London, 1822, p. 85.
2 Thackeray, *The Virginians: A Tale of the Last Century*, Harper and Brothers, London, 1859, p. 24.
3 Hagberg and Jost, *A Companion to the Philosophy of Literature*, John Wiley & Sons, New Jersey, 2009, p. 517 .
4 Bligh and Christian, *The Bounty Mutiny*, p. 251 [tense changed].

5 Bligh and Christian, *The Bounty Mutiny*, p. 251.
6 Bligh and Christian, *The Bounty Mutiny*, p. 251.
7 *The United Service Journal*, p. 191.
8 Kennedy, *Captain Bligh: The Man and His Mutinies*, p. 115.
9 Christian, *Fragile Paradise*, p. 192.
10 Brodie, *Pitcairn's Island and The Islanders in 1850*, p. 62.
11 The Bible, King James Version, Book of Luke, Chapter 5, Verse 35.
12 Brodie, *Pitcairn's Island and The Islanders in 1850*, p. 52.
13 Brodie, *Pitcairn's Island and The Islanders in 1850*, p. 64.
14 Mackaness, *The Life of Vice-Admiral William Bligh*, p. 214.
15 *Mutiny on the Bounty 1789–1989*, p. 125.
16 Nicolson and Davies, *The Pitcairners*, Angus & Robertson, Sydney, 1964, p 54.
17 Preston, *Paradise in Chains*, p. 274.
18 Kirk, *Pitcairn Island: The Bounty Mutineers and their Descendants*, McFarland & Co., Jefferson NC, 2008, p. 51.
19 Macklin, *Dark Paradise*, Hachette, Sydney, 2013, p. 114.
20 Author's note: These are generic commands, consistent with the terminology of the time.
21 Barrow, *The Mutiny and Piratical Seizure of HMS Bounty*, p. 219.
22 Barrow, *The Mutiny and Piratical Seizure of HMS Bounty*, p. 219.
23 *The United Service Journal*, p. 192.
24 *The United Service Journal*, p. 192 [reported speech].
25 Barrow, *The Mutiny and Piratical Seizure of HMS Bounty*, p. 220.
26 *The United Service Journal*, p 193.
27 *The United Service Journal*, p 195.
28 *The United Service Journal*, p 194.
29 Bligh and Christian, *The Bounty Mutiny*, p. 240.
30 Bligh and Christian, *The Bounty Mutiny*, p. 240.
31 *The United Service Journal*, p. 196.
32 Barrow, *The Mutiny and Piratical Seizure of H.M.S. Bounty*, p. 319.
33 Pipon, *Interesting account of the mutineers of H.M.S. Bounty – original account of the finding the home of the Mutineers – on Pitcairn Island – 1814*, SLNSW, p. 13.
34 *The United Service Journal*, p. 197.
35 Pipon, *Interesting account of the mutineers of H.M.S. Bounty*, pp. 4–5.

Epilogue

1 Milton, *Paradise Lost*, Dent, London, 1920, p. 104.
2 Camus, *The Rebel: An Essay on Man in Revolt*, Knopf Doubleday Publishing Group, New York, 2012, p. 49.
3 Mackaness, *The Life of Vice-Admiral William Bligh*, pp. 138–42.
4 Mackaness, *The Life of Vice-Admiral William Bligh*, pp. 138–42.
5 Dening, *Mr. Bligh's Bad Language*, p. 60.
6 Chambers, *The Letters of Sir Joseph Banks: A Selection 1768 to 1820*, Imperial College Press, London, 2000, p. 261.
7 Mackaness, *The Life of Vice-Admiral William Bligh*, p. 434.
8 Mackaness, *The Life of Vice-Admiral William Bligh*, p. 468 [reported speech].
9 Mackaness, *The Life of Vice-Admiral William Bligh*, p. 507.
10 Heywood, *Innocent on the Bounty*, p. 204.
11 Heywood, *Innocent on the Bounty*, p. 204.
12 Heywood, *Innocent on the Bounty*, p. 204.
13 Heywood, *Innocent on the Bounty*, p. 205.
14 Heywood, *Innocent on the Bounty*, p. 206.
15 Barrow, *The Mutiny and Piratical Seizure of HMS Bounty*, p. 131.

16 Belcher, *Mutineers of the Bounty*, John Murray, London, 1870, p. 8.
17 Beechey, *Narrative of a Voyage to the Pacific and Beering's Strait*, H. Colburn and R. Bentley, London, 1831, p. 67.
18 Beechey, *Narrative of a Voyage to the Pacific and Beering's Strait*, p. 67.
19 Beechey, *Narrative of a Voyage to the Pacific and Beering's Strait*, p. 115 [reported speech]
20 Alexander, *The Bounty*, p. 372.
21 *United Service Journal and Naval and Military Magazine*, p. 589.
22 Alexander, *The Bounty*, p. 376.
23 Mackaness, *Fresh Light on Bligh*, p. 62.
24 Gall, *In Bligh's Hand*, National Library of Australia, Canberra, 2010, p. 151.
25 Salmond, *Bligh: William Bligh in the South Seas*, p. 225.
26 *The Journal of the Polynesian Society*, Volume 11, 1964, p. 259.
27 Darwin, *Journal of researches into the natural history and geology of the countries visited during the voyage of H.M.S. Beagle round the world*, London, Murray, 2nd edition, 1845, p. 404.
28 Mark Twain, 'The Great Revolution In Pitcairn', *The Atlantic Monthly*, Vol XLIII, March 1879, p. 298.
29 Quoted in Christian, *Fragile Paradise*, pp. 149–150.
30 Christian, *Fragile Paradise*, p. 179.
31 Bach, *The Bligh Notebook*, p. 213.
32 *The Quarterly Review*, February to May 1810, John Murray, London, 1810, p. 24.
33 Kennedy, *Captain Bligh: The Man and His Mutinies*, p. 300.
34 Mackaness, *The Life of Vice-Admiral William Bligh*, p. 218.
35 Barrow, *The Mutiny and Piratical Seizure of HMS Bounty*, p. 233.
36 Hill, *A Coleridge Companion*, Macmillan, London, 1983, p. 263.
37 Barrow, *The Mutiny and Piratical Seizure of HMS Bounty*, p. 233.
38 Barrow, *The Mutiny and Piratical Seizure of HMS Bounty*, p. 233.
39 Barrow, *The Mutiny and Piratical Seizure of HMS Bounty*, p. 234.
40 Barrow, *The Mutiny and Piratical Seizure of HMS Bounty*, p. 234.
41 Barrow, *The Mutiny and Piratical Seizure of HMS Bounty*, p. 234.
42 Alexander, *The Bounty*, p. 406.
43 Freemantle, *Loyal Enemy*, Hutchinson & Co, London, 1938, p. 13.

BIBLIOGRAPHY

Books

Alexander, Caroline, *The Bounty*, HarperCollins, London, 2003

Bach, Jon, *The Bligh Notebook*, Allen & Unwin, Sydney, 1987

Barney, Stephen [compiled by], *Minutes of the Proceedings of the Court-Martial held at Portsmouth, August 12, 1792 on ten persons charged with mutiny on board His Majesty's Ship the Bounty*, J. Deighton, London, 1794

Barrow, John, *The Eventful History of the Mutiny and Piratical Seizure of HMS Bounty*, Folio Society, [John Murray], London, 1831

Beaglehole, John, *The Journals of Captain James Cook on his Voyages of Discovery*, Vol. II, Part 1, Cambridge University Press, London, 1967

Beaglehole, John, *The Life of Captain James Cook*, Stanford University Press, USA, 1992

Beechey, Frederick, *Narrative of a Voyage to the Pacific and Beering's Strait*, H. Colburn and R. Bentley, London, 1831

Belcher, Diana, *Mutineers of the Bounty*, John Murray, London, 1870

Bligh, William, *A voyage to the South sea, undertaken by command of His Majesty, for the purpose of conveying the bread-fruit tree to the West Indies, in His Majesty's ship the Bounty, commanded by Lieutenant William Bligh*, G. Nicol. London, 1792

Bligh, William, *A Voyage to the South Sea*, Hutchinson, Richmond, 1979

Bligh, William, *A Narrative of the Mutiny on board his Majesty's Ship Bounty*, William Smith, London, 1838

Bligh, William, *The Mutiny on Board HMS Bounty*, Airmont, New York, 1965

Bligh, William and Christian, Edward, *The Bounty Mutiny*, Penguin, New York, 2001

Bligh, William, *Mutiny on Board HMS Bounty*, Bloomsbury Publishing, London, 2014

Bowker, R. M. and Bligh, William, *Mutiny!! Aboard H.M. Armed Transport 'Bounty' in 1789*, Boerker and Bertram, Sussex, 1978

Brodie, Walter, *Pitcairn's Island and The Islanders in 1850*, Whittaker and Co., London, 1851

Brunton, Paul, *Awake, Bold Bligh!*, Allen & Unwin, Sydney, 1989

Byron, George Gordon, *The Works of Lord Byron Complete in One Volume*, H.L. Brönner, Frankfurt am Main, 1837

Camus, Albert, *The Rebel: An Essay on Man in Revolt*, Knopf Doubleday Publishing Group, New York, 2012

Chambers, Neil, *The Letters of Sir Joseph Banks: A Selection 1768 to 1820*, Imperial College Press, London, 2000

Christian, Glynn, *Fragile Paradise*, Book Club Associates, London, 1983

Clune, Frank, *Journey to Pitcairn*, Angus & Robertson, Sydney, 1966

Coleridge, Samuel Taylor, *The complete poetical works of Samuel Taylor Coleridge*, The Clarendon Press, Oxford, 1912

Cook, James, *First Voyage Around the World: Captain Cook's Journal*, Salzwasser, Paderborn, 2013

Cook, James, *The Voyages of Captain James Cook*, Vol. 2, W. Smith, London, 1842

Darwin, Charles, *Journal of researches into the natural history and geology of the countries visited during the voyage of H.M.S. Beagle round the world*, John Murray, London, 2nd ed., 1889

Defoe, Daniel, *The Life and Adventures of Robinson Crusoe*, Thomas Kelly, London, 1822

Dening, Greg, *Mr Bligh's Bad Language: Passion, Power and Theatre on the Bounty*, Cambridge University Press, Melbourne, 1994

Dickens, Charles, *A Tale of Two Cities*, James Nisbet and Company Ltd, London, 1902

Dolan, Edward, *The Old Farmer's Almanac Book of Weather Lore: The Fact and Fancy Behind Weather Predictions, Superstitions, Old-time Sayings, and Traditions*, Yankee Books, New Hampshire, 1988

Edwards, Edward, and Hamilton, George, *Voyage of H.M.S. 'Pandora' Despatched to Arrest the Mutineers of the 'Bounty' in the South Seas, 1790–1791*, Francis Edwards, London, 1915

Falconer, William, *Falconer's Marine Dictionary*, T. Cadell, London, 1815

Forster, Georg, *A Voyage Round the World: in His Britannic Majesty's Sloop, Resolution, commanded by Capt. James Cook, during the years 1772, 3, 4 and 5*, Vol. II, B. White, London, 1777

Freemantle, Anne, *Loyal Enemy*, Hutchinson & Co, London, 1938

Gall, Jennifer, *In Bligh's Hand*, National Library of Australia, Canberra, 2010

Galloway, James, *The Bounty Mutiny Courts Martial: William Bligh, The Carpenter, Edward Edwards, The Mutineers*, James Galloway Ebook, 2014, [no page numbers]

Hagberg, Garry and Jost, Walter, *A Companion to the Philosophy of Literature*, John Wiley & Sons, New Jersey, 2009

Hamilton, George, *Voyage Round the World in His Majesty's Frigate Pandora*, W. Phorson, London, 1793

Hall, James Norman and Nordhoff, Charles, *Mutiny on the Bounty*, Little, Brown and Company, New York, 1932

Harland, John, *Seamanship in the Age of Sail*, Bloomsbury, London, 2015

Heywood, Peter and Heywood, Nessy, *Innocent on the Bounty*, McFarland & Company, London, 2013

Hill, John Spencer, *A Coleridge Companion*, Macmillan, London, 1983

Hobbes, Thomas, *Leviathan*, Collier, New York, 1972

Hough, Richard, *Captain Bligh and Mr Christian: The Men and the Mutiny*, Cassell, London, 1979

Jarves, James, *History of the Hawaiian or Sandwich Islands*, Tappan and Dennett, Boston, 1843

Kemp, Harry, *Chanteys and Ballads, Sea-chanteys, Tramp-ballads and Other Ballads and Poems*, Brentano's Publishers, New York, 1920

Kennedy, Gavin, *Captain Bligh: The Man and His Mutinies*, Duckworth, London, 1989

Kirk, Robert W., *Pitcairn Island: The Bounty Mutineers and their Descendants*, McFarland & Co., Jefferson NC, 2008

Ledyard, John and Sparks, Jared, *Travels and Adventures of John Ledyard*, Henry Colburn, London, 1834

Lee, Ida, *Captain Bligh's Second Voyage to the South Sea*, Longman's Green and Co, London, 1920

Lumis, Trevor, *Pitcairn Island: Life and Death in Eden*, Routledge, London, 1997

McArthur, John, *A treatise of the principles and practice of naval courts-martial, with an appendix, containing original papers and documents illustrative of the text, opinions of counsel upon remarkable cases, the forms preparatory to trial, and proceedings of the court to judgment and execution*, Whieldon and Butterworth, London, 1792

Mackaness, George, *Life of Vice-Admiral Bligh Sometime Governor of N.S.W.*, Vol. 1, Angus & Robertson, Sydney, 1931

Mackaness, George, *The Life of Vice-Admiral William Bligh*, Angus & Robertson, Sydney, 1951

Mackaness, George, *Fresh Light on Bligh*, Review Publications, Dubbo, 1976

McKay, John, *The Armed Transport BOUNTY*, Conway Maritime Press, London, 2001

McKinney, Sam, *Bligh!: The Whole Story of the Mutiny Aboard H.M.S. Bounty*, Touch Wood Editions, Canada, 1999

Macklin, Robert, *Dark Paradise*, Hachette, Sydney, 2013

Maiden, Joseph, *Sir Joseph Banks: The 'Father of Australia'*, William Gullick, Sydney, 1909

Milton, John, *Paradise Lost*, Dent, London, 1920

Moore, A.W., *Nessy Heywood*, Brown and Sons, Douglas, 1913

Morrison, James, *After the Bounty*, Potomac Books, Dulles, 2010

Mundle, Rob, *Bligh: Master Mariner*, Hachette, Sydney, 2010

Nicolson, Robert and Davies, Brian, *The Pitcairners*, Angus and Robertson, Sydney, 1964

Oliver, Douglas, *Return to Tahiti*, University of Hawaii Press, Honolulu, 1988

Phillip, Arthur, *Historical Records of New South Wales*, Vol. I, Part 2, 1783–1792, Charles Potter, Government Printer, Sydney, 1892

Preston, Diana, *Paradise in Chains: The Bounty Mutiny and the Founding of Australia*, Bloomsbury, New York, 2017

Robertson, George, *The Discovery of Tahiti: A Journal of the Second Voyage of H.M.S. Dolphin Round the World, Under the Command of Captain Wallis, R.N., in the Years 1766, 1767 and 1768*, Volume 98, Hakluyt Society, London, 1948

Rutter, Owen (ed.) *The Court Martial of the 'Bounty' Mutineers*, William Hodge and Company, Glasgow, 1931

Rutter, Owen (ed.), *The Court-Martial of the 'Bounty' Mutineers*, Canada Law Book Company, Toronto, 1933

Rutter, Owen (ed.), *The Voyage of the Bounty's Launch as related in William Bligh's despatch to the Admiralty and the Journal of John Fryer*, Golden Cockerel Press, London, 1934

Rutter, Owen (ed.), *Bligh's Voyage in the Resource*, Golden Cockerel Press, London, 1937

Salmond, Anne, *Aphrodite's Island: The European Discovery of Tahiti*, University of California Press, Berkeley, 2009

Salmond, Anne, *Bligh: William Bligh in the South Seas*, Penguin, Harmondsworth, 2011

Shakespeare, William, *Julius Caesar*, H. Altemus, Philadelphia, 1890

Shakespeare, William, *Macbeth*, Lyons and Carnahan, New York, 1913

Shedd, William (ed.), *The Complete Works of Samuel Taylor Coleridge*, Harper and Brothers, New York, 1853

Tagart, Edward, *Memoir of the late Captain Peter Heywood, R. N.*, Effingham Wilson, London, 1832

Tennyson, Alfred, *The Complete Works of Alfred, Lord Tennyson*, Frederick A. Stokes, New York, 1891

Thackeray, William Makepeace, *The Virginians: A Tale of the Last Century*, Harper and Brothers, London, 1859

Tobin, Beth, *Colonizing Nature: The Tropics in British Arts and Letters, 1760–1820*, University of Pennsylvania Press, Philadelphia, 2004.

Tobin, George, *Captain Bligh's Second Chance*, UNSW Press, Sydney, 2007

Williams, David, *Mutiny on the Bounty & Pandora's Box*, Two Moons Rising, New York, 2014

Williams, Glyndwr, *Captain Cook: Explorations and Reassessments*, Boydell Press, Suffolk, 2004

Wordsworth, William, *William Wordsworth: The Major Works*, Oxford University Press, UK, 2000

Manuscripts

Sir Joseph Banks Papers, State Library of New South Wales

Banks, Joseph, The *Endeavour* Journal of Joseph Banks (25 August 1768 – 12 July 1771), SLNSW, Papers of Sir Joseph Banks, Section 2, Series 03.01, http://www2.sl.nsw.gov.au/banks/series_03/03_231.cfm

Banks, Joseph, 'Manners and Customs of the South Sea Islands' in The *Endeavour* Journal of Joseph Banks, 25 August 1768 – 12 July 1771, SLNSW, Papers of Sir Joseph Banks, Section 2, Series 03.354, http://www2.sl.nsw.gov.au/images/banks/digitised/60399.jpg

Banks, Joseph, 'Instructions for a Vessel from Botany Bay,' circa. February 1878, SLNSW, Sir Joseph Banks Papers, Series 45.03 http://www.sl.nsw.gov.au/banks/section-08/series-45/45-03-instructions-for-the-vessell-from

Banks, Joseph to George Yonge, Letter, 9 September 1787, SLNSW, Sir Joseph Banks Papers, Series 45.08, http://www.sl.nsw.gov.au/banks/section-08/series-45/45-08-copy-of-a-letter-received-by-banks-from

Bligh, William to Joseph Banks, Letter, 6 August 1787, SLNSW, Sir Joseph Banks Papers, Series 46.02

Bligh, William to Joseph Banks, Letter, 15 September 1787, SLNSW, Sir Joseph Banks Papers, Series 46.03

Bligh, William to Joseph Banks, Letter, 3 October 1787, SLNSW, Sir Joseph Banks Papers, Series 46.05

Bligh, William to Joseph Banks, Letter, 20 October 1787, SLNSW, Sir Joseph Banks Papers, Series 46.07

Bligh, William to Joseph Banks, Letter, 5 November 1787, SLNSW, Sir Joseph Banks Papers, Series 46.08

Bligh, William to Joseph Banks, Letter, 18 November 1787, SLNSW, Sir Joseph Banks Papers, Series 46.09

Bligh, William to Joseph Banks, Letter, 9 January 1788, SLNSW, Sir Joseph Banks Papers, Series 46.20

Bligh, William to Joseph Banks, Letter, 24 May 1788, SLNSW, Sir Joseph Banks Papers, Series 46.22

Bligh, William to Joseph Banks, Letter, 13 October 1789, p. 5, SLNSW, Sir Joseph Banks Papers, Series 46.27, http://www.sl.nsw.gov.au/banks/section-08/series-46/46-letter-received-by-banks-from-william

Bligh, William to Joseph Banks, Letter, 24 October 1790, SLNSW, Sir Joseph Banks Papers, Series 46.31

Bligh, William to Joseph Banks, Letter, 17 July 1791, SLNSW, Sir Joseph Banks Papers, Series 50.05

Bligh, William to Joseph Banks, Letter, 30 October 1793, SLNSW, Papers of Sir Joseph Banks, Series 50.32

Clerke, Charles to Joseph Banks, Letter, 23 November 1776, SLNSW, Sir Joseph Banks Papers, Series 11.03, p. 2, http://www.sl.nsw.gov.au/banks/section-04/series-11/11-03-letter-received-by-banks-from-charles

Howell, William to Molesworth Phillips, Letter, 25 November 1792, Papers of Sir Joseph Banks, SLNSW, Series 48.01

Lord Selkirk to Joseph Banks, Letter, 14 September 1787, SLNSW, Sir Joseph Banks Papers, Series 45.11

Bligh Family Collection, State Library of New South Wales

Bligh, William to Elizabeth Bligh, Letter, 19 August 1789, SLNSW Bligh – Papers relating to HMS Bounty, 1787–1794, Safe 1/45

Bligh, William to Duncan Campbell, Letter, 10 December 1787, in William Bligh – letters sent, 1782–1798, chiefly to Duncan Campbell, with correspondence of W.D. Campbell, 1895–1896, SLNSW, Safe 1/40 (Microfilm: CY 178, frames 254–344)

Bligh, William to Duncan Campbell, Letter, 22 December 1787, p. 1, in William Bligh – letters sent, 1782–1798, chiefly to Duncan Campbell, with correspondence of W.D. Campbell, 1895–1896, SLNSW, Safe 1/40 (Microfilm: CY 178, frames 254–344)

Bligh, William to Duncan Campbell, Letter, 9 January 1788, p. 3, in William Bligh – letters sent, 1782–1798, chiefly to Duncan Campbell, with correspondence of W.D. Campbell, 1895–1896, SLNSW, Safe 1/40 (Microfilm: CY 178, frames 254–344)

Bligh, William to Duncan Campbell, Letter, 26 May 1788, in William Bligh – letters sent, 1782–1798, chiefly to Duncan Campbell, with correspondence of W.D. Campbell, 1895–1896, SLNSW, Safe 1/40 (Microfilm: CY 178, frames 254–344)

Bligh, William, Notebook and list of mutineers, 1789, NLA, MS 5393, 30 May 1789, No page numbers, http://nla.gov.au/nla.obj-233757365/view

Morrison, James, Journal on HMS Bounty and at Tahiti, 9 Sept. 1787–1791, written in 1792, SLNSW, William Bligh – Papers relating to HMS Bounty, 1787–1794, Safe 1/42

Morrison, James, *Memorandum and Particulars Respecting the Bounty and Her Crew*, in William Bligh – Papers relating to HMS Bounty, 1787–1794, undated, State Library of NSW, Safe 1/33

Other

Bligh, William, Extract from the logbook HMS Bounty (16 August 1787 – 20 August 1789), The National Archives, Kew, ADM 55/151, http://discovery.nationalarchives.gov.uk/details/r/C2976823

Bligh, Log of the Proceedings of His Majesty's Ship Bounty in a Voyage to the South Seas, (to take the Bread-fruit plant from the Society Islands to the West Indies,) under the Command of Lieutenant William Bligh (1 Dec. 1787 – 22 Oct. 1788), 23 January 1788, SLNSW, Safe 1/46 (Microfilm CY247), http://archival.sl.nsw.gov.au/Details/archive/110368599

Bligh 'Log of the Proceedings of His Majesty's Ship Bounty Lieut. Wm Bligh Commander from Otaheite towards Jamaica, signed "Wm Bligh", 5 Apr. 1789 -13 Mar. 1790', 17 September 1789, SLNSW, Safe 1/47 (Microfilm CY 274), http://archival.sl.nsw.gov.au/Details/archive/110339148

Burney, James, Journal, State Library of NSW, Safe 1/64; Safe 1/79, Vol. 3

Cook, James, Journal of H.M.S. Endeavour, 1768–1771, 3 June 1769, NLA, MS 1, http://nla.gov.au/nla.obj-228983242/view

Edwards, Edward, Admiralty Library Manuscript Collection: Papers of Edward Edwards as Captain of HMS Pandora, 1790–1792, MSS 180

The Flinders Papers: Letters and documents about the Explorer Matthew Flinders (1774–1814), National Maritime Museum, http://flinders.rmg.co.uk/DisplayDocument0a25.html

Heywood, Mary, Letter-book, mainly concerning Peter Heywood, 1790–1792; and verse, 1786–1795, SLNSW, MLMSS 5719 (Safe 1/127), http://archival.sl.nsw.gov.au/Details/archive/110317966

Macquarie, Lachlan. *Journal No. 1: 15 December 1787 – 24 March 1792*, 13 June 1788, SLNSW, A768-2 (Safe 1/353), [Microfilm Reel CY299 Frames #48–59], http://archival.sl.nsw.gov.au/Details/archive/110342434

Pipon, Captain P, *'Interesting account of the mutineers of H.M.S. Bounty – original account of the finding the home of the Mutineers – on Pitcairn Island – 1814'*, State Library of NSW, DLMS 341

Samwell, David, *A Narrative on the Death of Captain Cook*, G.G.J. & J. Robinson, London, 1786, held at SLNSW, C694

Stephens, Ph, 'Secret Instructions for Lieutenant James Cook Appointed to Command His Majesty's Bark the Endeavour', 30 July 1768, NLA, MS 2, p. 1, https://www.foundingdocs.gov.au/scan-sid-252.html

Periodicals/Journals

British Critic, December 1794, F and C Rivington, London, 1794

Critical Review, March 1795

The Derby Mercury, 18 March 1790

The Edinburgh Magazine, 'Narrative of the Adventures of the Mutineers aboard his Majesty's Ship Bounty', June 1792

The Journal of the Polynesian Society, Volume 11, 1964

The London Chronicle

Mutiny on the Bounty 1789–1989 [Magazine], Manorial Research PLC, London, 1989

The Quarterly Review, February to May 1810, John Murray, London, 1810

The Scots Magazine, March 1790

Sydney Gazette

Twain, Mark, 'The Great Revolution In Pitcairn', *The Atlantic Monthly*, Vol. XLIII, March 1879

United Service Journal and Naval and Military Magazine, London, H. Colburn, 1829, Pt II

Walker's Hibernian Magazine, Part Two, R. Gibson, Dublin, 1794

Speech

Beaglehole, John, *Captain Cook and Captain Bligh*, The Dr W.E. Collins Lecture delivered at the University on 3 August 1967, The Victoria University of Wellington, 1967

INDEX